Forging a Nation

Forging a Nation

PERSPECTIVES ON THE CANADIAN MILITARY EXPERIENCE

BERND HORN

EDITOR

Vanwell Publishing Limited

St. Catharines, Ontario

Vanwell Publishing acknowledges the financial support of the Government of Canada through the Book Publishing Industry Development Program for our publishing activities.

Design: Linda Moroz-Irvine
Cover Painting: *Montcalm Congratulating his Victorious Troops, July 8, 1758*, watercolour by Harry. A. Ogden, 1931. Courtesy Fort Ticonderoga Museum.

Vanwell Publishing Limited
1 Northrup Crescent
P.O. Box 2131
St. Catharines, Ontario L2R 7S2
sales@vanwell.com
phone 800.661.6136
fax 905.937.1760

Printed in Canada

National Library of Canada Cataloguing in Publication Data

Horn, Bernd, 1959-
        Forging a nation : perspectives on the Canadian military experience

Includes bibliographical references and index.
ISBN 1-55125-090-X

1. Canada--History, Military. 2. Canada--Military policy--History. I. Horn, Bernd, 1959-

FC226.F66 2002   355'.00971   C2002-901062-4
F1028.F67 2002

TABLE OF CONTENTS

FOREWORD

AT THE BEGINNING of his classic study of *Canada's Soldiers*, noted military historian and member of the faculty at the Royal Military College of Canada, Professor George Stanley, concluded that "Canadians ... are not a military people." Not only are we not war-like, but most Canadians assume that because armed conflicts have, in the last century at least, happened "over there," the nation has been untouched by war. And yet not only did Canada immediately declare and demonstrate its support for the United States after the unprecedented terrorist attacks of 11 September 2001, Canadians applauded Prime Minister Chretien's announcement a month later that the nation would contribute what he described as the largest contingent of armed forces since the Korean War to the campaign against terrorism.

Canada's support of Operation Enduring Freedom is not an anomaly. It is but the most recent chapter in what is a distinct and rich national military experience. For more than two centuries Canadians have taken up arms to defend the nation and our national ideals, to support our allies and to maintain peace in far flung parts of the world. And armed conflict has left an indelible mark on the nation. Canadian participation in wars in the 20th century was accompanied by domestic turmoil and uncertainty; wars were a catalyst for profound social, economic, political and cultural change. And these wars also exacted a significant personal toll on individuals and families. Of the 620,000 who served in the First World War, 60,000 were killed and another 172,000 were wounded. During the Second World War, the whole nation mobilized and 1.1 million Canadians served in uniform; 42,042 never returned home; 54,414 were wounded. A scant five years later, 26,971 Canadians were again deployed overseas—this time to Korea; 516 were killed and 1,072 were wounded. And for the last half of the century, Canadian involvement in peace support operations has cost the lives of 108 personnel and permanently transformed the lives of tens of thousands of others—in and out of uniform. At the end of each conflict or tour of duty, we fervently hoped that such sacrifice would never again be needed; but when a new crisis arose, Canadians responded.

The deployment of ships and aircraft in the fall of 2001 is but the most recent manifestation of the Canadian military experience. Our aim, as the Governor General stated, is to "help maintain and protect the values that have made us what we are—tolerant, peaceful and free." It is an aim that binds together the 2000 service personnel deployed in direct support of Operation Enduring Freedom with the hundreds of thousands of Canadians who took up arms throughout our history. These sentiments are captured in many of the essays in this collection. So too is the realization that our military experience was an important element in forging our nation into the society it is today. It shaped how we as Canadians saw ourselves, as well as how we saw others. At times, it dictated economic and political priorities; and it has earned us international recognition and respect. Although this is all too often ignored, if not forgotten, we are a country with a rich and proud military history. Part of that story can be found in the following pages. Significantly, if not appropriately, the stories are told entirely by faculty members of the Royal Military College or those who are closely associated with the College.

Jane Errington
Chair, History Department
Royal Military College of Canada

ACKNOWLEDGEMENTS

ANY PROJECT OF THIS SCOPE AND MAGNITUDE owes its completion to the extraordinary efforts of a large number of people. Initially, I would like to thank Jane Errington, the Chair of History at the Royal Military College of Canada (RMC), for her support and assistance. Next, I would be remiss if I did not thank the wide array of contributors who took the time and effort to put their research and thoughts on paper. Their diligence made this book a reality.

In addition, I would like to acknowledge the assistance and support of Dr. John Cowan, the Principal of RMC, and his administrative assistant, Maggie Shepherd, for their support of the project. I would also like to thank Michel Wyczynski of the National Archives of Canada for his help in sourcing many of the pictures that appear in the book. As well, although too numerous to mention individually, I must also thank collectively the staffs of the Directorate of History and Heritage, the National Archives of Canada, and RMC, for their stellar co-operation and assistance.

Finally, I wish to express my gratitude to Angela Dobler and her design team for taking the manuscript and photographs and turning them into a polished final product.

INTRODUCTION

THERE OFTEN EXISTS A PERCEPTION that Canada's military history is devoid of drama, excitement or great martial feats. Quite simply, many consider it tame if not boring, particularly when compared to the more turbulent and violent heritage of our nation's southern neighbor, the United States of America. This is not overly surprising; after all, George Stanley, a prominent Canadian historian, labelled Canadians an "unmilitary people." This is not hard to understand. We take great pride in the orderly development of our frontier and place an inordinate emphasis on the herculean feat of building the railroad through the Rocky Mountains, and on the respect shown to the serge red tunic of the North West Mounted Police, as opposed to the Wild West image of our American neighbours who revel in their legacy of conflict and Indian wars.

But the fact that Canadian military history is habitually marginalized is a function of ignorance, as well as our culture. Canadians rightfully delight in their reputation as a polite and tolerant society. Adrienne Clarkson, the current Governor General of Canada and Commander-in-Chief of the Canadian Armed Forces, stated Canadians "are basically a forgiving and compassionate people." She went on describe Canada as "a peaceable kingdom."[1] More recently, in the wake of the September 2001 terrorist attacks, she praised "our ability to maintain justice and do what is right, to bring peace to those far and near." She went on to say that this "is difficult. It is trying. This is a role which history has allotted us."[2] Not surprisingly, our tradition and achievements in peacekeeping have come to define us as both a people and a nation. Yet, the perception of our national military history as benign and quiescent is simply fallacious. Much of this is because Canadians have been fortunate that they have not had to live with the direct impact of war in Canada in living memory. As a result, there is a tendency to forget the nation's military legacy and tradition.

Nonetheless, although not a warlike people, Canadians have carved out a reputation as courageous and capable soldiers who earned the respect of their allies and opponents alike. This justifiable reputation was earned as a result of the country's military experience. What is often forgotten is the extent to which Canada was forged and shaped by conflict. New France lived a precarious existence for decades in its struggle for survival against the Iroquois nations. The eventual cessation of hostilities was short-lived as North America was quickly engulfed in the struggle between the competing British and French Empires. Not surprisingly, the First Nations and early Canadians became adept at warfare, particularly fighting suited to the harsh and rugged environment in which they lived.

Military exigency continued even after the fate of the continent was sealed on the Plains of Abraham in 1759. Fewer than twenty years later, the American Revolution not only brought war once again to Canadian soil, but it also established a hostile and at times belligerent neighbour to the south. The War of 1812 and the Fenian Raids of the 1860s were but the most blatant manifestations. As if the threat posed by the Americans was not enough, throughout the nation's history, internal disputes and insurrections required the government to order the application of military force to resolve the issues. But overall, the horror of war became distant to most Canadians. As Canada and the United States learned to co-exist, both tensions and the requirement for strong military presence waned. Protected by the country's geography and the Royal Navy, the country seemed secure, if not invulnerable.

Nonetheless, alliances and allegiance to the British Empire ensured the continuance of a distinct Canadian military tradition. As such, conflict overseas imprinted an indelible mark on the maturing nation. The Boer War in South Africa at the turn of the twentieth century stamped the necessity of national command and control of its forces while serving as part of the British Army overseas. This sentiment was cemented through the painful experience of two world wars. In both cases, Canada's achievements were laudable and earned the country its place among nations. However, the cost was staggering in the loss of Canadian lives, economic resources and at times national unity. Consequently, the national military experience clearly had a dramatic impact in shaping our country's perception of itself, the world and Canada's role therein.

This perception was reinforced in the postwar world. Through a combination of political opportunism and altruism, Canada used its military to further its own interests, as well as make the world a more secure and stable place. Although a staunch supporter of NATO, Canada was also able to shed its Cold War warrior mantle and carve out a distinct reputation as the pre-eminent peacekeeper in the world. This tradition continued in the post Cold War era when the Canadian Forces experienced an operational tempo in the 1990s that strained its very foundation. However, once again, this participation in the plethora of peace support operations was critical in that it defined how we saw ourselves, as well as how Canadians saw the world they lived in. It was also part of the veiled dues demanded by members of the international community if Canada wanted a seat at the table.

Undeniably, Canada's military history is strong and has had a dominant impact on the forging of our nation. This book attempts to capture the drama of this experience. It is divided into four functional parts that are both chronological and thematic. Part I covers the colonial era. It begins with an examination of the First Nations, initially as feared enemies and later as allies in the struggle for colonial North America. The first chapter examines the culture shock and subsequent adaptation of the Régiment Carignan-Salières upon their deployment to New France in 1665 to secure the new colony against the Iroquois menace. The second chapter describes how, despite competing cultures and alien methods of war, as well as the Europeans' loathing of the Indian method of fighting, Canada's First Nations were invaluable in the struggle for the wilderness empire. Finally, on a dramatic departure from the first two chapters, Part I concludes with a look at Canadian participation in the first real conflict of the industrial age—the American Civil War—as well as an examination of the lessons pulled from the Boer War.

The next focus of the book is the impact of the two world wars on Canada. The key questions of national mobilization, in terms of resources, industry and manpower, as well as the financing of the war effort, are probed in detail. What falls out is the lasting impression that these two monumental events made on the country. From a more operational vantage point the experience of Canadians in Bomber Command is also revealed, as is the assessment of the Canadian strategy that guided the nation's participation in the Second World War.

Part III moves from a chronological to a thematic base, specifically the notion of national security in a Canadian context. Key issues such as developing and maintaining an indigenous munitions industry, the marginalization of our maritime defence and the importance of securing the North are all examined in depth. Moreover, the distinct Canadian way of war, born of our tradition and experience, is identified and explained. In the end, the impact of our military heritage, particularly how it helped shape the society we are today, becomes clearly evident.

The final segment of the book carries this thematic approach to the international arena. Not surprisingly, the first topic dealt with is Canada's historic reliance on alliance relationships. This overview is subsequently amplified by an analysis of Canadian military involvement in non-traditional regions, namely the Caribbean and Latin America, as well as a provocative assessment of the nation's Cold War experience. In a similar vein, the book finishes with a penetrating appraisal of the nation's peacekeeping legacy.

Taken together, the diverse essays form an image of the overwhelming impact that our military history has had on forging the nation. Whether rooted in survival, defence of the Empire, an attempt to maintain international stature and trade opportunities, or simply as a crusade to make the world a more secure and stable place, Canada's military tradition and achievements have been instrumental in shaping our country, and defining the way we see ourselves.

Notes for Introduction

1   Her Excellency the Right Honourable Adrienne Clarkson, Governor General of Canada, convocation address at Royal Military College of Canada, 18 May 2001.

2   "Clarkson says Canada a nation of peacekeepers," *Calgary Herald*, 16 October 2001, A7.

PART I

From the Colonial Era
to the Turn of the
Twentieth Century

Champlain battling the Iroquois near the present town of Ticonderoga, New York, 30 July 1609. (National Library [NL] 6643)

CHAPTER 1

New Horizons, New Challenges

The Carignan-Salières Regiment in New France, 1665-1667

Michel Wyczynski

THE HISTORY OF NEW FRANCE is one of conflict, hardship and struggle. Despite the chain of trading posts established in Canada by the French to exploit the fur trade, colonization was slow if not tenuous. By the mid-seventeenth century Canada's entire population was less than 2,500 people, consisting mainly of explorers, fur traders, missionaries and settlers.

Those intrepid souls that attempted to settle in the rugged North American wilderness faced untold challenges—severe climate, arduous terrain and hostile natives, notably the Iroquois confederacy. To meet these challenges and exploit the economic gains to be had from the wilderness, the French befriended and entered into alliances with a number of tribes who also happened to be enemies of the Iroquois. These friendships upset the status quo and earned the bitter enmity of the Iroquois. The war of annihilation that followed was beyond the military capability of the embattled French colonists.

The ensuing struggle threatened the virtual existence of New France. Desperate merchants hired small groups of soldiers to protect their interests while colonial administrators appealed for military assistance. During this troublesome period, France, however, was embroiled in its European conflicts and showed little interest in colonial matters. Nonetheless, by 1663 the French monarch, Louis XIV—who was in the midst of reorganizing his army—was displaying a growing concern for matters overseas. He realized that in order to save New France, particularly his economic ventures there, measures would have to be undertaken to eradicate the Iroquois menace. The only viable option was to deploy a large military force. The King ultimately selected the Régiment de Carignan-Salières for this important task. However, these soldiers were trained and equipped to operate and manoeuvre in the vast open plains of Europe, against an enemy who respected and prescribed to the accepted European manner of war. New France, on the other hand, was entirely different. It presented an incredible series of unprecedented military challenges. The soldiers were forced to adapt and live in a harsh and unforgiving environment with its extremely hot and humid summers and cruel severe winters. In addition, they had to learn to use completely new means of transportation, develop engineering skills, and create radically new tactics to battle their cunning and elusive foe. This entailed mastering how to travel quickly and safely through the rugged terrain and savage wilderness of the New World. Despite these hardships and challenges, the resiliency and tenacity of the men of the Carignan-Salières Regiment enabled them to successfully adapt to the new art of North American warfare. These soldiers provided the required stability and protection that ultimately enabled New France to become a viable self-sufficient colony.

But the beginnings were questionable at best. New France's vast territory and climate presented a series of never ending difficulties that constantly tested the French settlers. The dense and far-reaching woodlands forced the colonists to master the handling of various water craft to travel, as well as transport goods, the great distances between Quebec, Trois-Rivières and Montreal. Conversely, those who chose to journey by land had to develop other skills such as fishing, hunting, and navigation just to ensure their survival in the unforgiving wilderness. Compounded to these requirements was the necessity to remain ever vigilant to avoid or repel the roaming Iroquois raiding parties.

Each season tested the settlers' endurance and initiative and required them to discover new ways to overcome the many adversities that they faced. During spring, high water increased the flow of treacherous currents. Furthermore, heavy rains turned some ground and shorelines into muddy quagmires. Summer was humid and stifling while swarms of mosquitoes added to the discomfort of travelling through the woodlands. Fall also presented its particular inconveniences. The cold, dampness and heavy rains added to the discomfort of long journeys. But worst of all was the bitterly cold winter, whose deep snow limited the speed and desirability of extensive prolonged travel. All these factors hindered the vital communication lines between the distant settlements.

Additionally, back breaking work had to be done without the proper tools and equipment, in order to clear parcels of land required to sow crops. Because only meagre supplies were sent from France, the much anticipated fall harvests were vital to the survival of the settlers and their families during the long winter months. Undeniably, endurance and resilience were fundamental qualities required to conquer the various aspects of New France's wilderness.

However, the Europeans also quickly realized that knowledge derived from Indian allies was also fundamental if they were to enhance their ability to survive, not to mention to prosper economically. As a result, the French actively nurtured friendships and established crucial alliances during the sixteenth century with the Abenaki, Algonquin, Huron, Montagnais, and Outaouais. These new allies were instrumental in the education of the French. They taught them the medicinal power of various plants and what wild foods could be harvested as well as fishing, hunting and survival techniques. In addition, they taught how to manufacture specific footwear and clothing to counter the hostile elements, as well as how to use snowshoes and toboggans for winter travel. They also passed on skills and knowledge such as handling birch bark canoes and portaging techniques. Equally important, they served as guides and translators during explorations into the uncharted wilderness and during expeditions against the Iroquois. With this assistance the settlers slowly adapted and with time were able to become self-sufficient in their new surroundings.

In exchange, the Hurons persuaded the French to join them in a series of expeditions against their nemesis, the Iroquois. On 20 July 1609, Samuel de Champlain, the first governor of New France, led the first combined French, Algonquin and Huron force against the Iroquois. Armed with his arquebus, Champlain opened fire and his first volley killed two Iroquois chiefs. Stunned by the deadly efficiency of this new weapon, the Iroquois warriors broke ranks and fled. However, this small pyrrhic victory caused irreparable damage to French–Iroquois relations. The humiliated members of the Iroquois Confederacy became the sworn enemy of the French.[1]

The fierce Iroquois Confederacy consisted of five tribes. The Mohawks, the deadliest and most aggressive members of the Confederacy, lived in the southern region of the Richelieu River. Further west were the Oneidas, Onondagas, Cayugas, and the Senecas. The Iroquois, a semi-sedentary and semi-agricultural people, lived in a protected area of southern Ontario and western New York. Their homeland was strategically well chosen. It provided the Iroquois with an extensive series of natural obstacles that protected their villages and farmlands. Yet, the Iroquois themselves experienced no difficulties travelling on estuaries and waterways used to attack, at will, locations within the French colony. Furthermore, Iroquois contacts, initially, with the Dutch colony and later with English traders, provided them with a regular supply of much needed muskets and powder.

During 1648 and 49, the Iroquois launched major offensives that ultimately led to the complete destruction of Huronia in 1650.[2] After this victory, they focussed their attacks on isolated French settlements along the St. Lawrence Valley. For the next fifteen years the viciousness of the Iroquois raids horrified the French settlers. The intensity of the onslaught was such that an Iroquois chief boasted, "We plyed the French home in the war with them, that they were not able to goe over the door to pisse."[3] This taunt was more than just bluster. "The Iroquois used to keep us closely confined," acknowledged a Jesuit priest, "that we did not even dare till the lands that were under the cannon of the forts, much less go to a distance to ascertain the points of excellence of a soil which hardly differs at all from that of France."[4]

The more daring settlers organized themselves into small armed groups hoping to counter the Iroquois raiding parties. However, despite this brave initiative, the tactics employed by these bands proved unsuccessful. Lacking both military experience and weaponry, they were forced to be largely reactionary—stand their ground and resort to ineffective defensive tactics. There were, however, a few isolated victories that raised morale. The most famous was the battle of Long-Sault in May 1660, when Adam Dollard Des Ormeaux and his force of a few comrades, sixteen Frenchmen, forty Hurons and four Algonquins bravely fought off a large Iroquois war party for almost seven days.[5] Their actions, according to historians, saved Montreal from an Iroquois attack. Notwithstanding this success and the overall resistance offered by the French colonists, the exhausting effects of this war of attrition were telling.

In an attempt to stem the casualties and the drain of resources that the continuing war with the Iroquois represented, French colonial officials analyzed and studied Iroquois strategies and tactics. Pierre Boucher, Governor of Trois-Rivières, recorded his observations on the Iroquois art of war in a book titled *Histoire veritable et naturelle des moeurs et productions de la Nouvelle-France vulgairement dite le Canada*. It included among other things astute insights into Iroquois operations and tactics.[6] Boucher explained that there was a pattern to Iroquois behaviour. He observed that Iroquois war parties were always preceded by *découvreurs*, (scouts), that they handled their firearms efficiently, preferred quick raids or ambushes, never fought in open ground and always withdrew quickly after striking. In addition, he noted that all attacks were initiated with a series of sudden, intimidating and soul piercing screams. He also noted that when outnumbered they retreated promptly or simply aborted their attacks.

Boucher found they possessed great endurance and stamina that enabled them to travel great distances swiftly regardless of the terrain. Moreover, their detailed knowledge of the immense territory and waterways, he determined, increased their mobility and range. Their fieldcraft skills, such as their personal camouflage, added to their efficiency. "They set up ambushes everywhere, " he wrote, "and all that was required was a small bush to hide 6 or 7 warriors, or should I say to prepare their assault. Then without warning they pounced on you unexpectedly while you were working or travelling to your work site."[7]

The Governor of Trois-Rivières also argued that the French could only counter these small mobile raiding parties if they themselves mastered the ability to travel through the wilderness, adapt to the different seasons and develop clothing to endure the harsh North American conditions.[8] Boucher concluded that the only way to subjugate the Iroquois nation was to deploy a large force of eight or nine hundred soldiers.[9] More importantly, he strongly recommended the assistance of regular soldiers. The Governor and colonial leaders regularly pleaded for help, but the King's troops and resources were committed elsewhere.

Since 1635, France had been embroiled in a series of long conflicts and its rulers did not deem the defence of distant colonies as a priority. By the late 1650s, multiple campaigns had taken their toll on a now tired French Army. The young French monarch, King Louis XIV, showed a great interest in military affairs and he implemented a plan to completely reorganize his army.[10] During these difficult times only limited resources and manpower could be temporarily diverted to protect colonial possessions. Between 1604 and 1663, the Minister of Colonies occasionally sent small military contingents, ranging between thirty and two hundred soldiers. Their presence provided temporary relief, but their overall operational efficiency was low. As a token gesture, the *Compagnie des Cent-Associés,* responsible for the development of New France, also periodically hired small groups of professional soldiers.[11] However, upon arrival, these men were ordered to protect the *Compagnie's* business interests rather than the settlers' farmlands. These costly, short term deployments cut into the shareholders' profits. To minimize expenses, the soldiers were retained for a few months and returned to France.

Concurrently, the colonial administrators examined the possibility of raising their own troops. But the colony was simply too small. In 1663, New France's population totalled 3,035 inhabitants settled in three distant locations: Quebec, 1,976; Three-Rivers, 462; and Montreal, 597. The male population numbered approximately eleven hundred, of which maybe seven

The deadly efficiency of the Iroquois raiding parties was further enhanced by the acquisition of metal hatchets, knives and muskets. These new tools of war complemented the Iroquois warriors' lethal bows and dreaded wooden bludgeons. (Courtesy of Francis Back, Montreal)

hundred were capable of bearing arms. Of these, very few had military experience.[12] Moreover, the lack of specialized tradesmen and the absence of small industries able to manufacture military ordnance, weapons and supplies severely restricted all attempts of outfitting any proposed force. Furthermore, married men were reluctant to leave their families unprotected. As time passed, it became apparent that the colony could not defend itself and if the bitter war of extermination persisted, the future of New France would be in grave peril. By 1663, the *Compagnie des Cent-Associés* could see no financial benefits in pursuing future operations and opted to end its activities in New France. As an interim measure Louis XIV intervened and became directly involved in overseeing all facets of colonial affairs. He immediately assessed and evaluated the military options as well as what was needed to ensure peace and stability in his colonies.[13]

The French monarch and his Minister of Colonies were briefed on the demands for military assistance that were included in the annual reports dispatched from New France. The first pertinent insights into how to deal with the Iroquois menace were listed in a memoire dated 22 January 1663. "The Iroquois, " wrote a colonial official, "should be annihilated because they hinder the settlement process and trade. Eight hundred men led by competent officers should be sent and an additional 200 soldiers should be recruited in Canada. The Iroquois must be attacked in their territory.... They could either be killed or sent to France as galley slaves."[14] Two important conclusions were brought forward in this report. The first was that a large regular force led by experienced officers must be sent to the colony to conduct the operation. A small colonial contingent was to be raised only to augment this force. The second point stressed the importance of attacking the Iroquois in their own territory in order to destroy their villages and food supplies, as well as to inflict heavy casualties. Prisoners were to be sent to France to serve as oarsmen in the galleys. Thus, the French strategists believed that the key to victory lay in offensive action to destroy not only the Indian warriors but their base of support, namely their villages and crops. It was believed that such a strategy would also provide the colonial authorities with the necessary time to strengthen existing defensive positions, build new fortifications in strategic locations and increase immigration.

French officials carefully analyzed all incoming correspondence and compiled additional information that would assist in the continuing war against the Iroquois.[15] A series of colonial memoranda, drafted in 1663 and 1664, identified additional important details. One report described the current state of defensive positions and recommended sites for new strongholds. However, they explained that because of the immense territory to be protected, the building of stockades similar to those in France would prove impractical and costly. They, moreover, did not have the required manpower to occupy and defend them. Rather, methods of transportation and the careful planning of rates of advance, routes and logistics would be required to allow future troop deployments over great distances, particularly any expeditions intended to invade Iroquois territory.

Innovative solutions to the problem were also suggested. One possible way to accelerate the movement of a large body of troops against the Iroquois was to travel through Dutch territories. In fact, Major Guebin, the Commandant of Boston, offered his services to destroy the Iroquois for 20,000 francs.[16] In addition, hoping to draw a favourable response from the King, the colonial administrators proposed various options that could provide settlers with better means of defending themselves. "We could, " suggested one administrator, "congregate the settlers in groups of ten or twelve, establish them in small communities, store supplies in a fort defended by soldiers who would protect them against the Indians."[17] Another alternative was to send three hundred men from France annually to settle in the colony and to provide them with sufficient funds for the purchase of a musket, a pistol and a sword. However, the report did stress the importance of selecting suitable settlers. For instance, colonial officials insisted that the peasants who had emigrated from Normandy lacked the required fighting spirit to confront the Iroquois.[18] Hoping to ensure a favourable response from the King, the colonial administrators framed the problem in such a way that the King could not help but be concerned. They explained that the Iroquois raids impacted directly on all commercial ventures. "Il serait important," they emphasized, "pour Montréal et le commerce d'exterminer cette tribu."[19] In early 1664 the Ministry of Colonies concluded that the only practical way to save the colony was to dispatch, as quickly as possible for a limited time, a regular infantry unit to eliminate the Iroquois.[20]

But as this option was being further evaluated, the French Army was in the midst of a major reorganization that transformed it "from a small rag-tag collection of semi-independent units to a very large and modern force controlled by central authority."[21] The King was assisted by the Minister of War, Michel Le Tellier, Marquis de Louvois, and military strategist Marshal Henri, Viscount de Turenne. As part of the reorganization they conducted intensive recruiting drives and they ensured the establishment of sound administrative control. They also instilled discipline and organized military training. The King insisted that his soldiers be issued with a uniform and equipment to enhance pride and esprit de corps in the army. In addition, the innovators experimented with, and issued, new weapons. They also developed and instituted new tactics. During the course of all these activities a directive from the King was drafted to initiate the selection process of a infantry regiment to be deployed to New France.

On 18 March 1664, Jean-Baptist Colbert, Privy Councillor and Intendant of Finance, confirmed that the King had selected a regiment. Colbert explained to Monseigneur de Laval that "His Majesty decreed that an honorable infantry regiment be sent to Canada ... in order to totally decimate the Iroquois."[22] This marked the beginning of the King's military commitment to protect his colonies. He authorized the dispatch of regular infantry units to Guyana and the West Indies in 1664, to New France in 1665 and Madagascar in 1666.

And so, on 23 January 1665, the Régiment de Carignan-Salières was ordered to redeploy to La Rochelle for its upcoming sojourn to New France.[23] In its short twenty-year history, this would be the unit's first and only overseas mission. The regiment was raised in Italy in 1644 by Thomas Francis of Savoy, Prince de Carignano. Following the Treaty of Westphalia in 1648, the unit continued to serve in Italy for an additional five years. Deployed briefly to Paris, during the 1652 Fronde civil war, the regiment was quickly returned to Italy and remained there until 1658. However, at that time, unable to keep up with the escalating costs required to maintain it, Prince de Carignano turned the regiment over to the French Army. At that point it was renamed the Régiment de Carignan. Shortly after, the French high command undertook it's grand reorganization. Many units were disbanded while others were consolidated. The Régiment de Carignan was amalgamated with the Régiment de Salières, which had been raised by Johann von Baltazard at the beginning of the Thirty Years War, but who had recently retired. And so, in 1658, the unit two units were combined and re-designated the Régiment de Carignan-Salières.

The Regiment now consisted of fifteen companies and was subsequently redeployed for garrison duties on the northeastern French border.[24] Isolation and boring guard details eroded the soldiers' morale and discipline. The news of the upcoming deployment did not alleviate the discontent. Many of the officers voiced their concerns and displeasure regarding their new mission. Nevertheless, the regiment marched from Marsal in Lorraine and Arras to the port of La Rochelle, where it was to be outfitted with equipment prior to its departure for North America.

The unit's administrative move to La Rochelle, in early 1665, was marred by a series of disciplinary incidents: confrontations with hostile populations; theft; the murder of Sergeant Hivras from the Rougemont Company and the murder of a magistrate and a civilian of the town of La Mothe-Saint-Héray, south of Poitier, to name a few.[25] Surprisingly, this litany of events was considered normal behavior during these long administrative marches. When passing through towns, the troops were normally greeted by belligerent townsfolk. But this negative reaction is not surprising. It was the result of the government's incessant demand that the populace provide, at its own expense, food, shelter and supplies to troops in transit. Nonetheless, Ministry of War officials were apprised of the Carignan-Salières disorderly conduct. All pending legal cases against the soldiers were dealt with swiftly and new orders were then issued to ensure the regiment reached its destination as quickly as possible without further incident.[26]

Amazingly, upon the regiment's arrival in La Rochelle in early February, a total of twelve lieutenants and sixteen ensigns were reported missing. Other junior officers tendered their resignations, which were refused outright. The King insisted that all experienced officers participate in this campaign. He ordered that "experienced officers partake in the Carignan Regiment's forthcoming campaign."[27] However, certain exceptions were made to permit a few of the older captains to remain in France because of their ailing health. Even though the

A soldier of the Carignan-Salières Regiment wearing his new uniform. This individual is still outfitted with an old matchlock musket. (Courtesy of Parks Canada. Reconstitution by Francis Back.)

absence of twenty-eight officers did initially cause concern, these positions were staffed through an accelerated promotion scheme authorized by the King. This expeditious staffing was possible because many companies carried supplementary personnel. Meanwhile, the soldiers and non-commissioned officers were loaded onto small vessels and transported to the nearby islands of d'Oléron and Ré. This seclusion was a blessing. The troops were isolated from the population, there was no opportunity to desert and there was nothing left to do but focus on preparing equipment and stores, loading the vessels, outfitting the troops and teaching them how to handle and shoot the newly issued flintlock muskets.[28]

The regiment's deployment to New France also coincided with the King's new colonization scheme. Jean Talon, the newly appointed Intendant of New France, joined the regiment during its preparations. Talon spoke at length to many officers and men about the benefits of settling in the new colony. Those who wished to stay in New France following the campaign, he explained, would be awarded funds and land grants.[29] Encouraged by their reaction, Talon wrote to the Minister stating that they were favourable to this proposal. "The officers of the Carignan Regiment" he reported, "stated that they were pleased to travel to Canada."

Others were given various sums of money to reward their loyalty and extra efforts during the regiment's readying for the upcoming deployment.[30] While these incentives and promises motivated the soldiers, the laborious preparations, on the other hand, caused many frustrations.

The Carignan-Salières Regiment was among the first infantry regiments to undergo the strict new administrative control system that now stressed accountability and rigid record keeping. However, this unit's seventy-year-old commanding officer, Colonel Henri de Chasterlard, marquis de Salières, who had a long and distinguished service record, took exception to the new protocol.[31] He continually argued with Colbert de Terron, the chief administrator of La Rochelle. Salières and his officers, being of noble extraction, resented taking orders or being subjected to regulations enforced by the new generation of civilian administrators. He considered Terron's requests for information and incessant unit inspections to be interference in his unit's administrative affairs.[32] Regardless, regimental and company commanders were now held accountable for the manner in which allotted funds were expended to outfit and supply their units.

While in La Rochelle, Terron conducted numerous inspections, uncovered a myriad of flaws in the soldiers' uniforms, listed missing equipment and challenged discrepancies in the companies' reported nominal rolls. For too many years the army had endured countless cases of corruption, misuse of funds and mismanagement. Ultimately, it was the soldier who suffered the consequences. The new reforms aimed at halting this abuse. Having no other recourse, Salières corrected all the deficiencies brought to light.[33]

The administrators in La Rochelle worked diligently to ensure that the regiment was equipped in accordance with the army supply standards and requirements for a European deployment. However, no provisions were made for possible winter operations or to increase the quantities of certain items in the event the regiment was tasked to operate at company level. This lack of foresight, if one wishes to be generous, can be attributed to the fact that those overseeing the regiment's deployment to New France were not given any information on the colony's harsh climate or geography. Quite simply, no regular military unit had ever been sent to New France. All previous regular troop deployments were to colonies with more hospitable climates. Thus, there had never been a requirement to alter the type or scale of equipment issued to French troops.[34] Unfortunately, no concerted effort was made by the Ministry of War to contact the staff at the Ministry of Colonies or any of the religious orders who operated missions in New France, or any current or previous administrators who were serving or had served there. Although existing information was limited, the reports, documents and first-hand accounts that did exist contained details that could have been used to brief and prepare the soldiers and officers of the regiment. Regrettably, the troops were forced to make do with what they were given and adapt to situations as they arose.

And so, in the spring of 1665, twenty companies of the Carignan-Salières Regiment, totalling twelve hundred men, finally sailed from La Rochelle. Among the passengers were the colony's new Governor, Daniel Rémy de Courcelle, and the Intendant, Jean Talon.[35] Concurrent with the deployment from France, a contingent of four companies drawn from the Chambellé, Lignières, Poitou and d'Orléans Regiments, totalling approximately two hundred men commanded by Alexandre de Prouville de Tracy—who had been appointed Lieutenant-General of French possessions in North America—left Guadeloupe for Quebec aboard two vessels. The previous year, Tracy had conducted a successful campaign in Cayenne and had driven the Dutch out of the West Indies.[36] The two squadrons reached Quebec between 19 June and 12 September 1665. The voyages went swiftly and the regiment's overall health was excellent, with the exception of about one hundred men or more who had travelled on the ship *La Justice* and were afflicted by various maladies. The ailing soldiers were transferred to hospitals, churches and nearby dwellings to prevent the spreading of the sickness.[37] The number of ill and the required recuperation period, as well as the staggered arrival of vessels and supply ships, which in turn upset arrangements to prevent the spread of the disease, made it impossible to mount an operation that year. This meant that co-ordinating and preparing a late summer or fall expedition against the Iroquois was a forlorn hope.

Nevertheless, Tracy and Courcelle refused to remain idle. While carrying out their initial inspections, they immediately noted that the majority of the settlers were still reluctant to confront the Iroquois. However, the assertiveness and aggressive attitude displayed by both men quickly gained the confidence of the colonists. It also set a positive example for the soldiers who became eager to begin the campaign against the Iroquois. A Jesuit chronicler witnessed the Governor's impatience and forceful frame of mind. Impressed by this new and much needed leadership trait, he wrote "he focuses on war and immediately set forth to carry out his Majesty's requests."[38]

From the outset Tracy and Courcelle gave no indication of being intimidated by the Iroquois, the terrain or the climate. Despite their age and poor health, the sixty-two-year-old Tracy was suffering from gout and Courcelle, at thirty-nine, was afflicted with a nerve disorder. Nevertheless, both men actively participated in all expeditions and operations in spite of the asperities they entailed. Their determination, coupled with Talon's efficient administrative support, were instrumental in creating the new atmosphere required to stabilize the French presence in North America while wrenching the initiative from the Iroquois.

Notwithstanding their numbers and superior weaponry, the new French force was still blissfully unaware of the combat effectiveness, not least viciousness, of the Iroquois warrior. This soon changed. Shortly after their arrival, the regiment's younger soldiers became unnerved by stories of the Iroquois' cruelty and martial prowess. This had tragic consequences. For instance, while on sentry duty, an apprehensive soldier accidently shot and wounded one of his officers who had ventured out into some bushes.[39] However, the Iroquois too were unsure of their new foe. As a result, during the fall months of 1665, an uneasy peace seemed to prevail. The Iroquois maintained their distance and observed the newly arrived and well armed troops. This temporary lull enhanced the soldiers' confidence and enabled them to adjust to their new surroundings and prepare for the upcoming campaign.

But the inactivity of the soldiers also bolstered the courage of the Iroquois. Monitoring the French deployments, the now audacious Iroquois executed a series of lighting raids and ambushes against Carignan-Salières personnel during the following spring and summer. These attacks, as well as the horrific wounds inflicted during frenzied hand-to-hand confrontations suddenly unveiled to the French soldiers the deadly efficiency of the North American way of war. Their confidence was momentarily shaken. Salières logged the following gruesome entry describing the brutal death of one of his soldiers. "People rushed to the scene," recorded the commanding officer, " to find the remains of a scalped body, two bones in one leg were shattered by a musket shot, a sword wound close to the heart, another in the shoulder and the skull had been smashed with an axe."[40] The lesson was clear. While in New France, the soldiers could never let down their guard.

There was good reason for this. Whenever the opportunity presented itself, the Iroquois struck swiftly and without warning. On 8 June 1666, two soldiers were ambushed and killed while working near a wooded area despite Salières strict orders not to venture into the forest.[41] The Iroquois' mobility, stealth, and deadly use of long-range and close-quarter weapons were attributes against which the soldiers had no established defensive tactics. The exact positions of the Iroquois raiding parties could never be confirmed and when they were, the enemy seemed to vanish into thin air. The French soldiers quickly came to believe they could never equal the Iroquois's effectiveness in this type of illusive guerilla warfare. Thus, for the moment, the only option to limit the Iroquois effectiveness was to travel in large heavily armed groups, operate in open terrain and use the waterways carefully.

Tracy realized that the key to mobility on this continent was in mastering the use of the countless waterways. He recognized that European practice of relying heavily on the use of roads and wide open terrain was impossible at that time in North America. Therefore, his first priority was to devise a method for enabling large contingents to travel quickly and safely in the vast wilderness. He studied the techniques and means used by the settlers and experimented with how these could be adapted and used by his troops. Regrettably, the number of boats in Quebec was limited. Only ten shallops, a flat bottomed vessel designed to navigate through rapids, were available. Needing to deploy large groups of soldiers as quickly as possible, Tracy immediately ordered that another twenty be built by 20 August 1665. Each shallop was designed to transport twenty soldiers and supplies, and could be carried by six soldiers during a portage. Despite the novelty of this form of travel, the Carignan-Salières personnel quickly exploited these new means of transport. One added benefit of water travel was that it negated the need to march through dense forests, thus denying the Iroquois the opportunity to ambush them.

Salières and his officers, who had no prior amphibious experience, quickly adapted to the use of waterways, and the various indigenous vessels that plied the wilderness rivers and lakes. In fact, they quickly became dependent on them to complete their engineering and operational activities. Rafts were built to float timber from cutting areas to building sites and canoes were used to maintain communications and reconnoitre Lake Champlain.[42] The soldiers quickly mastered these new skills and soon operated all sorts of vessels without assistance from friendly Indians or colonists.[43]

While these new means of transportation provided the regiment with much needed mobility, Tracy and Courcelle were still faced with the complex challenge of defending the colony. Having assessed the military situation in New France, Tracy and Courcelle agreed that the top priority was to suppress Iroquois incursions. This would be achieved by establishing and maintaining a strong military presence in the Richelieu Valley. Historically, this area had been the Iroquois' main invasion route, providing them with a direct and unchallenged access to the French colony.[44] But troops were still needed to guard the various settlements. Therefore, in order to carry out these two vital concurrent activities, Tracy decided to divide the Carignan-Salières Regiment into a series of smaller, more mobile combat forces. Some companies were ordered to defend towns and settlements while others were tasked to build and occupy three forts on the Richelieu River. Tracy's logical and innovative plan to multi-task the regiment upset Salières. Being from the old school, the regiment's Commanding Officer adamantly protested the fragmentation of his unit. By doing this, Salières would no longer be considered as the unit's central command figure and he himself would be deployed with a smaller force. A disgruntled Salières wrote in his diary, "that this was not the manner to employ a regiment."[45] Tracy's and Courcelle's unconventional approach infuriated Salières and led to a series of endless arguments during the regiment's stay in North America. But undeniably, company level operations enabled younger company commanders to assert themselves in an active leadership role, allowed them more liberty and initiative, accelerated in-theatre decisions and instilled a sense of urgency in the rank and file to acclimatize themselves quickly to their new surroundings. Even though Salières and Tracy argued incessantly about the deployment of troops, Tracy's manner of conferring responsibilities was nevertheless well received by Salières' subordinates.[46] Significantly, there was another positive result from the splintering of such a large force. The Iroquois were now pressured into splitting their own forces to scout out the troop dispositions and monitor their activities.[47]

But Tracy's reforms went even deeper. He dispensed with the old ineffective command structure predicated on pedigree, rank, and years of service. His latest operational experience in Cayenne, and the challenges of this new deployment, required that he surround himself with competent officers who possessed stamina and displayed initiative as well as aggressive and

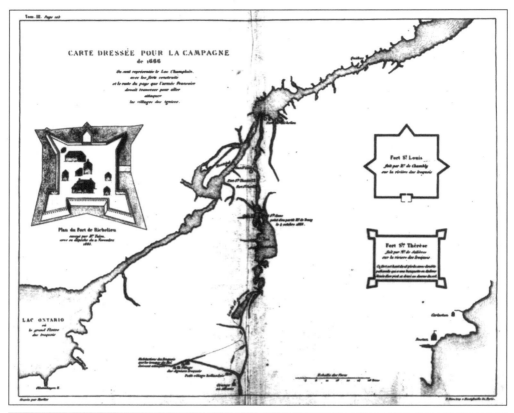

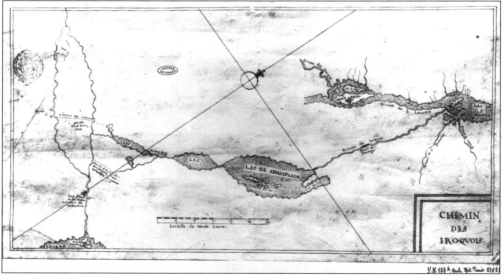

Top: Outline of the three forts built by Carignan-Salières personnel in the fall of 1665, and the location of Fort Sainte-Anne built in the summer of 1666. (National Archives of Canada [NA], NMC 6384)

Bottom: Early French map showing the location of the Iroquois villages and routes used by their raiding parties to attack habitants in New France. (NA, C-16146)

innovative leadership. Much to Salières's displeasure, Tracy even went so far as to state that if he so decided he would appoint a lieutenant to command captains.[48] Tracy's ideas had merit. However, Salières also correctly recorded that in many instances the high command's hasty planning and preparations were detrimental to his soldiers' well-being. It became evident to Salières that he and his men were seen as expendable. What ultimately mattered was the mission's success. Nevertheless, Salières—being a professional soldier—began in earnest to oversee the preparations of his soldiers for their upcoming deployment to the Richelieu Valley.

And so, on 23 July 1665, only six weeks after the arrival of the first troops from France, Tracy ordered Captain Jacques de Chambly and four companies to take up positions about sixty kilometres up the Richelieu River, with one hundred local settlers and Indians, a fur trader and two Jesuit missionaries. Chambly began in earnest to build Fort Saint-Louis near the Richelieu Rapids. About a month later, on 25 August, Captain Pierre de Saurel and his company were tasked to rebuild Fort Richelieu, originally built by Huault de Montmagny in 1642, located at the mouth of the Richelieu River.[49] A week later, Salières was dispatched to build Fort Saint-Thérèse at the entrance of Lake Champlain. It would be the most advanced structure and was located approximately twelve kilometres from Fort Saint-Louis.[50]

Building these fortifications presented a new challenge to the Carignan-Salières officers and men. They had little or no engineering or construction experience. However, Saurel did have one advantage over his colleagues, in the fact that he could study the layout of the ruins of the previous fort which had been built twenty-three years earlier. This provided him with a template for the positioning of buildings and palisades. Salières commenced work on Fort Sainte-Thérèse on 2 October. The major portion of the structure was completed approximately two weeks later. The grim necessity of building shelters for the upcoming winter and protection against marauding Iroquois ensured that the troops were motivated to work quickly. However, the inclement fall weather, the lack of warm clothing and footwear, proper tools and cooking utensils complicated an already daunting task. It quickly became evident that certain vital items had not been supplied in sufficient quantities. A bitter Salières had predicted this and angrily recounted "a few unsatisfactory tools ... three hundred men of which a large number were ill due to the flu caused by the heavy rains, the cold, poor clothing and bare feet. Furthermore, they did not have cooking pots to cook their lard and prepare their soup."[51] Nevertheless, strong leadership and the willingness of the soldiers to endure these hardships were instrumental in the completion of these three important forts.

Once completed, they served a dual function. First, their strategic locations denied the Iroquois easy access into New France and the use of the Richelieu River. By manning these positions, the French forced the enemy to seek alternate land routes and waterways, thus extending the time and distance required to conduct raids. The building of these forts provided the French colony with a much needed first line of defence. But equally, these structures provided the French forces with secure advanced assembly points and supply depots. This would reduce considerably the distance they would have to travel to conduct offensive operations.

The presence of the Carignan-Salières personnel in the Richelieu Valley had an immediate settling effect on the Algonquin allies. Marie de L'Incarnation reported that "our Christian Algonquins and their families set up camp in the vicinity of the forts and the soldiers who manned them."[52] The Algonquins were reclaiming the lands they had been forced to abandon because of incessant Iroquois attacks. Their arrival and subsequent settlement in the vicinity of the forts also enhanced the morale of the troops. They no longer felt so isolated. In addition, the renewed hunting and fur trading activities of the friendly natives were welcomed by the garrison commanders. Both groups benefitted greatly from each others' presence and activities. More importantly, the soldiers and the Algonquins helped each other. One letter revealed "the French and the Savages helped each other: The French protect the Savages, and the Savages in return supply the French with the meat of the animals they killed, after having removed the fur which they bring to the colony's stores."[53] Off-duty soldiers spent much time with their new neighbours learning how to survive and prosper in the wilderness. There was also an economic windfall. With the Algonquins now providing the troops with fresh meat and fish, the colony's feeding and lodging costs were greatly reduced.

Despite the occupation of these forts and the resultant strengthening of the French position in the Richelieu Valley, many settlers had hoped for more aggressive action. Even though there was a marked increase in military activity and troop deployment in the Richelieu Valley, the local population wanted immediate offensive action against the Iroquois. Many were concerned that the Iroquois would bypass the French troops, rendering the forts useless. Dollier de Casson, a member of the Saint-Sulpice Order based in Montreal, also questioned the high command's decision of dispatching so many Carignan-Salières companies to carry out garrison duties in his town and other major locations. He agreed that this strategy had proven useful in the old country but argued it was inefficient in New France. He would much rather see them patrol the countryside to counter raids and protect the settlers. Casson observed that "they were brave and good soldiers and noteworthy officers, however, their European defensive doctrine, was useless in this country. They still lacked the necessary experience [with regards to North American warfare]. In the meantime, the enemy was still killing our people."[54]

Casson's observations were valid. However, he failed to realize that while the troops in Montreal and elsewhere were conducting defensive garrison duties, the other companies posted in the Richelieu Valley now constituted the first line of defence between the scattered civilian population and the Iroquois. In the event that some raiding parties did slip through, the Iroquois warriors now had to contend with a second line of defence, composed of other companies on garrison duty in Quebec, Montreal, Trois-Rivières and other locations. For the moment, they could no longer attack isolated and defenceless inhabitants at will. They also had to be wary of these well armed company sized units that moved about with confidence. The positioning of the French troops and their superior firepower forced the Iroquois to temporarily revise their offensive plans. However, the warriors quickly observed that the French forces did not venture too far from their forts. Thus, for the moment it was evident that the soldiers did not pose a threat. Furthermore, with the arrival of the fall season came heavy rains, colder weather and less daylight. Taking into account these climactic changes and the distant location of their villages, the Iroquois concluded that an imminent French attack was highly unlikely. For the meantime, the wise Iroquois warriors preferred to enjoy the comfort and warmth of their longhouses, stocking their food reserves and hunting before the arrival of the first snow.

But, as both the Iroquois and French troops were preparing for a long and cold winter, Tracy continued to increase his knowledge of Iroquois tactics. Algonquin and Huron chiefs provided Tracy with additional insights. The first concerned the Iroquois' personal dress. A Jesuit priest, attending these discussions wrote, "He was alluding to the warriors' preparations for upcoming attacks, and the custom of applying various colors on their body, especially black: thus like an army of demons they launched their attack with terrible shrieks and horrifying screams."[55]

From a pragmatic point of view, the use of black paint, for whatever motive, enabled the warriors to blend in with the shadows cast by towering trees and dense brushes. They could move about undetected and close in on unsuspecting victims. The second point explained the Iroquois' use of sudden high pitched screams at the outset of their attacks. This caused a momentary surprise, bewildered the settlers and provided the warriors with a few vital extra seconds to pounce on their confused victims.

During the course of their deliberations, the Indian chiefs also informed Tracy that the uniforms of the soldiers of the Carignan-Salières, as well as their personal equipment would be detrimental to the soldiers' movements during operations in the forests. They explained to Tracy that whenever possible the Iroquois preferred travelling and fighting in or near densely wooded areas. The members of the raiding parties struck without warning and fell back quickly. What enhanced their lighting speed during attacks and withdrawals was their ability to run through heavily wooded areas and underbrush. The Jesuit priest described in great detail the Iroquois tactics:

> The enemy put half of his courage in running skillfully: he fights usually in the nude, armed only with a musket in hand and an axe attached to his belt. This is done to expedite his ability to pursue a retreating enemy, or to enable him to withdraw swiftly. You may have defeated him, but you will not have captured him; especially taking into account the way you are clothed. This will hamper and impede your pursuit through the brush and the undergrowth. Here is a belt that will enable you to tie down your bulky clothing. Also, this belt and the advantage of being dressed will enhance your movements while pursuing the enemy through the woods.[56]

The chiefs presented Tracy with a belt to tie down the soldiers' equipment; thus, they believed, enhancing the mobility of troops in wooded areas. However, for unknown reasons, the French soldiers did not alter their summer dress or the manner in which they wore their personal equipment or carried supplies during their forced marches to their objectives.

Despite the continuing study of their Iroquois enemy, a perception of success was evident. Following an inspection of the new forts during a period absent of any Iroquois raids, Governor de Courcelle ordered the creation of a road between Fort Sainte-Thérèse and Fort Saint-Louis. In addition, soldiers were directed to clear another road from Fort Saint-Louis to Montreal. Since Iroquois raiding was nearly non-existent, it was deemed an opportune occasion to further expand military control and communications among the forts and major towns. These roads were essentially wide cleared paths that enabled the movement of large groups as well as the possibility of using carts pulled by oxen. If attacked, these oversized paths permitted soldiers to deploy and carry out their musket drills that could not otherwise be conducted in a wooded area. It also made navigation easier and increased the speed with which a force could deploy from one fort to another. The roads also provided flexibility to the French, as they were not constrained by river conditions or the availability of watercraft.

Nonetheless, this back-breaking work caused great hardship to the already exhausted troops. In his diary entry of 26 October, Salières recorded that he had argued vehemently against this project conducted under terrible working conditions. "The Governor ordered me to oversee a work detail of thirty six men and six officers or sergeants, " he wrote, "to clear a path from Fort St Louys to Montreal through woods and a swamp, despite the fact that many of the men were ill. I pointed out that it would be easier to clear this path during winter while the swamp was frozen, rather than now when the men would be up to their waist in water. Regardless, he insisted that they carry out this task."[57]

Courcelle's obstinance prevailed. In the end, it allowed the French troops to deploy to their various locations either by land or by water. In less than four and a half months the soldiers of the Carignan-Salières Regiment had accomplished a series of incredible feats, in a difficult terrain and hostile environment, without proper equipment and support. Their hard work and initiative also provided a much needed relief from the tedium of garrison duty and created additional confidence in themselves. This in turn enhanced the level of confidence of the allied Indians and settlers who were now more willing to join the soldiers in the upcoming expeditions against the despised Iroquois.

However, the French hoped to avoid further conflict. Lieutenant-General Tracy during the past months had exhausted all possible diplomatic venues attempting to negotiate a peace treaty with all the tribes of the Iroquois Confederacy. Frustrated and unaccustomed to dealing with aboriginal ambassadors, Tracy authorized Governor Courcelle to prepare a punitive expedition. Witnessing the rigours of the winter climate, Courcelle was convinced that a well co-ordinated rapid winter attack coupled with the destruction of the enemy's villages and provisions would have a devastating effect on the Iroquois nation.[58] Initially, many factors led him to believe that such an enterprise was possible. First, the colony's storehouses were full of provisions after a good harvest.[59] Second, enthusiastic volunteers dressed and equipped to travel and operate in winter were eager to participate. Third, travel could be accelerated because all the waterways were frozen, thus dispensing with long and difficult portages. Fourth, several Algonquin Indians were ready to act as guides and provide his troops with fresh meat. And finally, the Iroquois rarely fought during the winter, giving the French the initiative as well as surprise. Regrettably, Courcelle's impatience damaged the expedition's preparations. In addition, his lack of winter campaign experience, the inability or failure to properly outfit his troops for winter, as well as neglecting to confirm the exact locations of the enemy's villages, all ultimately contributed to the campaign's failure.

Nonetheless, the effort was formidable. A force totalling five hundred men—three hundred soldiers from various companies of the Carignan-Salières Regiment and two hundred colonial volunteers—left from various points during the second week of January 1666 and assembled at Fort Saint-Louis. These initial deployments already severely tested the poorly equipped and clothed regular soldiers. Some were in such poor health by the time they arrived at the fort that they had to be replaced by men from the garrison. The *Jesuit Relations* paints a grim portrait of the voyages to the fort: "Despite being hindered by snowshoes which constitute a dreadful impediment as well as the heavy loads that everyone was forced to carry, we had to travel three hundred *lieues* through the snow, cross over the icy surfaces of lakes and rivers, risking to fall with very step; sleeping on the snow, in the middle of forests and suffering from the intense cold which surpassed many times that of our most rigorous European winters."[60]

Upon his arrival at the fort, a discouraged Salières described the poor state of his men. "When I wanted to confirm and evaluate the state of readiness of our soldiers for this venture," he wrote, "I noted the poor preparation. Soldiers did not have snowshoes, very few axes, one blanket per three men, no cleats, only one pair of Indian shoes and one pair of leggings, when in fact they should have had three to four pairs of each."[61] François de Tapie de Monteil, a captain with the Régiment de Poitou who participated in this campaign, is representative of the poor state of affairs, specifically in regard to the distribution of supplies and clothing by Intendant Talon for the use of his company. Monteil was allotted a paltry total of two *capots* (hooded coats) and fifteen *pelliques* (fur coats). It is possible that the other companies garrisoned in the towns were issued with a similar small number of coats. It seems that these were allocated to units rather than to individual soldiers. This enabled selected personnel to dress warmly during sentry duties or patrols. Some of these items may have been loaned by company commanders to officers or non-commissioned officers who had been selected to participate in this winter expedition.[62]

Salières also mentioned the lack of proper winter clothing to Father Raffeix, a Jesuit priest, who accompanied the force. Raffeix and others confided to Salières that a merchant had been willing to rent fifty pairs of snow shoes, but Courcelle found the fee too extravagant. Yet, each soldier and officer was ordered to carry a heavy load of provisions including "between 25 to 30 pounds of biscuits, blankets and other required provisions."[63] More importantly, the Algonquin guides had not yet arrived and no one had seen them. Courcelle was growing increasingly impatient while his soldiers waited in their makeshift shelters in the fort and surrounding areas. He was also concerned that this period of inactivity, coupled with the bitter cold, could cause difficulties in motivating his men to move out of the staging areas.

As a result, Courcelle decided that he would leave without the guides, hoping they would eventually join him. Not surprisingly, within the next few days many soldiers suffered serious cases of frost bite. Others suffered cuts and abrasions resulting from multiple falls on the river's icy surface, once again because of the lack of adequate footwear, namely cleats.[64] Certain officers nevertheless favoured walking on the treacherous ice rather than having to forge through deep snow.

While the soldiers of the Carignan-Salières suffered terribly, the Canadian volunteers faired well. Governor Courcelle was impressed by their resiliency and fervour and he used his Canadians wisely. Their superior winter clothing and footwear and their use of snowshoes enabled them to travel quickly and with little effort while seeming impervious to the cold. Courcelle ordered them to take the lead, "during the advance they took the lead and upon our return they acted as the rearguard force. Not many could have been entrusted with such honorable responsibilities during these perilous deployments in forests of which our troops had little knowledge of ... he called them his *Capots bleus* ... the Governor had noted and remarked that the people of this area were always the first to answer the call and always ready to march."[65] During the march the volunteers acted as an advance guard. They also prepared trails by packing down the snow with their snowshoes. This helped to a certain extent the main body's advance. Nonetheless, the cold and tired Carignan-Salières soldiers still moved with a considerable slowness. Within a few hours of their departure, wet footwear and clothing further added to their misery. At night the soldiers built makeshift shelters using branches and blankets. In small groups, they huddled close to camp fires which were used to dry their footwear, warm up tired limbs and prepare their meagre meals of sagamite, a type of pasty broth made of water and corn flour supplemented with biscuits.[66]

On 20 February 1666, after a nightmarish twenty-day trek, the dispirited French force reached the outskirts of the Anglo-Dutch colony of Schenectady. Thinking they had finally reached the Iroquois village, Courcelle and Tracy gave the order to attack. Upon hearing the shouts and musket fire, a nearby group of Mohawks who were trading with the Dutch settlers deployed and counterattacked. In a short skirmish the French incurred losses of one officer, five soldiers and one volunteer killed, with a further three officers and one volunteer wounded. Despite having to manoeuvre in deep snow, the French soldiers' volley fire accounted for four Mohawks killed and six wounded. During this confrontation, the enemy's efficient use of snowshoes enabled them to glide over the snow, altering their position while the French soldiers stumbled and floundered in the deep snow. A French officer impressed with the mobility of the Mohawks recounted his observations to Salières, who later recorded, "the English, and even the Iroquois were astonished. They could not comprehend why they [the French Forces] would even dare to set out on such a voyage."[67] When the action subsided, a confused and embarrassed Courcelle met with the head of the Dutch colony, bought provisions and retreated the next day under the cover of night.

Using the same route to speed his return, Courcelle ordered the volunteers to carry out the duties of a rear guard. Their warrior spirit dampened, the exhausted soldiers marched in pairs, in column formation, through three and a half feet of snow. Another blow to the soldiers' morale was the disheartening discovery that the previously prepared food caches had been looted. Luckily, a group of Algonquins met up with the French force. Courcelle ordered them to hunt and supply his troops with fresh meat. These fresh rations supplemented the soldiers' remaining supplies. The warriors also taught the soldiers some much needed winter survival techniques that made the trip more bearable.[68] The trip lasted approximately two weeks, during which long periods of rain further tested the endurance of the soldiers. The small force returned to Fort Saint-Louis on 8 March 1666. Tactically, the operation was a total failure. The expedition's objective had not been accomplished and the French had sustained heavy losses, not from the action of the Iroquois but from the effects of the cold.[69]

Nevertheless, this ill-fated winter expedition, the first of its kind, had a rippling effect throughout North America. Unknowingly, Courcelle's initiative had opened up a new operational dimension. The soldiers of the Carignan-Salières Regiment and auxiliary colonial troops had demonstrated that a large body of men could in fact operate, survive and travel in adverse winter conditions. Suddenly, the traditional protection provided by the cold weather, snow, rough terrain and geographical isolation no longer ensured one's security. Organized warfare in North America could now be conducted in all four seasons. Courcelle's winter expedition had caught both the Iroquois and the English off guard. Marie de L'Incarnation captured their reactions: "at the great astonishment of both the English and the Iroquois, they could not understand how they [the French] even dared to plan such a voyage."[70] Later, the Governor of Albany voiced his concerns to Tracy regarding such operations: "it was in some measure of surprise in February last, with the news of so considerable a force so far advanced into these his majesties Dominions without my knowledge, and consent or at least notice given of your intentions."[71]

Even though this incursion into enemy territory forced the English to re-evaluate their plans for winter military operations, French colonial officials did not look upon such future expeditions favourably. Intendant Jean Talon, responsible for the colony's budget, tallied the expenses incurred by the French troops. The costs were high and the anticipated return, the destruction of the Mohawk villages, had not been attained. It had been eight months since the first soldier of the Carignan-Salières Regiment had landed in New France and the Iroquois threat had still not been resolved. Time was now of the essence. Intendant Jean Talon met other officials and prepared a study enumerating the positive and negative factors affecting military operations in each of the four seasons. His goal was to identify the most economical time frame in which Courcelle could launch his next expedition.

NEW HORIZONS, NEW CHALLENGES

The Intendant's detailed and well-thought-out observations were submitted to Tracy and Courcelle for their consideration. The winter campaign had proven too costly, and so physically demanding that it had rendered troops inefficient. A spring campaign was also discouraged because the colony's food supplies would be low after the long and harsh winter. Furthermore, water levels would be very high, causing swift currents that complicated the maneuvring of canoes and boats and the building of suspended bridges. Following the spring thaw, wooded areas became soggy and marshy, hampering the soldiers' rate of advance. In late spring and summer, the heat and the plague of black flies and mosquitoes could also incapacitate soldiers. Talon explained, "mosquitos bites caused such great swelling, that they sometimes rendered soldiers ineffective for combat."[72] He concluded that the best time to prepare and conduct an expedition was during the fall following the harvest. The weather was ideal, food was plentiful and auxiliary troops could be raised, because the harvest and concurrent farm activities were completed. All agreed with Talon's recommendations. And so preparations for a fall deployment were begun.

However, in the interim peace overtures were once again made. The people who were posted in the Richelieu Valley had adapted very well to their new surroundings and with the assistance of friendly Indians had learned to become self-sufficient. Soldiers also used their spare time to clear parcels of land, sow crops, fish and hunt. They grew attached to their new homesteads and enjoyed this invigorating life.[73] However, the temporary tranquility was shattered by a series of sudden, as well as extremely bold, Iroquois attacks on Carignan-Salières personnel. Between March and July 1666, a total of seven soldiers were killed near Montreal and during the construction of the new Fort Saint-Anne, in the Richelieu Valley.[74]

This renewed raiding took place as Tracy was negotiating conditions for a peace treaty with Mohawk and Onondaga chiefs. Frustrated by the fruitless, never-ending discussions and apparent stalling, Tracy ordered the troops to prepare for an operation deep into Iroquois territory. He dispatched orders during the summer of 1666 to the commanding officers of all three forts informing them of the upcoming operation. The garrisons were placed on a state of high alert. Reconnaissance patrols journeyed along the shores of the Richelieu River and monitored Iroquois movements. Provisions arrived and were stockpiled.

Tracy authorized Courcelle to proceed with a punitive expedition against the Mohawk villages. A 1300-man invasion force was raised, composed of 600 soldiers from the Carignan-Salières Regiment, 600 volunteers and 100 Hurons and Algonquins.[75] In an attempt to intimidate the enemy, Tracy formed up his forces and showed them to Bâtard Flammand, a captured Mohawk chief. While they marched, Tracy pointed to his troops and stated, "Now we are going to your land, what do you have to say for yourself now? Tears streamed down his [Bâtard Flamand's] cheeks as he observed these well drilled troops."[76] The news of this expedition spread throughout the colony like wildfire while final preparations were being made simultaneously in Quebec and the Richelieu Valley.

Additional work was done to strengthen the forts in anticipation of possible Mohawk counterattacks. A series of redoubts was also built between these forts in case retreating soldiers needed protection or were required to conduct delaying actions. Brush and trees were cut down to improve troop movements between these new redoubts. As the final phases of engineering were completed throughout the Richelieu Valley, contingents of soldiers arrived in late September 1666 at Fort Sainte-Anne, which was the newest and farthest French fort on the river.

Courcelle immediately gathered the first groups and formed them into the expedition's advance party. Refusing to wait for the remaining groups, he left the fort toward the end of

September. Tracy arrived shortly after, organized the main body and left a few days later. De Chambly and Berthier, two officers of the Carignan-Salières Regiment, were ordered to wait for the last contingents. These troops were to act as the expedition's rear guard. They left Fort Saint-Anne four days after the departure of Tracy's main body.

This staggered order of march actually assisted the advance of such a large invasion force into uncharted enemy territory. Smaller groups were easier to control and manage when traversing dense wooded areas. This type of advance also complicated the enemy's reconnaissance operations and delaying tactics. First, the Mohawks experienced difficulties in gauging accurately the invaders' numbers, locations and intent. Second, attacking such a large body of well armed men could trigger counter-attacks resulting in being outflanked, surrounded and captured. Third, the Mohawks had never encountered a regular unit and were unwilling to expose themselves to its superior firepower. Strategically, however, Courcelle and Tracy knew that such a deployment negated all possibility of surprise. To compensate, they opted to use speed, hoping to reach the objective as quickly as possible. Regardless of the rough terrain, Courcelle maintained a gruelling tempo. This kept the troops alert and hopeful of a swift outcome.

Regardless of the planning, preparations, and high morale of the troops, the North American wilderness always tested the stamina of soldiers. In addition to carrying their regular combat loads and equipment, the French infantrymen transported more than three hundred light boats and canoes, as well as two small cannon to be used against the Mohawks' defensive structures and villages. Each canoe could transport up to six soldiers and their equipment.[77] Nonetheless, this time morale and stamina were excellent throughout the expedition. Marie de L'Incarnation reported, "our French soldiers are so zealous that they fear nothing, and there is nothing they would not do or carry out. They took it upon themselves to carry artillery pieces on their backs over falls and through difficult portages: They even carried boats which in itself was an incredible feat."[78]

Furthermore, the energy displayed by the young Canadian volunteers was impressive to many. "Our young French-Canadians," noted Sister L'Incarnation, "who are very vigorous, sprint like the Savages through the woodlands."[79] The coming generation of Canadian volunteer troops was acquiring much needed experience. As the French force approached its objective, the weather suddenly took a turn for the worse. The temperature dropped while cold rain raised the level of the marshes and swamps. Certain wooded areas were so thick with trees and exposed roots that the soldiers were forced to advance in a single column. Rations were running low but luckily the soldiers were able to live off large quantities of nuts.[80] After enduring many days of hardship and tedious marching the soldiers finally received their first taste of action.

Mohawk reconnaissance parties skirmished with Courcelle's advance group. Their heavy firepower forced the Mohawk warriors to retreat. Since the enemy had confirmed their location, time was now of the essence. Tracy ordered a forced night march, hoping their accelerated advance would disrupt the enemy's efforts to improve their defences. The French force reached the outskirts of the first Mohawk village on 5 October 1666. The soldiers were formed up at the edge of the woods, and upon a given signal marched at a slow pace in a simple but effective frontal advance. A Jesuit priest described the initial advance, "Our troops advanced, beating their drums, wanting to charge head on without resorting to trickery or shrewdness."[81] Approaching the village the French soldiers were both surprised and impressed by the Mohawks' intricate palisade fortification. Marie de L'Incarnation provides a detailed description: "Their village was surrounded by three twenty-foot-high palisades and four bastions, with incredible food supplies and large bark water containers designed to extinguish fires."[82] Despite these defensive structures the enemy seemed unsure of how to react to the tactics of the French.

Prior to the French advance, nervous scouts informed the chiefs of the size of the French force. Marie de L'Incarnation recounted that Mohawk prisoners had been intimidated by the vast numbers of French soldiers and allied forces. The order was given to abandon their villages without a fight. She wrote, "let us flee, everyone is against us ... they spread terror in the enemy's minds, thus seizing victory without having to fight."[83] This great show of force enabled the French troops to overrun their objectives without sustaining casualties. Furthermore, the invaders' unhindered advance had been helped by the loud and unnerving rattle of their war drums. The uninterrupted beat of the marching cadence caused panic in the enemy camp. Sister L'Incarnation described its effects on the defenders. "They found an old man hidden under a canoe, " she recorded, "he hid there when he heard the drum rolls, thinking that they were Demons. That is how they referred to our drums. They knew that the French did not want to lose, and they used their Demons to terrify and pursue the fleeing enemy."[84] Confused, the Mohawks elected to withdraw deeper into the safety of the neighbouring wooded hills.

Occasional volleys were exchanged, but the distance between the combatants rendered them ineffective. Having overrun the first village, the French force employed the same tactic and entered three other villages unopposed. Tracy then proceeded to raise a cross bearing the Royal Coat of Arms. Following a short ceremony, he proclaimed that this land was now part of the French King's colonial possessions. Soldiers were then authorized to replenish their food stocks by looting each village. During the pillaging an officer observed that the Mohawks had stockpiled enough provisions to feed the entire French colony for two full years.[85] Disappointed by the enemy's unwillingness to fight, the soldiers proceeded to vent their frustrations by systematically setting fire to all the shelters, fortifications and food supplies. Even though the Mohawks had not sustained casualties, they now had to contend with the grim reality of facing the hardships of a fast approaching winter without their homes and provisions.[86] Once again, the expedition failed to achieve its stated goal, namely inflicting heavy casualties on the enemy. But the plundering and destruction of the villages was a great morale booster for the French soldiers and volunteers and catastrophic to the Mohawks.

Having accomplished what he could, Courcelle assembled his men and ordered them to return to the safety of the Richelieu Valley. The travelling conditions during the regiment's return trip were miserable. Heavy rains made marching even more arduous, while high winds created problems on the rivers. High waves caused two canoes to tip and drowned eight soldiers.[87] Notwithstanding the difficulties, after fifty-three days in the field the triumphant French troops received a hero's welcome upon their arrival at Quebec on 5 November 1666.[88] The menace of the Iroquois Confederacy had been momentarily stymied. This provided the small French colony with the time to attract new settlers and tradesmen, develop small industries, become self-sufficient, explore and settle new lands. More importantly, it augmented the confidence of the French settlers to resist future Iroquois predations. Talon, pleased with the last expedition's outcome and the influx of new immigrants, felt confident that the Iroquois Confederacy had been intimidated and could be dealt with efficiently in the future.[89]

Notwithstanding the problems encountered in adapting to their new operational theatre, the Carignan-Salières Regiment had accomplished a large part of its mission. Although the Iroquois nation had not been annihilated, the soldiers had stabilized and bolstered the colony's military position and curtailed the Iroquois raids. In the end it was the regiment's formidable

The allied Indians were quick to point out that the uniforms and equipment of the French soldiers would hamper their mobility against the Iroquois warriors in dense brush or wooded areas. (Courtesy of Parks Canada. Reconstitution by Francis Back.)

size that was its greatest asset. The Iroquois had never before seen so many uniformed and heavily armed soldiers. Intimidation played a large role in the regiment's success.

Moreover, during a meeting with an Indian chief, Tracy realized that the use of noise was an effective way to instill fear. The Indian chief revealed that "when you are in enemy territory, load your muskets well, thus, when you will fire a volley, the noise will be such that you will frighten these Barbarians."[90] As a result, Tracy used noise and firepower on many occasions. In a show of force, he ordered Salières to greet with musket fire the arrival in Montreal of a large Iroquois delegation. Five companies were lined up and in unison fired a thunderous volley. As the smoke cleared, a booming cannon was fired for additional effect.[91] The Iroquois chiefs were bewildered. They had never before encountered such a large contingent of troops, nor such an impressive display of firepower.

Another unusual stratagem employed by the French was forced night marches.[92] During the 1666 fall expedition, Tracy marched his troops all night under the cover of heavy rains, high winds and thunderstorms to reach the Mohawk villages.[93] A few factors may have contributed to enforcing this method of travel. Inclement weather and the lack of proper bivouacking equipment may have encouraged Courcelle to use this as a alternate means of keeping his men warm and under control, while maintaining an accelerated rate of advance. Whatever the motive, this tactic caught the Mohawks off guard. In general, Indians rarely travelled or fought at night. Superstition may have been a factor. But possessing excellent survival skills, they knew how to build shelters and preferred to enjoy a good night's rest and start fresh the next day. These night marches also proved that even if French troops travelled in enemy territory they could feel safe in great numbers and thus dispense with stealth, camouflage and the element of surprise. Regardless of the type of mission given to the regiment, this unit had shown the Iroquois that the Confederacy was now vulnerable to attack. The balance of power had shifted.

It was now time to recompense the infantrymen who wanted to remain and allow those who wished to return to France to do so. Of the1,200 members of the Carignan-Salières Regiment who landed in 1665, 446 settled in New France and 200 returned with Salières to their homeland. Of the four companies of 200 men that had arrived with Tracy, one in eight chose to return to France. Losses through accidents, drowning, illness, enemy action and the dreaded winter campaign, although difficult to confirm, totalled somewhere between 500 and 600 men. Those who chose to remain and settle in New France were greeted with open arms. Intendant Jean Talon stated that the presence of these new citizen-soldiers would bolster the colony's ability to fend off future Iroquois raids. He wrote, "integrate the soldiers and the settlers so that they may teach each other how to farm and help defend themselves in times of need."[94] Even though the Intendant relied heavily on the soldiers' military background for possible future operations, their contribution as an organized force would be limited. The soldiers settled in widespread locations. Furthermore, a great percentage of their flintlock and matchlock muskets were returned to France. Their success had been made possible by their numbers and their firepower. This would no longer be the case. Enjoying their new lives as landowners, merchants, tradesmen or coureurs de bois, the ex-members of the Carignan-Salières Regiment had no inclination to leave their wives, families and estates to once again chase the illusive Iroquois.

Overcoming countless challenges, displaying great stamina, resiliency, versatility and an adventurous spirit, the soldiers of the Carignan-Salières Regiment left behind a proud military legacy. Even though they failed to subjugate the fearless Iroquois nation, they demonstrated that a large organized force could operate and be deployed in all four seasons in the rugged North American wilderness. They were the first to successfully counter the vaunted warriors of the Iroquois Confederacy. In doing so they operated as a large force deep within enemy territory and ultimately destroyed the enemy villages. Furthermore, the mobility displayed during the course of the winter and fall expeditions of 1666 sent a clear message to the neighboring Dutch and English colonies. Distance and the wilderness would no longer guarantee their security.

The soldiers of the Carignan-Salières successfully combined many aspects of French military doctrine while incorporating new procedures, techniques and equipment to increase their operational capabilities in the vast North American continent. It was evident, however, that a new doctrine was required for operations in New France. This challenging task would be undertaken and perfected by the Canadians themselves. They would combine the use of European weaponry with the mobility and tactics of *la petite guerre*, which they learned from their Indian friends as well as enemies. They had little choice. The fragile peace between the French and the Iroquois Confederacy, which had been achieved at great cost, quickly began to disintegrate. The defence of New France would once again fall largely on Canadian shoulders.

Notes for Chapter 1

1   The following year, on 19 June 1610, Champlain led another successful expedition. He expelled an Iroquois raiding party from the Richelieu Valley. Four years later, in October 1615, he confronted a well barricaded Iroquois war party on the east side of Lake Onondaga. After a few days Champlain ended his unsuccessful siege and returned to Quebec. Marcel Trudel, "Samuel de Champlain," in *Dictionary of Canadian Biography* (DCB), General ed. George Brown (Toronto: University of Toronto Press, 1966), Vol 1, 186-199.

2   The Iroquois' motives for the destruction of Huronia were fuelled by the despised French-Huron economic and military alliance. More importantly they wanted to monopolize the fur-trade. In order to do so, the Hurons had to be annihilated. Between 1648 and 1650 a series of deadly raids were conducted against the following Hurons villages: 1648, Village of Saint-Joseph (Teanaostaiaë—700 killed); Spring 1649, Village of Saint-Ignace (Taenhatentaron—400 killed); Autumn 1649, Village of Saint-Jean-Baptiste (Cahaigué—500 families killed). These as well as other

smaller raids eliminated the Hurons. The Iroquois then hunted freely throughout this vast territory and sold their pelts to the highest bidder. Furthermore, they could then focus all their military efforts and resources on the systematic destruction of the French settlements. Marcel Trudel, "New France, 1524-1713," in *DCB*, Vol 1, 31; René Chartrand, *Canadian Military Heritage, Volume 1, 1000-1754* (Montreal: Art Global Inc., 1993), 55-56.

3   W.J. Eccles, *Canada Under Louis XIV* (Toronto: McCelland & Stewart, 1964), 4.

4   Ibid., 46.

5   Adam Dollard Des Ormeaux, garrison commander of Fort Ville-Marie, set out on 20 April 1660 with his small force composed of sixteen Frenchmen to meet and escort a large fur convoy arriving from the northeast. He reached the foot of the Long Sault on 1 May 1660, where he was joined by forty Algonquins and four Hurons. The group settled in a small abandoned Algonquin fort that had been built the previous year. The following day, Des Ormeaux's position was discovered by a group of Iroquois scouts. They returned shortly after with the main force totalling approximately 300 warriors. During the next seven days this force, reinforced by an additional 500 Mohawks and Oneidas, launched four assaults. Between these attacks, the Iroquois kept the Frenchmen and their Indian allies pinned down with accurate heavy musket fire. In the final hours of the seven day siege, a desperate Des Ormeaux set fire to a powder keg and threw it in the direction of a group of Iroquois who had breached the palisade and entered the perimeter. The keg hit a part of the palisade, bounced back into the fort and fell to the ground. The keg detonated amongst the remaining defenders. Only five Frenchmen and four Hurons survived the explosion. They were taken prisoner and tortured by their captors during the course of the following days. This was the first time that the Iroquois warriors had encountered such fierce French resistance. André Vachon, "Adam Dollard Des Ormeaux," in *DCB*, Vol 1, 266-275; Chartrand, 59-60.

6   Pierre Boucher, *Histoire veritable et naturelle des moeurs et productions de la Nouvelle-France vulgairement dite le Canada* (Paris: Florentin Lambert, 1664), National Library of Canada, Rare Books Collection.

7   Ibid., 150, 152. (My translation, ed.)

8   Boucher further elaborated the various categories of terrain and waterways that hindered travel. The forests were dense; the rapids, waterfalls and turbulent shallow waters were treacherous and forced the use of canoes and *bateaux plates* and portages. The most dreaded season was the bitterly cold and long winter. To travel and operate in this cold climate for extended periods it was necessary to wear extra clothing and special items of dress such as *moufles* (heavy duty gloves). Thankfully, wood was plentiful for fuel and transportation was helped by using oxen to pull sleighs. Conversely, summers were very warm and swarms of mosquitoes and certain types of snakes made life unbearable in wooded areas.

9   Ibid., 141, 150, 152. The information provided by Boucher and others was regrettably never passed along to the French administrators overseeing the outfitting phase of the Carigan-Salières Regiment. Many factors contributed to this lack of foresight: Winter warfare was not part of the French Army's doctrine; the cost of winter clothing and required equipment was prohibitive; both the French and New France administrators were operating with limited budgets; and since the King had agreed to send a regiment, it was expected that the colony would provide supplies and equipment during the unit's time in the colony.

10 Louis XIV insisted on instilling discipline and organization at every level. From this moment on he demanded that his armies be large, impressive, and intimidating. René Chartrand, *Louis XIV's Army* (New York; Osprey Publishing, 1988), 8; Laurence Bradford Packard, *The Age of Louis XIV* (New York: Reinhart and Winston, 1966), 60-74.

11 In 1627, the *Compagnie des Cent-Associés* was granted the exclusive rights of New France's trade and resource development. In exchange, the company agreed to oversee all phases of immigration and colonization as well as establishing and expanding the colony's economic infrastructure, and sending troops when required to defend the colony and its operations. During the seventeenth century this company, colonial officials and the French government occasionally provided limited military support to New France. In 1604, trading companies hired soldiers to guard their depots and vessels. From 1609 to 1622, Samuel de Champlain led small forces on a series of expeditions to expand and protect the small colony. In 1627, the *Compagnie des Cents Associés* hired a small number of soldiers to guard its vessels. In 1642, France sent 40 soldiers to Governor Montmagny to build a fort at the mouth of the Richelieu River. In 1643-1644, Anne D'Autriche, the Queen of France, dispatched 60 soldiers to New France. Upon their arrival, they were formed into small groups and deployed to various locations throughout the colony. In 1652, the three main garrisons in New France were: Quebec, 15 soldiers; Three Rivers, 24 soldiers; and Montreal, 10 soldiers. In 1661, the *Compagnie des Cents Associés* sent 100 soldiers to assist the colony's new governor, Pierre Du Bois D'Avaugour, in his operations against the Iroquois. In 1662, another two companies were deployed to New France. In 1663, frustrated colonial officials decided to raise their own troops. The militia of the Holy Family of Jesus-Mary-Joseph was raised in Montreal on 27 January 1663. This unit totalled 139 men with very little military experience. They assisted the town's garrison of 12 soldiers in various defensive tasks. This militia unit was disbanded in 1665. Chartrand, *Canadian Military Heritage,* 45-62.

12 Marcel Trudel, *La population du Canada en 1663* (Montreal: Fides, 1973), 11, 23, 26, 150.

13 Déclaration que le roi reprend la Nouvelle-France, Paris, mars 1663, MG 1, Série C11A, Correspondance générale, Canada, vol 2, folio 5-7, microfilm F-2. National Archives of Canada (hereafter NA).

14 Mémoire de ce qui est à faire en Canada, dressé sur le rapport des vaisseaux revenus de Plaisance et de le rivière Saint-Laurent, La Rochelle, 22 janvier 1663, NA, MG 1, C11A, vol 2, folio 36-39, microfilm F-2. (My translation, ed.)

15 An increasing number of reports were sent by various colonial officials to the Minister of Colonies between 1660 and 1665. They explained in great detail the impact of the Iroquois raids on the colony's economy. If New France was to become a profitable economic venture, it was recommend-

ed that the Iroquois menace be dealt with once and for all. As time passed, it became evident to all concerned that a one-time major military operation conducted by a regular infantry regiment could resolve this issue and finally open up future trading venues across the continent.

Transcriptions and original microfilm copies of these reports are available at the National Archives of Canada. They are part of the following fonds: MG 1, Série C11A, Correspondance générale, Canada, vol 2, microfilm F-2 (Original documents), microfilm C-2374 (Transciptions).

16 Mémoire de ce qui serait à faire pour fortifier contre les insultes des Iroquois en Canada, 1663, NA, MG 1, Série C11A, vol 2, folio 46-48v, microfilm F-2.

17 Mémoire pour peupler et défricher le pays, n.d., NA, MG 1, Série C11A, vol 2, folio 45-45v, microfilm F-2. (My translation, ed.)

18 Réponse au mémoire sur le secours qu'il plaît au roi de donner au Canada, 1664, NA, MG 1, Série C11A, vol 2, folio 93-94v, microfilm F-2.

19 Ibid.

20 The colonial administrators as well as members of the clergy working in New France, were kept informed of the various military options being considered by the Ministry of the Colonies and the Ministry of War. Between late 1663 and early 1664, many stated in their correspondence that plans were underway to send a large military contingent to New France in order to destroy the Iroquois. Dom Guy Oury, *Marie de L'Incarnation, Correspondance* (Abbaye Saint-Pierre: Solemes, 1971), Lettre CCVII, Lettre à son fils, Québec, septembre-octobre 1663, 710-713; Mémoire du ministre à Tracy, 1664, NA, MG 1, Série C11A, vol 2, folio 99-105, microfilm F-2; Lettre de François de Laval, évêque de Pétrée, vicaire apostolique du Canada à La Propaganda Fide, Québec, 26 août 1664, NA, MG 17, Vatican, Archives de la Sacrée Congrégation de La Propaganda Fide, Série SOCG, vol 256, pièce 201, folio 21r-24v, microfilm K-244.

21 René Chartrand, *Louis the XIV's Army*, 3, 7-9. Following two lengthy campaigns, the Thirty Years War which ended in August 1648 and the war against Spain 1653–1659, Louis XIV seized the opportunity to review the state of his army. It was in total disarray and in need of a complete reorganization. With the assistance of Marshal Henri, Viscount de Turenne, a strategist and Michel Le Tellier, Marquis de Louvois, the Minister of War, the major problems and weakness had been identified. "Louvois found the army neither permanent nor regular. It was recruited, as taxes were collected, by farming. The Minister of War sold the commissions of the two most important administrative grades, those of colonel and captain. The colonels and captains, in turn, employed recruiting sergeants, who by any means whatever, sought to procure recruits; they got the men to enlist while they were drunk; they got them at any age, with almost any physical defects; they got them by any form of alluring promise as to pay and privileges. Colonels sold commissions to subaltern officers, captains were allowed by the War Ministry, for the maintenance and pay of their company, certain sums based upon the number of soldiers on the company rosters. Scandalous abuses existed, however, so that captains often drew funds for the upkeep of a full company, whereas there might be less than half of a full complement of men actually with the colours. When an inspection occurred, *pass volants* (filler) would be hired for the day from any available source, and put in line to deceive the inspectors. There was no regular training system. Most of the troops had no regular uniforms; certain units of Royal Guards wore special trappings, and sometime a unit might wear the livery belonging to household service of their commander. Discipline was almost non existent. Officers, being noble, resented taking orders or conforming to regulations. Pillage was ordinarily allowed to troops on Campaign." Packard, 60-64, 67.

22 Lettre de Jean- Baptiste Colbert à Mgr de Laval, 18 mars 1664, Lettre, Carton N, no 14, Archives du séminaire de Québec; Leonidas Hudon, *Vie de la Mère Marie-Catherine se Saint-Augustin, religieuse de L'Hôtel-Dieu du Précieux-sang de Québec, 1632-1668* (Paris: Éditions Spes, 1925), 209. (My translation, ed.)

23 Lettre de Colbert de Terron, Paris, 23 janvier, 1665, NA, MG 4, Série B1, Archives de la Guerre, Service historique de l'Armée, Archives historiques, vol 191, folio 191, microfilm reel F-466. For a complete listing and analysis of documents held by the National Archives of Canada pertaining to the Régiment de Carignan-Salières' activities and operations, please consult Michel Wyczynski's *Guide thématique des sources manuscrites ayant trait au Régiment de Carignan-Salières conservées aux Archives nationales du Canada*, Instrument de recherche no 1943, 1993; and Michel Wyczynski, "Sources manuscrites ayant trait au Régiment de Carignan-Salières conservées aux Archives nationales du Canada," *L'Archiviste*, Vol 6, No. 4 (juillet-août)1989), 10-11.

24 Etat des trouppes d'infantries de l'armée d'Italie, contenan la reduction et reformaon, Nevers, janvier 1659, NA, MG 4, Série B1, A1, vol 154, folio 65-65v, microfilm F-466; lettre du roi à MM. De Salières explicant la situation au suject de l'incorporation des régiments de Carignan et de Salières, Nevers, 22 janvier 1659, NA, MG4, Série B1, A1, vol 154, folio 112-113, microfilm C-12576; Louis Susane, *Histoire de l'ancienne infantrie françaises*,(Paris: Librairie militaire, maritime et polytechnic, 1851), V, 239-259, 410; VIII, 168, 355.

25 Correspondance ayant trait au comportement des soldats du régiment de Carignan-Salières lors de leurs déplacement vers La Rochelle, janvier-mai 1665, NA, MG 4, Série B1, A1, vols 191-193, microfilm F-466.

26 Lettre à M. de La Galissonnière, Paris, 27 janvier 1665, NA, MG 4, Série B1, A1, vol 191, folio 228, microfilm F-466.

27 Lettre à M. le marquis de Marins, Paris, 10 avril 1665, NA, MG 4, Série B1, A1, vol 192, 58, microfilm C-12576. (My translation, ed.)

28 The regiment was issued with 200 new flintlock muskets, 40,000 flints, 1,000 cleaning rods and 200 bayonets and sheaths. Matchlock muskets were also used by Carignan-Salières personnel during their operations in New France. Estat general de toutte la depense faite a cause des vingt companies du régiment d'Infantrie de Carignan Salliere et d'une compagnie de chacun des régiments d'Infanterye de Champbelle, Orleans, Poytou et L'Aillée, que sa majesté, entretient en Canada ou Nouvelle-France pendant l'année 1666, La Rochelle, 15 juin 1666, NA, MG 1, Série C11A, vol 2, folio 272-284, microfilm F-2.

29 Mémoire du roi pour servir d'instruction au sieur Talon qui vient d'être désigné intendant de la justice, police et finances dans la Nouvelle-France, Paris, 27 mars 1665, NA, MG 8, Série A1, Nouvelle-France: Correspondence officielle, Série 1, vol 1, 37-52, microfilm C-13574.

30 Lettre de Talon au ministre, La Rochelle, 22 avril 1665, NA, MG 1, Série C11A, vol 2, folio 124-124v, microfilm F-2; lettre de Talon au ministre, La Rochelle, 14 mai 1665, NA, MG 1, Série C11A, vol 2, folio 133-133v, microfilm F-2. (My translation, ed.)

31 Colonel Henri de Chastelard, Marquis de Salières was born around 1595. The marquis first joined the army in 1619. He was appointed colonel of the regiment when Colonel Balthazard retired. Following its amalgamation with the Carignan Regiment, he retained the position of active colonel. He deployed to New France in 1665 and returned to France in 1668 with what remained of his company and his regiment. He retired from the army in 1676 and died in July 1680 at the age of 85 and was buried at the Church of Saint-Sulpice in Paris. Paul Verney, *The Good Regiment, The Carignan-Salières Regiment in Canada, 1665-1668* (Montreal: McGill University Press, 1991), 181.

32 While in La Rochelle, Salières tempestuous character had been noted. In order to circumvent possible problems and personality clashes once deployed to New France, Salières received written orders advising him that he would report to and obey M. Rémy de Courcelle's orders. The letter stressed that "suivant l'usage du royaume Mons, de Courcelles doibt commander a toutes les troupes qui se trouveront dans l'estendue de son gouvernement de la mesme façon que le font en france Messrs les gouverneurs et lieutenants gens aux des provinces." Lettre à M. de Salières, Paris, 19 avril 1665, NA, MG 4, Série B1, A1, ol 192, folio 291, microfilm F-466.

33 The Regiment's uniform colours were predominately brown, grey and black. Detailed lists enumerating and describing various uniform parts, replacement issue and quantities are found in Estat general de toute la depense faite a cause des vingt companies du régiment d'Infantrie de Carignan Salliere et d'une compagnie de chacun des régiments d'Infanterye de Champbelle, Orleans, Poytou et L'Aillée, que sa majesté, entretient en Canada ou Nouvelle-France pendant l'année 1666, La Rochelle, 15 juin 1666, NA, MG1, Série C11A, vol 2, folio 272-284, microfilm F-2. René Chartrand, *The French Soldier in Colonial America* (Ottawa: Runge Press Ltd, 1984), Historical Arms Series No.18, 8. René Chartrand and Eugène Lelièpvre, "Carignan-Salières Regiment, Governor-General's Guards, Canada 1665-1668," Plate No. 493," *Military Collector & Historian* XXXII, Summer 1980, 2.

34 A detailed report prepared by Chamot, the Carignan-Salières Regiment's Quartermaster, confirmed that the stores and equipment issued to the unit were done so as if it were to be deployed in a European rather than a colonial theatre. État de toute la dépense faite pour les troupes d'infantrie entretenues au Canada par le Roi, La Rochelle, 15 juin 1666, NA, MG 1, Série C11A, vol 2, folio 272-284, microfilm F-2.

35 The soldiers embarked on six vessels which sailed from La Rochelle on three separate dates: *Le Joyeux Siméon*, 19 April 1665; *La Paix* and *L'Aigle d'Or*, 13 May; *Saint-Sébastien* and *La Justice* 24 May; and lastly the *Jardin de Holland*, which transported the regiment's supplies. Lettre de Talon au ministre, La Rochelle, 4 mai 1665, NA, MG 1, Série C11A, vol 2, folio 130-132v, microfilm F-2; Lettre de Colbert de Terron à Colbert, De Tonnay, 27 avril 1665, NA, MG 7, I, A6, Bibliothèque nationale, Département des manuscrits, Fonds Français, Série Mélanges Colbert, vol 128, 30, microfilm C-12868; Gazette de France, Recueil de toutes les gazettes, nouvelles, ordinaires et extraordinaires et autres relations, La Rochelle, 15 mai 1665, 510-511, University of British Columbia Library, microfilm 2427. For additional details describing the preparation of these vessels and their trips to New France, consult Germain Lesage, "L'arrivée du régiment de Carignan," *Revue de l'université d'Ottawa*, vol 35, No. 1 (janvier-mars 1965), 11-34.

36 Léopold Lamontagne, "Alexandre Prouville de Tracy," in *DCB*, vol 1, 554-557.

37 The reported losses vary depending on the sources consulted. Twenty soldiers died from an illness contracted during the trip to New France. Marie de L'Incarnation recorded that 20 soldiers had died, 30 septembre 1665, 754; the Jesuits were vague and reported that "many had died", vol 49,167; *Les Annales de L'Hôtel-Dieu* state that 35 had passed away, 147-149. Four others died at the Hôpital de Montreal, and one accidental death was reported in Three Rivers. Marie de L'Incarnation provides many interesting details and insights concerning the regiment's activities and operation. She obtained her information from her friend, Alexandre de Chaumont, Tracy's aide-de-camp. Dom Guy Oury, *Marie de L'Incarnation, Correspondence* (Abbaye Saint-Pierre: Solesmes, 1971), Lettre CCXVIII, Quebec, 30 septembre 1665, 754; Lettre du R.P. Rageneau à Colbert, 28 novembre 1665, 131-134, NA, MG 7, I, A6, vol 133, 131-134, microfilm C-12868; Rueben Gold Thwaites, *The Jesuit Relations And Allied Documents, Travels and Exploration of The Jesuit Missionaries in New France, 1610-1791* (New York: Pageant Book Company, 1959), Volume XLVIII, Lower Canada, Ottawas: 1662-1664, 161.

38 Thwaites, vol 50, 82; W.J. Eccles, "Daniel Rémy de Courcelle," in *DCB*, vol 1, 569-572. (My translation, ed.)

39 Oury, Lettre CCXVIII, Québec, lettre de Marie de L'Incarnation à son fils, 30 septembre 1665, 755.

40 Mémoire de M. de Salière des choses qui se sont passés en Canada les plus considérables depuis qu'il est arrivé, 1665-1666, NA, MG 7, Série A2, Bibliothèque nationale, Département des manuscrits, Fonds français ,Vol 4569, 14 mai 1666. (Hereafter Mémoire de M. Salières). (My translation, ed.)

41 Ibid., 8 juin 1666.

42 Mémoire de M. Salières, 2, 26-27 septembre, 21 octobre, 6 novembre 1665.

43 Two months later, Salières described a challenging canoe trip from Quebec to Montreal that was made solely by himself and his soldiers. He reported " ie souffris ces 9 iours que ie fus à faire 60 lieues de froid de tourmentes tout autant qu'on peut souffrir n'ayant pour gouverner le batteau que moy et mes noeufs soldats pour ramer." Ibid., 9 novembre 1665 and Thwaites, vol 50, 147.

44 Lettre du R. P. Paul Ragueneau à Colbert, 13 septembre 1665, NA, MG 7, I, A 6, vol 131bis, 81-82, microfilm C-

12868; Lettre du R. P. Paul Ragueneau à Colbert, 28 novembre 1665, NA, MG 7, I, A 6, vol 133, 131-134, microfilm C-12868; Oury, Lettre CCXV, Marie de L'Incarnation à son fils, Québec, 28 juillet 1665, 740. Marie de L'Incarnation, an Ursuline nun who showed great interest in the regiment's activities, noted Tracy's decision to occupy the Richelieu. She wrote, "a pris le devant pour se saisir de la Rivière des Iroquois et faire des forts sur ses rivages dans les passages les plus avantageux." Oury, Lettre CCXX, Marie de L' Incarnation à son fils, Québec, 29 octobre 1665, 760.

45 Ibid., 25 aôut 1665. My translation, ed.)

46 Many officers and non-commissioned officers who chose to remain in New France participated actively in various military capacities and future operations, including Jacques de Chambly, Michel-Sidrac Digué de Boisbriand, Hector d'Andigué de Grandfontaine, François Provost, Pierre de Joybet de Soulanges et de Mason, Pierre Bécart de Granville, Olivier Morel de La Durantaye, Phillpie Gaultier de Comporté, Pierre Lamotte de Saint-Paul, Philippe Dufresnoy Carion, Gillaume Richard (Lafleur) Arnoult de Broisle de Loubias, René de Gaultier de Varrennes, Jacques Labadie, Paul Dupuy de Lisloye, Pierre de Saint-Ours d'Eschaillons, and Hugues Randin. Rolle des soldats du Régiment de Carignan-Salières qui se sont fait habitans du Canada en 1668, NA, MG 1, Série D2C, Archives des colonies, Troupes des colonies, vol 47, folio 45-49v, microfilm F-582.

47 During the first year the companies were posted to the following locations. Quebec: Allier, Poitou, Orléans, Chambellé, Grandfontaine, La Motte, La Tour and La Noraye. Sainte-Famille, île d'Orléans: Maximy. Trois Rivières: Loubias, La Fouille and Froment. Chambly: Chambly and Petit. Sainte-Thérèse: Colonelle, Rougemont and Du Prat. Montréal: Salières, La Freydière, Contrecoeur, La Varenne and Du Gué. Depending on the nature of their tasks and their participation in operations, some of these companies would be relocated accordingly. Régis Roy and Gérard Malchelosse, Le Régiment de Carignan-Salières, son organisation et son expédition au Canada, 1665-1668 (Montréal: G. Ducharme, Libraire-Editeur, 1925), 67-78.

48 Mémoire de M. Salières, 25aôut 1665.

49 Jean-Guy Pelletier, "Pierre de Saurel," in DCB, vol 1, 602-603.

50 René Baudry, "Jacques de Chambly," in DCB, vol 1, 79-80.

51 Mémoire de M. Salières, 1 octobre 1665. (My translation, ed.)

52 Oury, Lettre CCXX, Marie de L'Incarnation à son fils, Québec, 29 octobre 1665, 758. (My translation, ed.)

53 Ibid., 760. (My translation, ed.)

54 Histoire de Montréal par Dollier de Casson, NA, MG 7, IV, Bibliothèque nationale, Département des manuscits, Fonds français, Bibilothèque Mazarine, vol 1963, microfilm C-12871. (My translation, ed.)

55 Thwaites, Reception des sauvages a M. de Tracy, 1665, vol 49, 230. (My translation, ed.)

56 Ibid., 232. (My translation, ed.)

57 Mémoire de M. Salières, 26 octobre 1665. (My translation, ed.)

58 The first snow covered New France on 10 November 1665. Thwaites, vol 49, 174.

59 In September 1666, Intendant Jean Talon prepared a report on the availability and quantity of food supplies for upcoming military expeditions. During the fall and the early winter months provisions were plentiful due to good harvests. By spring however, the quantity and quality of the remaining supplies was limited and it was impossible to feed a large group of soldiers for an indeterminate period. Mémoire de Talon à Tracy et Courcelles. Problems envoye par M.Talon au Sr. de Tracy et Courcelles pour servir s'il est plus avantageux au service du Roy de declarer le guerre aux Agnez que de faire la paix avec eux, Québec, 1 septembre 1666, vol 2, folio 211, microfilm F-2, NA.

60 Thwaites, vol 50, 132. (My translation, ed.)

61 Mémorie de M. Salières, 27 janvier, 1666. (My translation, ed.)

62 "Documents inédits, Le Livre de raison de François Tapie de Monteil, capitaine au régiment de Poitou (1661-1670)," Revue d'histoire de l'amérique française, Vol XIII, No 4, parties 1 et 2, mars 1960, 526-573; Vol XIV, No 1, juin 1960, 109-121. Because there was so little winter clothing, these coats were probably returned to the garrisons or quartermaster shortly after the survivors returned to Quebec. The after-death inventories of the personal belongings, uniforms and equipment of two officers, M. de Chazy, of the Carigan-Salières Regiment, and François Travestry, enseigne de la compagnie au sieur Vincent, capitaine au Régiment d'Orléans, listed no winter clothing items in their possessions. These two officers were killed in an ambush at Fort Sainte-Anne in July 1666. "L'embuscade du Fort-Sainte Anne en 1666," Le bulletin des recherches historiques Vol XXXVI, No. 3 (mars 1930), 129-130.

63 Thwaites, vol 50, 130. (My translation, ed.)

64 Ibid., 132; Lortie, Jeanne D'Arc, Pierre Savard and Paul Wyczynski, Les textes poétques du Canada français, 1607-1867 (Louisville: Éditions Fides, 1987), 53-68, René-Louis Chartier de Lotbinière, Sur le voyages de Monsieur de Courcelles Governeur et lieutenant général pour le roy en Nouvelle France en l'année 1666, Vers burlesques.

65 Histoire de Montréal par Dollier de Casson, NA, MG 7, IV, vol 1963, microfilm C-12871. Lortie, Savard and Wyczynski, 56, 63, 66. Courcelle referred to the Montreal volunteers as Capots bleus because of their oversize coats. These coats came with a large hood that when raised protected the individual's head and face from the cold winds. Its bulkiness enabled the volunteers to wear additional layers of clothing underneath. (My translation, ed.)

66 Lortie, Savard, Wyczynski, 63.

67 Mémoire de M. Salières, 6 mars 1666; Thwaites, vol 50, 182. (My translation, ed.)

68 Lortie, Savard, Wyczynski, 62.

69 Oddly enough, no precise figures regarding the losses sustained during this winter expedition were ever provided. The reported losses range from 60 to 400 men. Thwaites, vol 50, 183, the Jesuits stated that 60 men were lost. Capitaine François de Monteil de Tapie of the Poitou Regiment, who took part in this expedition, reported that 400 men were lost. Monteil, 112. No figures were logged in the official reports sent to France, possibly in an attempt not to hurt the possibility of future military assistance. For

unknown reasons, Salières, who had always been highly critical of Tracy's and Courcelle's decision making process never broached this issue. Taking into account the very cold weather and the lack of proper clothing and food, it is possible that the casualty rate ranged somewhere between 50 and 60 percent.

70 Oury, Lettre de Marie de l'Incarnation à son fils, 16 octobre 1666, 768. (My translation, ed.)

71 Letter of the Governor of Albany to M. de Tracy, 20 August 1666, NA, MG 11, Colonial Office 1, Colonial Papers, General Series, Series 1, vol 20, 102-104, microfilm C-1446.

72 Problems envoyés par M. Talon aux sr de Tracy et Courcelles pour servir s'il est plus avantageux de servir le Roy de declarer la guerre aux Agnez que de faire la paix avec eux, Quebec, 1 septembre 1666, NA, MG 1, C11A, vol 2, folio 207-231v, microfilm F-2. (My translation, ed.)

73 Oury, Lettre de Marie de L'Incarnation à son fils, 18 octobre 1667, Lettre CCXXX, 786-789.

74 Another seven soldiers had died from illnesses, drowning and accidents. Rolle de soldats du Régiment du Carignan-Salières qui se sont faits habitans du Canada en Canada en 1668, NA, MG 1, Série D2C, vol 47, folio 45-49v.

75 Thwaites, vol 50, 140.

76 Oury, Lettre de Marie de L'Incarnation à une de ses soeurs, 2 novembre, Lettre CCXXIV, 770. (My translation, ed.)

77 Thwaites, vol 50, 142.

78 Oury, Lettre de Marie de L'Incarnation à son fils, 16 octobre 1666, Lettre CCXXIII, 768. (My translation, ed.)

79 Ibid., 768. (My translation, ed.)

80 Ibid., Lettre de Marie de L'incarnation à son fils, 12 novembre 1666, Lettre CCXXV, 772-777.

81 Ibid., 773. (My translation, ed.)

82 Thwaites, vol 50, 145. (My translation, ed.)

83 Oury, Lettre de Marie de L'Incarnation à son fils, 12 novembre 1666, Lettre CCXXV, 774. (My translation, ed.)

84 Ibid., 774. Many hours before the French troops appeared, the Mohawk chiefs decided to evacuate the village of all elders, children and women. They hid in the adjacent wooded hills. Messengers were sent to the others villages, recommending a similar course of action. (My translation, ed.)

85 Ibid., 774.

86 Thwaites, vol 50, 143.

87 Ibid., 147. Some good fortune was present. Prior to crossing one of the lakes, soldiers uncovered large hidden canoes. They were left there by the Mohawks to cut down on portage time during their incursions into French territory. The soldiers put these to good use. Upon reaching the other shore, the canoes were then burnt, thus depriving the enemy of their much needed vessels that could have been used in the pursuit of the French rear guard. Oury, Lettre de Marie de L'Incarnation à son fils, Québec, 12 novembre 1666, Lettre CCXXV, 775.

88 Extrait d'un mémoire de Talon adressé à M. de Colbert sur l'état du Canada, Quebec, 13 novembre 1666, NA, MG 8, A1, Série 1, Nouvelle-France. Correspondance officielle, vol 1, 122, microfilm, C-13574.

89 A week after the troops' return, Talon received a request from Colbert de Terron, chief administrator of La Rochelle, to retrieve all the new flintlock muskets from the soldiers garrisoned in Quebec, Trois-Rivières and Montreal and ship them back to France in the most expeditious manner possible. Only the soldiers stationed in the forts were authorized to retain their arms. In France, the availability of new flintlock muskets was still very limited. Since the Carignan-Salières operations were coming to an end and a large number of troops agreed to settle in New France, Colbert de Terron, head administrator of La Rochelle, ordered that all muskets and slings be returned to France. France's involvement in the War of Devolution (France invaded the Spanish Flanders during late spring and summer 1667) meant these rare flintlock muskets were urgently required and they were immediately re-issued to other infantry units. Lettre de Talon au ministre, Québec, 13 novembre 1666, NA, MG 1, Série C11A, vol 2, folio 216-228v, microfilm F-2; Extrait d'un mémoire de Talon adressé à M.de Colbert sur l'état du Canada, Québec, 13 novembre 1666.

90 Thwaites, vol 49, 231. (My translation, ed.)

91 Mémoire de M. Salières, 19 novembre 1665.

92 The first forced night march took place during the 1666 winter expedition when Courcelle left the Dutch colony. The Jesuit chronicler describes the sense of urgency and the marching cadence, "decampa avec precipitation, on marcha toute la nuit et une partie du lundy" Thwaites, vol 50, 182.

93 Oury, Lettre de Marie de L'Incarnation à son fils, Québec, 16 novembre 1666, 773.

94 Lettre de Talon au ministre, Québec, 27 octobre 1667, NA, MG 1, Série C11A, vol 2, folio 308, microfilm F-2. (My translation, ed.)

CHAPTER 2

Terror on the Frontier

The Role of the Indians in the Struggle for North America, 1754-1760

Lieutenant-Colonel Bernd Horn

BOTH CANADA AND THE UNITED STATES OF AMERICA are proud of sharing the longest undefended border in the world. However, this was not always the case; the colonial North American frontier was anything but tranquil. From the arrival of the first Europeans onto the continent, conflict raged through the wilderness and along the frontiers of the early settlements. As the White population grew, the struggle evolved from one that pitted European against Indian to a succession of conflicts that were primarily focused on White against White, a virtual exportation of the power struggles of Europe. But, although the economic and political motives could easily be transported to the New World, the methods of warfare could not.

French trading post in *les payes en haut*. (NA, C-14253)

The Europeans brought their beliefs, attitudes and practices to a world that was totally alien to their culture. Their arrogance and their perception of the Indians as savages blinded them to the strengths of the Indian way of war in the forested wilderness of North America. Even painful lessons and experience had but a limited effect on changing these attitudes. "Unfortunately the regular soldier," explained noted Canadian historian George F. Stanley, "was slow if not positively loath to accept the Canadian militiaman or the Indian as his teacher—a form of professional conceit which was to bedevil Canadian military history for many years to come."[1] Although the Indians adopted European methods that they felt advantageous to their survival, the Europeans through sheer arrogance failed to acknowledge the superiority of certain aspects of Indian culture.

As the protagonists became European against European, the Indians were wooed and courted as allies. Despite a revulsion for certain Indian practices and behaviours, namely their unreliability and their penchant for torture and extreme cruelty, as well as their perceived cowardice, the more prescient colonial military and political leaders understood that the Indians were a critical element in the successful prosecution of war in the colonies. Their participation, or even neutrality, could represent the difference between victory and defeat. This was appreciated by very few, normally those who were born and raised in North America. However, with time it was also begrudgingly accepted as a necessary evil when campaigning in the New World by some of the military commanders who were sent from England or France to fight the wars of their Kings.

The relative ineffectiveness of the Europeans on the North American battlefield was largely a result of their arrogance as well as their deep-rooted cultural understanding of war. Armies consisted mainly of conscripts and social outcasts led chiefly by the country's aristocracy. There was little binding these two groups together. While the officers may have had a reason to fight for King and country, as a result of their position and stake in society, their soldiery did not. Their allegiance was to themselves. They did not fight, nor did they wish to die, for an ideological, political or philosophical cause. Their goal was to make a living. Not surprisingly, soldiers were neither expected nor trusted to operate as individuals or small groups because of their commanders' justifiable fear that they would desert or create havoc in the countryside, regardless of whether they were in friendly or enemy territory. This reality was one reason that commanders used only large formations in combat to ensure the troops remained in their place of duty and fought. This lack of cohesion in an army, in addition to the absence of a clear purpose the soldiers could identify with, requireded a reliance on iron discipline to create a unified and effective fighting force.

The need for harsh discipline also extended to the type of combat that the soldiers conducted. This was another reason for the use of large formations. The weaponry of the day, particularly the musket, had limited effectiveness. It was inaccurate and capable of only short-range engagements. During combat, battalions stood elbow to elbow in a solid line, three ranks deep, facing a mirror image of themselves no more than thirty to eighty metres away. On a given command, volleys would be exchanged with dev-

The French *courier de bois* and Indians fought a distinct Canadian way of war. (From L'Abbé H.R. Casgrain, *Les Français au Canada*. Québec: Maison Alfred Mame et Fils, undated.)

astating effect on the closely packed formations. Victory lay with the side that could deliver the most volleys in the shortest possible time and not break and run.[2] At eighty paces, there was little time to reload, and so the failure to ensure the volley struck home could lead to the necessity to withstand a bayonet charge by the enemy. As a result, repetitive training to turn the uninspired levy of reluctant combatants into an efficient mechanical fighting force was critical. Loading and firing a musket required approximately twelve movements, all of which were coordinated by drum beat or on word of command by an officer. Not surprisingly, it took at least eighteen months on the drill square to train the raw recruit, who normally represented the offal of society, to manoeuver and perform effectively on the battlefield.[3]

But equally important, severe discipline was also necessary for combat performance to ensure that soldiers maintained the advance under murderous fire or simply remained in position to deliver their volleys and accept the enemy's bayonet charge. Frederick the Great's dictum that a soldier "must be more afraid of his officers than of the dangers to which he is exposed," was not an idle rumination.[4] It was not uncommon for regulations to emphasize that "if a soldier during an action looks about as if to flee, or so much as sets foot outside the line, the non-commissioned officer standing behind him will run him through with his bayonet and kill him on the spot."[5] One veteran recalled "Col[onel] Prebble, who, I well remember, was a harsh man, swore he would knock the first man down who should step out of his ranks; which greatly surprised me, to think that I must stand still to be shot at."[6] The ridiculousness of this expectation was magnified by combat experience. "A man could not stand erect, without being hit," testified one wounded soldier, "any more than he could stand out in a shower, without having drops of rain fall upon him; for the balls come by hands full."[7]

Battle, therefore, in the European model became an elaborate set-piece manoeuvre much like a chess match. Formations of artillery, cavalry and infantry were carefully deployed and repositioned to gain the maximum amount of advantage over the enemy. Tactics relied almost exclusively on heavy infantry and cavalry. The courage of the soldiers to withstand the murderous volleys of the enemy was maintained by an iron discipline. The ability to pour a withering fire into the opponent's ranks was honed by constant drilling and training. The soldier was in many ways seen by his commanders as nothing more than an expendable automaton, albeit an expensive one to train. As such, virtually all European commanders shared a distinct contempt for the concept of light infantry fighting on their own, relying on their initiative and on engaging the enemy from behind cover.

The European method of warfare also included specific expectations of behaviour during and after a battle. Elaborate protocols for the conduct of sieges, surrenders and honours of war were followed. Courage and gallantry were respected. To honour one's word, to treat prisoners in a merciful manner, and to protect the civilian population, by the mid-eighteenth century were considered by most European commanders, under most circumstances, to be the accepted manner of waging war.

But the North American experience shattered this paradigm.[8] Colonists who endured and survived encounters with the Indians in the wilderness slowly began to realize the sagacity of their tactics. However, the regulars sent from Europe to fight the King's wars were reluctant to reject their philosophical and cultural understanding of war. "Such men [regular soldiers] may do very well in armies and garrisons where their duty is merely mechanical," remarked John Cleves Symmes, a renowned American frontiersman, "but it requires another sort of men to contend against Indians with success." He added: "It must be considered that every Indian is in fact a general in his way, and must be opposed by a combatant equally skilled in all their cunning and artifice."[9] Although it became apparent to some of the colonists as early as 1676 that reliance on closely packed columns and strictly controlled volley fire was futile against a enigmatic foe such as the Indians, the bloody lessons would be repeatedly ignored.

No event better exemplified the failure to learn, anticipate or adapt to a new environment or manner of waging war than Major-General Edward Braddock's crushing defeat at the Monongahela River on 9 July 1755. Braddock, with a force of approximately 1,200 regulars and 800 provincials, was en route to capture Fort Duquesne, a strategic western outpost held by the French. However, he was intercepted and soundly defeated by a smaller force of 250 French regulars and militia and 600 Indians.[10] This contest exemplified the cultural and philosophical divide between Old World and New.

Braddock's forty-five years of service had, predictably, endowed him with a deep-rooted comprehension of warfare that was reinforced by his own experience. He accepted as truth that the more disciplined and well drilled force would normally emerge victorious. In fact, Benjamin Franklin, writing fifteen years after the event, recorded that Braddock dismissed the threat posed by the Indians. According to Franklin, Braddock declared that "these savages may,

General Braddock's defeat. This romanticized engraving, although not accurate, does capture the turmoil and confusion of the one-sided battle. (NA, C-2644)

indeed, be a formidable enemy to your raw American militia, but upon the King's regulars ... it is impossible they should make any impression." This contumelious remark reveals his failure to fully appreciate his new environment.[11]

Braddock's failure, or inability, to adjust his European mode of combat led to the destruction of his army. In the end, Braddock's courage and steadfast belief that inevitably the undisciplined, motley opponent that faced his troops would break, combined with the training and discipline of his regulars to stand their ground regardless of the chaos that engulfed them, led to their ruin. Once ambushed, the closely packed troops were impossible to miss and they suffered horrendous casualties. Ironically, the provincials, particularly the Virginians, immediately sought cover and began to return fire against their phantom antagonists. Their actions provided some hope of staving off defeat. However, Braddock, incensed at this lack of courage and discipline, ordered them back into line using both oaths and the flat of his sword.[12] The contrast between the European and Indian way of war was never sharper. Tom Faucett, a bitter veteran who served with the Provincials, scathingly reminisced:

> You [Braddock] tried to put shame on th' names o' brave men. We was cowards, was we, because we knowed better than to fight Injuns like you red-backed ijits across the ocean is used to fight: because we wouldn't stand up rubbin' shoulders like a passel o' sheep and let the red-skins made sieves outen us!...And them boys— th' ole Virginny Blues—you made git from behint th' trees and git kilt; and them other you cussed, ...and cut down with yer saber, my own pore brother, Joe, amongst 'em!—Why ef I hadn't stopped ye with a shot, ye'd had us all massacred and scalped![13]

Despite the exhortations of the officers and the discipline of the regulars, as the ranks were continually thinned by a steady and deadly fire from a foe that could not be seen, the regulars lost their steadiness and eventually succumbed to an uncontrollable panic. "And when we endeavoured to rally them," recounted George Washington, then a young officer assigned to Braddock's staff, "it was with as much success as if we had attempted to stop the wild bears of the mountains."[14] The cost of the debacle was enormous. The French lost approximately five percent of their engaged force. The British lost seventy percent of theirs, including sixty out of eighty-six officers.[15]

But the lessons were not immediately absorbed. British officers still clung to their beliefs. For instance, James Wolfe wrote:

> Your Grace heard of Braddock's defeat with surprise I am sure; because you cou'd not conceive that the soldiers of this country cou'd behave in the infamous manner that those Rascals did—it surpasses all that is gone before, & yet the whole blame is thrown upon the General—whereas if that canaille, had obey'd his orders, or followed his example, I believe there wou'd have been no great room for censure ... but people of this Country are corrupt enough to patronise cowardice & disobedience, in opposition to discipline & courage; they are at pains to excuse the most unheard of treachery, rather than suppose or acknowledge, that subordination in an Army is necessary to its success—they have no idea of a free born English Soldier's marching, working or fighting, but when he thinks proper; and these notions of theirs will sometime or other bring on their ruin.[16]

Moreover, exactly four years after Braddock's rout, General Orders at the British camp at Lake George stated, "ye men to be acquainted that Is As ordered As ye enemy has but very few Regular troops to oppose us And that No yelling of Indians nor fire of Canadians Can possible beat 2 Ranks If ye Men Are Silent Attentive And obedient to their officer who will Lead them to ye Enemy—their Silence will terrifey ye Enemy more than husaying or nois they can make which ye Gene Abselutly forbids."[17]

Although the British regulars on the whole were slow to appreciate the wilderness tactics, the victory over Braddock, in the eyes of the French and many of the English colonists, seemed to underscore the superiority of the Indian way of war. Being economically and numerically inferior to the British, in both regular military forces and civilian population, the French also had a pragmatic reason to support it. Nonetheless, the Indian's conduct of warfare was in stark contrast to the European emphasis on mass, rigid discipline and volley fire. Conversely, the Indians placed great reliance on guile, stealth, the use of cover and especially marksmanship.

This focus came naturally. These were the attributes of a successful hunter. To ensure game was killed required exceptional fieldcraft. The more clever and stealthy the hunter, the greater were his chances of success. Firearms merely provided a more efficient and lethal technology with which to kill. Clearly, all these skills were transferable to making war. "So stealthy in their approach, so swift in their execution, and so expeditious in their retreat," noted a Jesuit missionary, "that one commonly learns of their departure before being aware of their arrival."[18]

The Indians took full advantage of their mobility and knowledge of the terrain and forests. They used cover to its fullest benefit, deliberately choosing not to make themselves an obvious target. "In all the Time," recounted one lucky survivor of Braddock's defeated force, "I never saw one nor could I on Enquiry find any one who saw ten [Indians] together." He added, "If we saw five or six at one time [it] was a great sight."[19] Furthermore, they used deceit to achieve as much surprise as possible. But, most of all, they capitalized on their marksmanship. Some contemporary writers felt that it was the unerring fire of the Indians that made them such a threat.[20] Undeniably, their proficiency with weapons was superior on the whole to that of the Whites. They often carved grooves into the stocks of their weapons so they could take better aim by being able to align their eyes along the barrel and in line with the target. Moreover, they aimed at single targets, specifically at officers who were easy to identify by their dress and position on the battlefield.[21] Captain Pouchot, a member of the French Béarn Regiment that fought with distinction in North America, wrote in his memoirs that the Indians were excellent marksmen who "very rarely fail to shoot their man down."[22]

But it was not just their fieldcraft or marksmanship that set the Indians apart from the Europeans. For the warriors "taking up the hatchet"—or more simply put, going to war—was largely a personal endeavour. It was meant to prove a warrior's courage and skill and to earn prestige through achievement in combat. The individual warrior was subordinate to no other. He saw neither shame nor dishonour in abandoning the field if the odds of easy success were against him. Moreover, if individuals tired of the campaign or simply failed to support a plan of action, their departure was seldom condemned by their peers.[23] They were not interested in a fair fight, but only one in which they could achieve their aims with a minimum of casualties. Ambushes, raids and terror were the preferred methods of conducting war. In short, the Indians practised what became known as the "skulking way of war."

"The art of war," declared Tecaughretanego, a Kahnawake chief, "consists in ambushing and surprising our enemies, and in preventing them from ambushing and surprising us."[24] Abbe H.R. Casgrain, the prominent nineteenth century French Canadian chronicler of the Seven Years' War, summarized the Indian way of war:

> Often brave to the point of recklessness, [they] did not understand bravery in the same manner as the Europeans, they fought in the manner of the savages, that is to say as guerillas. For them, to withdraw was not a flight, nor a disgrace, it was a means of falling back to occupy a better position. Their discipline endangered the regular armies, who were left in vulnerable positions when they [natives] left [the battlefield]; also they [natives] were preferably used—for scouting expeditions and raids.[25]

But, not all were as generous. Early American colonist Reverend William Hubbard's assessment was far more scathing. "[T]he Indians, notwithstanding their Subtility and Cruelty, durst not look an Englishman in the Face in open Field, nor even yet were known to kill any Man with their guns, unless they could lie in wait for him in an ambush, or behind some Shelter, taking aim undiscovered."[26] Similarly, Brigadier François-Gaston, chevalier de Lévis, the Marquis de Montcalm's second in command, wrote, "The savages, unnerved by the cannon's roar, as well as the effect of those loaded with cartridges and the howitzers, fired their first volley and took flight; the Canadians were next to break ranks, and others followed suit, leading to a total collapse."[27] The Indian way of waging war also elicited an unfavourable comment from Edward Abbot, a Lieutenant-Governor of Vincennes during the colonial period. "It is not people in army's that Indians will ever daringly attack; but the poor inoffensive families ... who are inhumanely butchered sparing neither woman or children."[28] The memoirs of one French soldier included a note that stated, "Of them [Iroquois] it has been said, they came like foxes, attacked like hares, and fled like birds."[29]

These comments, however, illustrate the chasm between European values and those of the Indians. The latter's definition of success diverged substantially from that of the White man. A victorious campaign was determined by the accumulation of prisoners, scalps and plunder. The Indians deemed a campaign successfully completed when a victory, regardless of how inconsequential, was won.[30] Moreover, as already noted, casualties were totally unacceptable. Furthermore, the capture of territory, forcing an enemy to abandon a strategic fortification or

Iroquois Warrior by Jacques Grasset de Saint-Sauver, engraver J. Laroque, circa 1795. (NA, C-3163)

postpone an offensive simply did not resonate with the Indians. It was only through tangible actions such as the accumulation of valuable commodities, such as prisoners, scalps or plunder, that individual warriors could show their achievement in battle. In addition, these items were also very valuable. For instance, in 1747, Massachusetts paid out a bounty of £35 for the scalp of a male Indian or Frenchman and £10 for that of a woman. However, an even higher price was paid for prisoners brought in alive. A man would fetch 40 and a woman or boy under twelve, £25.[31] Almost ten years later, in July 1756, De Lévis offered 150 livres for a scalp upon his arrival at Carillon.[32] Similarly, the French also paid hefty ransoms to buy back English prisoners in an attempt to spare them from a hideous death by burning or torture. Not surprisingly, with these monetary inducements, there was very little incentive to risk one's life for the strategic gains of a European power, or to fulfill a code of honour that was diametrically opposed to their understanding of war. Amazingly, this was apparently missed by the military commanders who continually lamented the unreliability of the Indians.

A further difference in the Indian conduct of war, and one that caused great consternation to their White allies during the Seven Years' War, was the torture and cruelty shown to prisoners, whether military or civilian, and regardless of gender or age. This predated the Europeans. The early writings of the Jesuits portray the shock and horror they felt when they witnessed the display of scalps, the torture of victims and the practice of cannibalism. Champlain's observation of his Indian allies torturing and subsequently drinking the blood and eating the hearts of their victims in 1609 caused him a similar revulsion and horror.[33] These cruelties continued during the Seven Years' War.[34] "They kill all they meet," wrote a French priest, "and after having abused the women and maidens, they slaughter or burn them."[35] Women were often forced to burn their husbands and watch their babies roasted over slow fires. Prisoners were normally forced to endure running the gauntlet, beatings, slow death by torture, and burning at the stake.[36] Both English and French consistently protested, with an element of truth, that they were unable to control their Indian allies. However, their exploits undeniably assisted the efforts of their White allies.

The Indian way of war, however, did have one major weakness that was beyond their ability to control. Their Achilles heel became their reliance on European technology and trade goods. Once their stocks of lead, powder and firearms were depleted, they could be easily brought to terms. The long history of conflict and skirmishes with the First Nations in America had demonstrated how effective an embargo of strategic trade goods could be on Indian resistance.[37]

For example, one Indian chief loyal to the French cause arrived at Fort Niagara after its capture by the English in the summer of 1759. "We are asking you for gunpowder & shot for hunting, and also for garments," he declared, "but we have not come to form an alliance with you; as we are still under the wing of our father." He conceded, "We are at war with you but necessity forces us to solicit our needs from you."[38]

Clearly, the contrast between the Indian understanding and philosophy of conflict and that of the Europeans was striking in both the motives for, and manner of, waging war. "Instead of stealing upon each other, and taking every advantage to kill the enemy and save their own people, as we do," explained an Indian veteran, "they marched out, in open daylight, and fight, regardless of the number of warriors they may lose!" He added, "After the battle is over, they retire to feast, and drink wine, as if nothing had happened."[39] To the Indian, the quintessential victory was that which was won with minimal casualties. Once this was achieved, and the individual warriors had gained proof of their martial prowess through prisoners, scalps or plunder— which also carried a significant economic benefit—the Indians were satisfied to end the campaign lest they push their luck.[40] Furthermore, they saw themselves as allies and not as levies. Therefore, if they felt a plan or manoeuvre was ill-advised they simply chose not to participate.

But the Europeans failed to fully appreciate, if not comprehend, Indian aims and expectations. Instead, they tried to impose their understanding of war. Both powers undertook military operations with a view to influencing and limiting the possible actions of their opponent. Campaigns were undertaken to either capture territory, seize strategic points or destroy the enemy's field

Iroquois going on a Scout
by Jacques Grasset de Saint-
Sauver, engraver J. Laroque,
circa 1796.
(NA, C-3165)

army, all of which had direct impact on the enemy's ability to prosecute war in a successful manner. To achieve these aims, particularly when attacking fortifications, commanders were prepared to suffer heavy losses. To them, the Indians' refusal to participate represented a lack of the discipline and courage needed of soldiers. Moreover, they were seen as unreliable. And so, the Seven Years' War in North America was fought by two distinct and competing cultures.

But there is an obvious paradox. The Europeans held the Indians in contempt. The journals and memoirs of officers and soldiers are replete with condemnation. European commanders characterized the Indians as an unwanted burden, if not a nuisance. "They drive us crazy from morning to night," exclaimed Baron Dieskau. "There is no end to their demands," he added, finally concluding that "in short one needs the patience of an angel with these devils, and yet one must always force himself to seem pleased with them."[41] Another French commander, De Bougainville, agreed. "One must be the slave to these savages, listen to them day and night, in council and in private, whenever the fancy takes them, or whenever a dream or a fit of vapours, or their perpetual craving for brandy, gets possession of them; besides which they are always wanting something for their equipment, arms, or toilet"[42]

Yet despite these criticisms the Indians were aggressively wooed and showered with lavish gifts of equipment and food. Major-General William Shirley, Chief of His Majesties Forces in North America in 1755, actively lobbied the War Office to support a policy of luring the Indians to the British, or at a minimum securing their neutrality. He requested the appointment of commissioners for each of the western provinces, and money to defray the cost of the treaty obligations and inevitable presents that would be required. For instance, he promised to build a fort at an Onondago Castle and then was required to pledge the same for the Oneidas, including a garrison and artillery pieces. The Cayugas demanded men to plough their lands and gunsmiths to repair their weapons. Furthermore, Shirley stipulated that the treaty must clearly articulate rewards for every prisoner or scalp the Indians delivered to a designated location.[43]

The British wasted little time. Shirley quickly gave instruction to his subordinates to assure the Indians that they would be "supplied with arms, accoutrements, clothes, provisions and pay...[and] that they shall have besides these a reward for every prisoner or scalp taken from the enemy and every other reasonable encouragement all which to be ascertained to their satisfaction."[44] The direction even made allowances for the Indian warriors to bring their women and children, who would be fed and protected by the British.

The English efforts to gain the allegiance, or at least neutrality, of the Indians was not lost on the French. "The governors of Virginia and Pennsylvania," wrote Montcalm in his journal, "put all their efforts in luring the savages [away from the French] and obtaining, at least their neutrality."[45] He further observed that the English used every means possible, including the provision of supplies and alcohol, to win over the Indians. Similarly, Le Chevalier Le Mercier warned the French Ministry of Marine that failure to supply the Indians would result in their deserting the French cause.[46]

This fierce competition for the goodwill of the Indians created a vexing situation for the Europeans. In an attempt not to upset them the most wanton outrages were often accepted. One French officer decried the tolerance shown to their Indian allies. "You could see them running throughout Montreal," he recorded, "knife in hand, threatening and insulting everyone."[47] Montcalm confided to his journal that the Indians "are extremely insolent; they wish our fowls this evening. They took with force some barrels of wine, killed some cattle, and it is necessary to endure all."[48] French officers claimed that it proved very expensive to maintain their allies because they "exhausted so much provisions" and "could not be stinted to allowance taking everything at pleasure and destroying three times the Quantity of Provisions they could eat."[49] The Indians had no sense of rationing and would consume a week's allocation of provisions in three days and then demand additional replenishment. Consistently, the Europeans denounced their allies as disruptive to their campaigns and a drain on valuable resources.

But the far more serious menace was their duplicity. The Indians often delayed committing themselves to either side until they determined who the likely winner would be. Moreover, they often switched allegiance if momentum or success swung to the opposite side. The noted

Canadian historian, W.J. Eccles, stated that the Indian nations, impressed with the French show of strength, specifically the dispatch in 1753 of 2,000 troops to Lake Erie to build a road to the headwater and a chain of forts at strategic points, began to sever their trade connections with Anglo-Americans.[50] The subsequent success of French arms over Major George Washington's force at Fort Necessity in July 1754, and Major-General Braddock's army a year later, merely reinforced their proclivity to support the French. In fact, after Braddock's defeat, the Indians rejected British overtures to remain neutral and replied, "It is not in our power to comply with it, for the French & we are one blood, & where they are to dye we must dye also."[51]

However, this noble sentiment was mere rhetoric. As the fortunes of war shifted, so too did their loyalty. "An offensive, daring kind of war," wrote Major-General James Wolfe to his commander, "will awe the Indians and ruin the French." He added, "Blockhouses and a trembling defensive encourage the meanest scoundrels to attack us."[52] And so, as the British swung to the offensive, bringing their massive advantage in economic, naval and military power to bear, the last sinews of French strength began to break. The destruction in 1758 of Fort Frontenac and Fort Duquesne, two of France's most strategic fortifications, was a watershed in the fealty of the Indians to the French. By the summer of 1759, the Indians were actively conspiring to assist with the capture of Fort Niagara. For instance, the French officer responsible for the resupply of the fort was intentionally led into an ambush by his Indian guides. Although they remained neutral during the initial engagement, once the supply column collapsed the Indians "fell on them like so many Butchers."[53] Furthermore, Captain Pouchot, the commandant of the fort, was assured by his allies that "if we learn that the Englishman is plotting anything against you, we shall inform you immediately, so that you are not taken by surprise."[54] Yet, in little over a month an entire army passed through the Iroquois territory and appeared without warning before the fortress. To add further insult, once the fort had fallen the Indians most well known to the French garrison swarmed in to pillage and plunder the fort, even attempting to strip the French soldiers, their former compatriots, of their arms and possessions.[55]

It would only get worse for the French. As the English noose tightened around Quebec those few Indians who remained loyal took advantage of the situation. "The savages ... are a scourge for the inhabitants,"confided Abbe Jean-Félix Recher in his journal, "they kill [inhabitants] with impunity and pilfer all types of foodstuffs from their homes, take their animals, especially the oxen, cows, sheep, poultry, and horses."[56] Abbe Casgrain would later write that the Indians were "more to be feared [by the Canadians] than even the enemy."[57] By August 1759, as the English siege of Quebec continued, Montcalm wrote "we have a few savages, [we are] almost all alone."[58]

The wavering nature of the Indians' allegiance, however, had other implications which irritated the Europeans. Because no one wished to offend putative allies, they were given unrestricted access to both camps. The Indians in turn used this freedom of movement to spy and report on the preparations and plans of a belligerent to their respective enemy. The information provided was normally rendered for payment or to demonstrate fidelity to a given side. "The Five Nations ambassadors who descended to Montreal," recorded Montcalm in his journal, "he met with them, and quickly concluded that they came here as English spies rather than ambassadors."[59] Montcalm's second-in-command, de Lévis, reached a similar conclusion, observing that the ambassadors who came to provide information on British preparations had also likely come to conduct a reconnaissance on those of the French.[60] For this reason, Montcalm and de Lévis consciously disseminated false information and plans among the

General William Johnson's victory over General Dieskau, near Crown Point, Lake George, New York, 1755. (NA, C-6488)

Indians.[61] Even the Governor of New France, Le Marquis de Vaudreuil, who normally praised the Indians and Canadians, wrote to the Ministry of Marine and conceded that there was no doubt that the Indians spied on their supposed French allies. He added that he reproached them for their treason and warned them of the consequences should they continue such conduct.[62] The British perspective was no different. Major-General Jeffery Amherst, who was appointed the British Commander-in-Chief in 1759, wrote, "If the Indians know them [operational plans] the French will have it; it is their business to give intelligence to both sides."[63]

Skulduggery aside, there were also immense limitations on the employment of the Indians. In particular was their propensity to desert once they felt the campaign was over, notably when they were successful in securing prisoners, scalps and plunder, or when they felt the plan was ill-advised and would result in too great a risk of incurring casualties.[64] "Upon leaving, the savages always promised a lot," wrote de Lévis to Vaudreuil, " however, I found that they do not keep their promises." [65] This reality frustrated Montcalm as well. The Indians' consistent departure after the smallest of victories ensured that they would never inflict a lasting defeat on the English. This was also known to the British. "I have never heard," reassured John Campbell Loudoun, the British Commander-in-Chief in North America in 1756, "of any Instance of Indians remaining of either side, after they have either lost any people, or got any Booty, but have constantly returned Home."[66]

The other major limitation was the inability to control the Indians after a battle was fought or surrender negotiated. This problem was exacerbated when alcohol was involved. Baron Dieskau, in his General Orders prior to his attack against the British on Lake George in the late summer of 1755, specifically ordered that Indians were not to "amuse themselves by taking scalps until the enemy had been completely defeated." He explained that one could kill ten enemy in the time it took to lift one scalp.[67] However, no exhortations by either the English or the French were entirely effective. These were two competing cultures, with two completely different sets of expectations. As a result, pillage, scalping, the taking of prisoners and torture, regardless of articles of surrender agreed to by the Europeans, continued throughout the conflict.[68]

Top: English capitulation at Oswego, 1756. (NA, C-799)

Left: Wooing Indian allies. Formal councils, following a rigid proto-col, were continually undertaken by both the French and the English in an attempt to gain the support, or in the case of the English, at least the neutrality of the natives. (NA, C-299)

Nevertheless, despite all the aforementioned limitations, troubles, and differences in the philosophy and practice of waging war, the British and the French both actively sought, throughout the conflict, to recruit and use Indians as allies. Clearly then, they must have filled a significant role in the conflict. If not, why was so much effort made to recruit them? And why was so much tolerance shown to them? The fact that the Europeans showered them with gifts and provisions despite their unreliability and treachery is in itself testimony to the value of the Indians in the wilderness battles of North America.

In essence, they were an important component in the successful prosecution of war in the colonies. Their participation or even neutrality often represented the difference between victory or defeat. There are several reasons for this. The first is identified by Montcalm's rhetorical question, "what good are the savages?" He correctly answered, "not to have them against you." It was a question of security. Former governors of New York, fully cognizant of their capability, consistently warned of the danger. One stated that the loss of the Indians as allies would "tend to the utter Ruin of all the English settlements on the Continent."[69] Another admonished that "...the loss of them must be the loss of all the King's interest on this continent."[70] One contemporary writer also cautioned of the danger to the frontier if the Indians were enemies. "They would likewise surround the colony of New England on all sides," he wrote, "the only strength we have in America, which must be at their mercy; as all our other colonies would be open and exposed to them on every side, without the least security or barrier against them."[71] Even the Canadians feared their supposed allies. Many inhabitants claimed that they would have submitted to the besieging British early on had it not been for the "fear of the savages."[72]

This deep-rooted and often usurious fear was as much based on the cruelty and savagery of the Indians as it was on their efficiency and effectiveness when allowed to practise their form of warfare. George Washington, in the aftermath of Braddock's defeat, realized "without Indians we shall never be able to cope with those cruel foes to our country."[73] John Askin, an experienced American frontiersman, declared that in the forests, one Indian warrior was equal to three White men.[74] "Here in the forests of America," wrote one journalist, "we can no more do without them than without cavalry on the plain."[75]

Herein lies the second reason for their importance: they provided manpower, particularly to the French, and they were extremely effective in the tactical battle. With a population of only 60,000, New France faced the danger of being engulfed by the southern English colonists, who numbered approximately 1,500,000.[76] Indian allies represented an effective means to make up this shortfall of combatants. Moreover, they were proficient practitioners of *la petite guerre*. As bush fighters they were unsurpassed. They were able marksmen and possessed remarkable fieldcraft skills such as concealment, mobility and stealth. Casgrain wrote that they "glide from tree to tree, stump to stump ..."[77] They would appear as phantoms in ambushes or hit-and-run attacks, and despite their small numbers would often inflict a disproportionally high number of casualties on the enemy.[78] This has an utterly paralyzing effect on the opposing combatants. For instance, after a brief but bloody engagement with Indians, recalled a frontier veteran, "at night there was a Hundred men upon gard or more for feare of there coming a Gain in the Night."[79] Soldiers simply hated to go into the woods for reconnaissance or foraging because of the fear of being killed and scalped by the Indians.

Their prowess in the woods also made them adept at flank security. The Indians acted as an economy-of-effort force by creating diversions, pinning down other forces and, most importantly, cutting off the enemy's lines of communication. They were so continually successful at this that even Montcalm, normally a strong critic, praised them. During the attack on Oswego in August 1756 the Indians had isolated the garrison to a degree that Montcalm called "brilliant and decisive."[80] Another noteworthy example occurred during the siege of Fort William Henry, when a courier with a message for the beleaguered fort commandant was intercepted by the Indians. It was subsequently handed to Lieutenant-Colonel Monro by Montcalm with conditions of capitulation.[81] But these examples are not aberrations. Movement for the English was so constrained that they could neither gather intelligence, nor ensure communications among their forces. "It is not possible to conceive the situation and danger of this miserable country," deplored Washington. "Such numbers of French and Indians are all around that no road is safe."[82]

And so, the Indians developed a fierce reputation among the White soldiers and colonists. What the Indians lacked in strategic acumen they made up for in tactical skill. Their abilities in the woods, combined with their brutality and cruelty, soon paralyzed their opponents. The mere presence of Indians, or the sound of their war cry, created a prodigious panic in the enemy ranks. The "ravenous hell hounds," as they were often labelled by their European counterparts, consistently had a decisive psychological effect. "The yells of our Indians," wrote Montcalm to his mother, "promptly decided them [the English garrison at Oswego]. They yielded themselves prisoners of war to the number of 1,700, including eighty officers and two regiments from England."[83] Vaudreuil recounted the same story. "The cries, threats, and hideous howlings of our Canadians and Indians," he boasted, "made them quickly decide." At the prelude to the attack on Fort William Henry, the ambush of a British supply flotilla produced the same effect. "Terrified by the sight of these Monsters, their agility, their firing, and their yells," recalled Bougainville, "they surrendered almost without resistance."[84]

Overwhelmingly the mere thought of battling the savages unsettled both the British regulars and the American militia. "The men from what storys they had heard of the Indians in regard to their scalping and Mawhawking," wrote a British officer in his journal, "were so pannick struck that their officers had little or no command over them."[85] George Washington recounted an escort from Winchester to Fort Cumberland. At the first firing from the Indians, he stated, the men broke and ran back to Winchester, with less than half the force even stopping to fire a shot.[86] Even the stout Highlanders were overcome by the "appalling yells of the Canadians and Indians" at Fort Duquesne in 1758 and broke away in a wild and disorderly retreat.[87] "We have seen that our regulars do not fight well in woods," wrote a British official to the prime minister. "The yell is horrid to their ears, and soon throws them into confusion."[88]

The importance of Indian allies in the tactical battles for the wilderness becomes clear. However, there was yet another essential role that they performed. Their unsurpassed skills in the woods, combined with their knowledge of the country, made them indispensable as guides, scouts and gatherers of intelligence. They were often the only ones who could penetrate the deep wilderness of the frontier successfully. Vaudreuil often instructed the leaders of his expeditions against the English that if the Indians abandoned the foray, they were to return to Canada without completing the mission.[89]

But equally important was the void of similar services to the enemy. The lack of allies, or the effectiveness of the opponent's Indians in shutting out hostile reconnaissance parties repeatedly had a calamitous effect on the British. "I am ashamed," confided one British colonel, "that they have succeeded in all their scouting parties and that we never have any success in ours."[90] This state of affairs continually blinded the British command and deprived them of intelligence of French preparations or plans. Understandably, this often led to poor and untimely decisions laden with unfortunate consequences, whether the ambush of a British column or the loss of a strategic fort.[91]

The final role that the Indians filled, very adeptly and with great import to the prosecution of the war for the French, was that of frontier raiding. New France, having endured such a plague during its early years, was fully versed in its effects. "The Iroquois," stated Louis XIV in 1666, "through massacres and inhumanities, have prevented the country's population from growing."[92] An Iroquois Sachem boasted: "We plied the French homes in the war with them that they were not able to go out a door to piss."[93] The French now turned this manner of war against the English colonies. It provided a successful means of diverting British attention and draining resources that, if not focused on ensuring their own security, would most likely be aimed at attacking Canada. Governor Vaudreuil was very clear on his aim. "Nothing is more calculated to disgust the people of those colonies," he explained, "and to make them desire the return to peace."[94]

It was a strategy that was carried out year round and it was cost effective and fruitful. It clearly represented an economy of effort. Small parties of Canadians and Indians, led by French—and in some cases Canadian—officers could in this manner make an effective contribution to the war effort. The Indian raids terrorized the frontier and tied down large numbers of troops for rear security. The plight of the settlers and colonists could not be ignored. The incursions into Virginia alone caused the governor there to raise ten militia companies (1000 men) to try and impede Indian progress.[95] Moreover, militiamen were reluctant to undertake remote campaigns when they felt their families were at risk at home. The barbarity of the raids further fuelled perceptions and added to the psychological impact the Indians had on their opposition, who often fled or surrendered at the mere sign of an Indian presence. Furthermore, their destruction of settlements, farms and livestock, as well as the murder or capture of colonists, ate away at the economy of the Thirteen Colonies. Crops could not be sown or harvested. Grains could not be stored for the winter or to feed the army on campaign. This created privations for both soldier and citizen alike. Quite simply, the impact on the frontier was devastating.[96] The ferociousness of the raiding was such that it would stain relations between Whites and Indians for generations to come. Although an effective strategy for the outnumbered French, it was only successful as a delaying action. It did not, as Vaudreuil had hoped, bring the English to the peace table.

So in the end, the role of the Indians in the Seven Years' War was substantial. In many cases their participation or neutrality in a campaign was the difference between success and failure. Their effectiveness as bush fighters, compounded by the reputation they earned for cruelty and savagery made them an opponent that inspired fear and panic in their enemies. They performed many critical tasks such as scouting and intelligence gathering, cutting enemy lines of communication, and supporting major assaults through skirmishing and attacks on the opponent's flanks. In addition, they conducted deep penetration raids that inflicted economic, physical and psychological damage on the enemy. However, as Montcalm accurately assessed, they did not, nor could they—because of their numbers, dependence on European technology and their cultural and philosophical understanding of war—impose a lasting defeat on their enemy.

Furthermore, the fastidiousness of the European methods of war slowly seeped into the consciousness of the regular military commanders. "It is absolutely necessary for his Majesty's Service," extolled William Shirley, "that one Company at least of Rangers should be constantly employ'd in different Parties upon Lake George and Lake Iroquois [Lake Ontario], and the Wood Creek and Lands adjacent ... to make Discoveries of the proper Routes for our own Troops, procure Intelligence of the Enemy's Strength and Motions, destroy their out Magazines and Settlements, pick up small Parties of their Battoes upon the Lakes, and keep them under continual Alarm."[97] Similarly, several years later Major-General James Wolfe explained, "Our troops must be employd in a very different manner from what has been the Practice hitherto." He added, "They must learn to live in the Woods as the Indians do—keep 'em in a continual apprehention of being attack'd to acquire a perfect knowledge of the Lakes & Rivers, & Hunting Grounds of the Savages."[98]

This sage advice was taken to heart. Companies of Rangers, the most famous being those of Major Robert Rogers, were raised as a direct answer to the British lack of Indian allies. In addition, in 1756, the Royal Americans 60th Foot were organized as light infantry to provide the British with a means of contending with the Indians. The regiment was intended to combine the qualities of the scout with the discipline of the trained soldier. Moreover, uniforms and tactics were adjusted to the reality of the wilderness. Musket barrels were made blue or brown to "take off the glittering." Commanders also directed that the coats of the light infantry were to be quite plain, adding the advice that "the less they are seen in the Woods the better."[99] One of the Highland regiments gave up their kilts for breeches and many officers gave up wearing gorgets and sashes. Astoundingly, some even went to such extremes as to wear the same tunic as those worn by privates.[100]

The change in philosophy was also clear in the manner in which the Europeans adapted their tactics. Rangers and scouts were always included in the advance party of any moving force. Furthermore, Wolfe in his instruction to his army embedded many of the lessons learned. He directed that all detachments and outposts fortify their camps by either entrenching or building palisades. Sentries were never to be placed in musket range of woods unless hidden behind rocks or trees themselves and he cautioned his commanders never to halt, encamp or pass through openings without first examining the area for a potential ambush or subsequent attack.[101]

Although slow in adapting, once the Whites adjusted to the Indian way of war, the significance of the Indians as allies and combatants was substantially reduced. Despite the martial prowess and skill of the warriors, in the long term the superior discipline and organization, as well as technology of the Whites, always prevailed. And so, although the participation or neutrality of the Indians often affected the success or failure of a particular campaign, they did not, nor could they, influence the outcome of the Seven Years' War in North America.

Notes for Chapter 2

1   George F. Stanley, *Canada's Soldiers. The Military History of an Unmilitary People* (Toronto: The Macmillan Company of Canada Limited, 1960), 17.

2   Emphasis in training was placed on speed and not accuracy of firing. The maximum effective range of a smooth bore musket was approximately 200 yards, but successfully striking anything was near impossible. The average soldier was capable of reloading and firing about two to three shots per minute. See Hew Strachan, *European Armies and the Conduct of War* (London: Routledge, 1991), 16-25; Robert Leckie, *A Few Acres of Snow—The Saga of the French and Indian Wars* (Toronto: John Wiley & Sons, 1999), 52-3 & 280; Geoffrey Parker, ed., *Warfare* (Cambridge: Cambridge University Press, 1995), 176-8 & 185; R.R. Palmer, "Frederick the Great, Guibert, Bülow: From Dynastic to National War," in Peter Paret, ed., *Makers of Modern Strategy* (Princeton, NJ: University of Princeton Press, 1986), 93-94; Carl Benn, *The Iroquois in the War of 1812* (Toronto: University of Toronto Press, 1998), 68; and Patrick M. Malone, *The Skulking Way of War* (Lanham, Maryland: Madison Books, 1991), 56-58.

3   W.J. Eccles, "The French forces in North America during the Seven Years' War," in *Dictionary of Canadian Biography, Vol III, 1741 to 1770* (Toronto: University of Toronto Press, 1974), xvi.

4   Parker, 178.

5   Palmer, 99-100.

6   David Perry, "Life of David Perry, (Chelsea, Vermont, 1819)," *The Bulletin of the Fort Ticonderoga Museum,* Vol 14, No. 1, (Summer 1981), 6.

7   Ibid., 6.

8   One veteran asserted, "Those who have experienced only the severities and dangers of a campaign in Europe can scarcely form an idea of what is to be done and endured in an American War. In an American campaign every thing is terrible—the face of the country, the climate, the enemy." *The Conquest of Canada, Vol II.* (New York: Harper & Brothers, 1850,) 18.

9   Leroy V. Eid, "American Indian Military Leadership: St. Clair's Defeat," *The Journal of Military History,* Vol 57 (January 1993), 86. See also Malone, 60 & 92.

10 Paul E. Kopperman, *Braddock at the Monongahela* (Pittsburg: University of Pittsburg Press, 1977), 30; Noel St John Williams, *Redcoats along the Hudson. The Struggle for North America 1754-63* (London: Brassey's Classics, 1998), 76; Fred Anderson, *Crucible of War* (New York: Vintage Books, 2001), 96-97; and Strachan, 28.

11 See Anderson, 95; Thomas Fleming, "Braddock's Defeat," *Military History Quarterly,* Vol 3, No. 1, (Autumn 1990), 90; and Martin L. Nicolai, "A Different Kind of Courage: The French Military and the Canadian Irregular Soldier during the Seven Years' War," *Canadian Historical Review,* Vol 70, No. 1 (1989), 60. Franklin also wrote, "this general was, I think, a brave man, and might probably have made a good figure in some European war. But he had ... too high an opinion of the validity of regular troops; too mean a one of both Americans and Indians." Quoted in Kopperman, 95-96 & 101; and Major James H. Silcox, "Rogers and Bouquet: The Origins of American Light Infantry,"*Military Review,* Vol 65, No. 12, 65.

12 Francis Parkman, *Montcalm and Wolfe* (New York: The Modern Library, 1999), 111and 117-118; Leckie, 284-285; Anderson, 102-103; and Kopperman, 79. Tragically, as the provincials moved forward to take cover and engage the enemy in the woods they were cut down by volleys from the British regulars, who seeing the smoke of discharges coming from the brush at the side of the road mistook them for enemy..

13 Kopperman, 139 and Annex E. In regard to the accusation that Braddock was killed by his own men, Kopperman's book is by far one of the best sources.

14 Stanley, 66. See also Kopperman, 70.

15 Strachan, 28; Anderson, 105; and Stanley, 66.

16 Wolfe to Charles, 3rd Duke of Richmond. "Some Unpublished Wolfe Letters, 1755-58," *Society for Army Historical Research Journal,* Vol 53, 1975, 68.

17 "The Josiah Goodrich Orderbook," *The Bulletin of the Fort Ticonderoga Museum,* Vol 14, No. 1 (Summer 1981), 44.

18 K.L. Macpherson, *Scenic Sieges and Battlefields of French Canada* (Montreal: Valentine & Sons, 1957), 4.

19 Anderson, 100. The veteran also recalled them "Either on their Bellies or Behind trees or Running from one tree to another almost by the ground." At the battle at Lake George

20 Benn, 71; and Malone, 59-60.

21 A Native veteran observed that in combat "the right men [Indian leaders] concealed themselves, and are worst clothed than the others." Eid, 81.

22 M. Pouchot, *Memoirs on the Late War in North America between France and England* (Yverdon, 1781), 160 & 476.

23 See Robert F. Berkhofer, "The French and Indians at Carillon," *The Bulletin of the Fort Ticonderoga Museum,* Vol 9, No. 6, 1956, 137-138 & 147; D.P. MacLeod, *The Canadian Iroquois and the Seven Years' War* (Toronto: Dundurn Press,1996), 21; Benn, 82; Eid, 81; and Nicolai, 60.

24 MacLeod, 34-35.

25 H.R. Casgrain, *Montcalm et Lévis—Les Français au Canada* (Québec: Maison Alfred Mame et Fils, undated), 43.

26 Ross Brian Snyder, "Algonquin Warfare in Canada and Southern New England 1600-1680." Unpublished M.A. (History) Thesis, University of Ottawa, 1972, 157.

27 François Gaston Chevalier de Lévis, *Journal Des Campagnes du Chevalier De Lévis* (Montreal: C.O. Beauchemin & Fils, 1889), 39.

28 Jack M. Sosin, "The Use of Indians in the War of the American Revolution: A Re-assessment of Responsibility," *The Canadian Historical Review*, Vol 66, No.2 (June 1965), 120.

29 Sylvester K. Stevens, Donald H. Kent and Emma E. Woods, *Travels in New France by J. C. B.* (Harrisburg, Penn: The Pennsylvania Historical Commission, 1941), 25.

30 Pouchot writes in his journal that "even if there are three hundred of them & they were to take only one or two scalps, they would not begin another operation, even were they capable of devastating an entire territory and killing other men." Pouchot, 477. See also Nicolai, 59; and Benn, 53.

31 See Letter William Shirley to British War Office, 22 December 1755, New York, Public Record Office (hereafter PRO), War Office 1/4, Correspondence, 1755-1763; "John Henry Lydius, Fur Trader at Fort Edward," *The Bulletin of the Fort Ticonderoga Museum*, Vol 11, No. ,(December 1964), 272-273; Benn, 54; and Parkman, 211.

32 Berkhofer, 157; and Anderson, 112.

33 Le Comte Gabriél de Maurès de Malartic, *Journal des Campagnes au Canada de 1755 A 1760* (Paris: Librairie Plon, 1902), 130; Leckie, 75; Anderson, 197; Brigadier R.O. Alexander, ed., "The Capture of Quebec. A Manuscript Journal Relating to the Operations Before Quebec From 8th May, 1759, to 17th May, 1760 Kept by Colonel Malcolm Fraser," *Journal of the Society for Army Historical Research,* Vol 18 (1939), 141; and A. Doughty, *The Siege of Quebec and the Battle of the Plains of Abraham, Vol II* (Quebec: Dussault & Proulx, 1901), 200.

in early September 1755, Baron Dieskau's French regular officer and men, who remained in the open, suffered horrendous casualties against the New England men who fired from behind logs. They lost nearly all their officers and approximately half of their soldiers. Conversely, the French Canadians and Indians remained behind cover and suffered negligible losses. Anderson, 158-159.

34 The North American component of the global Seven Years' War is often referred to as The French and Indian War (1754-1760).

35 Parkman, 168. Although they normally showed no mercy to anyone regardless of age or gender, this description is somewhat misleading. Prisoners were too valuable to just burn. In addition, few sources allude to wholesale rape. Highly superstitious, the warriors seldom dared to offend the Master of Life while on operations.

36 Snyder; Pouchot, 480; Leckie, 158; "Père Roubaud, Missionary Extraordinary," *The Bulletin of the Fort Ticonderoga Museum*, Vol 12, No. 1, (March 1966), 67-68; St John Williams, 105 & 115; Raymond Scheele, "Warfare of the Iroquois and their Northern Neighbours," unpublished PhD (Political Science) Thesis, Columbia University, 1950, 44; Koert Burnham, "Notes Regarding the First White Fur Traders on Lake Champlain," *The Bulletin of the Fort Ticonderoga Museum*, Vol 14, No. 4, (Fall 1983), 199; Casgrain, *Les Français au Canada*, 182-183; and Kopperman, 91-92. See also Fredrick Drimmer, ed. *Captured by the Indians. 15 Firsthand Accounts 1750-1870* (New York: Dover Publications Ltd., 1961), 19 & 9-104; and Ian K. Steele, *Betrayals. Fort William Henry & the Massacre* (New York: Oxford University Press, 1990). Although there was an element of entertainment involved with the torture it also fulfilled a spiritual and emotional need. Torture was often seen as a consolation for the death of a relative or a means of quieting the soul of the deceased. It also provided a means of allowing an enemy to display his courage. When an opponent did so in a gallant manner, his heart was often eaten because of a belief that it would render those consuming it more courageous.

37 Anderson, 454, 469 & 545. See also Letter William Shirley to Principal Secretary of War, 20 December 1755, New York, PRO, War Office 1/4, Correspondence, 1755-1763; *The Northcliffe Collection*, 71.

38 Pouchot, 285.

39 Benn, 67.

40 For example, a group of Indians having successfully executed an ambush that yielded both supplies and prisoners, without incurring any casualties, decided to return home. "The Master of Life has favoured us," they explained to the French commander, "here is the food, here are the prisoners, let's return." MacLeod, 35-36.

41 Doughty, Vol II, 202; *The Northcliffe Collection*, 138; and Berkhofer, 146.

42 Berkhofer, 146; and Anderson, 204.

43 Letter, Major-General William Shirley, Chief of His Majesties Forces in North America, to British War Office, 22 December 1755, PRO, War Office 1/4, Correspondence, 1755-1763; Letter, Major-General William Shirley, to Principal Secretary of War, 20 December 1755, PRO, War Office 1/4, Correspondence, 1755-1763.

44 Letter, "Additional Instructions to Major-General William Johnston relative to the Indians of the Six Nations under his care," from William Shirley, 13 January 1756, PRO, War Office 1/4, Correspondence, 1755-1763.

45 H.R. Casgrain, François Gaston Chevalier de Lévis Collection des Manuscrits, *Journal du Marquis de Montcalm Durant Ses Campagnes en Canada De 1756 à 1759, Vol VII* (Québec: L.J. Demers & Frère, 1895), 335. See also *Lettres Du Chevalier de Lévis Concernant La Guerre du Canada, 1756-1760* (Montreal: C.O. Beauchemin & Fils, 1889), 144.

46 H.R. Casgrain, ed. *Extraits des Archives des Ministéres de la Marine et de la Guerre A Paris—Canada— Correspondence Générale—MM. Duquesne et Vaudreuil Gouverneurs-Généraux, 1755-1760* (Québec: L.J. Demers & Frère, 1890), 150.

47 Louis de Courville, *Mémoires sur le Canada depuis 1749 Jusqu'à 1760* (Quebec: Imprimerie de Middleton and Dawson, 1873), 97. See also Doughty, 202-203; and Benn, 136.

48 Quoted in Berkhofer, 147. See also Casgrain, *Journal du Marquis De Montcalm*, 385; Parkman, 238. The sentiment of "enduring all" is a recurring one. During campaigns the largest portion of the armies were deployed, leaving the major centres virtually undefended. The spectre of large numbers of uncontrollable Indians going on a rampage haunted the governor. Prudence was continually the watchword. See Doughty, Vol I, 192; and George F. Stanley, "British Operations in the American North-West, 1812-15," *Army Historical Research*, Vol 22 (1943-44), 96.

49 Steele, *Betrayals*, 132-133; Parkman, 238; Berkhofer, 156; and Allen, 144.

50 W.J. Eccles, *The French in North America* (Markham, Ont: Fitzhenry & Whiteside, 1998), 201; and "Unrest At Caughnawaga or The Lady Fur Traders of Sault St. Louis," *The Bulletin of the Fort Ticonderoga Museum*, Vol 7, No. 3 (December 1963), 155. A similar mentality existed during the War of 1812. The initial British successes at Michilimackinac and Detroit induced a large number of tribes and nations of Indians to rally to the British standard. See Stanley, "British Operations in the American North-West," 93-94; Allen, 138, and Benn, 49.

51 Theodore Burnham Lewis, Jr., "The Crown Point Campaign 1755," *The Bulletin of the Fort Ticonderoga Museum*, Vol 13, No. 1 (December 1970), 37. See also O'Meara, 114; and Courville, 90.

52 Casgrain, *Wolfe and Montcalm*, 74-75. The concept of strength is a critical one—the Indians considered weakness, or being a weakling, the greatest of all insults. Richard A. Preston and Leopold Lamontagne, *Royal Fort Frontenac* (Toronto: University of Toronto Press, 1958), 206.

53 Letter from Albany of 6 August 1759, published in *Pennsylvania Gazette*, 23 August 1759, quoted in Pouchot, 231. See also Malartic, 268.

54 Pouchot, 183.

55 Pouchot, 229-231. The capture of Fort Frontenac was similar. Once the fort was captured the Indians arrived to plunder and scalp. However, Lieutenant-Colonel Bradstreet forbade the killing or scalping of prisoners or wounded. He was able to achieve their agreement by turning over most of the booty to the Indians. *An Impartial Account of Lieut. Col. Bradstreet's Expedition*, 8-9 & 20-22.

56   Jean-Félix Récher, *Journal du Siège de Québec en 1759* (Quebec: La Société Historique de Québec Université Laval, 1959), 36.

57   Casgrain, *Wolfe and Montcalm*, 130-131 & 203.

58   H.R. Casgrain, ed., *Lettres de M. De Bourlamaque au Chevalier de Lévis* (Québec: L.J. Demers & Frère, 1890), 339. See also Pouchot, 231; *Conquest of Canada, Vol II*, 99; Parkman, 332; Preston and Lamontagne, 269; *Impartial Account of Lieut. Col. Bradstreet's Expedition to Fort Frontenac.* (Toronto: Rous & Mann Ltd, 1940), 8-9; St John Williams, 219; and Maurice Sautai, *Montcalm au Combat de Carillon, 8 Juillet 1758* (Paris: Librairie Militaire R. Chapelot, 1909), 42-42.

59   Casgrain, *Journal du Marquis De Montcalm*, 88.

60   Casgrain, *Journal Des Campagnes du Chevalier De Lévis*, 174-175.

61   Casgrain, *Français au Canada,* 63; Berkhofer, 136 & 141; Stevens, 57; and Nicholas Beyard, *Journal of the Late Actions of the French at Canada by Col. Nicholas Beyard and Lieut. Col. Charles Lodowick* (New York: Joseph Sabin, 1868), 41.

62   H.R. Casgrain, ed., *Extraits des Archives des Ministéres de la Marine et de la Guerre A Paris—Canada—Correspondence Générale—MM. Duquesne et Vaudreuil Gouverneurs-Généraux, 1755-1760* (Québec: L.J. Demers & Frère, 1890), 72-73.

63   St John Williams, 197; and Parkman, 188.

64   Examples have already been cited. However, see also Casgrain, *Journal du Marquis De Montcalm*, 374-375; Parkman, 114, MacLeod, 30-31 & 69; Doughty, Vol I, 208-9; H.R. Casgrain, ed., *Guerre du Canada. Relations et Journaux de Différentes Expéditions* (Québec: L.J. Demers & Frère, 1895), 174; Sautai, 13, 18 & 80; H.R. Casgrain, ed., *Lettres du Chevalier De Lévis concernant La Guerre du Canada (1756-1760).* Montreal: C.O. Beauchemin & Fils, 1889), 21 & 75; Nicolai, 60; Steele, *Betrayals*, 49-50, 73; Anderson, 151; and Pouchot, 115. In addition see Stanley, George F. "The Indians in the War of 1812," *Canadian Historical Review,* Vol 31, No. 2 (June 1950), 153; and Benn, 82 (During the War of 1812, at the battle of Queenston Heights, under fire fifty percent of the warriors deserted, and at the subsequent Battle of Fort George, seventy percent of the Indians deserted); and Stanley, "British Operations in the American North-West," 95-6.

65   Casgrain, *Lettres du Chevalier De Lévis concernant La Guerre du Canada,* 75.

66   Steele, *Betrayals,* 126.

67   Casgrain, *Extraits des Archives des Ministéres de la Marine et de la Guerre A Paris*, 40-41.

68   Examples have already been cited. However, see also Casgrain, *Journal Des Campagnes du Chevalier De Lévis,* 101-102; Émile Lonchampt, *Pourquoi L'Amérique du Nord n'est pas Française?* (Paris: Challamel Aîné, 1888), 47; Eid, 77; Casgrain, *Les Français au Canada,* 102; and George Chalou, "Red Pawns Go to War: British–American Indian Relations, 1810-1815," Unpublished MA Thesis, Indiana University, 1971, 86.

69   Casgrain, *Journal du Marquis De Montcalm*, 591. A Whig leader in the Mohawk Valley during the Revolutionary War summed up the question in a similar manner. Because the Indians would be fighting, he stated, "for somebody and that they may better be fighting for us than against us needs no argument." Sosin, 121.

70   W.J. Eccles, "Frontenac's Military Policies, 1689-1698. A Reassessment," *The Canadian Historical Review,* Vol 37, No. 3 (September 1956), 204. Lord Bathurst, the British Secretary of War in 1812, correctly assessed, "If not retained as our friends, they will act against us as enemies." Chalou, 101.

71   Impartial Hand, *The Contest in America Between Great Britain and France, With its Confequences and Importance* (London: A. Millar in the Strand, 1757), 83.

72   *Conquest of Canada, Vol II*, 189. See also George F. Stanley, "The Indians in the War of 1812," *Canadian Historical Review,* Vol 31, No. 2 (June 1950), 155; and Benn, 47.

73   Silcox, 65.

74   Benn, 64.

75   Parkman, 241; and Anderson, 189.

76   Stanley, *Canada's Soldiers,* 61; Eccles, "French Forces ," xx; Leckie, 103; Doughty, Vol I, 158; and Fleming, 87.

77   Casgrain, *Français au Canada,* 87.

78   Casgrain, *Journal du Marquis De Montcalm*, 252; "Fragments of a Journal in the Handwriting of General Wolfe, 1759 (Wolfe's Journal 19 June—16 August 1759). Held in Royal Military College of Canada Library, Rare Book Collection, 17, 25, and 27 July; *The Northcliffe Collection,* 216; Thomas Haynes, "Memorandum of Colonial French War A.D. 1758," *The Bulletin of the Fort Ticonderoga Museum,* Vol 12, No. 3 (October 1967), 8; Casgrain, *Wolfe and Montcalm*, 40; Pouchot, 118; and Doughty, Appendix, Part I, 261.

79   "Amos Richardson's Journal, 1758," *The Bulletin of the Fort Ticonderoga Museum,* Vol 12, No. 4 (September 1968), 278; and *Governor Murray's Journal of the Siege of Quebec, from 18th September, 1759 to 25th May, 1760.* (Toronto: Rous & Mann Ltd, 1939), 14.

80   Casgrain, *Français au Canada,* 91.

81   Anderson, 194; and Parkman, 250.

82   Parkman, 168. See also Extract of a letter from Sir William Johnson to General Shirley, 10 May 1756, PRO, War Office 1/4, Correspondence, 1755-1763; O'Meara, 84; and Doughty, Vol I, 167. The tight grip on movement was also effective in catching deserters. See Malartic, 217; and Pouchot 136.

83   Casgrain, *Wolfe and Montcalm*, 35; Anderson 102; and Parkman, 207.

84   Parkman, 241.

85   O'Meara, 147.

86   Ibid., 177.

87   Parkman, 333.

88   *Conquest of Canada,* 153. See also Casgrain, *Wolfe and Montcalm,* 117; and Parkman, 112.

89   H.R. Casgrain, ed., *Lettres et Pièces Militarires. Instructions, Ordres, Mémoires, Plans de Campagne it de Défense 1756-1760* (Québec: L.J. Demers & Frère, 1891), 50; and MacLeod, 25. See also Berkhofer, 136; Pouchot, 476; and Malone, 84.

90   O'Meara, 85.

91   "Memoir on the Defense of the Fort of Carillon," *The Bulletin of the Fort Ticonderoga Museum*, Vol 13, No. 3 (1972), 200-1; Steele, *Betrayals*, 96; and Anderson, 187.

92   Quoted documents, display, Fort Chambly National Historic Site of Canada, Chambly, Quebec. Accessed 23 August 2001.

93   Ibid.

94   Anderson, 151; and Parkman, 214. See also *Conquest of Canada,* 93.

95   Letter from General Shirley to Major-General Abercrombie, 27 June 1756, PRO, War Office 1/4, Correspondence, 1755-1763.

96   Anderson, 637; and Leckie, 101. Statistics exist on the ruin caused by Indians raids in New York during 1780. These provide an idea of the scope of destruction: 700 houses and barns burned, 330 people killed or captured and nearly 700 cattle driven off. Don R. Gerlach, "The British Invasion of 1780 and 'A Character ... Debased Beyond Description," *The Bulletin of the Fort Ticonderoga Museum,* Vol 14, No. 5 (Summer 1984), 311. See also Letter From William Shirley (New York) to Principal Secretary of War, 20 December 1755, PRO, War Office 1/4, Correspondence, 1755-1763; Parkman, 173; Casgrain, *Lettres du Chevalier De Lévis*, 75; Ian K. Steele, *Guerillas and Grenadiers,* (Toronto: Ryerson Press, 1969), 24; Casgrain, *Journal du Marquis De Montcalm*, 110-111; Malartic, 52-53; Kopperman, 232; O'Meara, 161; and Gavin K. Watt, *The Burning of the Valleys* (Toronto: Dundurn Press, 1997), 73.

97   John R. Cuneo, *Robert Rogers of the Rangers* (New York: Oxford University Press, 1959), 33.

98   *Northcliffe Collection,* Vol IX, 110.

99   "Monypenny Orderly Book," *The Bulletin of the Fort Ticonderoga Museum*, Vol 13, No. 2 (June 1971), 170.

100 Anderson, 410; Leckie, 309; Strachan, 28; and St John Williams, 79 &143.

101 *General Wolfe's Instructions to Young Officers: Also His Orders for a Battalion and an Army* (London: J. Millan, 1780), 72-73.

CHAPTER 3

The Participation of Immigrants in the American Civil War

The Case of the French Canadians[1]

Jean Lamarre

CHARLES BOUCHER fought in the American Civil War. Born in Quebec in 1840, he enrolled at Manchester, Michigan, on 28 February 1862, for three years. Assigned to the 1st Michigan Infantry Regiment, he fought in the battle of Mechanicsville, Virginia in June of 1862. After a summer in Virginia, his regiment marched in September to Antietam, in Maryland, to face the enemy there. But they did so without him. On 30 August 1862, during the Second Battle of Bull Run, Charles Boucher was killed in combat after only six months of service. He was twenty-two years old.[2]

French Canadians, like many of the other soldiers who fought during the American Civil War, did not all meet such a tragic fate. Nevertheless, this fratricidal conflict—which lasted four years, mobilized four million soldiers and killed more than 600,000 people—deeply upset the lives of all those involved. During the four decades that preceded the conflict, the United States had welcomed more than five million immigrants. When war broke out, tens of thousands of them enlisted. They made a significant contribution to the war effort yet, American historians have long neglected to study their role in the conflict. This chapter attempts to shed some light on how the participation of immigrants has been dealt with throughout history, and particularly, it looks at how history has recorded the role of French Canadians.

Few events in American history have received as much attention as the American Civil War, which lasted from 1861 to 1865. This epic struggle, which has assumed a mythic character in the history of the United States, continues to fascinate a great number of Americans as well as Canadians, and it is the subject most written about in the US. More than 50,000 books and articles have been published on the war. These studies have dealt with all aspects: the causes, the forces involved, the various military campaigns, strategies employed, as well as the socio-economic and political impact on American society. The research has also analyzed the ideology of the protagonists, that is to say, that of Northerners who presented themselves as defenders of an industrial society and against slavery, and that of Southerners who represented an agricultural society that was conservative and depended on slavery.[3]

However, historians have long depicted this war as above all an *American* war; a war pitting brother against brother. But a significant number of immigrants from various backgrounds also took part. Of the five million people who came to the United States between 1820 and 1860, ninety-five percent came from Northwestern Europe, and three percent from North America. Of this number, more than one and a half million were from the German states. There were 967,366 from Ireland, 302,665 from England, 208,063 from France and 117,142 from Canada.[4] All were fleeing the political or economic problems of their countries. They chose the United States, at the time entering its first phase of industrialization, because of the promise it offered for greater political freedom and better employment. At the beginning of the war the US was home to 1,611,304 Irishmen, 1,301,136 Germans, 431,692 British, 249,970 Canadians and 109,870 Frenchmen[5]. It is estimated that in 1860, the free states of the North had 3,903,672 people who were foreign-born, compared to only 233,650 in the slave states that joined the Confederacy.[6] Not surprisingly, given that eighty-seven percent of these immigrants had settled in the industrial north, the great majority of immigrant enrollees joined the Union armies.[7]

Although the American Civil War ended in April 1865, more than 80 years passed before historians began to look at the contribution made by immigrants. In the wake of the claims of the Afro-American movement that developed after the Second World War, and the sharper awareness of the presence of various cultural groups within the United States, historians began to work on a wider and more inclusive re-interpretation of American history. Some approached the American Civil War with the objective of freeing it from its purely White-Anglo-Saxon-Protestant context in order to clarify the participation and the contribution of others, notably immigrants.

American historian Ella Lonn was the first to become interested in the participation of immigrants in the American Civil War. She published two monumental studies, the first in 1940 and the second in 1951, relating to the immigrant presence in the armies of the South and North.[8] Using documents from the War Records Office at the State Department, reports of the adjutants and ethnic newspapers, Lonn analyzed the contribution of the immigrants to the various regiments they were assigned to. She especially looked at the participation of German and Irish immigrants, who were by far the most numerous in the armies of the North. She also looked at the contribution of the smaller groups of Frenchmen, Scots, Scandinavians, Swiss and Mexicans. Lonn looked at immigrants' attitudes toward the war, and their motivation for joining the war effort. She highlighted the leadership that certain members of these communities demonstrated. Finally, she tried to recreate the everyday life of the soldiers in the camps and on the battlefields. Even though she attempted in her conclusions to establish a hierarchy of contributions made by immigrant groups, Lonn actually revealed the remarkable contribution they made as a collective whole. In her 1951 study she found that the Union Army was far from being the homogeneous army that was normally depicted. She also discovered that it was the most "representative of American armies," since its ranks well reflected the ethnic diversity that defined American society at the time. Lonn stressed that each ethnic group contributed in its own way to the victory of the North over the South.[9]

In the wake of Lonn's massive work, American historians have put increasing emphasis on the contribution of certain immigrant groups to the American Civil War effort. Numerous studies have been done of the participation of German and Irish immigrants. Other studies have used regimental histories to retrace the presence of immigrants and their unique contribution.[10]

In 1988, William L. Burton published a work which to some extent summarized the knowledge acquired since the research carried out by Lonn.[11] Based on military correspondence, regimental stories and other primary sources, Burton sought to account for the everyday life of the immigrant soldier, the ethnic tensions within the various regiments and the motivations that animated those tensions. The author considered the contribution made by all immigrant groups involved, giving priority, however, to the largest. Burton updated the information available on the subject and placed the immigrant contribution within a broader framework, specifically the interaction between the diverse ethnic groups present within the various regiments.

Social historians have not remained on the sidelines. Until recently, they had been especially interested in the process of industrialization during the nineteenth century and its impact upon society, workers, immigrants and the family. However, since 1990, the American Civil War has attracted their interest. Their work has revealed some lesser-known aspects of the war, particularly its impact on small multi-ethnic communities, and the role of volunteer work.[12] Immigrants and their contribution are now categorically included in almost all research that is conducted in regard to the American Civil War.

Canadian Participation

Although they were fewer in number than other groups that took part in the war, Canadians, whether of British or French origin, also fought. Most likely for geographical reasons, the majority enrolled in the Union Army, although some fought for the Confederacy.[13] At the time that the civil war broke out, approximately 250,000 Canadians were living in the United States. However, the number of French Canadians is difficult to establish. It is known that New England accounted for nearly 37,000[14] and it is believed that approximately 20,000 French Canadians were living in the American Midwest, including 9,000 in Michigan alone.[15]

Incredibly, it took a long time for Canadian historians to become interested in Canadian participation in this war. This is surprising because of the large number of Canadians who were living in the United States. In addition, Canadian newspapers at the time, both English and French, reported widely on the war, covering such issues as Canadian enrolment, the impact on the economy and Anglo–Canadian relations.[16] In English Canada, the first academic articles were published in the 1920s. These studies did not, however, look at the global picture of Canadian participation, nor did they try to evaluate it. Rather, they provided lengthy analyses of a particularly shocking aspect of the conflict that had been given spectacular coverage in the newspapers during the war, namely, the forced enlistment of Canadians by professional American recruiters representing both the American North and South.[17]

There are no studies that deal specifically with the French-Canadians. In 1936, E. Z. Massicotte and Lionel-A. Lapointe highlighted the French-Canadian contribution to the civil war by publishing lists of a few dozen French Canadians who had taken part in the conflict. These lists were created from information provided by close relatives of the combatants. However, the information was never confirmed.[18]

It was only in 1960 that the first exhaustive work was published on the American Civil War that included the participation of Canadians and its impact on the country. This study by Robin W. Winks remains the most substantial work on the subject. It deals with the origins of the conflict, the political tensions created between England and the United States as a result of the struggle, and Canadian opinion regarding the war. Winks also devotes several pages to direct Canadian participation.[19] He found that a significant number of French Canadians as well as English Canadians enrolled in the armies of the North and South. He noted that until then, the most widely reported estimates of the number of Canadian participants had varied between 40,000 and 53,000.

The first estimate came from Father David-Hercule Beaudry, who was the parish priest at Saint Constant, Quebec. In February 1865, during a funeral oration held in Montreal to commemorate the French Canadians who had fallen during the war, he stated that 40,000 French Canadians had taken part in the conflict, 14,000 of whom had lost their lives. Others later repeated this estimate. For example, in 1904, John A. MacDonald repeated it in a commentary concerning Canadian enrolment in the armies of the North.

The second estimate came from a study by Benjamin A. Gould, who in New York in 1869 published *Investigations in the Military and Anthropological Statistics of American Soldiers*. It was based on a survey that was carried out among a thousand Federal officers who were asked to indicate the place of birth of soldiers under their command. Gould concluded that 2.65 percent of the soldiers of the Union Army had been born in the British colonies to the north. Gould applied this percentage to the total number of combatants and concluded that 53,532 Canadians had enrolled in the Union Army during the American Civil War.[20]

However, these calculations were criticized by Winks. According to him, Beaudry's estimate was far-fetched and had no empirical basis. Winks pointed out that Beaudry never specified the source of his information. Winks also blasted Gould's assessment. He questioned the validity of the answers provided by the officers, since they were based on approximation, without the officers actually asking the soldiers to specify their birthplace. Winks believed, without proving his conclusions, that the Canadian contribution was much lower than the estimates that had been put forward. He felt that because of the poor quality of the archives, the carelessness of the personnel in charge of registering recruits, and the difficulty in isolating French Canadians whose names were often misspelled by unilingual officials, it was impossible to accurately determine the number of Canadian participants.[21]

Winks's work was not followed up. It was not until the 1990s that new interest in this subject surfaced. Books by Jim Cougle, Fred Gaffen, Danny R. Jenkins, and Greg Marquis—whose study is the most exhaustive research to date on the participation of the Canadians from the Atlantic provinces in the American Civil War—and articles by Tom Brooks and Lois E. Darroch have significantly improved our knowledge of the contribution made by English Canadians.[22]

As for the French Canadians, it has only been through research on their emigration to the United States that their participation in the war has been analyzed. In 1958, Robert Rumilly came to the conclusion, like Winks, that the number of French Canadian participants was much less than that put forward by Father Beaudry and by Gould. However, he neglected to provide his own assessment. Rumilly spent much time examining the quick enrolment of French-Canadian volunteers and highlighted, as did his English-Canadian predecessors, the forced enlistment that they had been subjected to, as well as their acting as substitutes. Furthermore, at the cessation of hostilities in 1865, according to Rumilly, many French-Canadian veterans were granted lands from the Federal government and settled in the State of New York and in the New England region.[23]

In 1968, the American geographer Ralph D. Vicero, in his doctoral thesis on the emigration of French Canadians to New England in the nineteenth century, also dealt with this subject. Vicero also questioned the figure of 40,000, but stressed that it would be impossible to know the full extent of the phenomenon. He indicated that the onset of war had changed the migratory dynamics and that some French Canadians had changed their minds about emigrating whereas others, already in the United States, decided to return to Canada.[24] But, according to Vicero, after the first several months of the conflict, requirements for war materiel stimulated certain economic sectors and restarted the migratory process. Predictably, some sectors of the American economy were greatly affected by the war. The wool and shoe industries were significantly stimulated, while the cotton-manufacturing sector experienced a major decline. These changes accelerated for some their return to Canada, whereas for others they caused a displacement from the declining sectors to those in expansion.[25] In parallel, Vicero stressed that many French Canadians left Canada to enroll in the army of the North, some as volunteers, others under the pressure of military recruiters who presented themselves as industrial recruiters. Vicero emphasized that this illicit recruitment was so successful that the archbishop of Quebec found it necessary to issue a bulletin in 1864 warning French Canadians about it.[26]

Nonetheless, French-Canadian participation in the American Civil War has never been the topic of specific studies and the sparse information that exists on the subject remains fragmentary and incomplete. Moreover, the historian Yves Roby, in his 1990 study on Franco-Americans in New England, deplored the lack of information on this major episode in the history of French-Canadian emigration to the United States.[27]

In the next section, more light will be shed on this aspect of French-Canadian participation. First, an estimate of the number of French Canadian participants in the war will be proposed. This will be followed by an analysis of newspapers published at that time to examine the motives of those who volunteered. The issue of illicit recruitment of French Canadians will also be addressed. Finally, the section will conclude by describing the different experiences of the Franchophone soldiers. This will be based on the military files of the combatants of the American Civil War.[28]

A New Estimate of the Number of French Canadian Participants

Researchers have tried in various ways to evaluate the number of Canadians who participated in the war. Until the end of 1950s, the figure put forth varied between 40,000 and 53,000. However, these estimates have been strongly criticized by many researchers without any valid alternatives being offered in their stead. Danny R. Jenkins in his 1993 Masters thesis took up the challenge of evaluating the number of Canadian participants in the war.[29] Jenkins used the American federal census of 1860 as a statistical base. This census indicated that 246,940 British North Americans, that is, individuals born in the British colonies to the north, lived in the free states of the North in 1860. According to these same statistics, forty-nine percent of the total population of these states was male. By using this data and applying it to the proportion of British North Americans, Jenkins concluded that the free states included 121,000 males born in Canada. The same census indicated that sixty-six percent of the population of the North were between 18 and 45 years old. Transposed to the British North Americans, these statistics meant that 80,000 of them were of the right age to enrol. In general, according to Jenkins, the studies dealing with enrolment concluded that half of all eligible

Americans actually enrolled. These same studies stressed that immigrants had been under-represented in the ranks of the Union army. In fact, immigrants accounted for thirty percent of the population but for only one quarter of all enrollees. Jenkins reasoned that if British North Americans acted in the same way as immigrants in general, forty-two percent of the 80,000 British North Americans who qualified would have actually enlisted. Therefore, he surmised that 34,000 British North Americans would have enrolled in the Union Army. This number, however, does not include those who crossed the border during the war to volunteer, which leads to the conclusion that the real figure was higher.

Jenkins used another tool to assess the number of Canadians who joined the Federal forces. It is known that 29 British North Americans received the Congressional Medal of Honour for exceptional services rendered during the American Civil War. In all, 1,200 medals were awarded to Union soldiers. Of these, 2.417 percent were awarded to British North Americans.[30] Therefore, if British North Americans had been honoured in proportion to their number and at a level comparable to that of other Union soldiers, then they accounted for 2.417 percent of the Union Army. Knowing that the Union army had between 2 million and 2.3 million men in its ranks, this army would have included between 48,000 and 55,000 British North Americans.

Jenkins concluded that the number of British North Americans who fought for the Union varied between 34,000 and 55,000. This methodology and estimate can be used to evaluate the number of French Canadians who joined the struggle. If French Canadians behaved in the same manner as English Canadians and the distribution according to age was similar among the English-speaking and French-speaking people of Canada, it is possible to estimate the number of French Canadians. The census of 1860 indicated that there were 246,940 Canadians present in the free states of the North. In addition, according to the American census of 1890, we know that the American Northeast[31] and Midwest[32] regions accounted for almost all of the French Canadians present in the United States.[33] As already noted, in 1860 there were 37,420 French Canadians living New England[34] and nearly 20,000 living in the Midwest. Unfortunately, no figure for the French Canadian population of the states of New York and Pennsylvania, which are part of the Northeast area, could be found. Taking into account that New York has a common border with Eastern Canada and that it was the destination for many nationalist refugees after the Rebellions of 1837-38, and that from 1830 to 1850 this state dominated forestry—an industry many French Canadians had been joining since the beginning of nineteenth century everywhere else on the continent—it is possible to contend that this state attracted as many French Canadians as did Maine (7,490), an adjacent state that dominated forestry during the first decades of the century. As for Pennsylvania, a state without a common border with Eastern Canada but one that dominated the forestry sector at the end of the 1850s, it probably attracted as many French Canadians as the more distant New England States, notably Rhode Island (1,810) and Connecticut (1,980), which had started their industrial development at that time. In this context, the state of New York would have had 7,500 French Canadians and the state of Pennsylvania, 1,800, for a total of 9,300. Therefore, by adding this figure to the known number of French Canadians in New England and the Midwest (57,420), the French Canadians in the free states of the North in 1860 can be calculated to approximately 66,720. This French-Canadian presence would be equivalent to twenty-seven percent of the Canadian contingent in the United States in 1860. If one agrees with Jenkins that the number of Canadians who took part in the war ranged between 34,000 and 55,000, it can be argued that the number of French Canadians who fought for the

Union Army ranged between 9,000 and 15,000.[35] This estimate, which excludes French Canadians who crossed the border during the war, seems closer to reality than the 40,000 proposed by Father Beaudry.

Voluntary Enrolment

At the very start of hostilities in 1861, Great Britain passed legislation declaring its neutrality in the conflict. This law forbade any British subject to enroll, without permission of Her Majesty, in the service of a foreign country or to help in any way the foreign warring factions, either through enrolment or by providing war supplies, under penalty of seizure and imprisonment.[36]

Despite the neutrality of Great Britain, the French-Canadian population was generally sympathetic to the abolitionist cause, even if, as Winks reminds us, this sentiment was never unanimous and varied according to the political situation.[37] It must be remembered that for several years the American anti-slavery movement had sought support in Canada and anti-slavery pamphlets were distributed in Canadian intellectual circles. The publication in 1852 in Toronto and Montreal of Harriet Beecher-Stowe's novel *Uncle Tom's Cabin* and its strong popularity in Canada—it sold one thousand copies and continued to sell well during the war—also contributed to informing Canadians of the merits of the abolitionist movement. It also gained their sympathy and support for the Union cause.[38]

Regardless, from the very beginning of hostilities, it appears that many French Canadians were indifferent to the sanctions threatened by London and crossed the border to enrol in the Union Army. The Quebec City newspaper *Le Canadien* reported in its edition of 22 April 1861 that "there is much enthusiasm developing within Canada for the North, and already, 600 men from Quebec City, and a good number from Montreal, have left for Boston to enrol in the Army of the United States."[39] As well, the *Montreal Gazette* reported at the end of April 1861, that a group of Montrealers had left the city for Boston to enrol in the Union Army.[40]

This voluntary enrolment, which continued throughout the war, also appeared among French Canadians who resided or who were travelling in the United States. In its edition dated 25 September 1861, *Le Canadien* reported that a significant number of French Canadians who had been established for several years in the border towns of Plattsburg, Champlain, Chazy and Rouse's Point, in the State of New York, had joined the Union Army. The anonymous journalist, who had spent some time in the area, stated that some of them had anglicized their names since arriving in the United States in order to ease their integration into American society. The Boisverts became the Greenwoods; Boismenu changed to Smallwood; Grandpré evolved to Widepark and Oliginy became Olena. It was while staying with the family of Raphaël Olena, established in Chazy, New York, for 25 years, that the journalist of *Le Canadien* had collected his information. He reported that one of the sons, Raphaël, 22 years old, born in Chazy, had enrolled at the beginning of the war in the 16th Regiment of New York. The journalist reported that the son had fought in the battle of Bull Run and that he was now stationed in Alexandria, close to Washington, D.C. and that he corresponded regularly with his family, to whom he sent his monthly pay of $17.[41]

Other French Canadians present in the United States also enrolled very early in the Federal army. An article published in *Le Canadien* reported that the 9th Regiment of Massachusetts, created on 11 June 1861 in Boston, had been sent to protect Washington. It added that this regiment included French Canadians who formerly worked in a cotton mill in the state and who had lost their employment when the owners could no longer secure raw material from the southern states.[42]

Recruitment

American agents quickly moved to take advantage of the willing volunteers. At the end of 1861, French-Canadian newspapers reported that there were American recruiters on Canadian soil looking for soldiers for the Union Army.[43] This recruitment, considered to be illegal, was severely condemned by observers. The Canadian government alleged that the American authorities, while not responsible, were not taking all the necessary steps to discourage the practice. These criticisms also obliged the American Secretary of State, William Henry Seward, in October 1861 to state that "any foreigner who has come on his own accord, in a spirit of loyalty, to offer his services to the Union, has been accepted; but there are no others in the Army of the United States."[44]

At the same time, American industrial recruiters were travelling the territory and offering employment to French Canadians. The war had seriously affected cotton manufacturing in New England. Many cotton mills employing French Canadians had to close their doors, forcing some to return to Canada.[45] But other sectors such as the wool and mining industry, as well as those directly connected to the war, were functioning at full capacity and required new workers to replace those who had been called to arms. It was thus with some confusion that American recruitment was occurring in Canada. Warnings appeared regularly in the newspapers in 1862 and 1863 calling upon French Canadians to act with prudence.[46] Although the presence of military recruiters was denounced, the newspapers provide no evidence of any arrests or arraignments of these recruiters before the courts.

Illicit Recruitment

The pressure to find recruits, however, was severe. From the moment that conscription was implemented in the northern states in March 1863, quotas imposed on each state forced recruiting to become more aggressive. Given the substantial premiums offered by states and municipalities to encourage enrolment and to fulfill the quotas, obtaining new recruits proved to be very lucrative for the recruiters. The newspapers of the day reported that these agents told French Canadians they could make lots of money if they enrolled. Some recruiters then took advantage of the more naive and pocketed part of the signing incentive.[47]

In the United States, some French Canadians had little choice. Recruiters did not bother to find out whether or not they were American citizens. In her 1951 study, Lonn reported that a French Canadian residing in Louisville, Kentucky, complained to the Canadian consul in July 1863 that he had been enrolled even though he had documents that exempted him. Many others had to obtain documents from Canada or from British authorities in the United States that proved their nationality.[48]

By 1863 American recruiters had become more numerous in Canada, and the means they were using to enrol French Canadians were often unconscionable. Contemporary newspapers published an impressive number of articles warning their readers about the unscrupulous recruiters. In April 1863, *Le Canadien* pointed to agents in Quebec City, who, under the pretence of hiring dock workers for the port of New York, were in fact recruiting for the Union Army.[49] A similar situation occurred in January 1864. Nearly 150 French Canadians were recruited to work in the mines near St. Louis, Missouri, for wages ranging from $25 to $30 per month. However, in June 1864, *Le Canadien* announced that the mining company had simply abandoned these recruits, that they had been reduced to poverty and were unable to pay their way home, had therefore no choice but to join the Union Army.[50] These abhorrent activities led the archbishop in Quebec City to issue a bulletin in January 1864 warning French Canadians about this practice.[51]

In some cases, the recruiters used special means of persuasion. Newspaper accounts reveal several occasions when the recruiters encouraged young men to consume alcohol, or even used drugs, to get them to sign a contract of enrolment. Others were kidnapped and bound before being transported to the United States and then turned over to the military authorities.[52] Most of these recruiters were Americans. But in some instances, to thwart the growing mistrust of the French Canadians, the American recruiters hired the services of French Canadians such as Louis Verbois, Michel Rochon, Hilaire Couture and Israel Dufresne, to name just a few, who recruited for the Union Army.[53]

However, as recruitment became more intense, the Canadian authorities succeeded in apprehending and arresting some recruiters. For example, George Washington Waitt and Samuel Perry were arrested in November 1863 in Quebec.[54] Upon his apprehension, Waitt had in his possession a letter indicating that he was authorized to pay up to $500 for each recruit. Other agents were arrested in 1864 and 1865. Despite these arrests, the recruiters remained active and continued to make headlines in French Canada until the end of the war.[55]

Motivation of the Volunteer

Whether they enrolled freely or under pressure from the recruiters, French Canadians undoubtedly had specific reasons for wanting to enlist and put their lives in jeopardy for a war that had little impact or influence on their daily lives. Winks suggests some reasons why Canadians enrolled.[56] But, to fully comprehend the rationale for French-Canadian involvement, it is necessary to place this participation within its historical context. During much of the nineteenth century, French Canadians were confronted with serious economic problems at home. The free market economy, combined with the increasing indebtedness of farmers, along with successive bad harvests and a lagging industrialization, led an increasingly large number of French Canadians into poverty. Some chose forestry work, others left for the city, and some departed for lands that needed to be cleared and settled. But many chose, often after these first efforts had failed, to migrate temporarily to the United States, particularly to New England.[57] It is likely that the start of the war south of the border, the need for soldiers, the wages offered, and the substantial joining premiums that were instituted in 1863, are what motivated so many French Canadians to enlist in the Union Army.

Upon enrolment, soldiers received wages varying from $15 to $30 per month.[58] From 1863 when conscription was implemented, premiums for enrolment were paid to the new recruits by various levels of government in order to reach the quotas imposed by the federal administration. These premiums generally varied between $100 and $400, but in certain cases, they reached nearly $1,000. Part of the premium was paid upon enrolment and the balance upon expiry of the contract. Not surprisingly, several French Canadians sought to benefit from this system of premiums without having to fight. Men who tried this tactic were called Bounty Jumpers. George Fisette, a 32-year-old sailor, was one such individual. He enrolled for three years on 28 April 1864 in Frankenmuth, close to the forestry town of Saginaw. Upon signing his contract, Fisette received a premium of $38 and was assigned to the 16th Michigan Infantry Regiment. However, Fisette never appeared. He was regarded as a deserter and would have incurred severe penalties if he had been caught. But Fisette was never found by the military authorities.[59]

Under the conscription law of 1863, the American federal government also made it possible for conscripts to avoid enrolment if they paid $300 or if they found a man who would replace them and to whom they would have to pay an amount of money. This was another way for some to profit financially from the scarcity of recruits. As Rumilly highlighted, several French

Canadians agreed to replace American conscripts in exchange for a substantial amount of money. For example, 20-year-old Joseph Beron, who enrolled in Detroit on 31 March 1865, took the place of Lyman C. Fisk in the 15th Michigan Infantry Regiment for a sum of $430.[60] Leon Borch, also 20, enrolled as a substitute on 27 March 1865, taking the place of Lewis A. Clark, who paid him the sum of $335.[61] Finally, Charles Brillant, 21 years old, a blacksmith by trade, enrolled on 28 March 1865 in Kalamazoo. He joined the 15th Michigan Infantry Regiment as a substitute for Frederick Zierle, who paid him $855.[62]

Some French Canadians enlisted in the Union Army to fight to free the slaves. It is difficult, however, to know to what extent they were aware of the debate that for the previous thirty years had marked American socio-political life. Anti-slavery literature had been distributed in Canada, but it is unclear how widely this literature would have been distributed among the French Canadian population. Moreover, it should be remembered that until September 1862, the emancipation of the slaves, although discussed, had not been considered seriously by Lincoln and his advisers.

The search for adventure could also explain why they volunteered. But it is difficult to find the evidence. Nevertheless, the war was tempting. It meant adventuring into the unknown, a reality a thousand leagues away from a boring rural existence. For many, the war was a challenge, driving them to the very limits of their abilities and ultimately putting their lives on the line. Finally, the conflict generally made it possible for soldiers to experiment with a certain social mobility. They could obtain special status during the war as well as certain social and financial benefits when the war was over. There could also have been family reasons as well. A large number of compatriots were living in the northern United States and they could have encouraged relatives, near or far, to enrol to support them in their war.[63]

One War, Several Roads

Not surprisingly, for financial and geographical reasons, French Canadians mainly enlisted in the bordering American states. Therefore, many French Canadians served in regiments of states of Maine, Vermont and New York. But several pushed further on, enrolling in Michigan, Wisconsin, Pennsylvania and even Arkansas.[64]

French Canadians who enrolled did so knowing they were risking their lives. Some came out unharmed, others were seriously wounded, and some were killed. Louis-Philippe Bouffard was one of the lucky ones who came out of the war physically unharmed. Born in Canada and a miner by trade, he was assigned to the 1st Michigan Sharpshooters on 4 July 1863 at the age of 21. He fought in the battle of the Wilderness, which took place 5-7 May 1864 and in the action at Spotsylvania during the following four days. He also participated in the attack on the town of Petersburg on 2 April 1865 and in the pursuit of General Robert E. Lee's forces later in the month. Bouffard was discharged on 28 July 1865.[65] Frank Picard and John Nollett, both 24 years old, enrolled as privates in August 1862 at Detroit. Both were assigned to the 2nd Michigan Regiment. They were among those who were entrusted with defending the city of Washington D.C. until October 1862. They took part in the battle of Fredericksburg from 12-15 December 1862, then in the battle of Chancelorsville from 2-5 May 1863, and finally in the well-known action at Gettysburg in July of the same year. Picard and Nollet survived three years of service and were both discharged on 30 June 1865 in Detroit.[66]

Not all were as fortunate. Canadian-born Cyrille Ledouc enrolled on 24 October 1861 and was assigned to a foot regiment in Michigan. He was wounded by a bullet in the battle of Stone River in Tennessee on 2 January 1863 and spent four days in the hospital at Murfreesboro before dying of his wounds. He was 31 years old.[67] The war was also cruel for many. Some remained permanently disabled. Joseph Duccat, originally from Montreal, 17 years old and a logger by trade, had enrolled on 30 July 1862 at St. Claire, Michigan. He was assigned to the 2nd Michigan Infantry Regiment. During the battle of Chickamauga, in September 1863, he was hit in the hand by a bullet, and lost a thumb. He was taken to St. Mary's hospital in Detroit and discharged a few days later by the military authorities, who had decided that he was no longer fit to serve.[0] Another case was Julius Sauvé, a day labourer born in 1846. He enrolled on 16 September 1861 and was assigned to the 1st Foot Regiment of Michigan. His regiment took part in several major battles, including Mechanicsville in June 1862 and the battle of Bull Run in August of the same year. It was during this last battle that he was seriously wounded. He was sent to the hospital in Washington where he remained for more than two years until his three-year contract expired on 16 September 1864. He was released from hospital but would require many more months of convalescence. He remained seriously disabled as a result of his wound.[69]

Finally, others died on the battlefield. This was the case for Toby Boivin who was born in Canada in 1846 but lived in Marquette, Michigan. He enrolled on 31 July 1861 in the state's 1st Foot Regiment. Initially considered as missing in action after the Battle of Meadow Bridge in August 1862, Boivin was finally found, lying on the battlefield, seriously injured by a bullet. He was sent to a hospital near Manassas where he died on 29 August 1862. He was 26 years old.[70] Samuel Bissonnette also met a tragic end. He enrolled on 20 June 1861 in Adrian, Michigan. He was 22 years old and one of those who fought at Gettysburg, Pennsylvania. He died there on 2 July 1863.[71] Jerome Lefebvre was another. At 24 years of age, he enrolled in Detroit on 28 June 1862 and was assigned to the 2nd Michigan Infantry Regiment. He too died during the Battle of Gettysburg.[72]

But death did not always come by bullet alone. The rudimentary hygiene of military camps added to the misery of those who were already sick. In fact disease accounted for more casualties than the battles themselves. For example, the 2nd Michigan Infantry Regiment lost 399 men during the war. Of this number, 310 (nearly seventy-eight percent) died of disease, while only 89 died in battle.[73] Théo Bouchard, a member of this regiment, was included in these statistics. A single farmer, aged 21, he enrolled in Pontiac, Michigan on 5 April 1865. Several weeks later, he was admitted to the General Hospital in Chattanooga, Tennessee, suffering from constipation. He died there two months later.[74] Jos Benway, a 19-year-old labourer born in Saint-Jean, also perished. He enrolled in the 51st Massachusetts Infantry Regiment on 21 March 1864. Five months later he was admitted to the Armory Square Hospital suffering from diarrhea, a common disease that was generally caused by the poor quality of food and water. He remained there until 5 August 1865, when he died from an intestinal infection.[75] Finally, Joseph Paradis, 18 years old, enrolled on 13 July 1861 as a sergeant. He was assigned to the 5th Foot Regiment of Maine. Paradis re-enlisted on 2 February 1864 after the end of his first service contract. Four months later, he was admitted to hospital at Cold Harbor, Virginia. He died on 18 June of blood poisoning.[76]

Some French Canadians were taken as prisoners during the war and lived under very austere conditions. The Southern armies had many unhealthy prisons but the one in Andersonville, Georgia, was considered the worst. Nelson Peyette died there. A 42-year-old farmer originally from Montreal, he had enrolled on 22 August 1862 in Pontiac and was assigned to the 2nd Foot Regiment of Michigan. He was captured during the Battle of

Chickamauga in September 1863 and taken to Andersonville. He remained there for ten months and developed diarrhea. He died in prison on 29 July 1864 from this disease.[77] Daniel Bourassas went through a similar experience. He enrolled in Detroit on 13 August 1863 at the age of 29. He served with the 2nd Foot Regiment of Michigan until August 1864, when military authorities reported him missing in Yellowtown. It was later discovered that he had been taken prisoner during a skirmish and was being held at a prison in Salisbury, North Carolina. It was in this prison that he developed the diarrhea from which he died a few days later.[78]

Others, however, survived the ordeal of prison. Canadian born, 22-year-old Clement Boudrie enlisted in Monroe, Michigan, on 16 September 1864. He was assigned to the 15th Michigan Infantry Regiment. During a skirmish near Raleigh, North Carolina in April 1864 he was taken prisoner by Confederate forces. He remained in prison until freed by the Union Army on 18 August 1865.[79]

The dangerous and rudimentary existence prompted many French Canadians to reflect on their decision to volunteer. Some came to the conclusion that they no longer wished to live the military life. This was probably the case for John Beauchesne and Alex Beaudry. The first, 21 years old, was born in Coteau-Landing and enrolled on 21 June 1862 in Winooski, Vermont. The second, born in Saint-Hilaire, was 22 and had enrolled two weeks earlier in Ruthland, Vermont. Both were assigned to the 9th Vermont Infantry Regiment and they served together for a few months. But military life quickly lost its appeal. As a result, while their regiment was stationed in Chicago they deserted, the first on 3 February 1863 and the second on 3 April of the same year.[80]

Promotions

In general, the French Canadians had no military experience and were mainly recruited as privates. But some obtained promotions, generally due to their courage on the battlefield or to their ability to handle their responsibilities well. This was the case for 27-year-old Vetal Bochamps, who enrolled as a private on 12 August 1862 in Marquette, Michigan and was assigned to Michigan's 27th Foot Regiment. In July 1863 he was admitted to hospital at Camp Dennisson, in Ohio, but re-joined his regiment three months later. He fought in several battles, including the Battle of Blue Springs in October and then in the siege of Knoxville, Tennessee at the end of the year. He was also in the battles of the Wilderness and Spotsylvania in May 1864, and in the action at Appomattox in March 1865. His regiment was among those pursuing General Lee in April 1865. Bochamps seems to have performed well because he was promoted to corporal before being discharged on 26 July 1865.[81] Lewis Chevalier was another who was promoted during the war. He enrolled as a private on 7 July 1863 in Ontonagon, Michigan at the age of 27. He served with the 27th Michigan Infantry Regiment until October 1863, when he became ill and was confined to Knoxville. He caught up with his regiment in July 1864 and fought in the attack on the town of Petersburg. He appears to have distinguished himself during the battle, being promoted to corporal two months later. Chevalier was discharged on 26 July 1865.[82] Stephen Loranger also performed well. At the age of 24, Loranger enrolled as a private on 4 August 1862. Assigned to the 27th Infantry Regiment, he served throughout the state of Kentucky from April to June 1863. He was promoted to corporal on 22 April 1863, only eight months after enrolling. In July his regiment took part in the destruction of the Mississippi Central Railroad and subsequently saw action at Knoxville, Tennessee in November and December of the same year. On 1 January 1864 Loranger was again promoted, this time to the rank of first sergeant. On 6 May 1864, during the battle of the Wilderness, he was struck in the knee by a bullet. He was consequently discharged on 6 January 1865.[83]

A few French Canadians, however, did have military experience. This was the case for Joseph Lefebvre, who was mentioned earlier. He enrolled on 28 July 1862 in Detroit as a corporal in the 24th Michigan Infantry Regiment.[84] This was also the case for Cyprian Millard, who enlisted on 20 June 1861 in Lake Linden and was assigned to the 9th Michigan Infantry Regiment with the rank of captain.[85] Dosite Chartier, who at the age of 22 also volunteered, was assigned to the 2nd Michigan Infantry Regiment. He also was given the rank of captain.[86] It is difficult to ascertain where they gained their military experience, but it seems probable that they were veterans of the British Army.

In April 1865, General Robert E Lee, commander-in-chief of the Confederate Armies, signed the terms of surrender. The North had won; the war was over. After the celebrations, the soldiers of the Union Army were discharged and returned home. It seems that the majority of the French Canadians who had crossed the border to enlist during the war remained in the United States. The hard years of combat appear to have created within them a feeling of belonging to the country for which they had fought. Some would join relatives already established in the United States. Others took advantage of land grants from the Federal government. In this, they read the situation in the same way as thousands of French Canadians had before them and as thousands would afterward. That is, they chose to settle in the United States rather than return to live under the difficult economic conditions that prevailed in Canada. The war was for them an opportunity to migrate and improve their lot, even if it was at the risk of their lives.

Conclusion

Approximately ten thousand French Canadians fought in the American Civil War. Faced with a difficult economic situation at home, they viewed this war and the wages it offered as an opportunity to improve their fortunes. At the risk of severe penalties under British authorities, many French Canadians crossed the border voluntarily and registered at recruiting offices in the bordering states. Others in Canada and the United States succumbed to the persuasion of the military recruiters. Many were the victims of unscrupulous American agents who promised fortunes to gain their signatures on a contract and pocket a share of the premium. And, many French Canadians who had settled in the United States, whether they had American citizenship or not, enlisted in the Union Army to support the cause or simply to display their patriotism for their adopted country.

Once enrolled and assigned to their regiment, the French Canadians met widely varying experiences. Few wrote anything of substance that revealed the social and military reality into which they were plunged. But we know that from the moment they signed on, their destiny depended on factors over which they no longer had any control. Many survived the war, others were seriously wounded with permanent scars and disabilities. Some died in combat while others were only wounded and died on the battlefields for lack of assistance. Still others contracted diseases and died for lack of adequate care. Some even made the decision to desert, knowing that they would be subject to prison sentences or execution if they were caught. Finally, for others, the war was an opportunity to distinguish themselves in combat and earn glory, as well as promotions. But beyond their various experiences, French Canadians had been deeply marked by this war. Whether they returned to Canada or settled in the United States, they carried with them the vivid memories of their experience in the monumental struggle of the American Civil War. Much remains to be learned about these men who lived this brief and bloody aspect of French Canadian history.

Notes for Chapter 3

1   I would like to thank Kira Zoellner, student in the department of history at the Royal Military College of Canada for her invaluable collaboration, and Roch Legault, a professor with the department, for his comments and suggestions. This chapter is the result of a research project subsidized by the Academic Research Program (ARP) at the Department of National Defence.

2   National Archives and Records Administration (NARA), Washington, D.C. Records Relating to Volunteer Soldiers. Civil War, 1st Michigan Infantry Regiment. Military file for Charles Boucher.

3   There are many books. Some examples include: Bruce Catton, *Bruce Catton's Civil War* (New York: Fairfax, 1984); James M. McPherson, *Battle Cry of Freedom: The Civil War Era* (New York: Oxford University Press, 1988); and by Philip S. Paludan, *A People's Contest. The Union and Civil War, 1861-1865* (Lawrence, Kansas: University Press of Kansas, 1996).

4   United States Census Office, *Eighth Census, 1860, The Statistics of the Population*. xxii, xxix. One must be careful when using figures concerning Canada since this country generated not only emigration but also played host to European immigrants in transit heading for the United States. We employ the term "Canadian" to designate individuals born in the British colonies in North America.

5   United States Census Office, *Eighth Census, 1860, The Statistics of the Population*, xxix.

6   Ella Lonn, *Foreigners in the Union Army and Navy* (Baton Rouge, Louisiana University Press, 1951), 1.

7   Ibid.

8   Ella Long, *Foreigners in the Confederacy* (Gloucester, Mass., Peter Smith, 1940); and *Foreigners in the Union Army and Navy* (Baton Rouge, Louisiana University Press, 1951).

9   Lonn, *Foreigners in the Union...*, 662.

10 See as well, Earl J. Hess, "Sigel 's Resignation: A Study in German-Americanism and the Civil War." *Civil War History*, vol 12 (March 1966), 43-53; Joseph Hernon Jr., *Celts, Catholics and Copperheads: Ireland Views the American Civil War* (Columbus: Ohio State University Press, 1968); Valentino J. Belfiglio, "Italians and the American Civil War," *Italian Americana*, vol 4 (Spring-Summer, 1978), 163-175; Cynthia H. Enloe, *Ethnic Soldiers: State Securities in Divided Society* (Athens, Ga.: University of Georgia Press, 1980); William L. Burton, "Irish Regiments in the Union Army: The Massachusetts Experience," *Historical Journal of Massachusetts*, vol 11 (June 1983),104-119. See also Philip S. Paludan, *A People's Contest. The Union and Civil War, 1861-1865* (Lawrence: Kansas, University Press of Kansas, 1996); James M. McPherson, *For Cause and Comrades. Why Men Fought in the Civil War* (New York: Oxford University Press, 1997).

11 William L. Burton, *Melting Pot Soldiers. The Union's Ethnic Regiments* (Ames: Iowa State University Press, 1988).

12 See Maris A. Vinovskis, ed., *Toward a Social History of the American Civil War* (Cambridge: Cambridge University Press, 1990).

13 Research at the National Archives in Washington in the personal files of French-Canadian soldiers having fought during the Civil War revealed that they also fought in the Southern regiments, notably those of Florida and Louisiana.

14 Ralph D. Vicero, "Immigration of French Canadians to New England, 1840-1900: A Geographical Analysis," Unpublished Doctoral Thesis (Geography), University of Wisconsin, 1968, 163.

15 Jean Lamarre, *Les Canadiens français du Michigan* (Sillery: Éditions du Septentrion, 2000), 37.

16 Many articles and reports from American newspapers such as *Le Courrier des États-Unis* were regularly published during the entire war in *Le Canadien* in Quebec City, *La Minerve* in Montreal and the *Globe* in Toronto.

17 Wilfrid Bovey, "Confederate Agents in Canada during the American Civil War," *Canadian Historical Review*, vol 2, No. 1 (March 1921), 46-57; W. F. Raney, "Recruiting and Crimping in Canada for the Northern Forces, 1861-1865," *Mississippi Valley Historical Review*, vol X (June 1923), 21-33. And in the 1940s, Marguerite B. Hamer, "Luring Canadian Soldiers into Union Lines during the War between the States," *Canadian Historical Review*, vol 57, No. 1 (1946), 150-162.

18 E. Z. Massicotte, "Les Canadiens français et la Guerre de Sécession," *Bulletin de recherches historiques*, vol 42 (1936), 538-540, 667-668; Lionel-A. Lapointe, "Les Canadiens français et la guerre de Sécession," *Bulletin de recherches historiques*, vol 42 (1936), 684-686.

19 Robin W. Winks, *Canada and the United States: the Civil War Years* (Baltimore: The John Hopkins Press, 1960). This author two years previously had written an article titled "The Creation of a Myth: Canadian Enlistments in the Northern Armies during the American Civil War," *Canadian Historical Review*, Vol 39 (March 1958), 24-40, in which he studied estimates of Canadian participation in the war.

20 Benjamin A. Gould, *Investigations in the Military and Anthropological Statistics of American Soldiers*, (New York: Sanitary Commission, 1869). The lack of scientific rigour is evident.

21 Winks, *Canada and the United States...*, 178-185. Andrew Moxley and Tom Brooks argued that 50,000 Canadians have served. Others like James Robertson, in his book, *Soldiers Blue and Gray* (Columbia: Warner Books, 1991), 28, reduce the number to 15,000. It is difficult to take part in the debate, especially when researchers do not define clearly the term Canadian. See Andrew Moxley and Tom Brooks, "Drums Across the Border: Canadians in the Civil War," *Canadian Military Then and Now*, Vol 1, No. 6 (November 1991), 59-60.

22 Tom Brooks, "British North Americans (Canadians) in the American Civil War, 1861-1865," *Camp Chase Gazette*, June 1991; Lois E. Darroch, "Canadians in the American Civil War," *Ontario History*, vol 83, No. 1, March 1991, 55-61; Danny R. Jenkins, "British North American Who Fought in the American Civil War," Unpublished MA Thesis (History), University of Ottawa, 1993; Jim Cougle, *Canadian Blood, American Soil, The Story of Canada's Contribution to the*

American Civil War (Fredericton, 1994); Fred Gaffen, *Cross-Border Warriors. Canadians in American Forces, Americans in Canadian Forces* (Toronto: Dundurn Press, 1995); Greg Marquis, *In Armageddon's Shadow: The Civil War and Canada's Maritime Provinces* (Halifax: Gorsebrook Research Institute for Atlantic Canadian Studies, Saint-Mary's University, 1998).

23 Robert Rumilly, *Les Franco-Américains* (Montreal: by the author, 1958), 36-38.

24 Vicero, 201.

25 Ibid.

26 Ibid., 202.

27 Yves Roby, *Les Franco-Américains de la Nouvelle-Angleterre, 1776-1930* (Sillery: Éditions du Septentrion, 1990), 57-58.

28 These files are available at the National Archives and Records Administration (NARA) in Washington, D.C. *Records Relating to Volunteer Soldiers*, Civil War. Tha author has already sorted through nearly one thousand.

29 Jenkins, 17-23.

30 *The Medal of Honor of the United States Army* (Washington, United States Government Printing Office, 1948), 469; Jenkins, 17-23.

31 In the *American Federal Census*, the geographic reality of the Northeast is designated by the expression North Atlantic States, and includes the six states of New England, as well as the states of New York and Pennsylvania.

32 In the *American Federal Census*, the geographic reality of the Midwest is designated by the expression North Central States, a territory that includes the states of Illinois, Indiana, Michigan, Minnesota, Ohio and Wisconsin.

33 United States Census Office, *Eleventh Census of the United States, 1890, Population, vol 1* (Washington Government Printing Office: Washington 1895). Considering the migratory trends, it is quite possible that this percentage had increased since 1860.

34 Here is the estimate for the French-Canadian population of New England in 1860, by state, according to Vicero, 163. Maine: 7,490; New Hampshire: 1,780; Vermont: 16,500; Massachusetts: 7,780; Rhode Island: 1,810; Connecticut: 1,980; Total: 37,420.

35 1860: 246,940 Canadians, including 66,720 French Canadians or 27 percent. If 34,000 Canadians participated in the war, 9,180 French Canadians did the same. If 55,000 Canadians participated to the war, 14,850 French Canadians did the same, excluding those who crossed the border during the war and those who were sojourning south when the war began. The weakness of this operation lies in the fact that overall, the economic situation in Canada East was more difficult than in Canada West at this time, which could mean that Canada East might have experienced a greater migration that Canada West.

36 *Le Canadien*, May 27, 1861, 2; *United Kingdom Statutes*, 24 Vict. C. 69.

37 Winks, 184.

38 Ibid., 10-11, 232.

39 *Le Canadien*, April 22, 1861, 5. Newspapers used in supporting the statements in this section are *Le Canadien* (Quebec City) and *La Minerve* (Montreal), two conservative newspapers known for being sympathetic to the Southern cause and critical of the actions of the American Federal government.

40 *La Minerve*, April 20, 1861, 3.

41 *Le Canadien*, September 25, 1861, 3.

42 *Le Canadien*, July 21, 1862, 2.

43 *Le Canadien*, December 9, 1861, 3.

44 *Le Canadien*, October 14, 1861, 2

45 *Le Canadien*, May 6, 1861, 2; September 18, 1861, 2.

46 See especially *Le Canadien*, April 16, 1863, 2.

47 See also *La Minerve*, November 17, 1863, 3.

48 Lonn, *Foreigners in the Union...*, 436-478.

49 *Le Canadien*, April 16, 1863, 2; July 13, 1863, 2.

50 *Le Canadien*, January 13, 1864, 2; June 13, 1864, 2.

51 *Mandements des évêques de Québec, 1850-1870*, Vol IV, 468. Bulletin of January 14, 1864.

52 *La Minerve*, November 17, 1863, 2; *La Minerve*, March 9, 1865, 2; Lonn, *Foreigners in the Union...*, 436-478.

53 *Le Canadien*, December 21, 1863, 2; *La Minerve*, February 27, 1864, 2; June 4, 1864, 2.

54 *Le Canadien*, November 20, 1863, 2.

55 *La Minerve*, September 1864, 2; October 1, 1864, 3; March 9, 1865, 2; March 18, 1865, 3; *Le Canadien*, January 18, 1864, 2; March 18, 1864, 2; June 30, 1864, 2; March 15, 1865, 2.

56 Winks, *Canada and the United States...*, 185. Winks evokes the love of adventure, the struggle against slavery, the lure of fortune, all of which translated into a fight for the cause; or simply because the Canadians had nothing else to do. To learn about the Americans' motivations see the exhaustive study by James McPherson, *For Cause and Comrades*.

57 See the first chapter of Lamarre.

58 These are the figures obtained upon analysis of the personal files for the French Canadians.

59 NARA, Washington, D.C. Records Relating to Volunteer Soldiers, Civil War, 15th Michigan Infantry Regiment. Personal file for George Fisette.

60 NARA, Washington, D.C. Records Relating to Volunteer Soldiers. Civil War, 3rd Michigan Infantry Regiment. Personal file for Joseph Beron.

61 NARA , Washington, D.C. Records Relating to Volunteer Soldiers. Civil War. 15th Michigan Infantry Regiment. Personal file for Leon Borch.

62 NARA, Washington, D.C. Records Relating to Volunteer Soldiers. Civil War, 15th Michigan Infantry Regiment. Personal file for Charles Brillant.

63 This information concerning motivation is based on hypotheses put forth by the author based on motivations generally expressed to explain enrolment by United States born soldiers and the particular situation of French Canadians in the United States.

64 These facts have been gathered from the personal files of French Canadians who fought in the Civil War. NARA, Washington, D.C. Records Relating to Volunteer Soldiers, Civil War.

65 NARA, Washington, D.C. Records Relating to Volunteer Soldiers, Civil War, hereafter NARA Records, 1st Michigan Sharpshooters. Personal file for Louis-Philippe Bouffard; Frederic H. Dyer, *A Compendium of the War of the Rebellion*, New York, Thomas Yoseloff, vol 3, 1280-1281.

66 NARA, Washington, D.C. Records Relating to Volunteer Soldiers. Civil War, 24th Michigan Infantry Regiment. Personal file for Frank Picard and John Nollet.

67 NARA, Washington, D.C. Records Relating to Volunteer Soldiers. Civil War, 1st Michigan Infantry Regiment. Personal file for Cyrille Ledouc.

68 NARA, Washington, D.C. Records Relating to Volunteer Soldiers. Civil War, 1st Michigan Infantry Regiment. Personal file for Julius Sauve.

69 NARA, Washington, D.C. Records Relating to Volunteer Soldiers. Civil War, 22nd Michigan Infantry Regiment. Personal file for Joseph Duccat

70 NARA, Washington, D.C. Records Relating to Volunteer Soldiers. Civil War, 1st Michigan Infantry Regiment. Personal file for Toby Boivin.

71 NARA, Washington, D.C. Records Relating to Volunteer Soldiers. Civil War, 4th Michigan Infantry Regiment. Personal file for Samuel Bissonnette.

72 NARA, Washington, D.C. Records Relating to Volunteer Soldiers. Civil War, 24th Michigan Infantry Regiment. Personal file for Jerome Lefebvre.

73 Dyer, 1291.

74 NARA, Washington, D.C. Records Relating to Volunteer Soldiers. Civil War, 22nd Michigan Infantry Regiment. Personal file for Theo Bouchard.

75 NARA, Washington, D.C. Records Relating to Volunteer Soldiers. Civil War, 51st Massachusetts Infantry Regiment. Personal file for Jos Benway.

76 NARA, Washington, D.C. Records Relating to Volunteer Soldiers, Civil War, 5th Maine Infantry Regiment. Personal file for Joseph Paradis.

77 NARA, Washington, D.C. Records Relating to Volunteer Soldiers. Civil War, 22nd Michigan Infantry Regiment. Personal file for Nelson Peyette.

78 NARA, Washington, D.C. Records Relating to Volunteer Soldiers. Civil War, 24th Michigan Infantry Regiment. Personal file for Daniel Bourassas.

79 NARA, Washington, D.C. Records Relating to Volunteer Soldiers. Civil War, 15th Michigan Infantry Regiment. Personal file for Clement Boudrie.

80 NARA, Washington, D.C. Records Relating to Volunteer Soldiers. Civil War, 9th Vermont Infantry Regiment. Personal files for Alex Beaudry and John Beauchesne.

81 NARA, Washington, D.C. Records Relating to Volunteer Soldiers. Civil War, 27th Michigan Infantry Regiment. Personal file for Vetal Bochamps.

82 NARA, Washington, D.C. Records Relating to Volunteer Soldiers. Civil War, 27th Michigan Infantry Regiment. Personal file for Lewis Chevalier.

83 NARA, Washington, D.C. Records Relating to Volunteer Soldiers. Civil War, 27th Michigan Infantry Regiment. Personal file for Stephen Loranger.

84 NARA, Washington, D.C. Records Relating to Volunteer Soldiers. Civil War, 24th Michigan Infantry Regiment. Personal file for Jerome Lefebvre.

85 NARA, Washington, D.C. Records Relating to Volunteer Soldiers. Civil War, 9th Michigan Infantry Regiment. Personal file for Cyprian Millard.

86 NARA, Washington, D.C. Records Relating to Volunteer Soldiers. Civil War, 22nd Michigan Infantry Regiment. Personal file for Dosite Chartier.

"Lost Opportunity"

The Boer War Experience and its Influence on British and Canadian Military Thought

Lieutenant-Colonel Bernd Horn

The present war has in fact been a valuable illustration of the necessity for organizing the defence of the Empire against far graver contingencies. Unless such preparation is made, the continuance of the Empire is doubtful, if not improbable, and it is essential to preparation that it should be definitely known in peace what forces can be relied on in war.[1]

—Sir Aylmer Haldane, British Secretary of State for War, 1902

THE BRITISH SECRETARY OF WAR'S revelation was born of the painful experience of the Boer War of 1899-1902. Great Britain entered the conflict with much confidence and little concern. It had been challenged on numerous occasions throughout the breadth of its Empire and it had never failed to demonstrate its capacity for martial greatness. However, this misplaced confidence would soon be lost and the South African experience seared into the very soul of the Empire. The war was initially contemptuously dismissed. The Boers, perceived as simple farm folk of no great military capability, inflicted a series of humiliating and costly defeats on the British Field Force

A typical British bivouac located outside Bloemfontein. (Photographer unknown. NA, C-3477)

which quickly demonstrated that the Imperial Army was woefully inadequate to the challenges of modern warfare. Military blunders on the battlefield that led to excessive British casualties and unmitigated Boer victories quickly revealed the flaws in British leadership, organization and training. The requirement to dispatch more forces into the theatre of operation, however, soon uncovered Britain's greatest weakness: the inability to field an adequate expeditionary force.

The Royal Navy was always considered the only real requirement to defend the Empire and as a result, the Army existed in its shadow as a protector of coaling stations, Imperial fortresses and as an occasional colonial enforcer when the need arose. However, the challenge posed by the Boer commandos was such that England was left virtually undefended and stripped of all its equipment to fulfill the requirement to field sufficient force to beat the citizen army of the Free State and the Transvaal.

This experience shocked Britain, as well as the rest of the world. Stunned by its vulnerability and inadequate army, the British quickly reflected on the lessons that had been learned. These were subsequently examined to determine the extent of the necessary reforms. Key concepts emerged that were used to shape a revitalized army. One such theme was the immense potency of modern weaponry that resulted in an enormous increase in the power of the defence and thus required changes to tactics and fieldcraft. The modern rifle also bred a reverence for individual marksmanship skills, which in turn fuelled an unrivalled focus on musketry training. Military theorists and commanders also realized that the modern battlefield required more mobility, comprehensive co-operation between all arms, greater communications, and more importantly, well trained, educated leaders and soldiers who had greater initiative and who were capable of individual action. The end product was nothing less than the foundation of a professional, modern army.

The Boer War also affected Canadian military thought, but in a distinctly different way. Although many concepts were mutually embraced, such as the importance of musketry skills, mobility and better training, for Canadians the key lesson of the war was the strength of the citizen army. This reinforced the belief of the Canadian military and political elite that there was little difference between a regular soldier and a citizen who could shoot. As a result, Canadian military development entrenched the viewpoint that the Militia was more than adequate to meet national defence requirements, a conviction that differed greatly from the British model, which moved toward a better trained professional army.

Despite the philosophical and practical differences the Boer War clearly had a great impact on British and Canadian military thought and practice. The debate that ensued, combined with the lessons that were carried forward, captured the essence of modern warfare. The overwhelming power of advanced weaponry, particularly when combined with entrenchments, was well understood, as was the folly of the unsupported attack in the open. The importance of neutralizing fire and the essence of fire and movement, fieldcraft, and all arms co-operation also emerged. Many of the ideas that arose were not unique, but the exhausting effort required of the Empire to vanquish such a feeble foe imparted a sense of urgency and credibility to concepts that had been largely ignored. The ideas and discussion that arose as a result of the war provided the keys to avoiding the slaughter that would become the First World War. Unfortunately, the Boer War experience was quickly redefined, lessons were reinterpreted and old preconceptions of war reinstated. The failure of the senior military leadership, both within the Empire and beyond it, to accept and heed the lessons that were initially so well understood, truly led to a lost opportunity.

The onset of the South African crisis was met with little apprehension in Britain since the Boers were viewed as little more than "the levies of two insignificant Republics whose forces

Infantryman of The Royal
Canadian Regiment, 1900.
(The Royal Canadian Regiment
Museum)

were but loose gatherings of armed farmers."[2] Lord Dundonald so doubted the capability of his opponents that he actually asked an officer of the locally raised scouts, on the eve of battle, if "the Boers would fight when they saw Her Majesty's troops."[3] However, these ill-conceived notions were soon shattered by hard reality. "The military situation is without doubt at this moment most grave and critical," reported Winston Churchill, the future Prime Minister, who was a correspondent at the onset of the conflict. "We have been at war three weeks," he explained, "[and] the army that was to have defended Natal, and was indeed expected to repulse the invaders with terrible loss, is blockaded and bombarded in its fortified camp." He added that "at nearly every point along the circle of the frontiers the Boers have advanced and the British retreated. Wherever we have stood we have been surrounded ... All this is mainly the result of being unready ... It is also due to an extraordinary under-estimation of the strength of the Boers."[4] The realization that the Empire was "unready" for modern war became quickly apparent. The decisive defeats during Black Week[5] revealed the shortcomings of the British Army, problems that would get worse as the campaign in South Africa played itself out.

Saddled with the experience of conflict against savages in the far corners of the Empire, few British officers paid attention to developments in modern warfare. The use of smokeless powder and the Boer expertise at the use of cover and concealment highlighted the inexperience of the British in this form of warfare. Initially, there was a simplistic belief that "there were no Boers about unless you could see them."[6] One bitter account stated: "It appears to me we attack the enemy first and then find out his position."[7] The failure of the British to properly determine the enemy's location repeatedly led to high casualties, low morale and embarrassing defeats on the battlefield. "Owing to insufficient reconnaissance," claimed the authoritative *Von Löbell Annual Reports* for 1901, "the British Generals were often badly informed of the enemy's movements, and, owing to indifferent measures of security, surprises throughout the whole war were the order of the day."[8] These observations were made again the following year. "Moreover," the report added, "large bodies of troops were taken by surprise, and suffered considerable loss from infantry fire at close range as a consequence of inadequate scouting."[9]

The shortcoming was also clear to the combatants. "We could hear the crackle of musketry to our front and flanks, but the first experience we had of being under fire was the little spurts of dust rising from the ground, now in front, now in rear, the soft swish of the bullet as it flew past one to strike among the men in the rear," reported one veteran of Colenso. "One thing I am certain of, no one in the regiment saw a Boer that day."[10] Another stated simply: "Once again the British had walked into the arms of the Boers they could not see and whose strength or position was a total mystery to them."[11] Other fiascos such as the advance at Colenso of the 5th Brigade in dense columns and the unlimbering of two batteries within 600 metres of the enemy (resulting in high casualties and the loss of the guns) and the careless advance of the Highland Brigade at Magersfontein, aptly illustrate a recurring problem.[12]

The failure to locate the enemy was only a symptom and not the root of the problem. The weakness of the British Army lay in its antiquated tactics and training as well as in its outmoded concept of warfare. Courage was revered and used as a substitute for the lack of professional skill and proper training. "They marched up to the muzzles of the Boer rifles with a calm and even stride," observed one participant, "which was the admiration of all who saw them. They were never steadier on the parade ground of Edinburgh Castle."[13] Another participant was equally impressed. "The attack," he stated with awe, "was pressed with a magnificent, and at times almost reckless courage."[14] But, nine officers and 87 soldiers became casu-

Members of the 1st Gordon Highlanders and Royal Canadian Regiment crossing Paardeberg Drift, 18 February 1900. (Photographer R. Thiele. NA, C-14923)

alties within moments of the assault. There was a fatal flaw in the adulation of courage at the expense of tactical acumen. For example, commentary on the initial assault at Paardeburg conceded that "it was superb as an exhibition of dauntless courage, but flesh and blood could not drive through the storm of rifle fire from the Boer trenches."[15]

But the British were caught in a trap of their own making. Their army was the product of outdated training that relied heavily on rigid drill movements and top-down direction that stifled independent initiative and action. One modern view is that the infantry "could not shoot straight, its fire discipline was rotten, and its old fashioned reliance on drill precluded the use of fieldcraft and battlecraft."[16] Foreign observers during the campaign remarked that "in no modern army does 'drill' flourish as in the British. We see everywhere the most exaggerated stress laid on uniformity and simultaneous action ... the British troops run in close formations into the effective fire range of the Boers, suffer great loss, and then begin their fire-fight."[17] Captain Slocum, an American observer, also noted the effect of the reliance on drill movements in the face of the enemy. "The fire," he wrote, "caused the troops, which were still partially in close formation, heavy losses. This brigade was practically put out of action in the first few minutes of the engagement."[18]

The systemic defects of the Army also extended to the lack of individual skills that became a noticeable handicap to successful operations. "Our men," admitted Lord Kitchener, "were not as quick and accurate as their opponents in shooting rapidly, but they had not been trained for this during peace time... Opportunities were also sometimes lost by the delay which almost invariably occurred before our men opened fire." He attributed this "to the strictness of fire discipline, which our system of training enforces."[19] British musketry skills were of such a low standard that the 1901 *Von Löbell Annual Reports* asserted that "their bad training in shooting led to their defeat in action."[20]

But the deficiencies extended further to such basic skills as adopting proper security and using the ground to the best effect for personal cover, or for the deployment of guns and large bodies of troops. Furthermore, digging in was considered loathsome and unsoldierlike and camouflage was unheard of. "The disregard of the British officer and soldier of all corps of ordinary precautions for his own safety is astonishing," commented an American observer. "The infantry," he stated, "never make rushes in their attacks, but march erect and calmly forward." He added, "I have seen mounted men under a hot rifle fire at short range halted, waiting for orders to advance, sitting erect on their horses, a perfect target... They have not the individuality and resources of our men, but for indomitable courage, uncomplaining fortitude, and implicit obedience, they are beyond criticism."[21]

No group, however, was blamed more than the officer corps as a glaring symbol of the army's decay and debility. The British, argued one foreign observer, "have excellent officers, penetrated with the idea of England's invincible greatness and possessed of a reckless daring brought about and nourished by a spirit of adventure. It is, however, a question whether training and skill in command of these officers are, especially as regards the infantry, on a level with their moral excellence." He believed that the "British officer has now become reckless, owing to constant wars and life of adventure in all lands, and inclined to solve all tactical questions by *l'audace, toujours l'audace*."[22] The criticism that the officer corps lacked depth in professional knowledge and training was universally accepted. In military and public circles, sentiments such as "the officers look upon military service as purely sport"[23] and "the British officer, in the main, is about as amateurish as it is possible for a man to be"[24] prevailed after the fiascos in South Africa.

The anti-intellectualism of the officer corps was widely criticised and calls for greater professional training and education grew louder. The public perception of the life of the ordinary officer was that of "an idle life" sheltered by the attitude that "anything new to be learned was shunned like the plague."[25] The need to improve one's knowledge was minimal and the average officer, "though occasionally compelled to read a little in order to pass examinations, merely 'crams' just enough to secure the defeat of the examiners."[26] The failure to nurture an officer corps that was knowledgeable in the evolution of warfare, and could in turn develop and apply a common and progressive doctrine, led to an army that had "no mental grasp of the requirements of a modern battle."[27]

The leadership shortfall was clearly evident in theatre. Unimaginative, outmoded and careless tactical deployments were made repeatedly with the same unnecessary wastage in human life. Most officers were not only unable but also unwilling to attempt alternate ways of overcoming the problems they faced on the battlefield. This underscored the fact that after fighting for half a century against disunited and ill-armed tribesmen in India and Africa, the generals were ignorant of the realities of large-scale war.[28] The Boer War reinforced a belief that the "British officer is too frequently compelled to rely upon his memory, instead of being encouraged to use his wits."[29] For example, General Symons, a believer in the "well tried virtues of close order and concentration," tried three times to force the enemy's position at Glencoe by frontal attack with the same tragic results.[30] This experience was replayed throughout the entire war.

Blame must also be levelled at the prevailing system. Drill, the reverence for conformity, centralized control and unquestioned obedience were valued over personal initiative and bold independent action. "The fear of once blundering in the choice of expedients was extraordinary," observed Major Balck of the German General Staff. "It led to inaction, and was the cause of many favourable opportunities being allowed to slip away by those in command ... the superior officers whose lack of initiative and fear of taking responsibility became a by-word."[31] Adding to this inertia was the fact that "nearly all the senior officers were moulded by a school of thought which made it virtually inconceivable for them to decentralize their authority."[32]

Pictured in the foreground are officers of the Royal Canadian Rifles, who along with the remainder of their column were advancing to the Orange Free State, February 1900. (Photographer James Mason Cooper. NA, C-173037)

But a much larger problem than the evident lack of proficiency of its officers and soldiers gripped the consciousness of the British people. The need to cobble together a field force large enough to overcome a loosely formed citizen's army had denuded England of her entire land force, leaving only the Royal Navy to protect her shores. Initially, the confident government of Britain was interested in colonial contingents only for their political value, to provide a united front of Imperial solidarity. When the Canadian fervour to support the Empire created independent offers to provide volunteers outside of any official Dominion contribution, Joseph Chamberlain, the British Colonial Secretary, quickly wrote to the Canadian Governor General and asserted "We do not want the men ... the whole point of the offer would be lost unless it was endorsed by the Government of the Colony."[33] The eventual offer of a second Canadian contingent on 20 October 1899 was discreetly deferred by Britain, who had no interest in taking on the expense of additional colonial troops of questionable value. However, after the events of Black Week the offer, which was now almost two months old, was eagerly accepted.[34] Moreover, the British government soon besieged its colonies with repeated requests for even greater numbers of men. Not surprisingly, this was quickly perceived by all as "an admission of the weakness of the British Army, unable to beat an armed peasantry."[35]

The reason for the crisis lay at the root of the Army's existence. The Royal Navy was traditionally viewed as the true defender of the Empire. In its shadow, the Army was hobbled with two main limitations. The first was that it must be a voluntary organization and, moreover, it "must not be extravagantly dear."[36] These limitations created a situation where a professional force of minimal strength was maintained for the provision of essential garrisons in the colonies; the supply of troops for coaling stations and naval bases; and the presence of soldiers in occupied territories. No provision was made for the emergency mobilization of forces on a scale greater than could be improvised from units normally in the United Kingdom.[37]

As a result, when the war in South Africa turned into chaos and frantic pleas for additional troops were urgently dispatched by the commanders in the field, the state of neglect of the army became obvious. The impact was well illustrated by comments to the War Commission by the Secretary of State for War. "The war," he confessed, "brought to light the melancholy extent

Canadian infantrymen engaging the Boers, 18 February 1900. (Photographer James Mason Cooper. NA, PA-181414)

of our deficiencies ... full of peril to the Empire."[38] The deficiencies in organization were legion and were summarized as:

a. Defective preparation, information and readiness for mobilization and embarkation.
b. Defective clothing for the field.
c. Defective equipment, notably in entrenching tools and in the sighting of small arms.
d. Excessive baggage and incumbrance.
e. Insufficient medical provision and transport.
f. Insufficient cavalry, mounted infantry and horses and defective equipment.
g. Insufficient artillery, both as to weight of ordnance and range.
h. Chaotic sub-divisions into divisions and brigades.
i. Unreadiness and unpreparedness of auxiliary troops.
j. Defective size and completeness of units.
k. Want of unity between the several Land Forces of the National Defence.[39]

The manpower shortage, however, was the defect that revealed most clearly the crisis the war had precipitated. By the spring of 1900, the last formed units of regular troops had left England. By September of that year, the auxiliary forces, which had been heavily drawn on to supply drafts to the regular battalions, were also exhausted.[40] This state of affairs was raised in Parliament, where it was noted that "We have got the whole organized army out of the country, and the War Office is face to face with the problem of how to make an army to take its place."[41]

The ad hoc nature of feeding the hastily mobilized units and formations into the theatre of operations provided another indication of a major weakness of the existing army structure. "Every formation higher than the unit," conceded the Secretary of State for War in 1907, "had to be improvised when mobilization was ordered."[42] The entire expeditionary force was composed of individual units that, except in the case of one of its six infantry brigades, had never trained together.[43] The inefficiency and ineffectiveness of this force soon became apparent. The conflict imposed a significant demand on Britain's manpower and public purse and, of equal significance, signalled the severe limitations of its army to the world. "The spectacle of a small race of peasants and herdsmen, whose total numbers fall short of the populations of towns like Munich or Cologne, maintaining a war for nearly three years against the first Power in the world," wrote General the Baron Colmar von der Goltz, "and compelling that Power to put forth the most extraordinary efforts to bring the war to a successful conclusion, is a matter which calls for earnest consideration, since we have to search carefully through the previous history of the world, in order to find anything at all analogous to it."[44] Another military analyst observed: "The shock to Great Britain was not so much the effect of the early defeats as of the impressive fact that this pigmy opponent had caused England's energies to be strained to the uttermost, that the mother country was exhausted to the point of defencelessness, and that its safety rested on its fleet alone."[45]

Britain's vulnerability was not lost on the nation; the ordeal created much reflection, debate and investigation. From the Boer War emerged reforms and ideas that became significant in the evolution of British military thought and the reconstruction of its land forces. The identification, comprehension and subsequent application of these key concepts laid the groundwork of a modern, professional British Army.

The impact of the modern rifle, with its greater accuracy, range, and rapidity of fire, was well absorbed and it was seen as bestowing monumental power to the defensive. An entrenched opponent, practically invisible with smokeless powder and a concealed position, could punish an attacker at great range with relative impunity. Military theorists and commanders determined that the attack normally lost its momentum approximately 600-900 metres from the objective, after an advance under fire of roughly 150-200 metres.[46] The imbalance of casualties paid testimony to the effectiveness of the defence. It was concluded that the Boers normally lost approximately one tenth the number of men as the attacking force (which was not always successful).[47]

As a result it was universally accepted that unsupported movement over open ground was folly and would succeed only in producing high casualties. The frontal attack, regardless of the mass of humanity it involved, was dismissed as futile. Most military authorities agreed that "the greater the masses the greater will be the defeat."[48] Discussion during the period 1899-1902 focussed largely on the sentiment that improvements in modern weapons had "rendered attack almost impossible even with a great superiority of forces."[49]

The much smaller ratio of defenders required to stymie the attacker was also testimony to the strength of the defensive. The range and rapidity of the modern weapon, combined with the protection of an entrenchment, allowed a larger frontage to be defended by a significantly smaller number of men than ever before. One leading military theorist went so far as to say "one salutary lesson above all others, is that numbers in war are not absolutely decisive ... The *rage de nombres* has had a damper."[50] One veteran explained the advantage. "It must be remembered," he insisted, "that the result of rifle or shrapnel fire against troops under cover is practically nil, and that all the time you are losing heavily while the enemy is securely sheltered from your fire and able to shoot without much danger."[51] However, it was the sheer volume of fire from the modern small arm that allowed for the imbalance in numbers. The "emptying of a thousand Mauser magazines, that had the force of machine guns gave the British the impression that they were facing twenty thousand Boers."[52] The machine gun itself was credited as counting for twenty-five men.[53]

The realization of the strength of the defence, proven by the indisputable reality of numerous costly defeats, was the catalyst for immediate change. It prompted Lord Roberts as early

Field Hospital at Paardeberg Drift, 19 February 1900. (Photographer R. Thiele. NA, C-6097)

as February 1900 to issue guidance in the form of a memorandum to his commanders which spoke of the Boers' skilful use of weapons and ground. "Against such an enemy any attempt to take a position by direct attack will assuredly fail," he warned. "The only hope of success," Roberts explained, "lies in being able to turn one or both flanks, or what would, in many instances, be equally effective to threaten to cut the enemy's line of communication .... the position must be carefully examined by reconnoitring parties ... and when advancing to the attack of the positions, infantry must be freely extended." This, he concluded, "will throw increased responsibility on battalion and company commanders."[54]

Although the memorandum failed to produce an immediate change in tactics and operational efficiency, it did represent a shift in philosophy. This change was noted by a German observer who asserted that, "it has proven conclusively how difficult it is to advance over open country without cover, in face of the rain of bullets from modern weapons, no matter how much bravery is displayed by the attacking force. More careful utilization of natural cover, and a still greater circumspection on the part of the leaders in bringing up their supports, are already receiving an amount of consideration, which is bearing fruit on the training grounds."[55]

Although the effectiveness of an entrenched enemy, armed with modern weaponry, should have been realized before the Boer War, it took the traumatic events of South Africa to force change in the British Army. In its wake a greater emphasis was placed on fieldcraft skills such as reconnaissance and the use of ground and concealment. The sweeping changes also ensured the demise of volley fire and the emphasis on rigid, close formations. Finally, the war began the evolution of new tactics and a greater reliance on the individual leader and soldier.

A second major theme that emerged from the Boer experience that had a strong impact on military thinking was the importance of individual marksmanship. To the British, the Boer War taught the lesson of "how easily a few resolute men armed, and trained to use, the modern small-bore rifle can successfully keep at bay a comparatively large force."[56] Related to this was the realization that their own musketry skills and small arms were sadly lacking.[57] As a result, a new pattern Lee-Enfield rifle (which was five inches shorter than the existing model) became the standard rifle of the British Army by 1902.[58] Furthermore, new emphasis was placed on small arms training that focussed on individual skill. Such emphasis was placed on the importance of shooting that a scheme of training individuals in Volunteer and Cadet Rifle Clubs was considered sufficient to train a home defence force which, by virtue of its shooting skills, could repel an invading army.[59]

The reverence placed on shooting was of such magnitude that some argued that the rifle had eliminated the difference between regular soldier and civilian. This prompted an emotional debate that polarized the professional soldier and the amateur. Based on his observations in South Africa, Winston Churchill "judged a militia army not very much less competent than a standing army."[60] He went on tell an audience that "nor was it soothing to their [cavalry] pride to find squadrons of Colonial Horse and South Africa Corps, raised at ten days' notice, considered as good as, and often better than, the finest and most zealous regiments."[61]

Professional military opinion, which eventually prevailed in England, drew completely different conclusions.[62] Experience had shown the regulars that the amateur soldiers lacked discipline, training and reliability. Their actual employment was only made possible, they thought, by the lack of Boer military expertise and the fact that the militia was used primarily to guard the lines of communication. It was only after lengthy experience in the theatre of operations that the military ability of the militia was seen as improving.[63] "I do not think," insisted Lord Roberts, "we could in the future venture to put an army into the field of the size we had in South Africa unless we had more trained troops."[64] Even the authoritative *Von Löbell Annual Reports* for 1902 claimed that "a doubtful conclusion drawn from the South African War experience is an overestimation of the value of Militia and similar levies."[65] Nonetheless, the debate that was triggered—as much by the effectiveness of the modern rifle as it was by the crisis of mobilization —provided another catalyst for army reform and restructuring.

A third major concept that emerged from the war and which drove the reform of the Army was the necessity of greater mobility on the modern battlefield. The Boers, who were all mounted, displayed a great ability for rapid movement and were consistently able to reinforce any threatened portion of their entrenched lines more quickly and more secretly than the British could assemble for the assault.[66] This led to the belief, as espoused by Winston Churchill in a letter from Colenso, that the Boer's advantage derived from his mobility was five to one over infantry. Some rated the advantage as high as ten to one.[67] The assertion created an emotional debate over the utility and future of the cavalry. Mounted infantry became all the rage and were seen by many as the key to the future. They "could apply themselves quickly to any spot in a fight, support and supplement independent cavalry actions and take over screening duties." Their greatest strength, proponents argued, was their ability to provide an overwhelming weight of dismounted fire and their ability to seize key terrain.[68] The British belief in mounted infantry became clearly evident, for they were the only European power to adopt such a force.

The cavalry provides an excellent example of the influence of the Boer War on British military thought. Despite the wails of anguish that echoed through the Empire, the cavalry lost its cherished lance and received instead the standard issue rifle. Furthermore, dismounted operations for scouting, and particularly marksmanship training, now became important elements of cavalry training. "The Battle tactics of the British Army, influenced by its recent experience, recede more and more from Continental practice," stated the 1902 *Von Löbell Annual Reports*. "They renounce almost entirely the Encounter Battle and look on their Cavalry as Mounted Infantry which they cannot entrust with a part in the drama of the battle-field."[69]

Relative to the major themes so far discussed was the realization that the battlefield had changed dramatically. This prompted a radical new importance of the individual. Training, initiative and common sense were conceded as superior to blind obedience and the slavish adherence to a rigid discipline that became an acceptable excuse for inaction. It also supported the abrogation of personal responsibility. The futility of a system "which acted as a paralysing agent on all ranks, and made the Army fit only to act according to stereotyped rules and formulas" was fully understood.[70] "We are entering upon a period," remarked General Sir Ian Hamilton, a veteran of South Africa, "when the efficiency of an army will depend far more upon the morale and the high training of individuals who compose it than upon the mere numbers of those who may be available."[71]

As a result, the concept of the dynamic battlefield and the importance of the commander's intent began to influence training. The idea was increasingly accepted that "fixed rules cannot be laid down beforehand for movements in presence of, and action against, an enemy, as these movements must vary according to the circumstances of each situation which must arise."[72] In a radical departure from tradition, the aim became one of educating and training both the officers and men to think for themselves, to use their initiative and to strive for independent action in the absence of higher direction. Although easier theorized than applied, the philosophical foundations were laid.[73]

The concepts that emerged were not limited to individual changes but were seen for what they were: interrelated elements of the modern battlefield. As a result, the British Army underwent sweeping reforms. The primary change was to the very structure of the army as a whole. The wastage of modern war was likely to be enormous and an effort was made to ensure that a system of mobilization was in place.[74] The war had clearly shown that Britain's professional forces had a limited ability to defend the Empire. A system was required that allowed for expansion beyond this narrow resource.[75] "We realized," reflected Sir Aylmer Haldane, the British Secretary of State for War, "that we had gone into that war without adequate preparation for war on a great scale, and that we had never fully apprehended the importance of the maxim that all preparation in time of peace must be preparation for war."[76]

As a result, the Haldane reforms of 1904 created a two tier army. It consisted of regular formations to provide a British Expeditionary Force (BEF) of seven divisions, and a Territorial Force of fourteen divisions organized for home defence. The BEF was described by Haldane as "the striking force ... designed to act swiftly, and ready to assist any portion of the Empire."[77] The Territorial Force was exclusively assigned home defence and was formed from the existing volunteer units. Members would only be sent abroad if they volunteered for foreign service. The significance of this Territorial force was that it freed up the BEF for overseas missions. More importantly, establishments were now the same as those of the regular force and it was mandatory for all units to undergo a specified period of annual training. Thus, a better trained and organized Territorial Force would provide a nucleus for mobilization in times of crisis.[78]

The restructuring went further and included the development of a General Staff that Haldane described as "a brain for the army ... which would be free to apply their minds wholly to war preparation."[79] But even this was not enough. The experience of perceived weakness and unpreparedness prompted Britain to attempt to mobilize the colonies for Imperial Service.

A group photo of members of the Canadian Scouts taken at Middleburg, Transvaal, 24 April 1901. (Photographer unknown. NA, PA-129350)

"The present war," recorded the proceedings of the 1902 Colonial Conference Relating to Defence, "has in fact been a valuable illustration of the necessity for organizing the defence of the Empire against far graver contingencies. Unless such preparation is made, the continuance of the Empire is doubtful, if not improbable, and it is essential to preparation that it should be definitely known in peace what forces can be relied on in war."[80] Britain stressed the importance of conformity in organizational structures and equipment throughout the Empire in order to ease what is now called interoperability. It also pushed for the exchange of staff officers. "Our great object," asserted the British delegation, "must be to make the General Staff an imperial school of military thought, all members of which are imbued with the same traditions, accustomed to look at strategical problems from the same point of view."[81] Although Britain was never successful in convincing its colonies to commit forces carte blanche to Imperial defence, its efforts displayed a grasp of the lessons the war provided. Britain was resolved to be prepared for its next challenge.

This determination was also evident in its development of doctrine and training. The criticism that Britain's defeats stemmed from the "absence of a clear, consistent and comprehensive doctrine of war" was not unanswered.[82] The Army soon issued new Field Regulations and Manuals such as *Firing Exercises, Combined Training* (1903); *Cavalry Training* (1904); *Infantry Training, Manual of Engineering* (1905); and *Field Artillery Training* (1907).[83] The concepts in these manuals, born from the experience of the war, were reinforced by training and practised in field exercises. "In the use of ground, careful methods of employing fire, fighting spirit, and in endurance," commented one foreign observer, "the British soldier, in the opinion of all who have seen him at work, is unequalled... The cavalry makes a thoroughly commonsense use of its rifle; it has, so to speak, the instinct for dismounted combat in its blood."[84] The 1904 *Von Löbell Annual Reports* offered similar praise. "In their manoeuvres," it wrote, "the British Infantry showed great skill in the use of ground. Their thin khaki-clad skirmishers were scarcely visible. No detachment even was seen in close order within 3,000 yards."[85]

The transformation was obvious and the descriptions fail to remotely characterize the army that fought so poorly in the Boer War. Its restructuring and the new emphasis placed on professional knowledge and training, rooted in doctrine, provided the foundation of a modern

British Army. The proof of its effectiveness came in August 1914, when the BEF was rapidly dispatched to France "where it fought most effectively and as a properly constituted army."[86]

Although the impact of the war on Canadian military thought was also profound, it failed to lead to such significant changes. All of the main concepts were also embraced by the Dominion. This is no great surprise since the nominal head of the Canadian Militia was a British General Officer Commanding (GOC) and the Militia was inherently influenced by British military practice. However, some lessons were interpreted in a vastly different manner, which created a distinctly Canadian response.

The reverence for the power of the modern rifle and the importance of individual marksmanship vividly demonstrate a polarized interpretation of lessons drawn from the war. In Canada, as in Britain, they triggered a debate on the merits of the citizen versus the professional soldier. However, in Canada, the lesson of marksmanship confirmed what the militia had known all along, namely that the citizen soldier who could shoot was equal to, if not better than, the regular soldier. A commentary in the *Canadian Military Gazette* in 1902 reflected a popular sentiment. "We proceed," it explained, "on the idea that the soldier, especially the Canadian soldier, is born, and that no making is necessary."[87] Sam Hughes, an outspoken Canadian veteran of the war, believed that South Africa had demonstrated that "long conflict and standing armies had given way to mobile, well-trained, and outfitted citizen-soldiers who could shoot straight and withstand hardship."[88] He went on to argue in Parliament that "all authorities on constitutional law and government agree that one of the greatest dangers to permanent stability of any nation is the maintenance of a large standing army."[89] His experience would have a profound impact on Canadian military affairs. When he became Minister of Militia and Defence in 1911, he followed a program of increasing support to the Militia at the expense of the small permanent force.[90]

Nevertheless, the importance of the "modern rifle" and individual shooting skills were embraced with a passion in Canada. The ability to shoot was perceived as fundamental for a soldier. It became the defining measure of whether an individual was trained or not. Frederick Borden, who was the Minister of Militia from 1896 to 1911, declared, "there can be no question as to the vital importance of rifle practise to the Militia. The fact is that without it the Militia amounts to nothing."[91] During the debates on the Militia Act Amendments (1904), Borden affirmed: "The lesson that has been taught in the recent wars is that the defence of the country is comparatively much more easy now than it was supposed to be in past times, and that if you have a really formidable body of men who are somewhat used to discipline and understand the use of arms it is a very enormous undertaking for a people of 40,000,000 or 50,000,000 to enter a country of one-tenth or one-fifth of that population and wage a successful war of subjugation."[92]

It was this reliance on the citizen marksman that fuelled additional innovations. *The Canadian Military Gazette* reflected the prevailing belief. "The education of every citizen to shoot straight and become an expert rifleman," it claimed, "is the foundation of Canada's defence, and the important feature in [GOC] Lord Dundonald's project of a force of 100,000 men in our first line, hence his desire for civilian marksmen."[93] To achieve the desired state of martial prowess, significant changes were made. An Inspector General of Musketry was appointed and a Royal Canadian School of Musketry, on the model of the Imperial School at Hythe, was established.[94] Furthermore, rifle associations and clubs were embraced as integral elements of Canada's defence structure. The government promulgated an edict that "Civilian

"Typical Canuks." Canadian Scouts at Drietfontein, Transvaal, May 1902. (Photographer unknown. NA, C-7987)

Rifle Clubs or Associations shall be established on the basis of the Reserve Militia-Land and Marine ... and that the Rifle Associations organized under these regulations shall be subject to the control of the Department of Militia and Defence."[95] The new regulations specified that "in the event of a national emergency, any person who is or has been duly enrolled in any Rifle Association in Canada shall be deemed to be already enrolled in the Reserve Militia of the Dominion."[96]

The pursuit of a thoroughly trained citizen force also encouraged cadet corps and military training in schools. To inculcate the youth of the country with military ideals and practical skills was seen as an efficient means of securing the nation against any future crisis. "I can imagine no easier way," declared Hughes in Parliament, "to maintain what would be the equivalent of a standing army, than the maintenance of a system by which the youth of the country would be thoroughly trained in rifle shooting, and in the simple necessary movements in drill which the new strategy and tactics require ...Wherever the young men of a country are drilled early in life, experience has proved that they maintain in after years their zeal and interest in military matters."[97] He maintained that the cadet corps was "the foundation of the volunteer force, and the foundation of the defence of the Empire."[98]

Hughes' musings were not isolated. The value of teaching children to shoot and perform simple military drill "in the same manner as they are taught to read and write"[99] gained widespread support. It prompted Frederick Borden to state "that a special effort is to be made in the near future to arrange some common basis by which all schools in the Dominion can be some how or other brought within the range of the influence of military training and rifle shooting."[100]

The Boer War not only influenced the structure and training of the Canadian military, it had a pivotal effect on Canadian military (and political) thought. The perceived impotence and apparent incompetence of the British Army had a dramatic effect on Canada's political leaders and military commanders. Successive defeats and repeated pleas by Britain for more troops destroyed the glowing image of the unconquerable Empire. It seemed that Sam Hughes might have been correct when he argued that "British regular soldiers were so incompetent that they would be defeated by the Boers ... If British officers persisted in their out-outmoded military ways, the old plugs of Boer farmers would surely defeat them."[101] Moreover, the shortcomings of the British Army in South Africa, particularly the failure to provide an adequate supply of food and proper medical attention, were not lost on the soldiers of the Canadian contingents. The entire experience led to an astute prediction by one contemporary writer who remarked that "an idol was shattered. One future effect of this will probably be to cause Canadians to resist any attempt at too great centralization of the military system of the Empire."[102]

The prophecy was correct. The war had provided Canada with confidence in itself and a realization of its own autonomy. The South African experience led to a determination that Canadians in the future would alway serve together as a homogeneous group and that any commander of that force would have a dual responsibility to both their British commanders in the field and to their national government in Canada.[103] Furthermore, the landmark Militia Act of 1904 established a Militia Council and confirmed the eligibility of a Canadian to be head of the Militia.[104] In response to questions in Parliament expressing doubt about the soundness of these changes, Sir Frederick Borden bristled and retorted: "The question is rather: Has Canada assumed such a prominent position by her growth, by the heroic acts of her officers at home and in the South African War, as to entitle her to appoint one of her own sons to the command of her militia? Has she not assumed a position when at least there should be removed from the militia of this country the reflection that we cannot rear a man competent to take command of our own forces?"[105]

A sense of independence which grew from the war also led Canadians to resist British attempts to raise an Army Reserve of an Imperial Force that would automatically embroil Canada in Britain's conflicts with little or no influence on the decision making process. The Prime Minister and his Minister of Militia consistently rebuffed any efforts to establish an Imperial Force for overseas commitments.[106] These strong feelings of autonomy and the desire to maintain control of its own forces, which were born of the South African experience, provided the foundation of Canada's distinct military contribution to the First World War. Although Canada swiftly rallied to Britain's side in 1914, it quickly became apparent—as a result of persistent and successful efforts to maintain administrative and organizational control of the Canadian Expeditionary Force—that the earlier experience was not lost.[107]

That the Boer War had a profound effect on British and Canadian military thought and subsequently on the military organizations of the two countries is indisputable. The lessons learned and the concepts taken away from that conflict embedded themselves in the very fibre of military institutions; in doctrine, organization and training. However, with time an insidious revisionism began to creep into the thinking of the military leaders of most nations. The lessons that were once eagerly consumed came increasingly under attack and their applicability was consistently questioned. Very quickly critics began to insist that the "Boer War is altogether on a different plan from what a war in Europe would be," and therefore "not much could be learnt from it."[108] The circumstances of the war were described by revisionists as so exceptional that no valuable lessons influencing the conduct of war could be gleaned from it. "Glorious in many ways, the campaign [in South Africa] certainly was," one commentator acknowledged, "but it is equally certain it was not 'War.'"[109]

Although reform continued, it was in the development of offensive tactics that the greatest amount of "progress" was lost to revisionism. Despite the fact that the lesson of the potency of an entrenched opponent armed with modern weapons was reinforced by other more conventional conflicts—the American Civil War (1861-1865), the Franco-Prussian War (1870-1871) and the Russo-Japanese War (1904-1905) among them[110]—old ideas of the battlefield once again reasserted themselves. The innovation and work done to avoid the inevitable heavy casualties of human wave mass attacks against modern technology were ignored. The Boer War confirmed that concepts such as fire and movement, neutralizing fire, and all arms co-operation would be critical to future operations. Yet, their application was later ignored.

Instructors at the School of Musketry in Hythe believed that "manoeuvre is essentially a fire problem, and that in war fire is everything."[111] An observer from the German General Staff who accompanied the British during the war supported this idea. "Tactical formations," he wrote, "are governed by fire effect, modern weapons govern modern formations."[112] As a result the principle of attaining "superiority of fire over the defence" became clear to the analysts.[113] One writer in 1904 vividly stressed the point. "The actual goal of the stormers," he noted, "must be so completely swept by rifle fire up to the last moment that the exposure of an eye or a finger in taking aim should be a serious risk to the defending troops."[114]

The realization of the effectiveness of modern weaponry resulted in the development of tactics to avoid the catastrophic casualties of the massed attack in the open. The 1903 Von Löbell Report stated that "Infantry must avoid open ground when within effective artillery range, choosing ground and formations which shall conceal their advance. Groups, not unbroken lines, must be formed, which, as long as they can do so, advance uninterruptedly without firing or lateral movement."[115] It was well documented that "successive waves of attack in the open are a source of weakness and not strength ... [ranks in depth] are exposed to just as heavy a fire as the front line once the fire-zone is entered, having probably just as many casualties."[116] Contemporary literature reverberated with the theme that formations advancing in waves or in close columns must now be replaced by "parallel or converging streams rushing forward, as the surface of the ground permits."[117] Military theorists argued that the actual assault depended increasingly on the strength of small unit commanders and the individual soldiers themselves, using the ground and supporting fire to work their way toward the objective. The modern military historian Paddy Griffith has explained the doctrine that emerged from the Boer War very well. "The Prewar army believed in a cautious approach" to the objective with fire and movement. "One would try to suppress the enemy's fire as much as possible by one's own fire, while the advancing riflemen used fieldcraft, short rushes and extended formations to protect themselves as much as possible," he explained. "Gradually a firing line would be established at around 200 yards from the enemy... Then, once the firefight had been won and the enemy's fire abated, the attackers would charge forward and finish the job with the bayonet."[118]

The importance of all arms co-operation was also well impressed on those who had studied the conflict. The 1902 *Von Löbell Annual Reports* explained that the Boer War indicated that "thorough preparation of the attack by artillery and infantry fire working together" was instrumental for success.[119] Soldier and scholar Colonel G.F.R. Henderson, in his writings and lectures prior to the Boer War, asserted that "against an enemy sheltered in trenches and concealed through the use of smokeless powder, the cost of using the old formations had become prohibitive. Under modern conditions a frontal attack could succeed only through close co-operation between artillery and infantry, and even then the best opportunities were to be found in envelopment."[120] This theme was reflected in other works that attributed much of the British failure in their attacks to an absence of co-operation between the artillery and the infantry. It was generally observed that the artillery usually supported the advance to within 400 to 300 metres of the objective but then became silent, thus allowing the defender to come out of his entrenchment and wreak havoc on the advancing infantry.[121] Better, closer co-ordination was shown to be extremely effective during General Buller's crossing of the Tuegla River in February 1900, when shells were sent "skimming over the heads of the creeping infantry, a creeping curtain of shellfire. Only a hundred yards ahead of them, the hillside foamed and thundered with rocks and earth and flying steel. While, on their side of the curtain, the sun still shone and the butterflies glittered on the rocks."[122] The *Canadian Military Gazette* claimed that the greatest contribution of artillery fire was not so much its destructive power, but rather its ability to keep the defender deep in his trench, or at least unnerved, so that his attention was not focussed on the advancing infantry.[123] Although one of the keys to unlocking the mystery of overcoming the power of the entrenched opponent was in the grip of the military leadership, it would not be properly applied until years of needless waste in the trenches of Europe had reinforced the message.

The failure to apply all arms co-operation stemmed from the overwhelming negative impression most commanders had of the artillery during the war. "The old theory that a great superiority of artillery is sufficient to silence the fire of entrenched men and prepare the way for infantry attack seems to be an illusion," was a sentiment widespread among veterans and observers.[124] General Douglas Haig ventured the observation that "artillery was only effective against demoralized troops."[125]

Another well understood and widely accepted concept was the futility of the human wave attack. It was well documented that "successive waves of attack in the open are a source of weakness and not strength ... [ranks in depth] are exposed to just as heavy a fire as the front line once the fire-zone is entered, having probably just as many casualties."[126] The futility of the tactic was obvious. "The art of war is becoming interesting," remarked one correspondent, adding prophetically that " It is perfecting itself in certain directions to a point that may yet shock the civilized world into its abolition and compel arbitration from a sense of common humanity."[127]

But the question must be raised: if the lessons were learned and the solutions to the slaughter of the First World War known, how then did the senior military leadership allow the tragedy to occur? Why was the opportunity lost? The answer can be found in the gradual redefinition of the experience of the war and a reversion to deep-seated ideas. The problem of the leadership was never one of accepting the new technology, but rather one of applying its effect to the field of battle. As a result, commanders dismissed some essential lessons of the Boer War as unique to that conflict.

The effectiveness of modern technology bred a belief that heavy casualties were now a foregone conclusion; large losses were not perceived as a sign of failure but rather one of determination and strength. This school of thought asserted that the factor of "cardinal importance in the conduct of successful attack is the grim necessity of sacrificing the lives of your men. No great result has ever been obtained over a determined enemy without incurring that penalty and the whole course of military history enforces this sad lesson."[128]

High casualties were regarded as inconsequential as long as a higher military purpose was being served. "A certain loss," argued proponents of the idea, "is inseparable from war; the degree of loss is almost immaterial so long as the morale of the troops and their desire to 'charge home' is predominant."[129] Some went so far as to ridicule a concern for losses as inherently hostile to military achievement. "Public opinion in England, which is all-powerful," lamented one such critic, "influenced by sensation-hunting ignorant correspondents, went even so far astray as to consider small losses the sign of good, tactical dispositions; and leaders, who have inscribed their names in history in iron characters, must give way to generals who subscribe to the precept that discretion is the better part of valour. It is conceivable that the English commanders were more or less influenced by this morbid flood, which hindered them from bringing the war to an end by summary, powerful blows."[130] The revisionism and failure to acknowledge the true root of defeat in South Africa is painfully obvious.

The acceptance of high losses was also wrapped in a larger belief in offensive action at any and all costs. This was, ironically, explained as a result of the recognition of the influence of firepower. "It is evident, therefore," wrote General Ferdinand Foch, "that the material superiority of firepower increases rapidly to the advantage of the attack."[131] Furthermore, the revisionists asserted that to win, one must attack. "Offensive strategy," they correctly argued, "entails offensive tactics, and to remain on the defensive is to suffer war, not to make it."[132] The idea that "the most insidious danger which can beset an army is disbelief in its own offensive power" became a recurring theme.[133]

The argument was based in part on a casualty time-exposed-to-fire relationship. It was claimed that the longer the troops were exposed to fire in the enemy's defensive zone, the greater was the likelihood of enormous casualties from the effectiveness of modern weaponry. Fire and movement was decried as a slow and ponderous process. Therefore, offensive action— meaning a rapid and unfettered assault—was rationalized as actually saving lives, since it limited the time that soldiers were exposed in the open to fire.

And so the old notion of the superiority of courage was resurrected. Steadfast courage and icy steel nerves were identified as the key determinant in conflict. Emotional arguments proclaiming courage as the most influential weapon on the battlefield quickly supplanted the actual experience of the war.[134] General Foch taught officers that "beyond everything, [there is] will: a steady will which does not dissipate its strength. There you have the whole thing—willpower."[135] Moreover, he insisted that "few battles are lost physically." Borrowing from the French philosopher Count Joseph de Maistre, he proclaimed that "Defeat is almost always a matter of morale. The real victor, or real loser, is the man who believes he has won or lost."[136]

The revisionists considered the firepower lessons of South Africa to be abnormal and therefore not representative of future warfare. Shortly after the conflict, the controversy over whether frontal attacks were necessary to ensure decisive action also re-emerged. "It is the fashion to talk of a frontal attack as a blunder," claimed the revisionists, "but without frontal attack there is no such thing as decisive action." They claimed that "the dictum as to the impracticability of frontal attacks is one that cannot be sustained."[137] Even the German editorial staff of the respected *Von Löbell Annual Reports* in 1903, reinforced the belief that "Nothing is more fatal than to inculcate the impossibility of frontal attack in the open as an unconditional principle. Now more than ever does the personal element assert itself side by side with fire effect."[138]

The commitment to offensive action; the invincibility of an army's courage, even in the face of modern technology; the perception that high casualties were inherent to modern battle, and in fact represented an army's worth and determination; all of these fuelled what came to be known as the "cult of the offensive." The belief was that "to advance is to win." This focus was on moving forward; the importance of "fire action" became secondary.[139] A fear soon grew among some commanders that concern with "fire action" could slow offensive operations to the point of stagnation, and thereby cause even greater casualties. Even as the effectiveness of fire-power was growing, a "swing against accepting that unsuppressed defensive fire made manoeuvre within 800 metres of the enemy prohibitive" was developed in parallel.[140]

This myopic re-interpretation of the lessons, based on a deep-seated but not necessarily accurate comprehension of warfare, led revisionists to re-examine the mass human wave assault. Many soon accepted the maxim that "a single line will fail; two lines will usually fail; three lines will sometimes fail, but four lines will usually succeed."[141] Major-General Webber, a veteran of South Africa, demonstrates the failure to absorb the lessons available. "A great many people say," he claimed, "that frontal attacks have been proved to be an impossibility. But that is merely wild talk."[142] He went on to declare that success was assured if one never "attacked with less than six-teen battalions line behind line, on a narrow frontage with great depth."[143] These men trivialized the new concepts of fire and movement, the use of ground, and all arms co-operation. They re-assessed the failures in South Africa and attributed them to the unique environment, the lack of stress on individual courage and the failure to concentrate sufficient mass in the assault.

This thinking led directly to the tragedy of the First World War. For the revisionists the human element of war was paramount and the introduction of new technology was not allowed to interfere with their preconceived notions of the battlefield. To key Allied generals like Douglas Haig, Ferdinand Foch and Joseph Joffre, battle was still a drama of successive independent actions: manoeuvre, preparation, attack and exploitation.[144] They still believed that the enemy was the main target to be attacked and that the opponent could only be defeated by the concentration of superior force at a decisive point. Moreover, they were convinced that success in battle depended predominately on the morale of the army and the quality of the commander-in-chief.[145] Haig was convinced of the necessity of a great battle of attrition, the victor being the one with the greatest "moral," meaning courage; quite simply the one who "stuck it out."[146]

The significance of the Boer War has often been overlooked. The South African experience transformed the British Army from a colonial custodian to a modern fighting force. The defeats suffered at the hands of the Boer citizen army underscored the weakness and archaic state of Britain's land forces. This led to dramatic reforms and changes that affected the structure, training and doctrine of the British Army.

The experience also influenced Canadian military thought and was responsible for numerous reforms and improvements to the Canadian military system. But it also confirmed the belief in the supremacy of the citizen soldier and the importance of individual marksmanship. More importantly, it laid the foundation for a greater sense of Canadian independence that would emerge during the First World War.

Of equal importance was the emergence of fundamental concepts and lessons that provided the key to avoiding the tragedy of the Western Front. The effect of modern firepower combined with entrenchments was well documented, as was the futility of unsupported attacks in the open. The futility of the massed human wave attack became evident, time after time, in the bloody experience of the British infantry in the Transvaal. The tactics needed to minimize the strength of the defensive—decentralized action, fire and movement, the use of ground, and co-ordinated fire support, particularly that of artillery to provide neutralizing fire until the final moments of the assault—were all documented and incorporated into manuals. The realizations that firepower dictated tactics and that unsuppressed defensive fire courted disaster were widely disseminated.

These lessons were not, however, universally embraced. With time a revisionism began to infil-trate contemporary military thought. The Boer War was dismissed as a unique experience that had no impact on future warfare, particularly on the Continent. This myopic approach ignored the universality of the lessons—confirmed by other contemporary conflicts—because of an insistence on clutching to preconceived ideas of the battlefield. Unbridled offensive action and the importance of courage became the answer to the power of the defence. Revisionists argued that modern technology made the battlefield more lethal, and that high casualties were therefore inherent to offensive action. They further asserted that the process of suppressive fire and movement was slow and ponderous and would ultimately lead to an even greater loss of life because the advance would stagnate and soldiers would remain exposed for longer periods of time in the fire-swept killing zone. Therefore, the answer lay in an unrestrained offensive spirit which emphasized a rapid advance and the well-tried combination of courage and discipline. After all, the revisionists repeatedly affirmed that any worthwhile military endeavour demanded sacrifice. The greater the number of dead, the greater was the perceived courage and determination of the army. To the revisionists, success would be decided by the commander who would persevere through heavy losses and continue to feed formations into the machine of destruction until the opponent lost courage or succumbed to attrition. As a result, the armies of the Great Powers entered into the furnace of the First World War, devoid of the lessons of the past only to repeat them on a colossal scale. The senior military leadership failed their soldiers because they turned their backs on the lessons of the Boer War. This was unforgivable. It truly was a lost opportunity.

> It was our own fault, and our very grave fault, and now
> we must turn it to use,
> we have forty million reasons for failure, but not
> a single excuse!
> —Rudyard Kipling, *The Five Nations*, 1903

Notes for Chapter 4

1 Colonial Office (UK), *Extracts from Proceedings of Colonial Conferences relating to Defence* (London, Colonial Office, 1909) 189.

2 "The British Army and Modern Conceptions of War," *The Journal of the Royal United Services Institute (RUSI)*, Vol 60, No. 40 (September 1911), 1181. See also Sanford Evans, *The Canadian Contingents* (Toronto: The Publishers' Syndicate Ltd., 1901), 36.

3 Gordon McKenzie, *Delayed Action. Being something of the life and times of the late Brigadier General, Sir Duncan McKenzie, K.C.M.G, C.B., D.S.O., V.D., Legion d'Honneur* (Private Printing, no date), 163.

4 Winston S Churchill, *The Boer War—London to Ladysmith via Pretoria, Ian Hamilton's March* (London: Leo Cooper, 1989), 31-32.

5 Black Week denotes the period when three separate British formations were decisively beaten at Stormberg, Magersfontein and Colenso, during the period 10-15 December 1899.

6 MacKenzie, 154.

7 Capt J.H. Ram, "Observations on the War in South Africa," *RUSI*, Vol 48, No. 311 (1904), 49.

8 LCol E. Gunter, "The Von Löbell Annual Reports on the Changes and Progress in Military Matters in 1901," *RUSI*, Vol 46, No. 296 (1902), 1311.

9 LCol E. Gunter, "The Von Löbell Annual Reports on the Changes and Progress in Military Matters in 1902," *RUSI*, Vol 47, No. 308 (October 1903), 1130.

10 A Regimental Officer, "Some Notes on the Lessons of the South African War," *United Service Magazine*, Vol 23 (1901), 64-65. A similar observation was made at the Battle of Spion Kop; "To our men they [Boers] were as usual, practically invisible." J.C. Hopkins and M. Halstead, *South Africa and the Boer-British War* (Brantford: The Bradley-Garretson Co. Ltd., no date), 421.

11 Rayne Kruger, *Good-Bye Dolly Gray* (London: Cassel, 1959), 139.

12 LCol von Lindenau, "What Has the Boer War to Teach Us, As Regards Infantry Attack," *RUSI*, Vol 47, No. 301 (March 1903), 320. See also Thomas Pakenham, *The Boer War* (London: Weidenfeld and Nicolson, 1979) and Carmen Miller, *Painting the Map Red: Canada and the South African War* (Montreal: McGill University Press, 1992). Another version of the debacle at Colenso noted, "Col Long's daring but unfortunate artillery movements...the Boer guns began a little later throwing shrapnel and the machine gun fired solid shot at them. But the gunners never floundered or winced." J. Birch, *War in South Africa Between the British & Boers* (London, Ontario: 1899), 421.

13 Hart-McHarg, *From Quebec to Pretoria* (Toronto: William Briggs, 1902), 211-212.

14 Maj J.E. Caunter, "From Enslin to Bloemfontein with the 6th Division," *RUSI*, Vol 44, No. 271 (September 1900), 1146. Correspondents also reported this tragic loss of life in valiant terms; "The Dublins and Connaughts advanced magnificently against almost overwhelming fire, men falling at every step." Hopkins and Halstead, 388.

15 R.C. Fetherstonhaugh, *The Royal Canadian Regiment 1883-1933* (Fredericton: The RCR, 1936), 109.

16 Shelford Bidwell and Dominick Graham, *Fire Power: British Army Weapons and Theories of War* (London: Allen & Unwin, 1982), 2.

17 LCol E. Gunter, "A German View of British Tactics in the Boer War," *RUSI*, Vol 46, No. 292 (1902), 805.

18 Ram, 47. A combatant observed, "the point that struck most of us was...the little opportunity any of us had of using our rifles, owing to the formation adopted." Regimental Officer, "Lessons of the South African War," 63.

19 "The South African Muddle," *The Canadian Military Gazette*, 17 November 1903, 11. LCol Gunter also wrote, "The want of careful individual training and the anxiety to pull his trigger the moment the word is given result in each man's firing without taking exact aim." Gunter, "A German View of British Tactics in the Boer War," 802.

20 Gunter, "The Von Löbell Annual Reports on the Changes and Progress In Military Matters in 1901," 1311. The weakness of the rigid system and low level of individual initiative and skill is illustrated in an example given of 35 British POWs. It was noted that although all had fired at the Boer positions as close as 350 paces, not a single soldier had the correct sight setting. In fact most of them had kept their sights fixed at 800 and 850 yards, because no order to change them had been given. Major Balck, "The Lessons of the Boer War and the Battle Working of the Three Arms," *RUSI*, Vol 48, No. 321 (November 1904), 1276.

21 Ram, 50. Major-General Sir Ernest Swinton remarked, "A marked feature of the first part of the war was the combination of ignorance as to the value of trenches and the ingrained aversion to the inglorious drudgery of digging." Extracted from John A. English, *On Infantry* (New York: Praeger, 1981), 4.

22 LCol E. Gunter, "A Retrospect of the War in South Africa," *RUSI*, Vol 45, No. 276 (February 1901), 41 & 46.

23 "The South African War of 1899-1900," *RUSI*, Vol 45, No. 281, July 1901, 853. Historian Denis Winter observed an impression of the period: "The Army...has so far been looked upon as a profession in which money will be spent rather than gained but one in which work is light and the amusements many. It has consequently attracted young men whose inclinations were towards an easy, pleasant life." *Haig's Command. A Reassessment* (London: Viking, 1991).

24 "Drill Reform," *The Canadian Military Gazette*, 1 April 1902, 10. Even within the Army itself, contempt was evident. One personal account noted, "The Army regarded most Generals and all Staff officers as pampered and stupid." Major E.T. Aspinall, "Recollections of the 2nd Battalion, South Africa—1899-1902," *The Rifle Brigade Chronicle for 1945*, 183.

25 Full Marks, "Getting Light," *The Canadian Military Gazette*, 18 March 1902, 12.

26 LCol Alsager Pollock, "Smokeless Powder and Entrenchments," *RUSI*, Vol 47, No. 305 (1903), 805.

27 Bidwell and Graham, 3. An article written by "Skipper" entitled "Officers and Professional Training," (*United Service Magazine*, Vol 25, 1902, 296-302) provides a window on the make-up and philosophy of the Officer Corps at the time. He states, "The question of the professional education and training of the officer is closely connected with his pay and social class. It has been generally recognized by the advocates for the exaction of harder work from officers that, beyond certain limits, it is vain to expect profitable work from men whose pay does not suffice for their living expenses. This difficulty has been met by the proposal to increase pay and cut down expenses, so that an officer may reasonably find his pay enough to live on. The proposers of these reforms have ignored the fact that such changes will at once open the commissioned ranks of the Army as a possible career to all classes of society."

28 Pakenham, 151.

29 Pollock, 808.

30 Gunter, "A German View," 804; and Pakenham, 129.

31 Maj Balck, "The Lessons of the Boer War and the Battle Workings of the Three Arms," *RUSI*, Vol 48, No. 321 (1904), 1276-1277.

32 Eversley Belfield, *The Boer War* (London: Archon Books, 1975), 31.

33 Joseph Schull, *Laurier - The First Canadian* (Toronto: MacMillan of Canada, 1965), 381. Brigadier McKenzie, a native of Cape Colony, believed that it was a serious mistake not to call out the colonists at the onset of the conflict since they were mounted and understood the Boer ways. He stated, "They would have been equal in every respect to the Boers themselves." *Delayed Action...*, 156. This is reinforced by Kruger who stated, "The British colonists and refugee Uitlanders were against the Army's obstinacy over volunteers, especially colonists who were apt not to be gentlemen. The Kaffir Wars had given the colony the highest proportion of fighting men in the world; they knew terrain intimately; the war was as keenly their concern as anybody." *Good-Bye Dolly Gray*, 154.

34 Miller, *Painting the Map Red* (Toronto: MacMillan of Canada, 1965),154. Kruger stated, "In England it was, says one authority, 'a succession of shocks and humiliations. Our national life and thought never were the same again.'" *Good-Bye Dolly Gray*, 144.

35 Ibid., 414.

36 LCol R.H. Morrison, "Lessons to be Derived from the Expedition to South Africa in Regard to the Best Organization of the Land Forces of the Empire," *RUSI*, Vol 45, No. 281 (July 1901), 796. Brigadier Dewing commented, "the feeling of safety from any land threat resulted in the constant determination to restrict the strength of the army to an absolute minimum." Brigadier R. H. Dewing, *The Army* (London: William Hodge & Company Ltd., 1938), 11.

37 Dewing, 11.

38   C.W. Dilke, "The Report of the War Commission," *RUSI,* Vol 68, No. 313 (1904), 224.

39   Col Sir Howard Vincent, "Lessons From the War For Immediate Application," *The United Service Magazine,* Vol 23 (1901), 28. The comment on the inadequate state of medical services is important to note. The Field Force was reduced by approximately 20% by disease alone in a comparatively healthy country. (Capt J. Rose, "Lessons to be derived from the Expedition to South Africa," *RUSI,* Vol 45, No. 279, May 1901, 572). Lady Edward Cecil also wrote to the Prime Minister in May 1900, "Far more people have been killed by negligence in our hospitals than by Boer bullets." (Pakenham, 374). See also LCol W. Hill-Climo, "Medical Lessons of the War," *The United Service Magazine,* Vol 21 (1900), 404-410.

40   J.K. Dunlop, *The Development of the British Army 1899-1914* (London: Methuen, 1938), 79.

41   Ibid., 81.

42   Secretary of State for War, "The Military System of the Future in the British Empire," *RUSI,* Vol 51, No. 355 (1907), 1068.

43   Belfield, 30. It was further noted that neither the Corps Headquarters itself, nor the four divisional headquarters possessed staffs trained to plan and co-ordinate the movement of the troops under their nominal control.

44   Gen the Baron Colmar von der Goltz, "What Can We Learn from the Boer War?" *RUSI,* Vol 46, No. 298 (1902), 1533-1539.

45   Gunter, "A Retrospect of the War in South Africa," 50.

46   "Military Observations on the War in South Africa," *RUSI,* Vol 46, No. 289 (1902), 357; and von der Goltz, 1533-1539. See also Fritz Hoenig, "The Lessons of the South African and Chinese Wars," *RUSI,* Vol 45, No. 277 (March 1901), 292. One veteran described the overwhelming power of defensive fire this way: "It was as though someone had pressed a button and turned on a million electric lights. And there was a great roaring in the ears as though a dam had burst its walls." Pakenham, 204.

47   Jean De Bloch, "The Transvaal War," *RUSI,* Vol 45, No. 286 (December 1901), 1434. As an example, casualties at Colenso were 165 killed, 760 wounded and 332 captured (British) against the loss of only 7 killed and 30 wounded for the Boers. Ram, 47-48.

48   Bloch, "The Transvaal War," *RUSI,* Vol 45, No. 286, 1417.

49   Bloch, "The Transvaal War," *RUSI,* Vol 45, No. 285 (November 1901), 1326. Other examples include "the leading of large bodies across open country will become almost or completely an impossibility" ("Military Observations on the War in South Africa," *RUSI,* Vol 46, No. 290, April 1902, 271) and "frontal attack will nearly always lead to a defeat when opposed to modern fire-arms" and "Forcing one's way through, as was Napoleon's custom, is as good as impossible in the present day." ("Military Observations on the War in South Africa," *RUSI,* Vol 46, No. 288, February 1902, 217-218).

50   Goltz, 1536. One example that incorporates a period widely studied at this time, illustrates the theme in question. At Waterloo, Wellington had some 35,000 men on each mile of ground. At Magersfontein, the Boers with some 6,000 men successfully defended 20 miles of front. (Bloch, "The Transvaal War," *RUSI,* Vol 45, No. 286, 1416).

51   A Regimental Officer, 66.

52   Pakenham, 231.

53   Ram, "Observations on the War in South Africa," *RUSI,* Vol 48, No. 312 (February 1904), 156.

54   Fetherstonhaugh, 104.

55   Goltz, 1535. The effectiveness of the Khaki uniform in reducing casualties, because of its earthy colour, led to the adoption (1903) of a single service uniform in peacetime which would also be worn on operations. By 1903 all troops were also issued with entrenching tools as part of their individual equipment. Hoening, 293; and Pollock, 806.

56   Morrison, 805.

57   Balck, 1276. See also the *Von Löbell Annual Reports*, 1901 and 1902.

58   Dunlop, 155. The 1907 pattern rifle was accepted, ultimately resulting in the SMLE No. 1 Mk III.

59   Ibid., 151. The importance of individual musketry skills became so ingrained in the British military psyche that they missed the opportunity afforded by the machine gun. Bidwell and Graham illustrate how the Germans concluded that even intense training would not make rifle marksmen out of conscripts, whereas they could teach them to produce accurate fire in great volume with machine guns. The British, however, continued to rely on the use of rifles to increase their strike rate, relying on fire discipline and individual skill, rather than adding to their scale of two machine guns per battalion. *Fire Power,* 22.

60   Tuvia Ben-Moshe, *Churchill Strategy & History* (Boulder: Lynee Rienner Publications, 1992), 10.

61   Winston S. Churchill, "Some Impressions of the War in South Africa," *RUSI,* Vol 45, No. 281 (July 1901), 843.

62   The Canadian conclusions differed and this sentiment was used as a rationalization for not maintaining a large standing professional army. Further discussion on the Canadian experience will be presented later in the chapter.

63   Field Officer, 274; "The South African War of 1899-1900," *RUSI,* Vol 45, No. 281 (July 1901), 855; and LCol Hallewell, "Notes on Mounted Troops," *The United Service Magazine,* Vol 29 (1904), 426.

64   "The South-African War Muddle," *The Canadian Military Gazette,* 17 November 1903, 11.

65   Gunter, the Von Löbell Annual Report, 1902, 1132.

66   Markham Rose, "Lessons to be Derived from the Expedition to South Africa in Regard to the Best Organization of the Land Forces of the Empire," *RUSI,* Vol 45, No. 279 (1901), 555.

67   LCol F.N. Maude, "Continental versus South African Tactics: A Comparison and Reply to Some Critics," *RUSI,* Vol 46, No. 281 (March 1902), 325. See also Sir Charles Dilke, "The Report of the War Commission," *RUSI,* Vol 48, No. 313 (March 1904), 239; and an Outsider, "The War: Some of Our Blunders," *The United Services Magazine,* Vol 21 (1900), 576-584.

68   BGen E.C. Bethune, "The Uses of Cavalry and Mounted Infantry in Modern Warfare," *RUSI,* Vol 50, No. 339 (May

1906), 622. See also Maj R.H. Carr-Ellison, "Mounted Infantry," *The United Service Magazine,* Vol 22 (1900-1901), 165-168; and Maj J.M. Macartney, "Mounted Infantry," *The United Service Magazine,* Vol 21 (1900), 8-13.

69 Gunter, the Von Löbell Annual Report, 1902, *RUSI,* Vol 47, No. 308 (October 1903), 1136. See also 1903 Report (*RUSI,* Vol 48, No. 320, October 1904, 1146).

70 Ram, 168. The Historical Section of the German General Staff placed inordinate importance on the concept of individual action and initiative. It wrote, "The rigid fettering with forms and rules, to which a false system of peace training had condemned leaders, avenged itself bitterly during the South African War. In this experience, so pregnant of warning for the future, is contained the most important lesson of the whole war." ("The British Army and Modern Conceptions of War," *RUSI,* Vol 60, No. 403, September 1911, 1183).

71 Tim Travers, *The Killing Ground* (London: Allen & Unwin, 1987), 46. The author demonstrates the polarity of the concept. He writes that LGen Sir William Gatacre thought that the individual should be trained into a "sharp fighting machine" as opposed to Lord Roberts who thought the solution was "training the men to act as individuals and not as machines."

72 Maj C.B. Mayne, "The Training of Infantry for Attack," *The United Service Magazine,* Vol 20, 1899-1900, 288.

73 See the Von Löbell Report, 1902 (*RUSI,* Vol 47, No. 308, October 1903, 1131-1133) and Field Officer, "The Reform of the British Army," *The United Service Magazine,* 1902, 271-274. Col Henderson noted in a report, in 1895, that "Foreign officers who have visited Aldershot have remarked...that our men did not seem to be able to act for themselves, but that they always required some one to tell them what to do; and it is evident that if officers have to look closely after their men, they will have little time to give to a consideration either of the ground or of the enemy." Extracted from Jay Luvaas, *The Education of an Army* (Chicago: University of Chicago Press, 1964), 236.

74 By the end of May 1900, 42,000 men were in hospitals (due to illness and wounds), representing nearly a fifth of the British total strength.

75 See Secretary of State for War, "The Military System of the Future in the British Empire," *RUSI,* Vol 51, No. 356 (October 1907), 1183-1189; and Victor Germains, *The Kitchener Armies* (London: Peter Davies, Limited, 1930), 4-10.

76 *Extracts from Proceedings of Colonial Conferences relating to Defence,* 189.

77 Ibid., 191. See also Dewing, 13-16. Under Haldane the BEF was approximately 156,000 men organized into six strong divisions of infantry and one cavalry division. (A. de Tarlé, "The British Army and a Continental War," *RUSI,* Vol 57, March 1913, 386).

78 Peter Simkins, *Kitchener's Army* (New York: Manchester University Press, 1988), 6-17.

79 *Extracts from Proceedings of Colonial Conferences relating to Defence,* 189.

80 Ibid., 119.

81 Ibid., 192 & 250.

82 "The British Army and Modern Conceptions of War," *RUSI,* Vol 60, No. 403 (1911), 1182.

83 Dunlop, 225-226; and "Firing Exercises," *The Canadian Military Gazette,* 1 April 1902, 7.

84 A. de Tarlé, 385.

85 Gunter, "The Von Löbell Annual Reports, 1904," *RUSI,* Vol 49, No. 333 (1905), 1281.

86 Belfield, 150. The author points out that of the four divisions which were deployed, unlike the Boer War, all had exercised together and most remained under their peacetime commanders. Capt B.H. Liddel Hart also believed that the Great War found the British Infantry the "best trained and best shooting infantry in Europe." Extracted from English, 7.

87 "The Rifle," *The Canadian Military Gazette,* 7 October 1902, 9. Much of the feeling also stemmed from praise received in the theatre of operations from British Commanders. After Paardeburg, Lord Roberts told survivors, that they "had done noble work, and were as good a lot of men as were in the British Army." John Marteinson, *We Stand On Guard* (Toronto: Ovale, 1992), 63. Roberts went on to say that "Canadian now stands for bravery, dash and courage." Miller, *Painting the Map Red,* 109.

88 R.G. Haycock, *Sam Hughes: The Public Career of a Controversial Canadian, 1883-1916* (Waterloo: University of Waterloo, 1986), 99.

89 Canada, House of Commons, *Debates,* 21 April 1902, 3156. F.W. Borden stated, "Let the permanent force understand that their office is to teach, we have no standing army and do not need to have one." Stephen Harris, *Canadian Brass: The Making of a Professional Army, 1860-1939* (Toronto: University of Toronto, 1988), 32.

90 See Haycock, *Sam Hughes* (Chapter 8 - The Peacetime Minister 1911-1914).

91 Canada, House of Commons, *Debates,* 11 March 1901, 1286. Hughes reinforced this image in the House when he stated, "The experience of the South African War is that the men who could shoot straight, mighty soon taught the Boers to fear them." (1287). See also "Dominion Rifle Association Meeting," *The Canadian Military Gazette,* 3 March 1903, 10. Shooting ability took on such importance that it would later determine the payment of the "efficiency pay" (75 cent per day wage of a militiaman). Hughes explained that the efficiency pay was paid "on the test for shooting,...on the record made at the target." Canada, House of Commons, *Debates,* 19 March 1912, 5463. Borden was knighted in 1902; Hughes in 1915.

92 Canada, House of Commons, *Debates,* 11 July 1905, 9180. Improvements which stemmed from the war included the establishment of a Militia Council, increase in Militia strength to 100,000, increased pay, appointment of an Inspector General, the Cadet movement, and the purchase of new rifles and artillery. See also "The New Militia Bill," *Canadian Military Gazette,* 26 July 1904; Miller, *Painting the Map Red,* 438; and Harris, 62-82.

93 "Encouragement of Rifle Shooting," *The Canadian Military Gazette,* 22 March 1904, 8.

94 Canada, Department of Militia and Defence. *Report of the Department of Militia & Defence, 1901,* 28.

95 *Report of the Department of Militia & Defence, 1903,* 5-6; and "The Rifle Clubs," *The Canadian Military Gazette,* 7 May 1901, 9.

96 *Report of the Department of Militia & Defence, 1903,* 6. Commentary in the *Canadian Military Gazette* remarked that "We trust that the day is not far distant when every city, town, yes and village, too, in the Dominion will have at least one range within easy reach." It also attacked the British Government for its reticence in financing suitable facilities for rifle shooting in the UK. It questioned , "Why are auxiliary forces kept up, if their efficiency is not regarded as of the first moment? Certainly they cannot be deemed efficient if skill with the rifle is absent." (7 October 1902, 9). The difference in support is due in large part to the difference, as noted early, in the priority put on the citizen force by the two different governments. The Rifle Clubs in Canada were given a substantial boost and by 1902 a total of 95 Clubs, representing 5,060 members, were in operation. In addition, 719 rifles and over 1.5 million cartridges were issued. *Report of the Department of Militia & Defence, 1902,* 2 & 32.

97 *Debates,* 21 April 1901, 3156-3157.

98 Carl Berger, *The Sense of Power* (Toronto: University of Toronto Press, 1970), 254.

99 Col J. Peters, "Teach the Boys to Shoot," *The United Service Magazine,* Vol 28 (1903-1904), 599. See also Reverend C.G. Gull, "Military Training in Secondary Schools," *RUSI,* Vol 45, No. 276 (February 1901), 115-120. He argues that, "The object in view is not to make soldiers, but to give all boys a military training of such a character as to enable them to take their place in the ranks in after years with but short preparation." A similar view stated, "With a knowledge of drill and the use of arms diffused among the youth of the country, England would in a time of danger, without conscription, have an entire male population ready to take their place with the regular army on active duty." "The Value of Cadet Corps," *The Canadian Military Gazette,* 3 February 1903, 6. See also "Military Cadet Organization," *The Canadian Military Gazette,* 9 February 1904, 8.

100 *Debates,* 11 July 1905, 9196.

101 Haycock, 70. When the prevailing GOC intimated that Hughes would be incapable of serving alongside British regulars, Hughes retorted, "Why, could I not retreat or surrender quick enough to the Boers?" Harris, 87.

102 Sanford Evans, *The Canadian Contingents* (Toronto: Publishers' Syndicate Ltd, 1901), 319-320.

103 Desmond Morton, *A Military History of Canada* (Edmonton: Hurtig, 1985), 117; and Miller, 437.

104 Robert Brown and Ramsay Cook, *Canada 1896-1921. A Nation Transformed* (Toronto: McClelland and Stewart, 1974), 167; and *Debates,* 11 July 1904, 6367.

105 Canada, House of Commons, *Debates,* 22 March 1904, 289.

106 *Extracts from Proceedings. Colonial Conferences relating to Defence.* This document covers the conferences of 1887, 1897, 1902 and 1907.

107 See Desmond Morton, *A Peculiar Kind of a War: Canadian Overseas Ministry in the First World War* (Toronto: University of Toronto Press, 1982) and Haycock, *Sir Sam Hughes,* for comprehensive accounts of the Canadian efforts to ensure national control over the CEF in the First World War.

108 Travers, 44. See also Field Officer, "The Reform of the British Army," 272 and Gunter, "A Retrospect of the War," 42.

109 Capt Evelyn Wood, "The Future Role of Cavalry," *The United Service Magazine,* Vol 21 (1900), 390.

110 The Russo-Japanese War reaffirmed the universality of the lesson pertaining to the power of the defence. Once again the efficacy of entrenchments and particularly the machine gun became apparent. *RUSI,* between 1904 and 1911 carried a wealth of articles pertaining to lessons [re-] learned. Some officers had already reached these conclusions prior to the Boer War. MGen Maurice believed as a result of the Franco Prussian War in 1870 that "assaulting troops must adopt flexible formations and make better use of ground; an attack in column is a thing no longer possible." Col Henderson deducted from his study of the American Civil War that "trench warfare greatly strengthened the defensive." See Luuvas, 177 & 231; and English, 2-8.

111 Bidwell and Graham, 29.

112 LCol von Lindenau, "What has the Boer War to Teach Us, As Regards Infantry Attack," *RUSI,* Vol 47, No. 301 (1903), 52.

113 Ibid., 54. One veteran developed a simple set of rules for modern combat: "If fired on, fire at everything and anything that may conceal an enemy...an appreciable diminution of the enemy's fire will at once result. Never rest until men have got cover. Always be prepared for rifle or gun fire *from any side*...The rifle which takes the shortest time to load and consequently can give a much intenser fire, is the weapon we should be armed with." (Regimental Officer, 72). The realization that the machine gun could develop far more fire economically and the fact that the "nerveless machine-gun in the hands of men with only two weeks training was worth forty rifles" was also well established. See Paddy Griffith, *Battle Tactics of the Western Front. The British Army's Art of Attack 1916-1918* (London: Yale University Press, 1994) and Travers, *Killing Ground.*

114 Cecil Battine, "The Offensive versus the Defensive in the Tactics of To-day," *RUSI,* Vol 47, No. 304 (1903), 661-662. The statement places a preponderance of emphasis on the rifle and very little on artillery to achieve the neutralization required. An officer from Sandhurst stated in 1914, "One of the main lessons of the Boer War was the immense value of the rifle handled by experts, so that the basic infantry training was to develop a very proficient rifleman with a bolt-operated weapon...we only had two machine-guns in a battalion...and they were not even taught at Sandhurst." Simkins, 305.

115 Gunter, The Von Löbell Annual Reports, 1903, *RUSI,* Vol 48, No. 320 (1904), 1140.

116 Regimental Officer, 66.

117 Battine, 663. The author used the French description of the concept known as the advance by petits paquets. He reaffirmed that "The ground and the ground alone can determine how close to one another the men move and fight." (666). The concepts were also put into practice. One officer reported, "By a method of advancing by rushes of small groups in succession from one flank only of the firing line, I found it possible to keep the greater part of the company constantly firing; the only men who were not firing at any particular moment being those on the move..." Col J.H. Verschoyle, "Training Infantry for the Fire Combat," *The United Service Magazine,* Vol 30 (1904-1905), 580.

118 Griffith, 49. See also Simkins, 305.

119 Gunter, "The Von Löbell Reports, 1902," 1130.

120 Luvaas, 238.

121 "Military Observations on the War in South Africa," *RUSI,* Vol 46, No. 289, 1902, 358; and Gunter, "The Von Löbell Reports, 1903," 1143. See also Churchill, 839.

122 Pakenham, 361-362.

123 "The Use of Modern Artillery in Battle," *The Canadian Military Gazette,* 5 May 1903, 10; and Jean de Bloch, "The Transvaal War," *RUSI,* Vol 45, No. 286 (December 1901), 1423.

124 Bloch, "Transvaal War," *RUSI,* Vol 45, No. 285, 1344. Other commentary of the time expressed the common assessment that artillery fire against entrenchments had practically no effect. (See Balck, 394-1397; Maude, 353; and A Hollander, "My Impressions of the British Army," *The United Services Magazine,* Vol 25, 1902, 407). A result of the marginalization of the artillery and a failure to apply the theory described resulted in a reliance on the infantryman and his rifle to overcome the enemy trenches. Historian Bill Rawlings described the process in 1915: "While infantry officers planned their attacks, the artillery made its own preparations in accordance with tactical notions now at least fifteen years old." *Surviving Trench Warfare* (Toronto: University of Toronto Press, 1992), 42. See also Griffith, *Battle Tactics of the Western Front.*

125 English, 7. A Boer's perspective differed greatly. Boer veteran Deney Reitz wrote, "All day long they shelled us with light and heavy guns while we hugged the sheltering bank. Shrapnel and lyddite crashed upon us, causing a great many casualties and we suffered a terrible ordeal." *Commando: A Boer Journal of the Boer War.* (London: Faber & Faber, 1983), 86.

126 356.

127 Birch, *War in South Africa between the British and the Boers* (London, Ontario, 1899), 269.

128 Battine, 656. See also Militär-Wochenblatt, "Frontal Attack and Infantry Fire-Superiority," *RUSI,* Vol 51 (January 1907), No. 347, 80-82.

129 Reiver, "Cavalry Training—Canada, 1904," *The United Service Magazine,* Vol 29 (1904), 416. Another account used the example of Von Bredow's desperate charge in August 1870, to make the point. It stated, "Out of 750 men, Von Bredow lost 16 officers, 420 men, and 485 horses. But he was successful in the object of his ride." Wood, 395.

130 Balck, 1274.

131 Gen Sir James Marshall-Cornwall, *Foch as Military Commander* (London: B.T. Batsford Ltd, 1972), 15.

132 Battine, 655-656.

133 Ibid., 656. In a similar vein the editor of *The United Service Magazine* noted the song of the Zulu Impis prior to battle, "If we go forward we die, and if we go backward we die, so it is better to go forward and die." He stated, "The sentiment is a very sound one that deserves to be followed." ("Offensive Tactics in Modern War," Vol 25, 1902, 391).

134 Gunter, "A Retrospect of the South African War," 49. Arguments such as the "moral [courage] of the troops is of primary importance," and "Courage is the best weapon—courage, which is infectious; therefore, every attack is accompanied by music," supplanted the actual experience of the war. As a result, as noted by historians Bidwell and Graham, "The British, would enter the First World War with the best marksmen in the world but fervently believing that a vigorous assault could be pressed home against rifle and machine-gun fire." Ibid., 49; Militär-Wochenblatt, "Frontal Attack," 82; and Bidwell and Graham, 2. The link between high losses, courage and success was also "statistically" proven. A comparison of British defeats during the Boer War was made against French and German successes in 1870. Percentage of casualties for the British defeats was given at an average of 5 percent compared to an average loss of 18 percent for German successes. French and Russian (1877) statistics (for select units) went as high as 50-75 percent. The numbers put forward argued that success was the result of courage which always entailed high casualties. Failure was the result of low "moral" which, of course, entailed very few casualties. See Hoenig, 293.

135 Marshall-Cornwall, 30.

136 Ibid., 30.

137 See Battine, 659 and Maj Balck, "The Lessons of the Boer War and the Battle-Working of the Three Arms," *RUSI,* Vol 48, No. 321 (November 1904), 1281. The concepts of frontal attack and decisive action are key to the argument of the casualty-time relationship.

138 Gunter, The Von Löbell Reports, 1903, 1140.

139 Bidford and Graham, 30-31. A criticism of the new generation of doctrine manuals highlights the revisionism and failure to study the lessons of the war in relation to other contemporary conflicts. One criticism observed that the new Cavalry Manual "enlarges on the defensive power of the rifle in true peace-time fashion." Reiver, 418.

140 Ibid., 30. This was rationalized on the basis of the casualty time-exposed-to-enemy-fire relationship. It was also often stressed that "fire is only a means to an end, and the end is the bayonet assault...The final advance in mass with the bayonet is the decisive act of battle." Mayne, 283.

141 Griffith, 49.

142 Maude, 349.

143 Ibid., 349. Simkins insisted, "The soundness of the principle of fire and movement was proved during the [Boer] war, but insufficient attention was paid during the training of Kitchener's army to its adaption to the special conditions of trench warfare and the domination of the open ground by machine guns and artillery." *Kitchener's Army,* 305.

144 Travers, 95-96. Brig Sir J.E. Edmonds wrote, "I have to write of Haig with my tongue in my cheek...One can't tell the truth. He was really above the average—or rather below the average—in stupidity. He could not grasp things at conferences, particularly anything technical." Luuvas, 393.

145 Travers, 86-88.

146 Bidford and Graham, 70. Winter's uncomplimentary assessment of Haig stated, "One response to a list of Haig's deficiencies as a director of battle is to link him with Marshal de Saxe's mules, which campaigned often and learnt little." *Haig's Command,* 157.

PART II

Canada and the
Two World Wars

CHAPTER 5

Canada and British War Finance

1914-1917

Keith Neilson

WHEN WAR BROKE OUT in August 1914, Sir Thomas White, the Canadian Minister of Finance, had just made an early return from his vacation in the United States.[1] This move was prompted by the impact that the international events of July 1914 had made on the world's financial markets, occurrences that led to White's being "exceedingly anxious about the Canadian situation." The finance minister was not alone. All across Europe, bankers and finance ministers, just as much as politicians, generals and admirals, were pondering what the outbreak of war would mean for the international banking and economic systems.[2] All hopes for a short war were shattered as the conflict became one that used up men, munitions and money at an unparalleled rate. With Britain acting as the banker for the Entente, the financial strain on Britain and the Empire was immense. Canada's role in this was of importance, and deserves more attention than it has been given, particularly as it pertains to British spending in Canada and the United States in the period before the latter entered the war.[3]

On the outbreak of war, there was dislocation in international financial markets, with the flow of gold interrupted and liquidity reduced.[4] In these circumstances, the Canadian government decided to borrow from Britain in order to finance the expenses incurred to maintain the Canadian troops in Europe. This borrowing took the initial form of a £7 million loan, concluded in September 1914 and stretching until the end of March 1915.[5] However, that sum rapidly proved insufficient, and, on 10 October, Sir George Perley, the Canadian High Commissioner in London, wrote to the British Treasury requesting a loan of a further £5 million for the same period, a request that was granted two days later.[6] Until the summer of 1915, this money was advanced to the Canadian government in twice-monthly increments, normally £1 million at a time.

By the time the period of this loan had ended, circumstances had changed. The military events of the first eight months of the war had ended all hopes of a short war, and its cost had expanded. Particularly important was the British need to purchase war materiel abroad, particularly in Canada and the United States.[7] In London, the *Commission Internationale de Ravitaillement* (CIR) had been set up to ensure that Allied purchases were properly co-ordinated and that they did not compete against one another in neutral markets. Canada, of course, was not a neutral, but the United States was, and purchases in the latter were intimately linked to both British and Canadian war finances. All this requires some further explanation.

By February 1915, it was clear that the Allies were going to need to co-ordinate their financial efforts in order to pay for the war. In the autumn of 1914, Russia had obtained a £12 million loan in London, and by Christmas they had requested a further £100 million.[8] At the beginning of February, there was an inter-allied conference in Paris in order to permit Russia both to raise money in the London and Paris markets and to obtain a further British loan. In Washington, the British government had appointed J.P. Morgan, the American banking firm, as its purchasing agent, in order to help the CIR carry out its task effectively. However, despite these efforts, the Allies continued to purchase (and thus spend) outside the structures set up to coordinate them.

In Canada, the British choice of the United States for munitions was annoying. The Dominion was in an economic slump in 1914, and Canadians did not see why their patriotism should not be recognized by the granting of contracts.[9] Sir George Foster, the Minister of Trade and Commerce, wrote to Prime Minister Sir Robert Borden on 22 September that the latter "should cable Mr. Harcourt [Lewis Harcourt, the British Secretary of State for Colonies] calling attention to rumours regarding the purchase of supplies in the United States and asking that Canada be given preference [over the United States] for any orders which cannot be filled in the United Kingdom."[10] Foster also wanted Harcourt to inform Britain's allies that Canada was open for business, one result of which was a disastrous shells contract placed by the Russian government early in 1915 with the Canadian adventurer and entrepreneur J.W. Allison.[11] The matter of imperial preference remained a sore point between the two governments, with many Canadian firms believing they had been overlooked by the British government and complaining that they found it difficult to make contact with the proper authorities in order to tout their wares.[12]

During the summer of 1915, difficulties arose in Allied finances. As a result of the enormous increase in Allied purchasing in the United States through the CIR (and unsanctioned orders outside it), in July and August there was an exchange-rate crisis on the New York and London money markets.[13] This had its impact on Canada. First, it was decided to delay the (now) monthly British loan increments of £1 million for three months, until the exchange rates were more settled.[14] Second, in October, the form of the loan changed. This was because of the difficulties with the gold standard encountered in the summer of 1915. At an inter-Allied conference held at Boulogne on 20 August, the British and French had agreed that each would hold £200 million in gold to ship if necessary to the United States in order to maintain the exchange rate.[15] This concern about gold meant that, when the British payments to Canada were resumed in November, the British Treasury suggested that the Canadian funds should no longer be backed by British gold especially earmarked for Ottawa.[16] Instead, two-thirds of the loan was backed by British three-month Treasury Bills, while the remaining one-third was "deposited with the British Treasury as a loan *at call*." This marked an important juncture. The Canadian government had gone from borrowing from the British government to, in effect, lending the money it had nominally borrowed back to the British in order that the latter could maintain Allied credit.

This reflected the changed economic circumstances of the Canadian government. The exceptional wheat crop of 1915 and the stimulus to the economy caused by war orders had increased the amount of money available in Canada.[17] As a result, White was able to float a $50 million domestic loan in November, an amount ten times larger than had ever been done before.[18] The loan was, in fact, over-subscribed, and the Canadian government was actually able to raise $100 million, with the extra $50 million being given as a credit to the British government for its purchases in the Dominion (for further on this, see below). Canada's well known contribution on the battlefield was now beginning to be matched by her contribution in the counting houses. Not for nothing did the British Chancellor of the Exchequer, Reginald McKenna, remark at the time: "Canada the borrower has become Canada the lender."[19]

That help, however, was not sufficient to shore up British (hence Allied) credit indefinitely. In 1916, the demands of the war continued to escalate, and the British had no recourse but to continue to place large orders in the United States and to raise money there to pay for them. Already, in the autumn of 1915, a special Allied mission had travelled to the United States in order to promote a loan for £100 million, an effort which had found the going difficult, leaving part of the loan unsubscribed.[20]

It was in these circumstances that the nature of Canada's economic and financial contribution to the Allied war effort underwent a significant change. Until the autumn of 1915, contracts for war materiel produced in Canada were largely in the hands of the Minister of Militia and Defence, Sir Sam Hughes.[21] Hughes' Shell Committee was controversial; allegations of corruption and political patronage were rampant. These were purely Canadian political matters, but they affected the production of munitions for the Allied war effort. Thus, they drew the attention of the British government. One result was that D.A. Thomas, a long-time political acquaintance of the British Minister of Munitions, David Lloyd George, visited Canada in the autumn of 1915 as part of his mission to improve munitions supply in North America. Thomas was blunt in his appraisal of the Shell Committee. It was, he told Borden, "not competent to handle this [munitions] business effectively."[22] The result was the formation of the Imperial Munitions Board (IMB), a Canadian branch of the British Ministry of Munitions.[23] The Chairman of the IMB was a wealthy Canadian businessman, Joseph Wesley Flavelle, and its liaison man in London—known as the Representative of the IMB—was R.H. Brand, a partner in the British merchant bank Lazard Brothers who had followed the example of many British businessmen and volunteered his services for the war effort.

While the IMB was a British institution, it was spending both Canadian dollars and pounds sterling, much of it in the United States. Thus, it was affected by the problems with foreign exchange outlined above. As a result, in the autumn of 1915 there was a shortage of available funds for the IMB's purchases. To help with this problem, White put the surplus $50 million from the November 1915 loan at the disposal of the IMB, the money to be disbursed in the period January to March 1916.[24] But this was merely an interim credit, and certainly not enough to serve as more than a stop-gap. Flavelle immediately sought other funding, as the British government made it clear in February 1916 that (because of problems with the exchange rate) orders in Canada would have to be curtailed unless they could be paid for locally. By the middle of March, Flavelle had been successful in persuading a consortium of Canadian banks to support the IMB. "I know you will have pleasure," he wrote to Brand, "in hearing that the banks have come to your way of thinking and have placed at the disposal of the Imperial authorities a credit for $75,000,000. The credit is to be available as required between now and midsummer."[25] This new money, plus the remnant of the sum that White had advanced, meant that, in Flavelle's opinion, the IMB would be able to meet its financial commitments well into the summer. And, he concluded optimistically, "I am under the impression that if in the Fall months, consideration has to be given to a further supply of moneys for the first six months of 1917, that the banks or the Government, or both, will be in a position to make further advances to assist in the payment of such munitions."

This was fortunate, for the British financial position in the United States continued to deteriorate in 1916. On 17 May 1916, McKenna informed the Cabinet of the seriousness of the situation.[26] British commitments until the end of September in the United States amounted to some $434 million and as much as $1.2 billion when, and if, all the Allied purchases, paid for by London, were delivered.[27] Thus the position of Canada and the IMB was crucial. Brand had made this point clear earlier, at the beginning of May, to Frederick ("Peter") Perry, another member of Lazards who acted as Brand's representative on the IMB's board.[28] Brand asked Perry to provide a clear estimate of what Canadian shell-producing capacity was, noting that many in London felt that "Canada is likely to be far behindhand," no doubt as a legacy of the problems experienced by the Shell Commission in 1915. Brand went on to outline the financial repercussions of shell contracts:

> At the present moment, the proposed extended big shell programme in the U.S. is hung up for Treasury reasons: in fact, the Treasury are kicking generally at the moment, both as regards our orders and Russian orders. I am bound to say that I think the people here have very little understanding of the gravity of the financial position. The American Exchange is, of course, on an entirely artificial basis, and sooner or later, the effects of our immense purchases will be seen.

While McKenna's memorandum for the Cabinet made the financial situation clear, clarity was by no means a solution.

In part, this was tied up with politics in Britain. Lloyd George had become Minister of Munitions in May 1915, and he had tied his political future to making a success of the new ministry, which had come into existence in many ways as a result of the Welshman's criticisms of the British munitions effort.[29] Further, one of the key elements in Lloyd George's attack on the War Office's handling of the matter had been that Russia, the fabled "steamroller" of pre-war military estimates, had not been provided with the supplies necessary to conduct the war effectively. As a result, Lloyd George, who had quarrelled often with Treasury officials when he was Chancellor, was not inclined to accept that any restrictions could be placed on orders in the United States, either for Britain or for Russia. The difficulty was paying for things in North America, both in Canada and the United States. This was why finding Canadian funding for the

IMB was so crucial. "If Canada can find means to lend us money, of course the problem, so far as she is concerned, is solved for the time being," Brand wrote on 15 May, "but if not, then it is as bad for us to order in Canada as in the United States, except that of course if a real crisis came, Canada and Great Britain might 'make a plan' easier than Great Britain and the U.S."[30]

Three days later, Brand wrote again to enquire about "the financial situation in Canada." He followed this up with another letter pointing out that, due to financial considerations and a belief that existing contracts would provide sufficient munitions, "no additional orders involving expenditure on new plant should be placed, either in the U.S. or Canada," although existing orders would be continued until the end of October.[31] This was somewhat galling to the IMB for two reasons: first, it transpired that some American firms were given longer extensions and, second, the IMB was optimistic that it would continue to receive sufficient funding from Canadian banks to carry out its activities—thus contracts should not be terminated precipitously.[32] Perry, in particular, was unhappy about what he saw as the Ministry of Munitions' lack of appreciation of Canada: "Cannot you make [the Ministry] see," he lamented to Brand on 5 June, "that Canada is in this war for all that she is worth, in money as well as men, and that it is just as silly to go on getting from the United States what they can get from Canada, as it would be to go on getting from the United States what they could get from Great Britain itself."

Despite this plea, the restrictions on further expenditure continued. Brand made it clear that this was not due to a lack of "a proper appreciation of the financial assistance given by Canada" either at the Treasury or the Ministry of Munitions.[33] The real problem was that, because of the exchange problems, "their policy is naturally, as far as possible, to avoid altogether further commitments in the U.S. and as far as possible Canadian commitments in Canada, until the present commitments are met."

This became a tangle. The British did not want to increase their commitments abroad unless someone else would pay the bill. Canadian banks were willing to give a free credit to the IMB largely to the degree that the British government would place orders in Canada to a similar value. Behind all this was the difference in the productive power of Canada and the United States. At the end of June, Brand informed Flavelle that E.W. Moir, the Ministry's representative in the United States, had told Lloyd George of "the danger of throwing off American manufacturers until he is absolutely certain of a sufficient and satisfactory supply [of munitions] from this country and Canada."[34] Moir had warned that the American firms might be lost if their contracts were terminated and "it is an extremely heavy responsibility for a Minister of Munitions here to take to turn off these big American firms when they have only just got thoroughly going" (and, one might add, dangerous to Lloyd George's career!). The only hope for Canadian firms was that the military estimates of what munitions were required should prove insufficient before the existing contracts expired at the end of October, 1916.

In Britain, the situation was a political football. At the end of May, McKenna argued in the War Committee that the British financial position was so desperate that "the time will come when I shall have to say to this committee that in three or four months' time we must make peace."[35] This was not accepted by Lloyd George. A month later, he ridiculed the idea that Washington might cut off supplies to the Allies, contending that the "lucrative" nature of the Allied contracts would result in American firms "making their own arrangements for financing these contracts on the joint credit of the three Allied countries."[36] Despite the Minister of Munitions' contentions, the Treasury did not agree, and the issue remained critical as an inter-Allied conference on finance opened in July.

Another of Perry's ideas, that Canadian bankers might be more readily induced to provide funds for munitions if a relatively small shipment of gold were sent to Canada, also fell afoul of the American situation. Sir John Bradbury, the Joint Permanent Secretary of the Treasury, told Brand that "while I see the advantages of Perry's suggestion and would urge its adoption," he could not do so as "the Yankee calls on our store of the yellow metal ... [are] so insistent."[37] Nor could exchange be used to finance matters, as it, too, was needed in the United States. Instead, he contended that "we must rely on the patriotism of the Canadian bankers to take risks in creating credit which would be quite unjustifiable in ordinary times." His conclusion was firm: it was "absolutely essential that the Canadian payments should be financed within the Dominion."

In these circumstances, White leaned on the banks. At the end of June, they agreed to advance a further $24 million, only about one-half of what Brand had hoped could be raised, but, as he noted, "a large sum and better than nothing."[38] But, the situation was desperate. Brand was only too aware of the state of British finances, and he pointed out to Perry that, in the existing state of affairs, "it may look absolutely impossible to meet both American and Canadian obligations."[39] He went on to warn Perry that the Canadian financiers had to realize the gravity of the situation. "Canada is in [the war], like we are, up to her last man and her last dollar; then obviously it is right that her banking community should fully realize what this may mean. It is no good," he noted ominously, "waiting until the damage is done and our credit is destroyed by a collapse in the Exchanges." Brand was convinced, however, that at some point the British would have to obtain further credit in the United States, and was optimistic that they could obtain "a considerable amount."[40] Even so, he made the point that the maintenance of British credit must come first, and that, should the exchange rate collapse, "Canada will be faced with the question as to whether she is to throw in her lot with us or the States." At the same time as he was making this clear, Brand was attempting to ensure that the Ministry of Munitions appreciated the magnitude of the IMB's efforts and the ways in which it had "cleaned up the inefficient work of the Shell Committee."[41]

At this point two things occurred. First, the war intervened. The earlier optimism that existing orders would provide sufficient munitions until the end of 1916 proved to be optimistic, as the Battle of the Somme, which began on 1 July, ate up shells at an unprecedented rate, collapsing British logistics.[42] Thus, the Ministry of Munitions won its on-going battle with the Treasury and was able to insist on orders being placed in the United States. Second, however, despite the orders being placed, the Treasury was still unwilling to pay for orders in Canada. A crisis ensued.

At the end of July, the IMB found itself without funds, but with commitments stretching to the end of the year. In London, Brand moved rapidly to attempt to deal with this problem. On 1 August he wrote to Bradbury at the Treasury to make clear the "delicate" situation.[43] The IMB was spending about $1 million per day, and this amount was "an enormous one for the Canadian Government suddenly to find, and, as I say, I don't think they can possibly do it, even with the best of goodwill." And, given that the IMB was a British institution "and in no way consults the Canadian Government" about the orders that it placed, "if the latter are to undertake the responsibility of payment, we cannot in my opinion possibly continue to place orders without their concurrence." He argued that the Treasury had erred in not informing the Canadian government earlier of its intentions, "but we did not do that and we have now placed the orders. It is a delicate matter, therefore, to shift the obligation on to the Canadian Government now, at any rate without full discussion and explanation."

In a revealing letter to Flavelle, Brand noted that the British government was so deeply enmeshed in negotiations with the Russian government, which was insisting that its financial needs be met, that the Treasury had "probably for the moment forgot the essentials of the Canadian position."[44] On the other hand, Brand was equally scathing in his comments about the willingness of Canadian bankers to take risks. "If we were all financial purists like the Bank of Montreal, we should have all stopped fighting months ago .... They forget that to lose the War is still worse than to inflate their currency."[45]

The result of all this was that the Treasury was forced to reconsider its position. Faced with Canada's inability to pay, the British government undertook to finance the IMB.[46] Over the three-month period from the beginning of August to the end of October, the Treasury provided some $80.5 million to ensure that the IMB remained solvent. During that time, White moved to raise a second government loan, this time for $100 million, of which half was to go toward providing funds for the IMB. But in the autumn of 1916, the Allied financial position in the United States continued to worsen. In early October, a joint Anglo-French financial committee met to discuss this issue.[47] The resulting report led McKenna to put forward a paper that painted a bleak picture for the War Committee.[48]

> There are two sets of circumstances, and in my opinion two only, which may
> deprive us of the liberty to fix for ourselves the time and terms of peace. One is the
> inability of a principal ally to continue. The other is the power of the United States
> to dictate to us .... If things go on as present, I venture to say with certainty that by
> next June or earlier, the President of the American Republic will be in a position, if
> he wishes, to dictate his own terms to us.

About five-sixths of all the money that Britain would spend in the United States in 1917, McKenna pointed out, would have to be found in that country. The result, as one member of the Treasury pointed out, was that Britain would have "not only to avoid any form of reprisal or active irritation [toward the United States] but also to conciliate and to please."[49] The situation was made even worse in late November. At that time, the American Federal Reserve Board, with the strong backing of President Woodrow Wilson, warned American banks not to invest in British Treasury bills, threatening the entire edifice of Allied credit.[50] The British moved quickly to head off disaster: no new British orders in either the United States or Canada were to be placed. In these circumstances, the Canadian point of view was not likely to be decisive.

In mid-December, relations between Flavelle and White deteriorated. This resulted from the fact that, just before the embargo on new orders, the Ministry of Munitions had told the IMB to issue shell contracts for the first six months of 1917 at a cost of $158 million, "subject to Treasury sanction."[51] Including orders carried forward into this period and possible further new purchasing, the total cost to the IMB for the period January to end June 1917 was $264 million. Given the overall financial situation in North America, it was obvious that direct Canadian funding was necessary. This exacerbated relations between the IMB and White. In mid-December, on the eve of a meeting with Canadian bankers and worried about the way in which the Canadian government had seemingly been forced to support the IMB without consultation, the Finance Minister informed the new British Chancellor, Andrew Bonar Law, that "no definite obligation rests upon the Dominion to supply any or all of the Imperial expenditures in Canada."[52] White went on to tell the head of the IMB that the "assistance which the Dominion Government and the Banks may be able to give will come by way of relief from time to time and not as a matter of express or implied obligation." This was too much for Flavelle. In a stiff letter, he informed

White that it "would be a matter of very great regret, as well as concern, to me, if this body of timid, fearful financial men [the Canadian bankers] are encouraged in their halting position."[53] In a slap at White and at the government generally, he pointed out that Canada's financial position was strong and that "courage and purpose" would make it stronger. "This country does not realise it is at war; no one has given them a convincing message to that effect, and no sustained effort has been made to educate our people to a knowledge of it."

Behind the scenes, he did more than exhort White. Before the Finance Minister's meeting with the bankers, Flavelle lobbied several of them, and "place[d] before them as clearly as I could what I considered to be the responsibility of all concerned in Canada to assist the Treasury over this period of stress."[54] The result was that the banks promised the Canadian government $25 million per month for the first three months of 1917, with the likelihood that similar amounts would be provided for April, May and June. This success led White to write a self-congratulatory and self-justificatory letter to Flavelle, detailing Canada's contribution (and, indirectly, his own) to the British financial war effort:

> This country's finance since the outbreak of the war has challenged the admiration
> of the world. Not only have we financed our own great effort but we have greatly
> assisted the finances of Great Britain as well. We have furnished two hundred mil-
> lion dollars in one year for Imperial expenditure in Canada. If any other Dominion
> or country has done better I am not aware of it. Before the war we were a borrow-
> ing community with a heavy adverse balance of trade and external interest indebt-
> edness. We have by our financial policy organized, equipped, sent forward and
> maintained forces in number away beyond the dreams of the most sanguine patriot
> when the war broke out. In Britain I know our military and financial effort is
> regarded with unmixed admiration.[55]

Flavelle was less impressed with White's effort than was the Finance Minister. As the Chairman of the IMB told Brand: "You will observe what White said in his letter: That the Bankers did it [gave the loan] without having him suggest it. Fortunately he did not block it."[56] In fact, while Flavelle recognized that White was an "able man ... I am beginning to fear," he told Brand, "that at the core he is fundamentally without courage and firm purpose."[57]

Early in January 1917, the bankers' promise of $75 million for the first three months of the year proved overly optimistic.[58] Instead, they could provide only $50 million in that period. This meant that there was a shortfall of some $8.33 million each month, and White was willing to promise that the Canadian government would make up the difference only for January. As to the hoped-for further $75 million in the second quarter of the year, White was doubtful that this would be forthcoming. Flavelle was more optimistic. However, he was aware of the need to massage White's *amour propre*, the Finance Minister's temperament and Canadian sensibilities. His explanation to Brand of financial affairs made this evident:

> It is impossible for White not to blow hot and cold according to immediate local sur-
> roundings. I am still hopeful that by one way or another it will be possible for
> Canada to assist with a sum approximating $150,000,000 for the first six months,
> but I think this should not be passed on to the Treasury, but rather let them count
> on the support which White will himself promise. He is more likely to do the large
> thing if he announces it himself and will probably be prejudiced if he thought I were
> attempting, through the Ministry, to tell the Treasury what the Canadian
> Government will do.

This was a delicate matter, and its importance was not lost on Brand.

However, the financial position for the Allies continued to worsen in the new year. In January, the British government used compulsion to acquire all foreign securities held in London, and Brand was convinced that the Treasury now took the "attitude that Canadian expenditure is as bad as American expenditure," to the detriment of new orders being placed in the Dominion.[59] While he was alive to White's concerns about the financial health of Canada, Brand felt that the country was not fully committed to the war in a financial sense. "One recognises ... how great Canada's burdens are and that for her to make the war one of unlimited liability like European belligerents do instead of one of limited liability, as I think it is not unfair to say she does at present on the financial side, might involve very serious financial embarrassments; those embarrassments every other belligerent has to face." In order to strengthen Flavelle's hand in discussions about finance and to overcome the wounded pride of the Canadian politicians scheduled to come to Britain for an Imperial War Conference, Brand arranged for the Treasury to compile figures comparing the relative financial efforts of Britain and Canada in the war.[60]

By the middle of February, hopes that the Dominion government could provide continued funding to the IMB grew. This resulted from the buoyant state of the Canadian economy. As Flavelle told Brand, "revenues are abundant; our trade continues to expand; the amount of money in circulation is without parallel in this country; the sale of merchandise is at maximum figures; the bank deposits are the greatest ever."[61] Even White was praised: "National financing has been well done." This was fortunate, for the situation in the United States continued to be dire. To help remedy this, the Treasury sent a mission to the US under the leadership of S. Hardman Lever, an Englishman expert in American finance (because of pre-war business experience there) and who had served successively in the Ministry of Munitions and the Treasury during the conflict.[62] Lever's goal was to shore up the shaky Allied credit and to obtain a large loan in New York to do so.

As part of this effort, he made a hurried trip to Canada in late February, after having been made aware of the health of the Canadian economy and the generally high opinion held of Flavelle in conversations in New York.[63] In Ottawa, he "had a very satisfactory interview with Sir Thomas White," after having been briefed by Flavelle on White's plans to issue a loan.[64] White "expressed complete readiness to assist" the Treasury's representative in his task, and Lever was pleased to note that "there is no doubt that he [White] will do his utmost to meet Mr. Flavelle's needs."[65] With respect to finance generally, White outlined his loan plans. These indicated the tensions in Anglo-American relations surrounding finance. White noted "that he was very much afraid of the Americans getting any strong control of American finance as he felt they might be ruthless in exploiting any power which they might obtain." He also "complained bitterly" that J.P. Morgan had prevented him from raising money in the United States in 1916 and insisted that Morgan be kept clear of the pending Canadian issue. But, Lever left Ottawa with only a favourable impression: "There is no doubt that we will receive all possible assistance from Sir Thomas White, who was most cordial."

At the same time, Lever was working to convert sterling issues held in Canada into dollars in order to ease the exchange difficulties. As part of this, he travelled to Toronto on 16 March in order to consult with financiers and officials there.[66] The following day, he had lunch with Flavelle, White and the leading lights of the Toronto financial world. White's speech to the gathering was positive, suggesting that his loan was progressing smoothly. The finance minister also indicated that "money would continue to be forthcoming in Canada for munitions expenditure."[67]

This impression was confirmed when White's highly successful loan for $150 million was concluded. This loan, of which the Canadian banks took some $60 million, allowed White to put $25 million at the disposal of the IMB in each of April and May, with the possibility of a further $25 million in June. But, neither Brand nor Flavelle had been confident that White would be so forthcoming, particularly as Canadian politicians were "still rankling" due to a belief that Canada had not been given a preference in munitions production over the United States.[68] To combat this, at the beginning of March, Brand had compiled a memorandum for the Minister of Munitions (of which he sent Flavelle a copy for use as he saw fit) "lay[ing] stress on the fact which is in general quite true that Canada is now getting a very distinct preference, and quite rightly, as against the U.S.A. and has on the whole nothing to complain of." However, at the same time, Brand also indicated that the Canadian finances were strong enough that "Canada ought to be able at least to advance to the British Government the sums necessary to meet the orders placed for munitions in Canada," something that "would have been thought impossible three or four years ago."

Flavelle agreed.[69] He, too, felt that Canada had "been treated with great fairness," and pointed out that "Canada did not show much faith in her own capacity" early in the war, when "neither Government nor manufacturers appreciated the opportunities which were before them." And, despite the fact that "the 'Powers that be' are still very sensitive at a suggestion that as a matter of right they should contribute" funds for munitioning, the IMB's chairman contended that "on the whole it is somewhat remarkable that Canada has done as much as she has having regard to the fact that we started many degrees below zero in the consideration of our capacity to render financial assistance." This feeling was multiplied by the end of March, when it became apparent that "White has scored a success [with the loan] of which he may well be proud."[70] With the promise of funds for the IMB in April and May, Flavelle was now generous in praise of the finance minister.

The entrance of the United States into the war at the beginning of April changed the British financial position. While in other ways, the problems with exchange and purchasing got worse over the summer of 1917, in some ways the issues concerning Canada evolved.[71] The primary difficulty became one of persuading the Americans that British credits could be used to finance war materiel produced in Canada. But, even when this was agreed to, the amount of Canada's funding was still in British hands, and the Treasury did not want to use its credit (just as it had not wanted to use its exchange earlier) for Canadian munitions. Flavelle caught the problem nicely in September 1917:

> One of the difficulties in the way [of sound Canadian financing of munitions] is that Canada is not a principal country. McAdoo [William Gibbs McAdoo, the American Secretary of the Treasury] has already advised White that the sum set aside for the Allies cannot legitimately be used for Canada except through Great Britain.
> Moreover, the position of the British Treasury has been so delicate that I presume they would not want White to jeopardize the amount which they would receive.[72]

Canada was now more and more dependent on the United States for the financing necessary to maintain its munitions industry, but not yet independent of Britain. The older phase of Anglo-Canadian financial relations had ended, but the shape of the future financial relations in the North Atlantic triangle was not yet clear.

Much of what occurred with regard to Anglo-Canadian war finance in the period from 1914 to 1917 parallelled what occurred with regard to Anglo-Canadian relations generally. In 1914, Canada was unprepared for war in every way—economically, financially and militarily. The growth of Canada's army is well known, as are Canadian struggles to obtain some sort of control over a national army subsumed within the British Expeditionary Force.[73] The case with finance and munitions was similar. Canada's contributions were considerable: by June 1918, $1.143 billion of munitions orders had been placed in Canada, of which the Canadian government had paid for $460 million.[74] However, the IMB was a British, not a Canadian institution, and there was bound to be friction between it and the Canadian government. The latter, not unreasonably, felt that if it were to be responsible for paying for munitions contracts, then it should be consulted as to the amounts involved. This combined with a belief that Canada was not being given a preference over the United States for munitions to produce latent hostility. For its part, the IMB was driven by the needs of its parent body, the Ministry of Munitions, and that department was in a constant struggle with the Treasury over the issue of funding the purchase of war materiel overseas. Given the relative productive capacities of Canada and the United States (and a certain belief that Canada, as a member of the British Empire and a co-belligerent, should be willing to risk more than neutral Washington), the Treasury tended to make keeping the Americans satisfied the cornerstone of its policy. As so often would be the case in the future, Canada was caught between two larger powers, convinced that neither was paying it the attention that was its due. Despite this, however, the goodwill and abilities of men like Flavelle, Brand, and White ensured that Canada was able to make a substantial contribution to Allied financing in the period from 1914 to 1917.

Notes for Chapter 5

1   This paragraph, except where otherwise noted, is based on Sir Thomas White, *The Story of Canada's War Finance* (Montreal, 1921), 5-10. The quotation is from page 5. White's memoir forms the background for this entire chapter.

2   For some specific cases, see John Lawrence, Martin Dean, and Jean-Louis Robert, "The outbreak of war and the urban economy: Paris, Berlin, and London in 1914," *Economic History Review*, Vol 45, No. 3 (1992), 564-593; and John Peters, "The British Government and the City-Industry Divide," *Twentieth Century British History*, Vol 4, No. 2 (1993), 126-48. The role of the British Treasury is in G.C. Peden, *The Treasury and British Public Policy 1906-1959* (Oxford, 2000), 73-127. There is an excellent overview of all the financial aspects of the war, which introduces the most recent literature, in Hew Strachan, *The First World War. Volume I: To Arms* (Oxford, 2001), 815-992.

3   The best accounts remain White, *Canadian War Finance* and three articles: F.A. Knox, "Canadian War Finance and the Balance of Payments, 1914-18," *Canadian Journal of Economics and Political Science*, Vol 6, No. 2 (1940), 226-57; J.J. Deutsch, "War Finance and the Canadian Economy, 1914-20," *Canadian Journal of Economics and Political Science*, Vol 6, No. 4 (1940), 525-42; and C.A. Curtis, "The Canadian Banks and War Finance," *Contributions to Canadian Economics*, Vol 3 (1931), 7-40.

There are glimpses of the interconnections between Canada and the United States with regard to finance in the following: Kathleen Burk, *Britain, America and the Sinew of War 1914-1918* (London, 1985); R.D. Cuff and J.L. Granatstein, *Canadian-American Relations in Wartime* (Toronto, 1975); and M. Bliss, *A Canadian Millionaire: The Life and Business Times of Sir Joseph Flavelle, Bart., 1858-1939* (Toronto, 1978). The best overview of the tangled relationship between the two countries is Greg C. Kennedy, "Strategy and Supply in the North Atlantic Triangle, 1914-1918," in B.J.C. McKercher and Lawrence Aronsen, eds., *The North Atlantic Triangle in a Changing World. Anglo-American-Canadian Relations, 1902-1956* (Toronto, 1996), 48-80.

4   See Strachan, *First World War*, 818-27 for an explanation of the gold standard and its impact on liquidity.

5   Outlined in Malcolm Ramsay (British Treasury) to Lewis Harcourt (British Secretary of State for Colonies), letter, 5 October 1914, Colonial Office (CO), 42/985, Public Record Office (PRO), Kew, United Kingdom.

6   See Perley to Sir John Bradbury (Joint Permanent Secretary, British Treasury), letter, 10 October 1914 and reply, 12 October, both ibid.

7   What follows is based on Burk, *Sinews of War*, pp. 13-54; idem, "The Diplomacy of Finance: British Financial Missions to the United States 1914-1918," *Historical Journal*, Vol 22, No. 2 (1979), 351-53; Keith Neilson,

"Managing the War: Britain, Russia and *Ad Hoc* Government," in M. Dockrill and David French, eds., *Strategy and Intelligence. British Policy during the First World War* (London, 1996), 96-100.

8   Keith Neilson, *Strategy and Supply. The Anglo-Russian Alliance 1914-17* (London, 1984), 54-57 and 66-68.

9   On the nature of the slump, see Deutsch, "War Finance," 525-28.

10 Foster to Borden, letter, 22 September 1914, Borden Papers, Manuscript Group (MG) 27, Vol 47, National Archives of Canada (NA), Ottawa.

11 Keith Neilson, "Russian Foreign Purchasing in the Great War: A Test Case," *Slavonic and East European Review*, Vol 60, No. 4, 1982, 572-90. For other examples of Canadian lobbying to secure contracts, see Henry Lambert (Colonial Office) to Perley's secretary, letter, 8 January 1915, Borden Papers, MG 26, Vol 47, NA and Perley's reply to Harcourt, 11 January 1915, and Perley to Borden, letter, 14 January 1915, both ibid. The Canadians seemed to feel that British attempts to co-ordinate matters through the CIR simply delayed things with "red tape and dead-weight of big governmental offices"; Perley to Borden, letter 12 February 1915, ibid.

12 See "Memorandum for Mr. Wintour," Borden, 11 August 1915, in which the Prime Minister made these points to Ulick Wintour, the former Director of the CIR and now Director of Army Contracts at the British War Office, Borden Papers, MG 26, Vol 47, NA.

13 Burk, *Sinews of War*, 62-67.

14 See Griffith (for Perley) to the Treasury, letter, 30 July 1915; Malcolm Ramsay (Assistant Secretary, Treasury) to Perley, 31 July 1915, both CO 42/991, PRO.

15 Neilson, *Strategy and Supply*, 105-07; Strachan, *First World War*, 969-72; Martin Horn, "External Finance in Anglo-French Relations in the First World War, 1914-1917," *International History Review*, Vol 17, No. 1 (1995), 63-5.

16 See the undated, unsigned ""Memorandum" and the accompanying letter from Sir John Bradbury (Joint Permanent Secretary, Treasury) to the Colonial Office, 29 October 1915, CO 42/991, PRO. Emphasis in the original.

17 On the sharp improvement in the Prairie economy in 1915, see John Herd Thompson, *The Harvests of War. The Prairie West, 1914-1918* (Toronto, 1978), 45-72.

18 White, *Canada's War Finance*, 22-27.

19 As cited in Strachan, *First World War,* 989.

20 Burk, *Sinews of War*, 67-76.

21 The rest of this paragraph, except where otherwise noted, is based on R.G. Haycock, *Sir Sam Hughes. The Public Career of a Controversial Canadian, 1885-1916* (Waterloo, Ontario, 1986), 225-57.

22 D.A. Thomas to Borden, letter, 3 October 1915, Borden Papers, MG 26, Vol 50, NA.

23 The best study of the IMB is P.E. Rider, "The Imperial Munitions Board and Its Relationship to Government, Business and Labour, 1914-1920," PhD Thesis, University of Toronto, 1974. Also very useful is David Carnegie, *The History of Munitions Supply in Canada 1914-1918* (London, 1925), 116 ff.

24 See "History of Canadian Munitions Finance," C.H. Jenkinson (Historical Records Branch, Ministry of Munitions), first draft, 21 December 1918, R.H. Brand Papers, A831, NA, for an outline of how the IMB was funded. This document underlies what follows.

25 .Flavelle to Brand, letter 14 March 1916, R.H. Brand Papers, A829, NA.

26 "[British financial liabilities in U.S.A.]," McKenna, 17 May 1916, Cabinet Office (CAB) 37/148/6, PRO.

27 Burk, *Sinews of War*,78.

28 Brand to Perry, letter, 3 May 1916, Brand Papers, A828, NA.

29 On this, see R.J.Q. Adams, *Arms and the Wizard. Lloyd George and the Ministry of Munitions 1915-1916* (London, 1978), 1-55.

30 Brand to Perry, personal letter, 15 May 1916, Brand Papers, A828, NA.

31 Brand to Perry, letter, 18 May 1916; Brand to Perry, secret & personal letter, 23 May 1916, both Brand Papers, A828, NA.

32 Perry to Brand, letter, 5 June 1916; Flavelle to Brand, letter, 12 June 1916 and Brand to Perry, letter, 12 June 1916, all Brand Papers, A829, NA.

33 Brand to Perry, letter, 12 June, Brand Papers, A829, NA.

34 Brand to Flavelle, private letter, 29 June 1916, Brand Papers, A829, NA.

35 Conclusion of the War Committee, 26 May 1916, Cab 37/148/36, PRO.

36 "Note," Lloyd George, 29 June 1916, Cab 42/15/14, PRO; minutes of the War Committee, 30 June 1916, Cab 42/15/15, PRO.

37 Bradbury to Brand, private letter, 30 June 1916, Brand Papers, A830, NA.

38 Brand to Perry, private letter, 30 June 1916, Brand Papers, A829, NA.

39 Brand to Perry, private letter, 1 July 1916, Brand Papers, A829, NA.

40 Brand to Perry, private letter, 30 June 1916, Brand Papers, A829, NA.

41 Brand's untitled memorandum, 18 July 1916, for Edwin Montagu (who had become Minister of Munitions on 9 July), Brand Papers, A829, NA.

42 For a useful discussion of the impact of the Somme on munitioning, particularly on the great increase in the need for larger-calibre shells, see Ian Malcolm Brown, *British Logistics on the Western Front 1914-1919* (Westport, Connecticut, 1998), 109-38.

43 Brand to Bradbury, letter, 1 August 1916, Brand Papers, A829, NA.

44 Brand to Flavelle, letter, 2 August 1916, Brand Papers, A829, NA. For the financial dealings with Russia, see Keith Neilson, *Strategy and Supply. The Anglo-Russian Alliance 1914-17* (London, 1984), 198-203.

45 Brand to Flavelle, 8 August 1916, Flavelle Papers, MG 30, A16, vol 24, NA.

46 "History of Canadian Munitions Finance," C.H. Jenkinson, 21 December 1918, Brand Papers, A831, NA.

47 "Report to the Chancellor of the Exchequer of the British members of the Joint Anglo-French Financial Committee," Lord Reading, R. Chambers, B. Cockayne (Deputy Governor of the Bank of England), and J.M. Keynes (British economist, seconded to the Treasury), 18 October 1916, in E. Johnson, ed., *The Collected Writings of J.M. Keynes*, XVI, Activities 1914-1918, The Treasury and Versailles (London, 1971), 201-09.

48 "Our Financial Position in America," McKenna, 24 October 1916, Cab 24/2/G 87, PRO.

49 "The financial dependence of the United Kingdom on the United States of America," J.M. Keynes, 10 October 1916, in Johnson, ed, *Keynes*, XVI, 198.

50 Burk, *Sinews of War*, 84-88.

51 "History of Canadian Munitions Finance, 1915-17," C.H. Jenkinson, 21 December 1918, Brand Papers, A831, NA.

52 As reported in White to Flavelle, letter, 14 December 1916, Brand Papers, A830, NA.

53 Flavelle to White, letter, 15 December 1916, Brand Papers, A830, NA.

54 Flavelle to Brand, letter, 16 December 1916, Brand Papers, A830, NA.

55 White to Flavelle, letter, 15 December 1916, Brand Papers, A830, NA.

56 Flavelle to Brand, 16 December 1916, Brand Papers, A830, NA.

57 Flavelle to Brand, letter, 29 December 1916, Brand Papers, A831, NA.

58 White to Flavelle, letter, 8 January 1917, Brand Papers, A831, NA.

59 Brand to Flavelle, letter 26 January 1917, Brand Papers A829, NA.

60 See Brand to Bradbury, letter, 12 February 1917, Brand Papers, A831, NA. This became "Financial Assistance to the Dominions by His Majesty's Government," secret, Treasury, nd, Cab 24/7/GT 173, PRO.

61 Flavelle to Brand, letter, 14 February 1917, Brand Papers, A829, NA.

62 On the Lever mission, see Burk, *Sinews of War*, 90-95.

63 Lever's diary entry, 12 February 1917, Hardman Lever Papers, Treasury Office (T) T 172/429, PRO.

64 Flavelle to Brand, letter, 23 February 1917, Brand Papers, A829, NA; Lever's diary entry, 23 February 1917, Hardman Lever Papers, T 172/429, PRO.

65 Governor General of Canada (for Hardman Lever) to Colonial Office, telegram, 26 February 1917, Hardman Lever Papers, T 172/420, PRO; Lever diary entry, 25 February 1917, ibid., T 172/429, PRO. The two following quotations are also from this source.

66 My account of this trip derives from Lever's diary entries, 16-22 March 1917, Hardman Lever Papers, T 172/429, PRO.

67 This was also Flavelle's impression; see his letter to Brand, 19 March 1917, Brand Papers, A829, NA.

68 Brand to Flavelle, letter, 2 March 1917, Brand Papers, A829, NA.

69 Flavelle to Brand, letter, 19 March 1917, Brand Papers, A829, NA.

70 Flavelle to Brand, 28 March 1917, Brand Papers, A829, NA.

71 On the circumstances in 1917 and 1918, see Burk, *Sinews of War*, 195-200; idem., "J.M. Keynes and the Exchange Rate Crisis of July 1917," *Economic History Review*, Vol 32, 3 (1979), 405-16; Strachan, *First World War*, 975-92.

72 Flavelle to Brand, letter, 11 September 1917, Brand Papers, A831, NA.

73 For a good survey, see D. Morton and J.L. Granatstein, *Marching to Armageddon: Canadians and the Great War, 1914-1919* (Toronto, 1979). More specifically, G.L. Cook, "Sir Robert Borden, Lloyd George and British Military Policy, 1917-1918," *Historical Journal*, Vol 14 (1971), 371-95.

74 Kennedy, "Strategy and Supply," 54.

The Battle of the Atlantic. Depth charge explosions astern of HMCS *Saguenay*, ca 1940.
(Photographer unknown, NA, PA-116840)

CHAPTER 6

The Canadian
Way of War

1939-1945

B.J.C. McKercher

*Canada is an unmilitary community. Warlike her people have often been forced to be;
military they have never been.*

—C.P. Stacey, 1955[1]

THE CANADIAN WAY OF WAR from 1939 to 1945 grew out of the relationship between civilian leaders and military commanders as they pursued the two crucial elements of wartime policy-making: developing national strategy and employing armed force to preserve and extend the national interest. This is not to downplay the significant achievement of the Canadian home front during the Second World War. With the country enmeshed in total war, and with the exception of a part of Francophone Quebec, men and women at all levels of society and the economy laboured hard and suffered personal loss and privation to provide Canada's contribution to the Allied defeat of Nazi Germany, Fascist Italy, and Imperial Japan.[2] However, the crucial element of Canadian war-making involved the use of the nation's armed forces by the civilian leadership to achieve specific foreign policy goals. As the Prussian philosopher of war, Carl von Clausewitz, famously observed: "[War] is not merely a political act but a real political instrument, a continuation of political intercourse, a conduct of political intercourse by other means."[3] Thus, while Canadian politicians harnessed the country's armed forces to help defeat the enemy powers, they also used the war to attain diplomatic objectives – not always successfully – that were being pursued before September 1939. Here, Prime Minister William Lyon Mackenzie King, in office from 1935 to 1948, is pivotal. Throughout this period, King dominated all aspects of Canadian political life including foreign policy, as he doubled as the Secretary of State for External Affairs.[4] His view of war-making, his view of the role of the military in shaping national policy, and his conception of the goals of Canadian foreign policy were all fundamental to the way in which Canada prosecuted the war. Mackenzie King's strategic goal was greater Canadian independence in international politics, especially in what had become known as the North Atlantic Triangle.

The Second World War in Europe began on 1 September 1939 when Nazi Germany attacked Poland. Because Britain and France had formally guaranteed Polish sovereignty five months before—a response to the German conquest of Czechoslovakia that violated the September 1938 Munich Agreement—London and Paris declared war on Berlin two days later.[5] Although Mackenzie King's government, which took office in October 1935, was isolationist in its foreign policy and had supported British appeasement of Germany after 1937 as the best way of remaining aloof from European Great Power rivalry, the Liberal-dominated Canadian Parliament declared war against Germany on 10 September. The reasons for this *volte-face* were simple: the abandonment of appeasement, which became necessary when Germany occupied Czechoslovakia in mid-March 1939; and given the overwhelming domestic support for Britain in English-speaking Canada, the strongly perceived duty of the senior Dominion to support the Mother Country in a moment of extreme peril.[6]

The Canadian Armed Forces were not at all ready for commitment to a struggle on the continent of Europe in September 1939. After the First World War, successive Canadian governments, but especially those of Mackenzie King, had allowed the country's armed services to run down through severe budget cuts. With minimal ground forces, a tiny navy and virtually no air force, Canada failed to contribute to initial Allied operations on the European continent in the autumn and winter of 1939-1940. However, by July 1940, following France's defeat by Germany and a British retreat across the Channel to the home islands, Canadian units in Britain were probably the best equipped forces there. The Allies faced two separate wars: one against Germany in the skies over and the waters surrounding the British Isles; and the second in North Africa, where Fascist Italy had launched land operations in September 1940 to conquer British-controlled Egypt and the vital Suez Canal. Canadian forces were committed to fighting Germany, and even after the conflict expanded to East Asia and the Pacific, Canada's fighting services battled mainly in the European theatre. Thus, for the next two years, while they trained and their numbers of men and arms grew, the Canadian Army stood ready to defend the British Isles against invasion.[7] At the same time, the Royal Canadian Navy joined the Royal Navy in the Battle of the Atlantic, chiefly anti-submarine operations to keep open lines of supply across the Atlantic Ocean.[8] And working with the Royal Air Force, the Royal Canadian Air Force played an important role in repelling German bombing attacks on British civilian and industrial targets.[9] To a significant degree, Canadian military involvement in the first years of the war helped the British to avoid defeat at the hands of the Germans.

Prime Minister W.L. Mackenzie King inspecting 1st Canadian Division, Surrey, England, 26 August 1941. (Photographer unknown. NA, PA-138264)

The political side of the war developed from Mackenzie King's desire to ensure Canadian independence from Britain in foreign policy, which had been his chief diplomatic goal between the two world wars. Although the prime minister had made great public displays of Anglo-Canadian unity of purpose in the first year of the war, he and his chief foreign policy advisor, O.D. Skelton, the Deputy Minister of External Affairs, decided consciously to avoid any hint of subservience to the British.[10] Therefore, when the Australians proposed in early 1941 to establish an equivalent of the First World War Imperial War Cabinet to appraise Commonwealth strategic issues, Mackenzie King engineered his Cabinet's rejection of the idea. He was reluctant to be removed from his Cabinet ministers, he was concerned about domestic political issues, and he was worried that the Canadian government would have "responsibility without power."[11] Happily for Mackenzie King, Winston Churchill, the British Prime Minister after May 1940, also proved lukewarm to the idea; he did want his own policy-making prerogative diluted. But the fact remains that the Canadian government baulked at working intimately with British leaders in prosecuting the war. Instead, as issues arose, Mackenzie King and individual Canadian ministers would deal with their British opposites on a case by case basis.

Indeed, one of the great achievements of Anglo-Canadian co-operation during the war, the establishment of the British Commonwealth Air Training Plan (BCATP) in 1939,[12] showed not only the Liberal Government's parsimony in war-making but the guarded nature of Mackenzie King's intra-Allied diplomacy. The BCATP was to train Commonwealth air crews in Canada but, because Ottawa funded the plan in Canada, Mackenzie King argued that the British government should underwrite the costs of the RCAF stationed in Britain.[13] Ironically, although RCAF air crews distinguished themselves in the air war in Europe, his policy led to the RAF determining largely where, when, and how Canadian airmen would fight. Canadian independent action against Germany, therefore, was greatly constrained. And what was so for the RCAF was equally so for the Canadian Army. This time, following the precedent set in the First World War, the British commander-in-chief was to be responsible for operational matters, while the Canadian commander-in-chief held the burden of organisation and administration.[14] This derived from a simple matter of *realpolitik*: Britain was a Great Power fighting for its survival; regardless of the rhetoric of independence, Canada was assisting in this struggle.

Still, Mackenzie King and his senior ministers were interested more in preserving and enhancing Canadian independence in foreign policy, both during the war and afterward. The Canadian military, therefore, was directed toward enhancing this autonomist element of the civilian-defined Canadian national interest. In policy-making terms, it meant keeping military advice in a perpetually subordinate position. In Britain, Churchill ran the British war with his two Chiefs of the Imperial Staff, Field Marshal Sir John Dill and, after December1941, Field Marshal Sir Alan Brooke. After the United States entered the war in December 1941, President Franklin Roosevelt ran the American war with General George Marshall, the Chairman of the Joint Chiefs of Staff. In Canada, long disdainful of the military, Mackenzie King directed Canada's war effort with Skelton; and, after Skelton's death in 1941, with another External Affairs mandarin, Norman Robertson.

The restricted influence of professional Canadian military advice is best seen in the composition of what was, in effect, the Canadian war cabinet—the Emergency Council (30 August - 5 December 1939) and then the Cabinet War Committee (5 December 1939 and afterward).[15] With Skelton and then Robertson as both advisors and the Prime Minister's point men, the committee was composed of senior ministers: James Ralston (Finance); Ernest Lapointe (Justice), who was also Mackenzie King's chief lieutenant from Quebec; T.A. Crerar (Mines and Resources); Norman Rogers (National Defence); and Raoul Dandurand (Government Leader in the Senate). These men were joined during the course of the war by C.D. Howe (Minister of Munitions), Charles Power (a newly-appointed Air Minister) and Angus MacDonald (Minister of Naval Services). Because of death and cabinet shuffles, Louis St. Laurent replaced Lapointe, Ralston replaced MacDonald, and J.L. Isley moved into the circle as finance minister. Only Ralston, a Minister of National Defence in the late 1920s, had military experience dating from the First World War. Neither he nor his colleagues had strategic vision; and even if some did, they followed Mackenzie King's lead in policy-making. The Canadian Chiefs of Staff (COS) were kept on the margins of this critical decision-making apparatus. As a recent analysis points out: "Unfortunately, early in the war, the Canadian COS were often ignored when they should have been consulted. They were rarely invited to attend the War Committee before 17 June 1942, when the latter agreed that 'for a stated period' they should attend the first and third meetings of each month."[16] In the event, the COS participated in only about a quarter of the Committee's deliberations. It follows that the direction of the Canadian war effort from 1939 to 1945 lay solely in political hands, hands lacking any real understanding of the battlefield. The Liberal government's domestic strength was solidified in the General Election of March 1940.[17]

For a year following the defeat of France, Britain and the Commonwealth fought alone against Nazi Germany and Fascist Italy on the periphery of Europe. In the latter half of 1941, however, the nature of the war changed completely. In June, believing it only a matter of time before German success in the Battle of the Atlantic forced Britain to sue for peace, Hitler unleashed his armies against the Soviet Union.[18] Although the first six months of this struggle saw the Red Army retreat to the gates of Leningrad and Moscow in the north and into the Ukraine in the south, victory eluded Hitler. By December 1941, the eastern war had transformed from one of mobility and manoeuvre into one of attrition. More importantly, Britain and its allies now had a power of the first rank as an ally confronting the Germans. Just as important in December 1941, Japan—mired in a renewed war against China since July 1937—decided to launch an all-out offensive to conquer the great European empires in the Far East. Throughout 1941, seeking to preserve the balance of power in East Asia, the Americans had used embargoes and diplomacy to restrict Japan's ability to wage war.[19] Believing that the United States was the main impediment to their imperial ambitions, Japanese leaders authorised a pre-emptive air strike against the US Pacific Fleet at Pearl Harbor on 7 December. Four days later, Hitler stupidly declared war on Roosevelt's America. With Japanese attacks on British interests in East Asia and the western Pacific, the Second World War had transmuted in

Bodies of Canadian soldiers lying among damaged landing craft and Churchill tanks of the Calgary Regiment following the raid on Dieppe, France, 19 August 1942. (Photographer unknown. NA, C-014160)

six months from a European-Mediterranean struggle between Britain and its allies, on one hand, and Germany and Italy, on the other, into a global struggle in which all the major powers were involved. And while new enemies now confronted the Commonwealth, this transformation brought new allies—important allies with, in combination, money, large armed forces and the industrial capacity to wage modern war.

Mackenzie King's government had not ignored the United States before December 1941; trade and shared concerns about hemispheric defence had brought the two North American nations together in the summer of 1940. After the fall of France, Roosevelt decided that for strategic reasons the United States had to support Britain economically in resisting Germany. More narrowly, he wanted to ensure North American security through a political mechanism that would allow for Canadian-American defence collaboration.[20] In mid-August 1940, he met a receptive Mackenzie King at Ogdensburg, New York, where they established the Permanent Joint Board on Defence (PJBD).[21] Charged with preparing plans for continental defence, Canadian and American delegations immediately began difficult negotiations to give form to their two leaders' aspirations. The chief Canadian representative was a civilian, a Liberal lawyer. In this context, the Canadians argued that while Washington could determine the strategic direction of defensive planning, Ottawa had to have latitude in commanding Canadian forces. Undertaking a series of complicated tasks like the defence of Newfoundland, the PJBD laboured for the rest of the war— in fact, it still exists today. And so, when the war expanded a year later, Canada already had established a formal defensive arrangement with the United States. In this sense, there is no irony in Mackenzie King's willingness to work closely with the Americans in the PJBD while rejecting a Canadian presence on any new Imperial War Cabinet. The irony, instead, lay in the fact that even while Canada was enmeshed in a war to defend Britain and its Empire, Mackenzie King and Skelton used Ogdensburg to augment their long held determination provide Canadian foreign policy with alternatives to what they saw as an over-weening relationship with Britain. Tied to Canada's growing military strength, and despite Mackenzie King's subsequent concern about becoming too close politically to the United States, their diplomacy further cemented the Canadian-American relationship.

President Franklin D. Roosevelt, Prime Minister Mackenzie King and Prime Minister Winston Churchill at the Quebec Conference, August 1943. (Photographer unknown. NA, C-014170)

Despite the flexibility that the PJBD gave Canadian diplomacy, the guarded nature of Mackenzie King's intra-alliance diplomacy before the end of 1941 precluded a strong Canadian voice in the Allied coalition once the war expanded. In the first phase of the war, over the opposition of a range of his civilian and military advisors, the prime minister refused to allow Canadian participation in the making of strategic decisions in the war against Germany.[22] The reason was that Lapointe and other Quebec Liberals wanted to weaken political links with Britain —in the 1940 General Election, Quebec gave the Liberals more than one-third of their parliamentary seats. One result of the prime minister's approach was recalled by Canadian historian C.P. Stacey:

> I ask myself, what was wrong? And the answer I get back is, lack of effective war leadership. What lift the country got, it got mainly from outside, from the broadcast voices of Churchill and Roosevelt. Canada had no equivalent. Nothing made Mackenzie King angrier than to hear Canadians speak of 'our leaders, Churchill and Roosevelt'.[23]

This issue might not have been telling before late 1941; but afterward when Churchill, Roosevelt, and Joseph Stalin, the Soviet dictator, dominated intra-Allied decision-making on the prosecution of the war and the determination of war aims, Canada's already weak voice became weaker. Thus, while Mackenzie King's conception of greater foreign policy independence was being transformed into practical diplomacy, that independence was not as great as it might have been.

As the war was transforming in 1941 and 1942, Canadian forces continued their work of helping to defend Britain from invasion and air attack and in keeping open sea-borne lines of communication. The RCN, particularly, found itself in stiff fighting against *Reichsmarine* submarine wolf packs; and the losses of merchantmen and convoy escorts were substantial.[24] Moreover, the RCAF not only continued bravely to meet Luftwaffe bombing attacks against British targets, it also participated in nascent RAF strategic bombing missions to weaken

Germany's war production and diminish its civil morale.[25] However, in the period before the Allies could take the offensive, the Canadian Army suffered two defeats. In October 1941, the Cabinet War Committee agreed to send Canadian troops to reinforce the British garrison at Hong Kong, part of a British strategy to deter Japanese aggression. Essentially newly-recruited soldiers with limited training, they became Japanese prisoners of war following the unexpected surrender of the Commonwealth forces there on 25 December.[26]

The second failure came in August 1942. Following Germany's attack on Russia, Soviet leaders immediately demanded that the British launch a second front against the Germans to draw away *Wehrmacht* forces from the Eastern Front; these demands increased over the winter of 1941-1942, especially after American entry into the war.[27] The Soviet definition of a second front meant a large-scale Allied amphibious landing in Northern France. Churchill and Roosevelt refused a cross-Channel attack in 1942 for a variety of strategic and materiel reasons, but chiefly because Churchill had won an Anglo-American debate about embarking on a peripheral strategy to defeat the Axis in the West. Allied armies would drive Italian and German forces out of North Africa and then take the fight into Europe from the south by invading Italy as a precursor to the invasion of Germany. This war by land and sea was to be coupled with an intensified strategic bombing campaign against the Axis to weaken the resolve of their peoples and reduce their economic infrastructure.[28] However, to show Canadians at home that their sacrifices and efforts were achieving something, the senior Canadian military leadership, chiefly General Andrew McNaughton and General Harry Crerar, pressed for their forces in Britain to acquire battlefield laurels—the Army had, in essence, been sitting and training for almost three years. The War Committee relented. In mid-August 1942, to test German defences on the north coast of France and possibly pave the way for a cross-Channel attack, Anglo-Canadian forces undertook a limited amphibious operation at the French port of Dieppe. Their mission was to land, briefly hold the town, and then withdraw. The Dieppe raid proved to be an operational disaster; of 5,000 Canadian and 1,000 British troops who landed, almost 4,000 were killed, wounded, or captured.[29] Although the raid is still controversial—Did the British use Canadian forces callously? Were Canadian leaders culpable thanks to their desire to have Canadian ground forces finally engage the Germans?—Allied planners learned tactical lessons that later proved important when the western Allies launched their cross-Channel invasion in 1944.

But that lay in the future. For the western Allies, 1942 proved to be a transitional year for the war in Europe. Whereas 1939-1941 had been a defensive struggle, 1942 saw the development of an offensive strategy, the mobilisation of the American economy for total war (in each theatre of operation) and the build-up of men and resources in Britain. For Canada, the RCAF continued playing a major role in the strategic bombing of Axis targets and, in an increasingly brutal Battle of the Atlantic, the RCN contributed substantially to meeting the German submarine campaign. Apart from preparing for what became the Dieppe raid, Canadian land forces in Europe continued to train for the assault on what Hitler called *Festung Europa*—Fortress Europe. Finally, in October and November 1942, the western Allies moved to clear North Africa of Italo-German forces. The British Eight Army launched an offensive against the enemy at El Alamein in Egypt.[30] After a week of hard fighting and, with the Axis in retreat across Libya, Anglo-American troops landed in French Algeria, secured the region, and then drove westward to crush the Axis in a pincer. Although it took longer than expected to drive Italian and German forces out of North Africa—until May 1943 rather than January 1943—the western Allies were ready to take the war into southern Europe by the summer. At the same time, the Soviet Red

Army had inflicted a punishing defeat on the *Wehrmacht* at Stalingrad.[31] The war had started to turn in favour of the Allies.

In this period, and later in 1944 and 1945, when the Allies were driving unflinchingly on Germany, the Canadian voice in Allied councils was weak or non-existent. After December 1941, the major decisions were made in high level discussions between what the newspapers called the Big Two (Churchill and Roosevelt) and among the Big Three (Churchill, Roosevelt, and Stalin). At Washington (December 1941-January 1942), Casablanca (January 1943), Quebec (August 1943 and September 1944), Teheran (November 1943) and Yalta (February 1945), these three leaders considered grand strategy, military objectives, the allocation of resources, issues of command and, in the last eighteen months of the struggle, war aims.[32] At the second level, in the western half of the alliance, stood the Anglo-American Combined Chiefs of Staff, established by Churchill and Roosevelt in December 1941 and headquartered in Washington. Composed of senior British and American officers and supported by large national staffs and sub-committees, it dealt with the minutiae of strategy and supply.[33] In reality, the Combined Chiefs of Staff directed the day to day running of all western Allied campaigns in Europe and the Pacific, although the latter was almost exclusively American. While Mackenzie King sought an important Canadian presence within this organisation almost as soon as it was formed, he and the War Committee had to be satisfied with the establishment of a Canadian Joint Staff in Washington with minimal influence on the British and Americans.[34] Despite some difficulties in Ottawa over having one Canadian senior officer represent all branches of the armed forces, the impediment blocking a strong Canadian voice came from the Americans. Seeing the Dominions as appendages of Britain, and unwilling to weaken their growing authority, the Americans blunted the efforts of the Canadians and Australians to have much influence on the Combined Chiefs. This was a domestic political problem for Mackenzie King. As he told Churchill at the time: "the U.S. and Britain would settle everything between themselves, and that our services, Chiefs of Staff, etc. would not have any say in what was to be done."

The Americans might be more responsive to Canadian concerns about hemispheric defence within the PJBD but, when it came to the higher direction of the war, Canada was a junior ally. Churchill had the same view; but for reasons touching good Anglo-Canadian relations, he let Roosevelt and Marshall take the lead in rebuffing Mackenzie King. Nonetheless, this junior status was the Canadian prime minister's doing. When Canadian forces were playing a vital part in resisting the Axis onslaught in 1939-1941, he avoided assuming the greater political responsibilities that Canada's position as Britain's principal ally allowed. Then, following Soviet and American entry into the war on Britain's side, Mackenzie King's influence within the alliance diminished further. Not surprisingly, as the Allies went on the offensive in Europe, Canadian soldiers, sailors, and airmen were essentially integrated into the Anglo-American forces that took the war to Germany. Still, in the Italian campaign, which began in July of 1943 and lasted almost until the German surrender in May 1945, Canadian fighting men distinguished themselves with skill, courage, and resolution.[35] And in the ten months following the invasion on 6 June 1944, when Allied forces landed on the coast of Normandy, established a beach-head, and then fought their way eastward to Germany, the RCAF, RCN, and Canadian Army showed as they had in 1914-1918 that Canadians might normally be an unmilitary community, but they could be warlike when necessary.[36] In this campaign, Canadian forces fought effectively in Northern France and then into the Low Countries within a force commanded by the British general Sir Bernard Montgomery.[37]

Top: Churchill and British Chiefs of Staff meet the Canadian War Cabinet, 15 September 1944, in Quebec. (Photographer unknown. NA, C-26946)

Bottom: Colonel, the Honourable J.L. Ralston, the Canadian Minister of Defence, meets General Dwight Eisenhower at SHAEF Headquarters, Paris, France, 12 October 1944. (Photographer Jack H. Smith. NA, PA-138433)

As the war progressed toward victory over the Axis, Mackenzie King and his advisors looked to exploit Canada's military contribution to augment as much as possible greater independence in international politics. The task was not easy and the results were less the product of careful calculation in Ottawa and more the luck of Canada being on the winning side. The milieu in which Mackenzie King and the War Committee laboured was problematical. Never warm to Britain, Quebec nationalists and their political representatives were willing to profit materially from the war effort by securing contracts in their province for supplying Allied forces; but they were largely averse to serving overseas to fight the enemy. As the Liberal majority in Parliament depended on support from Quebec, and with memories of the domestic divisions that conscription had created during the First World War, Mackenzie King and his advisors avoided introducing conscription to meet the needs of the armed forces. In fact, in the 1940 General Election, the Liberals had promised to rely only on the willingness of Canadian men and women to volunteer for service. But the D-Day invasion and its subsequent operations forced Mackenzie King to reverse himself, but not before Ralston was fired for supporting conscription and several senior officers had indicated that they would resign if the Cabinet did not reverse itself. This decision proved important in keeping the Canadian forces at fighting strength, but it produced outrage and rioting in Quebec and the resignation of Powers, who had a Quebec seat.[38]

Facing internal discord about fighting total war, Canadian diplomats worked on intra-Allied councils that were giving form to Big Three agreements about war aims and peace terms. In this way, Canadian representatives participated in laying the ground for the new United Nations organisation, in establishing and contributing to the United Nations Relief and Rehabilitation Administration, in creating the structures for post-war international trade and finance, mainly the International Monetary Fund and World Bank, and in preparing for the Allied occupation of Germany and Japan. Along the same lines, the Canadian government had representation in less spectacular but equally important negotiations about regulating post-war civil aviation; and within Commonwealth councils, Mackenzie King and Canadian diplomats never relented in arguing that Canada was a completely independent nation.[39] However, little doubt exists that for the most part, the senior Allies, and increasingly the United States and the Soviet Union rather than Britain, determined the shape of the post-1945 world. Constrained by Mackenzie King's unwillingness to risk the annoyance of his senior partners, the already weak Canadian diplomatic voice seems rarely to have been heard in the post-war planning process. As Mackenzie King remarked of his own delegation at the Paris peace conference of 1946: "If the effect of an effort to obtain amendments was a breakdown of the settlement, they would be defeating their own object .... It was preferable to accept an imperfect solution in order to make some progress."[40]

Built on the deployment of its armed forces overseas, Canada's support of Britain after September 1939 provided Mackenzie King and his government with an opportunity to use the Second World War as "not merely a political act but a real political instrument." Even if the prime minister and the War Committee had never read Clausewitz – and they probably had not – it would not have been difficult to provide substance to the autonomist rhetoric in foreign policy that had emanated from Liberal lips for so long. It only took political will to build on the efforts and sacrifices of Canadian soldiers, sailors, and airmen to give Canada an effective voice in international politics. Unfortunately, the Canadian way of war between 1939 and 1945 meant complete civilian control of policy-making, unlike the situation in both Britain and the United States. Unwilling to seize the initiative with Britain before mid-1941, the Mackenzie King government found its options limited when the war expanded. Therefore, while in most respects Canadian foreign policy had a higher profile abroad in 1945 than it did in 1939, it could have been higher. As for a more independent diplomacy, post-war international structures such as the International Monetary Fund and the United Nations, plus the Commonwealth, meant that aloof foreign policies of pre-1939 vintage were longer tenable. The war and the contribution of the Canadian armed forces to the Allied victory had brought Canada into the swirl of Great Power politics. As a new international order dawned, Canadian civilian and military leaders had to tread carefully. Given the policy-making process that had developed between 1939 and 1945, the military contribution would be negligible. The

Canadian way of war suggested only that the new dawn would be a cold one for Canadians who had sacrificed so much to defeat the Nazis.

Notes for Chapter 6

I would like to thank Professor Ronald Haycock, Dr. Daniel Byers, and Dr. Hugh Henry for their insight and valuable advice.

1   C.P. Stacey, *Six Years of War. The Army in Canada, Britain and the Pacific* (Ottawa, 1966 [originally published in 1955]), 3.

2   Cf. T. Copp and R. Nielson, *No Price Too High: Canadians and the Second World War* (Toronto, 1996); P. Marsden, "The Cost of No Commitments: Canadian Economic Planning for War, 1939," in N. Hillmer et al., eds., *A Country of Limitations: Canada and the World in 1939* (Ottawa, 1996), 199-216; D.B. Scott, *The Home Front in the Second World War* (Ottawa, 1995). Cf. C.D. Howe, *The Industrial Front* (Ottawa, 1944).

3   Karl von Clausewitz [E.M. Collins, editor and translator], *War, Politics, and Power. Selections from On War and I Believe and Profess* (Chicago, 1962), 83.

4   R.M. Dawson, *William Lyon Mackenzie King: A Political Biography* (Toronto, 1958); J.L. Granatstein, *Canada's War: The Politics of the Mackenzie King Government, 1939-1945* (Toronto, 1975); C.P. Stacey, *Canada and the Age of Conflict. A History of Canadian External Policies, Volume 2: 1921-1948 The Mackenzie King Era* (Toronto, 1981), esp. 164-373. Then see D. Owram, *The Government Generation: Canadian intellectuals and the state, 1900-1945* (Toronto, 1986).

5   The best studies of the origins of the war are D. Cameron Watt, *How War Came. The Immediate Origins of the Second World War, 1938-1939* (New York, 1989); and G.L. Weinberg, *A World At Arms. A Global History of World War II* (Cambridge, 1994), 6-47. On appeasement, see F. McDonough, *Neville Chamberlain, Appeasement and the British Road to War* (Manchester, 1998); R.A.C. Parker, *Chamberlain and Appeasement: British Policy and the Coming of the Second World War* (New York, 1993).

6   Cf. J.L. Granatstein and R. Bothwell, "A Self-Evident National Duty: Canadian Foreign Policy, 1935-1939," *Journal of Imperial and Commonwealth History*, Vol 3 (1975), 212-33; B.J.C. McKercher, "World Power and Isolationism: The North Atlantic Triangle and the Crises of the 1930s," in B.J.C. McKercher and L. Aronsen, eds., *The North Atlantic Triangle in a Changing World: Anglo-American-Canadian Relations, 1902-1956* (Toronto, 1996), 110-46.

7   Department of National Defence, *The Canadian Army at War. The Canadians in Britain, 1939-1944* (Ottawa, 1945); C.P. Stacey, *The Canadian Army, 1939-1945: An Official Historical Summary* (Ottawa, 1948).

8   M. Milner, *North Atlantic Run: The Royal Canadian Navy and the Battle for the Convoys* (Toronto, 1985); R. Sarty, *Canada and the Battle of the Atlantic* (Montréal, 1998). Cf. M.A. Hennessy, "World War II and the Rebirth and Death of Canada's Merchant Marine," *Journal of the Canadian Historical Association*, new series, Vol 6 (1995), 209-41.

9   B. Greenhous et al., *The Crucible of War, 1939-1945* (Toronto, 1994), Chapters 5-6; L. Milberry and H.A. Halliday, *The Royal Canadian Air Force at War 1939-1945* (Toronto, 1990). Cf. Historical Section Royal Canadian Air Force, *The R.C.A.F. Overseas: The First Four Years* (Toronto, 1944).

10   See W.L. Mackenzie King, *Canada at Britain's Side* (Toronto, 1941). On Skelton, see N. Hillmer, "The Anglo-Canadian Neurosis: The Case of O.D. Skelton," in P. Lyon, ed., *Britain and Canada: Survey of a Changing Relationship* (London, 1976). On Canadian interwar foreign policy, see J. Eayrs, *In Defence of Canada. From the Great War to the Great Depression* (Toronto, 1965); J. Hilliker, *Canada's Department of External Affairs. The Early Years, 1909-1946* (Montreal, Kingston, 1990), Chapters 4-7; Stacey, *Age of Conflict, Vol. I*, esp. Chapters 2-3, 5-6.

11   J.A. English, "Not an Equilateral Triangle: Canada's Strategic Relationship with the United States and Britain, 1939-1945," in McKercher and Aronsen, *North Atlantic Triangle,* 158.

12   F.J. Hatch, *The Aerodrome of Democracy: Canada and the British Commonwealth Air Training Plan, 1939-1945* (Ottawa, 1983); J. Golley, *Aircrew Unlimited: The Commonwealth Air Training Plan during World War 2* (Sparkford, UK, 1993).

13   This and the rest of this paragraph is based on W.S. Carter, *Anglo-Canadian Wartime Relations, 1939-1945: RAF Bomber Command and No. 6 (Canadian) Group* (New York, 1991).

14   See Appendix H: Memorandum on Organization and Administration of Canadian Forces Overseas, 7 December 1939, in C.P. Stacey, *Arms, Men and Governments: The War Policies of Canada, 1939-1945* (Ottawa, 1974), 561-63.

15   Except where noted, the rest of this paragraph is based on Stacey, *Arms, Men and Governments*, 112-22.

16   English, "Triangle," 160.

17   R. Bothwell, I. Drummond, and J. English, *Canada, 1900-1945* (Toronto, Buffalo, London, 1987), 317-21.

18   Weinberg, *World at Arms*, 187-205.

19   R. Dallek, *Franklin D. Roosevelt and American Foreign Policy, 1932-1945*, new edition (New York, 1995), 299-313; J.G. Utley, *Going to War with Japan, 1937-1941* (Knoxville, Tenn, 1985). Cf. N. Ike, *Japan's Decision for War. Records of the 1941 Policy Conferences* (Stanford, 1967).

20   On Roosevelt's motives, which also involved not allowing the RN to fall into German hands, see F.E. Pollock, "Roosevelt, the Ogdensburg Agreement and the British Fleet: All Done with Mirrors," *Diplomatic History*, Vol 5 (1981), 203-19; D. Reynolds, *The Creation of the Anglo-American Alliance 1937-1941. A Study in Competitive Co-operation* (Chapel Hill, 1982), 121-31.

21   The rest of this paragraph is based on J.L. Granatstein, "Mackenzie King and Canada at Ogdensburg, August 1940," in J.J. Sokolsky and J.T. Jockel, eds., *Fifty Years of Canada–United States Defense Co-operation: The Road from Ogdensburg* (Lewiston, NY, 1922), 9-29; Stacey, *Arms, Men and Governments*, 332-38.

22 See Hilliker, *Early Years*, 249-50; A. Preston, "Canada and the Higher Direction of the Second World War 1939-1945," *Journal of the Royal United Services Institute*, Vol 110 (1965), 35-40; Stacey, *Arms, Men and Governments*, 146-51. Cf. R.G. Haycock, "The 'Myth' of Imperial Defence: Australian–Canadian Bilateral Military Co-operation, 1942," *War and Society*, Vol 2 (1984), 65-84.

23 C.P. Stacey, "Canadian Leaders of the Second World War," *Canadian Historical Review*, Vol 66 (1985), 71.

24 M. Milner, *The U-boat Hunters: The Royal Canadian Navy and the Offensive Against Germany's Submarines* (Toronto, 1994); F.B. Watts, *In All Respects Ready: the Merchant Navy and the Battle of the Atlantic, 1940-1945* (Toronto, 1986).

25 The morality of Canadian participation in the aerial bombardment of Germany has lately become an issue in which even Canadian official military historians have questioned this part of Allied strategy. See Greenhous et al., *Crucible*, 533-622. For a balanced corrective, see S. Robertson, "In the Shadow of Death by Moonlight," in D.J. Bercuson and S.F. Wise, *The Valour and the Horror Revisited* (Montreal, Kingston, 1994), 153-79.

26 B. Greenhous, *"C" force to Hong Kong: A Canadian Catastrophe, 1941-1945* (Toronto, 1997). On Hong Kong and the controversy it has engendered, cf. J.R. Ferris, "Savage Christmas: The Canadians at Hong Kong," in Bercuson and Wise, *Valour*, 109-27; C. Vincent, *No Reason Why: The Canadian Hong Kong Tragedy–An Examination* (Stittsville, Ont, 1981).

27 M. Gilbert, *Winston S. Churchill, VII: Road to Victory, 1941-1945* (London, 1986), 110-13; K. Sainsbury, "Second Front in 1942: A Strategic Controversy Revisited," *British Journal of International Studies*, Vol 4 (1978), 47-58; M.A. Stoler, *The Politics of the Second Front* (Westport, Conn, 1978), 22-26.

28 Gilbert, *Churchill, VII*, 23-44; T. Ben-Moshe, *Churchill. Strategy and History* (Boulder, Colo, 1992), 179-80.

29 J. Campbell, *Dieppe Revisited: a documentary investigation* (London, 1993); D.W. and S. Whitaker, *Dieppe: Tragedy to Triumph* (Toronto, 1992). Cf. B.L. Villa, *Unauthorized Action: Mountbatten and the Dieppe Raid*, 2nd ed. (Don Mills, Ont, 1990).

30 Admiralty, *Operation "Torch": Invasion of North Africa: November 1942 to February 1943* (London, 1948); W.B. Breuer, *Operation Torch: the Allied Gamble to Invade North Africa*, 1st ed. (New York: St. Martin's Press, 1985); S. Brooks, ed., *Montgomery and the Eighth Army: a selection from the diaries, correspondence and other papers of Field Marshal The Viscount Montgomery of Alamein, August 1942 to December 1943* (London, 1991); J.L. Lucas, *War in the Desert: the Eighth Army at El Alamein*, 1st American ed. (New York, 1982).

31 A. Beevor, *Stalingrad*, 1st American ed. (New York, 1998); J.S.A. Hayward, *Stopped at Stalingrad: The Luftwaffe and Hitler's Defeat in the East, 1942-1943* (Lawrence, Kan., 1998); J. Mabire, *Stalingrad: la bataille décisive de la Seconde Guerre mondiale, juillet 1942-février 1943* (Paris, 1993).

32 Cf. A. Armstrong, *Unconditional Surrender: The Impact of the Casablanca Policy Upon World War II* (New Brunswick, N.J,

1961); R. Buhite, *Decisions at Yalta: An Appraisal of Summit Diplomacy* (Wilmington, Del., 1986); D. Clemens, *Yalta* (New York, 1970); P. Mayle, *Eureka Summit: Agreement in Principle and the Big Three at Tehran, 1943* (Newark, Del., 1987); K. Sainsbury, *The Turning Point: Roosevelt, Stalin, Churchill, and Chiang-Kai-Shek, 1943: the Moscow, Cairo, and Teheran conferences* (Oxford, 1986).

33 A. Danchev. *Very Special Relationship: Field-Marshal Sir John Dill and the Anglo-American Alliance, 1941-44* (London, 1986); J.M.A. Gwyer, *Grand Strategy*, Vol. I, Pt.1 (London, 1964), Chapters 14-15. Cf. Mark A. Stoler. *Allies and Adversaries: The Joint Chiefs of Staff, the Grand Alliance, and U.S. Strategy during World War II* (Chapel Hill, NC, 2000).

34 The rest of this paragraph, including Mackenzie's King's diary entry, is from Stacey, *Arms, Men and Governments*, 161-65. Cf. Appendix E: "Canadian Services Representation in Washington (Report by Canadian Joint Staff, 30 Jul 1942)," Ibid., 554-56. Then see S.W. Dziuban, *Military Relations Between the United States and Canada: 1939-1945* (Washington, DC, 1959). On Mackenzie King's marginalisation even at the Quebec conferences, see J.L. Granatstein, "Happily on the Margins: Mackenzie King and Canada at the Quebec Conferences," in D.W. Woolner, ed., *The Second Quebec Conference Revisited. Waging War, Formulating Peace: Canada, Great Britain, and the United States in 1944-1945* (New York, 1998), 49-63.

35 D.G. Dancocks, *The D-Day Dodgers: The Canadians in Italy, 1943-1945* (Toronto, 1991); R. Lamb, *War in Italy, 1943-1945: A Brutal Story* (Harmondsworth, England, 1950; Bill McAndrew, *The Canadians and the Italian Campaign, 1943-1945* (Montreal, 1996). Cf. S.R.G. Brown, "The Loyal Edmonton Regiment at War 1943-1945, " MA Thesis, Wilfrid Laurier University, 1984.

36 See G. Bernage, *Les Canadiens face à la Hitlerjugend (7-11 juin 1944): un voyage au bout de l'enfer* (Bayeux, France, 1991); C. D'Este, *Decision in Normandy* (New York, 1983); J.L. Granatstein and D. Morton, *Bloody Victory: Canadians and the D-Day Campaign 1944* (Toronto, 1984). In the initial assault and immediately afterward, the Canadian Army experienced some difficulties. On the debate about whether it was the quality of Canadian senior commanders or problems with ordinary soldiers, cf. J.A. English, *The Canadian Army and the Normandy Campaign: A Study of Failure in High Command* (New York, 1991); J.L. Granatstein, *The Generals* (Don Mills, Ont., 1993).

37 The best account is the multi-volume T. Copp and R. Vogel, *Maple Leaf Route: Falaise* (Alma, Ont., 1983); *Caen* (1983); *Antwerp* (1984); *Scheldt* (1985); *Victory* (1988).

38 R.M. Dawson, *The Conscription Crisis of 1944* (Toronto, 1961); M. Lubin, "Conscription, The National Identity Enigma, and the Politics of Ethno-cultural Cleavage in Canada during World War II," 2 volumes, PhD Thesis, University of Illinois at Urbana-Champaign, 1973.

39 Hilliker, *Early Years*, 296-309; D. Munton and D. Page, "Planning in the East Block: The Post-Hostilities Problems Committees in Canada," *International Journal*, Vol 32, 1977, 687-726. Cf. E. Reid, *On Duty: A Canadian at the Making of the United Nations 1945-1946* (Toronto, 1983).

40 Quoted in Stacey, *Age of Conflict*, Vol 2, 387.

The Industrial Front

The Scale and Scope of Canadian Industrial Mobilization During the Second World War

Michael A. Hennessy

CANADA MADE FIVE MAJOR CONTRIBUTIONS to the Allied assault against the Axis powers. Our Army fielded a fighting force of five divisions and played a significant role in the campaigns of Italy and Northwest Europe. Our Navy contributed hundreds of ships to the crucial Battle of the Atlantic, at one point providing virtually all the Atlantic escorts. Our Air Force grew to a strength exceeding 25,000 personnel in forty-eight fighter squadrons—some of which took part in the Battle of Britain—and a complete Bomber Group that took the air offensive to the heart of the Reich. The British Commonwealth Air Training Plan (BCATP) proved to be the fourth major contribution. This Canadian-run array of schools and airports trained over 130,000 pilots and aircrew for Commonwealth and Allied air forces. The fifth contribution, though no less important, has received perhaps the least attention. Canada became a major provider of war matériel in the form of industrial goods, raw materials and food stuffs. Indeed from July 1940 until December 1941, some eighteen months, Canada stood as Britain's principal and most potent declared ally. This chapter offers a brief summary of the development of Canada's industrial front to illustrate its scale, scope and consequences.[1]

Top: Eighteen-year-old Evelyn Turner doing light welding on a Bren gun magazine, May 1941. (Photographer unknown. NA, C-075212)

Bottom: Veronica Foster, known as the Bren Gun Girl, from the John Inglis Co. Ltd, operating a lathe on the Bren gun production line in Toronto, Ontario, 10 May 1941. (Photographer unknown. NA, PA-51587)

The general outlines of Canada's war effort are well known. The scale of Canadian war production was unanticipated in the years running up to the war, and there was no serious effort to harness Canada's full war potential until after the fall of France in the summer of 1940. Then Canada became Britain's chief co-belligerent. Neither Britain nor the Dominion government foresaw these circumstances, and pre-war discussions to prepare Canada's industrial base as the arsenal of the British Empire had come to nought largely because neither party was serious about it.[2] The loss of France meant the policy of avoidance also collapsed. Crash building programs aimed chiefly at exporting finished products, raw materials and artillery shells to Britain became a priority. The costs and related problems of turning on Canadian industry were enormous but have received little detailed attention. There is no published overview and statistical account of the entire Canadian effort comparable to the official histories produced in Britain, Australia, New Zealand and the United States.[3] Historian Michael Bliss argues that despite the centrality of industrial mobilization to Canada's wartime experience, and its importance to the post-war role of the state in the economy, the effort has received scant attention.[4] A good deal of attention has recently been paid to the mobilization of Canadian women and to the technical-scientific contribution. Beyond this the industrial front remains, in Desmond Morton's words, a "big historiographical gap."[5] To lay out the scale and scope of the Canadian industrial front, this chapter draws heavily on statistical material collected for an official history that was never published.[6]

Financial Arrangements

The war was nearly a year old before Canadian production began to move into high gear. But the initial months of the conflict were crucial to future production because of the many financial and institutional arrangements that were made to allow the full harnessing of Canada's war potential. These arrangements require a digression. Careful management of the financial aspects of the war was essential for the harnessing of Canada's latent industrial capacity. Within Canada, the Bank of Canada, the Minister of Finance, his Deputy Minister, and the Prime Minister, William Lyon Mackenzie King, played the major roles in controlling inflation, developing the tax base, seeking foreign orders and securing the Canadian balance of trade.

On the domestic front new tax sharing agreements were undertaken with most of the provinces in 1939 and 1940 to strengthen the tax prerogatives of the federal government.[7] As well, wage and price controls were developed to reduce the type of war-induced inflation that had proven a tremendous problem during the First World War. A comparison of price movements during the two wars illustrates the effectiveness of these controls. If the years 1935 to 1939 are used to establish a base value of 100, then wholesale prices rose from 83 in 1914 to 173 four years later, an increase of more than a hundred percent. During the six years of the Second World War, wholesale prices rose from a base of 100 to only 133. Similarly, the cost of living rose from 80 to 120 (an increase of fifty percent) during the first war, but from 100 to only 120 during the second, when wage and price controls were in place.[8] Parliament exercised little supervision in these matters as the government tended to impose restrictions by Order-in-Council without debate.

International finance proved more problematic. Originally the Dominion government required Britain to pay for all items produced in Canada. Payment came in the form of securities or gold sold in New York to raise American dollars. British-provided US dollars were essential for the financing of Canadian orders from the United States. Britain liquidated much of its gold reserve and undertook an elaborate divestment program of British owned Canadian and American securities and other assets. In all, Britain divested a greater value of Canadian securities than

American. Total British divestment totaled £1,118 million, about half of which went to the sterling bloc (the Empire less Canada); the USA received £203 million and Canada some £225 million. This divestment crimped British financial health for decades to come and reinforced its dependence on the sterling bloc; income from overseas assets fell from £230 million to £97 million. But the immediate liquidity crisis held dire implications for Canada's war effort. Britain had moved into a financial crisis by early 1941, its liquid reserves dwindling from £605 million to only £3 million by April 1941. Britain had already suspended payments to Canada at the end of 1940.[9]

Aware of Britain's developing liquidity crisis the United States announced the lend-lease program. This Congressionally supported plan authorized the American President to exercise his discretion in selling war materials to nations friendly to the USA. The Lend-Lease Act, however, would not be passed until the spring of 1941 and would take months to be acted upon fully. It superceded the earlier US "cash-and-carry" policy which itself superceded the non-intercourse measures of the US Neutrality Act. Although America's creeping belligerency on the side of Britain was strategically desirable for Canada, lend-lease posed several problems. It became clear Britain would take its business to the US, where it could buy on credit, thus not only eliminating work at Canadian plants but worsening Canada's US dollar shortage. That problem threatened to curtail production solely for Canadian needs as well, and so the government considered taking advantage of the terms of lend-lease. But the Cabinet recognized that if Canada had to liquidate Canadian held US assets in order to qualify for the aid, accumulating a large US dollar debt, Canada's post-war independence would be greatly reduced. Moreover, while there were balance of trade problems, Canada was not financially destitute like Britain. Canada decided not to make direct use of lend-lease to supply the Canadian war effort.

Direct intercession by Prime Minister Mackenzie King with President Franklin Roosevelt overcame this problem. Meeting in upstate New York, the two leaders signed the Hyde Park Declaration on 20 April 1940. The Declaration reads in part: "that in mobilizing the resources of this continent each country should provide the other with the defence articles which it is best able to produce, and, above all, produce quickly, and that production programs should be coordinated to this end."[10] Hyde Park ensured the continuation of Canadian production of war materials to British pattern and forestalled the need to retool, retrain and refocus US factories for producing a number of British pattern goods already being made in Canada. Moreover, the Americans agreed to purchase large quantities of war materials from Canada where they were readily available, rather than undertaking or awaiting US production. Finally, Canadian requirements for materials from the United States that would be worked into British destined goods would accrue to Britain's lend-lease debt. These general principles guided US-Canada defence procurement for the remainder of the war. The agreement solved Canada's US dollar shortage, increased Canadian sales to the United States, and ensured new British orders in Canada. Within months the United States had placed large orders for ships, aircraft, aluminum and raw materials. New merchant shipping was an American priority and British pattern 10,000-ton ships built in Canada helped fill their need. The ships also promised to be the major source of US dollars. By the end of 1942 the United States was taking steps to ensure their orders in Canada were maintained at the level necessary to satisfy Canada's US dollar needs.

The Canadian–American trade relationship under Hyde Park proved essential for maintaining the scale of the Canadian effort. Tables 1 and 2 shed light on this relationship. Table 1 reveals the volume and type of deliveries to the United States while Table 2 tracks the reciprocal receipt of American dollars.

TABLE 1 - VOLUME OF CANADIAN DELIVERIES OF MUNITIONS AND OTHER WAR EQUIPMENT TO THE UNITED STATES OF AMERICA, BY TYPES, 1941 to 1945

Description	1941[1]	1942	1943	1944	1945	TOTAL
Ships		85	48			133
Naval		13	30			43
Escort ships		13	20			33
Minesweepers			9			9
Landing craft			1			1
Cargo 10,000 - ton		72	18			90
Aircraft	6	659	2,368	1,555	508	5,096
Combat and patrol			62	1,005	423	1,490
Advanced trainers	6	452	1,212	501	85	2,256
Elementary trainers		207	1,094	49		1,350
Armoured Fighting Vehicles	4	4,349	2,434	110	542	7,439
Tanks and carriers	4	4,023	1,691	110	290	6,118
Wheeled vehicles		326	743		252	1,321
Guns and Equipment						
Field	50	2,768	990		711	4,519
Anti-aircraft		294	253			547
Naval						
Gun trailers		48	232			280
Loose barrels and forgings	1,819	6,915	25,588	1,561	9,721	40,604
Miscellaneous equipment [2]		4	272	17,562	15,066	37,904
Small Arms						
Rifles and pistols		100,524	150,843	28		251,395
Machine guns	1,750	12,649	11,650		2	26,051
Other		12,819	16,561	14,735		44,115
Magazines, tripods, etc...		12	11,960			11,972
Heavy Ammunition (000s)						
Filled rounds		8,010	10,590	2,734	10	21,344
Unfilled components						
Cartridge cases		4,145	9,604	12,349	3,799	29,897
Projectiles		1,359	887	558	1,175	3,979
Small arms Ammunition	17,502	189,357	303,064	18,452	182,890	711,265
.303 - inch	17,502	186,195	291,498	15,316		510,511
Other		3,162	11,566	3,136	182,890	200,754
Chemicals and Explosives						
Chemicals (000s of pounds)	641	8,627	37,735	77,208	24,486	148,697
Explosives (000s of pounds)	2,580	20,500	48,236	11,436	71,937	154,689
Pyrotechnics (000s)	0.5	181.1	16	101.1		298.7
Instruments & Signals Eqpt						
Instruments [3]		5,410	20,489	5,816	8,489	40,204
Signals equipment [4]		29,814	12,424	6,775	904	49,917
Cable, wire, etc. (miles)		400	620		500	1,520

Source: Unpublished History, table 12

(1) There were no deliveries of war supplies to the United States during 1939 or 1940.

(2) Including mussle-brakes, breech-housings, etc.

(3) Including compasses, maglips, range-finders, telescopes, binoculars, etc.

(4) Including wireless sets, installation kits, radar equipment, etc.

TABLE 2 - CANADIAN RECEIPTS OF UNITED STATES DOLLARS THROUGH DELIVERIES OF MUNITIONS AND OTHER WAR MATERIALS AND THROUGH AMERICAN DEFENCE EXPENDITURES IN CANADA, 1941 - 1945.

(Millions of U.S. Dollars)

| Calendar Year | Received for Deliveries under the HydePark Agreement | | | Sub-total | Special Capital Investment[4] | Total |
	Munitions[1]	Metal[2]	Other[3]			
1941	2	56		58		58
1942	273	54	4	331	25	356
1943	294	80	28	402	93	495
1944	421	90	30	541	28	569
1945	189	60	12	261		261
TOTAL	1,179	340	74	1,593	146	1,739

Source: Unpublished history table 13 based on Comptrollers Branch, Department of Munitions and Supply; War Supplies Limited; Commission for Defence Projects in Northwest Canada, Office of the Privy Council.

(1) Includes ships and aircraft.

(2) Includes a small amount of capital investment for base metal production.

(3) Includes synthetic rubber; lumber, wood pulp, and other forest products; and certain foodstuffs.

(4) Estimated American expenditures in Canada on the Alaska Highway and Canoil and air route projects. The cost of materials and equipment brought into Canada and other expenditures outside Canada are not included.

Despite the Hyde Park agreement, financing existing and impending British purchases through 1942 remained problematic. Large scale US orders and the resulting influx of American dollars took some time to arrive and Britain remained financially responsible for a number of orders placed or pending in Canada. However, after Britain suspended gold payments in December 1940, Canada developed a loan program for the British. Eventually termed Mutual Aid, it essentially wrote off the value of materials previously sold but not paid for, and then made a gift based on future orders in Canada of approximately one billion dollars' worth of "munitions of war" (which did not include ships, lumber, and metals). In the process, Canada took responsibility for providing promised British capital support to Canadian industries, and Britain transferred ownership of plant created in Canada with British financial support. That proved to be a major and contentious international undertaking.[11] It did help end American criticism of Canada for forcing Britain to pay while the US was "giving" lend-lease. Further Mutual Aid grants were made later in the war to help the transition to peace, and in the end total Canadian financial aid to Britain was on a per capita basis five times greater than American lend-lease.[12]

Administrative Arrangements

Unlike the United States and Great Britain, Canada created a centralized purchasing and production agency to administer the burgeoning war production effort. Steps to lay the foundations of this department were taken on the eve of war, but the Order-in-Council creating it was issued only in April 1940. Until that time orders were placed by a government agency, the War Supplies Board, which was eventually worked into the new department. Scandal had sparked the effort to create such an organization. As early as the 1937 Imperial Conference it was recognized that Canada could become the arsenal of the British Empire, because it would be impervious to aerial bombardment from Europe. Despite this and several efforts to survey Canada's war potential, few steps were taken to prepare Canadian industry.[13] Following the 1938 Munich Crisis, however, a Canadian entrepreneur, Major James Hahn of the John Inglis

Company, arranged to build Bren light machine guns under licence at his plant in Canada. The Canadian Army agreed to purchase several thousand weapons and offered a cost-plus contract. *Maclean's* magazine ran a piece critical of the relationship between the company and the government. Questions in the House of Commons taxed the Minister of National Defence, who muddied the issues. The tempest invigorated the Prime Minister's efforts to separate defence purchasing from the defence minister's portfolio and establish an organization to hold war production profits and profiteering in check.[14] Before adjourning on 12 September 1939, Parliament passed legislation to establish the Department of Munitions and Supply. C.D. Howe was appointed to head the new department in November.[15]

Howe, an American-born engineer educated at the Massachusetts Institute of Technology ran a successful heavy construction company in Canada before entering politics and winning election in 1935. Appointed the first Minister of Transport in 1936, Howe helped end its legacy of patronage and pork barrelling. That record, his practical construction experience and his knowledge of Canada's major industrial firms made him the most suitable candidate for the new post from within the Cabinet. Despite a series of run-ins and sometimes very vocal criticism of his methods, Howe retained the confidence of the Prime Minister in this portfolio throughout the war and would continue to serve in the Cabinet for many years. In 1940 Howe's immediate actions were to coerce experienced executives out of major corporations and place them on the government payroll at a nominal salary of a dollar a year (their parent company paid their regular salary) and to place work with large established firms. He did not initially see the war as an effort to transform Canada into a more modern industrial state, although the pace of events and the scale of the war soon greatly increased demands. By 1943 a number of very small plants previously judged unsuitable for war work were being drawn into production by the "bits and pieces program."

While Munitions and Supply bore responsibility for the industrial production program, a host of other government agencies and departments played important roles in the war effort. These included the Bank of Canada and the departments of Finance, Transport, Trade and Commerce, and Mines and Resources. Organizations such as the National Research Council and the National Film Board (formed to manage propaganda) also contributed and there were agencies and control boards too numerous to list to manage particular aspects of the war effort, such as rationing and manpower.

When the United States declared war in December 1941 steps were taken to further harmonize Allied production and mobilization programs. After several months of wrangling Canada joined two of the four major co-ordinating committees in Washington, the Combined Production Board and the Combined Food Production Board. These agencies helped co-ordinate American, British and Canadian production programs and established peak production and supply targets for late 1943 and mid 1944. Despite their often rocky relationship with the Anglo-American Chiefs of Staff, these boards clearly rationalized the programs of the three nations. Little further expansion of the industrial front proved necessary after their first and most influential year of operation.[16]

Patterns in the Industrial Front

The general pattern of demand and types of war product are shown in Chart 1. The smooth curve masks a number of major issues that arose during the early stages of the war which help explain its shape.

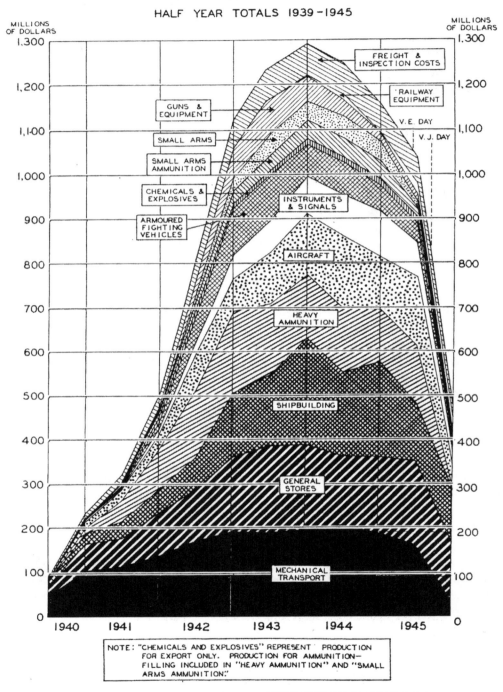

VALUE OF CANADIAN WAR PRODUCTION
IN THE MAJOR PROGRAMS

HALF YEAR TOTALS 1939-1945

NOTE: "CHEMICALS AND EXPLOSIVES" REPRESENT PRODUCTION FOR EXPORT ONLY. PRODUCTION FOR AMMUNITION—FILLING INCLUDED IN "HEAVY AMMUNITION" AND "SMALL ARMS AMMUNITION."

ECONOMIC RESEARCH BRANCH, DEPT. OF RECONSTRUCTION AND SUPPLY.

During 1939 and until the fall of France in June 1940—the period of the Phoney War—the Canadian economy was not seriously taxed by the war. There were few new orders calling for large scale or new fabrication and little more than pre-war demand for Canadian agricultural products or mineral resources. Neither Canadian nor Allied military requirements called for such increases, despite heated debates in the Canadian press and Parliament critical of the government for not doing more.[17] Britain did place small "educational" orders for small arms and light field guns in 1939 but these were very minor demands placed on only a few companies. Events in May 1940 brought forth a flurry of British orders and many from the Canadian military as it became clear the war would go on much longer than originally assumed.[18] The change is more clearly revealed in British orders in Canada before and after the evacuation of British forces from the Continent at Dunkirk. Following that retreat, nearly one third of the equipment required to rebuild the British Army was made in Canada. Table 3 illustrates the dramatic increase in demand consequent to Dunkirk.

TABLE 3 – British and Canadian Domestic Orders Before and After the Phoney War

Class of Equipment	Number of Units	To 30 Ap. 1940	To 31 Dec. 1940 UK Order	Cdn Order
Combat Aircraft	no.	450	1,075	315
Other A/C	no.	—		2,759
Warships (Corvettes and Minesweepers)	no.	10	22	108
Mosquito Air Craft	no.	—	12	24
Merchant Ships	no.	—	18	—
Tanks	no.	—	300	1,645
Other AFVs	no.	—	1,000	1,279
Vehicles	no.	—	72,434	23,414
Guns	no.	100	3,450	2,690
Small Arms	no.	5,000	155,900	66,122
Gun and mortar ammunition	Thousands	4,755	12,940	3,362
Small Arms ammunition	Millions	100	220*	
Aircraft bombs	Thousand pounds	—	50	9
Explosives and Propellants	Tons per annum	56,000	73,600*	

*Total Canadian and British domestic order.

Source: PRO CAB 102, file 794, "Procurement in North America Before Pearl Harbor," p. 35.

The unparalleled expansion of Canadian industry peaked in 1943, dropped gradually until the destruction of the Reich in May 1945, and came to an abrupt stop with the surrender of Imperial Japan in August later that year. The value in 1939 dollars of Canadian goods and services committed to the war from 1 September 1939 to the end of 1945 approached $20 billion—nearly one third of the Gross National Product for the period. Over that time the GNP increased from $5.6 billion in 1939 to nearly $12 billion in 1945. Total value of war production, not including agriculture, mining and forestry, exceeded $ 9.5 billion. Fully finished products included naval and merchant ships, landing craft, aircraft of all types, armoured fighting vehicles, motor vehicles, heavy and light artillery, small arms, shells, small arms ammunition, explosives, radios, radars, specialized optics and electronic fittings. Canada also became a major provider of foodstuffs, most notably meat, poultry and wheat to Britain, as well as semi-

Flower Class corvettes of the Royal Canadian Navy being built in Lauzon, Quebec, June 1941. (Photographer unknown. NA, PA- 105427)

finished products such as aluminum and plywood. Nominally sixty percent of this production went to Canada's allies, but some of that total undoubtedly found itself in the hands of Canadian troops overseas.[19] Even so, the majority of goods produced in Canada were consumed by Great Britain and the United States.

The pre-war Canadian economy was not geared to manufacturing. The country imported most heavy industrial goods and even the well developed automotive sector relied heavily on US-built engines. There were only small shipyards and automotive works. The engine of the Canadian economy remained the export of foodstuffs and raw materials. The war ushered in an unprecedented level of state intervention in the economy. By the exercise of creeping but widespread controls over the chief factors of production, principally capital, and labour but also plant and technology, Canada developed its military industrial base to the degree that more than fifty percent of Canadian war production would come from plants that did not exist in 1939. National steel ingot production capacity more than doubled. Aluminum production, vital particularly to British aircraft production, increased a thousand-fold, allowing Canada to provide one third of the aluminum required by the Allies for the war. New plants were built for the production of shells, artillery, small arms, ships, tanks, troop carriers and similar items.

In March 1941, Howe told the Cabinet that little further expansion of Canadian industry would be necessary. Late in1941 Howe informed the House of Commons that Canada was now producing all two thousand items needed to equip a modern infantry division at the pace of one division's worth every six weeks.[20] By late 1941 a number of plants had reached their productive capacity. However, after the US entry into the war in December 1941, production again increased and new problems had to be overcome.[21] Because American supplies of scrap metal, steel, machine tools and a number of finished products quickly became restricted, further expansion of Canadian plant and programs was undertaken. Despite early

C.D. Howe, the Minister of Munitions and Supply, sits behind the wheel of the 500,000th military vehicle produced in Canada, 19 June 1943. (Photographer unknown. NA C-068669)

calls to use the war as a national industrial program to spread factories and manufacturing skills the length and breadth of the country, Howe preferred to give work to companies with track records or at least with known managerial capacity. Consequently, there was considerable clustering of related industries. Clustering today is seen as beneficial but during the war Howe's policy was seen as favouring established firms and in the words of historian Ernie Forbes "consolidating disparity."[22] Undeniably Howe's initial efforts built on the nation's existing capacities and expertise. To expand it, work was subcontracted to small producers wherever appropriate machine tools and capacity remained under utilized. Through 1942 this became known as the "bits and pieces" program. "At the Minister's instigation, every effort was being made to expand the war effort and to harness all Provinces to the team," Howe's Special Advisor for Production later wrote, "The possibilities of each Province received individual and collective consideration."[23] For instance, a number of railway repair shops located across the country were taken over for war work. Table 4 shows the provincial distribution of war production.

TABLE 4 - EMPLOYMENT OF CANADIAN MANUFACTURERS, BY PROVINCES AS OF JULY 1, 1943*

Program	Prince Edward Island	Nova Scotia	New Brunswick	Quebec	Ontario	Manitoba	Saskatchewan	Alberta	British Columbia	Total Canada
Shipbuilding 141		15,255	3,299	42,629	24,934	640		103	39,184	126,185
Shipyards 23		13,574	2,970	26,980	10,167	67		3	32,967	86,751
Manufacture of parts 118		1,681	329	15,649	14,767	57		100	6,217	39,434
Aircraft		2,665	627	38,536	43,746	5,661	1,263	2,364	9,750	104,612
Assembly				19,586	15,700	1,061		6,073	42,420	
Overhaul and repair		760	627	2,660	2,600	2,837	1,243	2,328	1,314	14,369
Manufacture of parts		1,905		16,290	25,446	1,763	20	36	2,363	47,823
Automotive Equipment		10	12	8,953	64,588	488		37	39	74,127
Mechanical transport		10	12	1,500	50,095	276		37	33	51,963
Armoured fighting vehicles				7,453	14,493	212			6	22,164
Guns and Small Arms		931	129	6,530	33,907	190	989	1,053	1,092	44,821
Guns		931	129	5,938	13,327	190	740	1,053	1,092	23,400
Small Arms				592	20,580		249			21,421
Chemicals, Explosives and Ammunition		732	176	52,621	40,675	2,784	101	669	1,074	98,832
Small arms ammunition			15	23,614	3,310					26,939
Ammunition components		377	161	8,144	18,170	495		123	30	27,500
Shells		377	139	2,230	5,582	366		121		8,815
Bombs			19	1,939	3,650	129			26	5,763
Fuses				1,447	4,358			2		5,807
Cartridge cases			3	1,957	4,056				4	6,020
Pyrotechnics				571	524					1,095
Ammunition -filling				14,080	10,230					24,310
Chemicals and explosives		355		6,783	8,965	2,289	101	546	1,044	20,083
Explosive chemicals				4,253	4,250	2,122		405	42	11,072
Non-explosive chemicals		355		2,530	4,715	167	101	141	1,002	9,011
Instruments and Communications										
Equipment		20	22	10,434	24,508	32	218	248	1,048	36,530
Instruments		20	22	2,004	14,299	24	218	248	997	17,832
Communications equipment				8,430	10,209	8			51	18,698
General Stores 36		3,111	2,148	40,543	46,138	5,076	1,835	4,102	6,862	109,851
Food 34		1,013	1,182	5,906	8,582	2,762	1,554	2,636	5,488	29,157
Textiles 2		597	162	14,488	10,420	21			33	25,723
Clothing		782	427	11,975	13,762	1,668	9	265	331	29,219
Footwear and rubber clothing 117		160	4,880	2,832	100			50	111	8,250
Barrack stores		130	217	1,603	4,689	396	10	259	520	7,824
Office supplies				279	2,504	64		5	19	2,871
Oil and gasoline		460		732	1,690	58	262	887	332	4,421
Medical and dental supplies		12		680	1,659	7			28	2,386

SOURCE: Unpublished history, table 32.

The scale and rapid pace of new production entailed overcoming a number of technical, financial and administrative hurdles. There were shortages of machine tools, precision gauges, skilled fabricators, supervisors, and draftsmen. There were almost no technical drawings, and when Britain made large numbers of these available the conversion of British specifications to North American standards all taxed the initial effort. Britain supplied blueprints and often working examples and technical liaison personnel to help establish Canadian (and American) production. Britain not only contributed plans and designs but made available hundreds of technicians and experts who served as plant supervisors, advisors, inspectors and quality control personnel.[24] The importance of British technical assistance cannot be over stressed. Although such technical support was essential it was not sufficient alone to transform Canada's industrial base. In many cases capital assistance in the form of grants or attractive loans was all that needed to be added. All told, by late 1943 the government had provided over $1.3 billion in capital assistance and nearly the same amount was spent to expand infrastructure such as power generation and housing.[25]

However, when commercial interests could not or would not take up the work, Munitions and Supply struck on the war-time innovation of creating Crown corporations. In all, some twenty-eight Crown corporations were formed. These state companies became a post-war feature of the Canadian economy. Most ran small production enterprises but others served as clearing houses, purchasing bodies or co-ordinating agencies. In some cases Crown corporations simply provided the management to run operations, but in others private companies were nationalized for the duration of the war. Table 5 shows the role of Crown plant while Table 6 illustrates the clustering of these in production centres.

TABLE 5 - RELATIVE IMPORTANCE OF CROWN PLANTS AS MEASURED BY EMPLOYMENT, AT JULY 1, 1943

Description	Number of Plants	At Peak	At July 1, 1943		War Employment in All Plants At July 1, 1943	Employment in Crown Plants as a Percentage of Employment in All Plants At July 1, 1943
Shipbuilding	10	24,790	21,018	126,180	126,180	17
Aircraft	26	73,376	57,229	29,296	104,620	55
Automotive Equipment	1	5,154	4,378	15,029	74,130	6
Guns	8	14,630	12,509	11,578	23,400	53
Machine Guns and Small Arms	4	22,486	17,019	19,718	21,430	79
Ammunition Components	5	3,822	2,665	27,500	27,500	10
Small Arms Ammunition	7	28,979	24,972	nil	26,940	93
Ammunition Filling	7	33,201	23,927	12,330	24,310	98
Chemicals and Explosives	15	15,698	9,991		20,150	50
Instruments and Communication Equipment	6	9,083	8,802		36,530	24
General Purchasing	1	356	0		109,850	
Industrial Equipment	4	2,723	2,690		81,210	3
Basic	11	6,695	4,776		145,290	3
Total	105	240,993	189,976	821,510	821,510	23

Source: Unpublished history, table 35, data from Economics and Statistics Branch, Department of Munitions and Supply.

* Excluding government employees.

TABLE 6 - EMPLOYMENT OF CANADIAN MANUFACTURERS, BY PROVINCES AS OF JULY 1, 1943*

Program	Prince Edward Island	Nova Scotia	New Brunswick	Quebec	Ontario	Manitoba	Saskatchewan	Alberta	British Columbia	Total Canada
Shipbuilding	141	15,255	3,299	42,629	24,934	640		103	39,184	126,185
Shipyards	23	13,574	2,970	26,980	10,167	67		3	32,967	86,751
Manufacture of parts	118	1,681	329	15,649	14,767	573		100	6,217	39,434
Aircraft		2,665	627	38,536	43,746	5,661	1,263	2,364	9,750	104,612
Assembly				19,586	15,700	1,061			6,073	42,420
Overhaul and repair		760	627	2,660	2,600	2,837	1,243	2,328	1,314	14,369
Manufacture of parts		1,905		16,290	25,446	1,763	20	36	2,363	47,823
Automotive Equipment		10	12	8,953	64,588	488		37	39	74,127
Mechanical transport		10	12	1,500	50,095	276		37	33	51,963
Armoured fighting vehicles				7,453	14,493	212			6	22,164
Guns and Small Arms		931	129	6,530	33,907	190	989	1,053	1,092	44,821
Guns		931	129	5,938	13,327	190	740	1,053	1,092	23,400
Small Arms				592	20,580		249			21,421
Chemicals, Explosives and Ammunition		732	176	52,621	40,675	2,784	101	669	1,074	98,832
Small arms ammunition			15	23,614	3,310					26,939
Ammunition components		377	161	8,144	18,170	495		123	30	27,500
Shells		377	139	2,230	5,582	366		121		8,815
Bombs			19	1,939	3,650	129			26	5,763
Fuses				1,447	4,358			2		5,807
Cartridge cases			3	1,957	4,056				4	6,020
Pyrotechnics				571	524					1,095
Ammunition - filling				14,080	10,230					24,310
Chemicals and explosives		355		6,783	8,965	2,289	101	546	1,044	20,083
Explosive chemicals				4,253	4,250	2,122		405	42	11,072
Non-explosive chemicals		355		2,530	4,715	167	101	141	1,002	9,011
Instruments and Communications										0
Equipment		20	22	10,434	24,508	32	218	248	1,048	36,530
Instruments		20	22	2,004	14,299	24	218	248	997	17,832
Communications equipment				8,430	10,209	8			51	18,698
General Stores	36	3,111	2,148	40,543	46,138	5,076	1,835	4,102	6,862	109,851
Food	34	1,013	1,182	5,906	8,582	2,762	1,554	2,636	5,488	29,157
Textiles	2	597	162	14,488	10,420	21			33	25,723
Clothing		782	427	11,975	13,762	1,668	9	265	331	29,219
Footwear and rubber clothing	117	160		4,880	2,832	100		50	111	8,250
Barrack stores		130	217	1,603	4,689	396	10	259	520	7,824
Office supplies				279	2,504	64		5	19	2,871
Oil and gasoline		460		732	1,690	58	262	887	332	4,421
Medical and dental supplies	12			680	1,659	7			28	2,386

SOURCE: Unpublished history, table 32.

Bren gun, from raw material to finished product. (Photographer unknown. NA, PA-116367)

Naturally production bottlenecks occurred. Shortages of labour, management personnel, a lack of technical drawings, a scarcity of machine tools, and conflicting demands on manpower all took their toll. Many bottlenecks resulted from shifting assumptions about the course the war would follow. Originally, Britain and France acted on the premise that the war would not last three years. Placing orders in Canada that required a long start-up and even later delivery appeared imprudent. Moreover, much Canadian plant when closely examined was found to be antiquated, requiring greater capital assistance and technical aid than producers of comparable size in Britain. And priorities in Canada kept changing, as the shipbuilding and steel industries illustrate. During the initial stage of the war, Canada had primarily concerned itself with naval shipbuilding. The construction of large merchant ships only followed the fall of France and the dramatic increase in German U-boat activity across the Atlantic. Even then, the major production effort only came as a means to earn American dollars. The steel industry presents another example. Initially Canada was able to secure specialized steel plate from the United States so there was little perceived need to expand Canada's steel industry. When one major producer planned to expand its technical capacity without government financial assistance, it won from Howe the understanding that the government would not offer financial assistance for such modernization to its competitors. But the understanding had to be breached in 1942 when US steel became harder to obtain for Canadian needs.[26]

The pace of change to the course of the war also played havoc with rational planning. For instance, British plans to support production of 2-pounder anti-tank guns in Canada were well underway in 1939 and a number of subcontracts let when the War Office, following the fall of France, cancelled the work in order to focus on the production of a new and more powerful gun. It was then unable to provide detailed plans. This cancellation stalled the introduction of mass subcontracting of weapons component production in Canada for some eighteen months. Such mass production techniques were not generally used in Canada except in the automotive sector. The 25-pound field artillery piece was the first major system outside that sector to employ large scale subcontracting for components and became the model for other manufacturers.[27] The changing scale of the war hampered the orderly production of these weapons into 1942. The original orders anticipated one hundred guns at the rate of eight per month, commencing in 1940. French technicians on loan from a French gun manufacturer, however, sought repatriation following the collapse of the Third Republic in June 1940. The first guns were not completed until July 1941, by which time the plant was being geared to turn out seventy-five guns per month rather than eight. This plant at Sorel eventually became the largest of its kind in the British Empire and the only plant to produce finished guns from steel ingot. The plant began from scratch, lacked technicians, and in the throws of producing the first guns had to be reconfigured for a much greater volume of production, which could only retard progress, but these were conditions replicated in industries throughout Canada.

Beyond the many new strides made in manufacturing, Canada remained or became a chief provider of the foodstuffs and raw materials needed by both principal allies to continue the war. The production of raw materials and agricultural products was a significant part of Canada's overall contribution to the war. Chart 2 shows the relative weight of employment by type of war work while the output of raw materials and agricultural products is shown in Tables 7 and Table 8.

Canadian infantry with their Bren gun in Caen, France, 10 July 1944. (Photographer unknown. NA, PA-131404)

DISTRIBUTION
OF WAR EMPLOYMENT
AT PEAK

OCTOBER 1, 1943

TOTAL 2,163,000

AGRICULTURE 245,000

ARMED FORCES 752,000

ANCILLARY 306,000

MANUFACTURING 860,000

ECONOMIC RESEARCH BRANCH, DEPT. OF RECONSTRUCTION AND SUPPLY.

TABLE 7 - VOLUME OF PRODUCTION OF RAW MATERIALS

	Unit of Measure	1935 - 39 Annual Average	1940	1941	1942	1943	1944	1945	Total 1940 - 45
Aluminum+	Thousands of Pounds	101,505	218,289	427,747	681,193	991,130	924,130	431,426	3,674,284
Copper*	Thousands of Pounds	510,026	655,593	643,317	603,662	575,190	547,070	474,914	3,499,746
Lead*	Thousands of Pounds	388,357	471,850	460,167	512,143	444,061	304,582	346,994	2,539,797
Nickel*	Thousands of Pounds	193,968	245,558	282,258	285,212	288,019	274,599	245,131	1,620,777
Zinc*	Thousands of Pounds	360,043	424029	512,382	580,258	610,754	550,823	517,214	3,195,460
Pig Iron	Short tons	814,938	1,309,099	1,528,053	1,975,014	1,758,269	1,852,628	1,777,949	10,201,012
Steel Ingots and Castings	Short tons	1,344,055	2,253,769	2,712,151	3,109,851	3,004,124	3,016,162	2,877,927	16,973,984
Lumber	Thousands of board feet	3,627,230	4,629,052	4,941,084	4,935,145	4,363,575	4,512,232	4,514,160	27,895,248
Wood Pulp	Short tons	4,265,876	5,290,762	5,720,847	5,606,461	5,272,830	5,271,137	5,600,814	32,762,851
Crude Petroleum	Barrels	4,136,626	8,590,978	10,133,838[+]	10,364,796[+]	10,052,302	10,099,404[+]	8,482,796	57,724,114
Coal	Short tons	14,988,112[+]	17,566,884[+]	18,225,921[+]	18,865,030[+]	17,859,057	17,026,499[+]	16,506,713	106,050,104[+]
Synthetic Rubber#	Long tons					2,522	34,829	45,704	83,055
Asbestos	Short tons	315,209	346,805	477,846	439,459	476,196	419,265	466,897	2,626,468

Source: Unpublished history, table 7. *The Primary Iron and Steel Industry in Canada, 1945*, and *Preliminary Report on the Mineral Production of Canada, 1946*, Dominion Bureau of Statistics, and special information supplied by the Dominion Bureau of Statistics; Statistical Record of Forest and Forest Industries of Canada, Lands, Parks and Forests Branch, Dominion Forest Service, Department of Mines and Resources, Ottawa.

+ Primary.

* Refined and unrefined.

Butyl and GR-S types.

TABLE 8 - PRODUCTION VOLUME OF PRINCIPAL AGRICULTURAL PRODUCTS, 1935 -1945

Product	Unit of Measure (in millions)	1935 - 39 Average	1940	1941	1942	1943	1944	1945	Total 1940 - 45
Grain and Forage Crops									
Wheat	bu.	312.4	540.2	314.8	556.7	284.5	416.6	318.5	2431.3
Oats	bu.	338.1	380.5	305.6	652	482	499.6	381.6	2701.3
Barley	bu.	88.9	104.3	110.6	259.2	215.6	194.7	157.8	1042.2
Mixed Grains	bu.	38.5	43.1	48.7	68.6	35.7	57.4	46.9	300.4
Hay and Clover	ton	13.6	14.1	12.6	16.1	17.2	15.1	17.7	92.8
Alfalfa	ton	2.1	2.6	2.7	3.7	3.9	3.7	3.8	20.4
Dairy Products									
Milk	lb.	15,2284.1	15,999.30	16,549.90	17,488.60	17,519.10	17,624.00	17,626.80	102807.7
Creamery Butter	lb.	254.8	264.7	285.8	284.6	311.7	298.8	293.8	1739.4
Factory Cheese	lb.	119.9	145.3	151.9	207.4	166.3	181.9	188.7	1041.5
Evaporated Milk	lb.	90.2	135.9	166	185.8	178.4	184.3	200.5	1050.9
Condensed Milk	lb.	13.4	14.4	24.6	23.1	26.9	31	28.6	148.6
Milk Powder	lb.	26.1	33.8	34.8	37.8	37.4	46.7	50.3	240.8
Meats									
Pork	lb.	625.1	865.4	1,060.80	1,189.10	1395.7	1,504.60	1,112.80	7128.4
Beef	lb.	703.7	717.5	812.1	822.5	893	961	1,156.10	5362.2
Veal	lb.	122.2	130	134.1	123.6	118.5	126.1	141.6	773.9
Mutton and Lamb	lb.	61.6	52.6	58.6	56.7	62.2	63.5	73.4	367
Eggs and Poultry									
Eggs	dos.	219.5	235.5	244.5	280.7	315.6	360.9	374	1811.2
Poultry Meat	lb.	n.a.	219.1	220	258.7	265.4	315	307.1	1585.3
Fresh Fruits									
Tree Fruits	bu.	16.7	15.4	14	16.6	14.7	21.4	10.2	92.3
Berries	qt.	34.7	40.6	32.3	27.1	26.4	21.7	29.3	177.4
Grapes	lb.	42.8	52.7	47.2	74.9	53.8	60.9	66	355.5
Fresh Vegetables									
Potatoes	lb.	3,863.20	4,230.00	3,905.20	4,288.20	4,354.10	4,940.90	3,598.60	25317
Tomatoes	lb.	500	516.9	719.7	557.8	460.7	964.2	575.9	3795.2
Other Vegetables	lb.	1,060.00	1,017.10	1,052.10	1,508.30	1,129.00	1,411.10	872.2	6989.8
Oilseed Crops									
Flaxseed	bu.	1.5	3	5.8	15	17.9	9.7	7.6	59
Other Oilseed	bu.	n.a.	0.2	0.2	0.9	21.3	15.8	10.6	49
Seed Crops	lb.	28.4	24.8	37.8	40.6	52	54.9	52	262.1
Tobacco	lb.	76.6	64	94.2	89.7	69.1	105.4	92.3	514.7
Sugar Beets	ton	0.5	0.8	0.7	0.7	0.5	0.6	0.6	3.9
Maple Products	gal	2.7	3.1	2.3	3.3	2.3	3.1	1.5	15.6
Honey	lb.	35.7	28.2	33.2	28	39.5	35	33	196.9
Wool	lb.	16	14.9	15.3	16.5	17.8	19.3	19.6	103.4

Source: Unpublished history, table 6.

Labour became a closely managed commodity, and eventually restrictions were placed on certain job classifications. Labour mobility, however, was essential. Chart 3 illustrates appreciable interprovincial migration, most probably sparked by war work, the primary destinations being Ontario and British Columbia. Although it is not shown here, there was also considerable intra-provincial movement, particularly within Quebec and Ontario.

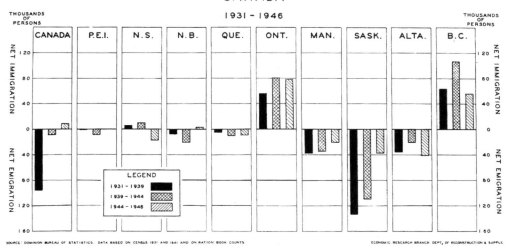

INTERPROVINCIAL MIGRATION
CANADA
1931 - 1946

SOURCE: DOMINION BUREAU OF STATISTICS. DATA BASED ON CENSUS 1931 AND 1941 AND ON RATION BOOK COUNTS.   ECONOMIC RESEARCH BRANCH DEPT, OF RECONSTRUCTION & SUPPLY.

Post-War Legacy

The long-term consequences of Canada's industrial war effort remain debatable. The immediate effects were real increases in Gross National Product and National Debt. The attenuation
of consumer demand and the accumulation of savings brought about by the war did generate
a flowering of consumer demand after the fighting stopped. In short, the war built up both savings and demand. Many industries, municipalities and provinces reduced their outstanding
debt—eliminating much legacy debt from the Depression. It is also clear that the war, and particularly how Canada financed war production, reduced British ownership of Canadian primary and secondary industries. At the plant level a number of small producers gained valuable
expertise in large- scale production, particularly in subcontracting, new production techniques
and financial controls. Many also modernized their shops and greatly improved their firm's
working capital position. Administrative and technical knowledge, however, remain intangible
assets to measure. Nationally, new departures were made in the fields of atomic energy and
research, radar production, communication electronics, optics, plastics, synthetic rubber, plywood fabrication and the production of special steels. Many essential items, such as tungsten-
carbide cutting tools and precision had never before been produced in Canada. The movement
of workers into war industries also accelerated the change from a rural to an urban Canada
and it helped break down barriers to the employment of women in production industries.

It is clear that Canada's whole contribution to defeating the Axis cannot be measured without taking into account the tremendous war production and supply effort made by the
Dominion. The contributions of some industries were decisive—Canadian aluminum in British
aircraft, or the motor transport of the Eighth Army in North Africa and Italy, to name only two.
For the last three years of the war, Canada provided Britain with nearly ten percent of all its
munitions. Canada as an overseas source of munitions supply was surpassed by only the
United States and dwarfed all other members of the Empire.[28] Moreover, Canada stood as the
strongest and most industrially potent co-belligerent during Britain's darkest hour. It was a role
of inestimable value.

Notes for Chapter 7

1 By war's end the Canadian Army numbered some half a million, 23,000 of which were killed in action; the RCN escorted 25,000 merchant ships and 200 million tons of supplies, destroyed approximately thirty-three U-boats, and lost two dozen ships; see Ralph Allen, *Ordeal by Fire. Canada 1910-1945* (New York, 1961), 369 passim.

2 On these efforts see C. Barnett, *The Collapse of British Power* (Atlantic Highland, NJ 1991), 210-228.

3 Cf. J.V. Baker, *War Economy. New Zealand in the Second World War 1939-45* (Wellington, NZ, 1965); or the extensive UK Civil Series histories such as D.K. Hall's *North American Supply. History of the Second World War* (London, 1955); or the US history, S.W. Dziuban, *Military Relations Between the United States and Canada* (Washington, 1959). On the Canadian front, C.P. Stacey's official *Arms, Men and Government* (Ottawa, 1970) touches in some detail on the issue but was primarily concerned with the Army and its use overseas; the closest Canada came to the civil series histories was the two volumes of J. De N. Kennedy's rushed and superficial *History of the Department of Munitions and Supply. Canada in the Second World War*, (Ottawa, 1950).

4 Michael Bliss, "Canada's Swell War," *Saturday Night*, (May 1995), 39-41, 64.

5 John Herd Thompson, *Ethnic Minorities During Two World Wars*, (Ottawa, 1991) part of the Canadian Historical Association (CHA) Series Canada's Ethnic Groups, and Ruth Roach Pierson, *Canadian Women and the Second World War*, CHA Historical Booklet (Ottawa, 1983), and Desmond Morton, *1945 When Canada Won the War*, CHA Historical Booklet No. 54 (Ottawa, 1995), 28.

6 Except where otherwise noted all the tables and charts reproduced here are extracted from the study "Canada's Industrial War Effort," Department of Reconstruction and Supply, copy 5 (Ottawa, 1947), found in National Archives of Canada (NA) RG 28 R2-R8, vol 862. This study is hereafter referred to as the "unpublished history."

7 A very complete discussion of the domestic economic front is found in David W. Slater, *War Finance and Reconstruction. The Role of Canada's Department of Finance, 1939-1946* (Ottawa, 1995)

8 Figures extrapolated from Indexes of Wholesale Prices and Cost of Living in Canada 1914-1948, p. 127, unpublished history.

9 Letter W. Eady, (UK Treasury) to Mr. Ilsley, Ministry of Finance, 24 February 1946, UK Public Records Office (hereafter PRO) CAB 102/38. The long-term implications of this divestment are beyond the scope of this chapter, however, the figures are reproduced here because they are generally unavailable.

10 For full text of the Hyde Park Declaration see, R. Warren James, *Wartime Economic Cooperation. A Study of Relations Between Canada and the United States* (Toronto, 1949), 20-21.

11 The details were very complex and entailed Britain giving assurances to Canada that it would not take advantage of the loan-gift to transfer liquid assets in payment to other nations. See W.A.B. Douglas and Brereton Greenhouse, *Out of the Shadows: Canada in the Second World War* (Toronto, 1977), 48. The Cabinet War Committee minutes are also very informative on this period. See NA, RG 2, 7c, Cabinet War Committee (CWC) Minutes.

12 NA, RG 2, 7c, CWC Minutes, 15-16 December. For detailed background see CWC Document #41, 3 December 1941.

13 Barnett, *The Collapse of British Power*, 210-228.

14 Contract cost control measures set a notional maximum of five percent profit but often resulted in considerably less. No comprehensive study has every been done on the subject but a good deal of original correspondence is available which demonstrates appeals were most often rejected, even when the cost overruns were the fault of government contracting parties. See for example discussion of the contract appeals process in NA, RG 28, vol. 129, files 3, c 29.

15 Robert Bothwell and William Kilbourn, *C.D. Howe A Biography* (Toronto, 1980), 120-123; Canada, *House of Commons Debates*, 9 February 1939, 771-75; George Drew, "Canada's Armaments Mystery," *Maclean's,* 1 September 1938.

16 On the origins and functioning of the Combined Boards, see S. McKee Rosen, *Combined Boards of the Second World War. An Experiment in International Administration* (New York, 1951).

17 For instance the Prime Minister in January 1940 called an election in face of criticism of Canada's mobilization voiced by the Premier of Ontario. Mackenzie King won a resounding re-election with 178 seats against 39 for the Conservative Official Opposition.

18 Anglo-French planners assumed until May 1940 that the war would not last more than three years.

19 Britain supplied from its depots a number of Canadian formations but no full accounting was kept of how much Canadian material sent to British forces was eventually passed on to Canadian users.

20 See Allen, *Ordeal by Fire*, 412.

21 NA, RG 2, 7c, CWC Minutes, 13 March 1941.

22 Professor Ernie Forbes, "Consolidating Disparity: The Maritimes and the Industrialization of Canada During the Second World War," in P.A. Buckner and David Frank eds., *The Acadiens's Reader, Volume Two* (Fredericton, 1988), 383-407.

23 PRO AVIA 22/3170, MS, 14.

24 See for instance David Zimmerman, *Top Secret Exchange. The Tizard Mission and the Scientific War* (Montreal & Kingston, 1996), passim, and Donald H. Avery, *The Science of War. Canadian Scientists and Allied Military Technology During the Second World War* (Toronto, 1998).

25 NA, RG 2, 7c, CWC Doc #675, 1 November 1943.

26 Leslie Thomson, "Steel Controller to Grant Dexter, 6 Jan.1942," in Frederick W. Gibson and Barbara Robertson, eds. *Ottawa at War. The Grant Dexter Memoranda, 1939-1945*, (Winnipeg,1994), Memo 41, 251-254.

27 At the request of C.D. Howe, Chrysler American Corporation loaned a vice president, Ledyard Mitchell, to the gun's producer, MIL of Sorel Quebec, and he effectively took over the production program. PROD AVIA 22/3170 MS, 32.

28 Cf. Table in Hall, *North American Supply*, 428.

CHAPTER 8

Canada's Zombies

A Portrait of Canadian Conscripts and their Experiences During the Second World War[1]

Daniel Byers

CONSCRIPTION WAS ONE OF THE MOST DIVISIVE POLITICAL ISSUES of the first half of the twentieth century in Canada. During the Second World War, it took on the most organized, long-term and comprehensive form it has ever had. Of the one million men and women who entered Canada's armed forces between 1939 and 1945, over 150,000, or fifteen percent, were conscripts called out under the authority of the National Resources Mobilization Act (NRMA) of 1940. Although the NRMA required those called up to serve only in Canada, some 60,000 of these men went on to volunteer for overseas service, accounting for ten percent of all Canadian Army volunteers. Another 60,000 conscripts were kept on permanent defence duty in Canada for up to four years and labelled Zombies by the public for their reputed lack of enthusiasm for military service. Little has been published about these men.[2]

The aim of this chapter is to provide a brief description of Canada's conscripts and their experiences during the war. It will present a statistical portrait of the NRMA men based on records collected by the Department of National Defence (DND) and other agencies at the time. In addition, it attempts to reconstruct a sense of the daily lives of the conscripts in training centres and operational units. It closes by discussing two of the key questions surrounding the NRMA and its impact during the war: the pressures put on recruits to volunteer for overseas service while they were in uniform and the reasons why many of them did not. Undoubtedly, a case study of the Zombies and their experiences adds an important perspective to our understanding of the war and its impact on Canadian society.

The story of conscription as a political issue during the Second World War is well known. Compulsory military service was authorized by the NRMA, which gave the federal government massive powers to control the war effort. The law was designed to meet calls for greater contributions to the war following a series of rapid German victories in the spring of 1940 while at the same time stressing that conscription would not be extended to overseas service, the cause of many problems in the First World War. Limiting the NRMA to home defence seemingly set the tone for compulsory military service for the remainder of the conflict. However, in April 1942, after further German advances in North Africa and Russia, as well as Japan's entry into the war, Canadians voted in a national plebiscite to release the federal government from its previous commitments on conscription. The section limiting the NRMA's powers was repealed, but Prime Minister Mackenzie King refused to take advantage of the change until he was convinced of its necessity. The scope of the law was slowly expanded until conscripts were required to serve anywhere in the Western Hemisphere. But none were sent overseas until November 1944, when shortages of volunteer infantry caused a crisis that nearly brought down the Mackenzie King government. Subsequently, 16,000 conscripts were ordered to Europe, although only about 2,500 made it to the front lines before the war ended a few months later.[3]

Responsibility for administering compulsory military service fell to the Department of National Defence. At first, the training was conducted in thirty-nine special camps located in smaller cities across the country. At this time conscripts were only required to serve for thirty days. In early 1941, facilities for compulsory training were merged with those for volunteers and the training period was lengthened to four months. For the rest of the war NRMA men and active service volunteers worked side by side for two months of basic training and two months of more specialized training. Shortly after the new scheme got underway, conscripts were told they would be required to serve for the duration of the war. As a result, they were posted directly to home defence units as soon as they completed their training.[4]

During the five years that the NRMA was in operation, a total of 157,841 men passed through the ranks of the Zombies.[5] It seems that many contemporary observers assumed that the NRMA consisted mostly of recruits who were French-speaking or "non-British" (presumably meaning recent immigrants or other members of minority ethnic groups). Recently discovered statistical data reveal how inaccurate that assumption was. What the numbers in fact show is that for the most part the Zombies reflected the larger society from which they were drawn (these statistics appear in the Appendix at the end of this chapter). It should be noted that when the information was collected, the number of men listed as NRMA recruits was slightly larger than the final postwar total, apparently due to a duplication of records. But this error is not large enough to invalidate the conclusions made here.[6]

Table I gives the dates of birth of all men who were called up for military training. By reading diagonally, one can estimate their approximate ages when they entered military service. Almost one-third of the Zombies were 21 to 22 years old, and nearly three-quarters were between 18 and 25. Only about ten percent of conscripts were more than 30 years old. As the war went on, the classes of men liable for compulsory service grew from single men 21 to 24, to all single men 18½ to 43, and finally to married men 18½ to 32 years old.[7] Unfortunately, it is not possible to differentiate between the number of single and married recruits, although, the majority of the NRMA men were undoubtedly young and single.

Tables II and III provide more interesting information. The first table lists the NRMA by place of residence and the second by place of birth. As they indicate, the proportion of conscripts from

A Second World War Recruiting Poster. (Canadian War Museum [CWM], 56-05-11-205)

A Second World War Recruiting Poster. (CWM, 56-05-12-334)

each province outside Quebec was slightly lower (particularly in Ontario) than the respective percentage of national population, while the number of men from Quebec was somewhat higher. The increase in figures for Quebec from year to year is especially noticeable. Nevertheless, even in late 1944, of the 60,000 men who were still in uniform as conscripts, roughly thirty-nine percent came from Quebec, twenty-four percent from Ontario, and thirty-seven percent from other parts of the country.[8] These numbers did not differ from the respective proportion of the larger population nearly as much as one might expect. Clearly, there were plenty of men in every province who were fit for service but had various reasons why they did not want to go overseas.

The number of conscripts from Quebec is even closer to its share of the national population when one looks more closely at the proportion of young single men in each province. According to the 1941 census, Quebec had slightly more single men between the ages of 15 and 24, in real numbers, than Ontario, the province with the largest share of the national population.[9] The same was true for men aged 25 to 34. At the same time, the number of married men in these age groups was considerably smaller in Quebec than in Ontario. Thus, relatively more Zombies would have come from Quebec than from Ontario or other provinces. As the war continued and the number of men who were suitable for training and who could be released from their civilian jobs shrank, more and more men had to be called up in order to pay the voracious manpower bill overseas. Demographic realities, combined with wartime stereotypes and perceptions, resulted in an increasing focus on Quebec to fill the gap. J.L. Ralston, the Minister of National Defence, repeatedly called on civilian authorities to make greater efforts to find men for compulsory training throughout 1943 and 1944. Since Quebec had one of the largest and most accessible manpower pools, Ralston wanted efforts concentrated there. He also called for tougher measures to locate defaulters who had not reported for their training when ordered. In both cases, Ralston seemed to be driven partly by his desire to find enough men to fill the Army's needs and partly by wartime perceptions that Quebec was not "doing its share" in the national war effort.[10] Given these factors, it is not surprising that the number of conscripts from Quebec grew disproportionately larger as the war went on.

Another notable feature of the NRMA was the range of languages spoken by its recruits. Table IV provides the languages listed by the men when they enrolled. Since each man is included only once, it can be assumed that he gave the language he was most familiar with; in other words, his mother tongue. The proportion of recruits who spoke French, or French and English, is actually fairly close to the national figures at the time. Even if the first language of all bilingual recruits was French, no more than forty percent of conscripts were francophones. The proportion of men who spoke English was lower than the national figures, and the number of languages other than English or French was considerably higher. Many Zombies were evidently members of minority ethnic groups. This conclusion is supported by the 1944 study of NRMA soldiers mentioned above, which found that twenty-eight percent of men remaining in compulsory service spoke English, twenty percent French, and twenty-three percent French and English. Twenty-five percent were recorded simply as "of other races." The 1944 report estimated that no more than thirty-seven percent of all NRMA men were French-speaking.[11]

Religion was another area where NRMA recruits reflected the general population fairly closely, in that a very large majority were members of Christian religious denominations. The only large difference was between Roman Catholics and Protestants, although it is not clear exactly why this was so. Quebecers made up slightly more than half of all Roman Catholic conscripts, but there were also considerable numbers from Ontario, New Brunswick,

Top: Members of the first class of National Resources Mobilization Act trainees in Brockville, Ontario, October 1940. (Photographer unknown. NA, C-143819)

Bottom: Thirty-day recruits in Camrose, Alberta, during the first compulsory training period, October 1940. (Photographer unknown. NA, C-144127)

Saskatchewan, and Manitoba, compared to the number of Roman Catholics in the general population of each province.[12] Thus, the majority of Catholic conscripts were probably French-speaking, but many were also Canadians of other origins. It is not clear how closely the number for "Other" religions mirrored Canadians in general, since the Army did not differentiate beyond the major religions listed in Table V. A comparable figure for the Canadian population as a whole would be from two to seven percent, still reasonably close to that of the NRMA.

The last four tables provide information on the occupations of conscripts before they entered military service. Table VI lists major industries and Table VII the type of work performed. Tables

VIII and IX compare the top twenty-five occupations for the NRMA and for Canadians more generally. The largest single group of recruits was clearly farmers, accounting for over twenty percent. Labourers made up another fourteen percent. In contrast, professionals and other self-employed or higher-paid workers seem to be under-represented, a conclusion that is not surprising. Many men in occupations classed as skilled or essential did not have to report for training. As already noted, a large majority of conscripts were young single men who probably had not been in the work force long enough to obtain more skilled or higher-paying jobs. As well, people with lower incomes may also have had more difficulty in challenging the large civilian bureaucracy that was created to mobilize the nation during the war. Nonetheless, all occupations were represented by at least a few of the NRMA conscripts.

Taken together, these statistics allow us to make some broad conclusions about the background of the Zombies. Like Canadians in general, most conscripts were born in Canada or other parts of the British Empire. They lived in all parts of the country before being called up. Conscripts were young and came from almost every occupation, although they were most likely to be farmers, labourers, or other skilled or unskilled workers. There was a somewhat higher chance that conscripts were French-speaking, or members of an ethnic minority, but not overly so. For the most part, NRMA soldiers reflected the larger society from which they came.

Describing the statistical background of the Zombies can only provide part of the picture. It is also necessary to see how they spent their months and years of compulsory service. Although few NRMA recruits left any record of their experiences voluminous official sources enable us to gain a broad sense of what they did while in uniform.[13] Since they often served alongside their General Service counterparts, especially as the war progressed, describing their experiences can also provide a sense of what Canadian soldiers underwent during training, as well as on their various home defence duties. From the start, training comprised the largest part of the lives of the Canadian conscripts. For the first few months of the system's operation, attitudes toward conscripts were reasonably lenient, since one purpose of the training was simply to make them familiar with the Army and less wary of being in uniform. But staffs in the camps took their responsibilities to train the men seriously and the training was at least as thorough as that of militia units. Recruits were instructed in foot drill, basic infantry tactics, fieldcraft, and the handling and firing of personal weapons. Most camps ended the thirty-day training period with a lengthy route march. Many trainees were in much improved health when they left the camps and reportedly expressed themselves satisfied with the experience.[14]

The early compulsory training camps also deliberately involved the citizens of their host communities. The most interesting example of this was a telegram from the Minister of National Defence, J.L. Ralston, to each host city, suggesting they all provide bands to the camps for training and entertainment purposes. Most replies were favourable and several towns arranged to supply musicians or instruments.[15] Nearby communities also did a great deal to help make the conscripts comfortable in their new surroundings. They donated books, magazines and newspapers and organized dances, concerts and other entertainment. In addition, every training centre had a Recreation Hut or Canteen that was created and run by one of the four national service groups that were given responsibility for providing for the comforts of Canadian soldiers during the war, namely the YMCA, the Salvation Army, the Canadian Legion, and the Knights of Columbus. Many local newspapers devoted space to describing the activities in the camps. Local radio stations, many of them still in their infancy and trying to fill air time, were also happy to broadcast talent shows and other events from the training centres.[16]

These activities were quite important because Zombies did have spare time. Training was scheduled five days a week, from early in the morning until late afternoon, but then their time was their own. Passes were provided to leave camp for the evening and everyone received at least one weekend pass to visit friends or family during their enrolment period. NRMA men were encouraged to participate in sports and teams were formed from various sub-units in the camps. Other teams competed in nearby city or military leagues. Saturday afternoons were often set aside for track and field competitions or other sporting events. Drill Halls doubled as gymnasiums for basketball, volleyball, boxing, or other pursuits. Almost every camp built a winter skating rink. Hockey was as popular among NRMA men as it was among all Canadians and recruits at one Toronto-area camp were even marched into the city to see a Maple Leafs game.[17]

Aside from community-sponsored events and sports, trainees had other ways to spend their leisure time. Most camps had some kind of movie theatre. Several training centres created camp newspapers to occupy personnel, and classes in French or English were provided in some locations, particularly in Quebec.[18] The religious needs of recruits were also looked after, perhaps more than some trainees wished. Church parades were held every Sunday for Protestant and Roman Catholic recruits on the parade ground, in the Drill Hall, or in local churches. They were usually compulsory. Arrangements were also made for Jewish services when numbers warranted. All camps had at least one chaplain and normally an interdenominational chapel.

After March 1941, the volunteer and NRMA camps were combined and compulsory service was extended for the duration of the war. Notwithstanding, much of the actual training and personal activities remained the same. NRMA camps became Basic Training Centres and the facilities used by those who volunteered for overseas service were converted into Advanced Training Centres. Training in the basic centres focussed on the elementary military skills and physical conditioning necessary to all soldiers. The Advanced Training Centres taught more specific skills—such as driving a tank or leading a patrol—required for the particular branch of the Army the camp supported. Sports and leisure activities continued to be an important component of camp life.

Predicably, the manpower shortage was felt in the training centres. Commanders did as much as they could to differentiate the Zombies and the others. This was done in an attempt to induce conscripts to volunteer for overseas duty. However, there is no evidence to indicate that NRMA men were openly barred from recreational or other facilities or from participating in other events as a result of their status.

At the end of their training, NRMA recruits found themselves posted to operational units across the country. For most of these men, training still seemed to be the main purpose of their existence. Canada was never subjected to a serious attack from land or air during the war, even though the threat existed. Soldiers on home defence duties underwent a continuous round of individual and unit training, as well as large field exercises. For most of the men, boredom was a big challenge. They were normally posted to small, isolated defence posts in British Columbia, eastern Quebec and Atlantic Canada where fewer opportunities existed to hold the concerts, dances, or other social activities they had been exposed to in the training camps. Units in remote areas of B.C. complained of the small number of movies available, and the length of time it took to receive recently released feature films.[19] Isolation was the worst for NRMA men whose first language was not English. Francophone recruits received training in English from the time they were called up and efforts were made to place as many of them as possible in French-speaking units, but there were virtually no other facilities in many areas for men to work in French or any other language other than English.

Trainees in Gordon Head, British Columbia conduct a march past for civilian and military authorities at the conclusion of the third 30-day training period, February 1941. (Photographer unknown. NA, C-144126)

The highlight of service for many conscripts came when four infantry battalions and other supporting units were selected to participate in the American liberation of Kiska, an island in the Aleutians, in 1943. All units spent months training for the task and the law was specifically modified to allow conscripts to serve outside Canada for this operation. They were in a high state of readiness when they landed on Kiska on 16 August, only to find that the Japanese garrison had evacuated the island under cover of fog and bad weather two weeks earlier. The men settled in as best they could and spent four months braving the approach of winter on the cold, barren, wind-swept island. They returned to Canada in late December. The operation marked the first time that Canadian troops had taken part in an operation under US command, as well as the first use of NRMA recruits in a combat situation. Despite their disappointment at finding the island abandoned, the Zombies were praised by Canadian and American commanders for their level of training and their conduct during the operation.[20]

The NRMA during the war years also raises a number of more social questions. One of the more significant issues was the pressure that was put on conscripts to volunteer for overseas service after the two training systems were merged in 1941. During the war, 64,297 NRMA recruits changed their home defence status and deployed outside Canada. The vast majority of these soldiers served in various branches of the Canadian Army.[21] Ralph Allen, a war correspondent for the *Globe and Mail* and a postwar editor of *Maclean's*, made many claims in two novels and a popular history, about physical and psychological abuse that occurred in the camps.[22] But few sources substantiate his charges. The written records of the Department of National Defence provide quite a bit of evidence that the Army realized the potential of the NRMA as a source of active service recruits from the beginning of compulsory training in 1940 and that it deliberately created the four-month training system with this benefit in mind.[23]

One of the best examples of what was considered acceptable behaviour in the camps comes from a commander in Cornwall, who described the first few days of training for one group of men:

> At 1400 hours, an appeal to the "R" recruits to go "Active" was made by me. It was explained to the men that they were in the army for the duration of the war. The benefits of going "Active" were explained. Those who were willing to go active were

Anti-conscription demonstration in Montreal, Quebec, March 1942. (Photographer unknown. NA, PA-108258)

told to form up ten paces in front of their respective companies. About 190 men responded immediately. Five minutes later on, the men were told that a long week-end would be granted to all those who were "Active." About twenty-five more men responded. ... The following day, about 25 more men went "Active." Out of a camp of 1020 men, only 47 remained in the "R" class.[24]

When public appeals and enticements failed to convince the final forty-seven recruits to go active, they were assigned to all the routine tasks of the camp, including cleaning, sentry duty and kitchen fatigues. What happened to them beyond that point was left to recruits to work out for themselves, and the commander of another camp admitted that many minor incidents occurred among recruits when officers were not present.[25]

More extreme evidence of what went on in the camps came in the fall of 1941, when two recruits swore legal affidavits describing their experiences. These included soldiers beating one of the NRMA men unconscious and inflicting an eye injury within sight of two non-commissioned officers. Both his company commander and company sergeant-major reportedly told him that such actions would continue until he volunteered. This case sparked a formal inquiry, which had to be repeated when the Commanding Officer of the training centre did not treat the first investigation seriously enough. No satisfactory explanation was ever found for the eye injury, but the two men eventually retracted their statements and refused to follow up on their accusations.[26] Whether this was due to a lack of honesty on their part, or to pressure on the men to drop their claims is not clear. But something had obviously happened. During the first few training periods in 1941, several camps reported up to one hundred percent of "R" recruits going active, not surprising if methods like those investigated were in regular use.[27] Other common complaints included discrimination in granting permission to leave camp, extra duties for NRMA men, and verbal or other abuse.

Further examples of pressures put on recruits to convert to active service emerged as the months went by. One early problem occurred because only active service volunteers could choose which part of the Army they would train for when they went on to Advanced Training Centres. Several men were misled into volunteering for overseas service in order to enter the branch they wanted, without being told clearly that they were volunteering by doing so.[28] One man's experience of advanced training was intercepted by censors and provides a good summary of events in the eyes of the NRMA men:

> The Commanding Officer has openly boasted that he intends to make it as tough as possible for those who do not intend to join. ... Today we were given a chance to again signify what branch of the service we wished to entered [sic]. Those who did not volunteer were taken on a route march without equipment and also without our water bottles. This is in line with their policy of tough stuff. ... I don't mind going away [to a home defence unit] but the thing that makes me so mad is the "Shit" that we will have to take between now and the time we are supposed to leave ... So far they have got about a third of the Company. I haven't done anything yet and I am at my wits end. God only know[s] how long the rest of the gang can hold out.[29]

As this and other examples show, mistreatment existed within the training camps after 1941, although it is still difficult to judge its extent. Every camp was different. Although it may be unfair to assume that everyone was treated poorly, it is also difficult to ignore the opportunities for abuse inherent in the system. After all, the evidence does indicate that it occurred.

Once the NRMA recruits were posted to home defence units, overt pressures to convert apparently declined. Isolation and lack of activity exerted their own influences. In April 1944, a recruiting drive was launched among home defence troops in eastern and western Canada that netted 2,000 new volunteers. During this campaign, several reasons were advanced to explain why so many other Zombies still refused to go active. It was during these investigations that several senior officers pointed to high numbers of French-speaking and "non-British" recruits among NRMA men. As indicated earlier, there may be some truth to these claims but the numbers were not nearly as large as these reports suggested.[30]

Another cause of resistance described by Army officers was opposition to the government's conscription policies themselves. Considering the accounts of the conscript experience cited above, it is not surprising that they felt this way. Some were also said to be resisting pressures to volunteer in order to force the government to send all able-bodied men overseas. These issues were aggravated by other public criticisms, especially about the large numbers of men who were thought to be evading military service without punishment, as well as other government policies that undercut the claim that military service was the most vital way one could contribute to the war effort.[31]

In May 1944, the Army interviewed 115 NRMA recruits in Southwestern Ontario to investigate why they would not go active. This study provides further insight into the motivations of the Zombies. Over half said that they would not volunteer for personal reasons such as their health or that of family members, pressure from parents or spouses to remain at home, or a personal fear of, or distaste for, the army. Of the remainder, most echoed some of the explanations advanced above and about fifteen percent refused to give any answer at all.[32] Thus, the motives that kept thousands of men in Canada as Zombies were many and complex and cannot be explained with simple answers like their racial or political backgrounds, or the (very real) fear of being killed. Their reasons were much more complicated than that.

In conclusion, Canada's Zombies were a large and varied group of men. Their experience was significant. Aside from remembering the NRMA men in their own right, a case study of them reminds us of the personal consequences of political decisions. These conscripts mirror the larger population of the country and their lives during the war reflect the huge scale on which even a peaceful society like Canada's can be mobilized in an age of total war.

APPENDIX, CHAPTER 8

TABLE I - Approximate Ages of NRMA Recruits on Enrolment
Year of Enrolment

Yr Born	1941	1942	1943	1944	1945	N.S.a	Total(Age)b	%
1899	-	1	-	-	-	-	-	-
1900	-	1	-	-	-	-	-	-
1901	1	9	8	-	-	-	-	-
1902	-	192	201	-	-	-	-	-
1903	-	245	267	1	-	-	-	-
1904	-	302	311	1	-	-	1(43)	0.0
1905	1	360	312	4	-	-	9(42)	0.0
1906	1	345	397	31	-	-	211(41)	0.1
1907	-	479	437	55	3	-	461(40)	0.3
1908	2	602	530	69	9	-	560(39)	0.4
1909	3	851	536	105	9	-	648(38)	0.4
1910	17	960	695	128	17	[1]	821(37)	0.5
1911	6	1202	683	136	21	-	861(36)	0.5
1912	6	1599	844	175	31	-	1132(35)	0.7
1913	5	2158	1117	957	89	-	1287(34)	0.8
1914	14	3098	1498	903	90	-	1715(33)	1.1
1915	137	4449	1607	763	65	-	1910(32)	1.2
1916	345	6142	1595	724	92	-	3110(31)	2.0
1917	1092	8254	1974	509	83	[1]	3690(30)	2.3
1918	4120	9231	1717	498	87	[2]	4517(29)	2.9
1919	14684	6308	1439	450	70	-	5517(28)	3.5
1920	11212	7512	1747	566	114	-	6654(27)	4.2
1921	246	7221	2945	734	129	-	8821(26)	5.6
1922	19	5392	3918	989	149	-	10880(25)	6.9
1923	4	2880	4677	1234	194	[1]	12457(24)	7.9
1924	1	41	4120	2553	294	-	13058(23)	8.3
1925	2	8	650	4998	480	-	26324(22)	16.7
1926	1	6	5	1123	1496	-	23879(21)	15.1
1927	2	5	-	3	5	-	13348(20)	8.4
1928	1	6	1	1	-	-	13513(19)	8.5
1929	3	5	1	-	-	-	1823(18)	1.2
-	-	-	-	-	-	-	51(12-17)	0.0c
N.S.	75	640	77	-	1	5	798(-)	0.5
TOTALS	32000	70504	34309	17710	3528	5	158056d	100.0

a   "Not Stated" on original documents used to compile table.

b   Ages estimated by comparing year of birth to year of enrolment.

c   These age numbers reflect errors apparently made in transcribing original information for tabulation. The total number of errors identified in this table is 386, or 0.2% of all NRMA records.

d   This figure differs slightly from official postwar totals of NRMA recruits due to later elimination of 215 incorrect records.

TABLE II - NRMA Recruits by Place of Residence on Enrolment

Province	NRMA	%	CANADA[a]	%
P.E.I.	919	0.6	95047	0.8
Nova Scotia	6255	4.0	577962	5.0
New Brunswick	7165	4.5	457401	4.0
Quebec	55402	35.1	3331882	29.0
Ontario	45158	28.6	3787655	32.9
Manitoba	9508	6.0	729744	6.3
Saskatchewan	12259	7.8	895992	7.8
Alberta	10475	6.6	796169	7.0
British Columbia	10903	6.9	817861	7.1
Yukon/NWT	-	-	16942	0.1
Newfoundland	3	0.0	-	-
United States	9	0.0	-	-
TOTALS	**158056**	**100**	**11506655**	**100**[b]

Province	1941	%	1942	%	1943	%	1944	%	1945	%
P.E.I.	248	0.8	596	0.8	52	0.2	21	0.1	2	0.0
N.S.	1539	4.8	2870	4.1	1214	3.5	608	3.4	23	0.7
N.B.	1360	4.3	3422	4.9	1782	5.2	469	2.6	132	3.7
Que.	9940	31.1	23270	33.0	11678	34.0	8307	47.0	2207	62.6
Ont.	9777	30.6	21368	30.3	9607	28.0	3956	22.3	446	12.6
Man.	2127	6.6	3664	5.2	2582	7.5	970	5.5	165	4.7
Sask.	2944	9.2	5811	8.2	2575	7.5	774	4.4	155	4.4
Alta.	2442	7.6	4188	5.9	2161	6.3	1390	7.8	294	8.3
B.C.	1621	5.1	5310	7.5	2657	7.7	1212	6.8	1103	3.0
Yukon/NWT	-	-	-	-	-	-	-	-	-	-
Nfld.	-	-	3	0.0	-	-	-	-	-	-
U.S.A.	2	0.0	2	0.0	1	0.0	3	0.0	1	0.0
TOTALS	**32000**	**100**	**70504**	**100**	**34309**	**100**	**17710**	**100**	**3528**	**100**

a   Source: M.C. Urquhart and K.A.H. Buckley, eds., *Historical Statistics of Canada* (Toronto: Macmillan, 1965), Series A2-14.

b   Some percentages do not actually total 100 due to rounding.

TABLE III - NRMA Recruits
by Place of Birth

Place of Birth	NRMA	%ᵃ	CANADAᵇ	%
P.E.I.	965	0.6	108423	0.9
Nova Scotia	6348	4.0	568797	4.9
New Brunswick	7393	4.7	463127	4.0
Quebec	54100	34.2	3155549	27.4
Ontario	36772	23.3	3123810	27.1
Manitoba	10405	6.6	570349	5.0
Saskatchewan	15145	9.6	667832	5.8
Alberta	9064	5.7	479098	4.2
British Columbia	5238	3.3	335554	2.9
Yukon/NWT	9	0.0	12267	0.1
Not Stated but Canadian	-	-	3002	0.0
TOTAL CANADIAN	**145439**	**92.0**	**9487808**	**82.5**
Newfoundland	112	0.0	25837	0.2
England/Wales	1649	1.0	635221	5.5
Scotland	870	0.6	234824	2.0
Ireland	344	0.2	86126	0.7
Australia	17	0.0	N/A	-
Tasmania	1	0.0	N/A	-
New Zealand	1	0.0	N/A	-
Union of South Africa	5	0.0	N/A	-
British Africa	4	0.0	N/A	-
British Guiana	3	0.0	N/A	-
British India	8	0.0	N/A	-
Other British Countries	27	0.0	21761	0.2
TOTAL BRITISH	3041	1.9	1003769	8.7
TOTAL BRITISH BORN	**148480**	**93.9**	**10491577**	**91.2**
United States	1899	1.2	312473	2.7
Mexico	2	0.0	N/A	-
Brazil	3	0.0	N/A	-
Cuba	2	0.0	N/A	-
Equador	1	0.0	N/A	-
Haiti	3	0.0	N/A	-
Argentina	4	0.0	N/A	-
Other South American	5	0.0	N/A	-
TOTAL AMERICAN	**1919**	**1.2**	**312473**	**2.7**
SUB-TOTALS	**150399**	**95.2**	**10804050**	**93.9**

Place of Birth	NRMA	%[a]	CANADA[b]	%
Poland	2091	1.3	155400	1.4
Russia	949	0.6	117598	1.0
Italy	653	0.4	40432	0.4
Czecho-Slovakia	593	0.4	25564	0.2
Hungary	578	0.4	31813	0.3
Germany	394	0.2	28479	0.2
Roumania	326	0.2	28454	0.2
Norway	273	0.2	26914	0.2
Sweden	221	0.1	27160	0.2
Austria	196	0.1	50713	0.4
Denmark	185	0.1	13974	0.1
Finland	163	0.1	24387	0.2
Holland	119	0.1	9923	0.1
Belgium	111	0.1	14773	0.1
Greece	81	0.1	N/A	-
Lithuania	81	0.1	N/A	-
France	40	0.0	13795	0.1
Switzerland	35	0.0	N/A	-
Syria	30	0.0	N/A	-
Bulgaria	15	0.0	N/A	-
Latvia	14	0.0	N/A	-
Turkey	12	0.0	N/A	-
Estonia	10	0.0	N/A	-
Iceland	6	0.0	N/A	-
Albania	3	0.0	N/A	-
Serbia	2	0.0	17416	0.2[c]
Luxembourg	2	0.0	N/A	-
Other	-	-	23298	0.2
TOTAL EUROPEAN	**7183**	**4.5**	**653705**	**5.7**
China	9	0.0	29095	0.3
Siberia	3	0.0	N/A	-
Japan	2	0.0	9462	0.1
Other Asian	6	0.0	5886	0.1
TOTAL ASIAN	**20**	**0.0**	**44443**	**0.4**
Non-British African	2	0.0	N/A	-
NOT STATED	452	0.3	4457	0.0
GRAND TOTALS	**158056**	**100**	**11506655**	**100**

a   Some percentages are not exact, due to rounding of decimals.

b   Source: Canada, Dominion Bureau of Statistics, *Eighth Census of Canada*, 1941 (Ottawa: King's Printer, 1950), Vol 1, Table 23, 668-69.

c   Census figures are for Yugoslavia, the only numbers available.

TABLE IV - Languages of NRMA Recruits

Language	NRMA	%	CANADA[a]	%	CANADA[b]	%
English	59255	37.5	6488190	56.4	7735486	67.2
French	30125	19.1	3354753	29.2	2181746	19.0
Both	33143	21.0	-	-	1474009	12.8
Neither	-	-	-	-	115414	1.0
German	6470	4.1	322228	2.8	-	-
Polish	3766	2.4	128711	1.1	-	-
Italian	3033	1.9	80260	0.7	-	-
Russian	1038	0.7	52431	0.5	-	-
Spanish	50	0.0	1030	0.0	-	-
Chinese	38	0.0	33500	0.3	-	-
Japanese	2	0.0	22359	0.2	-	-
Other	19310	12.2	1021546	8.9	-	-
Not Given	1826	1.2	1647	0.0	-	-
TOTALS	**158056**	**100**	**11506655**	**100**	**11506655**	**100**

a   Figures are based on mother tongues listed by census respondents, in F.H. Leacy, ed., *Historical Statistics of Canada*, Second Ed.(Ottawa: Statistics Canada, 1983), Series A185-237, and *Census of Canada, 1941*, Vol 1, Table 45, 710.

b   Numbers from *Census of Canada*, 1941, Vol 1, Table 38, 700-1, which provides information only on ability to speak Canada's two official languages, English and French.

TABLE V - Religion of NRMA Recruits

Religion	NRMA	%	CANADA[a]	%
United Church	20268	12.8	2208658	19.2
Methodist	813	0.5	N/A	-[b]
Congregational	6	0.0	N/A	-[b]
Anglican	13991	8.9	1754368	15.2
Lutheran	7428	4.7	401836	3.5
Presbyterian	7070	4.5	830597	7.2
Baptist	5381	3.4	484465	4.2
Salvation Army	172	0.1	33609	0.3
TOTAL PROTESTANT	55129	34.9	5713533	49.7
ROMAN CATHOLIC	91320	57.8	4806431	41.8
JEWISH	3479	2.2	168585	1.5
Other Protestant	-	-	231688	2.0
Greek/Ukrainian	-	-	325793	2.8
Other	6709	4.2	243466	2.1
TOTAL "OTHER"	6709	4.2	800947	7.0
Not Stated	922	0.6	17159	0.1
No Religion	497	0.3	-	-
TOTALS	**158056**	**100**	**11506655**	**100**

a   Source: Urquhart and Buckley, eds., *Historical Statistics of Canada*, Series A114-132.

b   Included in figures for United Church.

TABLE VI - NRMA Recruits by Industry Group[a]

Industry Group	NRMA	%	CANADA[b]	%
AGRICULTURE	38318	24.2	1062928	31.6
EXTRACTIVE INDUSTRIES	9451	6.0	236302	7.0
Forestry	3953	2.5	93313	2.8
Fishing and Trapping	1958	1.2	50533	1.5
Mining	3540	2.2	92456	2.7
MANUFACTURING	35184	22.3	735097	21.9
Food/Beverages/Tobacco	4079	2.6	87979	2.6
Leather and Rubber Products	1556	1.0	32392	1.0
Textiles/Clothing	2086	1.3	76294	2.3
Wood/Paper/Publishing	4531	2.9	160327	4.8
Metal/Machinery/Transport	15265	9.7	309763	9.2
Chemical/Petroleum/Minerals	833	0.5	51670	1.5
Other	6834	4.3	16672	0.5
TRANSPORTATION	18575	11.8	246835	7.3
Railways	5327	3.4	123514	3.7
Other	13248	8.4	123321	3.7
CONSTRUCTION	11663	7.4	218732	6.5
RETAIL AND WHOLESALE TRADE	6928	4.4	384046	11.4
FINANCE/INSURANCE/REAL ESTATE	731	0.5	61311	1.8
ELECTRICAL AND GAS UTILITIES	107	0.1	21134	0.6
SERVICE INDUSTRIES	11111	7.0	355657	10.6
Education	1824	1.2	35872	1.1
Health and Welfare	284	0.2	27998	0.8
Food and Lodging	2023	1.3	58312	1.7
Personal and Recreational	3999	2.5	59955	1.8
Government	896	0.6	111634	3.3
Other	2085	1.3	61886	1.8
NOT STATED/INSUFFICIENT DATA	25988	16.4[c]	41069	1.2
GRAND TOTALS	**158056**	**100**	**3363111**	**100**

a   Industrial classifications are from census guidelines in Canada, Dominion Bureau of Statistics, *Classification of Industries and Services*, Seventh Census, 1931, and *Classification of Industries*, Eighth Census, 1941 (Ottawa: King's Printer, 1931 and 1941).

b   Figures provided are for gainfully employed males. See Leacy, ed., *Historical Statistics of Canada*, Second Ed., Series D8-85.

c   Includes 19,511 unspecified recruits listed as Labourers or Workers, and 5110 clerks and other office workers.

TABLE VII - NRMA Recruits by Occupation[a]

Occupational Category	NRMA	%	CANADA[b]	%
Owners and Managers	2436	1.5	212460	6.3
Professional Occupations	3570	2.3	150379	4.5
Clerical and Sales Workers	14705	9.3	308342	9.2
Operatives	76047	48.1	1375879	40.9
Farmers and Farm Workers	38734	24.5	1061896	31.6
Labourers	21950	13.9	254155	7.6
Not Stated/Insufficient Data	614	0.4	-	-
GRAND TOTALS	**158056**	**100**	**3363111**	**100**

a   Occupational classifications listed in Canada, Dominion Bureau of Statistics, *Classification of Occupations*, Eighth Census, 1941 (Ottawa: King's Printer, 1941).

b   Includes only gainfully employed males, as listed in Leacy, ed., *Historical Statistics of Canada*, Second Ed., Series D8-85.

TABLE VIII - Top Twenty-Five Occupations of NRMA Recruits

Rank	As Listed by NRMA[a]	No.	%[b]	By Census Category[c]	No.	%[b]
1.	Farmer	31986	20.2	Farmers and Stock Raisers	32592	20.6
2.	Labourer	19482	12.3	Non-Farm Labourer	21950	13.9
3.	Truck Driver	8300	5.3	Truck Drivers	8300	5.3
4.	Clerk	4117	2.6	Office Clerks	6467	4.1
5.	Machinists	4054	2.6	Farm Labour (All)	5676	3.6
6.	Mechanics	3548	2.2	Mechanics and Repairmen	5234	3.3
7.	Farm Labourer	3178	2.0	Machinists (All)	4133	2.6
8.	Carpenter	2532	1.6	Store Salespersons	3918	2.5
9.	Other Miners	2468	1.6	Lumbermen (All)	3818	2.4
10.	Apple Packer	2157	1.4	Miners and Millmen	3245	2.1
11.	Store Clerk	2077	1.3	Carpenters (All)	2659	1.7
12.	Machine Operator	1947	1.2	Machine Operators	2100	1.3
13.	Fishermen	1774	1.1	Welders (All)	2088	1.3
14.	Painters	1669	1.1	Painters/Glaziers	1892	1.2
15.	Butcher	1629	1.0	Clothing/Textiles	1792	1.1
16.	Electricians	1528	1.0	Fishermen	1774	1.1
17.	Salesman	1436	0.9	Electricians (All)	1673	1.1
18.	Welder	1388	0.9	Retail Owners/Mgrs	1630	1.0
19.	Shippers	1343	0.8	Butchers	1629	1.0
20.	Students	1185	0.7	Shipping Clerks	1610	1.0
21.	Other Iron & Steel Workers	1101	0.7	Woodworkers and Turners	1334	0.8
22.	Woodsman	1071	0.7	Students (All)	1197	0.8
23.	Plumbers	909	0.6	Iron/Steel Workers	1101	0.7
24.	Logger	886	0.6	Sheet Metal Workers and Tinsmiths	988	0.6
25.	Lumbermen	877	0.6	Plumbers	909	0.6
TOTALS		**102333**	**64.7**		**119709**	**75.8**

a   This column ranks occupations by the individual titles under which they were listed in NRMA records.

b   Percentage of all NRMA recruits enrolled during the war (158056).

c   Information in this column is arranged using the 1941 census classifications (*Classification of Occupations*, op.cit.).

TABLE IX - Top Twenty-Five Male Occupations in Canada, 1941[a]

Rank	Occupational Category	Number	% of Workforce[b]
1.	Farmers and stockraisers	630709	18.8
2.	Farm labourers	431102	12.8
3.	Labourers (not farm, forest,fishing, or mining)	251889	7.5
4.	Office clerks	110043	3.3
5.	Owners, managers, dealers-retail	100756	3.0
6.	Carpenters	90470	2.7
7.	Truck drivers	81304	2.4
8.	Salespersons in stores	81270	2.4
9.	Lumbermen	74000	2.2
10.	Mechanics and repairmen	67246	2.0
11.	Miners and millmen	51503	1.5
12.	Operatives - metal products manu.	49052	1.5
13.	Machinists - metal	43077	1.3
14.	Painters, decorators, glaziers	39058	1.2
15.	Fishermen	33273	1.0
16.	Accountants and auditors	31384	0.9
17.	Owners and managers - manufacturing	30633	0.9
18.	Commercial travellers	29882	0.9
19.	Stationary enginemen	29792	0.9
20.	Operatives - clothing and textiles	25640	0.8
21.	Sectionmen and trackmen	24422	0.7
22.	Shipping clerks	23044	0.7
23.	Electricians and wiremen	22121	0.7
24.	Teachers-school	21988	0.7
25.	Guards and caretakers	20815	0.6
TOTALS		**2394473**	**71.2**

a   Source: Census of Canada, 1941, Table 61, 772-73.

b   Gainfully occupied males (total - 3,363,111).

Notes for Chapter 8

1   This chapter was originally presented as part of the 4th Military History Colloquium of the Université de Québec à Montréal, on 7 November 1997, and appeared in French as "Les 'zombies' du Canada: un portrait des conscrits canadiens et de leur expérience durant la Deuxième Guerre mondiale," *Bulletin d'histoire politique* 8, nos. 2-3 (2000), 184-204. The author would like to thank the participants of the conference and several other readers who have commented on previous drafts. Research for this chapter was aided by doctoral fellowships from the Social Sciences and Humanities Research Council of Canada and the Department of National Defence (Strategic Defence Forum).

2   Previous studies of conscription in the Second World War include: E.L.M. Burns, *Manpower in the Canadian Army, 1939-1945* (Toronto: Clarke, Irwin and Company, 1956); R. MacGregor Dawson, *The Conscription Crisis of 1944* (Toronto: University of Toronto Press, 1961); J.L. Granatstein, *Conscription in the Second World War: A Study in Political Management* (Toronto: Ryerson Press, 1969); C.P. Stacey, *Arms, Men and Governments: The War Policies of Canada, 1939-1945* (Ottawa: Queen's Printer, 1970); and J.L. Granatstein and J.M. Hitsman, *Broken Promises: A History of Conscription in Canada* (Toronto: Oxford University Press, 1977). For the two sides of the debate in Quebec, see also Norman Ward, ed., *A Party Politician: The Memoirs of Chubby Power* (Toronto: Macmillan, 1966); and André Laurendeau, *La crise de la conscription, 1942* (1962), transl. Philip Stratford, in *André Laurendeau: Witness for Quebec* (Toronto: Macmillan, 1973). Most of these accounts focus on the political implications of conscription, however, rather than more personal aspects such as how it affected the conscripts themselves.

3   Of the 2,463 conscripts who were posted to operational units, 69 died, 232 were wounded, and 13 became prisoners of war. For these numbers see Stacey, *Arms, Men and Governments*, 481-82, and Granatstein and Hitsman, *Broken Promises,* 234, which also provide the two best discussions of conscription during the war.

4   For a more detailed discussion of the Army's administration of conscription during the war, see Daniel Byers, "Mobilising Canada: The National Resources Mobilization Act, the Department of National Defence, and Compulsory Military Service in Canada, 1940-1945," *Journal of the Canadian Historical Association* Vol 7 (1996), 175-203.

5   Stacey, *Arms, Men and Governments*, Appendix T, 599-602. This number may not include some men called up for thirty-day training early on, although most were recalled for further training after the program was extended to four months in 1941.

6   These statistics are available in an unprocessed collection of material from the Canadian Army's Directorate of Records, which are held as part of the records of the Department of National Defence, Record Group 24 (hereafter RG 24), National Archives of Canada (NA), Ottawa, Ontario. I am indebted to Tim Cook and Paul Marsden of the National Archives of Canada for locating these records for me, which had not yet been formally accessioned or catalogued at the time of writing of this chapter.

7   For a detailed breakdown of the various age classes in use during the war, see Burns, 146, and Stacey, *Arms, Men and Governments*, Appendix N, 586. By government regulation, all men married after 15 July 1940 were considered to be "single" for the purposes of mobilizing men under the NRMA.

8   Figures available in Report of Cabinet Committee on Army Enlistment for General Service, 6 November 1944, General Staff Memoranda ... October-November 1944, Box 39, C.G. Power Papers, Queen's University Archives, Kingston, Ontario. Of the 37 percent of recruits from outside central Canada, 6 percent came from the Maritimes, 24 percent from the Prairies, and 7 percent from British Columbia.

9   Quebec had 304,420 single men between 15 and 24 and 111,916 aged 25-34 in 1941, or roughly 30 percent of all single male Canadians in each age group. Ontario's totals were 302,473 and 111,083—also 30 percent, or slightly less than the province's share of the population as a whole. For these figures, see Canada, Dominion Bureau of Statistics, *Eighth Census of Canada, 1941* (Ottawa: King's Printer, 1950), Vol I, Table 20, 641-52.

10 As one memorandum by wartime journalist Grant Dexter suggests, Ralston and other politicians were well aware of the equal division of manpower between Quebec and Ontario as early as December 1941. At that point, Ralston actually viewed conscription more as a way to put English-speaking men into uniform, since the Army had fewer facilities to train French-speaking recruits had more of them called up. Frederick W. Gibson and Barbara Robertson, eds., *Ottawa at War: The Grant Dexter Memoranda, 1939-1945* (Winnipeg: Manitoba Record Society, 1994), 231-33. On relations between Ralston and civilian mobilization authorities in 1943-44 and his increased focus on finding men from Quebec, see Stacey, *Arms, Men and Governments*, 413-15 and 430-32, and Granatstein and Hitsman, *Broken Promises*, 201-3.

11 Report of Cabinet Committee on Army Enlistment for General Services, in Power Papers.

12 Quebecers made up 56.4 percent of all Roman Catholic NRMA recruits, and 60.2 percent of Roman Catholics in Canada as a whole. Corresponding figures for Ontario are 18.4 percent and 17.8 percent; for New Brunswick, 5.1 percent and 4.6 percent; Manitoba, 5.6 percent and 2.9 percent; and Saskatchewan, 5.4 percent and 4.2 percent. For further details, see "N.R.M.A. All Ranks by Religion on Enrolment," Appendix G1 of Directorate of Records material, RG 24, NAC, as well as *Census of Canada, 1941*, Vol I, Table 50, 720-27.

13 Unless otherwise noted, this description of the NRMA is drawn from the War Diaries of various training centres and operational units where conscripts served during the war (including a complete reading of all Basic Training Centres for their first two years of operation, 1940-1942), all of which are located in RG 24 of the National Archives of Canada. For a more extended discussion of these issues, see also Chapter Two of my doctoral dissertation, "Mobilizing Canada: The Department of National Defence, the National Resources Mobilization Act, and Compulsory Military Service in Canada, 1940-1945," McGill University, 2001.

14 For example, see the following war diary entries and newspaper clippings: "Le Centre d'entrainement militaire de Chicoutimi," *Le Progrès du Saguenay,* 10 Oct 1940; Appendix II, War Diary, No. 51 Canadian Army (Basic) Training Centre [CA(B)TC], Chicoutimi, Quebec, October 1940, Vol 17233, RG 24, NA; entry for 29 October 1940, No. 71 CA(B)TC, Edmunston, New Brunswick, Vol 17258, RG 24, NA; 6 November 1940, No. 47 CA(B)TC, Valleyfield, Quebec, Vol 17225, RG 24, NA; "Trainees Opposed To Camp Life Change Opinions As Time Passes," unlabelled newspaper clipping, 7 November 1940, Appendix 4, No. 32 CA(B)TC, Peterborough, Ontario, October 1940, Vol 17194, RG 24, NA; "Report on Training," 9 November 1940, Appendix C, No. 130 CA(B)TC, Red Deer, Alberta, October 1940, Vol 17093, RG 24, NA; untitled clipping from *Le Petit Journal,* 10 novembre 1940, giving views of recruits from Montreal-area training centres, Appendix 4, No. 40 CA(B)TC, Farnham, Quebec, November 1940, Vol 17021, RG 24, NA; "A Nice Little Story About Militia Camp," *Camrose Canadian,* 20 November 1940, Appendix C, No. 131 CA(B)TC, Camrose, Alberta, November 1940, Vol 17290, RG 24, NA; entries for 22-23 November and 21 December 1940, No. 111 CA(R[eserve])TC [this title was used for all NRMA camps until March 1941—a few were then put to other uses and never changed to CA(B)TC], Gordon Head, British Columbia, Vol 17306, RG 24, NA; entry for 12 December 1940, No. 44 CA(B)TC, St. Jerome, Quebec, Vol 16912, RG 24, NA; "Report on Training," 22 December 1940, No. 110 CA(B)TC, Vernon, B.C., Vol 17277, RG 24, NA; and excerpts from camp newsletter (*Kamp Pain*): Appendix 8, December 1940, pp. 17-19, and Appendix 7, January 1941, pp. 14-15, in No. 132 CA(B)TC, Grande Prairie, Alberta, Vols. 17295-96, RG 24, NA.

15 For a copy of Ralston's telegram, see circular letter, Adjutant-General to District Officers Commanding various Canadian Military Districts, 19 September 1940, File HQ 1161-1-5, vol 3, in Vol 6571, RG 24, NA. This file also contains replies from various mayors, dated 19 September-3 October 1940, and other correspondence related to this subject up to 7 November 1940.

16 For two very good summaries of events in the training centres, see "Items of Interest During the Second Training Period," War Diary, No. 110 CA(B)TC, Vernon, B.C., December 1940, Vol 17277, RG 24, NA, and monthly summary of activities, Appendix D, No. 21 CA(R)TC, Long Branch, Ontario, January 1941, Vol 17304, RG 24, NA. See also comments in monthly summaries for October and November 1940, located in War Diary, No. 102 CA(B)TC, Fort William, Ontario, Vol 17269, RG 24, NA.

17 Entry for 29 January 1941, War Diary, No. 21 CA(R)TC, Long Branch, Ontario, Vol 17304, RG 24, NA.

18 For examples of newspapers, see first issues in the following War Diaries, all located in RG 24, NA: *Le "Petard",* 18 October 1940, Appendix 2, No. 42 CA(B)TC, Joliette, Quebec, October 1940, Vol 17205; *Le Chevalier,* 23 November 1940, Appendix 8, No. 44 CA(B)TC, St. Jerome, Quebec, November 1940, Vol 16912; and *Kamp Pain,* n.d. [December 1940], Appendix 8, No. 132 CA(B)TC, Grande Prairie, Alberta, December 1940, Vol 17295. Later examples include *Chins Up,* n.d. [April 1941], Appendix 5, No. 12 CA(B)TC, Chatham, Ontario, April 1941, Vol 17148; *Le Fort Richelieu,*

7 April 1941, Appendix V, No. 45 CA(B)TC, Sorel, Quebec, April 1941, Vol 17221; and *The Centurion,* 1 July 1941, Appendix 5, No. 100 CA(B)TC, Portage la Prairie, Manitoba, November 1941, Vol 17265. For examples of language classes, see War Diary entries for 2 May 1941, No. 53 CA(B)TC, Lauzon, Quebec, Vol 17236; 17 June 1941, No. 44 CA(B)TC, St. Jerome, Vol 16913; 25 September 1941, No. 42 CA(B)TC, Joliette, Vol 17207; and 21 January 1942, No. 51 CA(B)TC, Chicoutimi, Vol 17234.

19 See, in particular, the comment in the War Diary of the Assistant Adjutant and Quartermaster General, 6th Canadian Division, 6 May 1943, Vol 13802, Microfilm Reel T-10560, RG 24, NA. Also Headquarters, 13th Canadian Infantry Brigade, 19 January 1942, Vol 14164, Reel T-12398; 15th Canadian Infantry Brigade, 15 October 1943, Vol 14171, Reel T-12404; and 14th Canadian Infantry Brigade, 24 April and 13 May 1944, Vol 14169, Reel T-12403.

20 For a description of events on Kiska, see Brigadier H.W. Foster to H.Q. Pacific Command, 3 September 1943: "Report on KISKA Operation, 13 Cdn Inf Bde," File 595.013(D3), Directorate of History and Heritage [hereafter DHH], Department of National Defence, Ottawa, Ontario; G.W.L. Nicholson, "The Canadian Participation in the Kiska Operation," 11 December 1943, File 595.013(D4), DHH; and War Diary, 13th Canadian Infantry Brigade, June 1943-January 1944, Vol 14165, RG 24, NAC. Also C.P. Stacey, *Six Years of War: The Army in Canada, Britain and the Pacific* (Ottawa: Queen's Printer, 1955), 492-505, Reginald H. Roy, *For Most Conspicuous Bravery: A Biography of Major-General George R. Pearkes, V.C., through two World Wars* (Vancouver: University of British Columbia Press, 1977), 184-96, and two unpublished theses by Galen R. Perras: "An Aleutian Interlude: Canadian Participation in the Recapture of the Island of Kiska," M.A., Royal Military College of Canada, 1986, and "Stepping Stones on a Road to Nowhere? The United States, Canada, and the Aleutian Island Campaign, 1942-1943," Ph.D., University of Waterloo, 1995.

21 Stacey, *Arms, Men and Governments,* Appendix T, 600-602. Among NRMA men converting to active service, 58,434 went to the Army, 5,082 to the Air Force, 747 to the Navy, and 34 to other Allied forces.

22 See Ralph Allen, *Home Made Banners (*Toronto: Longmans, Green and Co., 1946), *The High White Forest* (New York: Doubleday, 1964), and *Ordeal by Fire: Canada, 1910-1945* (Toronto: Doubleday Canada, 1961), especially 393-94.

23 The remainder of this chapter relies heavily on the account provided in my earlier article, "Mobilising Canada," 184-202, as well as my larger doctoral dissertation, where these issues are developed in greater depth.

24 Lieutenant-Colonel R. Larose, Officer Commanding, Canadian Army Basic Training Centre #31, Cornwall, Ontario, to District Officer Commanding, Military District No. 3, 5 February 1942, in "Compulsory Training —NRMA, 1942: pressure on recruits to go active, regulations. April 1941-March 1942," Vol 68, Manuscript Group [MG] 27, III, B11, Papers of James Layton Ralston, NA.

25 Lieutenant-Colonel E.M. Ansell, Officer Commanding, No. 12 Basic Training Camp, Chatham, to Col. W.H. Kippen, Military

District No. 1, 19 February 1942, File HQ 1161-1-18, vol 2, Vol 80, RG 24, NA.

26 See statements by J. Albert Lefebvre and Joseph Robert Miville, 7 September 1941, Ibid., as well as reports by District Officer Commanding, Military District No. 3, 8 and 11 October 1941; Adjutant-General to District Officer Commanding, Military District No. 3, 30 October 1941; Adjutant-General to J.L. Ralston, 12 December 1941; Ralston to J.L. Thorsen, Minister of National War Services, 18 December 1941; and other documents on the same file related to this case.

27 For example, Cornwall, Ontario had 100 percent of NRMA recruits convert to active service in two successive training periods during 1941, and all but one recruit did so in another class a year later. Peterborough, Ontario also saw 100 percent of recruits go active in one training period in 1941, while Newmarket, Kitchener and Chatham all had rates of over 90 percent. See the following War Diary entries for these training centres in RG 24, NA: 2-5 July and 11 August 1941, and 21 April 1942, No. 31 CA(B)TC, Cornwall, Vols. 17189-90; 16 September 1941, No. 32 CA(B)TC, Peterborough, Vol 17195; 26 July 1941, No. 23 CA(B)TC, Newmarket, Vol 17168; 16 September, No. 10 CA(B)TC, Kitchener 1941, Vol 17145; and 26 November 1941, No. 12 CA(B)TC, Chatham, Vol 17149.

28 Several examples of such complaints are available in various correspondence for the period between 27 June and 9 October 1941 in HQ 1161-1-18, vols. 1-2, Vol 80, RG 24, NA.

29 Letter from Camp Borden, Ontario [details severed by censor], 9 July 1941, Ibid., vol 1.

30 On these events see papers in File 322.009(D50): "Brigade Groups—Pacific Cmd—Org & Admin— Sep 43/Sep 44," DHH, and particularly the report of Brigadier W.H.S. Macklin, Commander 13th Canadian Infantry Brigade, to General Officer Commanding-in-Chief, Pacific Command, 2 May 1944: "Mobilization of 13 Bde on an Active Basis." Also documents on file "Recruiting for Overseas 1944: Camp Vernon, B.C., Pacific Command, April-June," Vol 81, Ralston Papers, NAC; War Diaries, April-May 1944, for the Dufferin and Haldimand Rifles (Vol 15054, RG 24, NAC), Le Régiment de Joliette (Vol 15184), and Le Régiment de Montmagny (Vol 15189); Stacey, *Arms, Men and Governments,* 428-30 (where Macklin's report on recruiting is also reproduced in full, in Appendix "S", 591-98); Granatstein and Hitsman, *Broken Promises*, 204-7; and Roy, *Pearkes*, 209-16.

31 Macklin, "Mobilization of 13 Bde...". See also the appendices to Macklin's report, which give the views of various subordinates on the reasons why conscripts would not go active.

32 Records from A-29 Canadian Infantry Training Centre, 9-12 May 1944, "N.R.M.A.— MD 1 Nov/Dec 1944," File 161.009(D8), DHH. Of the 115 men interviewed, 21 replied that they had to stay in Canada to care for ailing parents or to help their families in other ways, and 12 would not enlist because of pressures from parents or spouses. Seventeen men reported that they had volunteered but been rejected by one of the military services, or that their health was too poor to withstand intensive training. Another 17 refused to answer any questions, and 11 more declared that they would not go active for any reason. Sixteen recruits said that they did not like the Army, or opposed enlisting as infantry. Seven explained that they wanted to remain in Canada and earn money as long as other men were able to do so, and 5 declared that they supported conscription, but wanted to force the government to send everyone overseas. Of the last 9 recruits, 3 agreed to go active, 3 said they would volunteer as soon as family problems were put in order in Canada, 2 agreed to reconsider, and the last was an American citizen who was prepared to enlist as long as it would not affect his citizenship. These restricted records were kindly provided to the author on condition that the contents be used only in anonymous aggregate form.

CHAPTER 9

Rallying Canada's Immigrants Behind the War Effort

1939-1945

N.F. Dreisziger

IN SEPTEMBER OF 1939 CANADA was unprepared for involvement in another world war. The country's military was not ready for overseas combat, or even for the defence of Canadian soil, had it been necessary. Furthermore, the country's economy was not in position to mount a war effort without first undergoing significant change and expansion.[1] But Canada was ill-equipped for involvement in a major international crisis in other respects as well. Her government had done precious little to prepare the Canadian public for the onset of war and the multitude of commitments that this implied. In particular, and this relates directly to the subject of this study, the administration of Prime Minister Mackenzie King had done nothing to prepare for the crisis the masses of immigrants who had come to the country since the previous war, often from lands that were, or would soon be, under enemy control. One of the aims of this chapter is to examine how the Canadian government came to realize this gap in its war preparations and how it tried to bridge it. Another goal of this paper is to point out that, just as the war resulted in massive intervention by the Canadian state in the country's economic affairs, it also brought intervention in the everyday lives of the country's population, including those of its immigrants. Much of this intervention manifested itself in police measures, but some of it was more positive in approach and concentrated not on compulsion but on persuasion. This study will focus mainly on the latter and will outline among other things how, after September 1939, government propaganda began to touch the lives of Canadians, including for the first time those of the foreign-born.

Although in retrospect the supplying of Canadian immigrants with "wartime information" appears to have been a haphazard and ineffective affair, by the time the war was over the government's pre-war *laissez-faire* approach to matters concerning immigrants had become discredited. The ultimate consequence of Canada's wartime experience in this respect was that in the post-war period the Canadian state was ready to embark on dealing with newcomers in a manner that was much more interventionist than had been the case before the war. Accordingly, this chapter will try to reinforce the argument that the interventionist Canadian state was born—re-born if we keep in mind the country's experience during the First World War—out of the ashes of the world conflagration of 1939-45.[2] This new interventionism was not confined to matters of high economic policy but touched myriad aspects of Canadian life, including the lives of the country's immigrants. The war therefore acted as an important agent in the forging of the modern Canada, and the policies toward immigrant groups that the conflict engendered presaged the time decades later when Canadian governments would endorse the tolerance of ethnic differences and undertake the promotion of multiculturalism. All of this seems to have started with a quest for winning the hearts and minds of Canada's immigrants during the darkest hours of the Second World War.

From the last decades of the nineteenth century to the middle of the twentieth, the Canadian strategy of forging a viable nation-state in the northern half of the North American continent was rooted in the national policies of tariff protection, immigration and railway development. These policies were interrelated and interdependent. The policy of fostering Canada's demographic growth through the encouragement of immigration[3] was an essential element of nation-building without which the other two national policies could not have been effective. Tariff protection, which was to promote the growth of industry and of local markets, would have been useless without the growth of the labour force and the creation of a substantial population. The development of railways could not take place without the influx of labour to supply a workforce for both railway construction and the secondary industries fostered by it. At the same time the railways' viability depended on the expansion of settlement and greater agricultural production as well as the expansion of natural resource extraction—all generating increased movement of goods and people throughout this vast country.

Canada's leaders, from Sir John A. Macdonald to William Lyon Mackenzie King, understood this perfectly well. With the exception of times of severe national or international crises, the administrations of all of Canada's major prime ministers encouraged immigration. The results, when looked upon from the perspective of three generations, can only be described as spectacular. It was in large part as a consequence of these policies that the Canadian West was peopled and the country's labour force doubled and then tripled. Canada's population grew from around four million at the time of Confederation to over 14 million by the time of the first census after the Second World War.[4] An indication of the substantial impact of immigration on these processes is the fact that from 1911 to 1931 every census revealed that nearly a quarter of Canada's population belonged to the category of "foreign-born."[5] Although in some parts of the country such as rural Quebec and the Maritimes the proportion of newcomers was low, in others, in particular the Canadian West and some industrial centres, it was very high.

At the time of Confederation and for some time after it, most immigrants to Canada came from the United Kingdom.[6] In the course of time, an ever increasing percentage of newcomers to Canada originated in parts of Europe other than the United Kingdom.[7] By the turn of the century, immigrants began to arrive from Central and Eastern Europe. Though much has been written about the "peasants in sheepskin coats" who came to the country from such hitherto unheard-of places as Galicia, Vojvodina etc., the non-British newcomers to Canada before the First World War were always in the minority. Nevertheless, the proportion of peoples such as Germans, Scandinavians and Italians kept steadily increasing, starting a trend which would eventually see the gradual alteration of the country's ethnic make-up.

These new trends persisted through the interwar years. Newcomers to Canada increasingly came not so much from the British Isles and Western Europe, but from Central and Eastern Europe. What would become important during the Second World War was the fact that so many of these newcomers originated in countries that would become Axis lands in the period from 1938 to 1941.

Mass immigration to Canada was slow to resume after the conclusion of the Great War in 1918. The post-war recessions and anti-foreigner sentiments stirred up by the war made the full re-opening of Canada's gates impossible. Only with the improvement of the economy and the gradual subsiding of nativistic feelings was a full-scale continuation of the national policy of immigration possible.[8] By 1925 economic expansion was outpacing immigration and the government in Ottawa implemented the notorious Railway Agreement that empowered the Canadian National and Canadian Pacific Railways to recruit and transport immigrants to Canada. Though the railways were supposed to encourage immigration from "preferred" lands such as Britain, the US and Western Europe, in their eagerness to increase the supply of cheap labour in the country, they brought people from wherever they could get them in great numbers.[9]

Recruiting prospective immigrants in Central and Eastern Europe in the second half of the 1920s did not prove difficult. The region had gone through the turmoil of war and post-war social and political upheaval, which had seen the collapse of the German, the Hapsburg and the Tsarist Russian empires, as well as the resulting massive re-drawing of political boundaries. The post-war peace treaties with Germany, Austria, Hungary and Bulgaria resulted in the transfer of millions of people to the newly-created or enlarged countries of Poland, Czechoslovakia, Yugoslavia, or Rumania (the latter three making up what was known as the Little Entente). Furthermore, in the early post-war years, many countries experienced large-scale political turmoil. The overall consequence of these developments was that more people were eager to leave these parts of Europe than before 1914.

More often than not, the members of this new immigration to Canada hailed from the newly-created ethnic minorities in the above-mentioned countries. In the interwar years minority Germans came to Canada from Poland and Czechoslovakia, German-speaking Austrians from northern Yugoslavia, and the Danube Germans (who had lived scattered throughout the former eastern Habsburg lands) from most of East-Central Europe. Hungarians who after the war had found themselves living under foreign rule came from all three countries of the Little Entente.

Minority Ukrainians emigrated from the impoverished provinces of southeastern Poland and northern Rumania, driven by a combination of political and economic motives.[10] An important reason for these newcomers not encountering major obstacles in leaving their native lands was precisely their minority status. The newly-emerged or enlarged states of Eastern Europe were reluctant to permit the emigration of members of the dominant nationality, but had no problem with, in fact might have been glad to see, the departure of members of potentially troublesome minorities.

By the early 1930s, Canada had become home to a great many Germans, Austrians, Hungarians, Ukrainians, Finns, etc., as well as other Central and Eastern Europeans (such as Italians and Rumanians) who were primarily economic migrants. Census data illustrates the rapid growth of these groups. In the 1921-1931 period, for example, the proportion of Canadian residents born in Germany rose by 55 percent; those born in Finland, by close to 150 percent, those born in Hungary, by over 280 percent.[11] The irony was that during the Second World War, a great majority of these newcomers, including even the Ukrainians, fell into the category of "potential enemies" of the Canadian, that is, the Allied war effort.

Perhaps the most useful statistics about the foreign-born element in Canada are provided in the census of the prairie provinces of 1936.[12] This census puts the number of people with German origin in Manitoba at 52,450, in Alberta at 90,961, and in Saskatchewan at 165,549. In this latter province they were the second largest "racial" group, outnumbered only by the English.[13] These numbers, however, do not tell the full story. While people of German ethnicity were numerous in the Canadian West, people born in the territories of the Third Reich itself were rather low in number. A large portion of the prairies' German settlers had in fact been born elsewhere, a great many of them in Canada; that is, many were second generation ethnics.[14] Only about 8,300 members of Saskatchewan's large German immigrant community, for example, had been born in Germany; the rest had come from "Russia" (17,182), Poland (4,129), Rumania (3,232) and other Central and Eastern European countries.[15] This trend of the members of a potential enemy alien group not having been born in the country that became an enemy nation during the Second World War was far less evident in the case of some enemy groups (for example the Hungarians) and was absent in the case of the Italians, Finns, Rumanians and others. Notwithstanding the fact that only a small portion of wartime Canada's "enemy ethnic" population would be Third Reich-born, the country's authorities and the members of its general public could worry after the onset of war about so many of the foreign-born in the country having links, through heritage, former residence or otherwise, to the enemy. Not surprisingly, the "enemy alien problem" became a major domestic issue during the war, especially at times when shadows were cast over the entire Allied war effort and a threat was perceived even to Canada's own territory.

While Canadian governments from the time of Macdonald to that of Mackenzie King were interested in promoting immigration to Canada, they were less interested in easing the acculturation processes that newcomers had to undergo after their arrival here. Once immigrants stepped off the train in Winnipeg or some smaller centre, in effect in most cases the various levels of government were no longer interested in them.[16] The integration of "immigrant communities into the larger life of the Dominion." writes historian Donald Avery, "was left to private agencies."[17] Since private institutions such as Frontier College and the YMCA touched the lives of very few newcomers, their role in the acculturation of the immigrant population was probably minimal. The Protestant churches, through their interior missions and the training of "ethnic ministers" to administer to the spiritual needs of immigrant congregations, probably accomplished a little more.[18]

The Canadian government no doubt hoped that whatever work the churches and private agencies could not accomplish, the public schools would in time complete. As Watson Kirkconnell, a keen observer of this age opined, the integration of immigrant communities into Canadian life was left to "the English-language school, supplemented at a later day by radio," which assured the assimilation of the second generation into Canadian mainstream culture.[19] A similar view was offered by a contemporary Canadian official: "the school... appears to be the most effective agency of promoting the use of English [among newcomers]." The ignorance of Canada's official languages would, in the mind of a Canadian authority, disappear very much as illiteracy would also be gradually eliminated: through death.[20] Canada's leaders then, were satisfied to leave the integration of newcomers into Canadian life to the churches, private charity, the public schools, and to the gradual physical extinction of the non-assimilated.[21] These attitudes spoke volumes about the Canadian government's complacency and their unshakable belief in the idea of the non-interventionist state. Such an approach did not really serve the interests of either the immigrants or Canadian society, but it could be tolerated in peacetime. The situation would change greatly with the onset of international crisis in 1939.

As war-clouds gathered on the horizon, especially during the crisis-filled year of 1938, Canada's leaders realized that preparations had to be made for the possible outbreak of another world war. As far as Canada's immigrant population of enemy origin was concerned, the first thoughts that came to the minds of decision makers in Ottawa were about the measures that had to be taken to assure the security of the home front. Their ideas were translated into action by a number of inter-departmental committees struck to work out plans for the contingency of war. The deliberations of these committees resulted in the formulation of the Defence of Canada Regulations (DOCR) which were to assure the security of the Canadian state and the success of the war effort at home.[22]

The DOCR regarding immigrant aliens were drafted by the interdepartmental Committee on the Treatment of Aliens and Alien Property. The members of this committee gravitated toward two almost diametrically opposite solutions. Some, especially the people representing the Royal Canadian Mounted Police and the Department of National Defence, argued for strict rules and their application to a large number of people, while the committee's civilian members were inclined to counsel moderation.[23] This disagreement over the nature of Canada's wartime regulations concerning newcomers from enemy lands intensified after the outbreak of war and especially after Hitler's invasion of northern and western Europe in the spring of 1940.

The regulations that were to govern enemy aliens in Canada during the war were Sections 24 and 25 of the DOCR. These divided enemy individuals into three categories: people facing internment, those having to comply with the requirements of a parole system, and those who were spared these restrictions. These people were granted "exemption certificates." Regulation 26, as originally drafted, provided internees with an appeal mechanism. Later this regulation was used to accommodate most of the changes and additions that government deemed necessary to control Canada's enemy alien population. Who was classified as an "enemy alien" depended on the individual's place of birth. At first only true aliens were to be affected but as public hysteria over potential fifth columnists grew, the regulations were revised to include people who were not really aliens but were in fact naturalized immigrants from enemy countries. In fact for some time it seemed that Canada's new experience in the treatment of enemy alien populations would resemble the patterns established during the First World War, when next to nothing was done to rally the country's immigrant groups from enemy lands behind the national war effort.[24]

But it was not to be. Already during the early phases of the war, attitudes surfaced that suggested the development of different patterns in this war from those that had prevailed from 1914 to 1918. The fact that in the Second World War the Canadian government would not satisfy itself with police measures only in its dealings with enemy immigrant minorities was very much the consequence of a few people among the Ottawa establishment who had good judgement as well as humane and compassionate convictions. These people included Norman Robertson of External Affairs, John F. MacNeill of the Department of Justice, Judge Thomas C. Davis of the Department of National War Services (established in 1940) as well as a handful of politicians. Among them were Icelandic-Canadian M.P. Joseph T. Thorson and especially James G. Gardiner, both of whom would be in charge of the new department for some time during the war.

Of all these people, Robertson would play the most important role. At the outset of the war he was Assistant Under-Secretary of State for External Affairs and a member of a few governmental committees dealing with the subjects of internal security and enemy aliens. After the death of Under-Secretary of State for External Affairs O.D. Skelton in 1941 Robertson was appointed to that position and became the most powerful civil servant in Ottawa. After the death of Mackenzie King's long-time confidant Ernest Lapointe (who was Minister of Justice) later that year, Robertson became Prime Minister King's closest advisor. Robertson was one of those rare members of Canada's elite who did not agree with the policy of disinterest in the country's immigrants. In an incomplete draft of a memorandum on the subject, he outlined in May of 1939 what should be done to integrate newcomers into Canadian life. He suggested the introduction of English classes and night school for them, and the provision of a social safety net until they established themselves, all carried out by the churches and voluntary organizations with government support.[25]

Another Ottawa official who would also have a great deal to do with the Canadian government's emerging wartime policies regarding immigrants was J.F. MacNeill of the Department of Justice. In the fall of 1939, he was working with Robertson regarding the details of imposing the regime of the DOCR on enemy aliens in Canada. The two saw eye-to-eye on many issues and tried to resist as best they could the RCMP's demands for the internment of more and more suspected Nazi and Communist sympathizers.[26] There can be no doubt that MacNeill, like Robertson, believed that neglecting immigrants was the wrong policy, and that relying purely on police measures to keep them behind the Canadian war effort was neither a humane nor a wise approach. In December of 1939, he set his ideas down in a memorandum which he gave to Walter J. Turnbull, one of Mackenzie King's aides, with the hope that it would be shown to the Prime Minister.

MacNeill began by describing how immigrants from Axis-controlled lands were apprehensive about what treatment they could expect in Canada during the war. He pointed out that while these people received next to no information about "our system of government" they were flooded with "Nazi, Fascist and Communist propaganda ... in their own language." Such propaganda had to be answered not "with repressive police measures ... [but] by reasoned argument." MacNeill suggested that everything should be done—even a "little time and money" spent and a few people hired—to make sure that the government's message about the war reached these people "in their own language ... distributed free of charge."[27]

Though King was impressed by what MacNeill had to say, the government was slow to implement his suggestions. It would not be until the summer of 1940 that, under the impact of the dramatic events in Europe, the government would begin to act and establish the Department of National War Services to handle the business of the war effort at home.[28] Until then, Ottawa pursued policies that were intended more to intimidate the country's enemy alien population than to rally them to the war effort. Hundreds of Germans, whose names had been placed on a list established by the RCMP precisely for such purpose, were rounded up and interned.[29] Beyond this, however, no drastic measures were taken against right-radical immigrants, no doubt because of the localized nature of the war in Europe in the fall and winter of 1939. The RCMP in fact probably spent more effort in keeping a tab on the activities of labour radicals than in ferreting out Nazis and fascists. Of course, by this time, communists were not only enemies of the capitalist order in Canada but also opponents of the war effort. The Soviet leadership had signed a non-aggression pact with Nazi Germany and the Communist International had instructed its membership throughout the world to oppose the "imperialist" war that had broken out in September. Not surprisingly, along with scores of German enemy aliens, numerous immigrant labour radicals were also interned by the RCMP.[30]

This preoccupation with left-wing radicals on the part of the men responsible for Canada's internal security inevitably turned Ottawa's attention to Canada's large Ukrainian community. This ethnic group was extremely fractured politically. The major split was along ideological lines, but even the Ukrainians who were not involved in the communist movement were hopelessly disunited. Moreover, Ukrainians were perceived by Ottawa authorities to be anti-Polish, and thereby potential enemies of an allied state and of the Allied war effort. They were also suspected to be sympathetic to the Nazi cause. Communist Ukrainians were allies of the Nazis, and their nationalist compatriots had been favourably impressed by Berlin's foreign policies when during the last months of 1938 the Nazis had patronized Ukrainian separatists in the eastern parts of the disintegrating Czechoslovak state. Though Hitler's courting of Ukrainian irredentism was short-lived,[31] the possibility of a future German-led crusade against Communism, which might result in the liberation of Ukraine from the Soviet yoke, remained on the minds of many ardent Ukrainian patriots.

Much had to be done to prevent the whole of Canada's Ukrainian community from becoming further mired in political attitudes hostile to the Allied war effort. The influence of the communists had to be curbed and the dangers of Nazi ideology and policies had to be explained to nationalist Ukrainians. Above all, the community had to be united behind leaders who understood and were sympathetic to Ottawa's position in the war. The accomplishment of this huge task was facilitated by a recent arrival, the Englishman Tracy Philipps. Philipps came to Canada in the spring of 1940 to begin a speaking tour explaining Allied war aims to the Canadian public. His tour was co-ordinated by Canada's National Council of Education and his lectures were sponsored by the Association of Canadian Clubs, which received a government grant for this purpose. At first Philipps' lectures had nothing to do with Ukrainian Canadians, but that had changed by the fall of 1940.[32]

During the summer the government of Mackenzie King had established the Department of National War Services (DNWS). Heading the department was James "Jimmy" G. Gardiner, the Minister of Agriculture. Gardiner was from Saskatchewan and was quite sympathetic to the plight of the Canadian West's masses of German immigrants. "During the last war," he explained at the time, "we did a great deal of damage to the citizenship of our country.... We

made those from Europe ... feel that they were not on an equal basis with our own people."
Gardiner was determined to create "an entirely different sentiment during this war..." through
his department's Bureau of Public Information and another branch that he was planning to set
up. The veteran politician promised that "a real effort [will be] put forth ... toward making
[European immigrants] feel that we welcome them as loyal citizens of this country."[33]

To help him handle the affairs of the DNWS Gardiner recruited a fellow Saskatchewan
native, Judge Thomas C. Davis, and made him associate deputy minister. When Davis came to
Ottawa, he was "astounded" to discover that in Central Canada immigrants from Europe were
not accepted as equals as they were in the West. "No attempt is made," he told an acquaintance, "to distinguish between Ukrainians, the Poles, the Swedes ... or anything else. If the
name of an individual happens to be something other than ... Anglo-Saxon ... he is immediately branded as a German."[34] Davis was determined to "create good feeling" among the foreign-born in Canada by distributing information among them and through other government
measures that would get them "behind the war effort," as he explained to Gardiner at the
time.[35] One of the several measures that Davis took was to arrange for Philipps to repeat his
lecture tour, talking this time to immigrant (mainly Ukrainian) audiences. But Davis had an
even more challenging task for Philipps: to convince the various Ukrainian organizations to
unite under an organization that could speak for all mainstream Ukrainian immigrants to
Canada. Using a combination of persuasion, cajoling and arm-twisting, Philipps accomplished
this at a meeting of the leading non-communist Ukrainian-Canadian organizations that took
place in early November 1940, in Winnipeg.[36] The result was the Ukrainian Canadian
Committee which would play a useful role as a link between Ottawa and one of Canada's
largest immigrant ethnic groups throughout the war.

In the meantime, plans for spreading the government's message also among other immigrant groups were under discussion in Ottawa. In October Robertson proposed that Canada
imitate the United States and begin radio broadcasts directed at the country's foreign-language
population. Another high-ranking Ottawa bureaucrat, Undersecretary of State E.H. Coleman,
countered by suggesting the government should use the immigrant presses that had been shut
down by the RCMP to publish pamphlets in various languages. To begin the publicity work,
Watson Kirkconnell of McMaster University was approached. He had command of several
European languages and had cultivated the friendship of immigrant organizations and leaders
while he had been teaching in Winnipeg. In the end radio broadcasts, prepared in consultation
with Kirkconnell, were also undertaken, but for the time being they were only in English and
French. The programs explained the Canadian war effort and exposed the falsehoods of Nazi
and Communist propaganda. They also described the dangers of Canadians becoming divided
against each other as a result of a war of words unleashed by the enemy. The broadcasts
included segments on "the cultural and historical achievements," to use Kirkconnell's words,
"of all the main national groups in Canada." The series was published in pamphlet form titled
Canadians All and nearly 400,000 copies were distributed.[37] Though intended mainly for the
Canadian general public, *Canadians All* was also designed to instill pride into immigrants and
make them feel important in their adopted homeland.

At about the same time, Canada's wartime Film Commissioner John Grierson (who had been
appointed in October 1939) and his organization the National Film Board were also at work producing "wartime information" for the Canadian general public. In March 1941 they, acting
through Associated Screen News Production, released the documentary film *People of Canada*. It

described some of the country's ethnic groups and showed their members working in their traditional occupations. The groups portrayed included French Canadians, Scots, Dutch, Germans, Scandinavians, Chinese and a few of the religious ethno-cultural groups. The film's message was that Canada was "becoming strong because of its tolerance" of ethnic and religious minorities.[38] *People of Canada* tried to assure English-speaking Canadians that the members of ethnocultural minorities in their midst were also good Canadians, but the film, not unlike Kirkconnell's *Canadians All,* also aimed to promote a sense of being acceptable and accepted, among members of Canada's ethnic and religious minorities, including the foreign born.

Gardiner, Davis and their advisors had even more ambitious plans, plans that went beyond the realm of propaganda in the media. They had in mind the establishment of a bureau within the DNWS that would carry out government publicity in the language of the various immigrant groups and, in general, would act as a liaison office between the Canadian government and immigrant communities. After lengthy discussions and many delays, the branch was set up in the winter of 1941-42. It was called the Nationalities Branch. An advisory body called the Committee on Cooperation in Canadian Citizenship (CCCC) was also established to act as a kind of board of directors.[39] Among its members were several prominent Canadians, most of them experts on immigration or immigrant groups, including Kirkconnell, Professor H.F. Angus of External Affairs, and author Robert England.

It seems that in the early winter of 1941, Ottawa's effort to find accommodation with the country's immigrants from enemy lands went into high gear and did not slow down for more than a year. Many steps were taken in this period that helped to improve relations between the Canadian state and the foreign-born. The creation of a bureaucratic machinery to handle contacts with immigrant groups was just one of these. Another was that labour radicals, (Communists) began to be released from internment camps. Then the government decided not to impose the full regime of the DOCR on Finnish, Hungarian and Rumanian immigrants when the home countries of these newcomers became involved in the war on Germany's side. In fact, instead of applying police measures, the government began organizing work among some of them on the pattern that had been established with the Ukrainians in 1940. And as a crowning point of this type of work came the decision of the government, just before Christmas of 1942, to rescind some of the amendments to the DOCR which in the summer of 1940 had made a great many long-term residents (in fact, citizens) of Canada "enemy aliens." The only group that would not benefit from this increasingly tolerant government approach to the foreign-born would be the Japanese, but even in their case some ineffective concessions would be made by the end of the period under consideration.[40]

The establishment of the Nationalities Branch of the DNWS, the bureau that was to act as the government's voice, was finally authorized early in 1942.[41] It was to be headed by Professor George Simpson, a Slavic studies specialist at the University of Saskatchewan. Tracy Philipps was hired as "European advisor," and a personal friend of his, the Ukrainian-Canadian scholar and activist Vladimir Kysilewsky, was put in charge of disseminating information to the ethnic press.[42] The CCCC also began its periodic meetings. Because Simpson did not take up residence in Ottawa, the branch's day-to-day direction was assumed by Philipps. For a while he continued to do what he had been doing throughout 1941: travelling, giving lectures, promote various schemes to further the war effort, and in general, acting as a lobbyist on issues of concern to Canada's immigrant groups. One of his most interesting undertakings was arranging a good will mission to Canada's Hungarian communities. In December of 1941, Hungary, along with Finland and Rumania, became enemy countries. This came about as a result of the decision of the Mackenzie King government to declare war on the minor Axis powers that had become involved in the Nazi invasion of the USSR. The decision was made collectively by the Commonwealth to appease Joseph Stalin, who had been pressuring the British government to act for some time. London in turn put pressure on Ottawa. The King administration declared war with a great deal of hesitation and after long delays. Though Ottawa at the time would have preferred not to issue any new declarations of war, it felt that it could no longer resist the British requests to do so. The government gave in but at the same time it decided not to apply the full force of the DOCR to Finnish, Hungarian and Rumanian immigrants to Canada.[43]

The concession probably went a long way to reassure members of the communities of the goodwill of the Canadian government toward them. Nevertheless, concerns about the future no doubt remained in the minds of many of these newcomers. To alleviate any fears, and to make sure that the largest of these communities, the Hungarian, did not come under the domination of radical elements, Philipps decided that a "mission" to Canada's Magyars should be undertaken. It would be on the pattern developed late in 1940 when he had toured the Ukrainian communities of the Canadian West.

To accomplish this task Philipps recruited a post- First World War arrival to Canada, a low-ranking insurance executive by the name of Béla Eisner. He had been active in Hungarian community life in Montreal, where only recently an umbrella organization of Magyar churches and clubs had been founded. Philipps evidently thought that such organizations would be useful in other Hungarian-Canadian centres as well and that eventually they could be brought under a federation of Hungarian associations for the whole of Canada, something Hungarians in this country had tried to establish before but never with lasting success.[44] Still another, though officially unstated, aim of this mission, was to bring Hungarian Canadians under leaders that could be politically trusted and who would support the Canadian war effort.

Eisner was borrowed from his Montreal employer and began his work in June of 1942. He at first contacted members of the Hungarian-Canadian elite—clergymen, newspaper editors, presidents of the various lay organizations, etc—to announce his plans and seek their advice in organizing his effort. Then he went on a speaking-tour of Ontario's Hungarian communities. Not having much luck, Eisner changed tactics before visiting visit the Hungarian centres of the prairie provinces. There he gave fewer speeches, but tried instead to convince local ethnic leaders to start preparations for the establishment of a Canada-wide Hungarian-Canadian umbrella organization. At the end of his tour Eisner was optimistic, but organizational work began to languish as soon as his mission was over and he had to return to work with his regular employer.[45]

While the DNWS was, through Philipps, engaged in getting the country's Hungarian communities aboard the Canadian war effort, more important measures were in the works regarding the government's relationship with Canada's German, Italian, and Austrian communities. The initiative came from Robertson. In October 1942 he approached Mackenzie King with a proposal for making further concessions to the country's immigrant communities from enemy lands. He called King's attention to the fact that the Roosevelt administration had stopped treating Italians as enemy aliens. He then suggested that new gestures of goodwill should be made by the Canadian government to the country's German and Italian ethnic groups. As a "first step" he felt that people of "former" German or Italian nationality—people of such background who had become citizens in Canada—should be removed from the enemy alien category.[46]

186

Robertson's suggestions were incorporated into a formal proposal by the Department of External Affairs. This in effect recommended that the amendment to the DOCR that had been passed in the summer of 1940, which had extended the definition of enemy alien to people whose naturalization had taken place after 1922, be rescinded. It also proposed that Italian aliens in Canada be treated the same way as Finns, Hungarians and Rumanians by granting them exemptions that freed them from the parole regulations. In early December the Cabinet approved these recommendations, adding that people of Austrian nationality should also be given the preferential treatment accorded to the citizens of the minor Axis allies living in Canada. These concessions were announced to the public in Mackenzie King's 1942 Christmas message to the nation.[47]

While the year 1942 had brought substantial improvements to the treatment of immigrants to Canada from enemy lands, the same cannot be said of 1943. To some extent, further improvement was difficult to achieve since the most important steps had already been taken. But there were other reasons for a marked slowing of the government's measures to bring Canada's immigrant masses around to the national war effort. First of all, it was becoming obvious that the vast majority of immigrants supported the war and that the very few who did not were either in internment camps or were doing little to show their anti-Allied sentiments. Second, it was also slowly becoming evident that, even if the war went on for years, a direct threat to Canada's shores that was perceived by the public as late as the spring of 1942, would probably not materialize. The government, furthermore, was preoccupied with pursuing the war on the economic and political fronts. Canada's leaders had to worry about larger issues such as labour shortages, a serious balance of payments deficit, and the even more threatening prospect of conscription for overseas military service. Under these circumstances it is not surprising that little was done to advance the work relating to the foreign-born in the country that had been started in the previous years.

Bureaucratically the most to suffer in 1943 was the Nationalities Branch. Aside from the general problems mentioned above, there were specific developments that combined to hinder the work of this small unit of the DNWS. Perhaps the most important was changes in personnel. In 1941 King replaced Gardiner as the minister in charge of that department. The new minister was Thorson, who soon fell out of favour with the Prime Minister and was replaced by L.R. LaFlèche, a veteran Ottawa soldier-bureaucrat whom Mackenzie King had decided to bring into the Cabinet.[48] Unlike his predecessors Gardiner and Thorson, LaFlèche had no interest in the work of the Nationalities Branch.[49] By this time Judge Davis had also been removed from the Ottawa scene: he had been appointed Canadian High Commissioner to Australia. The only man left to promote the cause of better relations between the government and Canada's immigrant masses was Philipps, but he had run afoul of a great many people in Ottawa and elsewhere. The leftist press attacked him asking whether it was appropriate to have an ardent anti-communist filling a position of influence during times of Soviet-Canadian friendship. He had also irritated people in External Affairs, including Robertson. Another Ottawa mandarin who was out to get Philipps was his countryman John Grierson of the NFB, who in the spring of 1943 had added the newly-created Wartime Information Board to his responsibilities. Grierson wanted to transfer the Nationalities Branch to the new board and conspired to replace Philipps with someone more in line with his own ideological inclinations. He even found a candidate for the position in the young Soviet and East European specialist H. Gordon Skilling.[50] But Grierson could not get his way. Though the branch remained with DNWS and Philipps stayed as its de facto head until

1944, his influence declined considerably. He was banned from public speaking and his office was denied an adequate budget. The work of the Nationalities Branch began to stagnate, as did that of the CCCC, which was also the subject of attacks in the leftist press.[51]

Though the work of winning Canada's immigrant masses for the war effort became less and less important as it was becoming evident that these people posed no danger to the Canadian state, the work that had been started in the first years of the war was not discarded by the government. The Nationalities Branch, instead of being disbanded as some had called for, was in fact reorganized in accordance with the suggestions of Robert England. It was renamed the Citizenship Division and was given a larger staff and budget. Frank Foulds, a veteran Ottawa bureaucrat, was appointed its director, while Philipps was encouraged to accept employment with the United Nations Relief and Rehabilitation Administration.[52] In the fall of 1945 the division was placed under the authority of the Secretary of State and in 1950 it was transferred to the Department of Citizenship and Immigration. A generation later it would become the administrative machinery of official multiculturalism.[53]

Although modern wars are fought primarily with weapons, they are also fought with other means designed to win the hearts and minds of combatants and non-combatants alike. The chief instrument of this latter struggle is propaganda: often euphemistically referred to as "wartime information." In 1939 Canada was ill-prepared for fighting a major war either with weapons or by other means. While some police measures were implemented from the very outbreak of the war to assure the security of the home front, the organization of wartime propaganda was painfully slow. The fact that some information work was undertaken by the Canadian state was in no small measure the result of fortuitous circumstances such as the presence in Canada of filmmaker John Grierson for whom the making of documentary films was a passion.

Grierson and his National Film Board, as well as the early wartime information apparatus of the King administration (the Bureau of Public Information), were meant to provide propaganda for all Canadians. Special measures had to be taken to explain Canadian war aims and to win the confidence of people who had emigrated from Axis or Axis-controlled lands,. The government of Mackenzie King, half-heartedly at times, did take steps to achieve these goals as well. That it did undertake measures to provide wartime information for and to win the goodwill of newcomers from Central and Eastern Europe was also the result certain individuals being present among the decision-makers in Ottawa who realized the need for these and who approached their task with conviction and determination. At the top political level Gardiner and Thorson supported such an approach, while among the mandarins of the Ottawa bureaucracy Robertson, Coleman, MacNeill and Judge Davis exerted positive influence. There were also advocates of such measures among Canada's intellectual elite: they included Kirkconnell and England.

The makers of Canada's wartime policy regarding the country's enemy alien population faced an uphill struggle. These groups had existed in pre-war Canada in a high degree of cultural isolation, and in near-total government neglect. In the years before the war they usually received their information about the world at large, the situation in their homelands, and even in their adopted land, from materials produced in Central and Eastern Europe. This meant that many of these immigrants were increasingly inundated by Nazi, Fascist or Communist propaganda. To counter all this for a government that up to then did not believe in dealing with newcomers to the country in any positive way was not an easy task. Indeed, the mere fact that Canada's wartime government began propagandizing and otherwise patronizing immigrant groups aroused the suspicion of many immigrants and hindered the effectiveness of the government's work.

Not even a vague assessment of the effectiveness of the government's wartime work concerning enemy alien populations is possible. William R. Young has argued that wartime information, as far as Canadian ethnic groups were concerned, was a "failure." At the end of the war, according to Young, anti-Oriental and especially, anti-Japanese prejudices were as virulent in Canada as they had ever been.[54] It must be admitted, wartime information in Canada for both the general public and the immigrants was limited. What government propaganda there was, was too little and often came too late. Even if it had been more efficient, it could not have affected public attitudes substantially, as prejudice takes a long time to abate. Nevertheless there can be no doubt that, as far as prejudices against European immigrants at the highest level of government was concerned, the war brought a change. The difference between how the Canadian state treated European immigrants in the two world wars is a testimony to the transformation of Canadian attitudes, at least at the official level, that transpired during the first half of the Second World War.

The most important change in the wartime treatment of immigrant minorities came in the realm of the regulatory regime designed to keep the enemy alien populations under control. The exemption of a number of immigrant groups, including Finns, Hungarians, Rumanians, and later, Italians and Austrians, from the more draconian provisions of the DOCR was a significant concession to these peoples and an undeniable move toward a more humane and sensible policy on the home front. The reversal of the 1940 provisions of Regulation 26 at Christmas time in 1942, which removed many naturalized Canadians from the enemy alien category, was another such move. These measures, more than any of the others, assured that fewer of Canada's residents were inconvenienced by the regime of the DOCR, and there were fewer cases of the Canadian state making enemies out of people who were not ill-disposed toward Canada and her war effort in the first place.

Of course, not all of the government's efforts in this direction, and beyond the provision of wartime information, were successful. We might recall the meager success of the goodwill mission to the Hungarians that the DNWS undertook in 1942. Some Hungarians could not believe that the government's new-found interest in them had no ulterior and sinister motives, such as a preparation for the conscription of Hungarian-Canadian young men for overseas service.[55] It is not surprising that the desired Hungarian-Canadian nation-wide umbrella organization did not materialize. True, the DNWS had had more luck with the Ukrainians in 1940, but in that case too, only the non-leftist organizations were united, and if we believe some scholars of Ukrainian-Canadian history—who contend that in the long term the Ukrainian Canadian Committee proved to be an ineffective organization[56]— we have to qualify the success of that undertaking as well.

The impact of wartime information on immigrant attitudes to the war cannot be assessed with any degree of accuracy. It is equally difficult to assess the long-term impact of these and some other policies and measures, and the impact of the mere fact that during the war the Canadian state mutated from being non-interventionist in the affairs of Canada's immigrant masses, to being highly interventionist.

In this connection a few words might be said about the long-term implications of Canada's new-found interventionism. Repeatedly throughout the war secret memoranda generated by the Ottawa bureaucracy identified one of the aims of the government's efforts as being the integration of immigrants into the wider Canadian society. Few of the authors of these pronouncements differentiated between the acculturation of immigrants and their assimilation. Apparently few people at the time realized the difference between these two processes and even fewer believed, as many students of the ethnic experience believe today, that while acculturation is useful and beneficial to all concerned, assimilation can have undesirable consequences both for the ethnic groups in question and the larger host society. In fact, some wartime propaganda did not clearly differentiate between the two. Kirkconnell's *Canadians All* praised the cultural differences that existed among Canada's ethnocultural groups and stressed "tolerance and cooperation," but in its conclusions rather ambiguously emphasized the need "to cultivate the consciousness that we are all Canadians," and repeatted the "vital importance" of unity.[57] The ending of the NFB's *Canada's People* was perhaps a bit less ambiguous in this respect. In the film's last scene the audience is told that there must be respect for the different beliefs of different peoples.[58]

Though Canada's wartime decision-makers did not discern, let alone debate, the respective merits and dangers of acculturation and assimilation, they implicitly accepted the notion that the state had a role to play in the integration of immigrants. In the post-war era the idea of leaving the acculturation of immigrant groups to chance, to the churches, private agencies and death, would disappear.

Post-Second World War immigrants to Canada would encounter a Canadian state that had a different approach to newcomers than its pre-1939 predecessor. Granted, there were other circumstances that contributed to the rise of new attitudes to immigration policies and the treatment of ethnic groups in general. The Second World War had served to discredit racism and intolerance everywhere. The post-war prosperity helped to dispel notions current in the depression-ridden 1930s that the state could not afford to embark on the building of a social safety net for the needy. And the emergence of the Cold War prompted Ottawa to keep up its propaganda work, and even engage in subtle political intervention in the affairs of immigrant organizations.[59] Despite the existence of these factors, there can be no doubt that the extent of the change that transpired during and immediately after the war was remarkable. While pre-war arrivals to Canada rarely received any help from Ottawa, or from lower levels of government, by 1956 a newcomer (such as the author of this chapter) could enjoy the hospitality of a government committed to making the shock of landing in a strange country easier. There was night school to learn English, as well as a social safety net to make the initial adjustment to life in Canada smoother. Norman Robertson's dream of May 1939 had come true.

Government support for the maintenance of ethnic heritages, the introduction of official multiculturalism, an apology to Japanese Canadians for their wartime treatment, had to wait for nearly another generation. But the seeds of these future developments were planted, not quite consciously in some cases, during the Second World War, when so much in this country changed or began to change, and when the modern Canada we know today began to be forged.

Notes for Chapter 9

The author would like to thank the various granting agencies that from time to time have supported his research on the subject of the Canadian state and immigrant minorities: the Multicultural Directorate, the Social Sciences and Humanities Research Council of Canada, and the Arts Research Program of the Royal Military College of Canada.

1   For a substantial collection of useful papers dealing with Canada in 1939 see Norman Hillmer, Robert Bothwell, Roger Sarty and Claude Beauregard, eds., *A Country of Limitations: Canada and the World in 1939/ Un pays dans la gêne: le Canada et le monde en 1939* (Ottawa: Canadian Committee for the History of the Second World War, 1996).

2   For historical literature dealing with or touching on the evolution of state interventionism in Canada during the Second World War see such works as C.P. Stacey, *Arms, Men and Government: The War Policies of Canada, 1939-45* (Ottawa, 1970); and Robert Bothwell and William Kilbourn, *C.D. Howe: A Biography* (Toronto, 1979). For a brief overview, Bothwell's paper "'Who's Paying for Anything These Days?' War Production in Canada 1939-45," in *Mobilization for Total War: The Canadian, American and British Experience, 1914-1945*, N.F. Dreisziger, ed. (Waterloo, Ont.: Wilfrid Laurier University Press, 1981), 57-69, is still useful.

3   For a fast-paced survey of immigration to Canada throughout the ages see Valerie Knowles, *Strangers at Our Gates: Canadian Immigration and Immigration Policy, 1540-1997* (Toronto and Oxford: Dundurn Press, 1997). See also the pertinent entries in the *Encyclopedia of Canadian Ethnic Groups*, Paul R. Magocsi, ed. (Toronto: University of Toronto Press, 1999).

4   For Canadian demographic development in general see Warren E. Kalbach and Wayne W. McVey, *Demographic Bases of Canadian Society* (Toronto: McGraw-Hill, 1979). For an overview of the subject, see Kalbach's article "Population," *The Canadian Encyclopedia* III (Edmonton: Hurtig, 1988), 2nd ed., 1719-22. Undoubtedly, much of the increase in Canada's population was the result of natural population growth. It is a fact that natural increase exceeded growth as a result of immigration during every "census decade" with only the period 1901-1911 constituting a near exception to this generalization (see ibid.). Nevertheless, the contribution of immigration to the nation's growth was very significant. One should also keep in mind the fact that natural reproduction rates for immigrants were much higher than for the general Canadian population, because immigrants tended to arrive in Canada at the outset of their highest child-bearing years. It could be argued that newcomers to Canada had contributed to keeping Canadian birth-rates much higher than birthrates in other developed countries.

5   See statistical data cited in Kalbach's encyclopedia article, 1721.

6   The British element in Canada's foreign-born were not really foreigners and were certainly not looked upon as such at the time. Reinforcing this fact was the absence of a separate Canadian citizenship. Canadians were British subjects, and so were immigrants from the UK.

7   There were also immigrants from the United States. As these were often returnees to Canada, or the children of people who had migrated to the US from Canada decades earlier, their arrival had little impact on Canada's ethnic makeup. The immigration of non-white populations from the United States was discouraged. Harold M. Troper, *Only Farmers Need Apply: Official Canadian Government Encouragement of Immigration from the United States, 1896-1911* (Toronto: Griffin House, 1972).

8   The number of newcomers was moderate in 1919 and 1920 (107,698 and 138,824 respectively, as compared to over 400,000 for the year 1913), sank to very low levels in 1921 and 1922, but improved in the following two years. In 1925 there was again a setback which probably played a role in a change in the King government's immigration policy. For annual immigration statistics see Table 1 in Jean R. Burnet

with Howard Palmer, *"Coming Canadians:" An Introduction to A History of Canada's Peoples* (Toronto: McClelland and Stewart, 1988), 40.

9   The railways often circumvented the requirement that newcomers from "non-preferred" countries could only be admitted if they were guaranteed permanent employment in Canada by creating fictitious jobs or pretending that temporary positions were actually long-term. John Herd Thompson with Allen Seager, *Canada, 1922-1939: Decades of Discord* (Toronto: McClelland and Stewart, 1985), 131f. See also Burnet with Palmer, *"Coming Canadians,"* 34.

10 Lubomyr Luciuk and Stella Hryniuk, eds., *Canada's Ukrainians: Negotiating an Identity* (Toronto: University of Toronto Press, 1991), especially the papers in Part I titled "To Canada: Immigration and Settlement." For a succinct overview see the subheading "Immigration of Ukrainians" in the entry by F. Swyripa, "Canada," in the *Encyclopedia of Ukraine*, Volodymyr Kubijovy, ed. (Toronto: University of Toronto Press, 1984), Vol 1, 344-358. In interwar Poland, an ethnic conflict, bordering occasionally on "quasi-guerilla warfare" existed between Ukrainians and the Polish state. Joseph Rothschild, *East Central Europe between the Two World Wars* (Seattle and London: University of Washington Press, 1974), 42ff. The Ukrainians in Rumania were "misgoverned... aggrieved" and were subjected to centralization by Rumanian authorities. (Ibid., 289f.)

11 W. Burton Hurd, *Racial Origins and Nativity of the Canadian People*, Census Monograph No. 4 (Ottawa: King's Printer, 1937), Table 13, 230.

12 The prairies had been the destination of the overwhelming majority of the "new immigrants." They had undergone extensive demographic changes both as a result of the immigration of the 1925-1931 period and as a result of the economic hard times of the early 1930s. These factors combined in the decision of the Canadian government to undertake a census of the three prairie provinces in 1936. The results of the 1941 census are probably less reliable as far as the foreign born are concerned because by then some newcomers tried to hide the fact that they had any association with Axis countries. In 1941 the tendency among German Mennonites to declare themselves Dutch probably increased, as did the likelihood of Germans who had been born in countries not at war with Canada to identify themselves not as Germans but as nationals of the country from which they had emigrated.

13 Canada, Dominion Bureau of Statistics, *Census of the Prairie Provinces, 1936* (Ottawa: King's Printer, 1938), Vol 1. Tables respectively for Manitoba, Saskatchewan and Alberta (pp. 90f, 500f, and 962f.). Another ethnic group with a large population in each of these provinces (raging from ca. 87,000 in Manitoba to 63,000 in Alberta) was the Ukrainian. (Ibid.).

14 Over 34,000 of those who resided in Manitoba, some 110,000 of those living in Saskatchewan, and close to 53,000 of the residents of Alberta. Ibid.

15 Ibid., Table 30 for Saskatchewan (pp. 500f).

16 There were exceptions to this. The most obvious took place in times of crisis when the state became interested in the immigrant as potential saboteur, or radical, or someone who

would try to become a "public charge." In such cases the state would intervene and would take steps to render the newcomer harmless to Canadian society through various means, the most extreme of which were internment or deportation.

17 According to Avery, to "Frontier College, the YMCA and the Protestant churches." Donald Avery, *"Dangerous Foreigners": European Immigrant Workers and Labour Radicalism in Canada, 1896-1932* (Toronto: McClelland and Stewart, 1979), 142.

18 I have traced the work mainly of the United Church of Canada and the Presbyterian Church of Canada among Hungarian newcomers in my *Struggle and Hope: The Hungarian-Canadian Experience* (Toronto: McClelland and Stewart, 1982), 103-94, 119-22, and 150-54. I point out that at least two of the "ethnic ministers" trained by these churches maintained Hungarian-language periodicals for the members of their congregations and often dispensed information on Canada and even on Canadian farming practices.

19 Watson Kirkconnell, *A Slice of Canada: Memoirs* (Toronto: University of Toronto Press, 1967), 261.

20 The official is not noted, but it was probably statistical expert W. Burton Hurd. Canada, Dominion Bureau of Statistics, *Seventh Census of Canada, 1931,* Vol XIII. *Monographs* (Ottawa: King's Printer, 1942), 681 and 684.

21 Among Canada's elite there were exceptions to this generalization. Among them was Norman Robertson of the Department of External Affairs, whose different ideas will be described later.

22 On the origins of the DOCR see Daniel Robinson, "Planning for the 'Most Serious Continency': Alien Internment, Arbitrary Detention, and the Canadian State 1938-39," *Journal of Canadian Studies,* 28 (1993), pp. 5-20; and Ramsay Cook, "Canadian Freedom in Wartime," *His Own Man: Essays in Honour of Arthur Reginald Marsden Lower*, W.H. Heick and Roger Graham eds. (Montreal and London: McGill-Queen's Press, 1974), especially p. 38. This study is based upon Cook's MA thesis: "Canadian Liberalism in Wartime: A Study of the Defence of Canada Regulations and Some Canadian Attitudes to Civil Liberties in Wartime," Queen's University, 1955.

23 This division of opinion is stressed especially by Robinson, "Planning for...". During the course of the war another type of a dichotomy seems to have surfaced. People of influence from the Canadian Prairies would tend to argue for moderation while some Central Canadians (foremost among them Minister of Justice Ernest Lapointe) took the opposite stance.

24 No comprehensive treatment exists of the subject of "enemy aliens" in Canada during the First World War, but brief introductions can be found in John Herd Thompson, *Ethnic Minorities during Two World Wars* (Ottawa: Canadian Historical Association, 1991), 4-10, and Burnet with Palmer, *"Coming Canadians,"* pp. 153-61 *in passim*. See also the relevant chapters in John H. Thompson, *The Harvests of War: The Prairie West, 1914-1918* (Toronto: McClelland and Stewart, 1978).

25 The Canadian Broadcasting Corporation and the National Film Board would also have to play active roles. Norman Robertson writing in May of 1939 in an incomplete and undated memo, found in the Papers of Norman Robertson, vol 12. file 134, National Archives of Canada. The memo is excerpted in J.L. Granatstein, *Man of Influence: Norman A. Robertson and Canadian Statecraft, 1929-68* (Ottawa: Deneau, 1981), 83. The memo's date has been established by Granatstein.

26 Granatstein, *A Man of Influence*, 84-89.

27 Memorandum by J.F. MacNeill to Walter J. Turnbull, 5 December 1939, enclosed in Trunbull to Arnold D.P. Heeney, 6 Dec. 1939, the Mackenzie King Papers, J1 Series, vol 273, National Archives of Canada. Heeney was Secretary to the Cabinet. See also Heeney's memo to King of 12 Dec. and King's handwritten notes on it.

28 Some of the delays are explained in Gary Evans, *John Grierson and the National Film Board: The Politics of Wartime Propaganda, 1939-1945* (Toronto: University of Toronto Press, 1984), 77-89; and in William R. Young, "Chauvinism and Canadianism: Canadian Ethnic Groups and the Failure of Wartime Information," in *On Guard for Thee: War, Ethnicity, and the Canadian State, 1939-1945,* Norman Hiller, Bohdan Kordan, and Lubomyr Luciuk, eds. (Ottawa: Canadian Committee for the History of the Second World War and the Canadian Government Publishing Centre, 1988), 32-33.

29 Robert H. Keyserlingk, "Agents within the Gates': The Search for Nazi Subversives in Canada during World War II," *Canadian Historical Review* 66, 2 [1985], 229f; also, the same author's "The Canadian Government's Attitude Towards German Canadians in World War II," *Canadian Ethnic Studies* vol 14, No. 1 (1984), 16-28. A plan for rounding up suspected Italian Fascists was abandoned at the last moment when it was realized that neither Canada nor Great Britain was at war with Italy in September of 1939. On the subject of Ottawa's attitudes to Italian-Canadians during the war see my study "L'Evoluzione dello Status degli italiana 'stranieri nemici' in Canada durante la Seconda Guerra Mondiale" [The Evolving Status of Italian 'Enemy aliens' in Canada during World War II], in *Il Canada e la Guerra dei Trent'anni*, ed. Luigi Bruti-Liberati (Milan: Guerini Studio, 1989), 229-39.

30 Aspects of this story are told, from the pont of view of the internees, in William Repka and Kathleen M. Repka, *Dangerous Patriots: Canada's Unknown Prisoners of War* (Vancouver: New Star Books, 1982).

31 Hitler's abandonment of the Ukrainian separatist movement in Ruthenia in the spring of 1939 caused bitter disappointment in Ukrainian-Canadian nationalist circles. The Fuhrer's motives for encouraging Ukrainian separatists in the Carpatho-Ukraine, and his abandonment of them later, had been motivated not by any feelings for or against Ukrainians but by considerations of power politics. In the fall and winter of 1939 Hitler by encouraging Ukrainian irredentism, wanted to put pressure on Poland and even the USSR, while his abandonment of this policy in March of 1939 was a signal to Stalin that under certain circumstances, co-operation between the Nazi and Soviet dictatorships might be possible. For discussion of Ukrainian-Canadian reactions to these events see my study "Tracy Philipps and the Achievement of Ukrainian-Canadian Unity," in *Canada's Ukrainians*, Luciuk and Hryniuk eds., 330f.

32 The purpose of Philipps' tour is explained in a pamphlet published by the National Council of Education. A copy of this can be found in the Papers of Tracy Philipps, vol 2, National Archives of Canada.

33 Copy of letter, James G. Gardiner to Ernest Lapointe, 9 Sept. 1940, Records of the Department of National War Services (RG 44), vol 36, National Archives of Canada. See also my study "The Rise of a Bureaucracy for Multiculturalism: The Origins of the Nationalities Branch, 1939-41," in *On Guard for Thee: War, Ethnicity, and the Canadian State, 1939-1945,* Norman Hiller, Bohdan Kordan, and Lubomyr Luciuk, eds. (Ottawa: Canadian Committee for the History of the Second World War and the Canadian Government Publishing Centre, 1988), 7-9.

34 Copy of letter, Davis to H.R. MacMillan of the Wartime Merchant Shipping Ltd., 28 Feb. 1942. Records of the DNWS (RG 44), vol 36.

35 Letter, Davis to Gardiner, 13 Nov. 1940, Records of the DNWS (RG 44), vol 36.

36 I tell this story in considerable detail in my study, "Tracy Philipps," 326-41 and 477-83. At the time Philipps saw the Ukrainian nation, with its forty million people, as a potential ally against the Nazi and Soviet dictatorships. He no doubt felt that getting the largest community of the Ukrainian diaspora in the New World on board, would be an essential first step in building a bridge between the Allies and Ukrainians.

37 Watson Kirkconnell, *Canadians All: A Primer of Canadian National Unity* (Ottawa: Director of Public Information, 1940). On all this see Kirkconnell, *A Slice of Canada: Memoirs* (Toronto: University of Toronto Press, 1967), especially p. 176, but also p. 276. Kirkconnell's pamphlet was re-published in 1941, expunged of its negative references to the Soviet Union. Kirkconnell, *A Slice of Canada,* 177. On Coleman's and Robertson's views at this time regarding propaganda among the foreign-born see my "The Rise of a Bureaucracy," 8-10.

38 Evans, *John Grierson,* 159f. Later documentaries along these lines produced by the NFB would include the films *Ukrainian Christmas* (1942), *Poland on the Prairies,* and *Ukrainian Dance, New Home in the West* (all 1943).

39 On the history of the Nationalities Branch and the CCCC see the lengthy report, written in the winter of 1945-46, of Robert England, "Advisory Committee on Co-Operation in Canadian Citizenship (Nationalities Branch)," copy of an undated manuscript, in the Records of Interdepartmental Committees (RG 35), ser. 7, vol 26, NA. For scholarly accounts see Leslie A. Pal, "Identity, citizenship, and mobilization: the Nationalities Branch and World War Two," *Canadian Public Administration,* Vol 32, (Fall 1989), 407-26; as well as Dreisziger, "The Rise of a Bureaucracy," especially pp. 13-20.

40 The story of the Canadian government's treatment of the country's Japanese community in the Second World War is not a completely unrelated development; however, because of restrictions of space, it cannot be considered here in any detail. It has been told many times before, recently and perhaps the most ably in the book by Patricia E. Roy, J.L. Granatstein, Masako Iino, and Hiroko Takamura, *Mutual Hostages: Canadians and Japanese during the Second World War* (Toronto: University of Toronto Press, 1990). For my own comments on the subject, and its implications on the general treatment of enemy aliens in Canada, see my study "7 December 1941: A Turning Point in Canadian Wartime Policy Toward Enemy Ethnic Groups?" *Journal of Canadian Studies,* Vol 32, No. 1 (Spring 1997), especially 102f.

41 One circumstance behind the delays in setting up the NB was the fact that King considered Gardiner's plans for the bureau profligate, because Gardiner wanted to hire too many people to handle the job. How many, the documents do not say. King felt he had to replace Gardiner as the boss of DNWS, a decision that caused delay. Given the fact that eventually three people were hired for the NB, we wonder if the "too many" Gardiner had in mind hiring was four. King's penny-pinching must have been frustrating to a great many bureaucrats in wartime Ottawa. See my "The Rise of a Bureaucracy," 14-20. The pitiful situation of the Canadian public service on the eve of and during the early period of the war, including the government's reluctance to hire new help, is ably described in Doug Owram, "Two Worlds: The Canadian Civil Service in 1939," in *A Country of Limitations,* Hiller, et al. eds., 182-198. It might be added that the American equivalent of the NB, the Foreign Nationalities Branch of the Office of Strategic Services, started with 35 full-time employees and an even larger team of volunteers. United States, War Department, Strategic Services Unit, History Project, *War Report of the OSS,* Kermit Roosevelt, ed. (New York: Walker & Co., 1976), 63-67.

42 At first, Watson Kirkconnell was offered the top job. He declined because he did not want to give up his newly acquired post at McMaster University. Ironically, Simpson was then hired with the understanding that he would not abandon his academic career. With his appointment to the press section, Kysilewsky began a long association with the Canadian public service, later with the Department of Citizenship and Immigration, where he would be known as Dr. Kaye.

43 In effect, the government created a new category of enemy aliens, people who were automatically offered the exemption certificates that Regulation 26 of the DOCR provided to aliens who were not deemed dangerous to the Canadian war effort. The man most responsible for this unique concession to a part of Canada's immigrant population was Robertson. For more detail see my "7 December 1941," 98-102.

44 The story of the earliest such federations is told in Martin L. Kovacs, "The Saskatchewan Era," in *Struggle and Hope: The Hungarian-Canadian Experience,* N.F. Dreisziger ed. (Toronto: McClelland and Stewart, 1982), 78-82; the experiments of the 1920s and 1930s in establishing such umbrella organizations are reviewed in my paper "In Search of a Hungarian-Canadian Lobby: 1927-1951," *Canadian Ethnic Studies,* Vol 12, No. 3 (Fall 1980), 84-86.

45 See my "In Search of," 86f. Eisner's tour is documented in detail in his papers that for the time being are in my possession. There is some evidence that Philipps had tried to arrange a similar goodwill mission to the Italian-Canadian community, but I have never found evidence that this tour got off the ground, let alone succeeded. Philipps' own publicity campaign to improve the employment prospects of

Canadians with Italian names had little effect, mainly because by 1942 there was such need for manpower that employers began hiring (or, rehiring) Italians regardless of public prejudices against them.

46 Robertson to [William Lyon Mackenzie King], 26 Oct. 1942, Records of the Privy Council of Canada (RG 2), series 18, vol 45, file D-15-2, NA.

47 It has been estimated that some 26,000 citizens of the country benefited from the new regulations and that, when this number is added to the number of those immigrants who had profited from the December 1941 changes to the DOCR, by late 1942 about 100,000 people had become exempted from the restrictions of the DOCR. Theoretically, the Dec. 1942 announcement exempted even some Japanese-Canadians from their enemy-alien status, but in practice their situation improved only slowly and modestly. For more details see my "7 December 1941," 103f.

48 Jack Pickersgill, who at the time was King's personal secretary, during his long career as Ottawa bureaucrat and politician had seen many people talk their way into the Cabinet, but met only one, Thorson, who had talked himself out of it, i.e. his habit of talking too much in Cabinet meetings irritated King. (Pickersgill to the author, private conversation, 27 August 1987).

49 At least, this is what Philipps claimed at the time and this is what is suggested by the record. LaFlèche's competence as an administrator has also been questioned. Owram, "Two Worlds," 194. King had brought LaFlèche into the government probably because of his background: a French-Canadian with distinguished military service.

50 The affair is discussed in William R. Young, "Chauvinism and Canadianism," 40-45. Skilling, who was interviewed for the job by Grierson, also mentions it in his recent memoirs, although he is mistaken when he writes that it was Watson Kirkconnell and not Philipps whom he was supposed to replace. H. Gordon Skilling, *The Education of a Canadian: My Life as a Scholar and Activist* (Montreal: McGill-Queenn's Press, 2000), 92f. Evans, in his *John Grierson*, does not mention the affair.

51 When the NB's press officer Kysilewski became ill, he could not be replaced and his work of sending press releases to editors of ethnic newspapers had to be put on hold, and when the NB's typist resigned, no replacement could be found. Finally even Philipps had to take sick leave while he recovered from a nasty fall. See my "Rise of a Bureaucracy," 21.

52 England, "Advisory Committee," 16ff. The NB's budget, which at one point had shrunk to about $18,000 a year, was increased to a little over $50,000 (ibid.).

53 For arguments to the effect that the NB and the Citizenship Division were direct bureaucratic ancestors of the Multiculturalism Directorate of the late twentieth century see the conclusions of Pal, "Identity, citizenship, and mobilization," and Dreisziger, "The Rise of a Bureaucracy," 21.

54 Young, "Chauvinism and Canadianism," 31-51.

55 Some Hungarians wondered why it was the DNWS that sponsored Eisner's tour. These and some other people were confused about the department's name, which they mistranslated as *Hadügyminisztérium* (War Department). See my *Struggle and Hope*, 172f.

56 Bohdan S. Kordan and Lubomyr Y. Luciuk, "A Prescription for Nationbuilding: Ukrainian Canadians and the Canadian State, 1939-1945," in Hillmer, *et al.* eds. *We Stand on Guard*, 88-89.

57 Kirkconnell, *Canadians All*, 20.

58 Evans, *John Grierson*, 160.

59 I cite examples of this in my *Struggle and Hope*, 200-02.

CHAPTER 10

Canadians and the Bomber Command Experience

1939-1945

Lieutenant-Colonel David L. Bashow

Tom, Dick and Harry, plain names and numbers,
Pilot, observer, and gunner depart.
Their personal litter only encumbers
Somebody's head, somebody's heart.
—John Pudney

DURING THE SECOND WORLD WAR, the combined Anglo-American strategic bombing campaign conducted against Germany, its allies, and its territories of occupation, was a formidable weapon in the destruction of Hitler's Thousand Year Reich and Mussolini's Fascist Italy. Further, while this Anglo-American campaign was fought in one form or another from 1942 until the cessation of hostilities in Europe during the spring of 1945, Britain, the Dominions and their European allies had stood against these totalitarian states for nearly two and half years before America's entry into the conflict. From the first day of hostilities until the last, Canadian airmen would serve with great distinction in Bomber Command as members of the Royal Canadian Air Force, the Royal Air Force, and other Allied units within the command.

Along with playing a significant role in the overall Allied victory, Bomber Command was, at the outset, the only weapon available to take the fight to the Axis; to demonstrate to friend and foe alike that Britain, her Dominions and her friends had no intention of acquiescing to the bullying demands of the totalitarian states. In taking the offensive, hope and pride were given to Allied servicemen and civilians alike. Later, it was a "poor man's second front" to the beleaguered Soviets when no Allied invasion of the European continent was yet possible. The bombing campaign tied down in the west or diverted significant German resources, thereby indirectly aiding the Soviet Union in its portion of the combined struggle against the Axis. It would accomplish all this without keeping massive armies in deadlocked confrontation with all the concomitant bloodletting, such as had occurred in the trenches of the Western Front during the Great War. It would also have a definite detrimental impact upon German morale. Along with effectively gutting the Axis oil industry and transportation systems, it did substantial damage to the enemy war industrial base, especially the aircraft and aviation support industries. It threw the Axis war strategy into disarray, forcing great diversions of economic effort to honour the threat of the bombers. And it paved the way for the Allied invasion of Northwest Europe in 1944 while effectively preventing any economic mobilization that could have concentrated on technological answers to Allied initiatives.

These victories did not come cheaply, although the costs of the western air offensive may seem to some very light in the context of up to 27 million Soviet war dead. There were, however, very heavy losses endured by the Anglo-American air forces: 81,000 airmen would be killed aboard 18,000 downed bombers.[1] During the entire war, of the 125,000 airmen who served with Bomber Command on operations, 55,573 were lost aboard 12,330 aircraft, including 47,268 personnel on operations and a further 8,305 in training or non-operational accidents.[2] Canada was by far the second-largest national contributor of men and materiel to Bomber Command, and 40,000 Canadian airmen, nearly one-third of the wartime strength of the Command, would serve either operationally or at operational training units therein. Of this number, over 10,000 would forfeit their lives, and many others would be wounded or injured or become prisoners of war.[3] At least 9,200 gallantry awards were bestowed upon 8,300 Canadian airmen overseas, including two Victoria Crosses and a George Cross.[4] Most of these awards were conferred upon Canadians in Bomber Command.

The Canadian contribution to the Allied strategic bombing offensive was unique and unlike that of the British and the Americans. In order to fully appreciate the human dimension of the Canadian participation, one must first understand how the Canadianization process affected that contribution. From the opening shots of the Second World War, individual Canadian airmen, either as members of the RCAF or as expatriates in RAF service (known as CAN/RAFs), were participating in combat operations with RAF units. They were the progenitors of what came to be called a Lost Legion of Canadian combat flyers. Eventually, indigenous RCAF units would be formed in all the RAF's commands. However, with the exception of 6 Group in Bomber Command, the largest RCAF unit would be a wing. Indigenous RCAF wings were established in the fighter-bomber, army co-operation/reconnaissance and day fighter disciplines, while RCAF night fighter, intruder, transport and maritime patrol squadrons operated within RAF wings.

Hampden EQ - H (AE 288) of 408 Squadron runs up at Balderton in Nottinghamshire, UK. This aircraft was shot down over occupied Denmark on the night of 8 May 1942. (CF photo PL 4715 courtesy of Air Command.)

Canadian airmen permeated Bomber Command, as they did the RAF in general, for the duration of the war. By January 1943 nearly one-third of all Bomber Command squadrons were designated either Allied or Dominion units: Canadians would comprise roughly a quarter of the Command's operational aircrew on strength at war's end.[5] They served in virtually every RAF bomber squadron and did so with distinction. In one such unit (76 Squadron equipped with Halifaxes) 85 members of the RCAF were killed on operations between May 1941 and May 1945, while at least 29 of their number were decorated for heroism during their tours.[6] And when 617 (Dambuster) Squadron under the legendary Guy Gibson breached the Möhne and Eder dams in the Ruhr on the night of 16/17 of May 1943, 30 of the 133 participants were Canadians. Thirteen were killed on the mission, and many of the survivors were decorated for gallantry.

However, profound social differences between the British and the men from the Dominions were a considerable source of friction in wartime Britain. These differences were often manifest in very different attitudes with respect to authority. The British military's small, pre-war regular force with its tradition-bound way of life—replete with public school values and class distinctions—treated British working class volunteers with a disdain that occasionally resulted in unfair treatment to non-commissioned airmen. While the new wave of British inductees was more inclined to accept these class distinctions as inevitable, the more egalitarian men from the Dominions found these attitudes rankling if not outright undemocratic. Leadership and command were felt to be questions of competence and substance and not a function of style and social status. Respect had to be earned, not assumed. Conversely, the British upper class view of North Americans and other "New Worlders" was less than flattering and potentially confrontational. Quoting from an RAF report of the day:

> The new world—American and Canadian alike—is impetuous, enthusiastic, sometimes childish, often self-assured and usually not a little boastful. It likes to seem tough and it likes to show off. One RAF officer, the CO of an RCAF squadron, told us that Canadians are erratic: they want quick excitement, but cannot settle down to a hard grind. Another RAF officer, the CO of an [Operational Training Unit], said that the Canadians are a pretty unsophisticated lot, who come over with a chip on their shoulder, and put on a tough exterior to cover up a sense of inferiority. A number of RAF officers told us that Canadians do not know how to hold their drinks.[0]

Additional comments on the same subject are also noteworthy:

> Canadians have no veneration for spit-and-polish. And they dislike discipline when it appears as the arbitrary will of a person in a superior rank. They must feel that discipline makes sense before they accept it wholeheartedly. When it goes flatly against common sense, they despise it.[8]

This British mind-set was manifest in much more preferential treatment of commissioned officers within the RAF. By comparison, the leaders of the United States Army Air Force, who were socially quite similar to the Canadians and the Australians, were much more egalitarian in their treatment of personnel, exemplified by the sharing of common mess halls and a predilection for all-ranks social functions.

One should note that the RAF executive harboured grave concerns about the large influx of Dominion aircrew, fearing a shift of influence, since their own service was eventually unable to take in "enough young men of the British middle and upper classes, the supposed natural leaders and 'backbone' of British society."[9] Many influential and respected British air leaders were noted for their condescending attitudes toward "the Colonials."[10] Even the most famous wartime Commander-in-Chief of Bomber Command, Sir Arthur Harris, feared what he termed an "alienation of the Service" by the men from the Dominions. Canadian historian Allan English elaborates:

> Harris worried that if most of the operational squadrons were manned by 'coloured troops,'" as he disparagingly referred to Dominion aircrew, he would lose operational control of his force, because the Dominions insisted on being consulted on personnel issues such as aircrew disposal and tour length. To hold on to what he saw as his operational prerogatives, Harris sometimes acted independently of Air Ministry policies. This and other RAF actions that undermined Canadian authority eventually forced the RCAF to take measures to ensure that its wishes were respected.[11]

Memories of the Great War, during which Canadian military formations were kept subservient to British higher authority, were still very fresh at the start of the Second World War. Therefore, when Prime Minister Mackenzie King signed the British Commonwealth Air Training Plan (BCATP) into being on 17 December 1939, Article XV of the agreement declared that graduates of the plan from the Dominions would be identified with their countries of origin through membership in Dominion units.[12] Specifically, Canada would be permitted to establish Canadian units and formations overseas as quickly as possible and man them to the greatest extent with Canadian aircrew. These RCAF units would be governed by RCAF regulations and procedures. Eventually there would be forty-seven flying squadrons overseas, including fourteen heavy bomber squadrons. One should note that Canada never sought operational autonomy from Britain, such as that enjoyed by American bombing operations conducted by the Eighth Air Force in England. Rather, while Canada designed the BCATP policy to provide the RCAF overseas with greater freedom from British control, this freedom was obstructed at various levels by the British government in general and the RAF in particular. One of the key issues concerned the commissioning of RCAF aircrew serving in RAF units. As Allan English explains:

> At higher levels it was perceived as the unwarranted political interference of a junior ally in operational matters where Canada had little influence. Consequently, some senior RAF commanders simply circumvented Canadianization when it suited them. At lower levels the policy was seen as disruptive to morale, and efforts were

made, especially with RCAF NCO aircrew, "to blot out" their Canadian identity by insisting that they belonged to the RAF once they left Canada.[13]

When the BCATP was renegotiated in June 1942, solicitations from the irate parents of RCAF airmen serving overseas with the RAF to Canadian Members of Parliament brought the commissioning issue to a head. Prior to the 1942 renegotiation, the BCATP policy had been to commission fifty percent of pilots and observers and twenty percent of wireless operators and air gunners; half at graduation and the other half based upon performance during operations. However, Canadian Air Minister C.G. "Chubby" Power disliked the quota system. He believed it was based upon the British concept that only members of a certain social strata were worthy of holding commissions.[14] "The Canadians drew attention to the sense of unfairness, 'damaging to morale,' to inequalities in pay, transportation, travel allowances and messing, and made a telling point by mentioning the effect of these inequalities on those unfortunate enough to become prisoners of war.... They dwelled on the injury to the team spirit when 'the crew, as an entity, is not able to live and fraternize, the one with the other, during leisure and off-duty hours.'"[15] Therefore, Canada insisted that the revised agreement should state that all pilots, navigators, air bombers and observers, who were considered suitable according to the standards of the Canadian government and had been recommended for commissions, were to be commissioned.[16] Canadian Air Minister Power's words on the issue to British authorities are revealing. "I gave these young fellows my word," he told the British, "but only after you agreed. I realize that Canadian and British ideas on commissions are not identical and that we may upset your officer-NCO balance in RAF squadrons. Nevertheless, I hope to live in Canada after the war, but you fellows will still be in England."[17]

However, the British refused to budge, and Canada eventually agreed to a compromise of commissioning all pilots and observers upon graduation, twenty-five percent of all other categories upon graduation, and a further twenty-five percent of this latter category at an unspecified later date.[18] And yet, British stubbornness persisted. In November 1942, Power learned that only 28.7 percent of RCAF pilots and observers serving operationally with the RAF under the old rules had been commissioned. Since field commissions were subject to British Air Ministry approval, and since the RCAF had been automatically commissioning a quarter of its pilots and observers upon BCATP graduation, that meant that the RAF was only commissioning a niggardly additional 3.7 percent of eligible Canadian airmen. "That reluctance did not extend to its own aircrew, however," notes the official Canadian history, "as on 1 September 1942, 57 percent of RAF pilots and observers were officers. The discrepancy was even greater in the (specific) case of pilots, as 67 percent of those wearing uniforms held commissions compared with only 29 percent in the RCAF."[19]

In the end, Canada simply circumvented this British intransigence by commissioning a greater number of its BCATP graduates. In fact, from 1943 onward, it would commission all its pilots, observers, navigators, and air bombardiers (similar to the American policy) although it adhered to existing quotas for commissioning the other air trades for the time being.[20] However, the Canadianization process would continue to meet stiff resistance within the RAF and the issue would dog the formation of a distinctly RCAF Group within Bomber Command.

As expatriate CAN/RAFs, hundreds of Canadian airmen were in action with Bomber Command from the first day of hostilities. They went to war as members of 23 front-line bomber squadrons equipped with 280 bombers in four groups; one each of Bristol Blenheims, Armstrong Whitworth Whitleys, Vickers Wellingtons and Handley Page Hampdens, all twin-

Top: Photographed beside a 408 Squadron Hampden at Balderton on 18 January 1942 are Sergeants Cornwall, Dunn, Manson, and Norton. (CF photo PL 7121 courtesy of Air Command.)

Bottom: A 6 Group Halifax V getting bombed up. On the bomb dollies are Small Bomb Containers (SBCs) and, nearest the tractor, a stalwart weapon of Bomber Command, the 2000-pound "cookie." (CF photo PL 19507 courtesy of Air Command.)

engined monoplanes. While these aircraft types were relatively modern, they were primitive in comparison to the four-engined types that would soon follow. All lacked electronic aids to navigation and possessed only the most primitive bomb sights. None of their performance characteristics—including top speed, service ceiling, maximum range, and bomb-carrying capacity—were particularly impressive. Perhaps most importantly at the time, their defensive armament had been woefully neglected.

British bombing policy was deliberately non-provocative for the first six months of the war. Bomber Command's objectives were limited to strategic reconnaissance, propaganda leaflet raids, and the destruction of enemy shipping at sea. Crews were repeatedly warned that the greatest care was to be exercised so as not to injure enemy civilians, and that there were to be no alternative targets to the German fleet. On the night following the British declaration of war, 3/4 September 1939, Robert Stevenson of Victoria, British Columbia, and John Sproule of Brandon, Manitoba, each climbed into Whitleys as part of the first ten-aircraft leaflet raid on German cities. Collectively, this tiny air fleet dropped 5.4 tons of leaflets, and assured their place in history as the first to drop materiel of any nature on Germany during the Second World War. That same night, Pilot Officer George E. Walker of Gleichen, Alberta, flew a reconnaissance mission over Germany in a Whitley from 58 Squadron. These three Canadians were actually flying operationally before the west coast of Canada woke up to the knowledge that Britain was at war with Germany. It would appear that Flight Lieutenant T.C. Weir was the first Canadian of the war to participate in an offensive sortie. Also on 3 September, he piloted a 44 Squadron Hampden on a North Sea search mission for German naval vessels. However, the first Canadian airman to actually engage in combat was Pilot Officer Selby Roger Henderson of Winnipeg. Henderson, piloting a Blenheim from 110 Squadron, was part of a gallant but ineffectual raid against German shipping on 4 September. He was awarded a Distinguished Flying Cross (DFC) early in the new year for his courage and determination in pressing home attacks during the war's opening phase, but he was killed in action in July, 1940. Even so, the dubious distinction of being the first Canadian to die in battle during this war fell to Sergeant Albert Prince of Vancouver. Prince was killed over Wilhelmshaven, Germany on 5 September, a full five days before Canada declared war.[21]

And so it began. From these humble beginnings a much more aggressive offensive posture would soon develop, and by the spring of 1940, the restraints with respect to the bombing of German population centres were irrevocably, albeit progressively, lifted. In May, Sir Charles Portal, the new Commander-in-Chief, Bomber Command, found himself agreeing with the new Prime Minister, Winston Churchill, that in order to support military operations on land, a more aggressive stance in the air was warranted. While indiscriminate bombing was still forbidden, any pressure that could be brought to bear onGerman communications, oil industries, aircraft plants and air force infrastructure was acceptable. Transportation targets were also considered fair game, and this limited mandate would soon be expanded to other industrial assets. Portal believed that concentrated, heavy attacks would also have a strong moral impact on the German population, adversely affecting their will to fight. His views would greatly influence the evolution of British bombing policy during the war years.[22] Churchill endorsed these views and, in the wake of the French capitulation on 17 June 1940, became "an enthusiast for bombing in the absence of any other means of attack."[23] A bombing offensive would serve notice to friend and foe alike that Britain and her allies could, and would, strike back.

Early on, draconian losses of Bomber Command aircraft on daylight raids forced a strategy shift to operating under the cloak of darkness. However, navigation and bombing aids and skills were so rudimentary that any form of precision bombing was out of the question for the time being. Thus, the inevitability of collateral damage to civilian populations in industrial centres was conceded in the early stages. This acceptance was undoubtedly influenced by repeated examples of indiscriminate bombing by the Germans and their totalitarian allies.

By the end of November 1940, the first graduates of the BCATP had made their way overseas. The initial 37 observers were joined by the first pilot graduates of the plan on 1 March 1941. This trickle would quickly become a steady stream and then a veritable torrent of aircrew, generated for the war against the Axis. The BCATP graduated 132,000 airmen of all categories during the war, including 73,000 Canadians.[24] These men of Canada included, in round numbers, 26,000 pilots, 13,000 navigators, 6,000 air bombers, 26,000 wireless operators/air gunners and 2,000 flight engineers.[25] A majority of these airmen served in Bomber Command. By mid April 1941, 1,680 graduates of the plan were already in England. By year's end, nearly 6,700 were serving overseas, and yet only 600 of them were in RCAF squadrons.[26] Canadianization was not going well, and in fact, nearly sixty percent of all RCAF airmen would serve in other than RCAF units throughout the course of the war. It should be noted that while many Canadians thought the multinational units provided the best of service experiences, many did not.

Although RCAF squadrons had been serving within the RAF since 1940 in the fighter and army co-operation disciplines, representation within Bomber Command was slower to evolve. That said, 405 Squadron (equipped with Wellingtons) was the first RCAF heavy bomber squadron to form, and it did so at Driffield in Yorkshire on 23 April 1941 under the command of 4 Group. They would fly their first combat missions in mid June, and by 24 June, 408 Squadron (flying Hampdens) had been activated at Lindholme, also in Yorkshire, as part of 5 Group. Since the creation of these two squadrons occurred within only six months of the bilateral, stage-setting Ralston-Sinclair Agreement between Canada and Britain—which dictated how Canadian airmen would be employed and treated overseas—practicalities demanded that initially the squadron commander, the flight commanders, and the first cadre of experienced aircrew would have to come from the RAF. At the outset this certainly held true, and when 405 Squadron commenced operations in June, only 16.5 percent of the pilots were Canadian. Only slightly better numbers were posted initially in 408 Squadron, where a quarter of all aircrew positions were occupied by RCAF members.[27] By late fall, however, the Canadianization rate had significantly improved, although many non-Canadians would continue to serve in RCAF heavy bomber squadrons, and Canadians in RAF squadrons, for the duration of the war. By year's end, two more heavy bomber squadrons, Numbers 419 and 420, had been activated, also with twin-engined Hampdens and Wellingtons.

The first of the four-engined heavy bombers, the Short Stirling, did not enter battle until February 1941. Its operational life in the bombing role was short and disappointing, fraught with problems. The true backbone of Bomber Command's eventual four-engined fleet was the Handley Page Halifax, which first flew operationally in March 1941, and the Avro Lancaster, introduced at year's end. Both were successful offshoots of earlier twin-engined aircraft. Both were capable weapons in their ultimate wartime configurations, although early Halifax variants were beset by significant troubles. Even the later Mark III model, flown extensively by Canadian squadrons, had a somewhat disappointing service ceiling and other flaws. At face value, there was little to distinguish these two aircraft in terms of speed and range. However, operational statistics compiled in mid-1943 showed that only one Lancaster was lost for every

130 tonnes of bombs delivered, while the delivery rate for each Halifax lost was 55 tonnes. That said, and due in no small measure to the location and number of emergency escape hatches and the formidable main wing spar of the Lancaster, which made internal movement very difficult, only eleven percent of Lancaster crews survived a shoot-down, while the corresponding survival rate for Halifax crewmen was twenty-nine percent.[28] Neither statistic compares favourably with the American successful egress rate from their mainstay heavy bombers, the B-17 Flying Fortress and the B-24 Liberator, which was roughly fifty percent for each.[29] However, along with being less likely to be mortally hit overall, the Lancaster was much more economical to produce. Therefore, as much as possible, the Lancaster was the Command's weapon of choice. Nonetheless, at least during the middle years of the bomber offensive, both were needed desperately.[30] Also, while the Mark II and the Mark V variants of the Halifax were both disappointing and dangerous to fly, the Mark III and subsequent versions overcame many of the shortcomings of their predecessors, and were generally popular with their crews.

Bomber Command policy was to re-equip its squadrons with four-engined types in order of unit seniority, and this virtually guaranteed an intermediate equipping with twin-engined medium bombers for newly-established units, including indigenous Allied and Dominion squadrons, until very late in the war.

Not only were the size and the technological face of the Command changing, so was bombing policy. An operational survey carried out in August 1941 by a member of the Cabinet secretariat, D.M. Butt, concluded that only a third of Bomber Command's sorties for June and July had bombed within five miles of their targets in Germany. His report significantly undermined confidence at the highest levels in the overall bombing strategy. After six months of argument, Policy Directive Number 22 was issued on 14 February 1942: it declared that henceforth, the primary objective of Bomber Command would be "the morale of the enemy civil population and in particular, of the industrial workers."[31] This policy was to be manifested as large raids on area targets in the major industrial cities of Germany, and while specific industrial aim points were virtually always identified and specified, collateral damage in terms of a "dehousing" of the civilian population was considered an acceptable, indeed desirable, adjunct to the bombing. The Ruhr area, particularly Essen, was singled out as being of primary importance. Berlin was also included on the preferred target list.

Ten days later, on 24 February 1942, the helm of Bomber Command passed to the man historically most closely identified with the bombing of Germany, a Rhodesian in RAF service, Air Marshal Sir Arthur Harris. Blunt, tenacious, and single-minded to the point of obsession, Harris had thoroughly absorbed the lessons of the Butt Report and was convinced that the bombing could only be effective when his forces were concentrated in mass to overwhelm the enemy defences, and when navigational and bombing techniques had vastly improved. These two preconditions became his focal points of the early years of his tenure.

> Above all he carried with him the conviction that no single target on the enemy side held the answer to German defeat. He remained hostile to what he called 'panacea' targets, not because they were difficult to hit—and the accuracy of Bomber Command operations increased remarkably over the war—but because he realized that an enemy economy and social structure could not be dislocated by an attack on just one of its many elements with the prospect of forcing a decision. Bombing was a blunt instrument during the Second World War, and Harris pursued a strategy that he believed would use that instrument to best effect.[32]

This strategy is telling, for it highlights the reality that while Bomber Command would eventually possess precision bombing specialists in the form of 617 (Dambuster) Squadron, the Command's precision capabilities were not widespread until the very closing months of the war.

As Bomber Command continued to expand and to adopt more sophisticated tactics and equipment, the Germans were quick to establish a countering chain of defences. These included early warning radars, a fleet of progressively more sophisticated night fighters, formidable high-intensity radar-directed searchlights, and a host of radar-directed anti-aircraft artillery (*flak*) emplacements. This defensive belt, called the Kammhuber Line, stretched unbroken and fifteen miles deep from the Scheldt estuary to the island of Sylt off the German-Danish border. Responding to this belt was a very rigid system of airspace control—called *Himmelbett* (Heavenly Bed)—in which the night fighters were assigned specific airspace sectors for patrol and engagement. The answer to this system was Harris' principle of the concentration of forces in the shortest possible time over the target to overwhelm the defences. To that end, he would introduce the concept of the bomber stream, the effectiveness of which was demonstrated very clearly on the night of 30/31 May 1942 over Cologne. Codenamed *Operation Millennium*, this was the first of the thousand-bomber raids, and it totally saturated the German defences. This ambitious operation completely monopolized the Command's still-limited resources, and even training aircraft were used on the raid to bring the striking force up to the required number. After this, the Germans would adopt much less restricted *Frie Jagd* (Free Hunt) or *Wilde Sau* (Wild Boar) tactics, that allowed the night fighters, and single-seat day fighters employed at night, much more freedom of movement.

As was the case on the North Atlantic in the submarine war, the night air war over Europe was very much a case of technological moves and counter moves by the opposing sides. New tactics were continuously developed to exploit these technological advances. On both sides of the fence, the airmen became increasingly dependent upon the scientists. The British scientific community provided increasingly sophisticated equipment to navigate, to bomb accurately, and to mask the bombers' presence, while the Germans proved to be very innovative in finding different ways to locate and engage the night raiders.

In early 1942, a new British navigational aid called *Gee* (Ground Electronics Engineering) was fielded. This electronic system and its derivatives would evolve and become a mainstay of Bomber Command for the rest of the war. In August, a specialized target finding andmarking force was introduced. Known as the Pathfinders, they were eventually concentrated in their own exclusive 8 Group. This innovative organization would employ increasingly sophisticated electronic aids and visual markers to pave the way for the main force and then direct and coordinate the raids, night after night, in fair weather and foul. They became an indispensable part of the bomber offensive. Many Canadians served in the Pathfinder Force and their 405 Squadron was a member of this elite flying fraternity from April 1943 onward. A lesser known body of experts was 100 Group, which specialized in all forms of electronic countermeasures to foil enemy detection and tracking equipment. Again, Canadian airmen would be well represented in this cutting-edge element of the electronic war.

Oboe would supplement *Gee* as a navigational aid after 1942, and an Air Position Indicator (API), which was linked to the aircraft's compass and airspeed indicator, provided a broadly accurate deterrent against crews getting hopelessly lost. *G-H* was an *Oboe*-like aid that was accurate but limited by its short range and vulnerability to enemy homing.[33] Perhaps the most versatile navigation and bombing aid was *H2S*, an airborne ground mapping radar that could

An RCAF Lancaster in flight. Note the H2S radar dome just forward of the tail wheel. The Americans did not have the market cornered on aircraft nose art. (DND file photo.)

double as a blind bombing device. It also would become a mainstay of Bomber Command operations from 1943 onward.

On the other side of the coin, the Germans used the enormous *Würzburg* and *Freya* detection radars to acquire and to track the bomber stream's nightly route. Bomber Command countered with *Window*, air-dropped aluminum foil strips cut specifically to the German ground radars' wavelength. This jamming technique was premiered with devastating effectiveness against Hamburg on the night of 27/28 July 1943. It completely blinded the defences and Hamburg was effectively reduced to a smoking ruin in the wake of a massive firestorm. All 78 Canadian crews participating—almost a tenth of the strike force that night—survived the mission.[34] *Window* was supplemented by *Mandrel*, an electronic way of jamming the early warning radars. The Germans then countered with *Freya-Halbe*, *Wassermann*, and *Mammut* radars, all with various anti-jamming capabilities. And the Germans had jammers of their own: *Heinrich* and *Bumerang* to counter *Gee* and *Oboe*, as well as *Naxos* and *Naxburg* to home in on *H2S*. With respect to airborne intercept (AI) radars, the Germans fielded *Liechtenstein* to find the bombers in all kinds of weather, and *Spanner*, an infrared device that detected the bombers' hot engine exhausts. The British then introduced *Monica*, an AI radar designed to warn the bombers of German night fighters sneaking up on their vulnerable stern positions. German countermeasures to *Monica* followed, as did British counter-counter innovations. One lesson that was only slowly and painfully learned by both sides was that most of this new electronic technology left an electronic signature of its source, thus providing an unintended marker of the transmitter's whereabouts. Many aircraft on both sides were lost because of this.

Bogus radio transmissions from England to German night fighters, codenamed *Drumstick*, *Fidget*, and *Jostle*, later supplemented by airborne *Tinsel* transmissions, further served to confuse and deceive. British bomb sights also improved to the point where the Mark XIV and Mark XVI systems were on a technological par with the vaunted American Norden sight. The bombs themselves also evolved, becoming much more reliable, robust, and purpose-built. Their explosive capability increased dramatically, culminating in the precision-developed 12,000 pound *Tallboy* and the 22,000 pound *Grand Slam* bombs of 1944 and 1945 respectively. "All these exotic tools and techniques came into play incrementally, spread over the length and breadth of the bomber offensive, each with its own grotesque identifier—*Cigar* and *Airborne Cigar*, *Corona*, *Dartboard*, *Grocer*, *Piperack*, *Perfectos* and *Shiver* on one side, *Donnerkell*, *Dudelsack*, *Erstling*, *Flamme*, *Laubfrosch*, *Lux* and *Sagebock* on the other."[35]

And on it went, seemingly without end. Yet while these innovations lent progressively more sophistication, accuracy and efficiency to the bomber war, it was the undisputed and sustained courage of the crews bringing these new technologies into play night after night that made the campaign a distinct albeit very costly success. In the judgement of Canadian historians Brereton Greenhous and Hugh Halliday, "the bomber offensive of 1942-43 and the first months of 1944 was the Second World War's equivalent of the First World War's Somme and Passchendaele."[36]

Canadianization within Bomber Command and elsewhere in the RAF proceeded throughout 1942 to include the formation of a fifth heavy bomber squadron, Number 425, a Francophone outfit, in June, and a further six squadrons in the latter half of the year.[37] Air Marshal Harold "Gus" Edwards, the new Canadian Air Officer-in-Chief of the RCAF Overseas, was much more nationalistic than his predecessor, Air Vice-Marshal L.F. Stevenson,[38] and he pushed Canadianization vigorously in attempting to establish a stronger measure of national control over Canadian airmen in theatre.[39] Indeed, by June 1942, seventy percent of the airmen in RCAF squadrons were Canadian, although the percentage was less in the bomber squadrons.[40] However, the drums were beating in Ottawa, and now overseas, to form the indigenous air equivalent of an operational Canadian army, and so it came to pass that 6 (RCAF) Group was established on 1 January 1943. Its creation coincided with a major bombing policy change mandated by the Casablanca Conference later that same month. The conference established the Anglo-American Combined Bomber Offensive. This massive co-operative effort, with the Americans operating by day and Bomber Command by night, would span the next sixteen months. It took as its mandate "the progressive destruction and dislocation of the German military, industrial and economic system, and the undermining of the morale of the German people to a point where their capacity for armed resistance is fatally weakened."[41] Codenamed *Pointblank*, the combined offensive gave targets the following priority:

1. German submarine construction yards;
2. German aircraft industry;
3. Transportation assets;
4. Oil plants and facilities;
5. Other targets within the enemy war industry.[42]

Number 6 (RCAF) Group initially comprised six twin-engined Wellington squadrons and three four-engined Halifax squadrons located on six, eventually ten, Yorkshire airfields, with operations being totally funded by the Canadian government.[43] The preponderance of twin-engined equipment in this new group is not unusual, since four-engined bombers were not yet available for all units. Also, the RAF believed in maintaining a homogeneity of equipment within groups as much as possible, for standardization and ease of logistics, training and maintenance.

Located between the Cleveland Hills to the east and the Pennines to the west, this area of quiet vales and rolling hills in the East Riding of Yorkshire put 6 Group the farthest away from the Continent, requiring thirty to sixty minutes more flying time to European targets than that for the more southerly-based groups.[44] Furthermore, because of the natural confinement of the bordering hills, many of the airfields had dangerously-overlapping traffic patterns. Southerly winds brought industrial smoke from the Leeds-Bradford area, while northerly winds brought smog from Middlesbrough. Also, given the high ground to the east, returning aircrew could not break cloud over the North Sea as could their fighting cousins in East Anglia and Lincolnshire. Living conditions at the 6 Group bases varied considerably. The few pre-war bases, such as Linton, were well-built and had comfortable dining, living, and recreational facilities. However, bases built during the war featured the ubiquitous Nissen huts. In contrast to Linton, Skipton-upon-Swale, a satellite station, was barren and dingy in the extreme, and at one time the airmens' showers were located a full mile from their lodgings. Tholthorpe, though a newly constructed station, had attractive lawns surrounding its Nissen huts and well decorated messes.

Not only were the locations and the accommodations of a decidedly mixed nature for the fledgling Group, but the RAF's equipment homogeneity policy became a significant source of dissatisfaction. While Canada wanted the Group to be equipped with Lancasters, partly because the nation would ultimately contribute Canadian-built Lancaster Mark Xs to the bombing offensive, the RAF saw this issue differently. Arguing that Canada could not produce enough Lancasters to supply her own needs, and "with no British-made Lancasters to spare, except at the expense of RAF squadrons, and the production of the unsatisfactory Stirling being phased out, Harris made, what was for him, the easy decision to equip the Canadians with Halifaxes."[45] This decision saddled 6 Group with the earlier Mark II and Mark V variants, and eventually some of the inferior radial-engined Lancaster Mark IIs; a condition that would not change until well into the last year of the European air war.[46] This was in spite of the fact that Power himself had promised the RCAF in April 1943 that he would "soon embark on a drive to secure better aircraft for Canadian squadrons—a drive which, in fact, never materialized."[47] Thus, there seems to have been some justification to Canadian claims that 6 Group was being discriminated against by the RAF in several subtle yet collectively damaging ways for being the showpiece of the RCAF Canadianization program overseas.

The combat record of 6 Group during its first year of operations was both disappointing and somewhat disturbing. Loss rates in Wellingtons had climbed to nine percent in June 1943, well above the five percent figure that Bomber Command had earlier reckoned to be the maximum long-term sustainable loss rate that would not be catastrophic for aircrew morale. While part of the losses were blamed upon 6 Group's location, which delayed the entrance of its aircraft into the main bomber stream and thus increased individual vulnerability to attack by German night fighters, a Bomber Command report of the time also implied that the Canadians were employing inferior tactics. Additionally the early return rate was cause for concern, with its implied lack of willingness to engage the enemy, and this same report suggested that the widespread deficiencies in training and maintenance stemmed partly from Canadians' failure to learn from their early apprenticeship under 4 Group.[48] However, the spring-1943 deployment of three Wellington squadrons to North Africa had included many of the more experienced crews. Ultimately, it was decided that most of the problems identified were attributable to the Group's lack of experience. By August 1943, both the loss rates and the early return rates had dropped measurably, at least for the time being.

However, 6 Group's first Air Officer Commanding, Air Vice-Marshal George E. Brookes, kept a rather remote detachment from those under his command. He also, in the eyes of some of his charges, unfairly blamed them for the relatively high "waverer" or early return rate. The aircrew started venting strong objections to being commanded by officers whose operational experience was limited, and who, they felt, were over-enthusiastically pandering to the British to the detriment of the airmen themselves. Eventually, this adversarial command situation was corrected, due in no small measure to inspired downstream leadership in 1944 from a new Air Officer Commanding, Air Vice-Marshal Clifford M. "Black Mike" McEwen.

The bomber offensive reached its apex in 1944 and 1945. Punishing losses during the winter of 1943-1944, particularly those associated with the Berlin raids, almost brought the

Command to its knees. In the spring, Harris reverted his forces to less-distant targets, which brought the loss rates back down to digestible proportions. And longer-term relief was acquired in April when the Command was seconded to Supreme Headquarters Allied Expeditionary Forces and General Dwight D. Eisenhower in support of the pending June invasion of north-west Europe by way of the Normandy beaches. For the next five months, Bomber Command would devote the bulk of its resources to closer-in transportation targets, significantly reducing 6 Group's loss rates still further when combined with the intensive new training regimen imposed by its new commander, Air Vice-Marshal McEwen. By the time Bomber Command reverted to control by the air staff in September 1944, and its priority was redirected against industrial targets in Germany, the back of German air resistance had been largely broken.

Except for a few isolated raids, losses would be relatively light during the last nine months of the European war, and it should be noted that most of the total wartime tonnage was dropped during this period. Also, the monthly average number of sorties had increased from 5,400 in 1943 to 14,000 in 1944, and the average payload per sortie had nearly doubled.[49] According to British historian John Terraine, eighty-five percent of the total bomb tonnage dropped on Germany was delivered after 1 January 1944, and seventy-two percent of the total after 1 July 1944, from which time forward the loss rates were greatly reduced.[50] In round figures, 13,000 tonnes were dropped on Germany in 1940, 32,000 in 1941, 48,000 in 1942, 200,000 in 1943 and nearly a million tonnes in 1944 by the American and British fleets together.[51] During the four effective months of 1945, nearly 200,000 tonnes were dropped by Bomber Command aircraft alone.

And what of the losses? The totals have already been mentioned but the loss rates require some clarification, since they were pivotal to aircrew morale. Here, hyperbole has played its part over the years, although this is not to suggest that Bomber Command losses were insignificant. In fact, one's chances of survival during the bomber offensive depended very much upon when one was flying. At a fairly early stage in the campaign, the RAF determined that an overall five percent loss rate would be the most that aircrew could endure on a sustained basis. However there were occasions when the loss rates were much higher, and conversely long periods, such as during the last year, when they were much lower. Overall, for every 100 men who flew operationally in the Command, 38 would be killed on operations, seven would be killed in operational accidents or in training, eight would become prisoners of war, three would be wounded in action, and three would be seriously injured.[52] Thus, fully 59 percent of all who served would become physical casualties.

That said, the Canadian results were considerably better, and for a number of reasons. The statistics are based on the determination that 40,000 RCAF airmen served operationally in wartime Bomber Command. Again, of every 100 who served, 21 would be killed on operations, four would be killed in operational accidents or training, five would become prisoners of war, two would be wounded in action and two would be seriously injured in operational accidents or in training.[53] Thus, only 34 percent of the RCAF airmen in Bomber Command became physical casualties. These figures, however, do not include more than five hundred CAN/RAF Bomber Command men who gave their lives during the war.

While CAN/RAF losses and those of RCAF aircrew serving in RAF units would mirror those of their British contemporaries, Canadians were not present in large numbers during the war's early phase when loss rates were relatively high. In 1942 the average loss rate per mission in Bomber Command was 4.1 percent; by 1944, it had been reduced to 1.7 percent per raid, and

This 419 Squadron Lancaster is loaded with 1000-pound high explosive bombs. On the left is Wing Commander Wilbur Pleasance, DFC and Bar, the Commanding Officer of the Squadron from October 1943 to August 1944. (CF photo PL 29078 courtesy of Air Command.)

by 1945, to 0.9 percent. And of the 364,514 Command sorties flown during the war, nearly two-thirds of them (213,186 sorties) were flown during 1944 and 1945.[54] Also, the largest part of the Canadian contribution to the bomber offensive is represented by 6 Group's operations from the beginning of 1943 onward. The neophyte group did stumble at the outset compared to the performance of its more experienced comrades. However, the high initial loss rate was mitigated when three of the group's Wellington squadrons were syphoned off between April and November 1943 to become 331 Wing in North Africa, flying in support of the Allied landings in Sicily and Italy. During this deployment, the wing flew 2,182 combat sorties but lost only eighteen aircraft, a pittance compared to the rest of 6 Group's losses over Germany during the same period.

Number 6 Group's overall wartime loss rate was two percent per mission, the lowest in Bomber Command. But, there were periods when the Canadian experience in 6 Group, as elsewhere in the Command, was much more fraught with risk. The group's Halifax II/V operations between March 1943 and March 1944 averaged a loss rate of just over six percent per raid, which equated to a terrifying 16 percent survival rate for an operational tour. The group at this time was also flying Lancaster Mark IIs, which were inferior to the Merlin-powered variants. With four radial engines, the Mark IIs were underpowered, and they displayed significant service ceiling limitations. The group's Lancaster II loss rate between August 1943 and March 1944 averaged five percent per mission, producing a concomitant twenty-one percent tour survival rate.[55] Worst of all was the group's Halifax II/V loss rate during January 1944, which, at the height of the Berlin raids, was a soul-destroying 9.8 percent per mission.[56] In round terms, this reduced the aircrew survival rate during the period to roughly one-in-twenty, a virtual death sentence.

Similar rough periods can be documented for the other groups. And yet while Bomber Command's morale faltered, it never failed. No other element of the western Allied combatants suffered the same enormous casualty rates over a sustained, long-term campaign; nor did they face "the mathematical certainty of their own deaths so routinely and so unflinchingly."[57] Specifically, less than one percent of the participants suffered combat stress so severe that it rendered them unable to carry on operations against the enemy, and even fewer were categorized in one form or another as lacking moral fibre.[58]

What caused them to prevail so steadfastly overall? American, British, Dominion and other Allied crews were motivated to join the war effort by a wide range of emotions, including patriotism and a sense of duty, and all of them were volunteers. For the British, having had their island ravaged by German raids early in the war, the patriotic sense of commitment was probably more pronounced than it was for American and Dominion airmen, for many "were far from their homes, and many did not feel the personal sense of commitment to the war that was possible for Englishmen."[59] The lure of flight and the thrill of service in a dimension considered glamourous by ordinary citizens were also compelling reasons. These were fit, specially selected and relatively well trained young men who for the most part started their operational tours secure in the belief that they were vital cogs in the war effort. All air forces did a very good job of fostering the elite status of their airmen through distinctive brevets or flying badges, and airmen were fiercely proud of these marks of distinction. However, the realities of combat, particularly the random nature of bomber casualties, dispelled a lot of the more glamorous notions. As the grim nature of the bombing campaign unfolded, motivations for continued engagement of the enemy had much less to do with patriotism and much more to do with pragmatic issues, ranging from self-esteem to simple survival. "Like the airmen of all nations, they were concerned about pay, privilege, rank and prestige to some extent. But ultimately their morale ... depended to a great degree on the quality of their equipment, the length of time they were kept in combat, the results they attained and the rate of attrition."[60]

Douglas Harvey, a distinguished Canadian Lancaster II pilot and DFC winner, has argued that while the military elite were preoccupied with strategic war aims, the goals of the aircrew flying the missions were generally much more narrowly focused, exemplified by the following comment referring to Sir Arthur Harris:

> At the time I knew nothing of Harris' grand design or of the horrible ordeal that lay
> ahead of me. His goal was the total aerial destruction of Germany. My goal, like
> that of other kids in Bomber Command, was quite simple: to complete thirty raids,
> the magic number that constituted a tour of operations.[61]

Combat motivations for the rank-and-file airmen centered around small unit and crew cohesiveness; the men wanted to get the onerous task at hand accomplished as soon as possible, not letting down their comrades in the process. "We were intensely preoccupied with our own crew and very strongly motivated not to let it down," explained one veteran. "Apart from our commanders and three or four other crews that were close contemporaries," he added, "we knew few other aircrew on the station as more than passing acquaintances."[62]

For the men of Bomber Command, the full risks of combat flying were generally not fathomed until they began operations. Relatively early in the bombing campaign, the RAF determined that "an average casualty rate of five percent per mission was considered to be the most that the bomber crews could bear without faltering over any prolonged length of time."[63] Also, experience gained from the Western Front during the Great War had driven home the value of front-line rotations and periods of rest from combat. "If men were going to be able to sustain themselves during night after night of arduous and extraordinarily dangerous flying, some sort of rotation policy was necessary."[64] Operational flying needed to be broken up into manageable periods of time, and there had to be a reasonable chance of survival. "It was generally accepted that it should be drawn at a point which offered a 50-50 chance."[65] The actual odds against survival, however, were held somewhat in confidence by the executive of the RAF during the war.[66] That said, those odds varied considerably at different times throughout the bombing campaign, and there is no evidence of a deliberate attempt to deceive the crews into believing that the odds of survival were actually better than reality. For one thing, the BBC Home Service accurately broadcast individual raid losses on a routine basis, and the crews would have known roughly how many aircraft had participated in any given mission.

With respect to specifying a tour length, Harris and his staff had grave concerns over the possible perception that a contractual agreement was being entered into with the airmen under his command. These concerns were not without substance. However, on 8 May 1943, Bomber Command did codify Main Force bomber service into two combat tours of thirty and a maximum of twenty sorties respectively, with an intervening staff or instructional tour of duty of normally not less than six months. "The tour of operations, with its definite promise of relief," wrote John Terraine, "was a sheet anchor of morale in Bomber Command. It made the unbelievable endurable."[67] However, the horizon of the average airman was extremely short, and few at the time grasped that their operational flying was not necessarily behind them after their first tour was over. This frame of mind was undoubtedly a psychological defence mechanism.[68]

Inevitably, there were some who could not face the continued stress, a problem usually associated with periods of extensive operations and high combat losses. The winter of 1942/1943

Lancaster DS 707 of 408 Goose Squadron, the day after D Day. Warrant Officer Bill Wade, the tail gunner, and Sergeant Doug Skingle, the mid-upper gunner, are leaving the aircraft after their seventh mission. (CF photo PL 29742 courtesy of Air Command.)

and the first few months of 1944, which corresponded with the battles for the Ruhr and Berlin respectively, were particularly problematic.[69]

In the RAF, considerable emphasis was placed on preventive treatment. Returning crews were met with fringe amenities—including hot drinks, cigarettes, doughnuts, bacon-and-egg meals and post-mission spirits—not always readily available to the rank and file. With a view to venting some of the most immediate reactions to combat, crews were encouraged to relax and to relate their combat experiences. Special leave of several days was given as often as operationally possible. Headquartered in London, the excellent Lady Ryder Leave Organization placed Commonwealth aircrew as honoured guests in many stately British homes, a generosity and hospitality that many veterans remember with great affection.

However, for some of those clearly in need of a respite, stronger measures were often required. These men were taken off flying duties for short periods and given additional food, warmth, drink and sedatives. The British emphasized the value of uninterrupted sleep, and so the administration of massive doses of sodium barbital was not uncommon. In a large number of cases this treatment was effective, since irrational fears and horrifying mental images were quickly diffused.[70]

Mark Wells (in *Courage and Air Warfare*) suggests that nearly two-thirds of all Bomber Command's stress casualties were successfully treated by these methods at a local level.[71] For those who required more formal treatment, there were several large neuropsychiatric centres, although RAF psychiatric specialists were always in short supply and extensive periods of time devoted to psychotherapy or psychoanalysis were impossible burdens on an unprepared system. The fundamental goal was to return as many airmen as possible to flying operations.

Yet, there was a small number of airmen who could not prevail. In the RAF during the Second World War, the Lack of Moral Fibre (LMF) designation was employed "as a means of handling aircrew who would not or could not fly for reasons that were considered unjustifiable."[72] The LMF Memorandum, issued first in 1941, and then in revised, somewhat clarified formats in 1943 and again in 1945, targeted "members of aircrews who forfeit the confidence of their Commanding Officers in their determination and reliability in the face of danger in the air, owing either to their conduct or to their admission that they feel unable to face up to their duties."[73] Aircrew who could not face the strain of operations were assigned to one of three categories. The first included those who were medically fit, but who had forfeited their CO's confidence without being subjected to exceptional operational stresses. The second category was reserved for those who were medically unfit solely on account of displaying nervous symptoms, but again, without having been subjected to exceptional stresses. A third category covered anyone who was medically unfit and did not qualify for the first two categories.[74]

Mild neurosis cases could be sent to the RAF Convalescent Depot Blackpool or to the Officers Hospital Torquay, but the more severe cases went to a Not Yet Diagnosed Nervous/Neuropsychiatric (NYDN) Centre for treatment by specialists. However, Bomber Command generally advocated a harsh approach to neuropsychiatric casualties. Although some doctors favoured immediate release from the flying services if the problem appeared to be constitutional or due to a faulty upbringing—psychotherapy would not likely be successful—their Principal Medical Officer expressed the opinion that "temperamentally unsuitable members of aircrews ... those lacking confidence...should be given no sympathy and should be dealt with by the Executive as early as possible."[75] The consequences of being branded LMF could be cataclysmic. And there is ample evidence to suggest that officers were treated more humanely than non-commissioned airmen; this was another by-product of the British class system and the presumption that the lack of public school values predisposed the NCOs to failure.

As was often the case when RCAF personnel overseas met the frequently heavy and class-absorbed hand of RAF administrative policies, "difficulties with the British LMF process became evident in Canada when the label of Waverer was applied to some RCAF airmen who clearly did not deserve it."[76] In a countering initiative, the RCAF (relying heavily upon its air force legal officers) drafted its own LMF policy in 1944 that emphasized the protection of individual rights and due process of law. "In adopting the creation of *clear and willful evasion of operational responsibility* as a basis for judging the behavior of aircrew, the RCAF regulations moved the LMF procedure away from the bureaucratic, operational and medical realms toward the political and legal arenas."[77] Although it was not promulgated until relatively late in the European air war, and affected only a small percentage of RCAF airmen, this distinctly Canadian policy signalled yet another small victory for Canadian national pride and political independence.

Perhaps the last word on this very emotional subject should fall to Murray Peden, an articulate Canadian pilot who won his DFC with Bomber Command, who reluctantly came to accept the LMF policy:

> Remembering those who had carefully refrained from risking their precious hides, who had carefully refrained from bearing arms for their country, in any capacity, I always felt that LMF was a dirty label to fasten on someone who had volunteered for dangerous duty and had tried to carry out his commitment. The harsh treatment was necessary simply because the strain was so great. If there had been an easy and graceful way to abandon operational flying, many crews would have found the temptation hard to resist as their tours went on and the bloodshed continued.[78]

However, it would be misleading to place too much emphasis on the importance of the LMF policies. During the entire war, less than 0.2 percent of all Commonwealth airmen were categorized as Lacking Moral Fibre, and even in the most arduous days of Bomber Command's operations, between July 1943 and June 1944, less than 0.4 percent were identified as being even possible LMF cases.[79] This was by any yardstick an enviable record under extreme duress.

If the LMF policy was the hammer that generated the will to persevere, inspirational leadership was the velvet glove. Fortunately for Britain and the Dominions, there was no shortage of inspirational leaders in Bomber Command. The home islands produced Guy Penrose Gibson, VC, the famous leader of 617 Squadron on the Ruhr dams raid in May 1943. Gibson was fearless, brilliant, inspirational and a jovial extrovert, possessed of unshakable courage, devotion to duty, and an abiding concern for the welfare of his crews.

Along with Gibson, Britain boasted the likes of Leonard Cheshire, who led his men night after night over the most dangerous targets with inspired example. By 1943, he had already completed two brilliant operational tours. His men would have followed him to hell and back, and frequently did. The Dominions produced Mick Martin and Dave Shannon from Australia, while Canada could point with pride to men such as Bob Turnbull, Reg Lane, and Johnnie Fauquier. Turnbull rose from Sergeant to Wing Commander as a pilot in just eleven months of bomber combat, winning many decorations in the process. He ended the war as a Group Captain and the Station Commander of Middleton St. George, having already commanded flights and squadrons in nearly four years of overseas service.[80] Reg Lane flew three full tours of operations, one of only 24 RCAF members of Bomber Command to do so. Two of those tours were completed as a Pathfinder, and Lane flew against virtually every vital enemy target in Europe. He served as Commanding Officer of 405 Squadron within 8 (Pathfinder) Group for the first half of 1944, and won the Distinguished Service Order (DSO), the Commonwealth's second-highest decoration for bravery, as well as two DFCs. Johnnie Fauquier won, among other Commonwealth and foreign awards, the DSO three times[81] during three tours of operations. He was the first Commanding Officer of 405 Squadron and then later voluntarily dropped two ranks for the chance to lead 617 (Dambuster) Squadron, which he did very successfully. Many people thought Fauquier was absolutely fearless. Instead, his bravery was reflected in the outstanding record he achieved even in the face of fear. "A fellow who isn't afraid lacks imagination," he once told a colleague, "And a guy who has no imagination can't be much of a combat pilot, and certainly never a leader."[82]

Another great example of sound leadership in the RCAF overseas came from a very high level. In its first year of operations, 6 Group lost 340 aircraft and the death toll would continue to rise, with a total of 814 Group aircraft being downed by war's end.[83] It is safe to say that 6 Group experienced significant morale problems in 1943. Nonetheless, in February 1944, Air Vice-Marshal Clifford M. "Black Mike" McEwen replaced Air Vice-Marshal Brookes as Air Officer Commanding, and the fortunes of the group changed dramatically. An inspirational leader who had proven his mettle during the Great War as a fighter pilot by downing 27 enemy aircraft, he was an unrepentant advocate of arduous training and stern discipline. No armchair commander, McEwen led fearlessly from the front, accompanying his crews on the toughest missions and against the explicit orders of Sir Arthur Harris. Knowing that their commander fully shared and appreciated the dangers of combat, the performances 6 Group soon became as good as any in Bomber Command. "McEwen's presence was soon taken for granted—he even became a good luck symbol. As the men saw it, when the man with the moustache was along, things were going to be fine. They felt drawn to this colourful airman who wanted to share their danger, and when ordered not to, could not sleep while his men were on a raid."[84]

Whatever the motivations of the men, and there were many, the bomber offensive was a magnificent effort, a true triumph of the human spirit. Canadians played a significant part in this drama and won lasting fame for their myriad contributions. It is perhaps most fitting to conclude with Sir Arthur Harris, the keeper of Bomber Command throughout its most arduous years:

> There are no words with which I can do justice to the aircrew who fought under my command. There is no parallel in warfare to such courage and determination in the face of danger over so prolonged a period, of danger which at times was so great that scarcely one man in three could expect to survive his tour of thirty operations ... It was, moreover, a clear and highly conscious courage, by which the risk was taken with calm forethought, for the aircrew were all highly skilled men, much above the average in education, who had to understand every aspect and detail of their task. It was, furthermore, the courage of the small hours, of men virtually alone, for at his battle station the airman is virtually alone. It was the courage of men with long-drawn apprehensions of daily "going over the top." They were without exception volunteers, for no man was trained for aircrew with the RAF who did not volunteer for this. Such devotion must never be forgotten.[85]

Notes for Chapter 10

1   Mark K. Wells, *Courage and Air Warfare* (London: Frank Cass, 1995), 2.

2   Richard Overy, *Bomber Command, 1939-1945-Reaping the Whirlwind* (London: Harper Collins, 1997), 200.

3   Ibid., 205, and Larry Milberry, *Canada's Air Force At War and Peace* (Toronto: CANAV Books, 2000), 2: 27.

4   Hugh A, Halliday, *RCAF Honours and Awards,* accessed August 2001; at http://www.achq.dnd.ca/handbook/hist2d.htm, 3.

5   Allan D. English, *The Cream of the Crop: Canadian Aircrew 1939-1945* (Montreal & Kingston: McGill-Queen's University Press, 1996), 122.

6   Larry Milberry, *Sixty Years: The RCAF and Canadian Forces Air Command 1924-1984* (Toronto: CANAV Books, 1984), 179.

7   Cited by Brereton Greenhous et al., *The Crucible of War: The Official History of the Royal Canadian Air Force, Volume III* (Toronto: University of Toronto Press, 1994), 49.

8   Ibid., 83.

9   English, 122.

10 Greenhous et al., 50, 95.

11 English, 122.

12 Milberry, *Sixty Years*, 98.

13 English, 106.

14 Brereton Greenhous & Hugh A. Halliday, *Canada's Air Forces 1914-1999* (Montreal: Art Global, 1999), 52.

15 John Terraine, *The Right of the Line: The Royal Air Force in the European War 1939-1945* (London: Hodder and Stoughton, 1985), 464.

16 At the Allied Air Training Conference of May 1942, and in order to bolster their arguments against broader aircrew commissioning, the British claimed that the Americans were then commissioning "80% of pilots, 100% of navigators, 50% of bombardiers, but no air gunners, radio operators or flight engineers." F.J. Hatch, *Aerodrome of Democracy: Canada and the British Commonwealth Air Training Plan 1939-1945* (Ottawa: Ministry of Supply and Services, 1983), 108. The USAAF would soon be commissioning virtually all of its pilots, navigators, and bombardiers, but virtually none of its gunners, radio operators or flight engineers. Wells, 123, 133.

17 Cited by Leslie Roberts, *There Shall Be Wings* (Toronto: Clarke Irwin, 1959), 156.

18 Greenhous & Halliday, 54.

19 Greenhous et al., 94.

20 Greenhous & Halliday, 54.

21 Norman Shannon, "The Cattle Boat Brigade." *Airforce,* October 1996, 9.

22 Overy, 44.

23 Ibid.

24 Greenhous & Halliday, 44.

25 Ibid., 55.

26 Ibid., 85.

27 Greenhous et al., 545.

28 Ibid., 94.

29 Wells, 54.

30 Greenhous & Halliday, 94.

31 Overy, 80.

32 Ibid., 69.

33 Greenhous et al., 712.

34 Greenhous et al., 694, and Greenhous & Halliday, 98.

35 Greenhous & Halliday, 100.

36 Ibid.

37 425 Squadron was the first RCAF heavy bomber squadron commanded from the outset by a Canadian.

38 Stevenson, an Anglophile, felt Canadian airmen could best serve the war effort in RAF units, and thus ran afoul of the Canadian political executive. He aided and abetted British foot dragging on Canadianization.

39 Greenhous et al., 7.

40 Greenhous & Halliday, 86.

41 Overy, 114.

42 Ibid.

43 Initially, 6 Group consisted of 408, 419, 420, 424, 426, 427 and 428 Squadrons based at Topcliffe, Leeming, East Moor, Middleton St. George, Dishforth, Croft and Dalton. By war's end, the group would consist of fourteen Halifax and Lancaster squadrons based at Linton-on-Ouse, East Moor, Tholthorpe, Leeming, Skipton-upon-Swale, Middleton St. George and Croft. Christopher Shores, *History of the Royal Canadian Air Force* (Toronto: Royce Books, 1984), 59.

44 Roberts, 161.

45 Greenhous et al., 603.

46 6 Group has been historically regarded as a Halifax group, once the transition to four-engined aircraft was completed. Although the group suffered with the severely-limited Mark IIs and Mark Vs for a long time, the Mark III gave yeoman service from early 1944 onward, in spite of remaining short-comings. However, by war's end, eight of the fourteen Canadian heavy bomber squadrons were flying Mark I, Mark III, or Mark X Lancasters, including four squadrons equipped with the new Canadian-made Mark Xs. The slow Lancaster re-equipment was mostly due to Canadian production delays in delivering Mark Xs to 6 Group. Ibid., 757.

47 Given the note above, this is somewhat of an overstatement, although the improved aircraft were certainly late in coming. Ibid., 94.

48 Ibid., 680.

49 Ibid., 831.

50 Terraine, 537.

51 Greenhous & Halliday, 62.

52 Overy, 204.

53 Ibid., 205

54 Ibid., 204.

55 Greenhous et al., 681.

56 Greenhous & Halliday, 114.

57 Wells, 115.

58 Ibid., 161.

59 Max Hastings, *Bomber Command* (New York: The Dial Press/James Wade, 1979), 214.

60 Wells, 116.

61 J. Douglas Harvey, *Boys, Bombs and Brussels Sprouts* (Toronto: McClelland & Stewart, 1981), 6.

62 David Oliver, a British Lancaster pilot, in Martin Middlebrook, *The Berlin Raids* (London: Penguin, 1988), 318.

63 Greenhous et al., 526.

64 Wells, 125.

65 Terraine, 522.

66 Bill Sweetman, "The Avro Lancaster," in Jeffrey Ethell, ed., *The Great Book of World War Two Airplanes* (New York: Bonanza, 1984), 399.

67 Terraine, 527.

68 A very important caveat to this policy was that the thirty sortie first tour requirement could be waived by group and squadron commanders if they were satisfied that the individuals involved had carried out their duties satisfactorily and were in need of a rest from operations. Ibid., 523.

69 In the words of one combat veteran, "The battering we received over the North German Plain cost us more than a thousand aircraft and between seven and eight thousand lives. Berlin wasn't worth it." Greenhous et al., 785.

70 Wells, 77.

71 Ibid.

72 English, 81.

73 Ibid, 84.

74 Ibid.

75 Cited ibid., 88.

76 Ibid., 128.

77 Ibid.

78 Murray Peden, *A Thousand Shall Fall* (Toronto: Stoddart, 1988), 416.

79 Greenhous et al., 787.

80 Arthur Bishop, *Courage in the Air* (Toronto: McGraw-Hill Ryerson, 1992), 215.

81 Fauquier was the only RCAF member to do so.

82 Cited by Bishop, 148.

83 Reader's Digest, *The Canadians at War 1939-1945* (Westmount: The Reader's Digest Association of Canada, 1986), 285.

84 Ibid.

85 Sir Arthur Harris, *Bomber Offensive* (London: Collins, 1947), 267.

PART III

Canada and the Question of
National Security

Richard Francis Foote, 1822. (NA, C-112062)

CHAPTER 11

British Military Business Practices in Canada

When Strategy and Cost Savings Shaped A Society, 1815-1832

Roch Legault

WAR AND MONEY have always been closely intertwined. Great Britain, at the beginning of the nineteenth century, used money strategically not only to buy allies and to support coalitions against Napoleon, but also to purchase provisions and services from his majesty's subjects, as well as foreigners, in a business-like fashion.[1] This practice was so successful in winning the Napoleonic wars that there seemed no reason to change it when doing business during times of peace. Moreover, it was only logical to implement this practice in Britain's major North American colonies.[2]

Britain's Canadian colonies, after the War of 1812, offer a perfect example of the difficult balance between cost savings and strategic considerations in military spending. If the rationale for spending on British forces in the first half of the nineteenth century had been primarily strategic, then decisions in that regard would have been dramatically different. But the strategic situation did not dictate every action or decision of the army's business process. Rather, the Treasury Board was a force of such significance that it not only influenced the strategic agenda, but was able to restrain that agenda. Absolutely no waste of money, and this was a deeply felt conviction of the decision-makers, was to be tolerated. As a result, the Treasury became a very powerful and frugal vehicle. It made certain that there was thought given to the cost of any scheme of strategic objectives. The aim of the system was simply to get the best strategic advantage at the lowest possible cost. This could only be attained by using the free market as often as possible. The colonial market was used in this respect, and it was also quickly realized that it was essential, and that its development should be encouraged and sustained.

Although various studies of the British Army and the colonial economy,[3] as well as some works done by social historians on the army and its contractors[4] have appeared, they have failed to reveal a comprehensive understanding of the British military's way of doing business. The aim of this chapter is to describe the British army's provisioning system in North America during a time of uneasy peace, where an effective defence was needed in combination with effective business practices to ensure that taxpayers' money was not wasted and that the market was used as an ally.

The Commissariat was in charge of provisioning the army in the colonies of the Empire.[5] It represents the very heart of the system and needs further elaboration. It was through this department that military demands were transmitted to the Treasury Board. Commissariat officers also received orders from the commander-in-chief of the colony in which they were stationed. Therefore, the Commissariat was well aware of the army's economic and strategic interests. But, what were its guidelines and its responsibilities? Its role as a military banker? The checks and balances on its daily work? What was the business personality of the department and how did it deal with contractors? And what happened when the Royal Engineers, concerned mostly with strategy, decided on a new relationship with the Commissariat? Answering those questions reveals the story of a military institution in time of peace that was very active in shaping the life of the Canadian business community, and Canadian society as a whole.

The British Army's Provisioning System: A Description

The establishment by the British government of a strong Commissariat branch in Canada in the early nineteenth century meant that the army was willing to tap local resources rather than wait for London to provide supplies. The question of provisioning in North America had been a long standing challenge for European armies, ever since the Spaniards had set foot in Florida. For example, the Spanish invaders were compelled to assess, to the best of their limited knowledge, the corn resources of the planned territory to be conquered before launching their invasion.[6] Similarly, by choosing to garrison Canada, Great Britain's supply system was, as Germans described it in the eighteenth century, the "Magazinssystem." Conversely, the alternative was the "Requisitionssystem " that was used mostly by the French during the Napoleonic Wars.[7] Therefore, the British system required the army to purchase its needs rather than to simply take them from the people.

The practice of using the market system and army contractors was imposed on the army by the Treasury Board. The Commissariat in Canada, in turn, played the role of its watchdog. The military officers would have been ready to comply with Treasury Board directives without any complaints had it not been for two reasons. First of all, the military work in peacetime was still difficult. In fact, the officers were preparing for the next war with the United States because the ending of the war of 1812-15 seemed to many to be merely a truce and not a real peace. Second, their environment was already burdened by the bureaucracy, in the creation of which the Commissariat played no small part. For instance, the officers of the Royal Engineers, charged with repairing chimneys in Ile Ste-Hélène were required to write a staggering seventy-four letters in four months from November 1825 to February 1826 simply to be able to carry out this routine task.[8]

The British army did business in North America according to the principles that public money had to be used wisely and provisioning of the army had to be done safely. It had faith in the marketplace, free competition and competitive bidding. Of course, not all commercial transactions of the army are well documented. The cases that were documented were those that caused problems for the armed forces, and these are the ones of interest to the historian, for they tell us much about questionable practices and difficult cases.

The Commissariat was guided by two sets of instructions issued during and just after the Napoleonic Wars.[9] Free and fair public competition was thought the only way to get the best value for public money. The market was considered the taxpayer's best ally. Compulsory announcements in the newspapers stated the needs of the army. When a complicated technical service was required by the engineers, a general announcement was made asking that the Commissariat or Engineer's Office be contacted about the details. The Commissariat gave ample time to the contractors to respond to the announcement. In Montreal, there was an average of nineteen days between the time the Commissariat published a military requirement and the close of bidding.[10] By allowing all interested contractors enough time to prepare a bid, the army avoided dealing with only the upper strata of the market. The very few big merchants were more likely to tap into the resources of the colony faster because of their extensive business network; higher prices for the army would have certainly followed.

The accepted bid had to be the lowest tendered. If not, the report submitted to the commander for his signature of acceptance had to explain clearly why the lowest bidder was not the one who won the competition. This rule was challenged on more than one occasion by the engineers, more inclined to check on the quality and less on the price. This happened most often because the best craftsman or most competent worker, according to the engineers, could not afford the lowest bid. On one occasion, the Commissariat was caught at his own game; the accepted bid was deemed much too high by Lieutenant-Colonel By, who reversed the commissary's decision and rewrote his public tender.[11] Most of the time, however, the Commissariat's decision prevailed.

Elsewhere in the Empire, some commissaries were advocating a less rigid attitude. For instance, one experienced commissary, Edward Farrington De Fonblanque, once wrote that security of provisioning was more important than ensuring that the lowest bidder always received the contract.[12] But the Commissariat stuck to the principle in Canada so firmly that one official complaint, launched by an unsuccessful bidder, stated that his bid was the lowest and if it were not accepted by the Commissariat, a precedent would be set in the colony. The frustrated bidder, however, did not convince the commander because the Commissariat pointed out that in a previous contract, the complainant was reluctant to replace six barrels of flour judged unfit by the army. Much tougher cases occurred when the lowest bidder could not supply all the army's needs. On one occasion, the Commissariat had tried to bring down the prices of the bidder who could fill all their needs as advertised. This did not work in the case of Stanley Bagg, who justly pointed out that his price was higher than his competitors because of the large quantity he was trying to assemble to fulfill the contract.[13] Sometimes a compromise could be reached by using two contractors together to bring down the price. For example, the Commissariat would buy as much as possible of the requirement from the lowest bidder and then complete the order by paying a higher price to the next lowest bidder for the remaining items that the first contractor was unable to supply.

Because Canada's market was in an early stage of development, some equipment could not be found in the colony. For instance, an eight-horsepower engine needed by the engineers in 1828 was not available in Canada and had to be bought in England or the United States.[14] As well, some advertised requirements went unanswered, although very rarely. This was less frequent in more remote areas or smaller cities where bidding was more often active than it was in the larger markets of Montreal and Quebec. This was probably due to the immaturity of those smaller markets where many people could still try to better their social position by venturing into business without having to face the fierce competition of established merchants. Unanswered tenders could embarrass the Commissariat, whose task it was to satisfy impatient for goods and services.[15]

The general feeling of the army's officers was that Canadian products were inferior to those available in England. Since services and products were bought locally, differences were noticed and rightly so. On occasion, the officers' judgements were tainted by prejudice. The testimony of Deputy Storekeeper General Robertson in 1817 indicated his belief that nothing of quality could be bought in the colony. "It is my anxious wish," he declared, "to prevent as much as possible the purchase of all Stores in this Country ... I am confident that the real interests of the service demand that the articles should be sent from England where if they cannot be made of good quality, they cannot in any part of the world."[16] Nevertheless, the price and not the quality consistently guided the choices of the Commissariat and the Treasury Board.

The approved procedure called for the unsealing of bids in the presence of the senior commissary officer. This procedure was taken seriously; Commissary General Gabriel Wood once tried to avoid it and was officially censored by London after the case was reported by the Deputy Commissary of Accounts.[17]

After the bids had been judged, a standard contract was made up to assure the army there would be no problems during the completion of the service or with the delivery of goods. A public notary completed it in the same way he would for any member of the business community. In the 1820s, the designated notary privileged to deal with the army was given the title of King's Notary. The position seems only to have bestowed prestige—a marketing advantage for the chosen notary—rather than bestowing on him a bona fida special status. After 1827, to save money the Commissariat dispensed with the position of the King's Notary but kept roughly the same contract format.[18] This did not stop the contracts from getting longer and longer, a result of the notary public being paid by the word as well as new provisions added to protect the army from dishonest or incapable contractors. The Commissariat was trying to prevent any errors in previous contracts from reoccurring. All the rules had to be clear, for the army wished to establish and maintain harmonious links with the colonial business community.

The Banker

The commissary officers also acted as bankers in Canada. In fact, they were the first in the country, well before the Bank of Montreal was established in 1817. Responsible for the military chest, the officers could count on a well-supplied war fund at all times. The British Army was never in real financial trouble in North America during the nineteenth century. Its main problem was not a shortage of paper money (because there was no difficulty in getting wealthy merchants to accept bank notes, money orders and such things) but of hard currency. The latter was rather scarce, and its scarcity had long been a handicap in the development of the colony. The problem had existed under the French regime and it persisted for some time after the period in question. The officers' main task as bankers in Canada, then, was to secure enough hard currency to pay the troops and occasionally the contractors. They were instructed to apply the same principles as those applied to other goods and services, that is to say, to proceed by public tenders. The procedure was surrounded by a wealth of security mechanisms, including a check on the limit of money levied and it was, of course, under the authority of the commander of the military forces in Canada. The aim of the British armed forces, here again, was to work through a market or at least to help create healthy competition in the local economy.[19]

In September 1825, an agreement was reached between the Treasury Board, the Board of Trade and the East India Company that simplified the Commissariat's affairs overseas.[20] The agreement, generated by the company, was well thought out and certainly helped the army a great deal. The proceeds of all tea sales were remitted to the military chest instead of being shipped home. Back in England, the receipt for the money was recognized by the Treasury Board and remitted to the East India Company. The company spared itself the travelling and insurance costs while the army enjoyed a much sought-after supply of hard currency at a flat rate determined by both parties.[21]

This arrangement was still not sufficient to meet the army's needs. The Commissariat had to call on the American money market as it had done before. The early importance of this foreign market is best illustrated by the decision of Commissary General Robinson to send an envoy to the United States as soon as the war between the two countries had ended. His haste was justified, he explained, by "considering our extreme distress for money, not having one thousand pounds in the Canadas."[22] In May 1815, the envoy wrote back to Robinson that the war had so greatly damaged the Boston and New York money markets that his mission was a total failure. Robinson's successors continued going to the United States because, as one of them acknowledged, "the Exchange here is entirely regulated by that of New York."[23] The Commissariat's public announcements of the money requirement in Canada, rather than articulating a clear procurement process, gradually became a matter of merely disseminating information on behalf of the army concerning how much money the colony could furnish and at what rate. The Commissariat had no hope of meeting its needs in Quebec, Montreal and Upper Canada.

Trying to work within an imperfect Canadian market actually backfired on the army. In the summer of 1825, the Commissariat was outraged when the Bank of Montreal used the New York money market and tried to get profits out of bank agents based in the United States.[24] These people were "speculators," according to the local Commissariat, because the bank was offering a much lower rate on letter of exchange than the one the Commissariat could get directly through its envoys in the same city. To deal with the Bank of Montreal meant to secure less money for the army. When forced by an order from London to accept the rate that the bank

Staff of the Commissariat, circa 1829-1846. (NA, C-139534)

was offering, the officer in charge could argue that, from that point forward, the Commissariat would never again be able to influence the market.[25] In this case, metropolitan authorities were trying to develop the Canadian economy. The army's reliance on the American market was deemed by the highest authorities in Great Britain a strategic weakness, and rightly so.

Checks and Balances

To ensure that commissary officers stayed within the spirit and letter of the regulations, financial controls were established. These were the Commissary of Accounts activities in Canada, the auditing of the Commissariat work in London by the Comptrollers' Office and the inspection of the military chest against Commissariat guidelines when entering a contract. The quality of these checks varied considerably during the period. The position of Commissary of Accounts was abolished in June 1830.[26] The number of audited documents in London had plummeted during the mid 1820s, sharply reducing the work required of the Commissariat to answer the auditors. This was where the strength of the British military administrative system resided: in its adeptness. Before leaving Canada, the Deputy Commissary of Accounts—since 1821, the highest rank in the department employed in Canada—was to enquire, under oath, from any Commissariat officers "as to any Accounts, Supplies, Expenses, or Charges, or any other Matters or Things whatsoever, relating to or in anywise connected with the Military Expenditure within the said Colony or Possession."[27] If an officer refused to comply, this could mean his dismissal or even his imprisonment. Of course, the cases reported by the Deputy Commissary of Accounts were related to the image of the army, although his office was not in contact with the public. The activities of the Comptrollers Office's changed after the mid 1820s from reporting minor details such as defunct contracts or omitted signatures to addressing broader issues of procedure and principle.

The regular inspection of the military chest—which contained all the money of the armed forces—began only in 1822.[28] Performed by a board of three inspectors chosen from among the officers of the army, the inspections had a serious drawback: the Commissariat officers were aware of the inspections well in advance. This weakness was stressed by an inquiry, but there was little that could be done to improve secrecy given the long lead times required to set up any board. The secrecy of the proceedings of the board was, on the other hand, improved to prevent the leakage of information regarding the financial state of the armed forces. Not surprisingly, this information was considered strategic by the British authorities.

The Friendly Commissariat

Commissariat officers have been cast in a very poor light by historian S.P.G. Ward:
> It is not to be wondered at if the men who came forward as commissariat officers were not over scrupulous, and in fact tended to come from the very worst elements of the commercial world. Many joined entirely with a view to the profits that could be made and the ease and comfort to be enjoyed from a life lived amongst piles of good food and embellished with a rake-off from the supplier or contractor... The number of commissaries who were dismissed for irregularities, both before and during the Peninsular War, was prodigious. There can have been few professions, crafts, or mysteries in the country which could point, as the Commissariat could, to two men of the highest rank who were serving a sentence in Newgate Gaol... It was almost expected of a commissary that he would defraud the public.[29]

These comments are not well documented, although Ward illustrated some of these qualities later in his book. The reality, however, gives no basis for such a damning judgement. Simply put, the British were winning wars, and the British system of provisioning was working. For obvious military reasons, the Commissariat officers had to be serious, trustworthy and obliging business partners. The army acted strategically to protect its sources of supply by preserving good relationships with potential contractors in Canada. The Commissary General, Isaac Isham Routh, believed "It is evidently the interest of the Government to establish a character of impartiality and it is the wish of the Commander of the Forces, as it is more particularly that of this Department and the principle of our instructions to take an equitable and dispassionate view."[30] Statements from other officers supported Routh's view: "It is never the intention that an individual should be ruined provided he uses all possible exertion to fulfil his engagement."[31] "It is the wish and maxim of the Government to give every fair and reasonable opportunity of redress to all claimants."[32] Routh went so far as to urge Commissary officers to mingle with the contractors to the point of almost sharing their views, because the talent and business skills of the officers "are of less value than the public reliance on your justice and integrity, and on your desire to consult, as far as your duty will permit, the interests and feelings of those with whom you are brought into communication."[33] These statements are not an indication of mismanagement, corruption and growing scandal. The historical reality was more complex. S.P.G. Ward drastically changed his original conclusions after a thorough study of some individual members of the Commissariat.[34]

Of course, close co-operation between civilians and military personnel led more than one officer into a conflict of interest. The guidelines could not stop the officers and the rank and file from trying to take advantage of the system. There were some cases of questionable activity reported. The most prominent one involved the senior financial and commercial officer of the army in Canada, Deputy Commissary James Craigie, who was disgraced in 1808. Having used government money to pursue personal activity, he was unable to remit the sum he had "borrowed" and was stripped of his responsibilities and sued.[35] He died soon after, having lost not only his money but also the social position he had gained in the colony.

It was argued in the political arena that the British Army practiced favouritism in Canada when doing business. The roots of this accusation are to be found in the years leading to the Rebellions of 1837-1838, when the patriots charged their political foes with having received special treatment from the colonial government and the army. For the historian to substantiate this with hard evidence, especially when characterizing the machinery of military spending as a whole, is quite difficult. Proving the contrary is actually easier, because the British system of tenders and bids was carefully designed to be even-handed. Although corruption could be found, and patronage was broadly accepted by society in general, Craigie's case does not tell the whole story.[36] The army had an agenda of its own, and it was strategic in nature.

The interests of the armed forces and the contractors did not always coincide. Routh was all too aware of this fact when he wrote that "too much confidence is not to be placed in contractors, who swarm about the Army when it is prosperous to prey upon its wants, but are the first to fly in the event of a reverse ... and [place] *no* reliance on those casual contractors with whom you have no fixed engagement."[37]

Contractors were generally treated well and fairly because the armed forces wished to project a favourable image to the Canadian business community. In 1829 in Montreal, the Commissariat officer in command of the station, Charles John Forbes, complained bitterly to the military secretary about how the Ordnance Department was dealing with a certain contractor. Payments were repeatedly late for work that was always completed. Forbes was worried about the Commissariat's reputation with the business community, because he had entered into the contract on behalf of the engineers. "I feel myself," he wrote, "imperiously called upon to express my regret that such a delay, which involves a breach of Contract with this Department, should have occurred as it cannot fail ... to operate strongly upon the public mind, and tend to destroy that confidence every Person transacting Business with Government Officers should feel in transactions with them.... I deem it to be a matter of the first importance, that where this Department is a party concerned in any obligation, that every Item of it should be most strictly fulfilled."[38] Forbes may have acted in part out of personal interest, because he had chosen to reside in the Canadian colony and his own reputation was also at stake; and he would not neglect his Canadian interests even when posted, later in his career, to the Caribbean.[39] Nonetheless, he was still defending the Commissariat and the army's way of doing business.

The Commissariat no longer advanced money to contractors as the British Army had done in Canada before the War of 1812.[40] Those days were gone now that the colony had merchants with substantial capital of their own. There was no need any more for the army to sustain the colonial economy in such ways.[41] Nevertheless, an understanding of the contractors' problems pointed toward what the army wanted in Canada: a full and straightforward exchange between the business community and the Commissariat. For instance, in 1827 one contractor, Smith and Anderson of Quebec, shamelessly complained to the Commissariat that their profit margin would be seriously reduced if the army agreed to the wishes of its soldiers to give them only beef during the summer and no salt pork. Smith and Anderson, the beef contractor for the army that year, feared having to buy more beef on unfavourable terms because, during the summer, their sub-contractors had usually already committed almost everything they had to offer.[42] Of course, the contractor required a reasonable profit, and so in this case the army was ready to take the contractor's complaint into consideration at the expense of its soldiers.

It was possible for the Commissariat to award financial compensation to army contractors who experienced problems fulfilling their commitments. Compensation was more common during the war of 1812 when keeping allies in the business community was crucial. After the war, in 1817, the Treasury Board stated clearly that reparations should be relaxed.[43] Public compensation should not reward unskilled merchants or provide guarantees against market fluctuations and imponderables. But the Commissary generals were ordered to continue helping distressed contractors even after the new guidelines were issued, if a strong case could be made.

On rare occasions, the Commissariat displayed impatience, invariably with the most humble of contractors. In one case, the Commissary general even considered a lawsuit against the widow of a bread contractor so that the department could recover the cost of changing bakers. Aware of the poor financial state of the woman, an army notary intervened and the Commissariat covered the amount itself, a mere £48 and change.[44] This case was handled so poorly by the army because of the trivial amount of money involved and the unimportance of the contractor. The Commissariat was much more inclined to treat well these contractors who could really be useful to the army in time of war or insurrection.

The Commissariat and the Engineers

The Commissariat had a monopoly on buying for the Crown in the colony, and the way it did business occasionally upset some other departments. The Navy conducted business on its own, but given the small scale of its establishment in Lower and Upper Canada, its business had far less impact on the colonies than that of the Commissariat. No clashes were recorded between the Commissariat and the Provincial Marine or the Royal Navy. By and large, the Navy applied the same business practices and principles when dealing with civilians. The same can be said about the Storekeeper General Department, the section of the army in charge of the stores. From August of 1816[45] until April of 1820,[46] this department was engaged in overseeing and issuing most of the commodities needed by the army. Soon after it was established, the officer in charge of the department started to question the Commissariat's way of doing business on the grounds that the Army's own department knew better than anyone else what was needed. The practices of the Commissariat were criticized, although the principle of using the marketplace was not.

Such was not the case with the Engineer Department. During the building of fortifications, or even worse, during the building of the Rideau Canal, the engineers were the people the Commissariat clashed with most often. The latter was concerned with savings, while the former was concerned with speed, the quality of work, and strategic planning.

The strategic context of Canada during this period meant that the Ordnance Department and its engineers were in the forefront. The Canadian border had to be fortified as swiftly as strategic considerations demanded. American economic and demographic expansion were threatening the British colonies.[47] The United States was involved in an extensive program to improve internal communications, and the program was an economic as well as a political and strategic challenge to the United Kingdom. The decision by London to adopt a "dig and wait" attitude in regard to the defence of Canada called for work by the engineers. They therefore played a much more important role than the infantry, the cavalry and the artillery, who remained idle, waiting for an invasion to occur. The engineers were, in a sense, in the first line of defence.[48] From 1815 to 1832,the security of the Canadian border was given serious attention by the Imperial authorities, and such important works as Fort Lennox (on Lake Champlain), the Citadel of Quebec, and the Rideau Canal were completed during this period.

As a result of the urgency of the situation, the engineers often contracted directly with colonial suppliers, contrary to Treasury Board directives. In some years more so than others, and in spite of repeated orders and warnings, contracts were repeatedly signed by the engineers without going through the Commissariat. This practice was difficult and in fact impossible to stop, in part because the engineers belonged to the Ordnance Department and not to the British Army as such. Channels of communication were not the same, staff kept changing, and military cultures differed.

A Commissariat officer working to secure a contract to purchase pickets discovered in December of 1819 that they had already been delivered. Trying to ascertain what had happened, he soon realized that he had been bypassed by the engineers. When complaining to the commander-in-chief at Quebec, he stressed that the Commissariat had been ordered to create a competition among contractors and he stated that the orders given to the engineers were not quite as clear.[49] This behaviour however was not atypical. In 1816, the engineers did not bother to use previous estimates before undertaking any new work. They did not send annual reports of activities to London either, although this had been compulsory since 1791. The Comptrollers' Office was blunt. "We cannot," it insisted, "consider the neglect of [the usual business rules] to be a good Reason for the continuance of it ... those Regulations have always appeared to us to have been framed with ... a view to and upon ... sound principles of Economy and responsibility in the Expenditure of Public Money."[50] As for the absent annual report, the commander-in-chief in Canada, Lord Sherbrooke, remarked that it was the usual practice in all British colonies.

Until 1824, the Engineer Department was under the scrutiny of all those responsible for money in Canada. They argued that they were tapping into the army's extraordinary funding, that they did not need to hurry in order to report these expenditures to Parliament, and that they could not always wait for the Commissariat to create a competition among contractors. These excuses were challenged several times. In July of 1822, in the middle of major work at Fort Lennox and elsewhere, the Commissariat stopped all payments to the engineers for the rest of the year.[51] An alarmed department pleaded its case to the military commander and governor of the colony in an attempt to avoid a major disruption to the scheduled work. Refusal to pay for work already underway occurred on two other occasions in 1824.[52] This forced the engineers to refuse building materials that were to be furnished by the contractor at an extravagant cost, and instead made them carry out a competition.

But 1824 was a watershed year for the engineers in Canada. After that year, they started drifting away from the control imposed by the Commissariat on orders received from the Treasury Board. An Inspector of Accounts for the Ordnance Department was sent to Canada to consummate an administrative divorce. This reflected the fact that, throughout the Empire, the

Ordnance Department was an expanding organization under the efficient leadership of the Duke of Wellington.[53]

The new freedom enjoyed by the department coincided with the Carmichael-Smyth Report advocating, among other things, a safe water connection between Montreal and Kingston by way of a canal. A major and expensive work, this cornerstone of the Canadian defensive system needed organizational and financial instructions before going ahead. But, because the military services and the Colonial Office were so worried about Imperial defence, these instructions failed to stress the importance of the sound business principles that had characterized earlier military activities in Canada. The Secretary of State for War and the Colonies gave carte blanche to Lieutenant-Colonel By, the officer nominated by the Ordnance Department to build the Rideau Canal. The direction was clear but devoid of fiscal restraint. The instruction stated, "his Lordship has no observation to make on the Instructions to be given to Lieutenant-Colonel By except his anxious hope that every exertion will be made to proceed in this important work ... without waiting for the passing of the annual grant [by Parliament]."[54]

The strategic decision-makers decided to give Lieutenant-Colonel By the freedom he needed to complete the work. Without having settled instructions for him, they immediately informed the commander-in-chief in Canada that By "should be entirely independent of the Commanding Engineer in Canada, except in such matters as may require his Assistance without prejudice to his own particular duties."[55] And, when instructions did come to the commanding officer, it was only to reiterate the need for speed regardless of the financial considerations: "the Secretary of State having strongly expressed his opinion and desire ... that the work should be carried on with as much dispatch as possible, and that no delay should arise in the Spring by suspending the Work till the arrival of the authorized Estimate for the Year 1827 and each succeeding Year."[56]

Other instructions from London would confirm the engineers' responsibility for public money, but savings were certainly not the priority. They were however urged to note the Commissariat's experience in dealing with Canadian contractors: "taking advantage in all arrangements and Agreements of the Experience which can be derived from the Contracts made for similar Works in Lower Canada, whereby the interests of the Public may be secured whilst any difficulty in the Shape of impediment may be avoided."[57]

The question of the engineers using Canadian contractors had to be addressed by Carmicheal-Smyth soon after he issued his report. He favoured, for reasons of speed and economy, using the Canadian market. Having to rely on the meagre resources of the armed forces in Canada would be detrimental to both the military and the project. According to the inspector, manpower could be found in Canada for excavating and building, making unnecessary any supervision by the Royal Engineers. After all, the Americans were doing precisely the same thing, and in Canada the Lachine Canal had proven that Canadians could indeed take on projects themselves. The fact that Wellington, while not resisting, had some hesitation about this showed how the leadership of the Ordnance Department was not altogether convinced of the efficacy of relying on the Canadian marketplace and that they considered Canadian businessmen anything but true allies: "I entertain some doubts ... whether it is expedient to confine ourselves to contracts in the execution of the Work. We shall be very much at the mercy of contractors if they should believe that we possess no other means."[58]

The Commissariat was deliberately kept at a distance. The Ordnance storekeeper was to have the credit line he desired even if it did not match the yearly estimate. This, of course, was to get around any possible question from the Commissariat. Furthermore, the Ordnance Inspector of Accounts was to compile all documents relating to the Rideau Canal separately and report every three months to the governor and commander-in-chief at Quebec. All departments at home or in the colony were to get their information only from this source; that is to say, the Ordnance Department was to control all the information. But even this was not enough. The Inspector of Accounts was ordered to terminate his duty in Canada on 30 September 1828; all accounts were to go directly to London, averting the possibility of their being questioned in the colony.[59] Another administrative impediment, in the view of some of the engineering officers, had been removed. However, apparently not content with the various arrangements made by his superiors, Lieutenant-Colonel By had further challenges to the established practice for doing business in Canada with the military.

The man in charge of building the Rideau Canal asked that the commander of British forces in Canada be authorized to tell the Commissariat which contractors to hire. By's opinion was undoubtedly that speedy arrangements with contractors and the judging of subtle technical details were beyond the capacity of the Commissariat or any other officers of the army. Although not happy about it, the commander gave By authorization to choose his own contractors, with the provision that he should not overspend. Nor did By get any real guidelines: "in cases ... where there may be an immediate and pressing necessity for the completion of an important object, within a short period, His Lordship will trust to the discretion of Lieutenant-Colonel By in making his agreements with Tradesmen, or Workmen, on terms that shall not be disadvantageous to Government, without an observance of the usual form of advertisement."[60] In Canada, engineers and colleagues of By, although siding with him on the matter, were so disconcerted by this open-ended instruction that they reacted in much the same way as the Commissariat, one stressing that this "might tend to shake the faith of individuals with government and prevent those advantageous offers being made which it is our duty to endeavor to procure."[61] Even the Ordnance Department in London admitted that "...this precedent is very objectionable."[62]

The first indication that normal precedures would re-assert themselves came in April of 1828, when the Treasury Board suggested that someone should tell the commander-in-chief in Canada that he was acting on his own when he authorized Colonel By to do as he wished. For, at this point, with regard to the Rideau Canal project, the Commissariat had been reduced to being able only to write down the verbal agreements reached by the engineers. Advertisements and tenders were being ignored—in short, the military was no longer using the Canadian market in a liberal way.

By 1829, Lieutenant-Colonel By was starting to lose whatever support he had had in England.[63] He lost the momentum that was there at the start of the operation when the sense of military urgency vanished. The conduct of the whole project was severely criticized when it was halted by a Treasury Board directive on 25 May 1832.[64] As a result, the rest of the military's business returned to normal established practice. The Rideau Canal episode was over. Cost saving became, once again, a primary concern of the military in Canada.

Conclusion

The British armed forces in Canada in the first half of the nineteenth century considered provisioning a highly strategic issue. The issue was dealt with by the Commissariat through a set of principles, guidelines, practices, checks and balances. The Commissariat took its work seriously, putting public money to good use by allowing the lowest price to dictate the winning bid. The Treasury Board's recommended procedures were even sometimes too closely followed.

Lieutenant-General Elias
Walker Durnford, RE.
(NA, C-97740)

lith. D. Weil Montreal.

From a Drawing in Crayon
Elizabeth Sewell.

They were certainly slow, frustrating military officers who were on many occasions more concerned with completing the task than counting its cost. The obvious lack of maturity of the Canadian marketplace no doubt also created some problems.

On the whole, the action of the army while doing business in Canada was determined by strategic advantage, and ultimately, the winning of wars at minimum cost. British military business practices, in combination with more traditional and familiar factors such as weaponry, tactics, intelligence and generalship, were undoubtedly instrumental in British military successes in North America and elsewhere. One cannot help but notice how modern, in using the market as it did, the British Army was in its procurement policy. The will to adopt such a course of action by London, an actual implementation of a set of well thought-out and proven rules, was a deliberate choice guided by the liberal ideology of British society, an ideology embraced by many career officers in the military. The Canadian approach to provisioning its armed forces has maintiained the essence of the British military model of the colonial era. In addition, by setting the rules, example and standards, the Commissariat had a direct impact on those who were provisioning the British armed forces, namely, the Canadian merchants, tradesmen, bankers, and craftsmen.

Notes for Chapter 11

1   The study of supply is not a popular theme in military history. Interesting works on the topic include Martin Van Creveld, *Supplying War: Logistics from Wallenstein to Patton* (Cambridge: Cambridge University Press, 1977); Julian Thompson, *The Lifeblood of War: Logistics from 200 BC to the Present* (London: Brassey's, 1991) and John Albert Lynn, *Feeding Mars : logistics in Western warfare from the Middle Ages to the present* (Boulder, Colorado: Westview Press, 1993). Professor Martin S. Alexander nevertheless sees a brilliant future for this genre. Logistics, he wrote, "may even displace intelligence as 'the new missing dimension' of the study of war. Without fuel, food, ammunition, medical supplies and transport infrastructures, whether by sea, air, road or rail, armed forces do not move—let alone fight, or fight effectively." "Military History in Great Britain 'Public passions and academic Ambiguities'" in *Cahiers du Centre d'études de la Défense, L'histoire militaire en Italie, en Allemagne, en Grande-Bretagne et aux États-Unis*, cahier no 4 (novembre 1997), 83.

2   This study focuses on Lower Canada and Upper Canada and not the Atlantic colonies.

3   George Raudzens, *The British Ordnance Department and Canada's Canals, 1815-1855* (Waterloo: Wilfrid Laurier University Press, 1979); Peter Burrough, "The Ordnance Department and Colonial Defence, 1821-1855" in *Journal of Imperial and Commonwealth History*, Vol 10, No. 2 (1982), 125-149; "Parliamentary Radicals and the Reduction of Imperial Expenditure in British North America, 1827-1834" in the *Historical Journal*, Vol XI (1968) 446-461; Elionor Kyte-Senior, *British Regulars in Montreal. An Imperial Garrison, 1832-1854* (Montreal: McGill-Queen's University Press, 1981), 288. All discussed the British armed forces and finance without going into very much detail.

4   Some attention to the military market in Lower Canada was given by George Bervin in *Québec au XIXe siècle : l'activité économique des grands marchands* (Sillery, Québec: Septentrion, 1991); Robert Sweeny, *Les relations ville/campagne: le cas du bois de chauffage* (Montréal: Éditions du Montreal Business History Project, 1988); and Gilles Paquet and Jean-Pierre Wallot, *Patronage et pouvoir au Bas-Canada (1794-1812)* (Montreal: Presses de l'Université du Québec, 1973). Glenn Steppler's unpublished Masters thesis, "A Duty Troublesome Beyond Measure, Logistical Considerations in the War of 1812," (Montréal: McGill University, 1974) has given the most detailed account of British business provisioning system for the War of 1812 to date.

5   In Great Britain, it was the sole responsibility of the Ordnance Department.

6   See Chapter 1 of Ian K. Steele, *Warpaths. Invasions of North America* (New York, Oxford: Oxford University Press, 1994).

7   Stephen George Peregrine Ward, *Wellington's Headquarters, A Study of the Administrative Problems in the Peninsula (1809-1814)* (London: Oxford University Press, 1957), 69.

8   National Archives of Canada (NA), Manuscript Group (MG) 13, Vol. 863, f.179, microfilm, reel B-2809.

9   Public Record Office (PRO), War Office (WO) 62, Miscellanea, Instructions to various Commissariat Officers in Canada, Bermuda and the Cape of Good Hope.

10 Roch Legault, *Le Commissariat de l'armée britannique et les dépenses militaires au Canada (1815-1830)*, PhD thesis, (Montreal: University of Montreal, 1995), 210.

11 For the biography of this very capable engineer but controversial figure see Robert Legget *John By: Lieutenant Colonel, Royal Engineers, 1779-1836: Builder of the Rideau Canal, founder of Ottawa* (Ottawa: Historical Society of Ottawa, 1982.) By would not be remembered for his frugality and would end up spending too much. The original price tag for the Rideau Canal waterway was set at £169 000 by Major-General Sir Carmichael-Smyth in his special committee's report of 9 September 1825 (NA, RG 8, II, 6 (2)). At the conclusion of the work in 1832, By's final bill was over £822,000, close to five times what had been envisaged. (Raudzens, 95)

12 E.B. De Fonblanque, *Treatise on the Administration and Organisation of the British Army* (London, 1858), 53.

13 NA, RG 8, I, vol. 135, f.82-83, microfilm, reel C-2687, Commissariat Office, Montréal, 5 March 1825, Edwards to Turquand.

14 NA, RG 8, I, vol. 141, f.152-153, microfilm, reel C-2689, Commissariat Canada, Québec, 15 September 1828, Routh to Cooper.

15 NA, RG 8, I, vol. 420, f.40 à 42, microfilm, reel C-2943, Royal Engineers Office, Québec, 24 August 1824, Captain Vavasour to Darling; NA, RG 8, I, vol. 134, f.77 and 80, microfilm, reel C-2687, Commissary General Office, Québec, 25 and 27 September 1824, Coffin to Darling.

16 NA, RG 8, I, vol. 122, f.279, microfilm, reel C-2683, Storekeeper General Office, Quebec, 25 September 1817, Robertson to the Storekeeper General in London.

17 "We must confess, We are surprised that the long experience of Mr. Wood in the Details of Commissariat Duties, should not have suggested to him the propriety of con-

ceding this Point, at once, to Mr Adams." [PRO, AO 17, vol.121, ff.97-98, Comptrollers' Office, 5 February 1821, Drinkwater and Rosenhagen.]

18 PRO, AO 17, vol. 123, f.259 to 261, Comptrollers Office, 29 February 1828, King and Drinkwater.

19 De Fonblanque, 232.

20 NA, RG 8, I, vol. 137, f.91-92, microfilm, reel C-2687, Treasury Chambers, 14 September 1824, Herries, Joint Secretary to the Treasury to Thomas Sack, Secretary to the Board of Trade.

21 It was important for the Commissariat that the currencies be accepted by the entire Canadian population, merchants and farmers alike. NA, RG 8, I, vol. 137, f.86 à 88, microfilm, reel C-2687, Québec, 3 September 1825, Forsyth and Richardson Co. to Turquand.

22 NA, RG 8, I, vol. 331, f.99, microfilm, reel C-2876, Commissary General Office, Quebec, 15 May 1815, Robinson to Foster.

23 NA, RG 8, I, vol. 138, f.80, microfilm, reel C-2688, Commissary General Office, Quebec, 25 July 1825, Turquand to George Harrison.

24 Ibid.

25 NA, RG 8, I, vol. 138, f.88, microfilm, reel C-2688, Commissary General Office, Quebec, 25 September 1826, Turquand to Dalhousie.

26 NA, RG 8, I, vol. 143, f.147 to 152, microfilm, reel C-2689, Commissariat Canada, Québec, 6 July 1830, Routh.

27 NA, RG 8, I, vol. 338, f.128, microfilm, reel C-2877, 1 and 2 George II, IV. Cap. 121, 1821.

28 PRO, AO 17, vol. 124, f.314 to 316, 12 November 1829.

29 Ward, 71-72.

30 NA, RG 8, I, vol. 438, ff.9-10, microfilm, reel C-2972, Commissariat Canada, Quebec, 17 December 1829, Routh to the Attorney General.

31 NA, RG 8, I, vol. 121, f.100 to 105, microfilm, reel C-2682, Commissary General Office, Quebec, 3 April 1816, Robinson to Foster.

32 NA, RG 8, I, vol. 438, f.8, microfilm, reel C-2972, Commissariat Canada, Quebec, 17 December 1829, Routh to Fortier.

33 Routh, London 1852, 42.

34 S.P.G. Ward, "The Peninsular Commissary" in the *Journal of the Society for Army Historical Research*, Vol LXXV, No. 304 (Winter 1997), 230-239.

35 Christian Rioux, *Dictionary of Canadian Biography*, vol V (Toronto: University of Toronto Press and Les Presses de l'Université Laval, 1983), 214-215.

36 See Gilles Paquet and Jean-Pierre Wallot.

37 Routh, 24.

38 NA, RG 8, I, vol. 49, f.186, 189 et 190, microfilm, reel C-2619, Deputy Commissary General Office, Montreal, 16 October 1829, Forbes to Sisson.

39 John Beswarick Thompson, *Dictionary of Canadian Biography*, Vol IX (Toronto: University of Toronto Press and Les Presses de l'Université Laval, 1977), 268-269.

40 Bervin, 177-178.

41 There were only two instances of money being advanced during the period from 1815 to 1832 in Montreal. See NA, RG 8, I, vol. 410, f.11 to 13, microfilm, reel C-2941, Montréal, 21 August 1821, Peter Rutherford's petition; and RG 8, I, vol. 1254, f.13, microfilm, reel C-3530, Headquarters, 15 September 1819, Bowles to Durnford.

42 NA, RG 8, I, vol. 139, f.48-49 et 50-51, microfilm, reel C-2688, Commissary General Office, Quebec, 7 February 1827, Turquand to Darling and Quebec, 2 February 1827, Smith and Anderson to Turquand.

43 PRO, WO 58, vol. 65, 235-236, 12 September 1817, Harrison to Wood.

44 NA, RG 8, I, vol. 136, f. 182, microfilm, reel C-2687, 16 May 1826, A. Campbell, Royal Notary to Turquand.

45 NA, RG 8, I, vol. 121, f.172, microfilm, reel C-2683, Downing Street, 7 September 1815, Lord Bathurst to Gordon Drummond.

46 NA, RG 8, I, vol. 125, f.109 to 113, microfilm, reel C-2684, Treasury Chambers, 8 April 1820, George Harrison to Dalhousie.

47 On this subject see Kenneth Bourne, *Britain and the balance of power in North America, 1815-1908* (Berkeley: University of California Press, 1967); J. Mckay Hitsman, *Safeguarding Canada, 1763-1871* (Toronto: Toronto University Press, 1968); and C. P. Stacey, *The undefended border: the myth and the reality* (Ottawa: Canadian Historical Association, 1953). For Canada's fortification program, the best account is to be found in André Charbonneau, Yvon Desloges et Marc Lafrance, *Québec, ville fortifiée du XVIIe au XIXe siècle* (Ottawa: Edition du Pélican and Parcs Canada, 1982) and André Charbonneau, *Les fortifications de l'Ile-aux-Noix* (Ottawa: Éditions du Méridien, 1994). The threat of invasion was less daunting for the already mighty United States, and most likely accounts for the fact that the American protection program related to its northern border has not been studied as well as its Canadian counterpart. But a good article is Dale Floyd, "Supervision of Fortification Construction (1794-1820)" in *Journal of America's Military Past,* Vol 20, No.2, 1993.

48 It was not quite clear as to why the Royal Staff Corps, the other engineering department of the armed forces, was not attached to Ordnance and did not benefit as much as the Royal Engineers from this policy in Canada. It might be that its bureaucratic establishment was no match for the Ordnance one in London.

49 NA, RG 8, I, vol. 125, f.124 and125, microfilm, reel C-2684, Royal Engineers Office, Fort Lennox, Isle-aux-Noix, 4 December 1819; Montréal, 20 April 1820, I. W. Clarke to George Bowles.

50 PRO, AO 17, vol. 118, f.172 to 183, Comptrollers Office, 6 December 1816, King and Drinkwater.

51 NA, RG 8, I, vol. 412, f.135-136, microfilm, reel C-2941, Commissary General Office, Québec, 8 July 1822, Wood to Darling.

52 NA, RG 8, I, vol. 418, f.140, microfilm, reel C-2942, Royal Engineers Office, Montréal, 21 February 1824, Romilly to Durnford and vol. 421, f.207-208, microfilm, reel C-2943, Royal Engineers Office, Montréal, 27 December 1824, Romilly to Durnford.

53 This phenomenon would originate in 1821 according to historian Peter Burroughs, "The Ordnance Department and Colonial Defence, 1821-1855" in *Journal of Imperial and Commonwealth History*, Vol 10, No. 2 (January 1982), 126 - 128.

54 PRO, CO 42, vol. 219, f.220-221, Downing Street, 18 April 1826, Horton to Griffin.

55 NA, RG 8, I, vol. 42, f.26-27, microfilm, reel C-2617, 21 April 1826, Gother Mann to Dalhousie.

56 NA, RG 8, I, vol. 44, f.5-6, microfilm, reel C-2618, no date, Instructions for the Respective Officers of the Ordnance at Quebec, Montreal, Kingston, and the Inspector of Accounts in regard of the mode to be adopted in making payments and keeping the Accounts of the Expenses of forming the Rideau Canal, Byham.

57 Ibid., f.6-7.

58 NA, RG 8, I, vol. 426, f.224, microfilm, reel C-2945, Copy of a Minute of the Master General of Ordnance on proposed new Works in Canada, 15 June 1826.

59 NA, RG 8, I, vol. 432, f.179, microfilm, reel C-2946, Office of Ordnance, 21 May 1828, Byham to the Ordnance Officers at Quebec.

60 PRO, WO 55, vol. 864, f.140, Quebec, 20 February 1827, Darling to the respecting officers.

61 Ibid.

62 PRO, WO 55, vol. 864, f.53-54, Office of Ordnance, 13 June 1827, Byham to the Ordnance officers, Quebec.

63 It has to be point out that, by and large, Ordnance finance was praised in London at that time. Peter Burroughs, 125.

64 Raudzens, 95.

CHAPTER 12

The Clash of Imperatives

Canadian Munitions Development in the Interwar Years, 1919-1939

Ronald G. Haycock

FOR NEARLY TWO DECADES after the end of the Great War senior military personnel in Ottawa had failed to convince their political masters of the need to have modern munitions facilities in Canada. But in February 1937 Canada's military equipment, like the armed forces themselves, was so obviously decrepit that even the over-cautious and usually anti-military William Lyon Mackenzie King was alarmed enough to start a modest rearmament. His conversion had been a painful one since being re-elected in the autumn of 1935. And his new defence policy announcement in the House of Commons that February was most welcome to the soldiers at headquarters and the defence minister, Ian Mackenzie. Indeed Mackenzie told the Prime Minister later in July that "there is really not very much now" to do save to decide on the policy of munitions production. This he saw as straightforward, as he told King. "It was only a matter of how far we should go by way of public ownership ... and how far we should go in control of private industry.[1] If Ian Mackenzie really thought it was that simple or that there were only these two aspects to consider in Canadian munitions policy, the next two years would prove him sadly mistaken. Canadian munitioning had never been that simple.

In order to fully understand what happened with munitions in the twenties and thirties it is necessary to quickly review what had gone before. This is particularly true of political sensitivities. In most countries, munitions development has always been the hardest in peacetime. Canada was no exception. The Dominion had established a public Cartridge Factory at Quebec City in 1879.[2] It was a state-owned and military-run facility for several reasons. No private Canadian manufacturers could be convinced to make any munitions because the product had no civilian application and the military production runs were too small to ensure either low cost or enough profit. Besides, the technical expertise required for the production of highly demanding munitions was not present in civilian industrial circles. In times of crisis, as a very junior partner in a large alliance structure of the British Empire, Canada had found that the mother country frequently could not, or would not, supply the Dominion with the best equipment or even equipment at all in time of crisis. And, when there was no perceived crisis the Canadians themselves said they couldn't afford it, or, more to the point, saw no threat so said they did not need it. Early politicians like "Old Tomorrow" (as Sir John A Macdonald's contemporaries sometimes called him) were reluctant to develop much in relation to an efficient military or its prime spin-off, munitions, lest it commit them to costly and divisive Imperial enterprises. This was especially so when there did not seem to be much of a threat and there was yet so much to do in expensive nation building at home.[3]

And so in the first thirty-five years Canadians had little more than a small publicly owned rifle cartridge facility politically placed conveniently in Quebec. It produced the small arms ammunition for the militia and some gun ammunition for the artillery. Its rationale was to be the schoolmaster for the future if an emergency ever induced private industry to expand. For all the rest of the munitions and ammunition and most of the raw materials, the country was completely dependent on Great Britain which, of course, insisted—as they did with doctrine and training—that all war materiel be of acceptable British patterns. To Canadian soldiers who were nearly all British-trained if not British themselves, it all made sense within the concept of the great Empire-alliance.[4] These factors would remain constants of Canadian munitioning for years to come. And they played a seminal role in the 1920s and 1930s.

The one exception to the idea of a military-run public system was the privately owned Ross Rifle factory created again at Cove Fields in Quebec City by the Laurier administration in 1902. Laurier's innovative militia minister, Sir Frederick Borden, was committed to expanding the munitions capability to include both private and public ownership, as well as military and civilian munitioning which in time would make Canada self sufficient in war supplies. Moreover, the Boer War had shown clearly that Great Britain could not supply the Dominion when she needed it with munitions, especially basic war materiel such as rifles. Like those before and after, Laurier wanted to encourage industrial development especially in Quebec. The industrial processes of rifle manufacturing fell nicely into building such expertise. So did the fact that the expansive and wealthy Scottish inventor and nobleman, Sir Charles Ross, was going to put up the facility at his own expense. As well, he offered what seemed to be a state of the art weapon at a time when the rifleman was still "queen of battle" on the field. Unfortunately, not much of the munitions optimism turned out to be justified.[5]

In the decade before 1914, the Dominion Arsenal, as it was re-named in 1902, never met plans for diversified production. Indeed, the rifle ammunition while often of good quality, was at other times very bad. The government did not want to spend the money to replace aging machinery and otherwise to pay for an expansion likely because it hoped to induce the private sector to pick up some of the production. By 1913, production problems caused the new Minister of Militia and Defence, Sam Hughes, to order a complete overhaul of the arsenal. He brought over British munitions experts from the Royal Arsenal at Woolwich to do it. Millions of rounds of Dominion Arsenal Quebec (DAQ) cartridges were declared unsafe to shoot. F.M. Gaudet, the French-Canadian superintendent, and his senior staff were quickly replaced and some newer machinery was added. But the factory was, as the report said, still right in the middle of a big city. Confined by its surroundings, it could not expand. It was unsafe for the citizens and was strategically vulnerable to seaborne attack.[6]

As for the Ross rifle factory, it had been built smack in the middle of the Champs de Battaille on the Plains of Abraham with a very generous land lease and substantial production cost advances; it was also plagued by late deliveries, cost over-runs, halting production and shortages of strategic materials and skilled workers. These criticisms were often the focus of embarrassing questions in the House of Commons. There was at least one attempted vote of non-confidence over the government's rifle policy. And there were more than just rumors that this new rifle jammed in rapid fire, to name just one of several technical problems. But most importantly for the future, its superb accuracy on military target ranges and in international competitions like Bisley in England saw it evolve over the decade toward a military target rifle and away from a general service weapon. Given that some of the other Dominions were flirting with buying the Ross rifle, War Office authorities did not like the fact that the Canadian rifle was winning on their own military ranges and that it did not conform to the Empire's small arms system based as it was on the Lee-Enfield family of small arms. With these factors all working, the rifle policy became inevitably so politicized by its detractors on one hand and its rabid defenders on the other, that there was no common ground for calm development. Significantly this pre-bellum politicization spawned doubt and distrust to the point where the uninformed volunteers of the Canadian Expeditionary Force (CEF) and the Canadian Corps in the 1914 war lost all confidence in the rifle. It was withdrawn from our armed force in the middle of the conflict and replaced by a British Lee-Enfield. The Ross factory was confiscated and rifle making stopped in Canada. Ross sued the government for three million dollars and finally settled for two million after the deputy minister of justice advised that Sir Charles had a good case based on the vagaries of the government's original contract. The lingering distrust of private weapons manufacturing held immense implications for later arms production. To make more than a pun, politicians especially became "gun-shy."[7]

And yet the Canadian munitions industry during the First World War was phenomenally successful if limited to mostly artillery shells. In the end it was tightly controlled. It made munitions not only for the Canadian government but also for that of Great Britain as part of its Ministry of Munitions. It involved private and public enterprise, profit controls and the novel idea of "national factories." It employed hundreds of thousands of Canadian men and women. The old Dominion Arsenal at Quebec City did yeoman service in both small arms production and in being an educator for civil industry thrown quickly into munitions production. Even a second arsenal was opened in Lindsay Ontario where it made rifle ammunition as well.[8]

Unfortunately, shortly after the Armistice in 1918, this wartime production feat was rapidly and almost without thought dismantled. The achievements of Sam Hughes' original Shell Committee and then Sir Joseph Flavelle's Imperial Munitions Board came to naught.

Canada's munitions pre-history was checkered and small. But during the First World War munitions experience in the main had been highly successful and the output was huge. It all indicates that munitions processes are far more complicated than usually acknowledged and always had been. Some observers have noted that there are a variety of factors—or as they call them "imperatives"—in all civil-military relations that are at the very centre of munitions policy. Above all, military personnel must meet the practical imperative of creating the most effective military tools to guarantee national security. For their part, the civilians, most markedly those in government, must satisfy the "societal" imperatives. There are a great many of these. For instance, a munitions factory owner must be concerned with the availability of skilled workers and with labour relations and with profit and loss. The mayors of towns want the employment that a munitions factory brings. They will lobby to get it and to keep it. Regions and provinces are affected by cultural considerations and perceptions of proportionate distribution of wealth. Federal politicians look beyond the confines of military security to national good and development. And in their minds, they must remain in power to do so.[9] There is no clearer case for this than in defence industrial preparation in the two decades after the Great War. Most of the time it was the social factors that dominated policy and production.

In 1919, for the discerning, there should have been several points to be made about the wartime experience of the arsenals. First, munitioning was complex, involving all segments of government and society. Organizations like the Shell Committee, the War Purchasing Committee and especially the Imperial Munitions Board (IMB) were essential to success. The public hated and politicians feared war profiteering and scandal. Central control by government was necessary in total war for a variety of reasons. Dependence on foreign sources for raw material, tools and expertise was a continuing and risky reality. And there was a much greater dependence on the United States for these things than had been anticipated. The Dominion Arsenals had provided vital services to mitigate that dependence but they could not by themselves answer war's demands. Allies looked after themselves first; production difficulties were assured unless peacetime industrial mobilization plans had been worked out; foreign or allied war orders were necessary to sustain full production even in war. If there was to be a defence industrial base after the conflict, foreign markets would be even more critical. And finally and most importantly, the Canadian government was not prepared to sustain any of this monumental effort after 1918. The IMB simply evaporated; National Factories were dissolved; stocks and machinery were promptly sold. And ideas died as memory faded. Yet in 1919 there were those who attempted to save expertise if not plant and process. One was Sir Joseph Flavelle, head of the IMB, who tried to get the minister to retain some of the National Factory plant for making ammunition then being offered by the British government at bargain prices. Another suggestion, through the voice of its vice president, came from one of the veterans of the private munitions effort, the Dominion Cartridge Company. It pleaded with the government to preserve and maintain a nucleus of small arms ammunition potential by placing small orders with selected war-experienced Canadian industries. But these exhortations were simply ignored.[10] The neglect would last for the next sixteen years.

But why was it so? On a higher plain reaction to the horrors of war, the international peace and disarmament movements, the appearance of Mackenzie King as Prime Minister in 1921, a general revulsion against the arms manufacturers—the supposed "Merchants of Death"—are but some of them. Recently Jonathan Vance has suggested another slightly different assessment of Canadians' memory of the First World War and the meaning they gave it. That generation, he says, not only refused to consider the horrifyingly technical conflict as just one of man-destroying machinery, but they also "avoided the machines of war" whereby "the individual is celebrated and the machines ignored." After the war, munitions were not the first consideration for many Canadians. There was also Senator Raoul Dandurand's "fire-proof house" made so by time and distance. The nation having just fought a "war to end all wars," many people had a faith in the new League of Nations. These are all part of the social imperatives. And there were still other factors including the lack of an enemy, at least for a while.[11]

After the war things spiralled down rapidly in the Canadian military. Their numbers remained small for two decades. In 1922, for instance, of an authorized establishment of 10,000, the Permanent Force consisted of only 428 officers and 3,215 other ranks. The Non-Permanent Active Militia fared no better; it was allowed to recruit to only half of its strength. In 1939, only about 47,000 went into the annual camps for training. It was less than had trained before the Great War. In general, the forces lived off the masses of surplus First World War munitions and each year these became more and more obsolescent. Stocks of ammunition dwindled and corroded into unserviceability. Outside of small arms ammunition and some gun shells, nearly all munitions going into service were procured abroad. Save for the two small public arsenals, Canadian defence industries had all but ceased to exist.

Yet two of the private companies held on for a while after the war. The Dominion Cartridge Company continued to make sporting ammunition for the civilian market, but its vital cordite explosive branch soon fell victim to a lack of government orders—and cordite was a British propellant that was not much used in North America and certainly not in commercial ammunition. As for the British, they did not yet accept military ammunition in peacetime loaded with anything but cordite. Canada's propellant capacity was severely hampered as a result.

The other firm was the Ottawa Car Company. It had been making a few gun carriages for the government even before 1914. During the war it had been in the vanguard of trying to establish artillery manufacturing in the Dominion. From the onset of the conflict the Canadians had agreed to a British munitions ministry prohibition on Canadian gun manufacture lest it divert the Dominion's massive ammunition effort. They also did not think Canadian steelmakers had the technical knowledge for making the regulation acid steel acceptable for gun barrels to the War Office. It was short sighted in as much as Canadians had already perfected a basic steel for artillery shell bodies which the British had reluctantly accepted. In addition, the War Office said it could not spare the necessary gunnery production experts to get manufacturing going. And by 1917, the British artillery industry could meet all the demands of the war and the Canadian government needed fewer than forty pieces of its own. So the usual imperatives applied: technology and alliance decisions pushed in their own direction, and unless the demand was large enough or the guns could be sold abroad, the munition was too expensive to make at home. Militia and defence personnel were disappointed in as much as they wanted the domestic gun production capability for both the current war and later peacetime strategic reasons.[12] But the conflict ended before it got off the ground. Soon after, the Ottawa company felt the pinch of no orders for a product that had no civilian application. While it did get a few government repair contracts in the early twenties, it was not enough to sustain the effort. With idle and expensive machinery taking up space, the company liquidated its munitions capacity. In 1923, the Quarter Master General (QMG), Major-General E.C. Ashton, tried to save it much like the president of the Dominion Cartridge Factory had suggested earlier, with some form of government subsidy, Ashton begged his minister "that every endeavor be made to keep them in existence as supplementary arsenals." The King government would not have it. After a long court case launched by the firm for breach of contract, and one final headquarters attempt to convince the government to buy the Ottawa Car Company and use it as a government gun man-ufactory, in mid-1928 the new Minister of National Defence, J.L. Ralston, exercised the Statute of Frauds defence to avoid a costly settlement. That ended the possibility of such gun manu-facture in Canada until the Second World War.[13]

While most of the above are aspects of the higher social imperatives, the two Dominion Arsenals had to contend with more down to earth functional imperatives. For one or two years after the war, these public facilities managed to secure small arms and gun ammunition orders from the United States. When these ended the government made no further attempts to find foreign markets. Yearly demands of the Canadian forces were too small; the ammunition plants were limited to producing only the annual expenditure and some small reserve stocks. Therefore unit costs were high. While its work force was experienced and its labour cheaper than in Ontario, the Quebec facility was old; its gun and small arms ammunition machinery was outdated and it had been heavily taxed by the war. It was also in the middle of a growing city and physically incapable of expansion and further diversification. It was also dangerous. There was no way it could be made completely safe; powder magazines had blown up before. The dangerous but necessary ammunition and explosives proof and accuracy testing could not be carried out efficiently. On the other hand, the Lindsay Arsenal had much newer plant and machinery even if housing and skilled labour were a problem. As it stood then, it made only rifle ammunition. But situated on the outskirts of a small town on good rail lines in Ontario, it was not as dangerous and could be expanded to do nearly all the things that DAQ could not, particularly if it received the latter's salvageable machine tools.[14]

The immediate post war questions quickly became "were both factories to be closed or just one, and which one?" Indeed, the superintendent of the Quebec plant advised the military headquarters (MHQ) at war's end to take advantage of the bargain opportunity to move the Quebec City plant into the recently closed national factory of the IMB at Verdun, Quebec on the island of Montreal.[15] But when Flavelle also pressed the point with the Militia minister, noth-ing happened for over a year. Part of the delay was that there was no discernable defence pol-icy coming out of the Union government. At the time, Sir Arthur Currie (and later Sir William Otter) were in the throws of reorganizing the Canadian militia into a new post war organiza-tion. No doubt the cabinet thought that things could wait for this new structure—whatever it was to be—before deciding such concomitant issues of munitionment.

Another reason was that the MHQ staff did not all agree on what to do with the arsenals. One group wanted to concentrate on Lindsay, another to retain the Quebec plant, and still another to keep them all open. Moreover, there was pressure from both urban centres to main-tain the existing facilities where they were. Meanwhile, the two plants had been ordered by MHQ to shift quickly to the lowest possible production rates. Both promptly let go nearly all their wartime employees. In fact once the US Small Arms Ammunition (SAA) contract was com-pleted in the spring of 1919, Lindsay was close to a skeleton staff, having been ordered to make the transition in less than thirty days. The Great War Veterans Association lobbied to get jobs in whatever peacetime employment there was, and at the same time insisted that excessive wartime profit from munitions be used to support veterans and veterans' widows.[16]

Once S.C. Mewburn, the Minister of Militia and Defence, bluntly rejected the offer of moving all the peacetime munitions work into one of Flavelle's vacant National Factories, the DAQ Superintendent, Colonel F.D. Lafferty, fought a brave rearguard action to save both the arsenals if possible. But as the senior superintendent he made a special case for his French-Canadian workers and their more experienced plant. The Quebec employees, he claimed were the only really skilled, longtime arsenal personnel in the country. During the war, they had been loyal to the Quebec factory in spite of the attraction of higher wages from munitioners in Canada and in the United States. Some of them had worked all their lives at the Quebec arsenal. They couldn't just be thrown onto the very uncertain employment market. Besides, if Lindsay was chosen over Quebec most of them would not move out of the province for cultural reasons, and those who did would be faced with strong local resentment from those who did not get hired, like the Ontario members of the veterans associations.[17]

While Lafferty was pushing for this course of action, some of his colleagues at MHQ simply thought the Quebec production should be closed down and all future peacetime munitions made at the facility in Lindsay. It appears that much of this came from the Master-General Ordnance (MGO), Major-General H.M. Elliott. He certainly was anxious to reduce the production of both plants quickly down to "peacetime" needs.[18] There would not be, he said, much need for manufacture given huge surplus war stocks of ammunition. Any solution was further delayed in late February 1919 when the militia minister refused to make a policy decision, saying that he was going to take the entire munitions question up to the Cabinet. If he did, no answer came from it for the next ten months. As a result, the two factories continued a very small amount of manufacturing simply to replace annual wastage, mostly of .303-inch rifle SAA and the completion of a few thousand rounds of medium field gun ammunition at Quebec.[19] The superintendents were told to divide up the production of ten million rifle cartridges and extend it over twelve months to keep both installations going until the spring of 1920. It was such a small amount that one of the factories could have produced it in a third of that time. One way to drag it out was to operate on minimal staff, and that is what they did.

By the fall of 1919 there was still no clear direction from the government. International politics were part of the reason. There were the Paris Peace Conferences where Canada had supported the Convention for the Control of Trade in Arms and Ammunition signed at Saint Germain in September that year; there were also the international debates over the proposed new League of Nations with its controversial articles on collective security.[20] In Britain, just days after the fighting stopped, committees were wrestling with questions about the future shape of the armed forces and imperial defence. The answers would have serious implications for Canada. Significantly, in 1919 there was a talented and determined Canadian professional soldier with excellent combat experience sitting on both the imperial defence re-organization panel and the army committee. This was Brigadier General J.H. Macbrien, who shortly was to become Chief of the General Staff in Ottawa. He was clearly enthusiastic about having a truly professional force in Canada, one efficient and well thought out with all the vital equipment necessary and conforming to the British Empire military model. There can be little doubt that he brought much of this enthusiasm home to Canada with him. Unfortunately, he did not make the transition from war to peace easily, a transition made even harder by the uncertainty and retrenchments that were affecting munitions so quickly.[21]

Before General McBrien took up his post in Canada, the munitions issue was going on apace with little resolution save down-sizing. In October 1919, Superintendent Lafferty put forward one more attempt to convince both the MHQ and the government to create a consistent and, at least in his opinion, viable peacetime munitions policy. This he called a "Militia System of Manufacturing Reserve." Under this commonsense scheme, a select group drawn from the private companies that had made munitions during the Great War would retain a nucleus of specialized machinery to do so again. The public arsenals would keep track of the latest munitions developments and ensure that each private company was kept up to date in machine tools, munitions developments and production processes. In short, the arsenals would be a militia school of munitions manufacture." To lend credibility to the idea for his military superiors at MHQ, and hoping also to convince the politicians, Lafferty hooked the idea to the defence needs of Canada. He pointed to her growing maturity and self-sufficiency and to potential Canadian contributions to future Imperial requirements. These were old arguments that MHQ soldiers and plant superintendents had been making ever since the Cartridge Factory had been established in 1879. Lafferty knew this, and so his recommendations to the MGO also noted the lessons of the war:

> It may not be in the policy of the Department to consider any such programme, but
> I also wish to go on record as recommending some such policy in view of the
> lessons that have been learned in the Great War. There is nothing original in the
> scheme, in the fact that the Germans,...were prepared...on just such lines; and
> while the war is still fresh in the memory of [our] manufacturers, it would be wise
> for a similar policy to be drafted...in Canada, not only to meet our local conditions
> but to assist in the efforts of the Empire.

If the Superintendent thought that all good ideas succeed, he was quickly disappointed. Lafferty's manufacturing reserve was immediately dismissed by Elliott, the MGO, with a curt "in abeyance for the present." Perhaps Elliott was not in a mood to accept this clear reliance on private enterprise. Certainly later MGOs were not: they wanted a full-blown public arsenal system run by the military.[22] Whatever the case, a month later to the day the MGO himself tried to get a policy statement on munitions from the minister through the Militia Council, but that too was put off. The minister, the secretary to the council said, "wished to look further into the whole question with a view to taking the same up in Privy Council."[23] Given that none of the greater strategic issues of the new peace treaties, the League of Nations or even Empire defence had yet been decided, the minister's response was hardly surprising. Besides, Admiral Sir John Jellicoe was then in Canada trying to drum up a very large Canadian commitment to Imperial defence. For Canadian politicians very sensitive to anything which might again embroil the Dominion in another European vortex, it was not a good time to do anything.

And so nothing was done. Moreover, there were signs of more of it to come. In the spring of 1921, when Hugh Gutherie, now the militia minister, tried to obtain a modest increase in the defence budget from the House of Commons, the new Leader of the Opposition, Mackenzie King, stifled the request with what was to be his refrain for many years to come:

> The minister thinks that...we ought to vote an amount equal at least to amounts
> that were being voted prior to the war. That is where I take issue with him.
> Conditions are wholly different today; there is no world menace. Where does the
> minister expect invasion from? The minister says that the expenditure is needed for
> the defence of Canada—defence against whom?[24]

At the same time, the new Liberal Party leader had a near complete ignorance of things military. Mackenzie King knew few soldiers and distrusted most of them. Moreover, he saw munitions as an evil commodity that could only harm Canada. One famous episode during the election campaign of that year demonstrates this clearly. While returning on the train from campaigning on the East Coast, King had to stop over at Levis, Quebec. While waiting for the next train, he was startled to see huge quantities of artillery shells being trans-shipped from boats to freight cars. He immediately took this to be evidence of a nefarious plot by soldiers and the British to make Canada, "without the consent of Canadians, into a vast munitions dump to serve the sinister purpose of imperialism." And he soon made the accusation into an election device.[25] In reality, Canada had bought no ammunition of any kind since the conflict ended and these artillery shells were simply the ammunition belonging to the Canadian Corps at war's end finally being returned to Canada. These facts did not seem to matter.

By late that year, King's Liberals were in power in Ottawa. And he was more than willing to carry out his policy of retrenchment. The Militia and Defence portfolio along with the navy and the new air services were among the first to feel the cut. By 1922, the armed forces may have been reorganized with more efficient government machinery, in the form of a new Department of National Defence (DND), but the Liberal government's motives were clear. In the Prime Minister's words, "if we are ever to have retrenchment in military and naval expenditures this is one moment in which it is possible to bring about something of that character." That year the military expenditures reached an all time low of $13,320,027, down from $335,525,512 in 1919-1920. For a decade after that military budgets hovered around the lower figure. They remained, at least in military minds, never enough for the professional needs of the armed forces in light of what they thought they would ultimately be called upon to do.

But in 1922, all of that was unknown. Nevertheless, one way for the military to carry out the new Liberal government's retrenchment policy was to cut munitions expenditure. The office of the Master General of the Ordnance was quickly abolished.[26] The MGO was the chief munitions officer on the MHQ Staff, and so from here on in the voice of munitions would be heard through others less senior. In the arsenals things also happened quickly. Much to the dissatisfaction of the Ottawa military and the local citizenry, the Lindsay plant was closed down. Part of the land was leased to the town as a park and some of the buildings were rented out as a temporary tannery under pressure from Lindsay's mayor and the Board of Trade to employ townsmen put out of work by a big fire. One success that the headquarters soldiers had was to convince the government not to sell the entire facility outright. To their mind the Lindsay Arsenal was still officially there and was just waiting at rest for vindication in a new crisis. While some of its newer machine tools went to Quebec to replace worn-out equipment, the remainder was mothballed in the remaining buildings which became a forlorn warehouse for surplus DND equipment.[27]

At the same time, the Quebec facility's work force and productivity shrank drastically. Little research and development took place in its cramped and outdated plant. Portions of its powder filling facility were moved to Cove Fields near the old Ross Rifle plant to do something about the danger. But there was a complete interruption in the manufacturing process, always anathema to production efficiency. Many citizens who believed in the sanctity of the historic plains were as upset with the powder filling station as they had been twenty years before with the location of the now defunct rifle factory in the same place. They wanted the land restored so that the whole Battlefield Park could be developed to its full potential as one of Canada's most significant places, and for both cultures. In December 1923, the *Montreal Gazette* reported that there was going to be a meeting between three federal Cabinet ministers about securing the land. It was rumoured, the paper claimed, that on the agenda would be the closure of the entire Quebec arsenal with a subsequent move to Lindsay. Three to four hundred French Canadians would be out of work. When the deputy defence minister, C.J. Desbarats, heard this he immediately quizzed the QMG. In spite of continuous debate since 1919, Ashton denied that the question of removing the arsenal had ever been "discussed." He quickly added that it was the opinion of "this department that this manufacture should be continued in Quebec for the reasons that this work has always been carried out in Quebec; the personnel are French Canadian, have been efficiently trained and are today turning out a finished article of high standard indeed."[28]

By the onset of the Depression, the factory had been temporarily shut down several times.[29] It was clear that to an unsympathetic government, always sensitive to the voters' mood, what little munitions were made in Canada were best made by public and not private factories. It was hard to imagine the Superintendent of the Dominion Arsenal as a "Merchant of Death." Besides, the government could control the arsenal directly, which was not always the case with private manufacturers, as the embarrassing experiences with the feisty Sir Charles Ross had proven.

All of this made the headquarters soldiers shudder. During the twenties the staff chiefs lamented, as MacBrien did in 1926, that "we have had no clear statement of military policy since 1905."[30] Such being the case, there could hardly be a munitions policy. By the end of the decade, these equipment shortages forced the Chief of the General Staff to cut training and militia numbers. Furthermore, most soldiers held little hope that private firms would be encouraged to get into the munitions business. As always, the public was not in the mood for that; neither was any government.[31] Orders were too small to attract entrepreneurs, and the toolage was too expensive.

But imperatives shaping Canadian munitionment in the decade of the twenties were not generated only on Canadian soil, just as they never were before it. The most salient factor from abroad was the infamous "no war for ten years" rule, an integral part of British foreign and therefore defence policy that had been practiced for all of the twenties but only officially adopted in 1928. It was to remain the guiding force for another six years in Great Britain. While never government policy of Canada, its effect on the Dominion's foreign and defence policy formulation was huge. On one hand, there was a Canadian military staff, British trained and battle experienced, that looked toward the War Office and Imperial strategists for guidance. To them, war on Canadian soil, that is, the direct defence of Canada, was a remote possibility. The far more likely threat would be to the Empire as a whole. Various Colonial and Imperial conferences before and after the Great War had confirmed for them several things; not the least was that they should be prepared to be active in defending that Empire should their government agree. There were also concomitants to this idea. There would be uniformity in doctrine, training, organization and munitions. Just after the Boer War (as Chapter 4 explains) Canada had accepted the principle of self-sufficiency where possible in manufacturing war materiel as part of both tour strategic and practical contribution to Imperial defence. The short of it was that all during the inter-war period Canadian senior military personnel thought in these terms.[32]

On the other hand, there were usually governments which, for one reason or another, were not going to commit Canada to any European imbroglios of the sort experienced after 1914.[33] They too espoused some of the tenets held dear by their soldiers but translated them completely differently. The most important was the lack of an enemy for Canada. The most obvious way to approach these concepts was to do nothing. As Sir Joseph Pope communicated in 1923 to the League of Nations Committee on the Reduction of Armaments, "Canada has no international obligations except in connection with her status as part of the British Empire."[34] Sometimes Mackenzie King said things at Imperial Conferences that were sufficiently vague and all encompassing so that some of the soldiers like MacBrien, or later perhaps A.G L. MacNaughton, may have thought they heard more supportive endorsement for their military views than was really the intent. Perhaps they were also just deluding themselves. For instance, at the 1926 Imperial Conference King spoke about Imperial and Canadian defence using such phrases as "the need of all parts of the Empire to keep abreast of the rapid changes and developments" in all armed services. A little later on, he noted that "for the most part, the principles laid down by the Imperial Organization Committee ... have hithertofore been followed ... in the department [of defence]." As we know General MacBrien was a member of this last group in 1919. King accepted the conference's draft resolutions on defence with a short "they are quite satisfactory, so far as we are concerned."

But it is also true that when King gave a synopsis of Canada's

Exterior view of the Ross Rifle Factory, Quebec City, ca 1900-1905. (Photographer unknown. NA. PA-107386)

defence posture to the Imperial delegates that year, he never once mentioned a very important aspect of what MacBrien had put in his memo on defence which formed the basis of notes for the Prime Minister's speech. The CGS had pointed out to King that "Canada is in a better position to lend support to other parts of the Empire than she has been at any time throughout her previous history" by reason of very experienced personnel and much more equipment "than ever before." MacBrien was at the conference; he must have recognized the significance of the omission. He also must have been disappointed when he heard his Prime Minister's comments on releasing conference statements about Imperial defence to the English press. King did not favour the practice because "misunderstanding is apt to be created [back in Canada] ... if they get the idea that the purpose of the Conference is to work out some Imperial scheme ... to which we are committed ... I wish to make it perfectly clear that I do not assert that anything of the kind is being attempted."[35] Whatever the case, James Eayrs is convinced that these soldiers took a remarkably long time to understand what was in the mind of their political chief.[36]

When MacBrien returned to Canada he drafted a long memorandum to J.L. Ralston, the defence minister. It listed all of the deficiencies of the country's defence. Among them was the warning that the munitions left over from the war were all but spent, and that much of the equipment was worn out or obsolete. He called for an industrial mobilization scheme including a comprehensive survey of what Canada could produce in a crisis. The forces desperately needed all kinds of modern mechanized equipment not now available to them, MacBrien argued. The office of the MGO should be revived to "form the nucleus of and arrange the plans for a ministry of munitions." Evidently the frustrated general held little hope for change. His memo was a *cri de coeur* and the frustrated MacBrien resigned shortly thereafter.[37]

If a lack of defence policy in Canada produced nothing more than a stunted and worsening munitions situation the deliberate defence policy of Great Britain produced the same result. As B.J.C. Mckercher has recently shown, British national security policy evolved through distinct phases from the victory in 1918 to the decision to rearm in 1936. The first phase was isolation from Europe and an emphasis on protection of the Empire with an assumption that no major war was likely in either scenario. Hence British defence budgets were cut and matched with radically reduced armed forces. Then there was the conference and treaty diplomacy after 1925, followed by disarmament attempts in and out of the League of Nations into the early thirties. When by 1933 these had failed, policy became directed toward rectifying the years of "defence deficiencies," and a hardening of the commitment to Europe. This led to British rearmament in 1936 in light of German, Italian and Japanese aggression and the apparent impotence of the League of Nations. These were profound environmental imperatives for Canadian politicians and soldiers alike.[38]

The external imperatives certainly discouraged Canadian official or private industrial munitions initiatives.[39] As late as 1935, Major-General A.G.L. McNaughton lamented that the infamous British ten-year rule had in political reality been in effect in the Dominion since 1919 such that there was virtually no modern military equipment in the country. Also, for years there had been a reluctance of English armaments firms to allow Canadians to produce British patented munitions if they were to enter the export market.[40] If any were to be made in Canada, the British preferred that they be made in the state factory. At the same time, the Canadian government had prevented the export of even surplus arms from Canada. On several occasions, in the twenties and thirties entrepreneurs had tried to buy surplus Ross rifles from the government. There was little doubt that if allowed, the export schemes would have fuelled what were then the hotspots of the world in China, Latin America, Ethiopia and Spain. Such proposals were quickly blocked by the soldiers in the Small Arms and Joint Staff Committees of MHQ. The existing stocks of British-made and now obsolete Lee-Enfield rifles on issue were wearing out. No domestic rifle manufacturing plant existed. And so with no apparent alternatives, the soldiers learned to look kindly upon the weapon that they had hated in the earlier war. By 1935, the situation in small arms was so bad that the new Chief of the General Staff, E.C. Ashton, warned the equally new minister of defence, Grote Stirling, that the "present rifle supply held limits Canada's rifle-armed troops to approximately 60,000 men, and this is only with the use of the Ross rifles for reinforcements, [and] training purposes." He lamented that there was no rifle manufacturing facility available. Even if there was ("while highly desirable") it would be very slow. So was the current practice of getting Enfields from England. He "strongly recommended that no consideration be given to the disposal of any rifle ... as ... our forces would be practically disarmed." The Lee Enfield that was in the hands of the troops was the 1907 pattern. At the end of the Great War, the Canadian Staff had said that it was obsolete and unsuitable for Canada. When queried from Ottawa MHQ on a more modern weapon, the British reported they would not decide on a new pattern for another decade, likely because their statecraft had not yet decided what kind of war they were likely to fight. By the time that Ashton wrote his memo in 1935, the War Office had still not decided or started on the final product. Canada was then caught between the Charybdis of no domestic production and the Scylla of imperial uniformity and no just-in-time delivery, to use a contemporary term.[41] And so with the exception of one important dalliance described later, the nearly 120,000 Ross rifles of various marks stored in grease in the old Quebec factory and at Lindsay remained sacrosanct.[42]

Interior view of the Ross Rifle Factory, ca 1900-1905. (Photographer unknown. NA, PA-107373)

But the real driver for the politicians in clamping down on munitions exports or imports was in not being seen to be supporting any international traffic in weapons, given Canadian support in the League for disarmament and the control of arms trading.[43] What embarrassed and perplexed everyone in Ottawa was that on several occasions Canada's Ross rifles showed up on international markets on their way to zones under interdiction by the 1919 St. Germain Convention. But it was the British and the Americans, not Canadians, who had sold them. In the American case, these weapons had been bought from Canada in 1917 when they entered the war. They were used for training and helped overcome an acute shortage of rifles at the time. After the conflict they were sold off in a variety of places.

Early in the war, the British had contracted with Ross for 100,000 of his Mk IIIB pattern also to address a rifle shortage. Many were used in the Royal Navy. At war's end, when the three Baltic states were established, the Foreign Office arranged to have at least parts of the Latvian Army outfitted with the Canadian-made rifle. By the mid twenties, the British had put 50,000 more on the market. Buyers, some of them Canadians, tried to have them trans-shipped through Canada to China. In 1928, one of the surplus Arms merchants also tried to set up a deal whereby the Chinese government would buy rifles directly from Ottawa. The request prompted an instant response from J.L. Ralston: it would not be "entertained." Even a German firm had some Ross rifles and offered to sell them back to Canada. Nevertheless, information about the sales of the British Ross rifles continued to perplex men like Cortlandt Starnes, the RCMP commissioner, and the military intelligence director at MHQ. They could do little about it save recommend keeping the shipments out of the country.[44] Rumour that Canadians were trying to sell large quantities of Ross rifles and ammunition continued to circulate from time to time for the next decade.[45] Such episodes likely made the government determined not to allow its own public factory to get involved in any way. At no time in the inter-war period was there any indication that the Dominion Arsenals would be allowed to seek the international contracts which would have promoted the arsenal's economy and diversification of production as well as increased domestic employment.

In reaction to all of these restrictions, the Ottawa military men, like their predecessors, saw salvation for munitions and supply in promoting the public aspect of the industry over the private. And by the late twenties, there were simply no private concerns that could make munitions; encouraging them was not a possibility even if there had been permission or money to do so. Making up the shortages of rifles was first among the equals in militia modernization and arsenal reform. But military attempts to modernize and expand the Dominion Arsenals into this area were equally rebuffed. As QMG in 1927, Ashton had tried to convince his Minister that there simply were not enough rifles to go around. Furthermore, a general mobilization would require 750,000 rifles for line, reserves and spares. These, the QMG pleaded, could be made on the existing Ross rifle machinery put in the Lindsay plant. But neither the minister nor the cabinet were convinced. All that Thacker, the new CGS and his Quarter Master General (who was now handling both supply and munitions) got from Ralston was a curt "No action this year." [46]

When A.G.L. McNaughton became the Chief of the General Staff in 1929, he also tried hard to get out of the downward spiral of obsolete and worn-out equipment. Like his predecessors, he believed in self-sufficiency in essential ammunition and weapons, as well as a great many other war materials. It was, he believed, an already agreed upon basic tenet of Imperial defence. Over the years, most political leaders, if somewhat vaguely, had agreed with the general principle. But the new CGS was also moving in a direction opposite to his political masters. For instance, in September of 1928, a little over three months before McNaughton became CGS, Mackenzie King had made Canada's political position clear when he told the full Assembly of the League of Nations that Canada's "public monies are saved and utilized for purposes of productive industry. There is the key to our prosperity. That is why we believe in disarmament." [47]

But the CGS was well aware that the condition of his equipment was at a dangerous level. So he kept up a constant barrage of memos to his minister imploring the construction of a more comprehensive arsenal structure, one in a more modern setting outside of Quebec City. In the summer of 1929, he struck an arsenal committee at MHQ; while personnel of this group had quietly been organizing the arsenal idea for well over a year, they immediately started to plan a comprehensive facility to be built well away from any urban area. The zealous CGS also made preliminary approaches to the British munitions experts at the Royal Arsenals at Watham Abbey, Woolwich and Enfield. About the same time, he was also encouraged by an opportunity that had arisen at Quebec City. This was related to the perennial and thorny question of what to do with the old Ross factory buildings and the arsenal filling and proof-testing facilities, all on the Plains of Abraham. The city wanted some of the land to build a water reservoir. The rest of it for years had been lobbied for by the National Battlefields Commission to extend the historic park. McNaughton also knew that if the old cartridge factory remained in its current location in the middle of the city near the St. Jean Gate of the upper town, a new arsenal would never be built. Very likely, all of this coalesced in the CGS' mind into a plan. Whether they realized it or not, he was aided by the politicians responding to some of the social forces. It seems they had given promises to remove the vexatious buildings for the park extension as soon as possible. It automatically raised the issue of what to do with the arsenal. McNaughton knew the answer: build an entirely new arsenal somewhere else. When the rumour mills started, there was the predictable lobbying by various towns wanting to be favoured as the chosen new site. And there was the old fear that the four hundred workers in the spread-out munitions works would lose their jobs. Even worse was the fear that the entire munitions group would be moved to Ontario. [48] The time looked right for a new munitions complex.

General Sir Sam Hughes arriving in France on his way to the front, August 1916. (Photographer unknown. NA, PA-704)

Yet as the depression set in military fortunes declined. By May 1930, the militia was five million dollars worth of ammunition short on reserves and was spending more than the Dominion Arsenal's total budget on British purchases and repairs. Vainly McNaughton tried to persuade Ralston to support the new arsenal. Without a comprehensive public production system, he pointed out, there would never be a technical cadre of experts in Canada to guide private industry in a mobilization. The general even used the argument that the facility could make money for Canada: "If we had not had the nucleus in 1914 for shell production, the business would have gone elsewhere, probably to the United States and Canada would have been denied hundreds of millions of dollars of external trade." This was to be an argument that the headquarters staff would use time and time again during the next ten years. But in 1930, it had little effect on the Liberal Cabinet or on Colonel Ralston.[49]

So frustrated by inaction under the Liberals, McNaughton nearly resigned that year over the munitions issue. He only stayed on because the general election brought in the R.B. Bennett Conservative government. In the meantime, McNaughton had sent an ordnance officer to a training course at Woolwich who was sending back a great deal of information on how to create and run an arsenal complex modelled after the great state-owned factories of England. Armed with this, the MHQ arsenal committee proposed the creation of an all new public facility to make essential munitions. It was to be located at Valcartier, north of Quebec City in the training area that had been established there by Sam Hughes in 1914. The complex was to cover ammunition production up to 4-inch guns and to make place for rifle and artillery manufacture. It cost was estimated at $35 million, or nearly three times the current defence budget.[50] The figure likely startled the financially hard-pressed Bennett Cabinet. As the depression worsened and unemployment rose dramatically, the general kept trying to get equipment for his force. One of his late 1930 memos to his minister suggested that purchasing Carden-Loyd armored cars and machine gun carriers would, he said, not only contribute to the long sought-after mechanization of the infantry and cavalry units, but they would also be useful as aid to the civil power in light of increasing social unrest.

But McNaughton convinced few in the cabinet or the Treasury to build either an arsenal or to fear the citizenry; he was forced to accept more budget cuts. In mid March 1931, Donald Sutherland simply told McNaughton that "it is not practicable to proceed with this at present, but the proposal is to be brought forward when next year's estimates are under consideration." The arsenal proposal was shelved as simply too expensive.[51] At the old Quebec City facility, in spite of the valiant efforts of the superintendent to keep his little factory in the best condition possible, he was forced to lay off non-essential people. In addition, wages were cut by ten percent; production was reduced by a million rounds of rifle ammunition a year and the factory put on caretaker status from time to time.[52] Indeed, the defence department was still spending a quarter of a million dollars in England annually simply repairing worn-out militia equipment and buying a bit of artillery ammunition.[53] Nevertheless, McNaughton's dream of having the arsenal was not forgotten either by him or his dedicated ordnance staff. One could say that it was simply driven underground; planning continued below the busy daily and primary activities at MHQ as other ways and means were explored to arrive at the arsenal goal.

Clearly, military expectations ran just the opposite to governmental ones. With the arsenal proposals on indefinite hold, McNaughton sought help from the British. The Arsenal Committee of the headquarters staff toyed with the idea of sending another ordnance officer to the Royal Arsenals in England to get detailed plans of rifle manufacturing. But in Ottawa the CGS was still making no headway with the defence minister or the Conservative government. Then in mid 1931 the creative McNaughton seized on an innovative idea. Why not sell all of those Ross rifles and use the money to build at least the rifle and artillery group of the arsenal? The idea may have come earlier that spring out of an offer from Sir Henry Pellatt to buy surplus Ross rifles at ten dollars each. It seemed like heresy when such strenuous efforts had been made in the past to protect the only weapons reserve there was. No doubt the immediate enthusiasm of the CGS reflected the very poor state of small arms in the force. It was also an indicator of the frustration at headquarters in not being able to do anything about the stalled arsenal project. But it was a risk. It would immediately destroy the strategic weapons reserve. And it raised the double-barrelled question: rifle sales to whom, and what will the government think?

Whatever debate went on in McNaughton's mind, at the end of July 1931 he personally discussed the scheme with Sutherland. Then he put it in memo form. The whole idea was predicated on the poor state of existing small arms. Selling 100,000 Ross rifles would net the ministry an estimated million dollars. Acting on the advice of the General Staff Officer Artillery, Nobel Carr, McNaughton claimed that if the existing Lindsay plant and the stored Ross rifle machine tools were used, the new factory would only cost about $250,000. The rest of the money could then be used to buy 20,000 new rifles from its production. The factory should make the latest pattern British Lee-Enfield that the MHQ staff had been told were about to be adopted by the War Office. In fact, McNaughton told Sutherland, the new Enfield was twice as good as any Ross. But the CGS made it clear that if the money realized from the sale did not go into a factory, he would not sell the rifle reserve. The general also gave the minister a written justification of how they could legally get by the restrictions on selling arms to foreign governments. This is interesting in light of Canada's signatures on the 1919 St. Germain Protocol and the 1925 Geneva Convention for the Control of the International Trade in Arms, Ammunition and the Implements of War. Six months later, in January 1932 as the rifle sales issue was still discretely moving, it must have seemed ironic to the few who knew about it that Prime Minister Bennett selected McNaughton to be one of three Canadian delegates to the Geneva Disarmament Conference. And while the general was away, the cabinet cut his budget.[54] Maybe that's why.

But back in July, in making the sales pitch not everything the CGS said to his Minister was exactly as it seemed. For instance, the War Office did not yet have a new sealed pattern Lee-Enfield ready for their own production, let alone Canada's; as it turned out they would not be able to produce it in Britain until 1940. And so in 1931 this was a big gamble. Moreover, McNaughton's own Director of Military Operations and Intelligence, Colonel H.H. Mathews, had cautioned his chief about the various disarmament agreements and even put a copy of the 1925 Geneva Convention into the Ross file. Evidently it was the Nationalist Chinese government which wanted the weapons. Mathews noted that sales to the Chinese had been prohibited since the Boxer Rebellion in 1900. He also pointed to the fact that in 1929, when Britain and several other governments had lifted the Chinese arms embargo, Canada had not. In 1930, after representations from several departments to follow the British lead, O.D. Skelton, the anglophobic Undersecretary of State for External Affairs had referred the question to the Privy Council. No doubt Skelton saw immediately that undoing the embargo could compromise Canada's neutrality, a position that he was constantly advocating. What his advice was to the Council is not known, but they refused to lift the embargo.[55] And yet the next year McNaughton suggested to Sutherland that this was the only thing that prevented Canada from selling the Ross reserves. Implicit in the comment was the suggestion to get it changed. Even though Canada had signed the Geneva Convention, it had not been ratified in the international community. Consequently, to use the later words of McNaughton's successor, without ratification "the Convention ... is without force or meaning." As McNaughton himself wrote to the minister, except for the Chinese embargo "there is no reason why these rifles should not be sold to a foreign government."[56] In light of contemporary politics and public opinion, he seems remarkably naive.

The defence minister must have thought the scheme had some merit and that he could convince the Cabinet to lift the interdiction on China because the project whirled around in several departments for the next eighteen months. Right at the start of this enterprise, the chief military intelligence officer had predicted to his general that the government would never approve the sale in light of the various international agreements to which the country was party. And he was correct. The government did nothing for nearly two years.

In the spring of 1933, when the Canadian trade commissioner in Shanghai resurrected the possibility of a rifle sale after direct communication from the Nationalist Chinese themselves, things picked up again. The approach to McNaughton originated in the offices of the Director of Commercial Intelligence at the Department of Trade and Commerce. A trade commissioner introduced an American company that was supposed to broker the deal. Almost immediately there was a separate bid from the well established New York firm of Griffin and Howe to buy the Canadian weapons for some unnamed South American customers. McNaughton could see the chance for increased revenue for his arsenal scheme. On 23 April he invited Griffin and Howe's legal representative to his office in the Woods Building. As soon as he arrived, the agent informed McNaughton and the defence minister's military secretary that his clients were prepared to buy a hundred thousand Ross rifles. Just as quickly McNaughton raised the price by thirty-five percent. He was now demanding about five dollars more per rifle than Pellatt had offered in 1931. As his after-meeting notes show, the CGS bargained hard.

The agent was told that before any action could be taken it would be necessary for him to make a firm offer supported by adequate financial guarantees, preferably from a Canadian bank in New York; that no offer less than $15.00 per rifle could receive consideration, as the rifles were very useful; and that no assurance could be offered that the price would not go higher.

If McNaughton thought he was finally going to get money for his arms or factory, he was mistaken. The Cabinet would make no decision on any sales to foreign states or to the "merchants of death." This inaction was in fact their policy statement. But evidently the general did not realize it yet. For politicians, South America held as many legal problems as did China. Shortly before these new offers came in, the British government had requested, and the Canadian government had agreed, not to ship war materiel to Paraguay and Bolivia who were then at war. No doubt that is where the Griffin and Howe rifles would end up. Nevertheless, the irrepressible CGS tried to show his minister that the new offer was well worth it, not only for the defence department but for the entire government. Instead of getting just a million dollars, he told Sutherland, the Griffin and Howe deal would net a million and a half. The extra $500,000 could therefore go "definitely to Treasury." Maybe the general thought that the siren lure of a half million dollars to a cash-starved government would soften their higher political ideals and clear the way for the sale. But it did not happen. The reasons were the same as they had always been.[57] The cabinet's inactivity was a policy statement, and it was a statement on two issues: no foreign sales and no arsenal. Over the next five years the defence ministry got offers from Poland, Estonia, Belgium, Mexico and Spain for the rifles. But the general staff never again tried to hook them to a method out of which they could get neither new rifles nor a rifle manufactory. Other ways would have to be found.

Until he could do so, McNaughton turned to other important areas. One of them was in supply and industrial potential beyond arsenals. Since there was no Canadian private munitions manufacturing and nothing was known of the country's industrial potential, the CGS was very anxious to create a Canadian supply organization. He wanted it modelled on the Principal Supply Officers Committee (PSO) of the Committee of Imperial Defence (CID) in Britain. The supply body, conceived in 1917 and re-affirmed in 1927, was meant to co-ordinate within Imperial strategy the raw resources and production facilities of each of the Empire's Dominions. By the early 1930s, all of the others had struck PSO Committees of their general staffs and had representatives sitting on the central body in London. But not the Canadians. The reason was most likely that Canadian politicians did not want to create another tie to the Imperial defence system. Furthermore, this new body could raise questions that would only point out the embarrassing state of Canadian military and industrial preparation. It could also suggest solutions too expensive to contemplate. For an anglophobe like O.D. Skeleton at External Affairs, such a committee if connected to the CID in London through the Imperial General Staff might further align Canada to Imperial policy or even lead the Dominion into another disastrous European commitment. Consequently, he scotched the appointment of any such Canadian position in Ottawa or London. Whatever the cause, no supply committee was created in the Canadian staff until the latter part of 1936. Iit was conspicuously *not* called a PSO Committee. In no way was it connected to an Imperial parent. Until 1936, the best the MHQ staff could do was to work through the Arsenal Committee, with its stifled aspirations and limited mandate while continuing to plan and to accumulate technical information.[58]

But given the drastic economic situation and the failure of the arsenal complex and Ross sales schemes, only incrementalism was possible. By the summer of 1932, there were over three-quarters of a million unemployed Canadians, many of them homeless and on the move. Clearly something had to be done; the government strained to find an answer. McNaughton had one. Why not use, he asked, the department of defence as a social tool to help alleviate the unemployment with useful works projects. The Prime Minister and the Cabinet were immediately impressed. And so in October that year, the military Depression relief projects began. The overall story is told by McNaughton's biographer and need not be repeated here. There is little doubt that the general was very worried about these homeless men. The future members of Canada's armed forces—and as Marx called them, the "industrial reserve army"—should be taken care of, even if only to head off the growing social unrest before it became violent.[59] Working closely with the Department of Public Works and with their budget (and some critics would say hiding the real military intent behind both), the CGS created a series of relief projects across the country. By the summer of 1933, McNaughton had expanded the program to include preparations on the site of the new Valcartier Arsenal complex: that is surveying, moving dirt, cutting trees, and constructing roads and some buildings. It was all done with the unemployed of Montreal and Quebec City.

Most of what the CGS did was to blend the military functional imperative nicely with the social imperative, making the former acceptable, or at least not so objectionable, to the latter. By the time the Valcartier project closed in 1936, it was employing nearly 2,000 men each year and putting much needed money into the local economy. The workers toiled for twenty cents a day and lived in barracks. All of the social problems that one would expect occurred at UER project 39, as the Valcartier effort was called. There were newspaper complaints that the men were working in some sort of military servitude. There was also a scramble of locals to get jobs and to sell goods needed for the project. Patronage expectations from the party faithful were present as well. On several occasions, French Canadians complained that all of the supervisors were anglophones and that the language of instruction was mostly English, while the workforce was primarily French. The local military personnel did a remarkable job in sorting it all out. Right at the start McNaughton warned his military managers of the "importance of absolute fairness between French and English Protestants and Catholics."[60] But the attempt to be scrupulously impartial did not always prevent arguments between ministers and priests, or successful and unsuccessful politicians and merchants.[61]

There is little doubt that this was the beginning of the realization of self-sufficiency in state-owned munitions. But McNaughton knew that it was just that, a beginning. There was still no government approval to embark on anything other than a Depression relief project. The defence minister had made that clear in the House of Commons in the summer of 1933 when he said that there was no intention of moving the ammunition plant out of the city and building a new one at Valcartier.[62] As things progressed through 1934, all of the Unemployment Relief projects across Canada were causing the Bennett government more and more criticism. By the fall of that year, the Prime Minister was very upset. He was convinced that McNaughton's camps were so unpopular that it would ruin his government's chances for re-election the following year.[63] Regardless of this threat, McNaughton knew that whatever work was done under the UER program was benefitting the military and that the politicians were now oriented toward a new arsenal at Valcartier. That, he felt, had its own momentum which would be useful later. So he continued to press his immediate goal to build first the most important parts of the arsenal, that is the ammunition filling and explosives storage facilities. Even with this incremental start, the CGS remained committed to a complete arsenal complex. If ever completed, he confidently told his minister, it would be a facility which in peacetime would "make Canada self-contained in armaments and ammunitions... [and] serve as a key plant to guide Canadian manufacturing in the event of it becoming necessary to undertake large scale production of munitions."

Unfortunately, in 1935 the tired Conservative government was in no way willing to accept the Arsenal Committee's costly proposal for a public munitions works, or for that matter any munitions facility.[64] That spring the Prime Minister was convinced that McNaughton could not continue as Chief of the Defence Staff, mostly because of the unpopularity of his unemployment relief schemes like Valcartier. So McNaughton was "seconded" to the National Research Council. In the summer, there was a strike by several hundred Valcartier UER workers, and that fall the Bennett administration lost the election. Mackenzie King's Liberals were back in power with a huge majority.[65] But the public arsenal complex remained uppermost in General McNaughton's mind even though he was no longer at military headquarters or in the Department of National Defence. Shortly before he left his post, he wrote a scathing condemnation directly to R.B. Bennett of the deplorable state of Canadian defence, especially of its supplies: "As regards reserves of equipment and ammunition, the matter is shortly disposed of. Except as regards rifles and ammunition partial stocks of which were inherited from the Great War—there are none."[66]

Fortunately, when McNaughton left office, he was replaced by a soldier dedicated to carrying on his predecessor's attempts to achieve self-sufficiency in essential munitions. Major-General E.C. Ashton would be the CGS until 1938. In the fall of 1935, when the Mackenzie King liberals were returned to power, it must have alarmed both generals. The outgoing Conservatives had not seemed to be against defence or public arsenals, they just did not have any money. But the Liberals had always been against defence and Imperial commitments and they still did not have any money. Immediately after the election contest, Ashton fired a secret and personal letter to his friend and former chief appealing for help. The response came the next day in a long and equally secret communication on the entire arsenal policy and the way ahead. It strongly advised the new CGS to continue the public scheme and to avoid private contractors. The point is that there was to be no discontinuity in arsenal policy at MHQ. During his tenure Ashton's own preference was to promote public facilities ahead of private ones but not to the latter's exclusion. His job was not easy. Most of his efforts were frustrated by government inaction and controversy.[67]

Four months after Ashton became the CGS, Liberal Ian Mackenzie was made the new Minister of National Defence. As Martie Hooker has shown, he turned out to be far more sympathetic, especially regarding equipment and supplies, than any of his predecessors since the days of Sam Hughes. A veteran of the Great War, Mackenzie knew the realities of military life and the need to plan. He was increasingly alarmed at the poor state of the Canadian armed forces and the deteriorating international situation of Ethiopia and Manchuria; he was also well aware that the British were vigorously trying to make up what they called their "defence deficiencies" and to rearm. Moreover, their defence and foreign affairs posture was progressively more and more oriented toward European commitment. The CID had identified "a war against Germany in 5 years from 1934." The Principal Supply Officers Committee was increasing its activities and urging the Dominions do the same.[68] Both Mackenzie and the Canadian general staff knew that the War Office had long made it clear that Canadians could not count on regular or immediate munition supply from Great Britain.

Soon after being sworn in, the new minister ordered Ashton to give him an appreciation of the state of the military services. Ashton needed no coaxing. On 12 November 1935 and again in April 1936, immediately after Hitler re-occupied the Rhineland, the CGS stated his case. Again pointing out that in terms of equipment, Canada "had none," he called for quick policy decisions on the completion of the filling and ammunitions groups at Valcartier, the establishment of a Canadian government factory for field and anti-aircraft guns, and of another one to manufacture rifles and machine guns. He also wanted supplementary budgets to increase small arms and artillery ammunition output at the Arsenal and to buy "smaller items such as trench mortar ammunition, a few Bren guns for demonstration and training, wireless equipment, the manufacture of gas masks, etc.," all from the United Kingdom.[69] Clearly Ashton was placing his bets on convincing his minister to build a strong public system for essential munitions as first among the equal necessities.

Mackenzie knew that what Ashton was saying was true. The question was how to do it politically. He also knew that outside the Dominion Arsenal—itself limited, worn-out and in a state of disruptive re-organization—only Canadian Industries Limited (CIL) in the private sector was finally producing small amounts of cordite, the British pattern explosive used in the Arsenal's rifle and gun ammunition. No other munitions firms existed. But the potential was there. Moreover, there was a resurgence of interest among hard pressed businessmen now that British industry was benefitting from the rearmament going on over there. The trouble was that no one in Canada had any idea of who could produce what. And knowing this was a vital first step in any munitions program.

Once Mackenzie got a grasp on the defence portfolio, he did two things in the spring of 1936. First, upon his soldiers' recommendation, he reactivated the MHQ position of Master-General of the Ordnance revealingly defunct since the defence department had been created a decade and a half ago. Second, he told the new MGO to form the "Navy, Army, and Air Supply Committee in order to prepare an inventory of national industrial capability." Clearly this was a satisfying response for both the MHQ staff and no doubt for Imperial planners of the CID and their Principal Supply Officers Committee. But the overworked and understaffed ordinance directorate in Ottawa could not respond for six months. Finally in September the new inter-service supply committee began to function.[70] Also that summer, Mackenzie convinced the Prime Minister to establish a long recommended Defence Committee of the Cabinet, an advisory body in which such questions as rearmament and supply could at least be aired before other ministers and their co-operation and consensus obtained. The following year, the Minister and Ashton succeeded in having a War Book adopted. All of these devices could make the course of any munitions policy easier once decided. Without mechanisms of planning and administration, as earlier defence planners well knew, policy and efficiency was hard to achieve.[71]

In the meantime, other events intervened. One was the attempt of a group of businessmen to get British munitions orders to revitalize their empty or flagging factories. But they did not know who to talk to over there. And thanks to the political fears of men such as Skelton and King, as well as a lack of money, there were few Canadian military liaison officers holding appointments in London who might be helpful. Yet, these business impulses coincided conveniently with the possibility that British rearmament programs could not be met by their own industries and that the War Office might need to place orders in the Dominions. Certainly all three service chiefs were anxious to have the British place orders in Canada, not only to encourage private industry to start up, but to get the unit cost of any associated Canadian orders down.[72]

There was also the need for Canada to meet new technological standards in re-equipping and mechanizing the Canadian militia. The most immediate was the case of the new light automatic machine gun, a Czechoslovak invention modified for the British .303 round at Enfield in the early 1930s. Called the Bren gun, this state-of-the-art weapon was to be the British standard.[73] For the sake of Imperial uniformity and simply to get any equipment at all, the Canadian soldiers had pushed for its adoption for several years. Another factor was a War Office impulse in the form of a Liaison Letter in April 1936 which informed the Canadian staff that British Bren gun production was about to start. It also noted the likelihood of long delays before any could be made available for the Canadian forces, indeed up to five years. The letter anxiously recommended that the Dominion try to produce it herself. Significantly, the War Office insisted that "such production must take place in a government-owned factory." This rider was typical of those intended to keep Canadian commercial firms out of competition with British ones. Conveniently, the condition also supported the Canadian soldiers' desire to produce essential munitions with state-owned arsenals. However, in July when the MHQ staff investigated producing light machine guns in a government facility, they were shocked to find it would cost about two million dollars, less toolage, and take three to four years. Moreover, the per-unit cost would be much higher because of smaller Canadian orders.[74] They only needed 7,000 Bren guns.

The same War Office Liaison Letter had also noted that the Canadian peace and wartime munitions potential was going to be an important subject of next year's Imperial Conference (1937). For many years, the Committee of Imperial Defence had realized that Dominion self-sufficiency would not only take pressure off English munitions industries but would be vital for what they could contribute to the British overall war effort. The letter asked Ottawa's MHQ for any details they could get on the subject and it encouraged the Dominion to place educational orders with Canadian industry to test its capability. Again, these suggestions triggered the MHQ staff to renew their pleas for industrial preparation. In July 1936, the MGO pointed out to the deputy minister, L.R. Lafleche, that beyond the old Arsenal at Quebec, only CIL was producing anything in the nature of warlike stores, (i.e., cordite). An additional Canadian contract for two million rounds of .303 rifle cartridges had been placed with the company in the spring to see if it could manufacture rifle ammunition of military quality. But the MGO declared that Canadian capacity with the exception of the Arsenal and CIL "is non-existent."[75] A month later, the CGS once again took the case for industrial mobilization directly to the minister; he even had conversations with Mackenzie King about the urgent need to encourage munitions production. One strong point Aston kept making to the politicians was the monetary benefit: the financial credits "built up in Canada by the supply of shells to the IMB in the Great War more than sufficed to meet the whole of Canada's wartime expenditure concurrent overseas." Such arguments were even beginning to seduce Mackenzie King.[76] In fact, since the spring when he had been surprised to learn about the poor condition of the armed forces, King had been worrying about defence capability. In late August he asked DND to give him a costed-out five year defence requirements plan. Yet it would not be soon or easily done. Social and military imperatives would have to come closer together and there was still much opposition within King's own caucus to re-armament and foreign commitments.[77]

All of these various forces started to coalesce in the late summer of 1936. While it remains pure conjecture, it seems likely that the defence department civilians pushed events by encouraging private concerns to seek business in England. By early September, both the defence minister and some private businessmen had lobbied King about securing British orders, one of them about making the Bren gun in his own idle factory. While presenting both the advantages and disadvantages for King, Ian Mackenzie emphasized the benefits of employment in Canada and also "the possibility of there being more supplies for Canada in the event of trouble." Perhaps later regretting his response, the Prime Minister wrote to one Member of Parliament representing Toronto business interests that "we see no reason why a Canadian firm established for the manufacture of munitions should be precluded from obtaining orders from the British Government. It would be necessary of course to see that it was distinctly understood that such orders ... were not at the instance of the Government of Canada."[78] The defence minister also recommended to King his five-year plan calling for spending some $200 million on all arms. Most of the other Dominions, he pointed out to the Prime Minister, had already instituted such proposals and "most have provided for local manufacture of arms and equipment." Mackenzie's scheme also activated the Navy, Army and Air Supply Committee, which was commissioned to prepare an industrial inventory.[79]

Interestingly, the documents revealed that inside the defence department there was an emerging difference between the soldiers led by Ashton and the civilians led by L.R. Lafleche, the deputy minister. Admittedly there had been no love lost between many of the MHQ officersand Lafleche since he had been appointed in 1932. McNaughton summed it up a few years later:

> I had no regard for his capacity and when his appointment had been forced on the
> Department I had seen to it by proper constitutional means that his authority had
> been so limited that he could do no harm to the great projects which were then
> under way. Since I had been transferred from the Defence Department ...this indi
> vidual had made himself de facto Chief of Staff and had broken the organization
> which I had laboured for years to build up in the public interest against a time it
> would be necessary to rehabilitate our defence forces.[80]

It seems that in 1936 the deputy minister was retarding the flow of military advice to the minister, or at least that's how some saw it, and perhaps the munitions question was one of those files. The MHQ staff wanted the rearmament program to centre on the Arsenal structure; the deputy preferred private enterprise. It would take many months to determine this debate, and the civilians would win. The reasons were several and old: to build a comprehensive arsenal system was too expensive and too slow, and it would not reflect the social imperatives necessary for political acceptance. [81]

This preference prompted Lafleche to encourage the more than willing J.E. Hahn, President of the John Inglis Company of Toronto, which since April 1936 had had an empty factory available, to seek British Bren gun orders. On the other hand, unable to get the government to build a weapons plant at Valcartier, the General Staff then tried to convince the department that the old Lindsay Arsenal, in mothballs since 1922, might be reactivated as a small arms factory. When that also proved too expensive, the soldiers had no other alternatives. Lafleche focused on Hahn's proposal in which the latter claimed that he could start production in a matter of months once toolage was available and adequate orders firm. Lafleche and Hahn also intended that the factory would go into rifle manufacturing. In short, the facility was a clear alternative to the public small arms complex preferred by the soldiers, and it was not just intended to make the new light machine gun. Hahn had already been in contact with King about the weapon. He and a group of other businessmen planned to go to England that fall to see what orders they could get. In October, the deputy minister secretly requested that O.D. Skelton make sure Hahn was introduced to all the right War Office people. No doubt feeling that he now had official endorsement from the government, Hahn left for England full of optimism.[82] It was premature.

Once there, Hahn got little co-operation from the British and would not for several months. There were two reasons. One was that the British had not yet overcome their insistence that the weapon be made in a Canadian government factory. Another part of the reluctance was that in England the planners were well ahead of the producers. British industry still had free capacity. Hahn had no official recognition because by now neither King nor Skelton wanted the Canadian government identified as a prime mover in the munitioning effort. Another businessman, namely Robert Magor of the National Steel Car Company of Hamilton, Ontario had managed to secure an order of 50,000 3.7-inch anti-aircraft gun shells. King himself had also gone to Europe that fall but for different reasons. Nevertheless, Canadian public opinion soon identified Magor's success with the government.

In November 1936, several national newspaper editorials were highly critical of the government, charging that such contracts would lead to a loss of neutrality and to profiteering. The *Toronto Star*, for instance, wanted to know how "the policy of encouraging or permitting large British munitions orders in Canada could be reconciled with the government's policy of no advanced commitments in British wars or how manufacturing munitions for foreign countries could be reconciled." From elsewhere came suggestions that the government was giving in to the "merchants of death" if it allowed a private munitions industry to start up. Hurriedly, Skelton advised King not to discuss the questions at all in public and to appoint a committee on controlling munitioning profits. Clearly, the under-secretary wanted little to do with any British-Canadian co-operation. But it was obvious that domestic rearmament had to take place at some time. The question was when. There would, Skelton advised King, "be a measure of increased prosperity if Great Britain places orders here." Extreme caution must be exercised however, lest Canada "forfeits her neutrality."[83] Significant about these comments is that King's growing yet soft and undefined sense of alarm about Canada's defence capabilities had started him on the path of accepting a domestic munitions industry. The military were in the equation, but not as a first factor; but homage to the social imperatives was.[84]

It did not take long to work out a way to pay that homage and raise hopes of doing something constructive for defence supplies. In January 1937, a secret Interdepartmental Committee on the Control of Profits on Government Contracts advised just that; by July 1937 Privy Council orders had quickly put the control mechanism into place along with new legislation limiting munitions exports; and on 2 August—all now conveniently de facto and de jure—the information was released to morning papers.[85] Two years later a Defence Purchasing Board was created, and modelled on the old War Purchasing Commission of 1915. As such, it demonstrated how mindful King was of the political dangers of any scandal similar to those levelled against Sam Hughes, the Shell Committee and even the Imperial Munitions Board during the earlier German war. King's new board was also clearly aimed at mitigating not only excess profits but patronage. One of its terms stipulated that the service chiefs would have to convince the board why any munitions ought to be purchased. It was one more step in divorcing the users from choosing their own munitions, a regulation device in civil-military relations.[86] King took the defence issue to his caucus in January 1937. That he chose to do it himself rather than let the defence minister carry the load revealed another step in King's slow conversion, but it also signaled that it would not be easy to convince his own party. King's assuming the file also showed who was in control.

> Our main task is to preserve the unity of Canada … We have today in Canada virtually no protection what ever; we are practically defenseless. You read what Meighen said in the Senate yesterday – that the amount of the [defence] estimates is not

enough, that we were concerned with the defence of the Empire as a whole, that the first line of our defence was the Empire's boundaries. We cannot accept that. But we can put our own house in order ... Meighen would do so much more, at least so he says—and Woodsworth would do nothing at all. The safe policy is the middle course between the two views—the safe policy is a national policy of domestic defence ... Let us explain that policy to our people and let us above all strive at all times to keep Canada united.[87]

When he repeated his caucus statement in the House of Commons the next month, it was the first public statement by the government that a cautious and modest re-armament would take place. But it would be a rearmament of a particular kind. Clearly this was a revitalized policy but only for the defence of Canada. It was the only way King wanted it. It was the only way that it could be sold to the Canadian people and to his own caucus.[88]

Four days after the Prime Minister met his caucus in January, Lafleche drafted a memo for King that signalled the ascendancy of the civilian position of private munitions over the military preference for a comprehensive public arsenal. As it turned out the memo also more accurately described the reluctant King government's preferences in armaments production. The free market, Lafleche advised, would provide the vast bulk of war stores, but essential munitions with only military use will have to be produced by specific private firms capable of doing so; the government will have to control them closely on a cost-plus basis avoiding excess profit. The Dominion Arsenal system should be encouraged to expand but not at the expense of new plant and "without creating heavy future responsibilities attendant upon the establishment of new communities." The munitions effort should be directed toward using buildings and machinery now empty and idle whether private or public and there should be a proper distribution throughout the country. The government should assume control of all private industry if needed in an emergency. The Customs Act should be made to control munitions exports. There must be close co-ordination between the Dominion Arsenal and private industry. The emphasis overall has to be to buy and produce in Canada. If all of this were done, Lafleche believed that it would "be fair, constructive and practical" and that it would "take the profits out of war" and thereby satisfy legitimate public opinion.[89]

Unlike the Chief of the General Staff's position, also restated that month, Lafleche's views were politically realistic and flexible. They did not deny the place of government factories, but he gave them a specific public role only where private industry could not respond. Here was a calm and practical compromise of all factors impinging upon munitions production. Furthermore, it did not, as Ashton's did, make a direct connection between arms production and Imperial policy and it emphasized civilian control, whereas the government factories recommended by the CGS would clearly be under the close purview of soldiers. Nor did Lafleche's proposal shy away from government control of industry profits and production if necessary. In the end, both civilians and soldiers agreed that there were financial off-sets, to use a contemporary phrase; that "continued dependence for supplies upon Great Britain is almost useless under present conditions" and that "a very large portion of the requirements of the Canadian forces can be and should be manufactured in Canada." Whatever the differences between them, Lafleche's position was one which the soldiers not only had to but could live with.[90]

However much it appears that Lafleche's 1937 memo acted as a guide for King's government, it did not mean either immediate or obviously positive action to carry out a dynamic munitions program. In fact, there were other considerations. Since September 1936, the Navy, Army and

Air Supply Committee (NAASC) had been working up an inventory of Canadian firms. For the first five months, it was hamstrung by a lack of funds and staff. According to G.F.G. Stanley, the committee was also "tied down by the old practice of political patronage and ... limited in its investigation to those firms whose names had been brought specifically to the attention of the Department of National Defence."[91] By the late fall, however the Canadian Manufacturers Association had given the NAASC a list of potential manufacturers while Trade and Commerce had provided the names of firms which had made munitions in the Great War. It took another two years and the recruitment of many civilian experts, but by 1939 the NAASC had compiled a list of 1,597 industrial plants which might contribute to large-scale war production.[92]

King's acute awareness of the public's distaste for arms merchants was an omnipresent factor. He also realized that rearmament had to come and the subsequent contracts placed in the private sector had a more therapeutic effect on the economy than could be accomplished by expensive government factories. King was also intensely sensitive to any commitment to Imperial policy, especially involving war in Europe and another Canadian Expeditionary Force; he did not wish to see the cataclysmic results of the earlier conflict repeated. Like it or not even the General Staff could not deny that Defence Scheme No. 3, with its expeditionary force role, was not unconnected to any industrial arms program for Canada then being encouraged by the British. King had read Ashton's memo of 24 August 1936 that clearly equated the two and in March 1937, the Prime Minister approved a revised Defence Scheme No. 3 that did the same thing.[93] It seems then that King was using munitions as one way to avoid getting trapped into an expeditionary force policy. This explains his enunciation in February of a "local defence" policy to counter the Imperial one preferred by his soldiers. Logically, his initial quiet approval of a domestic armaments industry also had a concomitant. His problem remained in trying to weave his way through the pitfalls of accepting British government orders in Canada on one hand, while on the other, not having the financial wherewithall to rearm. As for the military, they accepted the "Defence of Canada" policy for two reasons; first, they could do little about it and second, it was a road to rearmament they could live with. Most of the MHQ staff likely bet that when a European war came, Canada would be fighting at England's side. And so after 1937, the idea of an overseas force was lower on their planning scale but far from absent.

As we know, the Bren gun orders for Inglis had stalled in the fall of 1936. It would be another two years before any agreement materialized. Most of the aforementioned reasons were the cause. Mackenzie in National Defence had promoted Hahn in England far beyond King's policy of accepting British orders. But King himself had originally provided Hahn with letters of introduction. Public criticism of the National Steel Car ammunition deal had then caused the Prime Minister to publicly back off and proceed cautiously. He was also upset, as was O.D. Skelton, that the defence department was pushing contracts and that the soldiers were continuing to place munitioning firmly within the Imperial sphere. No better case was made than the decision to discuss Canadian industrial defence potential at the Imperial Conference in the spring of 1937, notice of which had come in the form of Liaison Letters from the Chief of the Imperial General Staff (CIGS) and the Canadian CGS.

The Liaison Letters had routinely passed directly between the CIGS and their Canadian counterparts since 1911. Besides containing a wealth of practical professional information and intelligence, they were one way that soldiers in both countries managed to promote issues which their governments preferred to ignore. King was embarrassed then in April 1937 to find out that the British wanted to talk about Canadian munitioning and that British authorities knew as much if not more about the state of the Dominion's military forces as he did. He was also afraid that these letters could commit Canada in some way to part of the British rearmament program and hence to another commitment to the killing fields of Europe. Indeed, Ashton's communication with the CIGS on 17 December 1936 implied exactly that. He proclaimed that Canada supported a "co-operative Empire policy" for the supply of munitions and that the "Empire should be considered a single economic unit for the production of war material." The CGS also stressed the helpful aspects of War Office munitions orders placed with Canadian firms.[94] One wonders how much more co-operative King would have been in the matter of munitioning if the soldiers had not used this particular vehicle as often as they did. But this time, Skelton was urging that something be done. In the end, King gained control of these communications by accepting his defence minister's compromise that in the future all Liaison Letters should pass through the Department of External Affairs.[95] This effectively short-circuited the flow of munitions information, among other subjects, between military headquarters in Ottawa and London. It would fall to the defence minister to explain the Canadian position on munitions to the Imperial Conference that spring.

Privately, Ian Mackenzie admitted that like his CGS, he preferred Canadian rearmament to come out of government facilities, but it was "very costly." The only real course, he felt, was to co-operate with the British:

> We should establish the principle in regard to private industry that only well-established enterprises be given orders and that no new private industrial undertakings should be established for the purpose of providing defence supplies alone. If such new undertakings must be established they should be government owned. The British can deal with respectable Canadian firms directly; we can deal with the same firms.[96]

In short, since well established private firms could be found, private industry was going to play a vital role, although not an immediate one because of the expense. It also seems that the Canadian government was willing to let a British demand attract Canadian industries into munitions production because it could then use those facilities without suffering the stigma of having created them.

Nevertheless, at the end of May 1937, Mackenzie announced at the Imperial Conference that Canadian policy on munitions expansion would be to give "government arsenals first priority," but the government would be prepared to co-operate with private industry and regulate it if necessary.[97] It was the latter part of his comments that struck reality. And it was around this time that he informed the Prime Minister that there was now not much to do in munitioning save get the mixture of public and private right.

Perhaps the defence minister's comments were only to stroke the public because the government did little about munitioning in any sector. Much of what was originally conceded in the estimates of 1936-1937 was later ordered deleted. This spawned several bitter complaints from Ashton about "obstruction" in government circles (presumable from O.D. Skelton at External Affairs) by men who ignored the stated policy of rearmament and Empire co-operation.[98] Moreover, given his minister's public statements about the priority of "government arsenals," the CGS continued to promote an expansion of the Canadian system; his model was an Australian program of self-containment based on a comprehensive government factory system.[99] The trouble was that in June 1938 when the MHQ staff countered Lafleches' idea with renewed arguments for their comprehensive Arsenal Group at Valcartier, the bill amounted to nearly $22 million. It now included plans to make aircraft engines and had an aerodrome

Meeting of the Defence Council, Ottawa, 13 August 1930. (L to R) Brigadier A.C. Caldwell, Commodore W.J. Hose, Mr. G.J. Desbarats, The Honourable J.L. Ralston, Major-General A.G.L. McNaughton, Brigadier A.H. Bell, Group Captain J.L. Gordon. (Photographer unknown. NA, PA-62488)

attached as well. This would also be run by the military. It all appeared to be a tight DND and military monopoly on industrial participation.

The King government instinctively shied away from commitment. One could argue that munitions production as an integral part of larger defence policy also has a national psychological component. If the larger non–military elements of society do not have a stake in it or cannot see that it serves their version of a national purpose, they are less likely to support it. At the same time, the government may have also been concerned that a commitment to a publicly owned arsenal it would divert limited resources away from civil industrial development already crippled by the depression and facing a highly competitive world.

This did not mean that no aspects of the public system went ahead. Parts of the Valcartier complex such as filling, testing, and inspection certainly did. And the old *cartoucherie* remained and some improvements had been made. Budgets began creeping upward after 1936. That year the factory went on full time production. Small arms ammunition output was increased. The new cartridge filling plant at Valcartier was nearing completion at the end of 1938 and the department announced a plan to re-open the refurbished factory in Lindsay. However, the arsenal had still not diversified much beyond small ammunition and components. And, it never approached the essential munitions industry of which men like McNaughton, Ashton or his MGO, Caldwell, dreamed. When that came it would be from elsewhere.[100]

While it was slow, the only apparent progress was with the Bren gun, whose negotiations had stalled in 1936 after revelations of government involvement in British orders for Canadian private industry. Nevertheless, behind the scenes the defence minister and his deputy continued to promote Hahn's efforts to secure British orders. Since they knew the only other way to get the gun built was by creating an expensive factory, which the government was unlikely to do, Hahn's group was the best bet for the time and money. Ashton had estimated that the Canadian forces would need only about 7,000 of the light machine guns. If the British could be convinced to give an order to a Canadian firm first, then not only would there be better economies of scale for both countries but the defence department could get a government commitment to order some for the Dominion. However, the British did not rush to order this item or many others because they still had not yet employed all of their own capacity and did not want to offend the sensitive Mackenzie King. Besides, as Sir Maurice Hankey, secretary of the CID, noted in early 1938, "Britain would be willing to spend money in developing industrial potential in Canada ... but we can't do that if there is the slightest risk of Canada adopting a 'neutrality set' or anything of the kind."[101]

After repeated efforts of Lafleche to get King to pressure the British to place a Canadian order, the Prime Minister finally said he would not do so. There the matter stayed all through 1937 and early 1938 with the officials of the defence department secretly continuing to promote an English contract for Hahn. About much of this the Prime Minister knew little. It was important for Lafleche to get the contract for Hahn because it would support his clear preference for private industry. Finally, in March 1938 with the rapidly declining international situation no doubt contributing to King's sense of obligation, he decided to approve the deal. But he did not like it. The contract was signed for 12,000 guns: 7,000 to Canada, 5,000 for the British, each with carefully worded separate contracts thus avoiding charges of Canadian government involvement in soliciting the order. Toolage was subsidized by both governments and Hahn got a contract for fixed costs plus ten percent. Putting the two contracts together saved about eight million dollars.[102] No other company was considered. In fact, when the British heard at one point that the deal might be put out to tender they lost interest, saying the process would be too slow and unpredictable. Lafleche justified the decision to use a private firm by arguing that a government factory for such a small order would take too long to build and cost too much. Besides, he advised his minister, one can "easily terminate" a private enterprise. The government lent Inglis all of the old Ross Rifle Company machinery. Yet, it took two years to get it all together and production started only in the spring of 1940, eight months into the war. By the end of the conflict, Inglis had produced nearly two million Bren guns.[103]

In spite of its caution, the government found itself under attack in September 1938 when Lieutenant-Colonel George Drew charged that it was patronage that got Hahn the contract and that the Bren guns could have been produced cheaper and faster in a government arsenal. Neither of these charges were likely true. But Drew had lots of information at hand when he made his statements. The relationship that the Conservative lieutenant-colonel—who had commanded artillery during the Great War and who would soon be in the Ontario Legislature—had with the former CGS, General McNaughton, is interesting. Earlier that spring, Drew had publicly attacked the failings of Liberal defence policy. Evidence remains sketchy about the collusion of the two men on the Bren gun charges. But they were kindred spirits in the need for munitions reform and in their opinion of the deputy minister, Lafleche. Drew's first swing at the Liberal policy came in late March in a three part exposé in the *Financial Post*. It had the eye-catching headlines "Canada's Defence Farce: No Tanks; Planes, Rifles, Obsolete—'Bow and Arrow Army Running out of Arrows.'" He followed it up with a speech at Brockille, Ontario a few days later. The articles spawned a personal letter of congratulations from McNaughton. "Every word is true," the general wrote. "There is no hope of manufacture in civil establishments ...We need a fully equipped Dominion Arsenal, and we will never get anywhere until we have it."[104] In a personal and confidential letter Drew asked McNaughton whether he was " in a position to give me some information ... I need hardly assure you, of course, that under no circumstances would the source of any of my information be disclosed." The general suggested that they meet in Toronto. Evidently they did because the general misplaced his walking

Major-General McNaughton visits Dominion Arsenals, ca. 1941. (Photographer unknown. NA, C-018228)

stick during the visit to Drew's house and that occasioned more correspondence revealing the meeting place. When the Bren gun deal was announced shortly after, Drew wrote again specifically asking for information on it:

> You have probably seen the notices in the papers ... that it is intended to make Bren guns at the Inglis Company here. Do you know anything about this, and also what is your opinion of the wisdom of making them in a private plant of this kind against making them in a government arsenal. The change in conditions has not in any way changed my opinion as to the desirability of avoiding private racketeering in army contracts and it seems to me that these guns could very well be made in a government arsenal without the invitation for graft that arises under the other plan.[105]

McNaughton quickly replied, "if you are in Ottawa, would you let me know so that we can meet and have a talk about things." Drew had previously told McNaughton that "I was more than shocked when I learned ... [about] ... the damnable things that are taking place under Lafleche." And the Bren gun deal was, more than any of the others, a Lafleche creation. What Drew and McNaughton said about it when they met remains lost. But that fall there was a heated debate in the press led by Drew about the controversial gun the likes of which had not been seen since the heady days of the Ross rifle.[106]

When the stories broke the King government safely distanced itself by quickly appointing a Royal Commission to investigate the Bren gun deal. That autumn, after two months of intensive examination, no guilt was found with anyone, save that King perceived that some members of the Department of National Defence had far overstepped his policy in their enthusiasm for the Bren gun. But the commission did recommend creating an expert advisory board to supervise all future munitions contracts. As we know that became the Defence Purchases Board in 1939.[107] But in 1938, the Bren gun affair more than any other sealed the debate over private and public supply.

Perhaps whatever equipment advances were gained by the military were offset by King's increasing assertion of political control over munitions, or simply undermined by his suspicions of soldiers and businessmen, especially in combination. For instance, the Ford Motor Company did not get British orders to produce aircraft engines on the explanation that the British thought the Canadian government did not want such contracts given. And in June 1939, King was cool to a delegation of the Canadian Manufacturers Association travelling to Britain that summer looking for contracts. But it did not matter much. By September everyone had run out of peace.[108] War for Canada and its defence industries came much like it had in 1914. No one was prepared.

Conclusion

If Ian Mackenzie thought munitioning was simple or straight forward when he made those comments to his Prime Minister in 1937, he was either naive or unversed in Canada's earlier procurement experiences. Both the soldier and the politician marched to different beats. The former had to listen attentively to the demands for military efficiency; but the latter had to hear the resonance of all the social factors. In writing about British rearmament in the interwar period, Norman Gibbs has noted that in peacetime planning, political calculations play a far greater role than they do once war starts. Canada was not exempt from this. All of the social imperatives were present and they resonated loudest with politicians. They took the form of veterans associations, constituent pressure, economic depression, pacifism and the new internationalism or isolationism; sometimes it was strong personalities with particular views, men such as Mackenzie King, O.D Skelton and McNaughton who had their own predispositions. And there was no obvious threat. All of them, to repeat Gibb's observation, are more active through political processes in Canadian interwar munitions development than in strictly military ones.

The interplay between the advocates of public or private munitions manufacture was omnipresent and at best tortuous. The military sought the creation of the public facilities to manufacture their equipment for many reasons. Not the least among them was the specialized nature of the equipment and the need to keep a mobilization base of munitions expertise. The bad experience of an earlier war with private concerns like the Ross Rifle Company convinced them that public manufacture was the only safe route. Moreover, it allowed the soldiers to exert a direct influence on the type and quality of the war materials they would use. It also let them conduct tests and experiments that would, at least in their minds, keep them up to date with the latest technologies of war. And Canadian military leaders wanted to associate themselves closely with the major ally, Great Britain. Their training and professional development had been linked for a long time, a link cemented by recent war-fighting experience. They believed in the tenets of Imperial defence. Collective military action abroad, in their opinion, was far more likely than ever fighting a major defensive war on Canada's soil. The armed forces were small. Highly specialized equipment and ammunition were usually not of interest to private manufacturers because of the intermittent nature of government contracts. Unit costs were high and for a variety of reasons there were no foreign sales that might have provided the profit or the stimulus for research and development; hence there was little Canadian expertise. Besides, it was the duty of any truly professional soldier to develop contingency plans based on the most likely scenario. No military person can be faulted for that. One final point about the soldiers of the period. In the twenties and thirties Canada had the best educated and professionally experienced body of military personnel in her history. These people were competent, articulate and well informed. They must have alarmed some politicians not used to having such a group to contend with. And while those soldiers of the thirties like McNaughton, Crerar and Ashton had more of the "cunning of restraint" that MacBrien obviously lacked in the twenties; still they had a lot to learn about the social imperatives that politicians must face.

Nor can the politicians be faulted for reacting the way they did. In their minds, two prime considerations permeated the entire interwar period: "defence against whom?" and "no commitments." The confusion in British security policy and it clearest manifestation, the infamous ten-year rule retarded the functional imperatives from approaching an accord with the social imperatives. When "the defence against whom" question slowly started to be answered in early 1937, munitions was allowed to respond in a similar fashion, but only after defence policy was directed to the politically feasible defence of Canada. The trick for the few politicians in the know was to convince the Canadian people, who had still not caught up to men like King or even the dogged Tory George Drew. One wonders how much quicker the transition would have been had the headquarters staff been less determined to have all their eggs in the one basket of a comprehensive public arsenal system.

Whatever the case, munitioning in peacetime is never simple or straightforward.

Notes for Chapter 12

1   Cited by James Eayrs, *In Defence of Canada, Appeasement and Rearmament, Vol II* (Toronto: University of Toronto Press, 1967), 145.

2   Canada, Parliament. House of Commons, *Sessional Papers*. "Annual Report of the Department of Militia,1879," Selby Smyth to the minister of Militia, 1 Jan 1880, xxii-xxxi. Hereafter cited *Militia Report*. See also the various descriptions of the new cartridge factory in NAC, RG 9, A1, "Report of the Committee on the Defences of Canada," vol485, "Organization of the Government Cartridge Factory from 1879." In 1947, the Dominion Arsenals published an uncritical and in places inaccurate brief history. See Dominion Arsenals, *The Dominion Arsenals at Quebec,1880-1945* (Quebec:1947)

3   R.G Haycock, "'Done in Our Own Country': the Politics of Canadian Munitioning," in B.D.Hunt and R.G. Haycock, eds., *Canada's Defence: Perspectives on Policy in the Twentieth Century* (Toronto: Copp Clark Pitman,1993); 44-68 analyses the munitions scene from Confederation to the Great War. Here the functional and social influences are quite evident. See note 9 below.

4   *Militia Report, 1894*, "Report of the Superintendent of the Government Cartridge Factory," 26 Nov 1894, 17-19. Haycock, "Done in Our Own Country," 44-53.

5   There is much written on the ill-fated Ross rifle. One of the latest which reprints Col. A.F. Duguid's comprehensive Appendix III from his 1938 official history of the CEF in the Great War is *A Question of Confidence: The Ross Rifle in the Trenches*, Clive M. Law, ed. Forward by Ronald Haycock (Ottawa: Service Publications, 1999), 1-48.

6   Canada. Royal Commission on the Sale of Small Arms Ammunition. *Report* (Ottawa: King's Printer, 1917) contains the details of the Arsenal purge. Also see Public Archives of Nova Scotia F.W. Borden papers, LLB, no.186, 17608, Hughes to F.W. Borden, 7 Aug 1913 where he says he was not prepared to blow the head off one Canadian Militiaman just to save the career of the incompetent Superintendent of the DAQ.

7   See R.G Haycock, "Early Canadian Weapons Acquisition: That Damned Ross Rifle," *in Canadian Defence Quarterly*, Vol14, No. 3 (Winter 1984/85), 48-57and fn 38.

8   Public Records Office (UK), Munitions Ministry, Records, Mun 5, 173, F1142 contains most of the documents on the Canadian Shell Committee and the IMB. In the National Archives of Canada (NA), RG 24 vol 2847, HQ5-3282 is a "History of the Operation of the Imperial Munitions Board" written at the end of the war. Peter Reider, "The Imperial Munitions Board and its Relationship to Government, Business and Labour," unpublished PhD thesis, University of Toronto, 1974.

9   For a discussion of the functional and "societal" imperatives, see Samuel Huntington's, *The Soldier and the State: The Theory and Politics of Civil-Military Relations* (New York: Vintage Books, 1957), 2-3, and for its application to Canada, M.A. Hooker, "Serving Two Masters: Ian Mackenzie and Civil-military Relations in Canada, 1935-1939" in *Journal of Canadian Studies*, Spring 1986, 38. The societal factors Huntington describes are " social forces, ideologies and institutions dominant within society." (p 2). These are collectively termed "social" in this chapter.

10   NA, RG 24, vol 6351 HQ 71-6-32, Flavelle to S.C. Mewburn, 25 Nov 1918. Flavelle wanted the militia minister to buy out the first of the Canadian national factories. Also see ibid., vol 1159, HQ 62-2-85, Brainert to MGO, 3 Oct 1919 and ibid., H.C. Brown to Brainert, 21 Oct 1919.

11   Jonathan Vance, *Death So Noble, Memory, Meaning and the First World War* (Vancouver: UBC Press, 1997), 142; Eayrs, vol I, *From the Great War to the Great Depression*, 3-27 and David G. Anderson, "British Rearmament and the 'Merchants of Death': The 1935-36 Royal Commission on the Manufacture and Trade in Armament," in *Journal of Contemporary History*, vol 29, (1994), 5-37.

12   NA, RG 24, reel c-5047, file HQC 46-1-50, "Proposed Manufacture of Ordnance in Canada." The file covers 1916 to 1937 but is mostly on the Great War period when most of the activity took place. This file points out the desire of military personnel at HQ to create a domestic capability that transcended by far the needs of war. And they hoped it would survive in the peace. The war time correspondence herein reveals that ideas of self sufficiency, national pride, the optimism of Canadian manufacturers believing that they could do anything that the allies could do, and an enthusiastic domestic inventiveness of a

new steel making process—are all among the reasons for manufacturing munitions in Canada. It did not happen!

13 NA, RG 13 Department of Justice, Acc.1897-88/103, vol110, file c-982, E.C. Ashton to MND, 15 August 1923. The file contains all of the correspondence of the trials of the company with the government, of the vain attempts by the soldiers to save it in order to have the vital gun making capability and of Ralston's intransigence in 1928. Six years earlier the company had been given partial government compensation on "moral" grounds, according to the Minister of Justice.

14 NA, RG 24 vol 2572 HQC 2948, 1, MGO to Minister of Militia and Defence, Memorandum regarding Dominion Arsenals at Quebec and Lindsay, 12 Feb 1919, confidential.

15 Ibid., vol 6351, HQ71-6-32, Superintendent DAQ to MGO, 9 Jan 1919 . Lafferty said that British Munitions Limited could make all the munitions from .303 up to 9.2-inch gun ammunition as well as the critical fuses that it made during the war. It would act as the munitions school for private industry in a crisis mobilization as DAQ had in the war but with much better equipment and facilities. He claimed that the present DAQ gun ammunition machine tools were worthless and that the British Munitions machines had "never turned a wheel" and were being offered by the British government at "scrap " value—it was a real bargain.

16 Ibid., vol 1146, HQ 54-21-57-11, GWVA Resolution, Vancouver, 4 July 1919.

17 Ibid., vol 25 72, HQC 2948, p1, Col Lafferty to MGO, 13 Feb 1919, confidential and Ibid., vol 6351,HQ 71-632, Mewburn to Flavelle, 5 Feb 1919.

18 Ibid., MHQ memo, "Dominion Arsenals" undated, unsigned, stamped received 17 Feb 1919. The two arsenal superintendents met with the MGO at MHQ to decide future activities of the plants in Ottawa, 28 Feb 1919.

19 Ibid., "decision # 272 of Militia Council, 19 Feb 1919. See Elliott's memo attached which says that there is only enough peacetime work for one arsenal. He suggests that DAQ is not in a good position to serve the rest of the country outside of Quebec, and that the facility should be in Central Canada. Also see ibid., MGO to Superintendent DAs, 10 Mar 1919.

20 C.P. Stacey, *Canada in the Age of Conflict: A History of Canadian External Policies, Volume 1: 1867-1921* (Toronto: MacMillan,1977), Chapter 9.

21 NA, RG 24, reel c-5060, File HQC, 2953, Dept.of Reorganization Cttee: Post Bellum Army of the Empire. See ibid., Reorganization Committee: Post Bellum Field Army, minutes of the first meeting, 21 Dec 1918. On MacBrien as the CGS, 1920-1927, see Norman Hillmer and William McAndrew, "The Cunning of Restraint: General J.H. MacBrien and the Problems of Peacetime Soldiering," in *Canadian Defence Quarterly*, Vol 8, No.4 (Spring, 1979), 40-47.

22 NA, RG 24, HQC 2948, vol 1, General Policy of Dominion Arsenals, SDAQ to MGO, 14 Oct 1919.

23 Ibid., memo on Future Policy to be Pursued in Regard to maintenance of Dominion Arsenals. MGO to Sec of the MC 14 Nov.1919 and ibid., Sec of the MC to MGO, 20 Nov 1919. Elliott also asked what levels of production were to be maintained in 1920-1921`. That too was evidently undecided and so left at wastage and reserve SAA and artillery ammunition production, both of which were very low.

24 G.F.G. Stanley, *Canada's Soldiers: The Military History of an Unmilitary People* (Toronto: Macmillan,1974), 341.

25 Eayrs, Vol I, 302-303.

26 Stacey, *The Military Problems of Canada*, 87 and Allan, "Make Ready Thine Arrows," unpublished MA (war studies) thesis, RMC, 1976, 47 et seq. On the MGO, see Stacey, *Arms, Men and Governments*, 69.

27 NA, RG24, reel C-5075, file HQC-5000, Policy re: Disposal of the Lindsay Arsenals.

28 *Montreal Gazette*, clipping in NA, RG 24, reel 5050, file HQC 171 vol 1, Leakage of Information from DND to Public. Also see in this file Ashton to the deputy minister, DND, 6 Dec 1923, confidential. The ministers who were to meet were W.S. Fielding (finance), E.M. Macdonald (DND) and Ernest Lapointe (marine and fisheries).

29 *Militia Report, 1919*, 37-46 and *Arsenals*, 53.

30 Eayrs, Vol I, 81.

31 M.A.Pope, *Soldiers and Politicians: The Memoires of Lt-Gen Maurice A. Pope* (Toronto: U of T Press, 1962), 90-91; and Stanley, *Canada's Soldiers*, 340-344.

32 NA, RG 24, vol1855, cn-ww1-65, Summary of Colonial and Imperial Conferences, 1887-1921. See those for 1897, 1907,1909, 1917, and 1921. And NAC MG 27, III, Ralston papers, vol 30, X-12, Defence problems for Imperial Conference, 1937, memo on PM's most secret communication, 2 Mar 1937, concerning Imperial Conference Papers E(37)2 and E(37)9 by Ashton, 8 Mar 1937.

33 Stacey, *Arms, Men and Governments: The War Policies of Canada,1939-1945* (Ottawa: Queen's Printer, 1970), 2 and 70-71.

34 Geneva, Archives of the League of Nations, Canada, 8/21328/20397, Box R218, Reduction of Armaments: Reply of Canada. Memo by Sir Joseph Pope, 17 May 1923. Hereafter cited League of Nations Archives.

35 Canada. Department of External Affairs, *Documents on Canadian External Relations, vol 4, 1926-1930* (Ottawa: Information Canada, 1971), doc.129, Extracts of Minutes of the Imperial Conference, 1926,15 November 1926, secret; doc. 216, Chief of the General Staff to the Prime Minister, 25 Oct 1926. Memorandum relating to Defence Matters.

36 Eayrs, Vol I, 80-81.

37 NA, RG 24,vol 2683, HQS 5121, Secret Report by the Chief of the Staff on the Defence Forces of Canada, 29 Jan 1927.

38 B.J.C. Mckercher, "From Disarmament to Rearmament: British Civil-Military Relations and Policy Making,1933-1934," in *Defence Studies*, vol 1, no.1 (Spring 2001), 21-48.

39 NA, Ian Mackenzie papers, MG 27, 41 B5, Vol 29, X-4,"The Defence of Canada: A Review of the Present Situation, McNaughton, 28 April 1935.

40 Stanley, *Canada's Soldiers*, 349.

41 NA, RG 24, vol 2740, file HQS 5740, v 1, Disposal of Ross Rifles and the Manufacture of New Pattern SMLE in Canada," See Memorandum on the Possible Disposal of Ross Rifles, Ashton to defence minister, 6 Sept 1935. The file contains correspondence on this subject from 1927 to 1938.

42 Ibid., vol 5942, HQ 516-1-36, Policy regarding retention of Ross rifles in Canada. This file covers the entire interwar period. The military policy seems to be laid down before 1924.

See ibid., QMG to CGS, 24 Jul 1924. The occasion arose when a Toronto businessman representing the National Cartridge Company wanted to buy Ross Mk IIs at $5 each to turn them into hunting rifles. The company was a post war creation that bought surplus .303 ball to convert to sporting ammunition by grinding off the nose of the military projectile to expose the lead core. This would theoretically make an inexpensive "expanding" hunting bullet. It was a very dangerous practice. The 18.5 tons per square inch of breech pressure of a firing .303 cartridge could blow the lead core out of the steel bullet jacket through the nose, leaving the steel jacket lodged in the bore of the weapon. The next round fired up the barrel would usually blow up the gun. Unable to get rifles, the company soon failed.

43 Ibid., reel 5060, file HQC 3103, Convention for the Control of International Arms Trade-1919, unsigned memo, Ottawa, 31 Oct 1923.

44 Ibid., reel C-5059, file HQC 1263, Exportation and Sale of Arms and Ammunition. All the mentioned correspondence is in this file.

45 NA, MG 30 E157 H.D.G.Crerar papers, vol 10, file Liason no.2, Correspondence with C.S.A. Ritchie and Dr. Riddell, Canadian Legation Washington, D.C." This file contains a series of memos about allegations of attempted Ross sales by Canadians emanating out of San Francisco.

46 NA, RG 24,v 2740, HQS-5470, v 1, Memo QMG to minister, 17 August 1927, and DM's memo to MND, 9 Sept 1927, minute by the minister.

47 NA, MG 30, E 133, A.G.L. McNaughton papers, S11, vol 107, *Montreal Gazette*, 8 Sept 1928, clipping reporting King's address to the League of Nations, Geneva, 7 Sept 1928. Hereafter cited McNaughton papers.

48 NA, RG 24, vol 2359, HQC 72-32-1, vol 1, Thomas Poulin, Secretaire, Le Conseil Central National des Metiers du District de Quebec to Ralston, 8 Feb 1928. Poulin wrote the factory "pourrait bien etre transferre en Ontario." He added " vous exprimer l'espoir qu'il n y a rien de fonde en elle et que cette cartoucherie sera reconstruite a Quebec." Ralston answered with a brief denial that any decision had been made, but Quebec would receive most careful consideration. Ibid., Desbarats to Poulin, 16 Feb 1928. This file contains the correspondence cited in the text

49 Eayrs, Vol I, 313-15. Also see NA, RG 24, vol 2359, HQC 72-32-1, pt.1 Memo on New Arsenal, CGS to minister, 12 May 1930.

50 NA, J.L. Ralston papers, MG 27, III, B11, vol 89, Bren Gun: Canadian General Staff Branch Memo re Bren Gun.

51 NA, MG30, E 133, SII, v 112, file Sutherland, Hon. D.M., 1930, 3 Dec 1930, Memo on mechanization of the Militia, CGS to Sutherland; and NA, RG 24 vol 2359, HQC 72-32-1, pt 1, memo by CGS on interview with minister, 19 mar 1931.

52 *Arsenals*, 58.

53 Eayrs, Vol I, 313-15.

54 NA, RG 24, vol 2740, HQS 5740, vol 1, CGS to the Hon. the Minister, 25 July 1931, secret; ibid., GSO Arty to CGS, 3 Sept 1931, secret; and John Swettenhan, *McNaughton* (Toronto: Ryerson Press,1968), vol 1, 264-268. McNaughton was very critical of the League of Nations disarmament attempts in 1932. He thought them doomed to failure when the various

delegates started to compare relative levels of armament. This, he said, led to an arms race as they tried to adjust to each others' levels instead of just getting on with finding a solution through debate on principles. He was probably right. See ibid., 266, note.

55 NA, RG 24, vol 2740, HQS 5740, vol 1, Memorandum on the Exportation and Sale of Arms, 27 July 1931. The 1925 Convention memo is herein. On the Lee-Enfield, see Ian Skennerton, *The British Service Lee: Lee-Metford and Lee-Enfield Rifles and Carbines 1880-1980* (Brisbane: Skennerton Press, 1982), 143. The British and Canadian forces went into WWII armed with the No. 1, Mk* SMLE, first introduced in 1907. The British lost so many of theirs at Dunkirk in 1940 that with the new pattern still only in limited manufacture, the Canadian government shipped over 75,000 Ross rifles which nine years before they had tried to sell to the Chinese. See the RG 24, vol 2740, f HQS 5740 for that 1940 shipment to outfit "Granddad's Army."

56 NA, RG 24, vol 2740, HQS 5740, vol 1, Ashton to Stirling, 5 Sept 1935, Memorandum Concerning the Disposal of Ross rifles. In response to a secret and confidential request from the minister, and ibid., CGS to the Hon. the Minister, 25 July 1931, secret.

57 Ibid., see memorandum by CGS on interview with Mr H.C.Bellew representing Griffin and Howe, 25 Apr 1933; and *ibid.*,CGS Memorandum for the Hon. the Minister, 6 May 1933. The remainder of HQS 5740, vol 1 covers all the rest of the events.

58 United Kingdom, Public Records Office (PRO), Cabinet Documents, Cab 60/4, Minutes of the CID Principal Supply Officers Committee contains all of the minutes of the PSOC. Also see Canada NA, Mackenzie Papers, vol 3, X-12 Defence Problems for Imperial Conference, 1937, memo by CGS Ashton, 8 Mar 1937, traces the fate of the PSOC and Canadian Supply Committee.

59 Swettenham, *McNaughton*, vol 1 chapter 8, and G.M. Lefresne, "The Royal Twenty Centers," unpublished (history) thesis, RMC, 1962.

60 NA, McNaughton papers, vol 22, HQ 1376-11-7-1, notes on telephone conversation, McNaughton to BGen McCuaig, 15 Apr 1933.

61 See NA, RG 24, vols 156, 366, 367 and 368 contain data relating to text. For a synopsis of the DND involvement in all the projects across Canada, see ibid., Report on the DND Unemployment Relief Scheme for Single, Homeless Men from the Inception of Scheme (8 Oct 1932) to 30 Sep 1935, Ashton (CGS) to the Hon. the Minister, 8 Feb 1936. Also see NA, McNaughton papers, vols 15a, and 22.

62 *Hansard*, 11 Apr 1933, clipping in NA, RG 24, vol3066, HQ 1376-11-7-1

63 NA, McNaughton papers, vol 100, memo of discussion with R.B. Bennett, 25 Oct 1934, McNaughton, 25 Oct 1934.

64 NA, Mackenzie papers, vol 29, X-4, The Defence of Canada: A Review of the Present Situation," McNaughton, 28 May 1935 and Parks Canada, *Arsenal*, 11.

65 NA, RG 24, vol 3066, Unemployment Relief Valcartier (Project 29) Training Camp, contains the details of the strike by 1900 men.

66 NA, Mackenzie papers, vol 29, X-4, The Defence of Canada: A Review of the Present Situation. McNaughton, 28 May 1935.

67 NA, McNaughton papers, vol 100, McNaughton to Ashton, 25 Oct 1935, secret and personal and ibid., Ashton to McNaughton, 19 Oct 1935, secret and personal.

68 PRO, Cab 60/4, PSOC, minutes of the 58th meeting, 4 April 1935.

69 NA, Mackenzie papers, Ashton to Mackenzie, 12 Sep 1937, Memorandum the Requirements of National Defence." Also Hooker in *Journal of Canadian Studies*, Spring 1986, 38-53.

70 NA, RG 24, vols 2772 and 2773, Navy, Army and Air Supply Committee: Department of National Defence, HQS 6619, vols. 1 and 2 contain much of the daily correspondence of this group.

71 Eayrs, Vol II, 137-138. Eayrs points out that the Cabinet Defence Committee was never given a chance and fell into disuse. See also Stacey, *Arms, Men and Governments*, 69-71.

72 NA, RG 24, vol 2684,HQS 5199, vol 3, SS for Dominion Affairs to SS External Affairs, Canada, secret, 12 April 1937. See ibid., JSC memo to minister, 27 April 1937.

73 Thomas B. Dugelby, *The Bren Gun Saga* (Toronto: Collector Grade Publications, 1986), chapter 2. The name " Bren" comes from the combination of the first two letters of where it was designed (Brno, Czechoslovakia) and the first two letters of where it was made (Enfield, UK), hence, "Bren."

74 NA, Mackenzie papers, vol 30, X-10, Supply of Bren Light Automatics, 3/7/36.

75 Ibid., vol 30, X-11, MGO to PM, 4 July 1936.

76 Ibid., vol 29, X-4, Requirements of National Defence: Report of the CGS, 24 Aug 1936.

77 NA, RG 24, vol 2693, HQS 5199-B, secret memo by Lafleche to CGS, 29 Aug 1926.

78 NA, Mackenzie papers, vol 29, 149-30. Mackenzie to Prime Minister, 4 Sept, 1936 and Ibid., King to Hugh Plaxton MP, 12 Sep 1936.

79 Ibid., Mackenzie to Prime Minister, 8 Sep 1936.

80 NA, McNaughton papers, vol III, memo to Dr. H.L.Keenleyside, 31 Jan 1939, private.

81 See NA, Ralston papers, MG27, III, B11, Bren Gun Files, MGO to CGS, 27 Jan 1936 and Ibid., CGS to Minister, 30 Jan 1936. Both these memoranda show the soldiers' preference clearly.

82 Ibid., vol 89, Report by Lieutenant. M.P. Jolley, RCOC, on Lindsay Arsenal as a possible Small Arms Factory, 25 Sep 1936, Ibid., correspondence: J.L.R. 1937, DCEMO to MGO, 29 Dec 1937, and Bren Gun Correspondence, J.L. Ralston, 1936, Lafleche to Skelton, 2 Oct 1936, secret.

83 NA, King papers, MG 26, J4, Vol 196, F1825. Skelton to PM undated memo likely Nov 1936, 1372-3 and Ibid., Skelton to PM, 20 Nov 1936, 137282.

84 Robert Bothwell, "Defence and Industry in Canada, 1935-1970," in B.F. Cooling, ed., *War Business and World Military Industrial Complexes* (Port Washington: Kennikat Press, 1981), 106-119.

85 NA, King papers, vol 196, F1825, Report of the Interdepartmental Committee on the Control of Profit on Government Armaments Contracts, 19 Jan 1937, secret, 139332-8.

86 NA, Mackenzie papers, vol 39, D77, Defence Purchases Board, Notes on Profit Control. See the entire file. Also see Eayrs, Vol II, 121.

87 Ibid., vol 29, X-6, PM's remarks at Caucus, 20 Jan 1937.

88 *Hansard*, 1937,vol II, 954-965 and 1142-1151.

89 NA, King papers, vol 196, f 1825, memo L.R. Lafleche to PM, 24 Jan 1937, 13732-41.

90 NA, Mackenzie papers, vol 29, X-4, Requirements of Canadian Defence: A Review of the Position as of 1 Jan 1937, by E.C. Ashton, secret. Ashton's frequent memos have an almost frantic tone to them, no doubt well warranted.

91 Stanley, *Canada's Soldiers*, 349.

92 Stacey, *The Military Problems of Canada*, 126-127.

93 NA, RG24, HQS 3498, vol 22, CGS to Mackenzie, 15 Mar 1937 and NA, King papers, vol 227, CGS to Mackenzie, 24 Aug 1936, Memo: Requirements of National Defence.

94 NA, RG24, HQS 3367 vol 28, Periodical Letter No. 5/1936, 17 Dec 1936. Also note NA, Mackenzie papers, Vol 29, X-6, Memo: An Appreciation of the Defence Problems Confronting Canada., 16 Nov 1936, secret. This noted that an expeditionary force "may again be necessary" (p. 11). It also calls for similarity in Empire training, equipment and organization.

95 NA, Mackenzie papers, vol 30, X-28, Mackenzie to PM, 10 April 1937.

96 Eayrs, Vol II, 118-120.

97 Ibid.

98 NA, Mackenzie papers, vol 20, X-4, Requirements of Canadian Defence, memo by Ashton, 1 Jan 1937 and ibid., vol 30, X-19, Observations on Canadian Defence Policy, 4 Oct 1937.

99 Ibid., vol 29, X-4, The Munitions Supply Organization of Australia, CGS to minister, 18 Oct 1937 and ibid., GCS Memo The Requirements of National Defence: Statement on Militia Supply and Armament, 23 Sep 1937, secret.

100 See the various *Annual Reports* of the Department of National Defence for much of this. For instance, *Annual Report*, 1936, 9; Ibid., 1937, 109 and Ibid., 1938, 81-84.

101 J.L. Granatstein, *Canada's War: The Politics of the Mackenzie King Government, 1939-45* (Toronto: Oxford University Press, 1975), 3. Also see Eayrs, Vol II, Chapter 4: "Empire and Reich."

102 Dugelby, 153.

103 Eayrs, Vol II, 119-122.

104 NA, McNaughton papers, ser 11, vol 116, McNaughton to Drew, 8 April 1938, personal and confidential. See also clippings in the same file.

105 Ibid., Drew to McNaughton, 7 May 1938.

106 Ibid., see all the correspondence in the file Drew, Lt-Col George A.

107 NA, Mackenzie papers, vol 39, D67, Notes on the Bren Controversy, contains a synthesis of the Royal Commission evidence.

108 Eayrs, Vol II, 121-123.

Canadian soldiers at Passchendaele, Belgium, 1917. (Photographer unknown. NA, PA-2084)

CHAPTER 13

The Canadian
Tao of Conflict

Sean M. Maloney

The Way is a specific and determinedly deliberate methodology. The ancient masters must be studied constantly without respite, even when the practitioner thinks he has grasped the knowledge. It is important to realize that technique is not the end of an art. Those good in technique, regardless of the art they pursue, are not necessarily able to teach the true meaning of an art.
—Miyamoto Musashi[1]

GEORGE STANLEY'S SEMINAL WORK, *Canada's Soldiers*, asserts through its subtitle that Canadians are an unmilitary people. Certainly this view was popular among certain academic and cultural elements when the work was published in its revised edition in 1960. Since Canada was apparently only a warfighting nation when pressed, and only then within an empire construct (the argument went) military policies were reactions to a world situation which was far away from Canadian shores and beyond Canadian control. The Trudeau Government's attempt to develop a post-colonial identity warmly embraced anti-militarism and it set about creating the myth that Canadians are morally superior to other people because they are peacemakers, not warfighters. This in turn gave further weight to Stanley's assertion over time. This view downplays, however, Canada's rich military heritage and the close proximity of violence to the creation of a truly unique Canadian identity. It amounts to wishful thinking of the type endemic to the 1960s and 1970s. Consequently, it has no real place in any considered analysis of whether or not there is a Canadian way of warfare. Let us therefore jettison such ideas up front.

There are several Canadian strategic traditions which, when combined, suggest that there is a Canadian way of warfare dating back to at least the 1800s, and possibly further. Searching for a uniquely Canadian way of warfare might be seen as a culturally insecure attempt to ape the work of a similar title on American warfare.[2] Why is such a quest important? What benefit could be derived from such a project?

Every nation was conceived under and exists within a unique set of circumstances, mostly geographic, usually ethnic, and definitely cultural and economic. Some factors do not change, although technology and the power of the state relative to others most certainly do. Can we, in fact, find any concepts, precepts, or ideas that transcend the different periods of Canadian history? If we can, they might be used to educate or at the very least provide context to the decisions made in the realm of warfare, decisions which Canadian leaders must make, however reluctantly. They might highlight long-standing stumbling blocks. They might even (shock!) point out areas in which self-deprecating Canada had a positive effect.

Let us first establish that there are several distinct periods of Canadian warfare.

The Colonial Era (pre-1867)

Confederation to the First World War (1867-1918)

The Second World War (1939-45)

The Cold War (1945-91)

The Stabilization Campaign (1990s)

War is here defined in its broadest sense: the use of military forces to achieve a political aim. Prior to the Cold War and for some time afterward it was fashionable to distinguish between the conditions of peace and war. Recognizing such conditions assumed, however, a functioning Westphalian state system. This system deteriorated during the Cold War and well into the Stabilization Campaign afterward, despite attempts to prop it up. Rigidly defining war as merely combat operations conducted during a legally and diplomatically recognized condition is far too narrow a position from which to view the national security activities of the world after 1945. Moreover, this represents nearly half of Canada's independent existence so far. Canadian historians and analysts must finally accept that the Cold War and the Stabilization Campaign were not periods of peace. They are only so when compared to the spectre of global thermonuclear warfare and the irradication of life on earth which, it could be technically argued, is also a form of peace.

Indeed, it is fashionable (and even Canadian Forces doctrine)[3] to recognize three distinct conditions: Peace, Conflict, and War. Yet, Canadian soldiers used lethal military force on many occasions when Canada has not been at war in the conventional sense (Cyprus in 1974, Croatia in 1993, Kosovo in 1999) but did not use significant lethal force during a formally defined war in the Persian Gulf in 1991. Labelling this "peacefare" is ridiculous, not to mention Orwellian, and is as ridiculous as the constant references in the media to Canadian soldiers as "peacekeepers." In any event, the Ottawa decision-making process from 1945 to today has not in practice differentiated between peace and war (although nuclear war is handled somewhat differently).[4]

What of continuity? Unlike the United States, which developed a system in the 1950s of codifying a coherent national strategy on paper and then re-examining it annually in the National Security Council,[5] Canada has only had coherent national strategy-making bodies during the Second World War and for about twelve years during the early part of the Cold War. Politicians tend to think no further ahead than the next election, while the professional bureaucracy was

Prime Minister Churchill surveying the Rhine River accompanied by his British and Canadian generals, Germany, 4 March 1944. He is accompanied by (l to r) General Crerar, Field Marshall Alan Brooke, Lieutenant-General Simonds, and Field Marshall Montgomery. (Photographer Barney J. Gloster. NA, 143952)

almost destroyed under the reign of Michael Pitfield in the 1970s.[6] As for the armed services themselves, they were new professional organizations during the first half of the twentieth century[7] and the effects of integration and unification in the 1960s and 1970s seriously disrupted their ability to think or transmit ideas over the long term.[8] How can the idea of a Canadian way of warfare be sustained? One might argue for Canada, as Russell Weigley has for the American case, that

> Throughout American history until [1941-45] the United States usually possessed no national strategy for the employment of force or the threat of force to attain political ends, except as the nation used force in wartime openly...The United States was not involved in international politics continuously enough or with enough consistency of purpose to permit the development of a coherent national strategy for the consistent pursuit of political goals by diplomacy in combination with armed force.[9]

We might seek answers to the Canadian situation in the realm of sub-conscious psychology. This would require, however, resorting to the long-discredited practice of pyschohistory as espoused by Erik Erikson.[10] Using Freudian constructions to explain Mackenzie King's motivations might be fun but it might have limited value here, since we cannot extend such an approach to cover all who influenced the policy-making environment.[11] Does Canadian literature offer insight into the Canadian soul and thus our motivations in national security policy? As Robertson Davies noted in *The Manticore*, "You'd better face it, Boy; Mackenzie King rules Canada because he himself is the embodiment of Canada—cold and cautious on the outside, dowdy and pussy in every overt action, but inside a mass of intuition and dark intentions."[12]

273

Then there is the debate over culture, values and their transmission over time. Can we assume that the values of 1867 remain operative today? Or those of the 1940s? Certainly Canadian interests do not really change: Canadians have always wanted economic and physical security. Although Maslowian in nature instead of Freudian, it is an accurate statement with which very few (Marxist academics and perhaps isolated religious orders or communes) can argue.[13]

The answer to the Canadian continuity conundrum is a *Fiddler on the Roof* one: Tradition. Naval historian Julian Corbett's analysis of British strategy in the 1700s and 1800s revealed that patterns of behaviour whether codified or not, emerge in those involved in making national security policy and serve as the basis for future activity. These patterns are usually interest-based.[14] As noted earlier, each nation's unique geographic, economic and cultural circumstances remain constant: Japan, for example, must still import raw materials as she did in the 1930s or Russia must control the oil fields of the Caucasus. The Balkans must collapse violently every fifty years because of its ethnic matrix. Similar factors apply in the Canadian case to also drive a Canadian strategic tradition. What are they?

Canada is a part of North America—geographically an island continent—and is dominated by a nation ten times its size in population. Canada is a vast, largely unpopulated land containing a great amount of natural wealth that cannot be defended by Canadian resources alone. Canada is not economically self-sufficient and must therefore trade. In part to avoid complete cultural and economic domination by its large closest neighbour, Canada conducts international trade and is thus involved in the free market economies of the world. But the Canadian people would never accept a Third World standard of living for the sake of avoiding trade with its largest neighbour. And Canada must accommodate Quebecois cultural and political sensitivities if it is to remain unified. These factors have remained constant in Canada for over one hundred years. In one way or another, they have influenced the national security policies of every Canadian government since 1867. One can debate the means or the skill with which they have been handled, but these factors are the basis of Canadian strategic tradition.[15]

One obstacle to finding continuity in Canadian national security policy is the language itself. Events of one period may be similar to events in another yet the vocabulary used to describe them may differ. This was particularly clear in the 1990s when politicized decision makers over-sensitized to media criticism called military operations using force "peacemaking" to avoid using that nasty "w" word. If we place past events in a modern context, the sophistication of Canada's national security policy from Confederation to the turn of the century is apparent.[16]

If one country harbours and overtly supports an armed and organized body of people who bear allegiance to a third nation which is occupied by a fourth country, and then permits these people to conduct guerrilla operations from it, we would call that state-sponsored terrorism. This is exactly what the Fenian Raids of 1866-67 were all about; IRA-affiliated groups attacked Canada in southern Quebec, New Brunswick, along the St. Lawrence River and across the Niagara Frontier. Canada mobilized its forces to successfully fight off this external threat and placed diplomatic pressure through London on the United States to cease and desist.[17]

The deployment of two Canadian battalions during the Red River Expedition in 1870 certainly counts as a show of force in an Aid of the Civil Power operation, while the Northwest Rebellion of 1885, involving a large military field force, could be compared with native disturbances in the 1990s at Oka, Ipperwash, Awkwasane or Gustafsen Lake or more exactly, the FLQ crisis of 1970. Ottawa's response in 1885 amounted to a counterinsurgency campaign. The creation of the paramilitary North West Mounted Police indicates that a colonial constabulary was necessary to project Canadian power into the vast space of the Northwest and to ensure that its constituent elements remained under Ottawa's control, not Washington's.[18] Indeed, these operations were conducted under the policy of what historian Michael Hennessy refers to as Canadian Turnerism: the Canadian national railroad as manifest destiny and a means to secure the Northwest.

Certainly the employment of the North West Mounted Police to combat American whisky traders at Fort Whoop Up in southern Alberta and at similar outposts in Saskatchewan resembles Drug Enforcement Agency operations against Columbian narco-para states in the late twentieth century. If we view the use of liquor by these American entities to incite the native population of these regions so as to destabilize Canadian control over the territory, we might even view this as an asymmetric threat.

The peace between Canada and the United States during this time was bolstered by British troops and Canadian-manned fortifications, with the promise of British strategic reinforcement from the home islands if the American hordes came across the border. This constitutes an early form of deterrence: think of it as a reverse version of NATO's situation in Europe during the Cold War. It was coupled to a strategic arms limitation treaty and a confidence building regime called the Rush-Bagot Agreement whereby major warships from both sides were scuttled in 1815 to de-escalate the situation.[19]

A critical component of Canadian national security policy in the nineteenth century was resource protection. Most of the Canadian-American disputes during the latter part of that century revolved around fishing stocks and boundary issues. The origin of what would become the Canadian navy, it could be argued, was a desire to ensure the economic viability of the Canadian fisheries.[20] On the Alaskan border, resource protection assumed equal importance. American prospectors were violating the boundary in the Yukon and threatening Canadian control over the gold fields of the region. The Yukon Field Force in 1898 conducted what could only be called a strategic deployment from eastern Canada. They were sent several thousand miles to deter illegal border activity and to provide Aid of the Civil Power to the North West Mounted Police.[21]

Once the nation was secured, Canadian policy makers looked to expanding power overseas. They have not looked back. The period before the First World War was one of globalization much like the 1990s.[22] Overseas trade was increasingly linked to overseas influence and Canada was not isolationist. Out of this milieu emerged the strategic tradition of Forward Security.

Forward Security involves the deployment of Canadian military forces overseas to ensure that violent international activity is kept as far away from North America as possible and that Canadian interests overseas are protected. Every Canadian military deployment outside of North America since 1898 has had a Forward Security component; even the Yukon Field Force expedition as well as the two rebellions were on the outer fringes of the Canadian empire and could be considered Forward Security.

It was fashionable in the 1960s and 1970s to portray Canadian involvement in overseas expeditions as reluctant deployments to satisfy the Imperial British demand for colonial troops. The reality was that Canada was part of a cultural and economic bloc and derived substantial security benefits from being a member of that bloc in the globalized world of the early 1900s. Threats to the economic well-being of the Empire had an impact on Canada. These threats came from the nascent American threat and from the ripple effect in the global economy if Germany, France, or others made too much headway. Canadian decisions to become involved in the Khartoum Expedition (1884-85) and in the Boer War (1899-1901) were driven by public support for the importance of the Empire. If the situation in South Africa deteriorated, for example, Germany might enter the war on the side of the Boers, which would have profound effects elsewhere.[23]

Canadian involvement in the First World War was essentially an extension of these policies, though Canada chose to confine herself to fighting on the Western Front. The disruption of the existing political and economic situation in Europe and the still-antagonistic relationship with the United States posed threats to Canadian interests which could be best countered by keeping the fighting contained in Europe and blocking German imperial ambitions.[24]

Canada's intervention in Russia (1918-19) was part of a larger project to prevent the emergence of a communist state that supported global revolution against the cultural and economic system of which Canada was part. Similarly, Canadian gunboat diplomacy in Central America during the inter-war period and well into the 1980s had distinct economic stability undertones.[25]

Canada's reasons for involvement in the Second World War within the context of Forward Security are straightforward: the Fascist totalitarian nations and their policies posed direct threats to the existence of the world as a politically and culturally free and economically stable environment. Canada herself was directly at risk this time (the Battle of the St Lawrence, for example) and the protecting coalition in which Canada had operated since the 1700s was in danger of complete collapse. To ensure Forward Security, Canadian forces kept the sea lines of communication open, conducted strategic air warfare, and mounted amphibious and airborne operations against the opposition throughout Europe.[26] Even the doomed Hong Kong expedition in 1941 had Forward Security ramifications, although they were somewhat dubious.[27]

Similarly, the Cold War period produced a plethora of Canadian operations calculated to ensure Forward Security, this time against Communist totalitarians seeking to impose their ideology on others. Sending land and naval forces to contain Communist aggression in Korea and then deploying land and air forces to serve in West Germany and France alongside other North Atlantic Treaty Organization forces was designed to deter Soviet adventurism against the reconstructed cultural and economic allies in Europe. Practically every Canadian UN peacekeeping operation conducted between 1948 and 1970 was directly related to Forward Security, as were the non-UN peace observation missions in Indochina. Since NATO could not operate outside of the defined alliance area, UN peace operations functioned as surrogate NATO activities to block Communist expansion into the newly-decolonized Third World.[28]

The second wave of decolonization, better known as the Stabilization Campaign of the 1990s, produced widespread anarchy as the world reordered itself after the central Communist Empire collapsed. Instead of containing monolithic totalitarians, Canada was involved in containing a regional one which was acquiring weapons of mass destruction and in attempting to stamp out brushfires in the Balkans before they could spread to newly freed Eastern Europe and beyond. The tradition of Forward Security was operating in these instances, though there will continue to be some debate over the efficacy of the operations.[29]

Closely linked with Forward Security is the tradition of Coalition Warfare. Canada has a relatively small population and, in the early years, had a limited industrial base. Given Canada's origins as a colony of the British Empire, it was natural that Canada initially operated within this context. The defence of Canada against American expansionism in the 1800s dictated a close relationship given the proximity of the threat and the need to demonstrate an effective deterrent posture.[30]

Farther away from home, Canadian involvement in the Boer War was an Empire exercise and thus conducted within a coalition context. Canadian interests were intertwined with British interests and there was no real requirement for independent operations. The struggle against Imperial Germany during the First World War demanded a unified effort, as did the defence against the Fascist totalitarians during the Second World War. There was no need for independent Canadian action given the global scale required for victory. Whereas the First World War was fought by Canada as part of a formal Imperial coalition, our Second World War effort was conducted within a coalition consisting of the declining imperial powers, their allies and dominions, and the United States.[31]

The struggle against the Communist totalitarians during the Cold War demanded a unified Western effort in many spheres to prevent nuclear war. The nature of the Cold War, a combination of deterrence and counter-moves in the Third World, dictated a different kind of coalition warfare. Standing alliances like the Permanent Joint Board on Defence (PJBD), the Military Cooperation Committee, NATO and the North American Air Defence Command (NORAD) were critical mechanisms to demonstrate deterrent solidarity. In these organizations Canada was an equal member and not a subordinate. The United Nations in the Canadian Cold War context was a mechanism to be used to contain Communist totalitarianism in conjunction with the more important NATO and Canadian-American relationships.[32]

Although there is a Canadian strategic tradition of coalition warfare, it would be a mistake to assume as many have that Canada never conducts independent operations. Canada has on many occasions deployed forces overseas to support diplomatic, economic, and military initiatives outside of formal coalition or alliance contexts. In many cases this included non-combatant evacuation operations in potentially hostile environments and various forms of naval pressure.[33]

The global nature of the Stabilization Campaign of the 1990s also demanded coalition operations, usually within the UN context and then NATO. The evolved nature of the UN in the post Cold War world raised expectations that Canada could join that international organization in its Quixotic quest for global peace. Unlike the Cold War period in which Canada used the UN, now the UN used Canada for its purposes until a serious decline in its credibility meant that NATO had to take over, particularly in the Balkans, while the United States took the lead in Haiti and Somalia. In the cases of NATO-led IFOR, SFOR, KFOR, and their air and naval counterparts, Canada was once more part of an alliance in which Canadian interests could be more clearly articulated.[34]

Within the Coalition Warfare tradition reside the complementary traditions of Operational Influence and Saliency. The idea that Canadians should have a say in what the coalition or alliance leadership does with Canadian forces assigned to them relates to issues of sovereignty and national pride. Indeed, Operational Influence—the ability to determine what deployed Canadian forces can and cannot do—evolved dramatically over the course of the 1900s. It was a pre-condition for service during the Boer War for the contingent to retain its Canadian character and not have it submerged in the khaki masses.[35]

The main problem was that the unwritten rules of coalition warfare dictate that the primary supplier of forces in any endeavour gets to command and control it.[36] Mass, particularly in an era where infantry dominated the battlefield, ruled. Canada, given the relatively smaller size of its contingents, had to develop means by which her soldiers, sailors and airmen would not be misused wantonly by the more cavalier elements in London. Canadian suspicions of British manipulations emerged during the Boer War but came to fore during the

Top: Brigadier J. M. Rockingham briefs platoon and company commanders of 1 PPCLI on their arrival in Korea, 7 October 1951. (Photographer unknown. NA, PA-128875)

Bottom: CF-104 Starfighter. (DND file photo.)

First World War when the situation produced massed infantry gunned down in unprecedented numbers during that mechanistic slaughter. Should others decide the fates of Canada's sons? Sir Robert Borden noted that "It can be hardly expected that we shall put 400,000 or 500,000 men in the field and willingly accept the position of having no voice and receiving no more consideration than if we were toy automata."[37] The best tactic, used in South Africa and in France, was to keep all Canadian forces grouped together under a single Canadian commander in the field.

Indeed, this problem was not solved during the Second World War. Canadian contingents were deployed under British command at Hong Kong and Dieppe with tragic results. The Canadian commanders in each instance were unskilled at coalition warfare, as were the politicians (both in uniform and out) and they did not insist on adequate protection of Canadian interests related to their employment.[38] Similar problems emerged with the strategic bombing forces and other RCAF units operating under Royal Air Force command and with Royal Canadian Navy forces operating in the Atlantic and elsewhere.

Operational Influence was finally codified in Korea when 25 Canadian Infantry Brigade Group, led by Brigadier J.M. Rockingham, determined that his forces were not prepared for combat and insisted that they not be deployed until they were, despite pressure from Ottawa and American quarters. In the case of 27 Canadian Infantry Brigade Group in West Germany, a British corps commander attempted to force his will on Brigadier Geoffrey Walsh and have Canadians conduct riot control duty against Germans. This move was resisted by Walsh, who cited his terms of reference that indicated that 27 Brigade was not an occupation force.[39]

It was readily understood by the generation of Canadian generals, admirals, and air marshals who fought the Cold War that Second World War experiences relating to the misuse of Canadian forces would not be repeated in the NATO, NORAD, or UN contexts. In every coalition that Canadians were involved in, Canadian staff officers occupied primary staff positions of the integrated coalition headquarters that controlled Canadian formations attached to them. In this way Canadians could at least observe and report to Ottawa and in many cases influence coalition planning involving the use of Canadian forces in ways which were not possible during the Boer, First, or Second World Wars. Indeed, in the 1960s Canadian staff officers were part of the super-secret Joint Strategic Target Planning Staff an American body that decided which targets would be hit with nuclear weapons if nuclear war were unleashed. The Deputy Commander-in-Chief (CinC) NORAD, a Canadian officer, at one time even had the ability to release American nuclear weapons for air defence if CinC NORAD were indisposed, surely the highest level of Operational Influence possible.[40]

Operational Influence improved again during the Gulf War of 1990-91 when a joint force headquarters was formed to protect Canadian naval and air forces operating in the anti-Iraq coalition.[41] Throughout Canada's long involvement in the Stabilization Campaign, Canadians occupied Sector Commander and Deputy Force Commander positions during the UNPROFOR period and division-level command in SFOR (both in the Balkans) while Canadians even commanded UNAMIR in Rwanda in 1994 and the Multinational Humanitarian Force in Zaire in 1996. In most cases Canadian units were only permitted to conduct high-risk activity after a thorough analysis of the risks involved and their relative importance to Canadian objectives in the regions.[42]

Saliency is another Canadian strategic tradition. The problem of Operational Influence or the lack of it in wars fought as part of the British Empire had political overtones in Canada. During the First World War, for example, and then after Dieppe in the Second World War, perceptions grew that Canadian troops were being used as colonial "cannon fodder." Why should Canada participate in such enterprises? As Canada's global position improved throughout the twentieth century and more and more autonomy was obtained from the Empire, the problem grew more acute as Canadian political leaders sought to influence their larger partners in alliance in matters of military strategy and the allocation of resources, particularly Canada's resources.[43]

Early attempts were made during the Boer War and the First World War to keep Canadian units in Canadian formations under Canadian command. Though less successful in the early parts of the Second World War, Canadian army units were kept together at the corps level. The ability of the Canadian government during these conflicts to exert significant influence in matters of strategy was not great. The problem was two-fold. First, Canadian diplomacy was in it

Brigadier-General Romeo Dallaire and Argentinean Major Miguel Martin (UN desk officer in New York) in discussion with members of the OAU observer group and a rebel brigade commander (in camouflage jacket), Rwanda, August 1994. (DND file photo.)

infancy and therefore the means to apply leverage in the circles of Imperial power were limited.[44] Second, Canada was deploying forces that could be used for cannon fodder: that is, Canada was not contributing something unique. Everybody from the Empire was sending infantry, for example. Canada's diplomatic and military efforts had to be connected so that the Canadian position in alliances and coalitions could improve.

The Saliency solution emerged during the Cold War. Canada's diplomats were seasoned after the fight against the Fascist totalitarians and saw the dawn of a new age of Canadian influence. Canada's military personnel had suffered at the hands of their allied commanders. After some failings, particularly with 25 Brigade in Korea, the two groups co-ordinated their efforts within NATO. Canada was an equal in the alliance, not a subordinate. To keep this position, however, Canada had to contribute forces to deter the Communist totalitarians and prevent a Third World War. The Cold War economic situation and the smaller relative size of Canada vis-à-vis the allies dictated that Canada could not send masses of troops to serve in Europe continuously. Ultimately, Canada contributed very high quality and well equipped forces. 1 Air Division of the RCAF contributed twenty percent of NATO's front-line fighter strength in the 1950s and was equipped with Canadian-built Sabre aircraft. On the ground, 27 Canadian Infantry Brigade Group and its successors consisted of volunteers, not conscripts, and were equipped with the best tank in the world, the Centurion. At sea, the Royal Canadian Navy deployed state-of-the-art anti-submarine warfare destroyers, the *St Laurent* class. Eventually, Canadian forces acquired a nuclear capability disproportionate to their contributions in NATO when the CF-104 Starfighters equipped with megaton-yield nuclear weapons were deployed and when Canada contributed a division's worth of Honest John nuclear-tipped rockets even though the deployed formation was only a brigade group.[45]

It was not enough to build these forces and then turn them over to NATO. Canada's forces had specialized roles in NATO planning and Canada got those roles because she contributed something unique, something that other NATO nations with mass could not. Providing credible forces to the alliance permitted Operational Influence to flourish in the integrated headquarters. Canada's contributions were protected from misuse. Now the diplomats had cards to

General Maurice Baril, former CDS, during the ill-fated OP Assurance, Zaire. (DND file photo.)

lay on the table, which they did with alacrity, particularly when they wanted to influence NATO nuclear strategy in the 1950s and early 1960s. Canada had Saliency.[46]

Saliency was also in effect in UN peacekeeping operations conducted during the Cold War. In an ironic twist, Canadian officers often found themselves commanding former colonial units deployed under UN auspices, thus taking over the British role of colonial master in coalition operations. Canadian troop contributions in Egypt, Cyprus, the Congo and elsewhere were deliberately calculated so that Canadian officers held the key positions in UN field headquarters in order to prevent the misuse of Canadian troops by figurehead Third World UN commanders. Canada also used Operational Influence to garner Saliency in UN circles on many occasions, but with fewer profound and noticeable effects than in the NATO realm.[47]

The Canadian-American relationship also functioned with Saliency as a prime Canadian method. It would have been easy to turn over sovereignty to the United States in matters of continental defence, but this was politically unacceptable to an emergent post-colonial nation. Canada was able to stave off American domination by providing, for their time, technologically sophisticated air defence surveillance and Canadian designed and built CF-100 interceptors. After the demise of the CF-105 Avro Arrow project, Canada acquired CF-101B Voo Doo interceptors equipped with nuclear weapons and deployed BOMARC anti-bomber missiles and their associated SAGE computers. These contribution assured Canada the Deputy CinC NORAD position referred to earlier and, along with provision of the CF-104 nuclear strike force in Europe, positions within the highest possible level of American nuclear strategy, the Joint Strategic Target Planning Staff.[48]

Saliency, Operational Influence, and Coalition Warfare continued as the basis of Canadian military operations well into the Stabilization Campaign period. The links between the military and diplomatic systems that were established during the early Cold War decayed, however. A new generation of diplomats and politicized leaders in uniform did not understand the carefully constructed web and they caused immense damage to it. Operational Influence continued as a principle of Canadian operations in the Balkans, specifically in UNPROFOR on the ground and during SHARP GUARD at sea, but the linkage between Saliency and higher Canadian objectives was lost. The new generation of diplomats refused to understand its utility in their quest for a Nobel Prize and a resurgence of Trudeau-era wishful thinking.

The linkage was only partially regained during the operations in Kosovo. The Canadian contribution to KFOR was deliberately driven by Saliency and Operational Influence. The Coyote reconnaissance squadron possessed capabilities that no other NATO nation had in theatre or elsewhere. Canadian CF-18s flew a disproportionately high percentage of bombing operations during Operation ALLIED FORCE. The Griffon helicopter squadron deployed with KFOR conducted airmobile operations that no other NATO contingent was capable of or willing to try. Salient and credible military forces, therefore, remain a Canadian strategic tradition.[49]

Not all Canadian strategic traditions are good ones, however. Lack of preparedness in both the political and military realms is readily apparent during a crisis, as is the tendency toward ad hoc and sometimes inadequate responses. The lack of a proper standing army and a reliance on various forms of mobilization meant that Canada had to take time to generate effective contingents for the Boer War and the First World War. The methods that Sir Sam Hughes used in creating, equipping and deploying the 1st Canadian Division to England in 1914 were nothing short of deplorable.[50] Similarly the disasters at Dieppe and Hong Kong were the product of hasty mobilization, inexperience and poor staff training as much as outside meddling. Early Canadian naval operations in the Battle of the Atlantic also suffered from rapid expansion and poor training.[51]

The problems with forming 25 Brigade for Korea in 1950 were legion. The Mackenzie King government drew down Canada's forces too far in the wake of the Second World War and did not ensure that a mobilization capability was fully maintained. Thus, when Canada needed to send something to fight and contain Communist aggression, the entire force had to be raised off the street since the existing army was too small. In the case of 27 Brigade, mobilized militia units augmented by elements of the small regular force had to suffice until the whole army could be expanded in 1954.[52]

In the case of the forced withdrawal of the United Nations Emergency Force I from Sinai in 1967, years of rhetoric about developing an amphibious and airmobile capability that never came to pass produced a Dunkirk-like humiliation. The Canadian UN contingent had to leave its heavy equipment behind and destroy its vehicles as the men clambered aboard RCAF transports designed for tactical operations. All of this was in the face of mid-intensity mechanized and air operations.[53]

The plethora of operations conducted during the Stabilization Campaign produced numerous instances of ad hoc responses. The primary humiliations were Somalia (1993-94) and Zaire (1996). Canada's Somalia force underwent at least two changes in mandate while its heavy equipment was at sea and closing in on the area of operations. The airborne unit was converted overnight into a mechanized force and vehicles had to be flown in by American transports.[54]

Top: Canadian soldiers as part of SFOR in Dvar, Bosnia, 24 April 1998. (DND file photo.)

Bottom: Canadians soldiers as part of KFOR in Kosovo, 1999. (DND file photo.)

As for Operation Assurance in Zaire(called the "bungle in the jungle" by the troops), Canada was unable to field a functioning multinational headquarters in part due to inadequate strategic communications capability and in part due to a lack of Canadian strategic airlift.[55]

Canadian frugality is another strategic tradition that has been less than helpful. The primary example is strategic lift. This long-term problem dates back to the Boer War when a hired steamer had to be used for the deployment. In the case of Hong Kong in 1941, an American transport ship was used to move the contingent's heavy weapons, ammunition and vehicles. Responding to American national authority, the ship was diverted to the Philippines en route and the contingent had to face the Japanese onslaught without their stores of heavy weapons and ammunition.[56] During the UN Congo operation in 1960, the vehicles of the Canadian signal unit could not fit onto Canadian Northstar and Yukon aircraft. A request for American Globemasters had to be made. The situation repeated itself eighteen years later in 1988 when Canada's UNIImog signals contingent had to be transported to Iraq and Iran by Soviet Antonovs.[57]

Canada's ability to contribute the better part of a mechanized brigade to a NATO extraction force for UN troops in the former Yugoslavia in 1995 was constrained by the lack of strategic sealift and our reliance upon unsuitable Auxiliary Oiler Replenishment ships (such as *Ames Preserver*) which were incapable of over-the-beach operations. Then there was the fiasco of the GTS *Katie*, when a contractor refused to return ten percent of Canada's armoured vehicle fleet in the redeployment of Operation Kinetic forces from Kosovo in 1999. Canadian naval forces had to board the roll-on roll-off ship and seize it.

A definite Tao of conflict emerges when one surveys Canadian military history. We are a unique nation with unique strategic requirements. We have certain strategic traditions that are used, either consciously or unconsciously, in the formulation and application of Canadian national security policy. Accepting a chaos theory of national security may be fashionable in the morally relative age in which we live, but the fact remains there are long-standing elements that we can use as guides for the future. It is up to those engaged in the formulation of policy to accept and adopt them.

Notes for Chapter 13

1   Miyamoto Musashi, *The Martial Artist's Book of the Five Rings,* trans. Stephen F. Kaufman. (Boston: Charles E. Tuttle, 1994), 5, 83.

2   For the purposes of full disclosure, I should add that I am Canadian and a former student of Russell Weigley, the author of *The American Way of War.*

3   Department of National Defence, *Canada's Army: We Stand on Guard for Thee* (Ottawa: DND, 1998), 73.

4   For Korea, see Herbert Fairlie-Wood, *Strange Battleground: The Official History of the Canadian Army in Korea* (Ottawa: Queen's Printers, 1966), chapters 1 and 2; for the Gulf War see Jean Morin and Richard Gimblett, *Operation FRICTION, 1990-91* (Toronto: Dundurn, 1997); see also Douglas Bland, *Chiefs of Defence: Government and the Unified Command of the Canadian Armed Forces* (Toronto: CISS, 1995); Sean M. Maloney, "Dr. Strangelove Visits Canada: Projects RUSTIC, EASE, and BRIDGE," *Canadian Military History* Vol 6, No. 1 (Spring 1997), 42-56.

5   See John Prados, *Keepers of the Keys: A History of the National Security Council from Truman to Bush* (New York: William Morrow, 1991).

6   John Ralston Saul, *Voltaire's Bastards: The Dictatorship of Reason in the West* (New York: Vintage Books, 1992), 91-93.

7   See Stephen Harris, *Canadian Brass* (Toronto: University of Toronto Press, 1988).

8   See Sean M. Maloney, *An Identifiable Cult: The Evolution of Combat Development in the Canadian Army 1946-1965* (Kingston: DLSC Report 9905, August 1999); Sean M. Maloney, "Purple Dawn: From Mobile Command to J-Staff, 1975-1991," *The Army Doctrine and Training Bulletin* (Spring 2002).

9   Russell F. Weigley, *The American Way of War: A History of United States Military Strategy and Policy* (Bloomington: Indiana University Press, 1973), xix.

10 Erik H. Erikson's model is developed in *Childhood and Society* (New York: WW Norton, 1963) and *Young Man Luther: A Study in Psychoanalysis and History* (New York: WW Norton, 1958).

11 My remarks should by no means deter anyone from reading Paul Roazen's *Canada's King: An Essay in Political Psychology* (Oakville: Mosaic Press, 1998).

12 As quoted in Roazen.

13 Sean M. Maloney, "Canadian Values and National Security Policy: Who Decides?" *Policy Options* (Fall 2001).

14 See Julian S. Corbett, *Some Principles of Maritime Strategy* (Annapolis: Naval Institute Press, 1911) which was the culmination of drawing lessons from British naval and maritime history.

15 Some short-sighted people argue that tradition is not important. Such a view contributes to the fragmentation of an already insecure Canadian culture. For an example see Janice Stein, "Policy is Messy Because the World is Messy. Get Used to It," *Policy Options,* Vol 22, No. 01 (Jan-Feb 2001), 73-78.

16 This list is adapted from an earlier study conducted by the author that was subsequently edited for publication. See Sean M. Maloney, "Helpful Fixer or Hired Gun: Why Canada Goes Overseas," *Policy Options,* Vol 22, No. 01 (Jan-Feb 2001), 59-65. See the IRPP website for the full version.

17 George Stanley, *Canada's Soldiers: The Military History of an Unmilitary People* (Toronto: Macmillan, 1970), 223-226.

18 See Bob Beal and Rod Macleod, *Prairie Fire: The 1885 North-West Rebellion* (Edmonton: Hurtig, 1984).

19 Roger Sarty, *The Maritime Defence of Canada* (Toronto: CISS, 1996), Chapter 1; C.P. Stacey, *Canada and the Age of Conflict, Volume 1: 1867-1921* (Toronto: University of Toronto Press, 1984), Chapters 1 and 2.

20 Sarty, *The Maritime Defence of Canada,* Chapter 1.

21 See Brereton Greenhous, ed., *Guarding the Goldfields: The Story of the Yukon Field Force* (Toronto: Dundurn Press, 1987); and Brereton Greenhous and W.J. McAndrew, "The Canadian Army Marches North: The Yukon Field Force 1898-1900," *Canadian Defence Quarterly,* Vol 10, No. 4 (Spring 1981), 30-41.

22 Thomas Friedman, *The Lexus and the Olive Tree: Understanding Globalization* (New York: Farrar, Strauss Giroux, 1999), xiii-xv.

23 Carman Miller, *Painting the Map Red: Canada and the South African War 1899-1902* (Kingston: McGill-Queen's University Press, 1993), Chapters 1 and 2; Norman Penlington, *Canada and Imperialism 1896-1899* (Toronto: University of Toronto Press, 1965), Chapters 1 and 14; Donald C. Gordon, *The Dominion Partnership in Imperial Defense, 1870-1914* (Baltimore: Johns Hopkins Press, 1965), Chapters 4 and 8; Thomas Packenham, *The Boer War* (New York: Avon Books, 1979), 260.

24 Stacey, *Age of Conflict Vol 1,* chapters 4, 6 and 7.

25 John Swettenham, *Allied Intervention in Russia 1918-1919* (Toronto: The Ryerson Press, 1967), Chapter 1; Serge Durflinger, "In Whose Interests? The Royal Canadian Navy and Naval Diplomacy in El Salvador, 1932" and Sean M. Maloney, "Maple Leaf over the Caribbean: Gunboat Diplomacy Canadian-Style?" in Griffiths et al, *Canadian Gunboat Diplomacy: The Canadian Navy and Foreign Policy* (Halifax: Dalhousie University Press, 1998).

26 C.P. Stacey, *Canada and the Age of Conflict, Volume 2: 1921-1948, The Mackenzie King Era* (Toronto: University of Toronto Press, 1981), Chapter 7.

27 Brereton Greenhous, *"C" Force to Hong Kong: A Canadian Catastrophe 1941-1945* (Toronto: Dundurn, 1997), Chapter 1.

28 See Sean M. Maloney, *War Without Battles: Canada's NATO Brigade in Germany. 1951-1993* (Toronto: McGraw-Hill Ryerson, 1997); and Sean M. Maloney, *Canada and UN Peacekeeping: Cold War by Other Means, 1945-1970* (St. Catharines: Vanwell, 2002).

29 See Maloney, "Helpful Fixer or Hired Gun?"

30 Penlington, *Canada and Imperialism,* Chapters 1 and 2.

31 See C.P. Stacey, *Age of Conflict,* Volumes 1 and 2.

32 Maloney, *Canada and UN Peacekeeping* and Sean M. Maloney, *Learning to Love The Bomb: Canada's Cold War Strategy and Nuclear Weapons, 1951-1968* (forthcoming).

33 Sean M. Maloney, "Never Say Never: Non-Alliance Operations in the Canadian Context," *The Army Doctrine and Training Bulletin,* Vol 2, No. 2 (May 1999), 29-34.

34 See Maloney, "Helpful Fixer or Hired Gun?"

35 Miller, *Painting the Map Red,* 49-51.

36 Sean M. Maloney, *Securing Command of the Sea: NATO Naval Planning, 1948-1954* (Annapolis: Naval Institute Press, 1995), Chapter 1.

37 Stacey, *Age of Conflict Volume 1,* 192.

38 Greenhous, *"C" Force to Hong Kong,* chapter 1; and Brian Loring Villa, *Unauthorized Action: Mountbatten and the Dieppe Raid* (Toronto: Oxford University Press, 1989).

39 Fairlie-Wood, *Strange Battleground,* 40-41; Maloney, *War Without Battles,* 28-29.

40 See Maloney, *Securing Command of the Sea, War Without Battles, Canada and UN Peacekeeping* and *Learning to Love the Bomb* for many specific examples.

41 See Gimblett and Morin, *Operation FRICTION,* chapter 5; Edward J. Marolda and Robert J. Schneller Jr., *Shield and Sword: The United States Navy and the Persian Gulf War* (Washington: Naval Historical Center, 1998), 128-129.

42 There were some occasions where these things were hotly debated by the British and Canadian commanders on the ground, particularly during one dangerous operation in Bosnia in 1994. See Sean M. Maloney and John Llambias, *Chances for Peace: Canadian Soldiers and UNPROFOR, 1992-1995* (St. Catharines: Vanwell, 2002) and briefings provided to the author at TFBH and MND(SW) Headquarters, SFOR, in May 2001.

43 C.P. Stacey, *Age of Conflict, Volume 1,* chapter 8.

44 For the best discussion of these fledgling efforts, see John Hilliker, *Canada's Department of External Affairs Volume 1: The Early Years, 1909-1946* (Kingston: McGill-Queen's University Press, 1990).

45 See Maloney, *Learning to Love the Bomb,* for a full exposition of these matters.

46 Ibid.

47 See Maloney, *Canada and UN Peacekeeping* and Sean M. Maloney, "Mad Jimmy Dextraze: The Tightrope of UN Command in the Congo," in Bernd Horn and Stephen Harris, *Warrior Chiefs: Perspectives on Senior Canadian Military Leaders* (Toronto: Dundurn, 2001), 303-320.

48 Maloney, *Learning to Love The Bomb.*

49 Sean M. Maloney and Scot Robertson, "The Revolution in Military Affairs: Possible Implications for Canada," *International Journal,* Summer 1999, 443-462.

50 Ronald G. Haycock, *Sam Hughes: The Public Career of a Controversial Canadian, 1885-1916* (Ottawa: Wilfrid Laurier Press, 1986), chapters 11, 12 and 13.

51 See Marc Milner, *North Atlantic Run: The Royal Canadian Navy and the Battle for the Convoys* (Toronto: University of Toronto Press, 1985).

52 Fairlie-Wood, *Strange Battleground,* chapters 1 and 2; Maloney, *War Without Battles,* chapter 1.

53 Maloney, *Canada and UN Peacekeeping,* chapter 8.

54 Charles S. Oliviero, "Operation DELIVERANCE: international Success or Domestic Failure?" *Canadian Military Journal,* Vol 2, No. 2 (Summer 2001), 51-58.

55 Michael A. Hennessy, "Operation ASSURANCE: Planning a Multi-national Force for Rwanda-Zaire," *Canadian Military Journal,* Vol 2, No. 1 (Spring 2001), 11-20.

56 C.P. Stacey, *Six Years of War: The Army in Canada, Britain, and the Pacific* (Ottawa: Queen's Printer, 1955), 449.

57 Maloney, "Purple Dawn: From Mobile Command to J-Staff,

HMCS *Shearwater* and HMCS *Rainbow* in Esquimalt, 1910. (Photographer unknown. NA, PA-29755.)

CHAPTER 14

Geography and History

The Six Fathom Line of Canadian Naval Policy

Lieutenant-Commander Gregg Hannah

Merely to face upon the oceans is not, ipso facto, to have maritime power, but only presents an opportunity. The test is what is done with it.
— Paul H. Nitze[1]

W.A.B. DOUGLAS in his article "Why does Canada have armed forces?" implies that the real question in Canadian defence policy is not what the roles and missions of Canada's armed forces should be, but rather what the fundamental reasons are for Canada having any armed forces at all.[2] Typically, Canadians have a remarkably unmilitary attitude and it shapes responses to this fundamental question. According to the renowned Canadian military historian C.P. Stacey, "Canada is an unmilitary community. Warlike her people have often been forced to be; military they have never been."[3] Fellow historian Desmond Morton points out that Canadians have not arrived at these unmilitary attitudes by "innocent illusion" or by accident, but rather "through the weight of historical experience," and that "unless this experience is understood, neither would-be defenders nor disarmers will ever understand the Canadian response to their respective programmes."[4]

Historians, observes W.A.B. Douglas, can "assist … in building policies on the rocks of fact rather than the sands of myth."[5] Sadly, however, Douglas also points out that "the people who matter in military policy-making often believe that the past simply does not apply and the questions that scholars ask tend to be ignored by men of action who demand quick solutions."[6] Therefore, failure to understand the historical determinants that create preferences for defence policy choices can only lead to frustration and unrealistic expectations. This is particularly pronounced for naval matters. The record of the treatment of the Canadian navy to date—nearly stillborn, abandoned and starved immediately after its creation, scorned for its lack of accomplishments in the Great War, threatened with extinction several times from 1918 to 1939, and reduced to neglected obsolescence during the 1970s—bears ample witness to this observation.

Notwithstanding, the starting point for all discussion of strategy is geography.[7] The basic realities of a country's physical geography are fundamental and unavoidable. Therefore, "geography always matters for strategic experience."[8] However, as much as geography is a distinct element of strategy in itself, it also helps shape strategy in every dimension; it is a truly pervasive factor.[9] Culture is another important and pervasive aspect of strategy. Colin Gray usefully defines "culture" as "the persisting socially transmitted ideas, attitudes, traditions, habit of mind and preferred methods of operations that are more or less specific to a particular geographic security community that has had a unique historical experience."[10]

There is, therefore, a direct linkage between geographical circumstances, historical experience, and cutlural attitudes.[11] The link is clearly evident in Desmond Morton's assessment that Canada is at once indefensible and invulnerable.[12] His assessment reflects geographical reality as well as a habit of mind born of historical experience. Canada is too remote and difficult to attack (and protected by powerful friends) and hence immune from direct assault. But should anyone actually decide to attack Canada, the size of the population, their available resources, and the extent of the landmass preclude any measure of effective defence, at least by Canadians alone.

The geographic feature implicit in Morton's assessment of Canadian invulnerability is the sea. C.P. Stacy attributes the characteristic Canadian unmilitary attitude in great part "to the happy accident of a … geographical situation that placed formidable barriers in the shape of ocean spaces … between Canada and potential aggressors."[13] Stacey sees no need to belabour the point nor a need to "account fully for the country's military outlook."[14] Is it sufficient, however, to attribute Canadian unmilitary attitudes simply to a vision of the sea as a barrier—an ultimate protection from attack?

There is no doubt that the sea figures prominently in Canadian history. Canada, says William Wood, "like other countries, may be looked at from many points of view but there is none that does not somehow include her oceans, lakes or rivers."[15] After all:

> Canada is the child of the sea. Her infancy was cradled by her waterways; and her
> lifeblood of her youth was drawn from the oceans, lakes and rivers. No other land
> of equal area has ever been so intimately bound up with the changing fortunes of
> all its different waters, coast and inland, salt and fresh.[16]

Entering the twenty-first century, Canada borders on three oceans, is one of only three countries in the world to do so, and all but two of her provinces or territories touch salt water. She borders only one other country by land. Canada is, therefore, both separated from and connected to the rest of the world by the oceans. This close connection with the sea is reflected in Canada's proudly proclaimed national motto *A Mari Usque Ad Mare*—From Sea to Sea. The oceans are a significant geographical feature of the Canadian imagination.

Naval strategist Alfred Thayer Mahan postulated that there were six principle conditions that affected the development of a nation's sea power.[17] Canada appears to enjoy the considerable advantages of at least two: Geographical Position and Physical Conformation.[18] As Mahan observed, however, the significance of oceans to a country is greater than simply having them wash the maritime boundaries. "The sea board of a country," he stated, "is one of its frontiers; and the easier the access offered by the frontier to the region beyond, in this case the sea, the greater will be the tendency of a people toward intercourse with the rest of the world by it."[19]

This is true of Canada where the oceans and the waterways connected to them penetrate to the interior of the country. They were the economic highways to the heart of the continent long before Europeans came, remained the great highways from Cartier to Confederation and continued to be vitally important despite the technological changes experienced from the late nineteenth century onward. The economic wealth of the oceans within Canada's jurisdiction has always been considerable and continues to grow. At the beginning of the twenty-first century more than one third of Canada's economy is based on international trade and much of it moves by sea to all parts of the globe.[20] Depending upon the criteria used, between twenty-five and forty percent of Canadians live in and/or work in coastal areas.[21] Clearly, "Canada's prosperity, security, and autonomy are largely defined by its ocean dimensions."[22] Given all of this, it seems reasonable to believe that Canadians would, as Canadian naval historian Gilbert Tucker suggests, view the sea "not as a barrier but a highway"[23] and have a significant interest in maritime and naval matters. From this it should follow that development of a navy would be important to the nation. However, few Canadians would "describe Canada as a great maritime state much less a sea power in the traditional sense."[24] Despite the obvious importance of the sea to Canada, "there has never been a strong national interest in developing more than token maritime forces."[25]

Canada's naval strategy, Nicholas Tracy argues, "is firmly rooted in experience dating back to the beginning of the century and beyond."[26] This experience shows that navies and sea power have always played an important part in the history of Canada.[27] The ability of the Royal Navy to maintain an unchallenged control of the St. Lawrence River, the Gulf of St. Lawrence and the Atlantic ocean contributed directly to the capture of Quebec and the fall of New France. Additionally, during the Seven Years' War, the American War of Independence, and the War of 1812, "naval operations of considerable importance were conducted on the interior lakes."[28] Nevertheless, "Canadian history is full of sea-power but Canadian histories are not."[29]

This should not be surprising because, as Ronald Haycock notes in *Teaching Military History: Cleo and Mars in Canada*, "up until the Second World War there was simply not much written on Canadian military history."[30] Writing in 1952 in the preface to the first official history of the navy, Gilbert Norman Tucker observed that "Naval history in the Canadian setting has hitherto received little attention from historians."[31] After the Second World War scholarship in Canadian military history increased significantly.[32] However, naval history continued to receive little serious scholarly attention.[33] A bibliography produced by W. A. B. Douglas revealed that in the 74 years prior to 1984 there were five volumes of official history of the Royal Canadian Navy, half a dozen theses on the history of the RCN, and several articles and a handful of additional books on Canadian naval history.[34]

But the seventy-fifth anniversary in 1985 of the founding of the RCN sparked a wide interest in Canadian naval history. As a result, the number of dedicated Canadian naval scholars has grown tremendously. Marc Milner observed in 1999 that "publications on Canadian naval history have mushroomed during the last two decades."[35] In recent general works of Canadian military history, however, naval topics still tend to be overshadowed by land-oriented ones.[36]

Mahan's analysis of the geographical elements of sea power offers some insight into why this is so. Mahan believed that "as regards the development of sea power, it is not the total number of square miles which a country contains but the length of its coast line and the character of it harbours that are to be considered."[37] Although Canada's seacoast is long, much of it, particularly on the Arctic Ocean, must be considered unsuitable or unusable for what Mahan terms "the tendency to trade."[38] This tendency to trade, he claims, is the "national characteristic most important to the development of sea power."[39] Although Canada has a large tendency to trade, the trade by sea is concentrated in a handful of ports on either coast and along the St. Lawrence River and in the Great Lakes.[40] Moreover, "the amount of overseas trade by Canadian registered ships is negligible" and what little Canadian owned shipping exists is almost exclusively engaged in trade with the United States across the Great Lakes.[41]

Mahan also insisted that "the extent of sea coast is a source of strength or weakness according as the population is larger or smaller."[42] Therefore, population size and distribution must also be taken into account. The size of the Canadian population relative to the landmass has always been small. Population that was once primarily concentrated in the coastal and waterway areas is now more dispersed farther inland and farther west. At the start of the twenty-first century eighty percent of the Canadian population lives in a long thin band about a hundred miles wide running along the southern border.[43] Therefore, far more Canadians live in proximity to the United States than the sea. Mahan held that "great shipping afloat" employs a large number of people in not only the crews of the vessels but in shipbuilding and other marine industries.[44] How many Canadians are actually involved in these? Census data from 1996 reveals that only about one half of one percent of the Canadian labour force is engaged in work related to marine activity.[45]

Although geography indicates that Canada is a maritime nation, there are also geographical factors that limit the development of Canadian maritime and naval interests. The statistical fact that a significant number of Canadians are in close proximity to the sea is overshadowed by the reality that as many or more Canadians are in fact a long way from the sea and few are actually engaged in occupations related to it. As a result, few Canadians have a first hand knowledge or experience of the sea and its impact on Canada. Thus, "although Canada was and remains a trading nation, and most of its imports and exports go by ship, the vast majority of Canadians have no contact whatsoever with the sea that girds their nation on three sides."[46] The majority of Canadians, then, are engaged in pursuits where wealth is generated by means other than the sea. As Mahan clearly shows, "where wealth is sought by other means it may be found; but it will not necessarily lead to sea power."[47] Mahan would argue that Canadian exposure to any significant maritime influence is too limited to permit the development of a strong interest in maritime or naval matters.

Simply put, "Canada is indeed a maritime nation, but not everyone understands this."[48] And as another naval historian sadly observed, "because of the nature of the country, few Canadians ever see the sea and, therefore, few see their navy or know much about it."[49] Thus, it seems that geography alone is sufficient to explain the Canadian lack of concern for maritime and naval matters. Stacey's claim that geography accounts for the Canadian unmilitary attitude—extended to combat at sea—would seem to be validated.

Nevertheless, there are still problems with accepting geography as the sole factor responsible for these unmilitary attitudes. As Colin Gray has shown, attitudes toward policy and strategy change only slowly. The obvious importance of navies and the sea in the past and its obvious continuing relevance to Canada cannot easily be squared with the current lack of Canadian interest in maritime and naval matters. The conditions described above which appear to have created and now sustain the current disinterest are relatively recent phenomena. Therefore, other factors must have influenced the development of an outlook that downplays maritime and naval matters.

The struggle for dominance of the North American continent was centered on the land campaigns to control strategic areas. Navies and merchant fleets transported the troops and the supplies necessary for these campaigns and prevented the enemy from doing the same. For more than two hundred years, Canadians lived in a state of real or expected war with invaders from the south – Iroquois, British, or Americans.[50] The naval operations that supported or generated these land threats were generally invisible to the inhabitants. Therefore, "the sea and all naval matters probably seemed largely irrelevant" to their immediate defence problems.[51] Thus, it can be seen that a habit of mind developed which discounted or downplayed the need for naval forces. Navies were seen by colonial inhabitants, at best, as enabling agents most often and best provided by someone else.

The predisposition toward discounting the need for naval forces was reinforced, for Canadians by the dominance established by the Royal Navy in the period following the end of the Seven Years' War in 1763. By 1815, the RN was undisputed mistress of the seas and *Pax Britannica* was fact. The effect of this was to "put an end to the struggle of European nations to control Canada" and remove from Canadian considerations the spectre of any credible overseas threat.[52] The chief instrument of Imperial defence became the Royal Navy[53] because "for almost the whole of the British Empire sea power was more vital than defence by land ... a decisive naval defeat ... would have enabled the enemy to attack with overwhelming land forces almost any part of the overseas Empire ... or to invade and conquer, or blockade and starve, the British Isles themselves."[54]

Because of the nature of maritime warfare the Royal Navy on its normal stations was, throughout the nineteenth century, in a position to cover Canadian coasts and trade routes.[55] It was rightly held to provide protection against any possible overseas enemies, for it guarded "Canada against hostile power projection, and the economic effects of hostile naval action against maritime trade and the exploitation of maritime resources."[56] Canadian maritime interests received this protection because the Canadas were British colonies and represented part of the all inclusive British Imperial interests of the period, not because Canadian interests were important in their own right.

After Confederation "the inclusive imperial responsibility of the Royal Navy were not regarded as having been circumscribed."[57] Confederation only conferred Canadian autonomy in local affairs. Great Britain continued to exercise full authority in foreign policy and Canada had no right to independent action and Canada had no authority to act autonomously outside her three-mile territorial limit. Therefore, from about 1815 until around 1900, Canadians had a sense that there were no maritime threats to their shores that would not and could not be dealt with effectively by the Royal Navy on their behalf.

After the American Revolutionary War, Canadians saw themselves threatened by the new republic to the south. With no enemy to worry about from seaward because of the Royal Navy's supremacy, local defence of British North America meant defence against the United States.[58] Although Britain provided regular troops for security, colonists were expected to shoulder some of the burden of defence. This took the form of volunteer militias, which saw service in the War of 1812 and the 1837 Rebellions. From these actions the perceived martial prowess of volunteers developed into the "militia myth" that argued that the militia, not regular forces, were the mainstay of the nation's defence.

After Confederation, the relationship with the United States continued to dominate Canadian defence considerations. The 1817 Rush-Bagot agreement resulting from the War of 1812 effectively eliminated the possibility of future naval confrontation on the Great Lakes, but not the possibility of land intervention.[59] But the war clearly demonstrated American willingness to take hostile action against British North America. This willingness was again demonstrated at the conclusion of the American Civil War in 1865. The Union's lingering resentment over British support of the Confederacy was expressed in a desire to seek redress through actions against the Canadas.[60] The apparent American willingness to do so and the availability of an army of about one million battle-hardened Union soldiers made it evident to Canadians that "there could be no successful rematch of the War of 1812."[61]

Both before and after Confederation, the relationship between Canada and the United States saw numerous disputes over various issues. The War of 1812 and the after-affects of the American Civil War provided a clear focus for the organization and prioritization of Canadian defence efforts. Additionally, friction between Britain and the United States, such as the Venezuela border dispute of 1895, continued to demonstrate that Canada could be caught in the middle and her security threatened.[62] Canadian governments also recognized that the American concept of Manifest Destiny expressed an interest in continental expansion to the north and west into Canadian territory. The Red River Rebellion in 1870 and, more seriously, the Northwest Rebellion in 1885 demonstrated an inability of the Canadian government to maintain stability and exercise effective control in these areas. The Americans could potentially respond by annexing the territories to provide stability and order. The Canadian government, therefore, saw that establishing "law and order in the Northwest would rob Americans of their most legitimate excuse to annex 'the Great Lone Land'."[63]

As a result, throughout the nineteenth century the uneasy relationship with the United States kept Canadian defence efforts firmly focused on continental defence. Most of these issues involved the protection of territory and, therefore, required land forces. Typically, apart from the military response to the Northwest Rebellion, Canada chose to react to these matters with minimum force. The creation of the paramilitary North West Mounted Police and its deployment to the west to establish and maintain national sovereignty illustrates this trend. The use of paramilitary forces in this fashion reinforced the belief that military forces were relevant only in extreme circumstances, and even then the militia could be called upon to deal with the situation. Thus, for Canadians, the tradition developed that "being 'military' implies a cast of mind unnecessary in a country whose myth of war emphasizes volunteerism and the prowess of amateurs."[64]

In sum, the focus was on the land defence of Canada against American aggression. However, as great a threat as aggressive American power projection was, there was also a threat posed by American economic interests to Canadian offshore resources.[65] While the Royal Navy was nominally charged with protection of Canadian maritime interests, quite often local events fell below their response threshold and "provincial marines had grown by necessity for local defence and to do all the chores the RN would not do. For years after the War of 1812 colonial governments chartered private vessels for essentials, from controlling smuggling to servicing lighthouses. Protecting the fisheries was a special problem."[66]

Convoy in the Bedford Basin, Halifax, April 1942. (Photographer unknown. NA, PA-112993)

In 1870, as a response to continued American fishing violations, the fledgling Canadian government acquired a small fleet of armed schooners and established a Marine Police. British policy in the latter half of the nineteenth century however was to avoid escalation of any issues that could lead to conflict with the United States; in many cases Canadian local interests were sacrificed to British Imperial interests. One such bitter disappointment with a significant maritime impact was the Treaty of Washington of 1871. The treaty contained fisheries provisions that resulted in the Canadian government's agreement to disband the new Marine Police. In 1885, however, the United States unilaterally abrogated the treaty's fisheries provisions and "Martimers watched angrily as the Royal Navy swung at anchor" and did nothing.[67] Canada acted. In 1886 the Fisheries Protection Service was created and armed vessels, in fact light cruisers, were acquired for patrol duties. When talks with the United States finally broke down in 1888 the Fisheries Protection Service became a permanent feature on the East Coast. The creation of such a national quasi-naval force was necessary at the time to "address the general problems of Canadian-American relations and to support Canadian jurisdiction in coastal waters."[68] Clearly it fit into the pattern of local continental defence and not that of Imperial defence.

Canadian attitudes toward defence developed in a two tiered concept of local and Imperial (or perhaps now better termed "forward") defence. Local defence was intimately tied to defence against threats from within the continent itself; it was inward looking. Local defence, therefore, has almost exclusively been land oriented and thus army-centric. Canadians, by weight of historical experience, were content to respond to such problems that arose with voluntary and part-time militia forces. The American impingement on local Canadian maritime interests, particularly the fisheries, also caused local maritime defence to become associated with this pattern. The voluntary or temporary nature of these efforts is reflected in the establishment of limited purpose provincial marines prior to Confederation and the provision for a marine militia in the Militia Act of 1868. That the Fisheries Protection Service became permanent can be attributed more to a recognition of the long term and continuing challenge to very specific Canadian economic interests rather than the need to provide for any broad Canadian maritime defence. In this way the creation of the Fisheries Protection Service can be seen as similar to the creation of the North West Mounted Police.

Imperial defence until the beginning of the twentieth century was almost exclusively maritime, outward looking and beyond the purview of Canadians. While Canadians, if somewhat

Top: A Consolidated Liberator G.R. V aircraft escorting a trans-Atlantic convoy, ca 1943. (Photographer unknown. NA, PA-107907)

Bottom: HMCS *Swansea* in rough seas, January 1944. (Photographer G.A. Milne. NA, PA-107941)

reluctantly, accepted the burdens of local defence, for a great part of their history they were not asked nor expected to shoulder burdens of Imperial maritime defence. After Confederation Canada was not "officially considered to be under any obligation to share in the support of the [Royal Navy]."[69] Nevertheless Canada enjoyed the benefits of the protection British warships provided and Canadians came to expect continued protection as a right of their membership in the Empire. At Imperial defence conferences through the last decades of the nineteenth century Canada often claimed that she met her share of the cost of the Royal Navy through efforts to open up and exploit the interior of the country. The building of the Canadian Pacific Railway was often cited as a significant outlay that improved Imperial security by making possible the rapid and secure movement of men and materials across the continent possible.[70] Thus, while Canadians were encouraged to see the need for local defence effort, and generally did, they were neither pressed, nor were many inclined to become involved in the defence of the Empire as a whole.

From the 1860s onward, however, it became increasingly clear that Britain could not, and would not, continue to provide complete Imperial defence on her own. Because of the overwhelming importance of maritime power to Britain and the sheer dominance of the Royal Navy the maritime effects of this policy were not felt or appreciated by Canada until very nearly the end of the nineteenth century. It was also becoming evident that British conduct of Imperial foreign and defence policy often sacrificed Canadian interests in favour of British ones.[71] Therefore, by the end of the Victorian era Canada was beginning to recognize a need to assert more independence from Great Britain.

The search for greater Canadian independence necessitated a shift in the long-standing balance between local and Imperial defence. Greater independence would mean a greater Canadian effort in areas that had hitherto been the exclusive responsibility of Imperial authorities. This effort could be made either entirely independently or within the Imperial system, and so two schools of opinion developed in the country. One school held that it was Canada's duty and obligation to provide support to Imperial defence and that this would be the price of gaining greater recognition and independence. The other pole held that participating in Imperial defence would draw Canada into British foreign adventures in which it had no business or national interest and thus participation would only serve to make Canada more subservient to Britain. In particular, many influential Québecois were concerned that Canada would pay in both blood and treasure by resorting to conscription to support British adventurism.

Over the last decades of the nineteenth century agreements were reached between Canada and Britain which saw Canada adopt Imperial standards of doctrine, equipment and training for its land forces. This was relatively easy to do and imposed no significant cost or obligation on the Canadian government. It reflected a continuing emphasis on the existing land oriented posture of defence thinking. Land contributions to Imperial defence were relatively easy for the government to control. The Canadian government could always choose the type, size and timing of any contribution. The requisite forces could remain primarily voluntary and always be available for call-up for local defence if required.

Naval contributions to the Empire, however, were another matter. Because of the nature of naval warfare of the period, forces-in-being were necessary and they had to be under the central control of the Admiralty. Thus, once naval forces were committed to Imperial defence the Canadian government would not have any control over their employment. As such, Canada could find itself obliged to become engaged in a conflict in which it had no interest. Additionally, Imperial naval units would not necessarily be available to provide local defence if the need arose. The assurance that the Royal Navy would ensure the security of the Empire as a whole could not easily be reconciled with the fact that Americans poached fish in Canadian waters with no recourse available to the Canadian government.

Canadian attitudes toward local and Imperial defence were already firmly established when in the late 1880s the debates began on Imperial defence and the Anglo-German naval arms race that preceded the Great War. The Boer War indicated a certain willingness on the part of Canada to participate in Imperial defence. Canada's contribution capitalized on the strengths of existing local defence and further served to reinforce the tradition of land campaigns fought by volunteers. But the Boer War also indicated that opinion was becoming polarized and it presaged the depth of feeling that would animate the debates to create a Canadian navy.

At the outset of the twentieth century, despite the threat of an ascendant, powerful German navy, "Canada was virtually immune to the threat of direct German power projection."[72] The threat to the security of Britain and the Empire and the challenge to the dominance of the Royal Navy, however, were real and they posed a very real danger to Canada's economic well-being by threatening her maritime trade. How Canada could best contribute to mitigating this threat while maintaining sovereignty in her own coastal areas was a delicate political as well as a naval problem.

Eventually, the Admiralty conceded that a fleet could be built which would be based in and operate in Canadian waters under Canadian control during peacetime but which could be turned over to the control of the Admiralty for operations during war.[73] While the direct cause of the establishment of the Royal Canadian Navy in 1910 was the perceived German threat, it was also as much to strengthen the "capacity of Ottawa to control Canada's waters and to define Canada's relationship with the United States."[74] Nevertheless, the debate over the establishment of a Canadian navy was arguably the most divisive political event since Confederation. The opinions illustrate the ambiguity and uncertainty surrounding naval policy that was born of the well established concepts of local and Imperial defence.[75] One body of opinion held that it was unnecessary for Canada to take any measures at all for naval defence. The belief was that Canada only required local land defence and that the Royal Navy would continue to protect Canadian maritime interests free of charge. A second body of opinion held that the naval defence of Canada would be best achieved by close co-operation with the Empire and participation in Imperial naval activity. This represented a recognition of the larger maritime aspect of Canada's position that historically had never been present. A third body of opinion held that to participate directly in Imperial naval activity would result in an undesirable subordination of Canadian interests. Naval policy, it was argued, should pursue a purely Canadian navy under the control of the Canadian government for the direct defence of the country. This opinion represents a continuation of the long established realization that local defence extended into the maritime sphere.

While the proposed new Canadian navy would operate in Canadian waters, it was clearly designed as a unit that could be integrated into the Imperial fleet. The emotions this raised were so strong that "Canada's infant navy was almost destroyed at birth because to some critics, it made Canada subservient to Britain."[76] The political wrangling over the *raison d'être of* the Royal Canadian Navy and the proper response to Imperial naval defence caused the election defeat of the Liberals under Laurier and the return of Conservative government under Robert Borden. Borden's initial opposition to the creation of a navy as well as severe pressure from party factions ensured that the Naval Service Act was never fully implemented. Borden

Destroyers of the Royal Canadian Navy serving with the United Nations in Korea. (L to R) HMCS ships *Athabaskan*, *Cayuga*, and *Sioux*, Hong Kong, 20 November 1950.

cancelled the contract for the building of the ships and instead attempted to contribute money for the construction of Royal Navy battleships. He encountered great opposition and was forced to abandon this approach. Canada took possession of the two training ships, HMCS *Niobe* and *Rainbow* but funding was severely cut and training restricted to such a degree that at the outbreak of the First World War, Canada had a navy only on paper.

The concept of naval warfare as the conflict began had been developed during the period of the Royal Navy's dominance and had been articulated in 1890 by Alfred Thayer Mahan in his seminal work *The Influence of Sea Power Upon History 1660-1783*. Although naval technology had changed dramatically by the end of the nineteenth century, the doctrine of naval warfare remained basically the same as that practiced at the time of the Battle of Trafalgar in 1805. The theory was centered on the idea of decisive battle wherein battle fleets would close with and engage each other with guns. It was through superior firepower and the ability to withstand an opponent's punishment that one side would see the capital ships of the other battered into submission and a decisive victory achieved, assuring the winners command of the sea for their own purposes. This was the doctrinal framework around which the Royal Navy was organized; the heart of the fleet, therefore, was the battleship. The Canadian navy as originally proposed but not then acquired would have fit into this battle fleet concept. The two old cruisers Canada did possess at the outbreak of the war could merely play a marginal role in operations to protect British shipping from German armed merchant cruisers. They could also assist with the disruption of German trade. They could not contribute to battle fleet operations.

It was genuinely believed that the war would be short. Although the German Navy was clearly powerful, there was complete confidence that the Royal Navy would prevail and win the decisive naval battle when it finally came. Therefore, when the Prime Minister of Canada asked the Canadian High Commissioner in London to determine from the Admiralty what course it would advise if Canada were to offer naval aid, the response was not surprising. The Admiralty felt ships would take too long too build; Canada should, therefore, concentrate on the army.[77] This advice was consistent with the well established Canadian focus on volunteer troops committed to the defence of Canada's border. Canada therefore busied itself with an army expeditionary force.

The war, of course, was not short at all. The stalemate that quickly evolved into trench warfare demanded massive numbers of men. The requirement to provide substantial numbers of Canadian reinforcements came before there was any significant change in the need for naval

Canadian Patrol Frigate replenishing at sea. (DND file photo.)

forces. Therefore, the primary Canadian contribution to the war effort became the Canadian Corps. The absolute horror of trench warfare and the sheer number of Canadians it involved focussed the attention of Canadians on the army. Indeed the efforts of the Canadian Corps in Europe provided an important lever to Canadian politicians demanding and receiving greater Canadian independence after the war.

On the oceans, the decisive battle never occurred. Instead, a new dimension of naval warfare appeared in 1917—unrestricted submarine warfare. Aimed at starving Britain into submission, submarine warfare was brought directly to the East Coast of Canada in the spring of 1918 when several long range German U-boats made successful patrols off the coast of Nova Scotia. The Canadian Navy, despite having realized the danger for almost a year, and having taken steps to increase its preparedness, was unable to effectively deal with the submarines. Several dozen ships were sunk. Although all but one of the ships sunk were quite inconsequential to the war effort, the Canadian public was outraged. The people considered the navy to have failed. The public reaction to this perceived failure would persist well into 1921 and would influence the parliamentary debates of the defence department's budget.

The experience of the Great War confirmed the already existing historical attitudes. Although this was an expedition overseas it was based on the volunteer system that served for local defence. The militia organizations not only seemed to work, but they garnered fame and glory in the process and increased the prestige and international position of the country. Conversely, the Royal Canadian Navy, in the eyes of Canadian citizens, had been an abject failure. It had even failed to protect Canadian home waters.

After the war Canada slipped back into its sense of isolation and security best illustrated by Senator Rauol Dandurand's remark to the League of Nations in 1923 that "We live in a fireproof house, far from inflammable materials."[78] This substantiates the historical perception that Canadians were only concerned with local defence. In 1933, the Department of National Defence was pressed hard to reduce its expenditures in the midst of the Depression. The Chief of the General Staff, Major-General A.G.L. McNaughton, suggested that if sufficient funds were not available to maintain an effective army, navy, and air force, one shold be sacrificed to save the other two. He considered the navy to be the least necessary and therefore the one to be cut; the army and the air force could be relied upon to deal with offensive action by an enemy on the coasts.[79]

"The potential depredations of a hostile cruiser or commerce raider," Desmond Morton observed, "still seemed remote to citizens of a country who essentially considered themselves an inland nation."[80] McNaugton's recommendation reflects the perception of the utility of Canadian naval forces based on the historical experience of continental land-oriented defence and reinforced by the shape of the First World War. Echoes of the opinion that Canada did not need a naval service of its own, expressed at the time of the creation of the Canadian Naval Service in 1910, could still be heard. Historical experience, expectation, and, to a limited degree, the reality that the Royal Navy would provide for the forward maritime defence of the country still held firm. Fortunately, the Chief of the Naval Staff, Commodore Walter Hose, convinced the Treasury Board that this course of action should not be adopted.

The Royal Canadian Navy survived the interwar years but remained a small coastal defence navy with units that could be integrated into Royal Navy fleet operations in times of war. This opportunity was not long in coming. Britain declared war against Germany on 3 September 1939 and the next day a German submarine sank the Cunard liner *Athenia*. Unlike the course of the Great War, the menace of submarine warfare was demonstrated and recognized at the very beginning of this conflict. The convoy system was implemented instantly and Canada took immediate steps to acquire a larger force of coastal escort vessels for local protection. The early result of this was the Corvette building program. Moreover, at the outbreak of the war the Canadian Navy quickly pressed to place its ships under the operational control of the Royal Navy. Prime Minster Mackenzie King refused to allow it. He stated, "It had been built for home defence and it would remain, under Canadian control in adjacent waters."[81] Both the corvette building program and the decision regarding the employment of the Canadian fleet once again reflected the long held attitudes of Canadians about the need for local security. Canada would provide for her own local defence and expected the Royal Navy to provide the global defence of ocean trade.

The fall of France in June 1940 and the subsequent threat of the invasion of England the government more open to a wider employment the Canadian fleet. British cruisers and later an entire Battle Squadron were based in Halifax for convoy escort duty, when the government relented and allowed Canadian destroyers to be deployed to Britain.[82] The employment of the corvettes as coastal escort forces held until early 1941, when it became apparent that combating the U-boats would require continuous transoceanic escort. Too few ocean-going escort vessels were available for the duties. Canadian corvettes, designed and built only for "a few days of inshore patrolling" were pressed into service to fill the demand for transatlantic escorts.[83] In both cases a clear threat and the need to react overruled the traditional Canadian preference for local defence. Canadian naval forces were soon committed to other distant operations that would eventually take them to the Arctic, the Mediterranean, and even the Far East.

The Royal Canadian Navy made a significant contribution to victory in the Battle of the Atlantic, and contributed forces to almost every other maritime theatre of war. Despite problems in training and equipment that arose from a rapid expansion (and which resulted in the withdrawal of Canadian ships from the Battle of the Atlantic at its height in the spring of 1943) Canadian naval efforts were recognized as being of great value. They resulted in the creation of the Canadian Northwest Atlantic Command under Rear-Admiral L.W. Murray on 30 April 1943. This was the only theatre in the Second World War to be commanded by a Canadian. The creation of this command set the precedent for a Canadian sub-area in NATO's Atlantic command structure. Despite the RCN's successes, German U-boats managed to penetrate the Gulf of St. Lawrence and attack Canadian shipping. Because of its distant commitments the RCN was unable to respond effectively to these attacks. This generated ill feeling and doubt in the Canadian public about the capability of their navy and the balance between local and extended defence. On balance, however, the RCN emerged from the Second World War with a good operational record and reputation.

During the Second World War, the largest Canadian effort was once again devoted to the army, an emphasis consistent with a long tradition. This time militia regiments themselves were mobilized for the land forces. In the case of the navy, the keys to the initial expansion of the RCN were the Royal Canadian Naval Reserve and the Royal Canadian Volunteer Naval Reserve. These naval organizations, established in the 1930s, drew upon the same traditions of citizen service the militia had always embodied. After 1945 most of these men returned to the civilian life they had come from. The attitudes that arose from the war, including the naval experience, were accommodated in the established traditions of citizen armies and local, continental defence.

The end of the war saw an attempt to reduce the size of the Canadian Forces to near their pre-war levels. This was consistent with the Canadian belief that large armed forces are only required in times of actual crisis. However, even as this reduction was underway it was becoming clear that the Soviet Union was a major threat. In response, Canada became a full and leading member of the North Atlantic Treaty Organization, the military alliance established in 1949 to counter the communist menace. The Korean War a year later generated fears that the Soviet Union was prepared to use force to achieve its aims in Europe. Faced with these very real and imminent threats—which included the possibility of nuclear warfare—Canadians opted uncharacteristicly for an extended defence regime. The Canadian Forces were re-armed and enlarged while substantial air and land formations were stationed in Europe. For the first time in Canadian history, Canadian defence policy was predicated on forces-in-being prepared to meet a danger that was not a direct threat to Canada.

The perceived menace of the Soviet Union and the potential for continued global conflict greatly influenced Canadian attitudes toward defence for little more than a decade. Initially, support for this policy was strong. But by the mid 1960s the heady days of expansion and the unconditional acceptance of such a security posture were clearly over and several things were becoming obvious. For instance, a nuclear war would make conventional forces irrelevant. Canadians recognized that there was no defence against intercontinental ballistic missiles and that Mutual Assured Destruction included them. They also realized that sharing the North American continent with the United States would prevent any direct conventional attack against Canada herself.

Throughout this period, it was also becoming obvious that modern military forces were becoming increasingly expensive. The prohibitive costs meant that Canada could no longer afford large forces. The reduced levels Canada could afford to maintain in Europe, however, would not be militarily significant in any balance of force calculations. Although Canada had seen it as a duty to assist in maintaining European security in the immediate post-war period—when most European nations were incapable of resisting a Soviet threat on their own— by the mid 1960s European nations had recovered sufficiently economically to shoulder a larger burden of their own defence. As a result, many questioned Canada's need to continue committing forces to what was essentially the defence of Europe.

Canadian Patrol Frigate on operations. (DND file photo.)

Thus, the better part of four decades were spent by Canadian governments trying to reconcile the dilemma caused by the need to meet defence treaty obligations they could not easily or unilaterally abrogate with the realization that these commitments were not consistent with the traditional Canadian attitudes toward defence. To solve this dilemma, they generally chose to pay lip service to the extended defence obligations. Consecutive governments spent the minimum amount necessary to meet them and otherwise reduced the Department of National Defence budget whenever possible by as much as possible. With the exception of the 1987 Defence White paper, *Challenge and Commitment,* the policy papers produced between 1945 and 1994 all demonstrate through their language and tone a desire to return Canadian defence posture to one more oriented toward local defence as opposed to extended defence.[84] The early 1970s and the Trudeau government's foreign policy document, *Foreign Policy for Canadians, 1970,* and the companion defence policy document, *Defence in the 70s*, signalled a very clear return to a more inward vision consistent with local, continental concerns. As a result, starting from about 1965, the entire armed forces suffered a process of equipment rust-out and resulted in a condition termed the commitment–capability gap. Canada had extended defence commitments but over time neglected to provide a credible capability to realize them.

The emphasis on peacekeeping that developed in this period can be seen as a minimum response to a wider military situation that demanded a Canadian contribution. The apparent lack of commitment to provide forces for NATO, it was argued, was offset by the Canadian commitment to peacekeeping. By engaging in peacekeeping Canadians reduced the possibility of the superpowers coming into direct confrontation, and, thus, the possibility of nuclear war. Therefore peacekeeping, it was claimed, should be considered an effective Canadian contribution to Western collective defence.

No doubt peacekeeping captured the unmilitary imaginations of Canadians because it was something non-warlike that could be accomplished with their military forces. Peacekeeping served to differentiate Canadians from Americans by capitalizing on the strengths of the essential Canadian characteristics beyond the military ones. To Canadians it represented more of the attributes of the ordinary citizen than employment in combat operations did. Thus, peace-keeping, even though initially carried out exclusively with regular force soldiers, can also be seen to fit into the tradition of the citizen soldier.

But this period also reflected another major change. Until roughly the Second World War, Britain had been Canada's guarantor of security. With the Royal Navy protecting Canada from foreign invasion, Canadians were free to concentrate on other matters. From 1900 onward, however, Britain's ability to guarantee Canada's security slowly diminished. At the same time the United States ceased to be a threat and began, by her mere presence as a neighbour, to provide some measure of security for Canada. When the Second World War broke out Canada recognized Britain's inability to continue to provide the necessary security guarantees and entered into a more formal defence relationship with the United States. This decision had long lasting ramifications.

During the Cold War there was no direct military danger to Canada but there was a clear threat to the United States. This menace, because it involved the possibly of nuclear attack, first by manned bombers and later by intercontinental ballistic missiles, constituted a threat to the continent as a whole. To make themselves secure against nuclear attack the United States required access to Canadian territory and air space. It was quite clear that the United States would take whatever action it felt was necessary with or without Canadian co-operation or permission. Canadian defence policy was required to look inward to continental defence in co-operation with the United States to counter the possibility of nuclear attack as well as to maintain a degree of Canadian independence from the United States. Eventually, Canadian–American defence plans for the security of North America were developed which involved land, air and maritime forces. However, the focus of military co-operation was air defence. This was reflected in the creation of the North American Air Defence Command, in 1958.[85]

Throughout the period commencing in 1945 the Canadian Navy was the orphan of defence policy. NATO and peacekeeping sustained a small requirement for ground forces and a certain level of air forces that governments could reduce to the absolute minimum but could not eliminate. Similarly, NORAD sustained a minimum requirement for Canadian air forces for the defence of continental North America. These force contributions were extremely visible to Canada's allies. Failure to live up to allied expectations affected other aspects of relations with them. For example, Prime Minister Trudeau discovered that Germany would refuse to conclude a trade agreement with Canada unless Canadian tanks in Europe were replaced. But, committed to NATO's Atlantic Command and tasked with participating in the anti-submarine defence of the North Atlantic sea lines of communications, Canadian naval operations were virtually invisible to both Canadians and their allies.

Furthermore, the bedrock of peacekeeping did not provide any foundation for naval policy. Peacekeeping is predominantly a land operation; there is very little call for naval peacekeeping forces.[86] Moreover, the aspects of peacekeeping that permitted Canadians to focus on and use their national characteristics for the advancement world peace are almost universally absent from any maritime operations. Therefore, the Canadian view of, and focus on, peacekeeping inevitably reinforced the bias toward land forces. The Canadian Navy had little visibility at home that could garner it even a minimum amount of support.

The relationship with the United States compounded this problem for the Navy as well. When the United States was considered a threat it was a land not a maritime one. As a guarantor of Canadian security, however, the maritime power of the United States is at least as great as Britain's was in the past. Thus, Canadians continue to feel assured that a great maritime power will provide the necessary maritime defence of the continent on their behalf. However, unlike the period of security association with Britain, most of Canada's trade with the United States is on land or through the inland waterways. Therefore, neither the defence nor the economic relationship with the United States requires the development of any measure of Canadian maritime interest.

Despite the change of guarantors of Canadian security, the basic attitudes of Canadians toward defence fundamentally did not alter. This was particularly true of attitudes toward naval defence. It was relatively easy for Canadian governments to ignore naval requirements and reduce the allocation of funds for shipbuilding. As a result, for about two decades from the mid 1960s until the mid 1980s, capital acquisitions for the Navy were almost nonexistent. The national unmilitary character and the tendency toward local self-defence remained strong. The commitment to NATO and the defence of Europe, an extended defence commitment, was an aberration that resulted from the exigencies of the onset of the Cold War following so quickly after the Second World War. While the commitment to NATO has never been officially abandoned, Canadians as a whole were always uneasy with their involvement and successive Canadian governments sought ways to minimize Canada's obligations. This entire process is again consistent with the pattern of historical experience that leads Canadians to believe that large standing forces in peace time are unnecessary and that defence expenditures should be minimized and restricted to only those which are absolutely necessary for the local defence of the country.

Canadian attitudes toward defence are shaped by geography and experience. North American wars and conflicts notwithstanding, the historical truth is that Canadians have lived through most of their history in a secure land on an isolated continent.[87] Canadians were prepared to go overseas to fight when necessary but they would not do it as a matter of course. Geography, then, has handed Canadians a unique circumstance that has allowed them to be less concerned about defence than many other countries can afford to be. "Military neglect has not led to armed invasion or disaster," noted Desmond Morton, who added that history "has justified the Canadian habit of neglecting peacetime defence in favour of economic and social development."[88] When not forced to respond to military events Canadians, by and large, have been content to focus their energies and attention inward, not outward. The problems of developing the country, not military operations, tended to absorb their interest and their wealth.[89] This has led to an aversion to large peacetime military expenditures and standing forces and the development of a reliance on volunteer forces raised when required. These attitudes discourage the development of maritime forces.

Nonetheless, there are obvious geographical characteristics that suggest Canada should be viewed as a maritime nation. However, there are other, much stronger geographical characteristics that prevent the development of such a maritime view. Additionally, there is little historical experience that suggests to Canadians that a maritime view of Canada is either important or necessary. Quite simply, Canadians are not naturally disposed toward naval forces. Geography and historical experience have led Canadians to develop a continental view of the country that puts the army at the centre of defence requirements. While this view is not conducive to the development of maritime forces, it has shaped our maritime history nonetheless.

Notes for Chapter 14

1 Paul H.Nitze, "Trends in the Use of the Sea," *Marine Corps Gazette,* March, 1965.

2 W. A. B Douglas, "Why does Canada have armed forces?" *International Journal*, Vol 30, No. 2, spring 1975, 259. He asks, " Why do we have - not why do we need but why do we *have* - armed forces?"

3 C.P. Stacey, *Six Years of War: The Army in Canada, Britain and the Pacific* (Ottawa: Queen's Printer, 1955), 3. This is the first volume of the Official History of the Canadian Army in the Second World War.

4 Desmond Morton, *A Military History of Canada: From Champlain to the Gulf War*. 3rd ed. (Toronto: McClelland & Stewart, 1992), x. See also Desmond Morton, "Defending the indefensible: some historical perspectives on Canadian defence, 1867-1987," *International Journal*, Vol 42 (autumn 1987), 626-643. For an example of the different responses see Peter Haydon, "Our Maritime Future," *Maritime Affairs* (Naval Officers Association of Canada, 1997) http://www.naval.ca/library accessed 15 August 2001, and his comments on Franklyn Griffiths, *Strong and Free: Canada and the New Sovereignty* (Toronto: Stoddart,1996).

5 W.A.B. Douglas, "The Prospects for Naval History," *The Northern Mariner*, Vol 1, No. 4, Oct 1991, 19. This should not be taken to mean, however, that military history is a panacea. See Michael Howard "The Use and Abuse of Military History," *Journal of the Royal United Services Institute*, Vol 107 (February 1962), 4-10. See also Michael Howards' book, *The Lessons of History* (Oxford: Clarendon Press Russell, 1991). Russell F. Weigley's comments in his Introduction to *New Dimensions in Military History* (San Rafael, California: Presidio Press, 1975) are also useful as is Jay Lucas's chapter "Military History: An Academic Historian's Point of View, " 19-36, in the same volume.

6 Douglas, "Why does Canada have armed forces?" 260. Note that Douglas does not single out a particular group for this criticism. It is fair then to assume that it could be applied equally to Government Ministers, Members of Parliament and senior bureaucrats as well as senior officers of the Canadian Forces.

7 For a discussion of the fundamental relationship between geography and strategy see Colin S. Gray, *Modern Strategy* (Oxford University Press, 1999).

8 Colin S. Gray, "Geography and Strategy, Geopolitics and Action," *The Journal of Strategic Studies*, Vol 22, No.2/3 (June September 1999), 172.

9 Ibid., 170.

10 Colin S. Gray, *Modern Strategy* (Oxford University Press, 1999) 131.

11 Gray, in *Modern Strategy,* shows that predominant attitudes and habits of mind become very deeply entrenched in a society. Nevertheless, Gray admits that counter or alternative attitudes can exist simultaneously, but that they normally exist at the margins of the society's consciousness. Gray allows that the predominant attitudes can change but that this occurs slowly over long periods of time. He also shows that even in the face of catastrophic events that indicate that the predominant attitude may be incorrect it is rarely abandoned quickly or completely. In some cases, an alternative attitude is adopted for the period of the crisis. The alternative attitude is abandoned and the old one returned to after the crisis passes. Take for example Canada's response to the Great War: "It is a remarkable fact that the First World War, which affected Canadian development so fundamentally in so many ways, had almost no long term influence on the country's military policy .... when the emergency was over the country reverted lightly and confidently to her earlier traditions , and reduced her armed forces to a level of insignificance almost as low as that of 1913." Stacey, *Six Years of War,* Vol 1, 4.

12 Desmond Morton, "Defending the indefensible," *International Journal*, Vol 42 (autumn 1987) 627-643. Also see Morton's arguments in "Providing and Consuming Security in Canada's Century," *Canadian Historical Review*, Vol 81, No. 1 (March 2000) 2-26.

13 Stacey, *Six Years of War*, 3.

14 Stacey,, 7. There is no reason, however, to expect Stacey to account any more fully for the Canadian attitude. His purpose was to describe the Canadian Army's operations in the Second World War.

15 William Wood, *All Afloat: A Chronicle of Craft and Waterways*. *Chronicles of Canada Part IX National Highways*, *Vol 31*, Eds. George M. Wrong and H.H. Lanagton (Toronto: Glasgow, Brook & Company, 1914), 7.

16 Wood, *All Afloat*, 1.

17 Alfred Thayer Mahan, *The Influence of Sea Power Upon History 1660-1783* (New York: Dover Publications, 1987. An unabridged, slightly altered republication of the fifth edition, 1894, Boston, Little Brown and Company, 1890), 25. All further references are to this edition unless other wise noted. For the list of Mahan's six principles see page 28. The other factors are Extent of (thickly inhabited) Territory, Number of Population, National Character, and Character of Government.

18 Mahan, *The Influence of Sea Power Upon History*. On Geographical Position see page 29: "It may be pointed out in the first place that if a nation be so situated that it is neither forced to defend itself by land or induced to seek extension of its territory by way of land, it has by the very unity of its aim directed upon the sea an advantage compared with one of whose boundaries is continental." On Physical Conformation see page 35.

19 Ibid., 35.

20 Glen Herbert, *Canada's Oceans Dimension: A Fact Book,* Niobe Papers, Volume 11 (Halifax: Maritime Affairs, 1999), 1.

21 Ibid., 4. Herbert estimates in 1996 that approximately 6.5 million people or 25 percent of Canadians lived in or worked in coastal areas.Working with population figures taken from *Canadian Global Almanac 2001* (Toronto: Macmillan Canada, 2000) a higher figure can be arrived at. The three largest Canadian cites, Toronto, Montreal and Vancouver, all are situated on or have access to the sea. Including these three cities, 11 of the 25 largest Canadian metropolitan areas are either on the sea or the Great Lakes. These cities represent a total population of about 12 million or about 40 percent of the population of Canada.

22 Ibid., 1.

23 Tucker, *The Naval Service of Canada, Its Official History: Origins and Early Years*, 1. Tucker discusses the relationship of Canada's geographical position and naval strategy in more detail on page 7. Tucker reflects Mahan's view of the sea as "a great highway … [or] a wide common, over which men may pass in all directions," Mahan, *The Influence of Sea Power*, 25.

24 Milner, *Canada's Navy: The First Century* (Toronto: University of Toronto Press, 1999), x. The traditional sense of sea power is described by Nicholas Tracy, "Canada's Naval Strategy: Rooted in Experience," *Maritime Security Paper No. 1* (Center for Foreign Policy Studies, Dalhousie University, 1995), 1: "The fundamental historical motive for state involvement in naval forces was for power projection across the sea, and for defence against such foreign aggression."

25 Fred W. Crickard and Peter T. Haydon, *Why Canada Needs Maritime Forces* (Nepean: Naval Officer's Association of Canada, 1994), 3. During the discussions concerning the establishment of the Canadian Navy in 1909, a comment was made by a Canadian politician that "a large portion of the population took no interest in naval developments," Department of External Affairs, Notes of Proceedings of Conference at the Admiralty between representatives of the Admiralty and the Dominion of Canada to work out a scheme for the establishment of a Canadian Navy, *Documents on Canadian External Relations, Vol 1, 1909-1918* (Ottawa: Queen's Printer, 1967), 244.

26 Tracy, "Canada's Naval Strategy," 59.

27 There were conflicting rights, claims, and jurisdictions about the waters long before the Dominion of Canada was ever thought of. Exploration, pioneering, trade, and fisheries all raised questions involving mercantile sea power, ultimately turned on naval sea power and were settled by the sword. Wood, *All Afloat*, 4-5. For a short description of the involvement of navies in Canadian affairs up to about 1913 see Ibid., 179-182.

28 Tucker, *The Naval Service of Canada*, 36.

29 Wood, *All Afloat*, 13.

30 Ronald Haycock, *Teaching Military History: Cleo and Mars in Canada* (Athabasca University, 1995), 3. Nor he observes was there much study of it either. *Teaching Military History* is a good reference for Canadian military history source material. The most comprehensive list of published material for the period 1867-1997 is O. A. Cooke, *The Canadian Military Experience 1867–1995: A Bibliography* (Ottawa: Directorate of History and Heritage, Department of National Defence, 1997). Also useful is M. Brook Taylor, ed., *Canadian History: A Reader's Guide: Volume 1: Beginnings to Confederation* (Toronto: University of Toronto Press, 1994) and Doug Owram, Ed. *Canadian History: A Reader's Guide: Volume 2: Confederation to The Present* (Toronto: University of Toronto Press, 1994).

31 Tucker, *The Naval Service of Canada*, xi. Tucker goes on to note that "Even that part of the subject which consists of high policy has been told only as a part of more general accounts and with most of the purely naval implications omitted."

32 See Haycock, *Teaching Military History*, page 6 on, for fuller details.

33 For example see C.P. Stacey, ed. *An introduction to the Study of Military History for Canadian Students,* (Ottawa: Queen's Printer, 1960). Stacey states in the Preface that the "pamphlet is designed to provide an introduction to the study of military history suitable for Canadian students and particularly members of the Canadian Officers Training Corp." While an excellent work, the volume contains no naval history and reflects the army centric bias of the state of Canadian military history of the period.

34 Douglas, "The Prospects for Naval History," 19. His findings were originally published as "Canadian Naval Historiography," *Mariner's Mirror,* Vol 70, No. 4 (November 1984), 349-362.

35 Milner, *Canada's Navy*, xi. Douglas also remarks of production of scholarly material of the same period that "the stream is turning into a torrent," Douglas, "The Prospects for Naval History," 19.

36 Take for example a commonly used introductory text for the study of Canadian military history, Desmond Morton, *A Military History of Canada: From Champlain to the Gulf War*, 3rd ed. (Toronto: McClelland & Stewart, 1992). This text contains only short paragraphs on the creation of the Canadian Naval Service, and is silent on the activities of the Canadian Naval service in the Great War. Only 4 fi pages plus one diagram out of 46 pages deal with the RCN in the Second World War. The majority of this deals with the Battle of the Atlantic. Naval participation in the Korean War and the Gulf merit only sentences. Similarly, there is little mention of Canadian naval activity during the Great War in Desmond Morton, and J.L. Granatstein, *Marching to Armageddon: Canadians and the Great War 1914-1918* (Toronto: Lester & Orpen Dennys, 1989).

37 Mahan, *The Influence of Sea Power*, 43.

38 Ibid., 53.

39 Ibid., 53.

40 In 1996, fifty percent of the 357.7 million tonnes (mt) of international and domestic cargo was handled by seven ports: Vancouver (71.4 mt), Sept-Iles (22.6 mt), Port Cartier (21.7mt), Saint John (20.6 mt), Montreal (19.2 mt), QuÈbec (16.9 mt), and Halifax (13.6 mt). Of the 17.9 million tonnes of containerized cargo handled in 1996 by Canadian ports, 95 percent of it was handled by three ports, Montreal (7.9 mt), Vancouver (5.1 mt), and Halifax (4.0 mt). See Herbert, *Canada's Oceans Dimension,* 34-36.

41 Herbert, *Canada's Oceans Dimension*, 34. "International trade through Canadian ports in the Great Lakes is almost entirely with the United States," Herbert, *Canada's Oceans Dimension*, 36.

42 Mahan, *The Influence of Sea Power*, 43.

43 Jospeh T. Jockel, *Security to the North: Canada–US Defence Relations in the 1990s* (East Lansing: Michigan State University Press, 1991), 18.

44 Mahan, *The Influence of Sea Power*, 46.

45 Statistics Canada, http:\\wwwstatscan.ca\english\census96\mar17\occupa\table3\t3p00t.htm accessed 5 Sep 01. Total work force –

14,812,700. Water transport – 19,795; incidental to water transport – 12,200. Fishing 39,380; incidental to fishing 4575. For an indication of the importance of the Canadian shipbuilding industry in the past see Tony German, *The Sea is At Our Gates: The History of the Canadian Navy* (Toronto: McClelland & Stewart, 1990), 19. For an indication of the current state of the Canadian shipbuilding industry see Herbert, *Canada's Ocean Dimension*, 36.

46 Milner, *Canada's Navy*, x.

47 Mahan, T*he Influence of Sea Power*, 53. See also Mahan's analysis of the elements of sea power: Number of Population, 44-49 and Character of the People, 50-58.

48 Herbert, *Canada's Oceans Dimension*, 63.

49 Milner, *Canada's Navy*, x.

50 Morton, "Defending the Indefensible," 629-30.

51 Tucker, *The Naval Service of Canada*, 16-17.

52 Tracy, *Canada's Naval Strategy*, 1.

53 Tucker, *The Naval Service of Canada*, 14.

54 Ibid., 65-6.

55 Ibid., 33.

56 Tracy, *Canada's Naval Strategy*, 1. Tucker makes a similar observation: "Through all those years, by day and by night, the most powerful fleets in the world sailed or steamed, or lay at anchor. A floating breastwork guarding Canada from serious assault or intimidation from across the sea." *The Naval Service of Canada*, 8. Morton also makes a similar comment, "If the coasts were menaced by other enemies, the Royal Navy stood guard," "Defending the indefensible," 632-3.

57 Tucker, *The Naval Service of Canada,* 33.

58 Ibid., 29.

59 Morton feels that the Rush–Bagot agreement "conceded American control of the lakes in any future war," *A Military History of Canada*, 72.

60 For example, the St Alban's Bank robbery and the acquittal of the perpetrators by Canadian courts raised Union ire and generated tensions.

61 Desmond Morton, "Providing and Consuming Security in Canada's Century," *Canadian Historical Review*, Vol. 81, No. 1 (March 2000), 5.

62 See C.P. Stacey, *Canada and the Age of Conflict, Volume 1:1867- 1921* (Toronto: University of Toronto Press, 1984), for a description of the crisis and its effect on Canada.

63 Morton, "Defending the indefensible," 630-1. For the fuller argument see Morton, "Cavalry or police: Keeping the peace on two adjacent frontiers, 1870-1900," *Journal of Canadian Studies*, Vol 12 (spring 1977).

64 Morton, *Military History of Canada*, ix.

65 Tracy, *Canada's Naval Strategy*, 3.

66 German, *The Sea is At Our Gates*, 20. Thomas E. Appleton, *Usque Ad Mare: A History of the Canadian Coast Guard and Marine Services* (Ottawa: Queen's Printer, 1969) provides a useful summary of the details and activities of Provincial Marines prior to Confederation.

67 German, *The Sea is At Our Gates*, 21.

68 Tracy, *Canada's Naval Strategy*, 3. Milner makes a similar

69 Tucker, *The Naval Service of Canada*, 33.

claim: "The need to police the fishing activities of Canada's great neighbour formed the essential basis for the development of a national naval force," *Canada's Navy*, 8.

70 The CPR would have been critical to Britain if she was unable to use the Mediterranean in time of war, Tucker, *The Naval Service of Canada*, 82. See Chapter Three, "The Imperial Defence Question, 1870-1902," 60-84 for a fuller discussion of other arguments.

71 The resolution of the Alaskan boundary dispute is a good example of this. See Stacey, *Age of Conflict Vol 1*, Chapter 4 for a discussion of it.

72 Tracy, *Canada's Naval Strategy*, 2.

73 Notwithstanding this concession, the Admiralty still had significant control over operations. For example, when it was proposed to take the Governor General on a cruise outside of Canadian territorial waters in one of the new naval units, the plan was vetoed by the Admiralty.

74 Tracy, *Canada's Naval Strategy*, 4.

75 The following discussion on the varying opinions draws heavily on material in Tucker, *The Naval Service of Canada*, 17.

76 Morton, *Military History of Canada*, x.

77 Department of External Affairs, Telegram Acting High Commissioner to Prime Minister, London October 10, 1914, *Documents on Canadian External Relations Vol 1, 1909-1918* (Ottawa, Queen's Printer, 1967), 52.

78 Cited in Norman Hillmer and J.L. Granatstein, *Empire to Umpire: Canada and the World to the 1990s* (Mississauga: Copp, Clark, Longman 1994), 88.

79 Tucker, *The Naval Service of Canada*, 342. Interestingly the air force, only just created, had apparently established a constituency for itself by its involvement in the civilian air industry and mapping and charting efforts throughout the country. The navy was either unable or unwilling to establish a similar type of constituency.

80 Morton, "Defending the indefensible," 632-3.

81 Cited by Milner, *Canada's Navy*, 81.

82 Ibid., 81.

83 See Milner, *Canada's Navy*, 90-91 for a discussion of this.

84 See Douglas L. Bland, *Canada's National Defence, Volume 1: Defence Policy* (Kingston: School of Policy Studies, Queen's University, 1997) for the text of the Defence White Papers and an analysis of them.

85 The name was later changed to North American Aerospace Defense Command to better reflect the organization's expanded responsibilities.

86 Michael Pugh, ed., *Maritime Security and Peacekeeping: A Framework for United Nations Operations* (Manchester University Press, 1994) presents numerous arguments in favour of maritime peacekeeping operations but fails to show convincingly how these operations could function in the same manner as land peacekeeping operations.

87 Tucker, *The Naval Service of Canada*, 1.

88 Morton, "Defending the indefensible," 629.

89 Tucker, *The Naval Service of Canada*, 16.

CHAPTER 15

Gateway to Invasion or the Curse of Geography?

The Canadian Arctic and the Question of Security, 1939-1999

Lieutenant-Colonel Bernd Horn

What is important to Canadians is not what we think the Russians will do; it is what we think the Americans think the Russians will do.[1]
—David Cox, Queens University, 1984

THE ARCTIC has a very special hold on the Canadian psyche despite the fact that very few Canadians have actually ever seen the North. Strategist Kenneth Eyre observed that the "North to Canadians is more of an idea than a place."[2] Nevertheless, it was not until the Second World War that Canadian apathy toward its Arctic was actually broken. The war led to the implementation of a continental alliance which dictated close co-operation between Canada and the United States in the defence of North America. It was also the catalyst that sparked a new surge of interest in the North.

The Canadian Camp at Kiska, October 1943. (Photographer unknown. NA, C-144121)

The looming Japanese threat to Alaska and the fear of a Nazi occupied Siberia, only a short distance away across the Bering Strait, raised American anxiety in regard to its security to an unprecedented high. The subsequent American mobilization to meet the perceived peril quickly spilled into Canada and transformed its northern region into a hive of activity. Unfortunately, the Americans placed little weight on the formalities of ownership and executed their tasks with a single mindedness that raised the concern that the long neglected Canadian North was actually under the control of the United States.

The growing American presence, coupled with their dominating attitude, worried Canadian politicians. This fear soon led to action to safeguard Canadian sovereignty. Canada had always been defensive of its claim to ownership of the Arctic archipelago and the growing occupation of the North by the United States was seen as a direct threat to Canadian proprietorship. The American presence, argued Canadian governmental officials, could be seen as de facto control. As a result, a policy was implemented to reimburse the Americans for their wartime developments in the North, irrespective of whether the Canadian government originally supported or wanted the subject projects. It was not lost on the politicians that sovereignty has a price. Equally clear were the consequences of not paying that price.

Canada's new wartime defence partnership underscored another inescapable reality. It became evident that any threat perceived by the Americans to the security of the United States, whether realistic or not, represented a genuine danger to Canada. The national political and military leadership promptly realized that it was critical that Canada be seen by its southern neighbour to be taking adequate steps to secure Canadian borders from any intrusion that could subsequently threaten the United States. This geographical reality was exacerbated at the end of the Second World War. New technology, weapons of immense potency and the emergence of two diametrically opposed superpowers—which sandwiched Canada between them—fuelled what would become a continuing challenge to Canada's efforts to maintain security and sovereignty of its Arctic regions.

It is this balance between security and sovereignty that cries out for examination. Was Canada's defence policy and northern focus driven by a real menace in the Arctic as a result of a belief that its security was jeopardized by the threat of invasion by an enemy? Or, was it geared to thwarting the perceived peril to its sovereignty by an ally? Careful scrutiny uncovers a Canadian defence policy that was focussed more on frustrating erosion to its sovereignty and minimizing American expansion into the Canadian Arctic than it was on meeting any real danger to its territory from hostile invasion. Although a degree of threat was always recognized, more so by the military than the political leadership, decisions taken on the defence of the North were primarily geared to countering American encroachment. This theme, which began with Prime Minister King in the Second World War, continues to the present.

Prior to 1939, Canadian politicians and their military commanders placed very little emphasis on the Arctic. The primary stimulus of the limited northern development conducted by the government during this period came from a select few individuals. Patrons such as J.A. Wilson, the Controller of Civil Aviation, and Major-General A.G.L. McNaughton, the Chief of the General Staff (CGS), sponsored initiatives that included the survey of suitable landing fields in the Arctic archipelago; a program of aerial photography for mapping purposes; and the establishment of a series of northern radio stations.[3] Not surprisingly, by far most growth in the North was civilian in nature. Canadian Airways and Mackenzie Air Service, two commercial airlines that began operations in the Arctic in the late 1920s, were instrumental in this process of opening up the North.[4] Nonetheless, eventually a series of civilian airfields and emergency landing strips, supported by the Departments of Defence and Transport, were established across the entire Dominion. These fields were primarily used by Trans-Canada Airlines but also yielded a network that could be used to concentrate military air strength in times of crisis.[5]

Much of this development was by Depression-era relief projects. However, interest in an air route to Alaska and Europe over the Arctic was always present and by 1935, technological and economic conditions merited a closer examination of the possibility.[6] Consequently, the government sponsored survey of northern airfields was conducted to determine whether expansion of existing sites was required and what additional landing fields were necessary.[7] Construction on this network of airfields was begun in 1939 and continued well into the Second World War. It eventually became known as the Northwest Staging Route and it proved instrumental in the defence of Alaska and in the supply of aircraft and equipment to the beleaguered Soviet Union.[8]

Despite the remarkable strides in aviation and the limited but growing commercial development of the North, both the military and political leadership shared the belief that an undefended Canadian Arctic represented a negligible security threat to the "fire-proof house" of Canada. In 1938, Prime Minister Mackenzie King asserted, "May I point out that undoubtably Canada is the most secure of all countries."[9] He dismissed "the launching of fantastic expeditions across half the world [by belligerents intending to attack Canada]" and stated that "at present danger of attack upon Canada is minor in degree and secondhand in origin. It is against chance shots that we need immediately to defend ourselves."[10]

Glider aircraft coming in for landing at Great Bear Lake, Northwest Territories (NWT), during Operation Musk-Ox, 29 April 1946. (Photographer Robert W. Morton. NA, PA-134305)

The Minister of National Defence (MND), Ian Mackenzie, agreed. "There is danger," he acknowledged, "but so far as Canada is concerned, it is, as I have already pointed out, an incidental contingency."[11] He maintained that the direct defence of Canada entailed the defence of "our coastal areas, our ports, our shipping terminals, our territorial waters, the focal areas of our trade routes adjacent to our harbour mouths."[12] Specifically, he felt that the threat consisted largely of raids by submarine, aircraft or other craft for the purpose of creating diversion and panic.[13]

The military perception was little different. "The idea of our having to fight a major war on our own soil," wrote Lieutenant-General Maurice Pope, "was absurd ... As the forms and scales of attack to which it was judged Canada might be exposed in the event of even a major war comprised only limited naval and air bombardment and minor raids against our defended ports."[14] This judgement changed little even with the commencement of hostilities. An army appreciation in February 1941 stated that "Canada's front line lies in and around the British Isles." [15]

The apparent lack of concern of any menace to Canada's security emanated from the nation's geography. A military analysis of Canadian defence problems noted that "the direct defence of the national territory ... owing to our fortunate geographical position ... has not been given a high degree of priority."[16] General Charles Foulkes reinforced this theme. "Prior to 1939," he explained, "Canada was able to derive a considerable amount of security from her geographical position. The then available weapons precluded a direct attack on Canada."[17]

Geography and history provided Canada with another important element in its defence, namely, a powerful neighbour to the south. The close proximity to the United States prompted Colonel E.L.M. Burns in 1936 to write that "we believe, reasonably or unreasonably, that our Southern neighbour would go to war before she would allow a foreign nation to establish itself on our territory."[18] The renowned Canadian historian C.P. Stacey reiterated this thesis in his examination of Canadian defence policy in 1940. "It has long been generally recognized in

The specific rationale behind the MSF and DCF was the Defence of the North. Soldiers from 9 Platoon of "C" Coy, The RCR exercise their MSF mandate by conducting training in the Arctic. (Photographer Fenn, NA, PA-204970)

Canada," he insisted, "that the most elementary regard for the security of the United States itself would render it impossible for that country to permit any aggressive power to gain a foothold on Canadian soil."[19]

These conclusions were not entirely visionary. In 1936 President Franklin D. Roosevelt raised the image of a benevolent neighbour when he declared, "We can defend ourselves, and we can defend our neighbourhood."[20] Two years later he erased any doubt with his famous declaration at Queen's University in Kingston. "The Dominion of Canada," he announced, "is part of the sisterhood of the British Empire. I give to you assurance that the people of the United States will not stand idly by if domination of Canadian soil is threatened by any other empire. We as good neighbours are true friends."[21]

Two days later King responded. "We, too," he declared, "have our obligations as a good friendly neighbour, and one of these is to see that, at our own instance our country is made as immune from attack or possible invasion as we can reasonably be expected to make it, and that should the occasion ever arise, enemy forces should not be able to pursue their way, either by land, sea or air, to the United States across Canadian territory."[22] These courageous words were uttered at a time when there were no perceived threats to Canada due to its geographical location and the naval might of both Britain and the United States. As a result, King's pledge to guard the flanks of his neighbour seemed effortless and easily enforced. However, his words would return to haunt him and take on the essence of a curse. World events and technological developments soon changed Canada's outlook on security forever, particularly in regard to its Arctic region.

The Second World War dramatically altered Canada's perception of its security and fuelled an unprecedented concern for its North. Paradoxically, northern security became focussed primarily on protecting national sovereignty from the encroachment of an ally rather than guarding an unprotected flank from hostile invasion.

The catalyst was the renewed American focus on Alaska. Originally, American politicians and military leaders shared a common apathy with their Canadian counterparts in regard to their northern territory. "In the halls of Congress, Alaska was described as a 'frozen waste,' much as strategic Guam was passed off by some Representatives as a 'grain of sand.'"[23] The military leadership shared a similar view. An official report tabled just prior to the American entry into the war argued that "there appears at present to be no necessity, from the viewpoint of national defense, of increasing the military garrison of Alaska."[24] Few acknowledged Brigadier-General W.B. Mitchell's observation that Alaska, "as the most central place in the world of aircraft," was subsequently the most strategic location on earth. He reasoned that "whoever holds Alaska will hold the world."[25]

It took the Axis juggernaut to galvanize American action in the North. The German attack on the Soviet Union in June 1941 "muddied the already seething situation in the Far East and seemed to bring closer to Alaska the danger that Alaskans had been advertising for years."[26] The realization that "in the possession of the enemy Alaska will furnish a jumping-off point for invasion by air of the United States," soon resulted in the restoration of money to expand Alaskan defence.[27] The Permanent Joint Board for Defence concluded on 26 February 1942 "that the effective defence of Alaska is of paramount importance to the defence of the continent against attack from the West, since Alaska is the area most exposed to an attempt by the enemy to establish a foothold in North America."[28]

Canadians quickly absorbed the idea of a northern threat via Alaska. "It was easy to believe," wrote Canadian military historian Desmond Morton, "as Japanese power spread irresistibly across Southeast Asia ... that it could also reach out easily to seize a foothold in North America. If the threat was far-fetched militarily, it was politically all too real."[29] Even Mitch Hepburn, the Premier of Ontario at the time, "predicted a Japanese assault on Alaska, and visualized the enemy infiltrating down the western coast of Canada."[30] Prime Minister King also believed that the Japanese represented a real danger. He warned his military officials that it would be foolish to discount their strength. Moreover, King cautioned his generals not to rule out the possibility of operations of a larger or more serious nature.[31]

Despite the dire admonitions, the military was not overly alarmed. Even the Japanese seizure of the Aleutian islands of Attu, Agatu, and Kiska in July 1942 failed to change their outlook. Their analysis confirmed that "the forms and scales of attack envisioned on the entry of Japan into the war remained unchanged."[32] The confidence of the military commanders rested on the premise that there were no military objectives of sufficient importance to justify other than very small tip-and-run raids which would have little military significance. In addition, the generals emphasized that the Japanese were already over committed. The Chiefs of Staff Committee clearly stated that an actual attempt to invade Canada's West Coast by Japanese forces was considered highly remote.[33]

Nonetheless, the chain of command took into account the anxiety of the public. "The question of increasing protection in British Columbia," asserted an army appreciation, "is one of vocal and increasing concern on the part of the civilian population. In view of the immense length of the coast line, greater mobility of Army personnel would seem a matter of urgent consideration and might do much to allay the present feeling of apprehension."[34] As a result, the West Coast was reinforced with artillery and manpower.[35] Lieutenant-General Pope, however, noted the nature of the real threat. "It was clear that if ... Canada should attempt to remain neutral and aloof," he explained, "our American neighbours would ride roughshod over us and make use of our territory and facilities as it pleased them."[36]

Pope's observation was the more accurate. The response of the United States to the new northern menace was representative of the energy and seemingly unlimited resources of a great power. The American reaction was swift and all encompassing. It created an intricate web that quickly entangled Canada. The expeditious American mobilization resulted in a massive influx of personnel to reinforce the Alaskan garrison, as well as to establish the logistical infrastructure required to support the new defensive effort in the North. By June 1943, more than 33,000 American soldiers and civilian workers had poured into Northwest Canada.[37]

The American "invasion" was driven by their perception of defensive steps required to protect the North. These included the expansion and upgrading of the Northwestern Staging Route, the construction of a land route to Alaska, and the assurance of petroleum for military forces in the North. These projects all encompassed development on Canadian territory and were, theoretically, subject to consultation and agreement between the two nations in accordance with the Ogdensburg Agreement.[38] This agreement was signed in haste, almost in panic, as a contingency for the imminent collapse of Britian. As the tide of war began to shift, the consequences of the agreement soon became apparent.[39] Although the projects signed under the auspices of the agreement were grounded in the noble pursuit of mutual defence, they quickly highlighted the dangers of a relationship between two unequal partners.

What were trumpeted as "projects of vital importance" to the security of North America very quickly captured Canadian attention. One such project, the construction of the Alaska Highway, was representative of the difficulties that faced Canada. As early as 1928, both Americans and Canadians had considered a land route to Alaska; but the exorbitant cost and "negligible military value" precluded any official support.[40] American military planners viewed a road link to Alaska as of little strategic importance and primarily of economic benefit to civilians.[41] The Japanese attack on Pearl Harbor abruptly changed the American perspective.[42] Overnight, the construction of an all-weather road was seen as "one of the most important steps toward making Alaska defensible."[43] Once the Americans decided what was necessary, they took prompt action with little regard for Canadian sensitivities.

On 12 February 1942, the Under-Secretary of State for External Affairs informed the Cabinet War Committee that the Americans had reached a conclusion that construction of a land route to Alaska on Canadian soil was necessary for continental defence, but they had not yet submitted a formal request to do so.[44] It was two weeks later (26 February) that the Permanent Joint Board for Defence (PJBD), as its twenty-fourth recommendation advised that the construction of the Alaska Highway should be undertaken. The Canadian dilemma was evident. The government was reluctant to proceed with the project. Nevertheless, a secret External Affairs memorandum conceded that "the United States Government is now so insistent that the road is required that the Canadian Government cannot possibly allow itself to be put in the position of barring the United States from land access to Alaska."[45] It commented further that the Canadian government would be in a completely untenable position if it prevented the construction of land communications to Alaska and subsequently, as unlikely as it may be, the Japanese were able to deny the United States access by sea.[46]

The alternative, however, was daunting. It required Canada "to expend some $80,000,000.00 on the construction, and about $1,000,000.00 per annum on the maintenance of a road that would be a monument to our friendship for the U.S. but would otherwise be pret-

Members of the DCF practice a winter deployment. (Canadian Airborne Forces Museum)

ty much of a 'White Elephant.'"[47] Cabinet concluded that Canada had little choice but to agree. War Cabinet Committee approval was subsequently given on 5 March 1942.[48]

But the Cabinet's approval was irrelevant. The actual decision to proceed had already been made in the United States. President Roosevelt considered the matter as a fait accompli. Consequently, he had allocated $10 million for the project from his emergency fund as early as 11 February.[49] As a result, American engineers arrived in Dawson Creek to begin construction on the road two days before Cabinet approved the request.[50] The highway eventually proved insignificant. By the fall of 1943, only fifty-four tons of supplies had been delivered to the Alaska Defence Command by motor transport.[51]

Nonetheless, the American presence quickly struck a chord with Canadians, particularly Prime Minister King. Alarming reports emanating from the North painted a grim picture for a country that laboured to maintain a decorum of independence. One account acknowledged that "the Americans in Edmonton are openly describing themselves as an 'Army of Occupation.'"[52] To King the spectre of American encroachment was very real. "I said," he wrote in his diary, "I was not altogether without feeling that the Alaska Highway was less intended for protection against Japan than as one of the dangers of the hand which America is placing more or less over the whole of the Western Hemisphere."[53]

The Alaska Highway was not the only source of concern. The CANOL project provided similar hazards to the Canadian hosts. Its aim was to provide a guaranteed supply of fuel to Alaska and military traffic en route by means of a pipeline from Norman Wells, in the North West Territories, to a refinery in Whitehorse, Yukon. By the time the project had been completed it had expanded to include a series of airfields, numerous construction camps, pumping stations, supplementary pipelines and additional roads.[54] Its utility and efficiency were questioned from the beginning and it has since been labelled a "junk-yard of military stupidity."[55] Lieutenant-

General Pope, who was a Canadian member of the PJBD, later said "the CANOL project as a defence measure has always seemed to me so far-fetched as to be absurd."[56]

Of greater concern was the fact that the decision to proceed with the project was once again taken prior to receiving the requisite approval from the Canadian government. Canadian historian Donald Creighton observed that "the United States army authorized the pipeline and signed a contract with Imperial Oil more than a fortnight before the Canadian government signified its approval."[57] Furthermore, additional airfields were constructed in support of the project without consulting the Canadian government.[58]

The American insensitivity to Canadian control led Vincent Massey, the Canadian High Commissioner in England, to an ironic comparison: "They have apparently walked in and taken possession in many cases as if Canada were unclaimed territory inhabited by a docile race of aborigines."[59] His diary entries made further disquieting observations. "The Americans," Massey recorded, "who unfortunately under cover of the needs of the war effort are acting in the North-West as if they owned the country ... We have for too long been far too supine vis-á-vis Washington and the only threat to our independence comes from that quarter."[60]

As the war progressed, all perceived threats to the North American land mass, particularly in the Arctic, diminished dramatically.[61] However, suspicions of American intentions did not. Malcolm MacDonald, the British High Commissioner in Canada, visited the northern projects and reported to the Canadian Cabinet War Committee that "it was quite evident that these vast undertakings were being planned and carried out with a view to the postwar situation. Canadian representatives in the area were few and quite unable to keep control or even in touch with day to day developments."[62] Civilian entrepreneurs also questioned the long-term motives of the Americans. J.K. Cornwall, an Edmonton businessman, remarked, "I visualize the U.S.A. controlling to a large extent the development of Canada's north land, due to their financial power and experience."[63]

But no-one was more suspicious than the Prime Minister. "Despite his close friendship with Roosevelt," disclosed the Prime Minister's secretary, J.W. Pickersgill, "Mackenzie King was never without suspicions of the ultimate designs of the Americans... He referred to 'the efforts that would be made by the Americans to control developments in our country after the war.'"[64] King's own diaries are testimony to these misgivings. "I viewed the Alaskan Highway," he wrote, "and some other things growing out of the war, which was clear to my mind that America had had as her policy, a western hemisphere control which would mean hemispheric immunity, if possible, from future war but increasing political control by United States Forces greater than those of any one country working to this end."[65] With regard to the Americans leaving when the war was over, he confided in Vincent Massey that "he had grave doubts whether international agreements on this which Canada had secured from the United States [would] provide any practical guarantee against the United States' claims and pretensions."[66] King went on to say that "Canadians were looked upon by Americans as a lot of Eskimos."[67]

This fear of "possible domination of post-war Canada by the Americans" led King to believe that it was necessary to displace the Americans from further development in the North and "keep control in our own hands."[68] The prevailing perception of American encroachment into Canada's North led directly to new initiatives to regain control and assert ownership. The Canadian government "now embarked on a vigorous programme intended to 're-Canadianize' the Arctic."[69] Clearly, the new focus on the Arctic was not inspired by security concerns but rather by the fear of losing jurisdiction over its territory. A military appreciation asserted that

James Richardson, the MND and General J.A. Dextraze, the CDS at Crocker Bay, Devon Island, NWT, surveying a possible location for a northern training centre, 26 July 1975. (DND File Photo.)

"it is of great importance that Canada should carefully safeguard her sovereignty in the Arctic at all points and at all times, lest the acceptance of an initial infringement of her sovereignty invalidate her entire claim and open the way to the intrusion of foreign interests of a nature which might create an ultimate threat to national security."[70]

Specific action to reclaim the North began with the appointment of a Special Commissioner for Defence Projects in Northwest Canada. His task was to supervise and co-ordinate the activities of the government and "to maintain close and continuous cooperation with all agencies of the United States government in the area."[71] The government's most influential initiative, however, was the policy of reimbursing the Americans for the cost of construction and development that was undertaken in the North.[72]

The tight-fisted King government realized that retention of clear ownership and title to its North required payment for those bases and facilities of a permanent nature that were built by the Americans. What made this decision more painful was the fact that most of the projects were never supported as necessary by the government and almost all were constructed to standards far in excess of Canadian requirements. Regardless, the need to buy back control was seen as primordial and a new financial agreement was reached between the two nations in June of 1944. It resulted in the acceptance of a further war debt of $123.5 million to reimburse the Americans for work that had been done.[73] The principle in question was simple. King himself, prior to the outbreak of war, pronounced that "domestic ownership, maintenance and control of all military stations and personnel is one of the really indispensable hall marks of national sovereign self government."[74]

This fundamental belief led the government, in the interest of sovereignty, to buy back the North and ensure clear title of Canadian ownership. As the *Final Report of the Advisory Committee on Post-Hostilities* advised in January 1945: "As time went on, it became increasingly apparent that the existence of major military installations in Canada built, paid for and operated by the United States might impair Canada's freedom of action. This difficulty has been mitigated, if not eliminated, by the Canadian Government's decision, agreed to by all the United States, to reimburse the United States for construction costs of all airfields and certain other facilities of continuing value erected in Canada by the United States."[75]

The lessons learned through painful experience during the war were not lost. "The war," wrote Desmond Morton, "had taught Canadians how swiftly the Americans could move when their minds were made up and how little weight Ottawa's appeals really carried in Washington."[76] A government report frankly stated that "if Canada had refused or failed to undertake projects which formed part of United States plans or measures in Canadian territory for the special protection of the United States, the United States was willing and even anxious to proceed alone."[77]

The realization that American security concerns represented a genuine threat to Canadian sovereignty was entrenched by the end of the Second World War. Nowhere was this more evident than in the Canadian North. "We had to discharge our obligations to make sure that nobody attacked the U.S. over our territory," explained General McNaughton. "If we had not done so there was the danger that the U.S. might have taken over the Canadian North in the interest of their own security."[78] This fear led to a new focus on the North and the acceptance of an enormous debt for unwanted infrastructure. The new geo-political reality was that Canada and the United States formed a strategic unit. As a result, American security was of vital interest to Canada.[79] "Because of the gateway which Canada opens to an enemy," King himself noted, "that the defence of this continent is bound to be increasingly that of the United States itself."[80]

This awareness, combined with the dramatic improvements in technology and the growing antagonism between the newly emerged superpowers, cast Prime Minister King's pre-war pledge in a new light. It now took on the likeness of a curse. Sandwiched geographically between the two rivals, Canadians quickly deduced the hazards and the potential penalty of attempting to remain aloof. A Canadian diplomat underscored the danger by pointing out that "the United States military men refer, whether nervously or menacingly, to the 'undefended roof of North America' and claim the right to return en masse to the Canadian Northland which they left so recently."[81] If the Second World War forced the nation's leadership to take a direct interest in the North for fear of losing Canadian control and ownership, then the post-war era burned the issue of Arctic sovereignty into their very souls.

Any respite from American encroachment in the North that the Canadian politicians had hoped to gain at the cessation of hostilities in 1945 quickly disappeared. The geographical reality was also highlighted in a 1946 classified US military appreciation on the problems of joint defence in the Arctic. It concluded that "the physical facts of geographical juxtaposition and joint occupation of the North American continent have at all times carried the implication that the defence of Canada and the defence of the United States cannot be artificially divorced. Recent technological developments rendering Canada's Arctic vulnerable to attack and thereby exposing both Canada and the United States to the threat of invasion and aerial assault across the northern most reaches of the continent have greatly heightened the compulsion to regard the defence of the two countries as a single problem."[82]

The Canadian assessment, although similar, was more blunt. Norman Robertson, the Under-Secretary of State for External Affairs, summed it up: "To the Americans the defence of the United States is continental defence, which includes us, and nothing that I can think of will ever drive that idea out of their heads. Should then, the United States go to war with Russia they would look to us to make common cause with them, and, as I judge their public opinion, they would brook no delay."[83] Prime Minister Louis St. Laurent quipped, "Canada could not stay out of a third World War if 11,999,999 of her 12,000,000 citizens wanted to remain neutral."[84]

Once again Canada was caught in the vortex of American security concerns. The North was perceived as an unprotected gateway to invasion that required immediate and costly measures to minimize its vulnerability.[85] Canadian politicians and their military commanders quickly supported the new emphasis on the defence of the North, but they did so to minimize American encroachment in the Arctic. The motive behind Canadian defence policy in the North was not security but remained one of countering perceived American penetration in the interest of sovereignty. Although an element of menace was recognized, Canadians consistently questioned their ally's assessments of risk. This difference in the threat perception is another indicator of the true reason for the government's focus in the North. By 1946, joint military planning committees warned of a serious threat, within a few years, to the security of Canada and the United States by means of attacks on North America by manned bombers equipped with atomic weapons.[86] The updated *Canada-U.S. Basic Security Plan* (revised ABC-22) more accurately reported that "up to 1950, the Soviets could use subversion and sabotage by internal groups; covert biological and chemical attacks; air attacks against Alaska, Iceland and Greenland and the use of airborne irregular forces ranging throughout the continent."[87] By 1952, military planners projected "the use of the atomic bomb delivered by long range aircraft and the occupation of Newfoundland, Alaska and Greenland for the forward basing of Soviet bomber aircraft and airborne forces."[88] As a result of those assessments the Americans maintained a worrisome interest in the Canadian Arctic.

Gladman Point Distant Early Warning station, King William Island, NWT. (Courtesy B. Horn.)

It was this American interest in the North, more than the threat posed by possible invasion, that concerned Canadian politicians. Their view of the risk of Soviet invasion was somewhat different. Scholars have pointed out that Canadian defence analysts were "less alarmist" than their American counterparts about Soviet intentions and the pace of technological advancement.[89] A Canadian intelligence report assessed that "the USSR is not considered capable at the present time of endangering, by direct action, the security of Canada and the United States."[90] It bluntly stated that the present American outlook gave an impression of a greater threat to the security of Canada and the United States than actually existed. It specifically disagreed when the Americans ascribed to the Soviets the ability to seize objectives in Alaska, Canada, or Labrador, from which they could operate to strike strategic targets in North America. The report commented that the Americans "credit a potential enemy with greater capabilities than we consider reasonable."[91] The British Foreign Office concurred. They affirmed that "Russia, so far as we can judge, is neither prepared for nor in the mood for war, and Stalin is a sober realist."[92] Canadian diplomats like Norman Robertson candidly agreed: "I hold that the scales of attack, to which it could reasonably be held we were exposed, were, are, and will be, almost insignificant."[93] So did the nation's military commanders. "I feel," conceded the Deputy Chief of the General Staff, "there is often a tendency for the Americans to place the worst picture before us in our discussions, with the result that our thinking is often along the lines of 100% protection and does not take into account a more realistic policy of calculated risk."[94]

Finally, Brooke Claxton, the Minister of National Defence, shared the same belief. He felt strongly that Canada faced no imminent threat. "On the information as is available to the Canadian government," he wrote, " it appears most unlikely that the Soviet Union would be in a position to wage another war in the near future, and for this reason it is highly improbable that the Soviet Government would run the risk of deliberately provoking such a war."[95] Claxton postulated that the Soviet Union would not be physically capable of war for at least another fifteen years.[96]

The skepticism of the actual risk was not a function of blind ignorance. The politicians maintained a belief that there was no peril to Canada even at the height of the demoralization of Communism in the early 1950s. They recognized an international threat but not one to Canada itself. Gordon Graydon, an MP who was part of the Canadian delegation to the United Nations, pointed in the House of Commons to the Soviet Union's "undisguised steps toward world domination."[97] Prime Minister St. Laurent and his Secretary of State for External Affairs, Lester B. Pearson, both went on record in 1951 as stating "the international situation was never more serious."[98] Other parliamentarians were more colourfully describing Communism as "a diabolical dynamic thing ... aiming at the destruction of all the freedoms and the inherent hard-won rights of man" and describing it as "the darkest and direst shadow that has ever fallen upon this earth."[99]

The international threat was such that Canada expanded its armed forces and dramatically increased its defence expenditures. This was to pay for an expeditionary force to fight the evils of communism in Korea, as well as to raise a special brigade for service in Europe.[100] Despite these concrete actions to combat the growing international menace, the actual danger to the Canadian Arctic was perceived as minimal. "The danger of direct attack upon Canadian territory," declared Claxton, "was extremely remote ... any attack on North America would be diversionary, designed to panic the people of this continent into putting a disproportionate amount of effort into passive local defence."[101]

This confidence was based on an assessment of practicality, probability and risk. Claxton explained the factors that were important in determining Canada's defensive posture. He insisted that consideration must be given to four above all: "the geographical position of Canada; the capacity of any possible aggressor to make an attack; the disposition of friendly nations; and what may be called the international climate."[102] Based on these criteria, the northern threat was quickly discounted. The government argued in the Commons that "we have to discard from any realistic thinking any possibility of an attack by ground forces on the area of Canada either by air or by sea. Anyone who has any knowledge of the terrain of the outlying parts of this country will realize that such an attempt would be worthless and useless and is not likely to be part of any aggressive plans which may be launched against Canada."[103] Furthermore, the government emphasized that invading the North "would in no way destroy our war-making potential nor would it have any decisive effect on winning a war on this continent by invasion ... you have only to look at this vast continent to see how formidable such a task is."[104] The historian R.J. Sutherland likened Canada's Arctic region to a strategic desert separating what he considered the two bastions of polar defence, Alaska and Northern Greenland. He concluded that there was no particular strategic value in the Canadian Arctic itself.[105]

The military assessment was similar. Army appreciations considered the likelihood of enemy airborne attack to be extremely slight because of the difficulties of re-supply and re- embarkation of the attacking force.[106] The official assessment contained in *Defence Scheme No. 3*, concluded that as a result of their extremely limited base facilities in eastern Siberia, the Soviets were not capable of more than isolated airborne operations, none totalling more than a few hundred men. Furthermore, it explained that the lack of fighter escort would make sustained operations impossible. More importantly, the official defence plan identified only Western Alaska and the Aleutian Islands as potential targets of enemy airborne forces.[107] Joint Intelligence Committee assessments argued that the data available "implies that the Soviet Union cannot land any airborne forces on Canadian territory."[108]

The marginalization of the North as a potential "gateway to invasion" gained further impetus in the Cabinet Defence Committee. It rationalized that "if the Soviets attempted to use a Canadian Arctic station as a bomber base, warning would be received and it was expected that such a base, which would have immense supply problems, could be immobilized rapidly."[109]

The double-edged nature of having facilities in the North was now exploited. Prime Minister King carefully weighed the Governor General's observation that bases in the Arctic "may become bases from which the enemy himself may operate were they not there."[110] He subsequently decided that "our best defence in the Arctic is the Arctic itself."[111] Claxton elaborated on the concept: "In working out the doctrine of defence of our north, the fewer airfields we have the fewer airfields we have to defend against the possibility of the enemy using them as stepping stones from which to leapfrog toward our settled areas. Indeed, were it possible the greatest single defence throughout our northland would be the rough nature of the ground and the extent of the territory itself."[112] General McNaughton agreed that "ice is something of a defence in itself" and Lester Pearson quickly dubbed the government's position the "scorched ice policy."[113]

In spite of it's position on the actual threat to the North, or lack thereof, the government continued to funnel resources into the Arctic. By 1956, a great deal had been done. The government established more weather stations in the far North; increased arctic research and built a permanent research facility at Fort Churchill; escalated the number of northern exercises; formed the Canadian Rangers among the Inuit to increase northern patrols; and co-operated in the construction, financing and manning of a series of early warning radar networks. It also restructured the permanent force of the army around an air portable/air transportable brigade (called the Mobile Striking Force) whose primary task was to counter enemy lodgements in the North.[114]

These actions were not based primarily on security concerns but rather were part of the government's active "re-Canadianization" program aimed at "keeping the Canadian Arctic Canadian."[115] Government reports highlighted the necessity of ensuring effective protection of Canadian sovereignty because of the continuing fear of American penetration. The Privy Council Office noted that "our experiences since 1943 have indicated the extreme care which we must exercise to preserve Canadian sovereignty in remote areas where Canadians are outnumbered and outranked... Of much greater concern is the sort of de facto U.S. sovereignty which caused so much trouble in the last war and which might be exercised again."[116]

Canadian concern for the North was aptly revealed by an editorial in *The Canadian Forum* of 1947. The intellectual magazine reminded its readers that "we must be certain that we defend [Canada] as much from our 'friends' as from our 'enemies.'"[117] Action was taken in the absence of a legitimate concern for security because, explained Norman Robertson later, "what we have to fear is more a lack of confidence in United States as to our security, rather than enemy action ... If we do enough to assure the United States we shall have done a good deal more than a cold assessment of the risk would indicate to be necessary."[118] In essence, this was the spark behind the continuing Canadian focus on its Arctic region.

The immediate post-war concern for the perceived northern Achilles heel eventually began to wane and by the mid fifties the menace in the Arctic was seen almost exclusively as an air threat. Political and military leaders generally agreed that "the only probable method of attack, is by air,"[119] and "that in the final analysis the task of Canadian defence is defence against aerial attack over the north pole."[120] This new assessment provided Canadian politicians with a welcome respite. The emphasis of military activity in the North shifted from active "defence" to simply "surveillance." Department of National Defence annual reports documented the subtle change. The stated threat no longer postulated surprise attacks in co-ordination with a campaign of aerial bombardment of North America. The yearly summaries of the later 1950s narrowly defined the danger as an air threat based on the manned bomber.[121]

The air threat itself evolved in step with technology and so the manned bomber was largely replaced by the intercontinental ballistic missile (ICBM). By 1963, Paul Hellyer, the MND, could state that "the air threat to North America consists of long range ICBMs, submarine or ship launched intermediate range ballistic missiles and manned bombers."[122] The new ICBM threat rduced the Arctic's military importance; its role now was simply to provide strategic depth. As General Charles Foulkes explained, this new reality meant that "we will have to rely on the deterrent and retaliatory effect of the U.S. strategic [nuclear] force. So that with the passing of the bomber, the Canadian contribution to the defence of North America will be greatly diminished and the importance of Canadian air space and territory in defence of North America will be seriously reduced."[123]

American interest in the Canadian North declined dramatically during this period. Not surprisingly, as the threat of American encroachment into the Arctic disappeared, so did Canadian interest. The navy gradually stopped its northern cruises in the summer. Surveillance flights were pared down. Armed exercises ceased. And the radio system as well as the Alaska Highway were turned over to civil departments of the government. Even the Canadian Rangers were allowed to languish.[124]

This lack of concern was further evidenced in the 1964 White Paper. It did not include a single reference to the Arctic. This silence accords with strategist Colin Gray's observation that "since the mid-1960s there has been no military incentive to urge the Canadian Forces to be active in the North. Reference to 'foreign incursions,' let alone 'lodgements,' should be treated with the contempt they merit."[125] But Gray missed the point: "military incentive" had always been absent. The rationale behind Canada's defence policy in the North was primarily political—to protect its sovereignty against perceived American penetration. Only when American interest died in the late 1950s did Canadian interest also wane. The need to assert Arctic sovereignty was always the driving force behind Canadian military action in the North.

The government was soon reminded of this. In 1969, the Americans announced that the supertanker *Manhattan,* belonging to the Humble Oil Company, intended to sail through the Northwest Passage to study the feasibility of transporting Alaskan crude oil through northern waters year-round. They did not seek Canadian permission. The United States considered the Northwest Passage international waters. Canada, however, asserted that the passage was within its territorial waters. As a result, the *Manhattan* incident sparked another frenzy of politically directed military activity in the North. Maxwell Cohen captured the essence of the challenge. "*Manhattan's* two voyages," he wrote, "made Canadians feel that they were on the edge of another American steal of Canadian resources and rights which had to be dealt with at once by firm governmental action."[126]

Members of 1 Battalion, The RCR, on a sovereignty exercise, Rankin Inlet, NWT, January 1984. (Courtesy B. Horn.)

The military was once again given the principal role of protecting Canadian authority in the Arctic. "Our first priority in our defence policy," asserted Prime Minister Trudeau, "is the protection of Canadian sovereignty."[127] This was followed by the external affairs minister's admission that the future role of Canadian forces would be "in the surveillance of our own territory and coastlines in the interests of protecting our sovereignty."[128]

The defence of the North, specifically the ability to rapidly deploy paratroopers to any corner of the nation's territory, represented the Canadian Airborne Regiment's most pervasive task from 1968 until its disbandment in 1995. (Canadian Parachute Centre)

Changes were rapidly implemented. Year-round training of soldiers in the North was resumed in March 1970. The following month a new permanent headquarters to co-ordinate all military activity in the North was established at Yellowknife.[129] A year later, a new defence White Paper emphasized sovereignty protection as the primary commitment of the Canadian Armed Forces.[130] The government cleverly used the need to bolster its defence of territory and sovereignty in the North to cover the withdrawal of half of its forces from NATO Europe.

Critics viewed the "whole emphasis on the North as a sham" and one editorialist wrote that "while Pierre Trudeau didn't invent the Arctic, he certainly seems determined to re-discover and exploit it for political purposes."[131] The accusation was appropriate. The White Paper emphasized the perennial distress over American encroachment instead of any concern over security. The military threat was never a serious issue. The NDHQ Directorate of Strategic Planning insisted that "apart from the threat of aerospace attack on North America, which can be discounted as an act of rational policy, Canada's geographic isolation effectively defends her against attack with conventional land or maritime forces."[132] Predictably, once the storm over the *Manhattan* died away, and the cuts to the Canadian Forces in Europe had been implemented, the emphasis on Arctic sovereignty was allowed to dissipate.

Concern for the Arctic ebbed with the tide and remained low for more than a decade. Then in 1985 the Americans triggered the hypersensitive nationalist sentiment once again. The announcement, with no accompanying request, of the impending voyage through the Northwest Passage of the U.S. Coast Guard cutter *Polar Sea,* incited shrill cries for the protection of Canadian sovereignty.[133] The military was once again sent to meet the non-military threat to the North. The *Canadian Strategic Review 1985-1986* noted that the government's decision "to underscore Canadian sovereignty in the north with an increased air and naval presence was reminiscent of the steps taken by the Trudeau government during the late 1960s and early 1970s."[134] The trip through Canadian waters of the U.S. Coast Guard cutter *Polar Sea* was linked by Melvin Conant to the "political receptivity of an increased defense effort."[135]

The magnified emphasis on defence was subsequently highlighted in the 1987 White Paper, *Challenge and Commitment*. Like its predecessor, this policy document established as "its first priority the protection and furtherance of Canada's sovereignty as a nation."[136] It stated: "After the defence of the country itself, there is no issue more important to any nation than the protection of its sovereignty. The ability to exercise effective national sovereignty is the very essence of nationhood."[137]

The Conservative government's initiatives included the North American Air Defence Modernization Program (North Warning System),[138] a proposed new northern training centre for the army, the designation of five northern airfields as Forward Operating Locations, the construction of the *Polar 8* icebreaker, and an ambitious new fleet of nuclear submarines.[139] These programs were rooted in a perceived challenge to sovereignty rather than in any actual military threat. The White Paper commented that technology had nullified the Arctic Ocean as a buffer between the superpowers and had made the Arctic as a whole more accessible. It warned that "Canadians cannot ignore that what was once a buffer could become a battleground."[140] But the underlying motive was explained by Perrin Beatty, the MND. "Our sovereignty in the Arctic," he admitted, "cannot be complete if we remain dependent on allies for knowledge of possible hostile activities in our waters, under our ice and for preventing such activities."[141] The protection of sovereignty was cited repeatedly to justify the cost of a fleet of nuclear submarines. The proposal did not reflect any belief in a potential Arctic battleground. This point of view is shared by Canadian military strategists who "have privately mused that ... it seems safe to assume the threat of attack on or through the ice of the Arctic Ocean against Canada is indeed negligible."[142] The political scientist Joseph Jockel asserted that "it is important not to overrate the importance of Canadian Arctic waters, a tendency that sometimes emerged in the Canadian SSN debate ... To the north, there are very substantial limitations to the firing positions SLCM-carrying submarines could take up."[143] Jockel underscored the political stimulus when he remarked that the emphasis on sovereignty protection "places a premium on the presence of Canadians, rather than on the fulfilment of a defence mission."[144]

Fiscal realities and the end of the Cold War quickly dampened the latest surge of interest in the Arctic. Many of the programs proposed, such as the fleet of nuclear submarines, the northern training centre and the *Polar 8* icebreaker were never implemented. However, the emphasis on sovereignty never waned. The *1994 Defence White Paper* echoed the sentiments of its predecessors and emphasized sovereignty as a vital attribute of a nation-state.[145] This was reinforced in DND's *Defence Planning Guidance* documents four years later which reiterated that "although Canada faces no direct military threat, it must have the ability to protect its sovereignty."[146]

The Arctic was never seen as a gateway to invasion. Prior to the Second World War little focus was centred on the North. With the exception of a few far-sighted individuals who envisioned the importance of a transpolar air route to Asia and Europe, as well as the national value of a network of northern airfields and communications sites, most considered the Arctic nothing more than a frozen wasteland. The question of the North representing a security risk was never considered.

The Second World War erased the Canadian apathy toward its Arctic region. The spectre of a Japanese or Nazi occupied Siberia from which attacks could be launched against North America stimulated a new American focus on Alaska. The American mobilization to protect its northern most frontier spilled into Canada and shocked Canadian politicians. American energy and resources quickly transformed the Canadian North into a hive of activity. Unfortunately, the Americans placed little weight on the formalities of ownership and executed their tasks with a single mindedness that suggested the long neglected North was under de facto United States control. For Prime Minister King the apparent loss of independence was intolerable and action was quickly taken, as it was put at the time, to "re-Canadianize the Canadian Arctic."

Canadians quickly realized that when it came to the defence of North America, the technological advancements in aircraft and weapon systems, as well as the reality of geography, made Canada and the United States a single strategic unit. Furthermore, it was evident that any American concern for Arctic security became a real danger for Canada. It was well understood that if Canada failed to take the appropriate action to ensure its frontiers were safe from any hostile action that could endanger the United States, the Americans would do so unilaterally. As a result, in an effort to maintain control and sovereignty over the North the Canadian government undertook an energetic and costly program to halt American penetration. The motive was strictly one of sovereignty. Security was never the over-riding issue.

The theme of sovereignty over security was replayed consistently during the post-war era. A decline in activity and interest in the North by the Americans was always parallelled by a welcomed reduction in the Canadian effort. However, Canadian energy was always quickly refocused by the appearance of any American challenges such as the voyages of the *Manhattan* in 1969 and the *Polar Sea* in 1985. In both cases, loud cries lamenting the loss of sovereignty in the North triggered visceral public debate. And in both cases the government reverted to its default setting and quickly increased military activity in the North. The use of the military was a symbolic and very effective way to reinforce sovereignty. But the Canadian Armed Forces were there merely to provide a presence, an exhibition of control and ownership, rather than to perform any real military mission in response to an actual military threat.

The North was never seen by Canada as a gateway to invasion. Instead, the nation's geographic location was often viewed as a curse. Canada was sandwiched between two rival superpowers and as the weaker ally of a more powerful, and at times even paranoid, neighbour it had little option but to do whatever was necessary to placate the security concerns raised by the United States, regardless of its own best interests. In the process Canadians became more concerned with defending their North from their close ally and neighbour than from any perceived threat of invasion. To the Canadian government it has always been a question of sovereignty, not security.

Notes for Chapter 15

1   Cited by Canada, *Canada's Territorial Air Defence* (Ottawa: DND, 1985), 35.

2   Kenneth Eyre, "Forty Years of Military Activity in the Canadian North, 1947-87," *Arctic*, Vol 40, No. 4 (December 1987), 293.

3   Trevor Lloyd, "Aviation in Arctic North America and Greenland," *The Polar Record*, Vol 5, No. 35 (January-July 1948), 36, 164; and John Swettenham, *McNaughton, Volume 1 1887-1939* (Toronto: The Ryerson Press, 1968), 210-214. In 1941, this established network of radio stations and air fields proved invaluable to provide communications for the many defence projects which were quickly undertaken. See also Shelagh D. Grant, *Sovereignty or Security?* (Vancouver:

UBC Press, 1988), 15. The cost of the radio stations was shared between the Department of the Interior and Defence.

4   H.W. Hewetson, "Arctic Survey," *Canadian Journal of Economic & Political Science,* Vol 11 (1945), 462-463. See also Vilhjalmur Stefansson, "The American Far North," *Foreign Affairs,* Vol 17 (April 1939), 517-521; and J.A. Wilson, "Northwest Passage by Air," *Canadian Geographical Journal,* Vol 26, No. 3 (March 1943), 107-115.

5   Stacey, *The Military Problems of Canada,* 112. See also Canada, *House of Commons Debates* (hereafter *Debates*), 28 February 1944; and Vilhjalmur Stefansson, "Routes to Alaska," *Foreign Affairs,* Vol 19, No. 4 (July 1941), 869.

6   The perceived importance of a transpolar route was rekindled in 1937, when three Soviet airmen flew non-stop from Moscow to Vancouver in 63 hours and 17 minutes. W.M. Franklin, "Alaska, Outpost of American Defense," *Foreign Affairs,* Vol 19, No. 1 (October 1940), 247. It was quickly noted that "On the maps of tomorrow's air age Canada holds a strategic position that can shape our future as a world power...In practise every plane from Europe or Asia reaching the United States by great circle courses will cross the Dominion." Trevor Lloyd, "Canada: Mainstreet of the Air," *Maclean's,* 3 April 1943, 34.

7   C.P. Stacey, *Arms, Men and Governments: The War Politicians of Canada 1939-1945* (Ottawa: Queen's Printer, 1970), 379-380. See also F.H. Ellis, "New York to Nome and Back," *The Beaver,* September 1949, 28-32.

8   Stacey, *Arms, Men and Governments*, 380. See also Stan Cohen, *The Forgotten War—Vol I* (Missoula, Montana: Pictorial Histories Publishing Company, 1988), 10-22.

9   W.L. Mackenzie King, "Canada's Defence Policy," *Canadian Defence Quarterly* (hereafter *CDQ*), Vol 15, (October 1937-July 1938), 135.

10   *Debates,* 16 May 1938, 3179.

11   *Debates,* 24 March 1938, 1644.

12   Ibid, 1644. See also *Debates* 19 May 1936, 2979; and "Royal Canadian Air Force," *The Royal Air Force Quarterly,* Vol 9, No. 1 (January 1938), 10-13.

13   *Debates,* 24 March 1938, 1650 and 26 April 1938, 3236-3237.

14   M.A. Pope, *Soldiers and Politicians. The Memoirs of Lt.Gen. Maurice A. Pope* (Toronto: University of Toronto Press, 1962), 83 & 93. See also C.P. Stacey, *Six Years of War. The Army in Canada, Britain and the Pacific* (Ottawa: Queen's Printer, 1966), Defence Scheme No. 3, 30-31.

15   CGS Appreciation of Military Situation, February 1941, Directorate of History and Heritage (hereafter DHH), File 112.3M2 (D496).

16   Joint Staff Committee, DND, 5 September 1936 (Army Records), as quoted in James Eayrs, *In Defence of Canada: Appeasement and Rearmament* (Toronto: University of Toronto Press, 1965), Document 1, 213.

17   Charles Foulkes, "Canadian Defence Policy in a Nuclear Age," *Behind the Headlines,* Vol 21, No. 1 (May 1961), 1. Stacey supported this claim. He noted, "All Canada's pre-war defence planning was implicitly conditioned by the knowledge that Canadian territory was protected by geogra-

phy and the naval power of the United Kingdom and the United States." Stacey, *Arms, Men and Government,* 130.

18   E.L.M. Burns, "The Defence of Canada," *CDQ,* Vol 13, No.4 (July 1936), 379.

19   C.P. Stacey, *The Military Problems of Canada* (Toronto: Ryerson Press, 1940), 29-30.

20   Ibid, 29.

21   Monica Curtis, ed., *Documents on International Affairs 1938 - Vol 1* (London: Oxford University Press, 1942), 416. See also *Canadian Annual Review of Politics & Public Affairs,* 1937-1938, 141; and *Debates,* 12 February 1947, 346. FDR's speech was made in Kingston, Ontario on 18 August 1938. There was a degree of pragmatism involved. It has been well established that "the American Army has always taken the position that an attack on Canada is equivalent to an attack on the United States. For it is axiomatic that such an invasion...would merely be the prelude to an assault on the industrial heart of this country." Edgar P. Dean, "Canada's New Defence Program," *Foreign Affairs,* Vol 19, No. 1 (October 1940), 236.

22   *Debates,* 12 February 1947, 346. The reliance on American protection led King to retort in Parliament, "The talk which one sometimes hears of aggressor countries planning to invade Canada...is, to say the least, premature. It ignores our neighbours." *Debates,* 24 May 1938, 3179. This is not to say that some alarmists did not raise the issue. The advances in aircraft technology and the development of transpolar routes raised the concern of aerial bombardment. It was postulated that industrial centres in Canada could conceivably be attacked from Europe by aircraft using the Arctic routes. These concerns however were largely ignored. See *Debates,* 13 February 1939, 861-871; Flight Lt. A. Carter, "It Can be Done," *Canadian Defence Quarterly,* Vol 16 (October 1938-July 1939), 54-58; and E.L. H-W, "The Trend of Air Power," *The Royal Air Force Journal,* Vol 10, No. 1 (January 1939), 1-6.

23   Jean Potter, *Alaska Under Arms* (New York: Macmillan, 1942), 35.

24   Franklin, 247.

25   Potter, 74. Despite Alaska's strategic geographic location, it was the last of the overseas departments to receive combat planes. S. Conn, R. Engelman, R.C, and B. Fairchild, *The U.S. Army in World War II. The Western Hemisphere. Guarding the United States and Its Outposts* (Washington D.C.: Department of the Army, 1964), 247.

26   Conn, 392. Alaska was described as, "Not exactly a soft under belly but rather the big toe an enemy can stand on while he slugs you." M. Young, "Defence Dilemma on North Frontier," *Saturday Night,* 13 Oct 1951, 28.

27   Potter, 35-36. It was noted that it took less than four hours to fly, in a bomber, from the southern Alaskan bases to Seattle. Ibid, 13.

28   Canada, *Documents on Canadian External Relations, Vol 9, 1942-1943* (Ottawa: External Affairs, 1980), 1180.

29   Desmond Morton, *Canada and War. A Military and Political History* (Toronto: Butterworths, 1981), 110.

30   Yarham, 227. This was reflected by the concern shown by the Minister of Parliament for Cariboo in Question Period

following the initial announcements of Japanese occupation of some islands in the Aleutians. He stated, "there will be much uneasiness in British Columbia, Alberta and other parts of Canada." *Debates,* 11 June 1942, 3257.

31 Galen R. Perras, "An Aleutian Interlude: Canadian Participation in the Recapture of the Island of Kiska," (Unpublished War Studies MA Thesis, Royal Military College, April 1986), 9.

32 An Appreciation of the Military World Situation with Particular Regard to its Effect on Canada (as of 31 July 1942), completed by the General Staff (GS), 4 August 1942, 7, National Archives of Canada (hereafter NA), Ralston Papers, MG 27, III B11, Vol 37.

33 Brief Appreciation of the Situation as of 24 Feb 1941, GS estimate 25 February 1941, 2; and Japanese Occupation of the Aleutians Islands, GS estimate 15 July 1942, 3, NA, Ralston Papers, MG 27, III B11, Vol 37.

34 Appreciation Re Air Landing Troops, 24 January 1942, 2. DHH 112.3M2 (D232).

35 Stacey, *Six Years of War*, 174-175. At its peak in June 1943, the army attained a strength of 34,316 men on the West Coast. See also Perras, 3-4.

36 Pope, 91.

37 Colonel Stanley W. Dziuban, *The U.S. Army in World War II. Special Studies. Military Relationships Between the United States and Canada 1939-1945* (Washington D.C.: Department of the Army, 1959), 199. The United States military strength in Northwest Canada in late 1942 exceeded 15,000, and in the next year, when some of the troops had been replaced by civilian workers, U.S. civilians alone exceeded that figure.

38 The Ogdensburg Agreement (18 August 1940) was a result of discussions, relating to the mutual problems of defence, between President Roosevelt and Prime Minister King. King stated, "The common approach of the governments of Canada and the United States to the problems of North American defence was formally recognized in the Ogdensburg agreement." *Debates,* 10 May 1943, 2504. The PJBD consisted of "four or five members from each country, most of them from the services." See J.W. Pickersgill, and D.F. Forster, *The Mackenzie King Record, Vol 1* (Toronto: University of Toronto, 1960), 137-142; and Dziuban, 22-30. See also "Canada-U.S. Permanent Joint Board on Defence—Twenty-Fifth Anniversary," *External Affairs,* Vol 17, No. 9 (September 1965), 384-388; and H.L. Keenleyside, "The Canadian-U.S. Permanent Joint Board of Defence, 1940-1945," *Behind the Scenes,* Vol 16, No. 1 (Winter 1960-61), 51-75. In regard to the North-West Staging Route, Howe described it as, "One of Canada's most important airways...composed of a chain of main aerodromes, with intermediary fields, extending form Edmonton to Alaska." *Debates,* 28 February 1944. A northeastern staging route, code named Crimson, was also developed which was used to ferry aircraft and supplies to Europe via northern Canada (The Pas, Churchill, Fort Chimo, Frobisher Bay, Northern Quebec), Labrador and Greenland. See Conn, 399-403; and Dziuban, 130-133.

39 Adrian Preston, "Canada and the Higher Direction of the Second World War 1939-1945" in *Canada's Defence.*

Perspectives on Policy in the Twentieth Century, eds., B.D. Hunt and R.G. Haycock, (Toronto: Copp Clark Pitman Ltd., 1993), 116. J.T. Jockel echoed this assessment. He noted, "Canada had been prepared to accept U.S. direction of continental defences in early plans which assumed a defeated Britain and a retreat to Fortress North America." Jockel, "The Military Establishments and the Creation of NORAD," in *Canada's Defence,* 166. See also Grant, *Sovereignty or Security?* 131. The impression of a "sense of panic" at the imminence of Britain's collapse (as well as a perceived lack of faith and loyalty) caused Prime Minister Winston Churchill to initially look upon the Ogdensburg Agreement in an unfavourable light. This was reflected in an uncomplimentary telegram to King. See Pickersgill, *Record, Vol 1*, 139-143; and Stacey, *Canada and the Age of Conflict, Vol 2* (Toronto: University of Toronto Press, 1984), 312.

40 Grant, *Sovereignty or Security?* 46.

41 K.S. Coates, and W.R. Morrison, *The Alaska Highway in World War II* (Toronto: University of Toronto, 1992), 25-26. This source provides an unrivalled account of the social impact of the "American invasion" on the Canadian North.

42 Dziuban, 53-54; Cohen, *The Forgotten War, Vol 1*, 16-17; Yarham, 227; G.L. Smith, "War Unlocks Our Last Frontier—Canada's Northern Opportunities," *Maclean's,* 3 April 1943, 11.

43 Stefansson, "Routes to Alaska," 868.

44 *Documents on Canadian External Relations, Vol 9, 1942-1943,* 1175.

45 *Documents on Canadian External Relations, Vol 9, 1942-43,* 1183. The author, H.L. Keenleyside noted, "I do not like the idea of Canada allowing the U.S. to construct a highway on Canadian territory (thereby acquiring a moral if not a legal right to its continued use, at will, in peace or war)."

46 *Documents on Canadian External Relations, Vol 9, 1942-43,* 1183. See also Keenleyside, 54-55.

47 Stacey, *Arms, Men and Governments,* 383.

48 Ibid, 348; and Dziuban, 220-221.

49 Stacey, *Arms, Men and Governments*, 348; Grant, *Sovereignty or Security?* 74-78; and Dziuban, 41.

50 Grant, *Sovereignty or Security?* 76.

51 Stacey, *Arms, Men and Governments,* 383.

52 Grant, *Sovereignty or Security?* 123.

53 *Mackenzie King Diaries*, Queen's University Archives (QA), File (Microfiche) T172 (21 March 1942).

54 Grant, *Sovereignty or Security?* 82-86; O.B. Hopkins, "The 'CANOL' Project," *Canadian Geographical Journal,* Vol 27, No. 5 (November 1943), 241; Cohen, *The Forgotten War, Vol 1,* 34-38; and W.O. Kupech, "The Wells and CANOL: A Visit after 25 Years," *Canadian Geographical Journal,* 1968, 137-139. The eventual price tag for the project was $134,000,000.00.

55 Coates, 36. See also Dziuban, 229; and Cohen, *The Forgotten War, Vol 2,* 30.

56 Pope, 219.

57 Donald Creighton, *The Forked Road* (Toronto: McClelland & Stewart, 1976), 73. See also D. Grant, "CANOL—A Ghost From the Past, *Alternatives,* Vol 9, No.2 (Spring 1980), 23.

58 Grant, "CANOL," 23; Dziuban, 214; and R.S. Finnie, "The Origin of CANOL's Mackenzie Air Fields," *Arctic,* Vol 33, No. 2 (June 1980), 274-277.

59 Vincent Massey, *What's Past is Prologue* (Toronto: Macmillan, 1963), 371.

60 Ibid, 372. Creighton commented, "All too often they behaved as if they were on their own soil, or on a separate but tributary and submissive part of the Empire of the United States." Creighton, 73. Stacey noted, "Canadian officials were often troubled by a tendency on the part of Americans to disregard Canadian sovereignty. American officers and officials...were sometimes as little disposed to worry about respecting Canadian national rights...and acted as if they were on their own soil." Stacey, *Arms, Men and Governments,* 385.

61 Stacey, *Six Years of War,* 145-183. Lieutenant-General Pope stated, "The threat to Canada was less than minor, and insignificant as it was, it was created almost entirely by the overwrought imagination of too many of our otherwise sane and sensible people." Pope, 180 & 219. See also Nils Orvik, *Canada's Northern Security: The Eastern Dimension* (Kingston: Queen's University, 1982), 2.

62 Stacey, *Canada and the Age of Conflict, Vol 2,* 362. Trevor Lloyd, assigned to the Wartime Information Board, reported that it was apparent that the Americans were far advanced in their study of the Canadian Arctic. He noted that the American Army "was deeply entrenched in the north and that they have first class research facilities and an Arctic information centre." He added, "We have nothing." Grant, *Sovereignty or Security?* 122. Norman Robertson exclaimed, "The American presence had been allowed to grow in a fit of absence of mind" and he recommended that "a good, competent Canadian staff would have to be sent to the area, capable of collaborating with and controlling American development activities." J.L Granatstein, *Canada's War: The Politics of the Mackenzie King Government 1939-1945* (Toronto: Oxford University Press, 1975), 322.

63 Cited by Coates, 36.

64 Pickersgill, *Record Vol 1,* 396.

65 *Mackenzie King Diaries,* QA, File T172 (18 March 1942).

66 Massey, 396. Minutes from the Cabinet War Committee meeting on 7 April 1943 recorded, "It was feared that despite these agreements the United States, after the war, might seek to base an equitable claim to special concessions upon these large expenditures in Canada. *Documents on Canadian External Relations, Vol 9, 1942- 43,* 1259. King also noted a similar conversation with Malcolm MacDonald in his diary. He wrote, "I said we're going to have a hard time after the war to prevent the U.S. attempting control of some situations. He [MacDonald] said already they speak jokingly of their men as an army of occupation." *Mackenzie King Diaries* (29 March 1943).

67 Massey, 396.

68 Pickersgill, *Record Vol 1,* 644.

69 *Documents on Canadian External Relations, Vol 18, 1952,* 1201.

70 "Sovereignty in the Canadian Arctic in Relation to Joint Defence Undertakings," 29 May 1946. DHH 112.3M2 (D213).

71 *Debates,* 10 May 1943, 2504. The commissioner, Brigadier W.W. Foster, reported directly to the War Cabinet Committee. See also Grant, "CANOL," 24.

72 Prime Minister King stated, "To carry out joint plans for the defence of this continent, and to facilitate the transportation of war materials to fighting fronts, the Canadian government has agreed to the stationing of United States military units at certain places on Canadian territory...It is not contemplated that the contributions which the United States is thus making to the common defence will give that country any continuing rights in Canada after the conclusion of war." *Debates,* 29 January 1943, 20-21.

73 Grant, *Sovereignty or Security?* 132; Conn, 403-404; and Stacey, *Arms, Men and Governments,* 381.

74 *Debates,* 1 July 1938, 4527.

75 *Documents on Canadian External Relations, Vol 11, 1944-45,* 1570. See also L.B. Pearson, "Canada Looks 'Down North,'" *Foreign Affairs,* Vol 24, No.4 (July 1946), 641-643. In 1969, SCEAND reiterated the importance of "paying your own way" and denounced the "free ride theory." The committee was convinced that Canada must be prepared to incur reasonable expenditures for its own defence in order to maintain its independence and freedom of action as a nation, and to ensure that Canadian interests are taken into account when continental defence measures are being taken. Cited in E.J. Dosman, ed., *The Arctic in Question* (Toronto: Oxford University Press, 1976), 90.

76 Morton, *Canada and War,* 156.

77 *Documents on Canadian External Relations, Vol 11, 1944-45,* 1570. Defence analyst R.J. Sutherland echoed those same observations seventeen years later when he observed, "Canada must not become through military weakness or otherwise a direct threat to American security. If this were to happen, Canada's right to existence as an independent nation would be placed in jeopardy." R.J. Sutherland, "Canada's Long Term Strategic Situation," *International Journal,* Vol 17, No. 3, Summer 1962, 202. A group of twenty influential Canadians (politicians, scholars, bureaucrats) reached this same conclusion in July 1940. They wrote *A Program of Immediate Canadian Action,* which stated in part, "A United States bent on large-scale preparations for its own defence and that of the hemisphere would be determined to take adequate measures wherever they might be needed. If concerned about the inadequacy of the meagre Canadian defences, it might and probably would insist on acting to augment them. Canada would have to co-operate voluntarily or involuntarily." Cited in Dziuban, 18.

78 Cited by Sweetenham, 176.

79 P. Buteux, "NATO and the Evolution of Canadian Defence and Foreign Policy," in *Canada's International Security Policy,* eds., D.B. Dewitt, and D. Leyton-Brown (Scarborough, ON: Prentice Hall, 1995), 160-161. R.J. Sutherland commented, "in the final analysis, the security of the United States is the security of Canada." Sutherland, 203.

80 Pickersgill, *Record, Vol 1,* 203.

81 Grant, *Sovereignty or Security?* 156.

82 *USAAF Study on Problems of Joint Defence in the Arctic,* 29 October 1946, quoted in Grant, *Sovereignty or Security?* Appendix G, 302-311.

83 *Documents on Canadian External Relations, Vol 11, 1944-45,* 1535.

84 M.A. Conant, *The Long Polar Watch. Canada and the Defence of North America* (New York: Harper and Brothers, 1962), 73. General Foulkes wrote, "Canada cannot negate geography. Canada is physically joined to the United States just like Siamese twins. If one of the twins gets hurt the other one suffers." Foulkes, 10. Even Nikita Khrushchev later stated, "This time Canada would not be geographically secure." Norman Hillmer, and J.L. Granatstein, *Empire to Umpire. Canada and the World to the 1990s* (Toronto: Copp Clark Longman, 1994), 221. Pearson observed, "In 1946 there is no isolation—even in the Arctic ice." Pearson, "Canada Looks Down North," 647.

85 The new perceived vulnerability was the result of "the principal advancements in the science of war," namely, "The increased range of application of destructive power and armed force resulting from the development of modern aircraft, amphibious technique, guided missiles, and advancement in technique of submarine warfare, as well as the increased destructive capacity of weapons such as the atomic bomb, rockets, and instruments of biological warfare." *Documents on Canadian External Relations, Vol 12, 1946,* 1617-1618.

86 J.T. Jockel, "The Canada-United States Military Co-operation Committee and Continental Air Defence, 1946," *Canadian Historical Review,* Vol 64 (1983), 352. During the 1947 May Day flyover of Red Square, the Russians revealed that they now had bombers (copied from an American B-29 that made an emergency landings in the U.S.S.R. during the war) capable of striking the United States. Ibid, 355. See also *House of Commons Debates Official Report—The Defence Programme,* 5 February 1951, 1.

87 *Documents on Canadian External Relations, Vol 12, 1946,* 1618-1623 and *Vol 15, 1949,* 1560-1561 & 1566-1567. See also Sean M. Maloney, "The Mobile Striking Force and Continental Defence 1948-1955," *Canadian Military History,* Vol 2, No. 2 (Autumn 1993), 76.

88 Maloney, 76. See also "If the Russians Attack Canada," *Maclean's,* 15 June 1951, 8-9 & 68.

89 See Ron Purver, "The Arctic in Canadian Security Policy," in *Canada's International Security Policy,* ed., D.B. Dewitt, 82. Colin Gray also stated, "There is no doubt that in the late 1940's Canadian-United States differences over the scale of 'the threat' were quite considerable." *Canadian Defence Priority: A Question of Relevance* (Toronto: Clarke, Irwin & Company, 1972), 71. Stacey observed, "Canadian ministers, officials and officers were probably somewhat less disposed than their American opposite numbers to believe that the USSR intended to attack the West." Stacey, *Canada and the Age of Conflict, Vol 2,* 406.

90 *Documents on Canadian External Relations, Vol 14, 1948,* 1581.

91 Ibid, 1581-1582. A memorandum from the MND to PM, in 1947, reiterated this belief. He wrote, "war is improbable in the next five or even ten years." Ibid, *Vol 13, 1947,* 1482. Furthermore, Ernest Ropes of the U.S. Department of Commerce stated that Russia's industrial production would be "insufficient to support a war against the U.S.A. for at least 25 years." J.W. Warnock, *Partner to Behemoth* (Toronto: New Press, 1970), 50.

92 James Eayrs, *Defence of Canada. Growing Up Allied* (Toronto: University of Toronto Press, 1985), 6.

93 *Documents on Canadian External Relations, Vol 11, 1944-45,* 1534.

94 "Intelligence Aspects–PJBD Canada–U.S.A.," 15 October 1946, DHH 112.3M2 (D213).

95 "Political Appreciation of the Objectives of the Soviet Foreign Policy," 30 November 1946. NA, Claxton Papers, MG 32, Vol 95, Box 5, File: Canada–U.S. Defence Collaboration.

96 Ibid.

97 *Debates,* 5 February 1951, 77.

98 *Debates,* 12 February 1951, 267.

99 *Debates,* 8 May 1951, 2833. The shrill screams of fear included claims that "We also have no reason to believe that the Russians have not at this time, somewhere in the north, set up camouflaged rocket installations. It is not entirely beyond the realm of possibility;" and "We have no reason to believe they could not send suicide bombing missions, and if they did central Canada would make a beautiful target." Ibid, 2834.

100 *Debates,* 12 February 1951, 260. The government program called for an armed force of 115,000 men and an expenditure of $5 billion. See also *House of Commons Debates Official Report–The Defence Programme,* 5 February 1951, 1-7; and *Canada's Defence Programme 1951-52,* 5-10; and Desmond Morton, *A Military History of Canada, 3rd ed.,* (Toronto: McClelland & Stewart, 1994), 233-237.

101 Eayrs, *Peacemaking and Deterrence,* 100, 107 & 401. See also D.J. Bercuson, *True Patriot: The life of Brooke Claxton* (Toronto: University of Toronto Press, 1993), 195; and *Documents on Canadian External Relations, Vol 11, 1944-45,* 1583.

102 *Debates,* 9 July 1947, 5270; and Canada, *Canada's Defence* (Ottawa: DND, 1947), 7.

103 *Debates,* 17 June 1955, 4925. One military officer stated, "In Canada's northern regions there was no place to go from a military point of view and nothing to do when you got there." Dosman, 23.

104 *Debates,* 8 May 1951, 2834-2835.

105 Sutherland, 209.

106 Composition of Mobile Striking Force for Defence of Canada, 3 December 1948; and Appreciation on the Mobile Striking Force, 13 May 1949. DHH 112.3M2 (D369).

107 *Defence Scheme No. 3–Major War,* Chapter V, "The Direct Defence of Canada," 16 September 1948, Appendix A, 2 & 4. DHH 112.3M2 (D10).

108 The Employment of the MSF for Reduction of Enemy Lodgements in Canada, 2 May 1950. DHH 112.3M2 (D400)

109 *Documents on Canadian External Relations, Vol 17, 1951,* 1249.

110 Pickersgill, *Record, Vol 3,* 370.

111 Eayrs, *Peacekeeping and Deterrence,* 344.

112 *Debates,* 15 April 1953, 3920.

113 Alan Harvey, "Scorched Ice Policy," *Globe & Mail*, 27 November 1948.

114 *Documents on Canadian External Relations Vol 12, 1946*, 1560; *Vol 14, 1948*, 1518; Canada, *Report on the Department of National Defence, 1949* (Ottawa: DND 1939), 12; Canada, *Winter Warfare Research Program. Exercise Eskimo* (Ottawa: DND, 1945); H.A. Halliday, "Recapturing the North. Exercises 'Eskimo,' 'Polar Bear,' and 'Lemming' 1945," *Canadian Military History*, Vol 6, No. 2 (Autumn 1997), 29-38; and Canada, *Winter Exercise Musk-Ox 1946* (Ottawa: DND, 1947); *Debates*, 24 June 1948, 5785 and 21 May 1954, 4953; *Canada's Defence Programme(s)*, 1949-1957; *The Defence of Canada, 1955*, 4-5; and Maloney, 75-86. *Report on the Department of National Defence, 1952, 53;* Doug Holmes, "The North's Own Canadian Rangers," *UP HERE*, February/March 1987, 60-63; and J. Honderich, *Arctic Imperative: Is Canada Losing the North?* (Toronto: University of Toronto Press, 1987), 31-33. Canada. *Canada's Territorial Air Defence*, 5; J.J. Sokolsky, "A Seat at the Table: Canada and its Alliances," in *Canada's Defence,* eds., Hunt and Haycock, 150-152; Purver, 85-87; Morton, *Military History*, 240. Participation in the Dew Line project elicited great storms of protest which raised the issue of military vassalage. A *Maclean's* editorial stated, "DEW is on Canadian soil, but it will serve primarily American rather than Canadian defence purposes." (6 August 1955, 2). Another article stated "For a sum of money that has been officially estimated at four hundred million dollars we have at least temporarily traded off our northern frontier. In law we still own this northern frontier. In fact we do not...In return for the luxury of not spending money on the Dewline we Canadians have surrendered something that for the last generation we have regarded as our greatest necessity, our independence." Ralph Allen, "Will Dewline Cost Canada Its Northland," *Maclean's*, 26 May 1956, 16-17 & 68-70.

115 *Documents on Canadian External Relations, Vol 15, 1949*, 1471.

116 Ibid., *Vol 18, 1952*, 1197-1198. It was noted that "U.S. activities now far surpass those of Canada, and there have been numerous incidents of U.S. military personnel throwing their weight about." Ibid., 1117 & 1195-1196. G.W. Smith noted "a massive and quasi-permanent American presence in the Canadian North such as we have seen during and since World War II could in due course lead, gradually and almost imperceptibly, to such an erosion or disintegration of Canadian sovereignty that the real authority in the region, in fact if not in law would be American." R.St.J. Macdonald, ed., *The Arctic Frontier* (Toronto: University of Toronto Press, 1966), 213. The Secretary of State for External Affairs, during a briefing to Cabinet reiterated the danger of de facto American control as a result of increased American activities in the Arctic which would "present greater risks of misunderstandings, incidents and infringements of Canadian sovereignty." *Documents on Canadian External Relations, Vol 19, 1953*, 1048.

117 *The Canadian Forum*, Vol 27, No.318 (July 1947), 75. Colin Gray claimed that "the only plausible challenger to the writ of Canadian law in the Arctic is Canada's principal ally, the United States." Gray, 128.

118 *Documents on Canadian External Relations, Vol 11, 1944-1945*, 1535.

119 *Debates*, 21 May 1954, 4951. See also Canada, *The Defence of Canada* (Ottawa: DND, 1955), 2; and Canada, *Defence 1959* (Ottawa: DND, 1959), 10. The emphasis on air was obvious. Proportion of monies for the different services was broken down as follows: navy - 15.7%; army - 15.7%; air force - 41.4% (remainder spent on mutual aid, research, and other), 6. *House of Commons Debates Official Report–The Defence Programme*, 20 May 1954.

120 *Debates*, 17 June 1955, 4925. It was also stated that "we have to discard from any realistic thinking any possibility of an attack by ground forces on the area of Canada either by air or by sea." The belief was that "any attack on Canada will be in essence part of an attack on the United States," (Ibid., 4925), and it would be part of "a world war, a total war." Ibid., 24 June 1948, 5783. See also *Canada's Defence Programme* 1949-50; Sutherland, 271; and A. Brewin, *Stand on Guard. The Search for a Canadian Defence Policy* (Toronto: McClelland & Stewart, 1965), 53-54.

121 The change was reflected in the *Canadian Defence Programme* annual reports. Reports from 1949-1955 spoke of the need to repel "surprise attacks." In 1956, the wording was changed and reflected the downgraded danger. It now ambiguously stated that forces were required to "deal with possible enemy lodgements." Another subtle change was in the focus of the aim of Canada's defence programme. Wording changed from "defence of Canada from direct attack" to "provide for the security of Canada."

122 *Statement by the Honourable Paul T. Hellyer, MND, to the Special Committee on Defence, June 27, 1963,* 1. See also Canada, *Territorial Defence*, 5-7; Macdonald, 271-272.

123 *Special Committee on Defence–Minutes of Proceedings and Evidence, 22 October 1963* (Ottawa: Queen's Printer, 1963), 503.

124 Eyre, 296.

125 Gray, 185.

126 Maxwell Cohen, "The Arctic and National Interest," *International Journal*, Vol 26, No.1 (Winter 1970- 1971), 72. The government tried to place a favourable spin on the event. Both Prime Minister Pierre Eliot Trudeau and External Affairs Minister Mitchell Sharp stated publicly that they "concurred with the project." Nevertheless, their approval was never sought and the research information was never shared. See *Debates*, 15 May 1969, 8721; and *Globe & Mail*, 18 September 1969, A7. Sharp explained that a large part of the problem lay in Canada's fear that its claims to the Arctic archipelago and adjacent waters, specifically the Northwest Passage which was disputed by the Americans, may be defeated in an international tribunal. Sharp stated, "the government continued to feel that a blunt declaration of sovereignty would invite a challenge from the United States, a challenge for which Canada, equipped only with legal and historical arguments of less than conclusive force, might be ill-prepared." *Canadian Annual Review For 1970*, 350. External Affairs had always candidly noted, "Due to the desolate nature of the areas in question, these claims have little support on the grounds of effective occupation, settlement or development. Thus while

Canada's claims to sovereignty to these regions have not heretofore been seriously challenged, they are at best somewhat tenuous and weak." *Documents of Canadian External Relations, Vol 12 (1946),* 1556. See also Grant, 178 & 307; L.C. Green, "Canada and Arctic Sovereignty," *The Canadian Bar Review,* Vol 68, No. 4 (December 1970), 740-775; *Globe & Mail,* 12 March 1970, A1; and Dosman, 34-57.

127 *External Affairs,* Vol 21, No. 6 (June 1969), 253.

128 *Globe & Mail,* 18 September 1969, A7.

129 *Canadian Annual Review For 1970,* 362; *Debates,* 21 May 1971, 6054; and Canada, *Defence 1971* (Ottawa: DND, 1972), 59-60. General J.V. Allard confirmed that the establishment of the new headquarters was a direct result of the *Manhattan* incident. J.V. Allard, *The Memoirs of General Jean V. Allard* (Vancouver: The University of British Columbia Press, 1988), 291. See also Dan G. Loomis, *Not Much Glory* (Toronto: Deneau, 1984), 69; Purver, 88-90.

130 Canada, *Defence in the 70s.* See also Canada, *Canada's Territorial Air Defence,* 31; and Nils Orvik, *Canadian Defence Policy: Choices and Directions* (Kingston: Queen's University, 1980), 1-2. He felt that the "so- called 'northern orientation' in Canadian defence policy was never well defined in terms of defence objective and deployments." Joel Sokolsky commented, "the general thrust of the Trudeau policies was to de-emphasize collective defence in favour of national sovereignty protection." J.J. Sokolsky, *Defending Canada* (New York: Priority Press Publications, 1989), 5.

131 *Canadian Annual Review for 1970,* 363. Professor Bland revealed that Donald Macdonald, the MND, "found military advice unhelpful, if not antagonistic. He directed the preparation of the 1971 White Paper without military advice." D. Bland, *The Administration of Defence Policy in Canada 1947-1985* (Kingston: R. P. Frye & Co., 1987), 213.

132 A Draft Study of the Future International Scene, 5 April 1968, 4 & 8. DHH 112.11.003 (D3), Box 3.

133 R.B. Byers, and M. Slack, eds., *The Canadian Strategic Review, 1985-1986* (Toronto: CISS, 1988), 126-128; Sokolsky, 13; and J.T. Jockel, *Security to the North. Canada-U.S. Defence Relationships in the 1990s* (East Lansing: Michigan State University Press, 1991), 30-31.

134 Byers, *Strategic Review 1985-1986,* 130.

135 M.A. Conant, "The Long Polar Watch: An American Perspective on Canada's Defence of Its Arctic," *American Review of Canadian Studies,* Vol 18, No. 3 (Autumn 1988), 373.

136 Canada, *Challenge and Commitment–A Defence Policy for Canada* (Ottawa: DND, June 1987), II.

137 Ibid., 23.

138 *Challenge and Commitment,* 55-56. Erik Nielsen (MND 1985) stated, "I want to emphasize the importance of fully exercising sovereignty in our north. The DEW Line has served Canada well, but Canadians do not control it...The North Warning System will be a Canadian-controlled system–operated, maintained and manned by Canadians. Sovereignty in our north will be strengthened and assured for the future." *Debates,* 13 March 1985.

139 *Challenge and Commitment,* 50-55 & 60; Byers, *Strategic Review 1985-1986*, 128-131 & *1987,* 106; and Honderich, 78-80.

140 *Challenge and Commitment,* 6.

141 Paul George, "Arctic defence too hard to handle?" *Globe and Mail,* 12 March 1987, A7.

142. Honderich, 90.

143 Jockel, *Security to the North,* 162. For a description of the difficulties of submarine operations in the North see W.G. Lalore, "Submarine Through the North Pole," *The National Geographic Magazine,* Vol 115, No. 1 (January 1959), 2-24; and J.F. Calvert, "Up Through the Ice of the North Pole" *The National Geographic Magazine,* Vol 115, No. 1 (July 1959), 1-41.

144 Ibid., 193. He also stated that "the emphasis on sovereignty protection can pose two long term future problems for the United States. First, Canada can devote its very scarce military resources to presence rather than military mission, knowing that the United States can be counted on, in the final analysis, for defence."

145 Canada, *1994 Defence White Paper* (Ottawa: DND, 1994), 15.

146 Canada, *Defence Planning Guidance 1998* (Ottawa: DND, 1997), 1-1.

PART IV

Canada and the International Community

Top: Canadian SFOR Patrol in Bosnia. (DND file photo.)

Bottom: Canadian soldiers contain a riot in Dvar, Bosnia, 1998. (DND file photo.)

NOT EVEN FOOLS RUSHED IN

The Canadian Military Experience in Latin America and the Caribbean

Hal Klepak

THIS CHAPTER LOOKS AT THE EXPERIENCE of the armed forces of Canada in Latin America and the Caribbean from colonial times to the present. As such it is an overview meant to stimulate interest in a little studied part of Canadian military history but one whose dimensions are growing steadily at the present time.

The lack of keenness exhibited by Canada and Canadians for these regions until the 1980s should not surprise us. Nor should the fact that if national interest in the area was slight, the defence element of that interest was slighter still. Latin America and the Caribbean were not vital to Canada's survival over the centuries; the colonies' wars, and then those of the nation, were rarely fought in any decisive way in those regions. Instead, it was of course in North America and Europe where Canada's future was decided even though New France was indeed given up because Versailles considered it of less value than Caribbean possessions of slight size but great wealth. And while Latin American and Caribbean issues were never absent from such wars, those issues were never central to Canada's war effort.[1]

Indeed, when it was asked why Canada was not interested more in the Americas south of the United States, the reply of a variety of governments tended to be in line with the thinking of the Canadian scholar and diplomat John Holmes. Holmes pointed out there was no reason why Canadians should be particularly interested in a region very far away with which they were not linked culturally, historically or politically, and with which they were only joined by an impassable isthmus.

Indeed, in most modern Canadian history, the extent of United States domination of the region was such that the very idea of somehow joining it at the expense of more comfortable Commonwealth and NATO contexts seemed to many observers little less than madness.[2] Both Lester Pearson and Vincent Massey, for example, were of this view.[3] This was especially true in the security field where our interests were seen as almost certain to clash with those of the U.S. and to do so on issues that were marginal to Canada but were often seen as vital by Washington.[4]

Thus Canada remained largely aloof until the late 1980s from any idea of a security linkage with Latin America. And while the Commonwealth ensured some connection to the West Indies, that relationship was hardly central to Canadian concerns. Haitian immigration eventually created an important community in this country, largely in Quebec, but issues from their land of birth were generally seen as even less vital to Canada than those of their anglophone Caribbean neighbours.

This having been said, there is a requirement for nuance here. Canadians did serve in the region on a number of occasions in the past and since the late 1980s the Canadian Forces have been repeatedly deployed to the area. But that is recent history indeed.

New France

New France enjoyed a special place within the French Empire, for Quebec and Acadia were the only significant colonies of France to be settled by white colonists. This was true for the whole history of the French Empire up to the conquest of Algeria in 1830 but even then the place remained overwhelmingly Arab.

In military terms, the continental colony in North America was exceptional. The nature of its defence problems, involving confronting a massively superior southern enemy on land, and usually at sea as well, made a large and relatively efficient militia absolutely essential. While distance from the English colonies, combined with a frightful climate, proved useful in deterring or defeating attempts at conquest, only a numerous and effective militia could make those advantages stick in the face of overwhelming odds that approached forty to one.[5]

The French West Indies were entirely different. Saint-Domingue, present-day Haiti, was a vitally rich element of the Empire providing Versailles with a huge percentage of its income. And colonies such as Martinique and Guadeloupe were important as well. Their role in the sugar economy of the seventeenth and especially the eighteenth century ensured them a priority with the French government that, as seen in 1763 at the peace table, totally eclipsed that enjoyed by New France.[6]

They were, however, not French except in terms of ownership. The white élite of the islands was miniscule when compared with the vast numbers of black slaves there.[7] Government officials, merchants and great landowners did not provide a base for a militia of any consequence and only regular soldiers from France were available for the defence of these colonies. This was a far cry from the situation prevailing in North America where the potential for mobilization of the male population was perhaps unmatched anywhere else in the Americas.[8]

Thus, the North American colony, while hardly a major centre of population, was the single most important source of white military manpower outside metropolitan France. Thus it should not surprise us to see a limited number of *canadiens* active in imperial defence outside their territory early in the seventeenth century.

For long after the founding of New France, Spain and France were enemies. The long-lived Hapsburg drive for European if not worldwide supremacy had made inevitable a clash with the dynasty in France. Thus the seventeenth century was marked, as the previous had been, by war and talk of war between the two countries. France never acknowledged the Spanish claim to dominion of the non-Christian world (shared with Portugal) granted by the Pope in the 1490s. Instead, its corsairs in war and its pirates in peace raided the new Spanish colonies without mercy and brought home to France both bullion and a further stimulus to territorial ambitions.

Indeed, while English pirates were to become the most famous on the Spanish Main, in the early sixteenth century and at many later stages, it was the French who were most feared in the Spanish Caribbean possessions.[9] It is unknown to what extent the colony to the far north was involved in this activity but individuals from it doubtless were. The maritime traditions of the colony, and the trading context especially of Acadia, ensured this.

In the dynastic diplomacy of the day, it was not long before raids were being replaced by more serious military campaigns and islands and other territories were changing hands regularly. Saint-Domingue, Martinique and Guadeloupe were soon to be French along with a number of smaller islands. Sugar was the king in the Antilles and this reinforced the commercial link with New France and especially with Louisiana.

The War of the Spanish Succession dramatically changed the diplomatic context. Beginning in 1702 and lasting until 1713, the war raged over whether the two crowns of Spain and France could be joined in one. The overwhelming potential power of this combination ensured the creation of an opposing alliance which included the British and which in the end prevailed, although only after long and costly warfare in which Canada's fate, as well as much of Spanish America's, was frequently in the balance.

While allied success ensured that one vast Franco-Spanish empire did not result, Versailles and Madrid were quick to establish a Family Pact which supposedly would unite their efforts in defence of joint objectives in foreign and imperial policy. Bourbons were on the throne of both countries and Spain and its empire were inundated by new ideas from France or from people trained, and institutions established, by the French.

In theory New France now had a considerable link with the Caribbean. Spain's enormous empire there included the whole coastline of that inland sea stretching in a vast arc from Florida to today's Venezuela, interrupted only by logging establishments set up by the British here and there on the inhospitable Central American coast. And with the exception of smaller islands the French, Dutch and British had wrenched from Spain since the discovery of the Americas, Madrid was still supreme in all the Greater Antilles including eastern Hispaniola, Cuba and Puerto Rico.

The days of raids on those colonies were largely past. The new threat as the eighteenth century developed was British sea power and its ability to reach virtually anywhere. Regular warfare would become the rule, even though corsairs remained a major part of Caribbean maritime conflict for well over a century.

The new alliance paid off for Spain in the sense that French successes in North America reduced the pressure on its own American possessions. Coalition operations could be imagined in the Caribbean between France and Spain, and who better to lead them than Canada's most famous soldier and sailor, Le Moyne d'Iberville. Born in Montreal in 1661, he was then governor of Louisiana and already a hero for his spectacular successes against the British in Hudson Bay, Newfoundland and Acadia.[10]

Iberville was in Havana in 1706 at the head of a major fleet, preparing it for a descent on the Atlantic seaboard. While there he and his men confronted a major cholera epidemic; he was himself taken ill with yellow fever and died in the city. He is buried in Havana and there are monuments to him around the city, notably in the central museum, the Palace of the Captains-General. It is uncertain how many other *canadiens* died.

These events represented what was almost certainly the most important presence of *canadiens* of whatever stripe ever seen in the region prior to the Second World War. Indeed, never again under the French regime did such a large force go south in support of Spanish or indeed French objectives in the Americas.

The greatest danger came to the French West Indies, as it did to New France during the Seven Years' War (1756-1763). Indeed, after Quebec fell it was the turn of several French islands to do the same. It was too late for the northern colony to provide even the very limited succour it had given in the past. St. Lucia, Grenada and the Grenadines, Guadeloupe and Martinique and other smaller islands all fell during the war to the British.

British Rule

Britain's acquisition of Canada meant a neater integration of the colonies of Nova Scotia and Newfoundland, now with the addition of Quebec, into the system of rule prevailing in the Thirteen Colonies to the south. There was no significant threat to British North America; France was reduced to the tiny holding of St. Pierre et Miquelon (off the south coast of Newfoundland) and its remaining few dependencies in the Caribbean. Only an enormously weakened and less threatening Spain gained in the Americas. Its Mexican territory grew with the addition of Louisiana and thus Spanish dominion was pushed east to the Mississippi. However, its loss of Florida in the peace of 1763—handed over to Britain for the return of Cuba—reduced its position in North America tremendously and meant the end of its presence on the Atlantic coast altogether.

The British could thus feel a degree of security never known since the foundation of their colonies in North America, a safety emphasized by the astounding victories of the war and the seeming invincibility of the Royal Navy. Indeed, that very security helped spawn the American Revolution a scant twelve years after 1763. The French threat from the north and west had long been a tangible reinforcement of loyalty to the English crown, but now that threat was gone.

The war was fought against a backdrop of increasing commercial ties between the West Indies and British North America. The Bourbon experiment allowing limited Cuban free trade encouraged commerce between that rich island and North America, and that trade continued even after British forces left it in 1763.[11]

In defence terms, however, the link was to be clearer still. The beginning of the great naval triangle West Indies-Bermuda-Halifax began to surface as the need for a series of bases for the blockade of rebel ports made itself felt.[12] Few Canadian militiamen served in the Revolution in ways that would have taken them to the West Indies or the Spanish or Portuguese empires in the Americas. And while doubtless some did—from Quebec, Nova Scotia or Newfoundland—these were individuals and very little is known of them.

The War of 1812 is another story. By now the links between the naval base at Halifax and its Bermudian and West Indian counterparts were as firm as the blockade the Royal Navy established through their use. In this war the Canadian militia was both large and dramatically engaged in the defence of the homeland. Troops and sailors served abroad, and in the West Indies specifically, on some scale.

The success of the defence of British North America in the War of 1812, however, led directly to a major change in the direction of United States expansionism in the Americas. Instead of driving northwest at First Nations, British and Canadian expense, the disastrous showing of the U.S. Army in its attempt at such conquest suggested the possible advantages of turning south against weaker Spanish possessions.

This happened just as the opportunities there were suddenly proving much more attractive. With the kidnapping of the royal family of Spain by Napoleon in 1808, Spanish dominions around the world were suddenly decapitated. They were also deprived of the bulk of their Spanish garrisons. And while the movements for independence spawned by these events were slow to develop, the United States was speedy indeed in profiting from the discomfiture of Spain, its former ally and a valuable supporter during its own recent revolution.[13]

The United States, taking the lead from Andrew Jackson, by 1815 had seized all of Florida while Spain was defenceless and prostrate. It was the first of a series of invasions, filibustering attempts, purchases and diplomatic moves that would lead to American domination of Latin America's north in the coming decades. Wary now of British power, Washington moved on from the acquisition of Florida—which then included what is now southern Alabama and Mississippi—to test the newly independent republics of Mexico and Central America. The British were troubled by this expansion in areas of traditional British importance but they could console themselves with the thought that at least the aggression was not against Canada.[14]

Direct linkages between Canadian interests and Mexican had to await the Oregon Crisis of 1846. Here Lord Palmerston's clear-headedness about the real possibilities of an Anglo-Mexican alliance in the face of Manifest Destiny's determination to acquire the Canadian Northwest and Mexico's Texan territories meant that each country faced U.S. expansionism essentially alone. The settlement of the Anglo-American crisis that year meant the United States had its hands free to face the Mexicans.[15] Within two years U.S. military strength had half the Mexican state and added not only Texas but California, Arizona, New Mexico and much else to the Union. British North Americans could only watch with some horror the continuing filibustering efforts of U.S. citizens, corporations and the government itself in Central America, Cuba, Hispaniola, and elsewhere.[16]

Sympathy for Latin America and its fate in the face of the United States began to grow in Canada. While it certainly found an echo in London, the benefits of attempting to stop it were not seen to be worth the risk of war with the United States. British concern over events was real enough but there was also a sanguine understanding that only major war could (perhaps) stop the Americans. And such a war would involve immense risks for Canada, the British Empire's only territory with a frontier on a land power of importance. Fears of such ambitions turning north again provided the bedrock of thinking on Canadian defence, as it was for so long to do, and thus they were an indirect link between events in Latin America and Canada's strategic position. But few Canadians wanted a showdown with the United States any more than their fellows in the United Kingdom did, even though on many occasions they appeared to do so on themes which touched Canada closely.[17]

The Dominion

The end of reciprocity with the United States in 1866 was, as is well known, linked to the drive for Confederation in 1867. A less well known effect was the dispatch of a trade mission abroad. That mission went to Latin America, felt to be a natural and essential place for Canadian trade in the light of reciprocity's demise.[18] Little came of this initiative: there was civil war in Mexico, political crisis in Cuba (soon to break out into the Ten Years' War of 1868-78) and more turmoil in much of the rest of the Caribbean and northern South America.

Dominion status did not change Canada's strategie relationship to Latin America. Britain still handled Imperial foreign policy and the Royal Navy protected the approaches to Canada. While Canadians served as soldiers and sailors wherever the Union Jack fluttered, they did so as adventurous individuals and not as representatives of Canada. The Sudan expedition and Boer War of the late nineteenth century changed this but they little affected Latin America and the Caribbean.

The major change there came with the Hay-Pauncefote Treaty of 1901 in which the British abandoned any rights in the partially completed Panama Canal.[19] Presaging the Anglo-Japanese Treaty of a year later, the British essentially conceded naval dominance in the Americas to the United States, London having confidence that this was not only inevitable but would cause little harm to British trade interests in the region.[20] In any case, it was necessary to reduce the risk of conflict with the United States, a thought increasingly unthinkable for the British Empire. The Venezuela Crisis with the United States, the Alaska Panhandle settlement and other American issues—but especially the diplomatic context of the Boer War—made settling accounts with the U.S. a priority, and one which could be addressed with little loss.

Canadian-U.S. relations improved along with those overall between the Empire and the United States. And the increasing likelihood of war in Europe reinforced the Atlantic orientation of Canadian defence planners; the threat to Canadian interest was not from the south.[21] This did not reduce the connection with Latin America and the West Indies. Rather, the opposite prevailed. The First World War began the same year the Panama Canal was opened, and despite Canada's superb railway structure and its proven military utility, much of the Canadian war effort also moved by sea and a considerable percentage of that went through this new inter-oceanic waterway. While in no way as important for Canadian defence as it was for that of the United States, the canal was nevertheless an asset of strategic value to Canada.

The war also brought co-operation in Imperial defence in the West Indies. For the first time, a Canadian force was deployed as far south as Bermuda (not of course strictly in the Caribbean but decidedly in the West Indies and refreshingly tropical). The Royal Canadian Regiment was sent to the island in order to free up the British garrison for service immediately on the Western Front in what was to be a dress rehearsal for a much larger deployment of this kind in the Second World War. And some Canadians serving with the Royal Navy got to know a few of their Brazilian counterparts. This occurred when Rio de Janeiro entered the war on the Allied side, as a result of the German sinking of neutral Brazilian merchant ships, and sent a squadron of three cruisers and four destroyers to co-operate in convoy escorts off Africa as well as South America.[22]

The Inter-War Years

With the return of peace in 1919, and against the backdrop of the isolationist Liberal government of Mackenzie King, Latin America once more dipped below the horizon of the Department of National Defence. And indeed so it would have remained had the Salvadorean crisis of the early 1930s not occurred. Conditions for the peasantry, never that good, had worsened in recent months in that country, and calls for reform were met with resistance from an autocratic government hard pressed by the Depression.

The events there had nothing to do with Canada but when fighting—massacres, to be more accurate—occurred in many parts of El Salvador the Admiralty found itself with no ships close to Central America in a position to protect British lives and interests. The West Indies squadron would normally have had the responsibility but El Salvador is the only country in the region not to have an Atlantic (or Caribbean) coast. And the fleet in the Far East was a much reduced force whose bases were far away.

The Commander-in-Chief America and West Indies had received reports from the British chargé d'affaires and consul in San Salvador of "well armed Communists" in the area of the capital. He was concerned for the safety of British subjects from a variety of Imperial territories and Dominions at that time in El Salvador, which was an important producer of coffee for export to Europe and a place where many foreigners (including Canadians) lived. The Dominions Secretary in London advised the Secretary of State for External Affairs in Ottawa on 22 January, 1932, that there was a "possibility of danger to British banks, railways and other British lives and property."[23] Because the only Royal Navy warship in the region was five days away, and as he knew that two Canadian ships were closer, he asked the Chief of the Naval Staff of the very much reduced Dominion navy if it could help.

There is some debate about what happened over the course of the next few days. The Chief of the Naval Staff quickly instructed Commander V.G. Brodeur (of the famous RCN family of L.P. and Nigel Brodeur), captain of HMCS *Skeena,* to proceed to the Salvadorean port of Acajutla. In a telegram sent from Ottawa at 1:30 a.m. on the 23rd, Cdr Brodeur was strongly warned that "No overt acts should be taken unless actual and immediate imperative necessity to save lives of British subjects."[24] Prime Minister R.B. Bennett was informed of the situation the following afternoon in a memorandum from the Under-Secretary of State for External Affairs. It referred to a further report from the British chargé in San Salvador speaking of the "likelihood of an outbreak tonight" but reassured the Prime Minister by saying that the United States authorities locally were less concerned.[25]

The record is lost at this stage. Two days later a message was received from Cdr Brodeur on board *Skeena* saying that he had gone ashore and spoken to the British Consul and even the President of the Republic. He had been shown around some of the troubled areas by the army on the 24th and had made the three-hour trip to the capital, San Salvador. While reporting the possible presence of "Communist Indians" in the neighbourhood of the capital and suggesting "propose remaining for present," he said the earlier reports of danger had been "greatly exaggerated." Of Indians, he reported "several hundreds already killed."

The captain went on to say that the President had given "definite orders that foreign armed parties are not to be landed." Nevertheless, "an armed platoon was landed yesterday (from *Skeena*) Sunday at repeated and urgent request of British Consul at San Salvador. Platoon remained at wharf but was withdrawn as soon as I reached San Salvador and ascertained that conditions in no way warranted such drastic action." He added "it is considered that refugees will leave ship shortly."[26] Thus it is clear that a Canadian naval party was indeed landed but hardly as an act of aggression. It is also clear that British subjects took refuge on the ship, and it appears at least five of them were ladies connected to a British-owned local railway company.[27]

What was to be termed the San Salvador Incident ended the next day and the RCN warships continued on their journey southward to the Panama Canal. On the 29th the Dominions Secretary wrote the Secretary of State for External Affairs to say the British "are most grateful for service rendered by the two Canadian ships and highly appreciate action of His Majesty's Government in Canada in responding so readily."[28] Thus, London was pleased and there were no major repercussions, positive or negative, in El Salvador or the region. The Salvadorans had other problems and the incident is now completely forgotten there. Apparently there was, however, unfavourable coverage of the incident in Mexico, a country at the time troubled about any foreign influence in Central America. "Adverse comment in the Mexican press" was mentioned by the consul, D.J. Rogers, in a note to London on 9 February.[29] He went on to tell his diplomatic masters how much the local government had been helping the British community of late, saying that the "prompt arrival of the destroyers [HMCS *Vancouver* had quickly joined *Skeena* in Acajutla] has been largely responsible for this eagerness on the part of the authorities," and insisting that the Canadians had been of the "greatest help."

Finally, Rodgers said that the British community, which of course included Canadians living in El Salvador, had prepared a message of thanks to External Affairs which he had sent on to Ottawa. Whether remembered today or not, the Royal Canadian Navy had technically intervened for the first time in the domestic affairs of a Latin American country.[30] It is perhaps just as well that the incident has remained forgotten.

World War II

The Second World War expanded Canadian contact with Latin America. War-related trade grew dramatically, indirect military link with the region began through the immensely closer alliance with the United States, and Canadian troops served in several British island and continental colonies. In addition, Latin American forces served in at least one theatre of war in which Canadian forces were active.

The fall of most of Europe to Nazi and Fascist forces not only cost Canada her sense of security—ensured for so long by the Royal Navy—it had effects south of the border that extended all the way to South America. Optimists in the United States felt that Britain would hold out and that therefore the only sensible approach was to find ways short of war to help sustain her. But pessimistic opinion, dominant in many military circles greatly impressed by Nazi successes (especially the *blitzkrieg)* suggested that indeed, as the French were saying, Britain would soon "have its neck wrung like a chicken." Therefore it was imperative, it was argued, that the U.S. retain all national defence capabilities at home, that being interpreted variously as in the United States or within the Western Hemisphere.[31]

Washington at first opted very much for staying at home, and it pursued a number of initiatives with Caribbean and Latin American countries, notably Brazil. But as the summer and autumn of 1940 gave way to the winter of 1940-41 and the Commonwealth showed no signs of surrender, the tide began to change in U.S. opinion. A variety of ways were found to help the beleaguered British and the Dominions.

Latin America was shaken as well by events in Europe. Democratic governments there had long been worried about Fascism, especially those parties able to exploit a traditional local populism widespread in the region. Brazil and Uruguay but especially Argentina had massive Italian immigrant populations, and while Germans were fewer in number, they often had remarkable local influence.[32] Military regimes and the military in general in Latin America were also impressed with German military prowess, on display especially during the early years of the war. Many military men, as in the United States, tended to see Nazi Germany as essentially unbeatable. Thus there were many pulls in the direction of finding a *modus vivendi* with the new forces dominating Europe.

German strategic incompetence helped deal with this. The growth of U.S. power and influence in the region did as well. The attack on Pearl Harbor, followed by what was viewed locally as Berlin's madness in declaring war on the United States, began to change opinions dramatically in northern Latin America. Most Central American and Caribbean states followed the attack in the Pacific with declarations of war in support of Washington. And while South American and other reluctantly pro-American states were often slower in doing so, unrestricted submarine warfare soon forced their hand. Even traditionally nationalistic and anti-American states such as Mexico found themselves with dead and wounded from their merchant marines filling the newspaper headlines.[33] Within a few months both Mexico and Brazil, Latin America's most populous states, had also declared war on Germany.

The Rio Conference of the Pan American Union, the political and economic organization linking all republics of the Americas, took place in February 1942 shortly after Pearl Harbor. It began a process of hemispheric defence co-operation that continues today. Interestingly, the map of the area of interest to the arrangements set up at this time included both Canada and Greenland, despite the fact that neither Ottawa nor, needless to say, occupied Copenhagen was consulted. An Inter-American Defence Board was set up to co-ordinate the military response of the hemisphere less Canada. A political body to co-ordinate the struggle against Fascist ideology, the Emergency Advisory Committee for Political Defence, was also established.[34]

Canada had three indirect links to all of this: Brazil's entrance into the war and its decision to take an active role; Mexico's joining the United States in a Permanent Joint Board of Defence (PJBD) on the U.S.-Canadian model of 1940; and the dispatch of Canadian troops to the British West Indies. Each was revolutionary in its own way.

Brazil was a vital if junior partner in the war effort. It was felt that only that country's eastward tip of the continent could provide the Allies with the air and naval bases necessary for the North African landings of 1942 and the successful conduct of the anti-submarine campaign in the South Atlantic. And her rubber supplies were essential to the Allies once Burma succumbed to the Japanese in 1942. In addition, the Brazilian acquisition of Italian submarines just before the war allowed Allied navies to train against them in a highly realistic fashion and this, given the size of the Italian submarine fleet, proved most useful.

Brazil also sent air and land forces to Europe, the only Latin American country to do so. A full infantry division was sent to Italy and served near the Canadians advancing on the eastern side of that peninsula.[35] But the connection appears to have been little more than the odd leave spent close together in Florence or thereabouts.

Mexico's entrance into the war brought the U.S. and thus the Allies unimpeded access to that country's agricultural and mineral wealth as well as to its important oil industry. It also meant the U.S. could recruit among Mexicans living in the United States and, perhaps more importantly, could import agricultural workers—in high demand with so many young Americans in uniform—on a temporary basis and in large numbers. Mexico also sent an air squadron to assist the Americans in the reconquest of the Philippines. The southern Permanent Joint Board on Defence co-ordinated this and much more as the U.S. was given access to Mexican defence installations and allowed to construct its own on Mexican soil.[36] All of this would have been unthinkable before the war. When Canada suggested a single, continental PJBD, the Americans decided to keep these relationships firmly bilateral and thus dominated by the bigger member.

London, hard pressed in ways never imagined during the First World War, had an even greater need of Ottawa's assistance. The West Indies garrisons were needed for front-line duty, especially after Dunkirk, the beginning of fighting in North Africa and the collapse of the British Empire in the Far East. Remembering the successful experience with the Royal Canadian Regiment in Bermuda at the beginning of the First World War, the British asked if the Canadians could send mobilizing militia infantry units from Canada to a variety of colonies in the Caribbean, freeing up Imperial regiments for service elsewhere. Ottawa agreed and a number of battalions set forth for this extraordinary garrison duty in what were later to become major tourist destinations for Canadians.

The possible impact of these deployments on Canada's future relations with Latin American countries played no role in the decision to deploy. Troops in both British Honduras and British Guiana, for example, were apparently only vaguely aware that they were garrisoning colonies partly or wholly claimed by their neighbours, Guatemala and Venezuela. Indeed in the second case, it had been less than half a century since a threat of a U.S.-Canadian-British war over the colony had existed, and the prospect of local fighting was far from unthinkable. Even where Canada declined the British invitation—in the case of the Falkland Islands—the decision to say no was not related to the claim of neighbouring Argentina, not a small state at the time, but rather to the possible reaction in Washington.[37] Thus, Ottawa showed some daring in sending such forces several years before formal bilateral relations with these countries were established.

In tandem with these moves came other political and economic developments. Canadian trade flourished in Latin America, reaching six percent of the country's total world trade, a figure unheard of in peacetime. The fall of Europe, the Allied blockade of the Nazi-dominated continent, the loss of Japan as a trading partner, and the transformation of the British economy into one geared for war all meant that Canada (not to mention the United States) had a golden opportunity to export to the region. At the same time, the absence of Latin America's traditional European markets forced them to seek new ones, including the Canadian. Latin America's importance as a source of strategic minerals was not lost on Ottawa either, especially after the Japanese did such damage to traditional sources of such minerals in Asia.

Politically, Canada debated the advantages and disadvantages of accepting its status as an American nation and joining the Pan American Union. Pressure from many Latin American countries to do so was evident, especially after Ottawa used resources freed up in Europe to staff new embassies in the region. After much soul searching, Mackenzie King decided to test the waters. Washington's quick rebuff settled the issue for years to come.[38]

The Post-War Years

The end of war brought a return to more traditional Canadian concerns and, of course, a demobilization which left the forces only marginally better off than they were before the war. At the same time, trade and investment became increasingly dominated by the United States which had noted with considerable misgivings the growth of Canadian trade with Latin America. Ottawa was frequently seen, even at this late date, as a stalking horse for the British in the region.[39]

Despite this, Canada succeeded in selling several of its famous corvettes, as well as some frigates, to several Latin American navies.[40] Some excess air and land war material was also sold to Latin American forces. A number of Latin American crews visited Halifax for hand-overs and some received training as well from the Royal Canadian Navy.

Except for some occasional naval visits, the military linkages of the war, weak as they were, were not maintained during the early years of peace. U.S. domination of the region was vastly increased with the advent of the Cold War, the signing of the Rio Pact in 1947, and the formation of the Organization of American States the next year, and this domination ensured that Canada remained lukewarm to invitations to join in security efforts at the hemispheric level. Canada made NATO—ideal as linking both mother countries with the U.S. in the preferred multilateral environment—the main pillar of its defence. Even its eventual peacekeeping role was explained to the military as part of this multilateral approach to security. There was little room for interest in Latin America, despite the wartime experience and the importance of the Panama Canal to Canadian shipping.

Only two events in the early 1960s disturbed this context during the long years of the Cold War. The first was the 1959 victory of Fidel Castro in his revolutionary struggle against the U.S.-backed Batista dictatorship in Cuba. A leftist government proposing deep reform of a Latin American country, including a drastic reduction in the role and influence of the United States, had taken power and quickly proven how serious it was. The second event was the Cuban Missile Crisis of October, 1962. This story is well told elsewhere but suffice it to say that with the Latin American scene changing so quickly, and with the world coming to the brink of nuclear war, it became obvious to Canada that a more comprehensive policy might be necessary for the region.[41] Successive governments in Ottawa refrained from taking a contradictory stance on things Latin American. The risks of annoying the U.S. were too great and the benefits too small for such independence in the superpower's backyard.

Central America's civil wars did what the Cold War's spillover into Latin America had not proved able to do: bring Canada closer to the region. And although Cold War issues were not absent from Canadian policy toward Central America in the 1980s, they were far from dominant. Instead it was Canadian public opinion, historically almost totally indifferent to Latin America, which was to pave the way for a greater role in the region. The public, and especially non-government organizations, became interested in Latin America as never before.[42]

Canada became involved in the national peace negotiations of El Salvador, Guatemala, and Nicaragua as well as in the overall peace processes known as Contadora and Esquipulas. The United Nations was usually excluded from the region by the U.S. but the disarray in American policy occasioned by the Iran-Contragate affair presented opportunity. Ottawa offered its support in the international organization's effort to broker peace.[43]

The Breakthrough—ONUCA

In the light of progress made by the UN and the Central Americans themselves toward a general peace, the world body asked Canada to organize a reconnaissance of the region in November 1989.[44] Planning was underway for a mission to each of the region's five countries with the goal of reducing inter-state tensions resulting from the civil wars and the involvement of neighbouring countries on one side or another.

Canada dispatched the reconnaissance team and was deeply involved in the full-scale mission that followed upon it early in 1990. Ottawa was eventually to provide a mission second-in-command and later a commander (Brigadier-General Lew Mackenzie) as well as the largest contingent and the only helicopter squadron. Canadians of all three armed services served in

Costa Rica, El Salvador, Guatemala, Honduras, and Nicaragua. Spanish-speaking capability within the Forces grew apace, fuelled as well by recruiting in Canada's increasingly multicultural cities. For the first time it could be said that the Canadian Forces were really getting to know Latin America, working with its forces and addressing its problems.

The Salvadorean branch of the Observer Mission of the UN in Central America (ONUCA) after its Spanish acronym was initially hamstrung by the inability of the FMLN guerrilla organization to guarantee the safety of its members. This was soon overcome and the organization used the time to prepare for a separate mission, ONUSAL, which was set up in 1992 in the wake of the peace agreement in El Salvador. As a result of partial agreements between the warring parties on the need to have a verifiable way of humanizing the war and respecting human rights, ONUSAL was assigned that role.[45] Here again the Canadian Forces were well represented. But the wide-ranging elements of the peace accords meant that electoral observers, judicial reformers, policemen and a host of others, many also from Canada, soon dwarfed the military element.

The Guatemalan UN mission that was finally set up after the accords of December 1996 were signed was smaller but still dramatic. However, here political factors limited the military presence. Nonetheless, a small number of Canadian Forces personnel did serve over time in this later mission to Guatemala.

All of this Canadian military presence—hundreds of personnel and much equipment—set the scene for the posting of a military attaché to the region. In the atmosphere of the North American Free Trade Agreement, the office was opened in Mexico City and given responsibility also for Central American countries where Canadians were serving.

The Expansion of a Canadian Defence Interest

Central America and Mexico were not the only countries of interest in the Latin American region. Canada's foreign ministers beginning with Joe Clark in 1989 have continued to refer to the Americas as "Canada's region." Free trade with the United States had shown Canadians how much they needed Latin America as counterpoise in order to avoid becoming American in the cultural sense as well as the geographic. A rapid decline in European political connections and the slow growth of new Asia-Pacific ones, combined with the failure of Mr Trudeau's Third Option trade diversification effort, all seemed to focus attention on Latin America.[46]

The first conference on Latin America and Canadian defence was held in 1992 at the Collège militaire royal de Saint-Jean. This was followed by several others at defence installations and universities elsewhere in the country.

Canada meanwhile moved cautiously closer to the inter-American security system. Prime Minister Brian Mulroney had announced in October 1989 that the country would be joining the Organization of American States in early 1990. But Canada specifically rejected the security aspects of membership embodied in Chapters V and VI of the OAS Charter that included the common security and mutual defence commitments. Canada also refused to sign the central pillar of the system, the Inter-American Treaty of Reciprocal Assistance, commonly known to as the Rio Pact. Ottawa would not join the Inter-American Defence Board, send officers as students to the Inter-American Defence College, or attend as other than observers the conferences of commanders of the armies, navies and air forces of the Americas. The reputation of the inter-American security system as the birthplace of dictators and the mechanism of U.S. domination of the hemisphere—combined with the unsavoury reputation Latin American admirals and generals had earned over the years—ensured that governments in Ottawa were wary of co-operation in defence with anything like the OAS.[47]

Once in the overall system of the Americas, however, it became increasingly difficult to suggest one wished to be active in all fields except security. How could one speak of anchoring democracy if one would not deal with civil-military relations, or with the defence of that democracy? How can one talk of creating a region of peace without addressing the security of the states in question? How could one deal seriously with the new and emerging security agenda, almost all of it of interest to Canada, without being inside the forums where it was being debated and formed?

Specific problems of security raised their heads at the time as well. The Haitian situation involved the possible use of force and indeed Canada was an advocate of a hard line on establishing democracy there. Mexican security also loomed large. As the United States moved toward the militarization of the struggle to contain illegal drugs as well as increasing tendencies to include illegal immigration, the illicit arms trade and even health and environmental issues under the security rubric, staying out of anything related to inter-American security was increasingly at odds with Canadian policy internationally and in this region in particular.

By 1991, Ottawa had changed its point of view. While still reluctant to join the overtly U.S.-dominated elements of the security system, it was proving more than willing to work in others and even create new ones.[48] Canada joined Argentina in pressing for the creation of a Special Committee on Hemispheric Security at the OAS. It continued a forward policy on Haiti. And it pressed for firm action on the defence of democracy in the region against the potential threat of unconstitutional actors.

Thus, the road was paved for more defence involvement, although the first campaign joined was the war on drugs. Ottawa approved a program to support Caribbean Commonwealth countries in their own efforts; equipment and small numbers of personnel were made available along with relevant training opportunities in Canada.[49] In addition, Canada sent a cash grant of $800,000 to the newly founded OAS office dealing with illicit drug control (CICAD after its initials in Spanish).[50]

These efforts proved to be only a beginning. Canada began to send formal delegations to the conferences of commanders of the armed forces of the Americas, groups that had enjoyed a very bad press indeed during the Cold War. Ottawa was active at the first Defence Ministerial of the Americas in Williamsburg, Virginia, in 1995. And most dramatically, but with major misgivings, Canada agreed to command and provide the largest contingent for the United Nations mission to Haiti. This replaced the essentially unilateral U.S. occupation force sent to the island some months before.

The United States initiative, while supported in many ways by the UN and even by Canada, was widely criticized as yet another unilateral military intervention. It was also felt that while most UN members wished to see order in Haiti and the country a democracy, many balked at the idea of the United States acting with its own forces alone. It was also widely felt that the intervention had more to do with voters in Florida and Haitian illegal immigration than it did with Washington's desire to see democracy prevail in Port-au-Prince. Ottawa wisely moved with caution but in the end accepted US and UN pressure to assume a leadership role.

The Canadian Forces would remain at significant strength in that unhappy republic for two years and contribute personnel for some time after that. In addition, the Royal Canadian Mounted Police became a pillar of the security reform program, training hundreds of policemen and providing a long-term presence in much of Haiti alongside contingents from other UN members.

Events continued to call for a greater Canadian role in defence issues of the Americas, a role permitted for the first time in the *1994 Defence White Paper*. Latin America had not been mentioned in any previous defence policy papers of this kind. But this time the white paper promised that "We will assist Latin American countries in such areas as peacekeeping training, confidence-building measures, and the development of civil-military relations." In general, "Canada's changing geographic priorities," were creating a need "to expand bilateral and multilateral contacts and exchanges with selected partners." The conclusion states clearly that the Canadian military "will become more actively involved in security issues in Latin America."[51]

The early and mid 1990s saw coups, and attempted coups in Guatemala, Haiti, Paraguay, Peru and Venezuela. There were continuing insurgencies in Guatemala and Peru and a worsening situation in Colombia. The defence of democracy, thus, came repeatedly to dominate the headlines from Latin America. And Canada's forward policy continued to be fed by the need to see Latin America democratic if this country was to feel comfortable with that region as in any sense "ours."[52]

The continuing view in Washington of the drug trade as essentially a security matter— declared indeed the No.1 security problem of the U.S. in 1986—also made Canada wary and forced her to take Latin American security seriously. American views often shared by Ottawa, and other elements of the new security agenda, kept National Defence with an ear to the ground in Latin America.

The 1994 explosion of the *Ejército Zapatista de Liberación Nacional* onto the Mexican scene put security into profile in that crucial Latin American country. The fact the fighting occurred against the backdrop of the official beginning of NAFTA lent urgency to a security solution in this new, close partner of Canada's in the Americas.

The outbreak of real interstate war in 1995 likewise put security front and centre. The myth that Latin America is a sort of commonwealth where conflicts between states are a thing of the past was once again destroyed in the six weeks of sharp conflict between Ecuador and Peru over territory along their border.[53]

All of this prompted DND to expand its Latin American contacts. Officers began to be sent to the Inter-American Defence College. A new defence attachés office was opened in Buenos Aires. Eligibility for the Military Training Assistance Plan was extended to several Latin American countries. The navy began to join the extensive Unitas exercise with several navies of the Americas.

In the arms control field, Canada was active in the opening moves of the successful initiative to negotiate a treaty banning anti-personnel land mines and was able to garner impressive Latin American diplomatic (although not always military) support for the idea. It likewise pressed to move forward with regional and sub-regional confidence building measures. National Defence personnel also supported inter-American initiatives in creating cultures of peace and peace education, white papers and exercises in civilian control of military forces, peacekeeping and peacebuilding, and much else.[54] The directorate at National Defence Headquarters responsible for Canada-U.S. defence relations was expanded to include the whole of the Americas and renamed Western Hemisphere Policy. Canada was becoming a nation of the Americas in defence terms as well.

Current Trends and a Conclusion

These trends still dominate Canadian defence involvement in the hemisphere. While Canadian Forces at the beginning of new century were not deployed in peacekeeping in the Americas, they are working alongside growing Latin American contingents in UN efforts around the world.[55] Ottawa has been pushing for more such involvement, as Latin American armed forces often have much to offer, while the Canadian Forces are over-stretched.

Canada in 2001 opened two more defence attaché offices, in Bogotá and Brasilia, a clear mark of the region's importance when several such posts in other parts of the world are being shut down to save money. Canada's Military Training Assistance Program has been offered to even more Latin American countries. Participation in most elements of the inter-American security system is now a given even though the thorny issue of Inter-American Defence Board membership remains unresolved. And the Canadian Forces have shown themselves capable of quick and resolute action in disaster relief, especially in beleaguered Central America.

Other issues also remain. The overwhelming dominance of the system by the United States leaves Canada uncomfortable at many levels since it has been rather spoiled in its bilateral relationship with that country and at the multilateral level has enjoyed unparalleled success in NATO and elsewhere in this regard. Instability and the difficulties of really anchoring democracy and civilian control of the armed forces of the region are also worrying. Colombia's horrifying level of violence and seeming inability to come to grips with its insurgency is a serious problem. And there are lingering doubts as to Mexico's potential to address its vast domestic panorama of problems. The main security problems of the region revolve around non-traditional threats such as the international narcotics trade, illegal immigration, international crime and the like, fields in which armed forces are justifiably nervous, in Canada or in Latin America.

Until the late 1980s it would have been easy to exaggerate the degree of Canadian military interest in this region so dominated by the United States and so foreign, or so it seemed, to our own national interests. For centuries Canadians and their armed forces have been indirectly linked to Latin America and the Caribbean, but these links were rarely seen to require any action. Instead other regions of the world, as well as North America itself, ensured that Latin America was little noticed.

This has changed. But it is too early to say to what degree this is so. Numerous Canadian Forces personnel, however, now speak a Latin American language, probably some two thousand have been posted there in the last decade, and many are interested in the region's issues. This is in its own way a small revolution for a country, a defence ministry, and armed forces traditionally Eurocentric. It is unlikely that this revolution will be reversed in the context of NAFTA, inter-American free trade, the decline of the European connection, the lack of bounce in political links with Asia, the fall in interest in the Commonwealth and even more dramatically in the Francophonie, the increasing role of the U.S. regionally and globally, and much more on the national agenda. The Canadian Forces are therefore likely to be in the region to stay.

Notes for Chapter 16

1   An argument could be made that this was not true of Central America during the Second World War because of the importance for the Canadian war effort of the Panama Canal. But British and then United States naval power were such during that conflict that there was little perception in Ottawa of the degree to which canal issues were vital to the war's success, this despite the large amount of Canadian trade and supplies which passed through that waterway. Very little indeed has been written on this. See Jock A. Finlayson, "Canada as a Strategic Mineral Importer: the Problematical Minerals," in David Haglund, ed., *The New Geopolitics of*

Minerals (Vancouver: University of British Columbia Press, 1989).

2 James Rochlin, *Discovering the Americas: the Evolution of Canadian Foreign Policy towards Latin America* (Vancouver: University of British Columbia Press, 1994), 27-29.

3 There was of course also a minority who held quite the opposite view from this. See, for example, Marcel Roussin, *Le Canada et le systme interaméricain* (Ottawa: Presses de l'Université d'Ottawa, 1959).

4 H.P. Klepak, ed. *Canada and Latin American Security* (Montreal: Mridien, 1993), 107-110.

5 W.J. Eccles, "The French Forces in North America during the Seven Years' War," in *Dictionary of Canadian Biography, Vol 3, 1741 to 1771* (Toronto: University of Toronto Press, 1974), xx; and George F. Stanley, *Canada's Soldiers* (Toronto: Macmillan Company, 1960), 61.

6 See Guillermo Calleja Leal and Hugo O'Donnell, *1762-La Habana inglesa: la toma de La Habana por los ingleses* (Madrid: Cultura Hispánica, 1999), 198-199; and Julian S. Corbett, *England in the Seven Years' War, Vol II* (London, Longmans, Green and Co., 1907), 331-390.

7 In Haiti, for example, there were some twenty-four slaves for every white inhabitant. See the figures given by Juan Gualberto Gómez in his "Cuba no es Haiti," in the newspaper *La Igualdad*, 23 May 1893, quoted in Aline Helg, *Lo Que nos corresponde: la lucha de los negros y mulatos por la igualdad en Cuba 1886-1912*, (Havana: Imagen Contemporánea, 2000), 71.

8 See Desmond Morton, *A Military History of Canada* (Edmonton: Hurtig, 1990), 18-23; and Allan Greer, *Brève histoire des peuples de la Nouvelle-France* (Québec, 1998), 140-141.

9 Francisco Mota, *Piratas y corsarios en el Caribe* (Havana: Gente Nueva, 1984), 19-22.

10 George F. Stanley, *Canada's Soldiers: The Military History of an Unmilitary People* (Toronto: Macmillan, 1960), 45-48; W. Stewart Wallace, ed. *The Macmillan Dictionary of Canadian Biography, 4th Ed.* (Toronto: Macmillan, 1978), 377. Morton, 17; and Greer, 34-39.

11 Calleja Leal and O'Donnell, 190-191.

12 This long process of beefing up these by British capabilities for a blockade of the United States is described in a highly useful Bermudan account Roger Willock, *Bulwark of Empire* (Bermuda: Bermuda Maritime Museum Press, 1988), 2-32. Also useful is Ian Stranack, *The Andrew and the Onions: the Story of the Royal Navy in Bermuda, 1795-1975* (Toronto: University of Toronto Press, 1993). It should also be mentioned, although not strictly part of this story, that Canada maintained for decades a small station at Bermuda until cuts forced its closure as the Cold War ended.

13 Jorge I. Dominguez, *Insurrección o lealtad: la desintegración del imperio español en América* (Mexico City: Fondo de Cultura Económica, 1985), 57-70.

14 Rory Miller, *Britain and Latin America in the 19th and 20th centuries* (London: Longman, 1993), 47-69.

15 Jesús Velasco Martínez, "La Separación y la anexión de Texas en la historia de México y Estados Unidos," in Josefina Zoraida Vázquez, ed., *De la Rebelión de Texas a la guerra del 47* (Mexico City: Nueva Imagen, 1994), 125-165, especially 51-162.

16 Filibustering in this sense meant expeditions largely by U.S. citizens to set up regimes in remote parts of Spanish America which would then usually call on the U.S. government to support them against imperial or local elements hostile to their implementation. The best work on this subject is probably Josefina Zoraida Vázquez and Lorenzo Meyer, *México frente a Estados Unidos: un ensayo histórico 1776-1988* (Mexico City: EFE, 1989). There were similar events in Canada over this period as well. See Donald E. Graves, *Guns across the River: the Battle of the Windmill 1838* (Toronto: Robin Brass, 2001).

17 See, for example, Charles P. Stacey, *Canada and the Age of Conflict. A History of Canadian External Policies, Volume 1: 1867-1921* (Toronto: University of Toronto Press, 1984), 17-30.

18 James Ogelsby, *Gringos from the Far North: Essays on Canadian-Latin American Relations 1866-1968* (Toronto: Macmillan, 1976), 9-39.

19 Age of Conflict p.100.

20 Demetrio Boersner, *Las Relaciones internacionales de América Latina* (Caracas: Nueva Sociedad, 1990), 188-194; and Pierre Queuille, *Les EtatsUnis, la doctrine Monroe et le panaméricanisme* (Paris: Payot, 1969).

21 This occurred despite a massive expansion of Canadian direct investment in Latin America, part of a wider imperial process but with a national dimension very much of its own. See Christopher Armstrong and H. V. Nelles, *Southern Exposure: Canadian Promoters in Latin America and the Caribbean* (Toronto: University of Toronto Press, 1988).

22 Adrian English, *Armed Forces of Latin America* (London: Jane's, 1984), 109; and Arthur Oscar Saldanha da Gama, *A Marinha da guerra do Brasil na segunda guerra mundial* (Rio de Janeiro, 1982), 1-12.

23 Dominions Secretary to Secretary of State for External Affairs, 22 Jan 1932, Canada, *Documents on Canadian External Relations, Vol 5, 1931-35* Telegram B.6, No.92, p.84. It should be said that a large percentage of British banks and other investments in Latin America were by this time in fact Canadian.

24 Chief of Naval Staff to Commander of *Skeena*, Telegram, 0130 hrs (E.S.T.), 23 January 1932, Ibid., No.93, p 84. The accompanying HMCS *Vancouver* meanwhile headed for the port of La Libertad down the coast from Acujatla and took no further part in the incident.

25 Memorandum of Under-secretary of State for External Affairs to Prime Minister, 2:30 p.m., 23 January 1932 titled San Salvador, Ibid., No.95, 85.

26 Commander of *Skeena* to Chief of the Naval Staff, Telegram, 15.21 hrs (EST), 25 Jan 1932, Ibid., No.96, 86. The dead Indians referred to the visible (to him) part of the gigantic massacre of native people undertaken by the army and Rural Guard in El Salvador as a means to smash all opposition to the Maximiliano Hernández Martínez dictatorship then in power. James Dunkerley, *Power in the Isthmus: a Political History of Modern Central America* (London: Verso, 1990), 95-97 and 109-110.

27   Hugh Francis Pullen, "The Royal Canadian Navy between the Wars, 1922-39," in James A. Boutilier, ed., *The RCN in Retrospect 1910-1968* (Vancouver: University of British Columbia Press, 1982), 68-69.

28   Dominions Secretary to Secretary of State for External Affairs, Paraphrase of Telegram 11 of 29 Jan, 1932, Canada, *Documents on Canadian External Relations, Vol 5, 1931-35*, No.99, p 87.

29   D. J. Rodgers to Sir John Simon, Despatch No.13, 9 Feb 1932, *British Documents on Foreign Affairs: Reports and Papers from the Foreign Office Confidential Print*, Part II, Series D (Latin America 1914-1939), VIII, Mexico, Central and South America, August 1931 to July 1932, Doc. 83, 111-112, A 1056/9/8.

30   See Peter McFarlane, *Northern Shadow: Canadians and Central America* (Toronto: Between the Headlines, 1989), for a description of this event which makes rather more of it than was really there, especially in terms of Canadian intentions in the area.

31   This context is superbly discussed in David Haglund, *Latin America and the Transformation of U.S. Strategic Thought* (Albuquerque: University of New Mexico Press, 1984).

32   Stanley E. Hilton, *Brazil and the Great Powers 1930-1939* (Austin: University of Texas Press, 1975), 42-43 and 173-174; and James R. Scobie, *Argentina: a City and a Nation* (London: Oxford University Press, 1971), 220-221.

33   Moyano, *1941: Mexicanos al grito de guerra!* (Mexico: Porras, 1992), 55-77.

34   G. Pope Atkins, *Latin America and the Caribbean in the International System* (Boulder: Westview, 1999), 230-233.

35   Rubem Braga, *Crónicas da guerra na Itália* (Rio de Janeiro: Editora Record, 1967).

36   See Héctor Aguilera Camín and Lorenzo Meyer, *A la sombra de la Revolución mexicana* (Mexico City: Cal y Arena, 1993), 195-6; Hal Klepak, "Crisis y oportunidades: dos lustros en las relaciones entre Canadá y México 1939-44 y 1989-94," in Mónica Verea Campos, *50 Años de relaciones México-Canadá: encuentros y coincidencias* (Mexico City: UNAM, 1995), 59-63; and Lorenzo Meyer, *Su Majestad Británica contra la Revolución Mexicana 1900-1950* (Mexico City: Colegio de México, 1991), 526-532.

37   Galen Roger Perras, "Anglo-Canadian Imperial Relations: the Case of the Garrisoning of the Falkland Islands in 1942," in *War and Society*, Vol XIV, No. 1 (May 1996), 73-97.

38   See James Ogelsby, *Gringoes from the Far North: Essays on Canadian Policy in Latin America* (Toronto, Macmillan, 1969), 49-53; Peter MacKenna, *Canada and the OAS* (Ottawa: Carleton University Press), 72-75; and Rochlin, 22-25.

39   Rochlin, 16-24; and Miller, 222-230.

40   Ken Macpherson, *Frigates of the Royal Canadian Navy 1943-1974* (St. Catharines, Ont.: Vanwell, 1988); and Ken Macpherson and Marc Milner, *Corvettes of the Royal Canadian Navy 1939- 1945* (St. Catharines: Vanwell, 1993).

41   John Kirk and Peter McKenna, *The Other Good Neighbor Policy: Canada-Cuba Relations* (Gainesville: University Press of Florida, 1997), 4-63; and Peter Haydon, "The RCN and the Cuban Missile Crisis," in Marc Milner, ed., *Canadian Military History: Selected Readings* (Toronto: Copp, Clark, Pitman, 1993), 349-367.

42   Liisa North, ed., *Between War and Peace in Central America: Choices for Canada* (Toronto: Between the Lines, 1990), 198-241.

43   Much of the Canadian side of the early part of this story can be found in Jack Child, *The Central American Peace Process 1983-1991* (Boulder: Lynne Rienner, 1992).

44   These matters are more fully developed in this author's *Verification of a Central American Peace Accord* and *Security Considerations Regarding Peace in Central America*, both published by the Department of External Affairs and International Trade, Ottawa, 1989 and 1990.

45   John Joly, "ONUCA: A Story of Success in the Quest for Peace," *Canadian Defence Quarterly*, Vol XX, No. 6, 12-19.

46   Edgar Dosman, "Managing Canadian-Mexican Relations in the Post-NAFTA Era," in Jean Daudelin and Edgar Dosman, eds., *Beyond Mexico* (Ottawa: Carleton University Press, 1995), 82-98, especially 88-90.

47   See H.P. Klepak, ed.*Canada and Latin American Security* (Montreal: Meridien, 1993).

48   G. Pope Atkins, *Latin America in the International Political System* (Boulder: Westview, 1995), 105-106.

49   Griffith, 269 and 282.

50   Rochlin, 209-219 and 222-223.

51   Canada, *1994 Defence White Paper* (Ottawa: Canada Communication Group, 1994).

52   John Graham, "Canada and the OAS: *Terra incognita*," in *Canada among Nations: Big Enough to Be Heard* (Ottawa: Carleton University Press, 1996), 301-318, especially 311-317.

53   This bit of wishful thinking, while by no means without some foundation, is widespread in Latin American and Latin Americanist circles despite the lack of historical evidence. Latin America is relatively free of war but totally free of the scourge it most surely is not. See it David Mares, *Violent Peace: Militarized Interstate Bargaining in Latin America*, (New York: Columbia University Press, 2001), 28-51.

54   This is treated in considerable length in H.P. Klepak, "The Inter-American Dimension of Canadian Security Policy," in *Canadian Foreign Policy*, Vol 2 (Winter 1998), 107-128, especially 110- 113.

55   For some idea of the scope of this connection, see the whole issue of Argentina's high quality defence affairs review, *Seguridad estratgica regional*, V, March 1994, "Hacia dónde van las misiones de paz?"

Officers of the 25th CIB examining a map, Korea, 9 November 1951. (Photographer P.E. Tomelin. NA, PA-115809)

CHAPTER 17

CANADA AND THE COLD WAR

The Maturation and Decline of a Nation

Sean M. Maloney

"It is DEW Line and NORAD emissions Soviet subs are recording and checking out to help them penetrate our defenses when the time comes. I also suspect scouting and ranging of submarine missile-firing positions. These are objectives worth tremendous risks. They are worth killing over…."

"Does anybody get hurt, Captain Finlander?"

"Fear hurts. Unrelenting tension becomes physical pain. Uncertainty and frustration can turn into crippling agony. But I suppose that to you, actual killing is the ultimate hurt, so I can truthfully answer: no, nobody has been hurt—so far."

This is the hard-core 'war' part of the Cold War. Here we clash in the privacy of a black, empty ocean with no audience but our own conscience; both parties want to keep it that way because the stakes are such that no compromise is possible. If you doubt me, ask yourself what the United States has left if its DEW Line and NORAD systems are cracked. What have the Soviets got if they never crack them? So both parties need secrecy to protect their freedom of manoeuvring against each other.

—Mark Rascovitch, *The Bedford Incident*

Mark Rascovitch captured the spirit of the Cold War in his naval pot boiler, though he was incorrect in stating that nobody had been hurt so far. By the time *The Bedford Incident* went to press in 1963, Soviet-inspired and supported totalitarianism was responsible for the deaths of millions.[1] These numbers included 516 Canadians killed fighting in Korea from 1951 to 1953, several hundred Canadian soldiers, sailors and airmen who died in accidents during training exercises which were part of presenting a deterrent posture against the Warsaw Pact, as well as the 70 Canadian soldiers who died during peacekeeping operations which were designed to keep Soviet surrogates at bay in the Third World. Ultimately, the numbers will also include those Canadians who participated in nuclear weapons trials in Australia and the United States who later died of unusual cancers and diseases brought on by accidental or deliberate exposure to radiation.

These Canadian deaths were incurred during a period that we know as the Cold War: the years 1945 to 1991.[2] The Cold War was, however, not just some convenient label or an umbrella title to encompass the varied events of those fifty-five years: The Cold War was a new type of conflict with its own rules, unique force structures, and deadly consequences. It also was a period in which Canada matured as a nation while under the pressure of the very real possibility of global nuclear annihilation.

What were the characteristics of that conflict? First, there was ideological antipathy brought on by Communism's intolerance of personal freedom and of the free market economy, both of which Western peoples deemed to be in their best interests. The maintenance of mobilized military forces equipped with nuclear and conventional weapons placed at high states of readiness was another characteristic, which in turn was linked to aggressive intelligence-gathering programs designed to provide early warning of attack.

The Cold War was also a period of chess-like moves and countermoves using subversion, insurgency, counter-insurgency and guerilla warfare to incrementally achieve political objectives in vital regions. Similarly, the Cold War was fought on a propaganda plane, with each camp attempting to seize the moral high ground and influence opinion in such forums as the United Nations and international media outlets. This conflict was also characterized by numerous crises and confrontations which, within the nuclear context, made every action on the global stage potentially the subject to the frightening consequences of nuclear escalation. Finally, the Cold War was an economic war that favoured those players who could best achieve the optimum balance between domestic and military spending.

It is somewhat fashionable to scoff at the threat posed to Canada during this time because, as some believe, nothing happened. There is a school of thought that seeks to downplay or excuse the nastier elements of Soviet-backed totalitarianism and its expansionist tendencies despite conclusive evidence to the contrary that has emerged in recent years. These obsolete views have no real place in any analysis of Canada and the Cold War. Indeed, the Canadian people and their military forces were significant espionage and nuclear targets. Canada's fate was linked to the fates of her European and North American allies, by geography as much as by a common heritage.

Canadian involvement in the Cold War had as its basis the events of 1918 when Canadian expeditionary forces were dispatched to Archangel and Vladivostok as part of a multinational effort to prevent the collapse of the Russian provisional government in the face of Bolshevism and to re-establish an Eastern Front. This operation was conducted to keep German forces engaged in the east and draw off the pressure on Canadian forces in the west. At another level, there was diffuse concern among the Allied powers that if Bolshevism took hold in Russia, it would spread in the post-war world and pose a threat to the liberal-democratic political system and its basis, the proto-globalized trading environment which emerged in the 1800s. Canadian gunners successfully supported American and British operations against Moscow-directed forces. War-weary Canada eventually withdrew her forces after the Armistice. Canada's first clash with Communism was over.[3]

As Stalin consolidated his position in the Soviet Union and its conquered adjacent areas in the Caucasus and the Baltic states, the defining characteristics of Communist ideological warfare and their relationship to Canada emerged between 1920 and the mid-1940s: aggressive hostility to democratic institutions, covert attempts to foment discord using all means of subversion short of open warfare, massive intelligence penetration of the intelligensia, and a reordering of economic reality based on but not limited to the Marxist model. Canada was slow to identify the increasingly sophisticated means by which Stalin's Soviet Union sought to achieve its aims and then slow to understand it as part of a coherent strategy directed at altering the political system in the western democracies. This produced rather ham-handed responses on the part of the security services well into the 1940s. In any event, covert funding was provided by the Soviets to Canadian Communists on a regular basis and, as the 1946 Gouzenko Affair aptly demonstrated, there was significant Soviet espionage and subversion activity in Canada directed against Canadian interests.[4]

It took the Gouzenko revelations and the probability that the Soviet Union would acquire nuclear weapons to bring home to Canada that victory in the war fought against Nazi Germany could be lost to another totalitarian state which used methods that were equally monstrous.[5] Despite the fact that the two nations had been allies of convenience in the war since 1941, the Soviet system which led to the deaths of 11 million subject people in the 1930s and now stood astride Eastern Europe was incompatible on a philosophical basis with how Canadians wanted to live.[6] Any form of totalitarianism crushed that fundamental reservoir of life and innovation, the individual, and systematically destroyed those institutions that ultimately supported people in the fulfillment of their lives.

On an economic basis, the new world order of the late 1940s with its hasty decolonization processes was vulnerable to Soviet-backed Communist parties operating under the guise of, and even alongside, legitimate nationalism. If the Western powers lost too much ground globally, they could very well find themselves isolated with no markets or raw materials. Economic recovery in Europe was dependent on stable trade with these post-coloniel areas. Attenuation of trade would produce the very conditions needed for Communist revolution in the newly-freed West.[7]

Canada could no longer remain isolated in North America, despite Prime Minister Mackenzie King's wishes. She demonstrated during the Second World War that totalitarian domination of her cultural and economic allies in Europe was unacceptable. New technologies, particularly long-range submarines, cruise missiles, ballistic missiles, long-range bomber aircraft and nuclear weapons ensured that Canada could be directly threatened with military force. The decline of British power further ensured that Canada could not revert to the days when the Royal Navy guaranteed secure seas for trade and defence against imperial battlefleets, nor could Canada rely exclusively on the Empire's economic system. Canada could no longer choose to ignore her former adversary and now ally to the south, the United States, particularly in matters related to defence in the nuclear age.

This new view was manifest in several ways. Despite the precipitous draw-down of Canadian forces in 1946, numerous structural improvements were made to guarantee Canadian access to the scientific and intelligence information necessary for independent military, economic, and diplomatic planning commensurate with an independent state. An alphabet soup of acronyms proliferated under the tutelage of Minister of National Defence Brooke Claxton, General Charles Foulkes, and their counterparts in the Department of External Affairs: These included the Defence Research Board (DRB), the Joint Intelligence Committee (JIC), the Communications Branch of the National Research Council (CBNRC) and the creation of a singular Department of National Defence (DND).[8]

Unlike the interwar years, Canada's approach to the Cold War rested in her relationship to several formal alliance systems designed to guarantee the protection of Canadian interests. The burgeoning American-Canadian relationship established during the Second World War formed the basis of a Cold War policy manifest in a re-vitalized Permanent Joint Board on Defence and its secret associate, the Military Co-operation Committee, which was established in 1946. Similarly, the American-British-Canadian (ABC) relationship established during the war to co-ordinate production, intelligence sharing and other matters took on new importance in the effort to plan for the probability that the Soviets would expand their empire after war. Canada was not subservient in these relationships and over time grew adept at maintaining her interests in these forums.[9]

Taken together, the creation and permanent manning of organizations designed to observe and plan for continued Canadian involvement in the new world order was a significant evolution away from the more ad hoc approaches of the years following the First World War.[10] Canada was hedging her bets and did not want to make the same mistakes that had been made in the 1930s.

Developments in the late 1940s indicated that merely anticipating and planning for a future war with global Communism was not enough. The destruction of the fledgling democracy in Czechoslovakia by Soviet subversion followed by Stalin's stranglehold on Berlin produced many a Munich analogy. Elsewhere, the Dutch lost control of Indonesia, the British were fighting in Malaya, the French in Indochina, all while Maoist forces were beating the Nationalist Chinese and forcing them to retreat to Formosa. The Greeks were in the process of ending a Soviet-backed insurgency, and the Turks were standing up to Soviet military and diplomatic pressure. The United Nations was incapable of containing Soviet expansionism and interference in countries of the emergent Third World. The demonstration of a Soviet nuclear capability in 1949 was the last straw. Despite the fact that Stalin essentially declared war on the West in 1946, Western powers including Canada wanted to reach some form of peaceful coexistence with the Soviet Union. After four years of aggressive Soviet activity, this was deemed to be no longer possible.[11]

One product of this was the North Atlantic Treaty Organization established in 1949. NATO was the cornerstone of Canada's approach to the Cold War, blending the bi-lateral and ABC relationships with those of a revitalized European defence identity, the Western Union Defence Organization. Even Canada's involvement with the Korean War was related to NATO: Korea was seen as a diversion to draw in Western resources so that the main Soviet effort could be made against Western Europe. However, a collective stand had to be made against Communism and Korea was selected to play a role. The dispatch of three destroyers and 25 Canadian Infantry

Brigade Group in 1950-51 highlighted Canada's military unpreparedness, as did the hasty dispatch of the combined regular-militia 27 Canadian Infantry Brigade Group to NATO in 1951.[12]

While Canadian soldiers were fighting Communist Chinese "volunteers" (as the Chinese called them) in Korea, Canadian policy makers realized that talking and planning was not enough. Credible and salient military forces were necessary to deter Soviet activity in Europe. The expansion of the defence program initiated in 1951 recognized force structure deficiencies and laid the groundwork for corrective action. During this time, however, the detonation of a test American hydrogen weapon and the subsequent demonstration of a more advanced Soviet capability produced what amounted to a revolution in military affairs. The order of magnitude increase in destructive power encompassed in a single bomb wedded to the means to deliver it intercontinentally generated some pause in Canadian circles. Canada was now directly at risk at home.

The Canadian strategic reappraisal that occurred from 1952 to 1954 produced Canada's first serious tri-service military strategy. Outside of nebulous mobilization planning conducted 1914 and during the interwar years, there had never really been a standing Canadian strategy. By the end of 1954, there was. Based on NATO strategic concept MC (Military Committee) 48, which was produced with significant Canadian input, Canada was now able to link the planning for the continental defence of North America with the protection of the Atlantic lines of communication with the forward defence of Europe. Equipment purchases, from anti-submarine destroyers to armoured personnel carriers, even modifications to airfield defences to survive nuclear attack, all were linked to the pattern of projected war established in MC 48. That NATO document and its successors served as the basis for Canadian strategic planning well into the mid 1960s.[13]

Indeed, the aim of Canada's Cold War strategy was to deter a nuclear war with a hybrid conventional and nuclear force structure in the NATO Area (which included North America) and then to fight a nuclear war if deterrence failed. Canada's initial commitment of forces to NATO was modified to accept up-to-date technology and re-trained to fight on a battlefield contaminated by nuclear weapons. The brigade group based in West Germany moved to dispersed peacetime locations, while the twelve interceptor squadrons assigned to NATO's 4 Allied Tactical Air Force practised escorting the USAF's 49th Air Division nuclear strike force to its targets in Eastern Europe. In time, both Canadian formations were altered so they could use nuclear weapons. The brigade group acquired Honest John launchers, while 1 Canadian Air Division relinquished its F-86 Sabres and CF-100 Canucks in favour of CF-104 nuclear strike aircraft which were then equipped with a variety of nuclear weapons, some of which were in the megaton-yield range.[14]

As for maritime forces, the emphasis shifted from a small balanced fleet to one specializing in anti-submarine warfare. The top-of-the-line St Laurent class destroyers and their follow-on classes were eventually equipped with Sea King helicopters capable of dropping a nuclear depth charge. The RCAF's maritime patrol aircraft fleet included the Canadair Argus and the Neptune, both nuclear-capable.[15]

An additional alliance was formed: the North American Air Defence Command. NORAD essentially formalized planning and command organizations that had been handled by the Permanent Joint Board on Defence and its offshoots. In time, the nine squadrons of CF-100 all-weather interceptors assigned to NORAD were replaced by CF-101 Voo Doos carrying Genie rockets and two squadrons of BOMARC nuclear-tipped ramjet cruise missiles.

All in all, Canada had a viable force structure capable of fulfilling all Canadian strategic requirements: sovereignty, operational influence and saliency, which produced strategic influ-

F-86 Sabre aircraft in formation, January 1951. (Photographer unknown. NA, PA-67557)

ence in the alliances Canada was a member of. More importantly, this force structure was an effective component of the West's deterrent system and would probably have fought well if deterrence had failed. The plethora of large-scale NATO exercises and the salient Canadian participation in them—from the battalion group in Allied Command Europe deployments to northern Norway to the never-ending CF-104 nuclear tactical evaluations to 4 Canadian Mechanized Brigade Group operations in corps-on-corps level manoeuvres in Northern Army Group—all demonstrated Canadian intent to NATO's enemies.[16]

The problems with implementing such a force structure were nearly all overcome until elements within the Diefenbaker government interfered with the acquisition of the nuclear weapons necessary to carry out the agreed-to tasks. In time this problem was rectified, but not before tremendous damage had been done to Canada's credibility with the United States during the Cuban Missile Crisis of 1962.[17]

One other notable aspect of Canada's Cold War strategy was National Survival. In accordance with the MC 48 strategy and its successors, the Canadian government embarked upon a comprehensive continuity-of-government program so that if deterrence failed, a large portion of the Canadian population would survive and government control could be re-constituted as quickly as possible. Canada's Project Bridge bunker system was the only hardened federal and provincial protective system in NATO. Protected by the NORAD air defence forces and warning systems and the National Attack Warning System sirens, it is conceivable that the Canadian people would have had a fighting chance in the event of nuclear attack, at least in the era of the manned bomber. When vast numbers of intercontinental ballistic missiles and submarine-launched ballistic missiles were deployed by the Soviet Union in the late 1960s, the system could be overwhelmed. However, if war had occurred during the 1961 Berlin or 1962 Cuban crises, the system was robust enough to do its job.[18]

Canadian military planners and diplomats realized as early as 1955 that generating a nuclear-based stalemate would induce the Soviets and their surrogates to move into areas not under NATO's protection. Conceptually, a Canadian strategy evolved which supplemented the one based on MC 48. UN and non-UN peace operations could be used to ensure that clashes and incidents in the Third World did not escalate into nuclear weapons while at the same time the forces deployed for peace operations could be used to block the extension of Soviet influence. Consequently, UN peacekeeping functioned as a NATO surrogate in the Congo, Cyprus and the Middle East. Every UN operation had strong Canadian representation that was deliberately designed to prevent Soviet-bloc powers from controlling the operations for their own purposes.[19]

The link between Canadian strategy and deployed credible and salient military forces in the NATO and UN contexts during the 1950s and 1960s gave Canada unprecedented influence in those corridors of power that she chose to operate in. Canadian military and diplomatic representatives were key figures in the adoption of NATO strategic concepts, particularly MC 48 and its successors. Canadian opinion was solicited and even acted upon. In terms of command and control, Dieppe and Hong Kong would not be repeated because Canada retained operational influence over her own forces and, moreover, influenced military planning which affected other allies including Britain and West Germany. Canada was even able to force the Kennedy Administration to back away from implementing provocative and unrealistic Berlin contingency planning in the early 1960s. In time, the high quality of the Canadian nuclear strike force—the RCAF's 1 Air Division in Europe—and the provision of nuclear air defence forces for North America gave Canadian representatives access to the secretive world of American nuclear weapons planning.[20]

Canada was able to generate significant influence within the UN. By providing high-quality military leadership for UN peace observation and peacekeeping operations as well as support personnel for Third World dominated UN contingents, Canada was able to make significant inroads into UN diplomacy during a period of massive change as the world decolonized. The knowledge that Canada was part of NATO and that she had close links to the United Kingdom and the United States bolstered Canadian credibility. During the 1950s and 1960s, Canadian forces possessed their own adequate strategic sea and airlift so that she could unhesitatingly deploy UN contingents in crisis situations without referring to other alliance partners. Again, this influence was used to maintain the West's position in the critical UN forum, particularly in times of crisis like Suez in 1956 and Cyprus in 1964.[21]

Sadly, this influence waned after 1970 when the Trudeau government decided that Canada would henceforth be the largest of the small rather than the smallest of the large. NATO's new strategy, MC 14/3 (better known as Flexible Response), had little Canadian input. Flexible Response placed new emphasis on conventional forces that would fight the first battle, and then escalate by stages to nuclear weapons if required. The government refused to build up conventional forces and even attempted to withdraw the existing formations from Europe. The Canadian Forces, which were structured to deter and fight nuclear warfare, were permitted to rust out. Military independence and capability eroded to the point where any Canadian influence was merely residual from the 1950s and 1960s. Without strategic lift, without salient and credible military forces, Canada was forced onto the sidelines of the Cold War, coming out occasionally for the odd peacekeeping operation. Even the hard-won influence with the Americans, built on the continental defence system, was jettisoned in favour of an adversarial trade and cultural relationship. It was only in the 1987 defence white paper that a Canadian government gave serious thought to rebuilding influence, but this momentum was lost with the inability to meet the policy's military goals with the 1989 budget. Significant steps were taken, however, to re-equip the force based in Europe: CF-18s replaced the aging CF-104s while 4 Canadian Mechanized Brigade Group was strengthened with better anti-tank capability and more soldiers.[22]

Canadian efforts in the field of international aid cannot be divorced from a Cold War context. The Commonwealth's Columbo Plan of 1950 was designed to offer development assistance to former colonies in Asia, Africa, the Caribbean and Latin America, that is, those areas at risk of Soviet subversion. By improving economic conditions in these areas, it was hoped, the constituent nations would not feel obligated to seek Soviet assistance. Canadian foreign aid was centralized in the Canadian International Development Agency in 1968 and used alongside military training programs and naval deployments to prop up the Canadian position in non-NATO areas. As the 1970s progressed and decolonization moved to completion, economic aid and military training lost their utility as significant Canadian elements of the Cold War. They became geared instead to more altruistic ends.[23]

The Canadian part of the intelligence war was not as glamorous as American or British involvement. Canada did, however, provide critical input to signals intelligence (SIGINT) and in the collection of information on Soviet and Chinese nuclear tests through seismic sensors and aerial sampling. The SIGINT aspects were the most important, particularly the role of the Alert station located at the northern tip of Ellesmere Island in the Arctic. It is from this and other sites that advanced warning of a Soviet nuclear attack would have been received and transmitted south. Indeed, the Canadian SIGINT capability today, a legacy of the Cold War, is still used for economic intelligence gathering. The Canadian portion of the CAESAR underwater listening system (called SOSUS) provided equally important information on underwater targets. And Canada was not immune to Soviet espionage: a top-level Canadian traitor, Hugh Hambleton, seriously compromised NATO economic intelligence in the 1950s, while a spy ring which included Member of Parliament Fred Rose and a number of military personnel was also uncovered.[24]

What other benefits were there for Canadians during the Cold War? The most obvious was the solidification of a Canadian identity. Canada was no longer British and was not subsumed into the United States. The complex web of Cold War alliance structures and Canada's role in them guaranteed Canadian independence, within the limits imposed by nuclear warfare. The deployment of Canadian forces to Europe and within the UN context kept Canada on the map. There were some problems, however. One of the more hide-bound Royal Canadian Navy leaders objected to the use of a Canada flash on the naval uniform, since the RCN was still royal. Conversely, the name of a Canadian Army unit—the Queen's Own Rifles of Canada—was used as an excuse for the Egyptians to prohibit the unit's deployment as part of the UN Emergency Force. A new national symbol, the Canadian flag as we know it today, may have in part been generated by the need to project an independent Canadian identity into the far flung battlefields of the Cold War.[25]

More controversially, the Cold War was in part responsible for dragging Quebec out of its self-imposed isolationism endemic to that province in the earlier part of the twentieth century. Louis St. Laurent's defence policy platform had national unity as an important plank, which implied that Canadian involvement overseas had to be acceptable to Quebec in order to avoid the unpleasentness of another Conscription Crisis.[26] Canadian involvement in NATO and NORAD could not really be seen as extensions of British Imperial policy, and they were not, even though Canadian Army formations served under a British corps headquarters in West

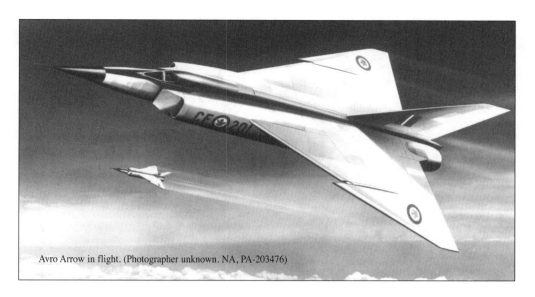

Avro Arrow in flight. (Photographer unknown. NA, PA-203476)

Germany from 1951 to 1970. That corps headquarters reported to a NATO headquarters which was infused with Canadian officers and thus operational influence was retained. The brigade sent to Korea had similar relationships to prevent the formation's misuse by non-Canadian commanders.[27]

It is possible that the Quiet Revolution might not have occurred had the Cold War not been fought. The repressive measures of the Duplessis government against real or imagined Communist influence were instrumental in generating support for reforms which in time succeeded in replacing *La Chef* with a left-wing government which, when it did not go far enough, produced FLQ offspring who used Marxist rhetoric and terrorist tactics to campaign for independence.[28]

It is fair to suggest that that the Cold War globalized Canada. Over 12,000 Canadian soldiers and airmen were stationed in Europe in any given year from 1951 to 1970, along with some 30,000 or more dependents (these numbers declined roughly by half for the 1970-1990 period). Constant rotations provided Canadian military and civilian personnel broad and enriching personal experiences throughout Europe, experiences that were brought home to Canada and shared. Canadian soliders and sailors deployed to exotic locations. In Laos, Yemen, the Congo, the Holy Land and many other places the inhabitants got a first look at Canadians in action. These deployments provided reciprocal cultural and economic benefits. Clearly this was a big improvement on the common characterization of Canadians as rural hewers of wood and drawers of water. Without Canadian participation in the Cold War, it is unlikely that such a high degree of diversification would have developed.

The Cold War also made Canada a smaller place for Canadians. The development of microwave communication systems for military purposes in the High North was quickly adopted for civilian use in the 1950s. In time, telephone microwave was the primary means of domestic communication. The maintenance and improvement of countless defence-oriented sites in the Yukon and Northwest Territories (initiated during the Second World War) dramatically accelerated northern development, strengthening Canadian sovereignty at the same time. Without the radar, signals intelligence, and Strategic Air Command refuelling bases scattered throughout this huge area, it is unlikely that the level of development we see today would exist. The same holds true farther south. The Mid-Canada Line, the Pine Tree Line and Ground Control Intercept radar sites as well as RCAF bases and dispersal sites provided a federal gov-

361

Major-General E.L.M. Burns inspecting Canadian members of the United Nations Emergency Force in Egypt. (DND file photo.)

ernment presence, and hence economic and social activity, in many remote areas. The improvement of Canadian airports to handle military traffic and the adoption of air traffic control standards to serve such traffic had similar effects across the country.[29]

In technological terms, the benefits that accrued to Canada from the Cold War are immeasurable. In addition to microwave technology, MUFAX fax machines—devices whose existence carried a Top Secret security designation—were first used in the Project Bridge "Diefenbunker" national survival system.[30] Computers proliferated within defence-oriented establishments, especially the National Research Council and the Canadian Armaments Research and Development Establishment, before spreading elsewhere into the Canadian government. Digital signals processing, used by the SOSUS underwater listening systems tracking Soviet submarines in Canadian waters, gained greater speed and accuracy to keep pace with the threat. Atmospheric and oceanographic information gathered by Canadian military research establishments had uses beyond the military.[31] The Semi-Automated Ground Environment (SAGE) air defence computer based at North Bay was linked to the plethora of radar sites and used phone lines and high frequency radio to relay targeting data to BOMARC missiles and manned CF-101 interceptor aircraft. The American SAGE system is credited with being the grandfather of the Internet and Canada was the only NATO ally to have access to this level of technology.[32] Canadian science and engineering was also a beneficiary of the space age, which itself is attributable to the Cold War. Canada was the third country to design and build a series of communications satellites, although they were put into orbit on American launchers.

The most spectacular Canadian technological advances were in the field of Cold War aviation, in part because of the large numbers of Canadians employed in cutting-edge aeronautical work. AVRO designed, built, and marketed its own jet interceptor, the CF-100 Canuck. This all-weather machine was the mainstay of North American air defence throughout the 1950s and also operated in Europe with both the RCAF and the Belgian air force. The superb North American F-86 Sabre, an American-designed and Canadian-built aircraft, was powered by an Orenda engine designed in Canada that made it the most potent day fighter in the world dur-

Armoured lifeline. Paratroopers in APCs rescue U.S. personnel on 19 August 1974, after an anti-American demonstration at the U.S. Embassy. (Photographer WO W.H. Cole. CFPU CNL, CYPC-74-156)

ing the 1950s. In time, practically every NATO air force used Canadair's Mark VI version of the F-86. When NATO members shifted over to the nuclear strike role, their selection of the F-104 Starfighter was influenced by Canada's decision to build the CF-104 at Canadair. Spares and simulators were available here and aircrew training was done in Canada by most NATO members under a training program similar to the British Commonwealth Air Training Plan of the Second World War.[33]

Canada's most spectacular national failure also was in the aviation industry. Designed to intercept Soviet bombers, possessing more than Mach 2 speed and capable of delivering nuclear air defence weapons, the CF-105 AVRO Arrow was a showcase of Canadian technology, ingenuity, and verve. The collapse of the program highlighted the inability of Canadian politicians to appreciate the increased importance of national pride during the Cold War. It was a blow from which Canadians never fully recovered. The AVRO Arrow has reached mythic proportions: there are more books on it than any other Canadian subject short of the First and Second World Wars.[34]

The inescapable fact is that the demise of the Arrow presaged the collapse of the Canadian Cold War system. After 1967, Canada no longer participated in Cold War nuclear crisis management, eliminated five of the six classes of nuclear weapons at her disposal, and drastically slashed forward-based deterrent forces. She also withdrew from most of her low intensity commitments (peacekeeping and military training) in the Third World while cutting back and redirecting economic aid to areas not threatened by Communist expansion. The defence of Canada was virtually turned over to the United States when the Trudeau government chose not to modernize Canada's forces in the 1970s. In doing so, Canada's influence in NATO, the UN, and more importantly, with the United States, declined precipitously. It got to the point where assertions of independence were limited to defying the Americans in what were essentially inconsequential matters played up to a domestic Canadian audience.[35]

It is evident from this survey that the effects of the Cold War on Canada were profound. Canada was no longer an appendage of the British Empire and was thrust into a world where sound independent judgements regarding Canadian security had to be made. Splendid isolationism or pseudo-neutrality were deemed inappropriate to a thermonuclear world. The formulation of a Canadian Cold War strategy and the means to implement it—including nuclear weapons, forward-deployed deterrent forces, strategic intelligence gathering, low intensity operations and the provision of economic aid to vulnerable areas—demonstrates that, in addition to providing for the security of Canadians against nuclear attack, Canada moved into a far more influential position than she had occupied in the First and Second World Wars. The technological, social, and economic benefits gained during the first twenty years of the Cold War built on the successes of the early 1940s: but they were not sustained into the 1970s and 1980s. Canada can take credit for helping stabilize the free world against the Communist threat in the first two and a half decades of the Cold War, but cannot do the same for the latter and equally critical twenty years. Thinking big and having the will to pursue interest-based aims leads to big things. Thinking small leads to irrelevance.

Notes for Chapter 17

1   For the best attempt at developing the numbers of deaths attributable to Communism, I would recommend *The Black Book of Communism: Crimes, Terror, Repression* (London: Harvard University Press, 1999) by a collection of French historians led by Stepane Courtois.

2   Brian Crozier, *The Rise and Fall of the Soviet Empire* (Rocklin: Prima Publishing, 1999), Chapters 44 and 45.

3   C.P. Stacey, *Canada and the Age of Conflict. A History of Canadian External Policies. Volume 1: 1867-1921* (Toronto: University of Toronto Press, 1984), 276-184; E.M. Halliday, *When Hell Froze Over* (New York: Simon and Shuster, 2000), Chapters 1 and 2; Melvyn P. Leffler, *The Specter of Communism: The United States and the Cold War, 1917-1953* (New York: Hill and Wang, 1994), 3-33.

4   Gregory S. Kealy, "Spymasters, Spies and Their Subjects: The RCMP and Canadian State Repression, 1914-39," in Kinsman et al, *Whose National Security? Canadian State Surveillance and the Creation of Enemies* (Toronto: Between The Lines Books, 2000), 18-36; Harvey Klehr et al., *The Secret World of American Communism* (New Haven: Yale University Press, 1995), 30, 198, 235-236; Crozier, *The Rise and Fall of the Soviet Empire*, Chapters 3 and 4; Courtois, *The Black Book of Communism*, Chapter16.

5   Denis Smith, *Diplomacy of Fear: Canada and the Cold War, 1941-1948* (Toronto: University of Toronto Press, 1988), Chapters 3 and 4; See also Oleg Sarin and Lev Dvoretsky, *Alien Wars: The Soviet Union's Aggressions Against the World, 1919 to 1989* (Novato: Presidio, 1996).

6   Courtois, *The Black Book of Communism*, 9-10.

7   See, for example, Andrew Rotter, *The Path to Vietnam: Origins of the American Commitment to Southeast Asia* (Ithaca: Cornell University Press, 1987), 49-68.

8   Sean M. Maloney, "General Charles Foulkes: A Primer on How to be CDS," in B. Horn and S. Harris, eds., *Warrior Chiefs: Perspectives on Senior Canadian Military Leaders* (Toronto: Dundurn Press, 2001), 219-236; David Jay Bercuson, *True Patriot: The Life of Brooke Claxton 1898-*

1960 (Toronto: University of Toronto Press, 1993), Chapters 9 and 10.

9   Sean M. Maloney, *Securing Command of the Sea: NATO Naval Planning 1948-1954* (Annapolis: Naval Institute Press, 1995), Chapters 1 and 2.

10   See, for example, Steve Harris, *Canadian Brass: The Making of a Professional Army 1860-1939* (Toronto: University of Toronto Press, 1988), 144-158; John Hilliker, *Canada's Department of External Affairs Volume I: The Early Years, 1909-1946* (Kingston: McGill-Queen's University Press, 1990), Chapter 5.

11   John Lewis Gaddis, *The United States and the Origins of the Cold War 1941-1945* (New York: Columbia University Press, 1972), 299-301; Don Cook, *Forging the Alliance* (New York: William Morrow, 1989), Chapters 5 and 6.

12   Sean M. Maloney, *War Without Battles: Canada's NATO Brigade in Germany, 1951-1993* (Toronto: McGraw-Hill Ryerson, 1997), Chapter 1.

13   Sean M. Maloney, *Learning to Love The Bomb: Canada's Cold War Strategy and Nuclear Weapons, 1951-1968* (to be published in 2002), Chapter 2.

14   Ibid., Chapters 4 and 5.

15   Ibid.

16   See Maloney, *War Without Battles* for a full exposition on the role of exercises in the NATO deterrent system.

17   Ibid., Chapters 8 and 9.

18   Sean M. Maloney, "Dr. Strangelove Visits Canada: Projects RUSTIC, EASE, and BRIDGE, 1958- 1963," *Canadian Military History*, Vol 6, No. 1 (Spring 1996), 42-56.

19   Sean M. Maloney, *Canada and UN Peacekeeping: Cold War by Other Means, 1945-1970* (to be published by Vanwell Publishing, 2002), Chapter 3.

20   Sean M. Maloney, "notfallplannung Fur Berlin: forlaufer der flexible response, 1958-1961," *Militargeschichte*, Heft 1, 1 Quartal, 1997, 7 Jahrgang, 3-15.

21   See Maloney, *Canada and UN Peacekeeping*; Sean M. Maloney, "Global Mobile: Flexible Response, Peacekeeping and the Origins of Forces Mobile

Command, 1958-1964," *The Army Doctrine and Training Bulletin,* Vol 3, No. 3 (Fall 2000), 20-34; "Global Mobile II: the Development of Forces Mobile Command, 1965-1972," *The Army Doctrine and Training Bulletin,* Vol 4, No. 2 (Summer 2001), 7-23.

22 Maloney, *War Without Battles,* Chapters 5 and 6.

23 David R. Morrison, *Aid and Ebb Tide: A History of CIDA and Canadian Developmental Assistance* (Waterloo: Wilfrid Laurier Press, 1998), 1, 27-29; Sean M. Maloney, "Maple Leaf Over the Caribbean: Gunboat Diplomacy Canadian-Style?" in Griffiths et al., *Canadian Gunboat Diplomacy: The Canadian Navy and Foreign Policy* (Halifax: Dalhousie University Press, 1998).

24 John Bryden, *Best Kept Secret: Canadian Secret Intelligence in the Second World War* (Toronto: Lester Publishing, 1993), Chapter 14; Mike Frost, *Spyworld: Inside the Canadian and American Intelligence Establishments* (Toronto: Doubleday, 1994); Christopher Andrew and Vasili Mitrokhin, *The Mitrokhin Archive: The KGB in Europe and the West* (London: Penguin, 1999), 218-220, 251, 259-260, 365.

25 Ann-Maureen Owens and Jane Yealland, *Canada's Maple Leaf: The Story of Our Flag* (Toronto: Kids Can Press, 1999).

26 Lester B. Pearson, *Mike: The Memoirs of the Rt. Hon. Lester B. Pearson Volume Two 1948-1957* (Toronto: University of Toronto Press, 1973), 29.

27 Maloney, *War Without Battles,* Chapter 1.

28 For information on the Marxist leaning of the FLQ, see Louis Fournier, *FLQ: Anatomy of an Underground Movement* (Toronto: NC Press, 1984), 14-29.

29. Shelagh D. Grant, *Sovereignty or Security? Government policy in the Canadian North 1936-1950* (Vancouver: UBC Press, 1988), Chapters 7, 8 and 9.

30 Maloney, "Dr. Strangelove Visits Canada," 42-56.

31 See D.J. Goodspeed, *DRB: A History of the Defence Research Boards of Canada* (Ottawa: The Queen's Printer, 1958).

32 Katie Hafner and Matthew Lyon, *Where Wizards Stay Up Late: The Origins of the Internet* (New York: Touchstone, 1996), 31, 74.

33 Larry Milberry, *The Canadair Sabre* (Toronto: Canav Books, 1986); and Larry Milberry, *The AVRO CF-100* (Toronto: Canav Books, 1981).

34 See The Arrowheads, *Arrow: Revised Edition* (Toronto: The Boston Mills Press, 1980) and Randall Whitcomb, *Avro Canada and Cold War Aviation* (St. Catharines: Vanwell Publishing, 2002) as two examples of this literature.

35 See Thomas S. Axworthy and Pierre Elliott Trudeau, *Towards a Just Society: The Trudeau Years* (Toronto: Viking, 1990), Chapter 1; Ivan Head and Pierre Trudeau, *The Canadian Way: Shaping Canada's Foreign Policy, 1968-1984* (Toronto: McClelland & Stewart, 1995); Brian Cuthbertson, *Canadian Military Independence in the Age of the Superpowers* (Toronto: Fitzhenry and Whiteside, 1977), Chapters 7 and 8. See also John Hasek's useful polemic *The Disarming of Canada* (Toronto: Key Porter Books, 1987).

Canadian and UN vehicles crossing the swollen Yongpyongchong River just north of the 38th parallel, Korea, 30 May 1951. (Photographer unknown. NA, PA-143955)

ALMOST A LEGACY

Canada's Contribution
to Peacekeeping[1]

Major David Last

PONDER FOR A MOMENT the curious and perhaps ambivalent legacy of Sir Percy Girouard.
The portrait that graces the building named for him at the Royal Military College of Canada
depicts an idealized hero under an incongruous fez—his youthful face and blond moustache
giving little hint of mature intellect. But a photograph from his days as Governor in Nigeria
tells a different story: a lined face, shrewd hard eyes, and a sense of more grey than blond. This
man was a problem-solver, a leader, and quite possibly a bit of a bastard. He drove 588 miles
of railway across Egyptian deserts in just two years to support Kitchener's campaign against
the Sudan.[2] He was director of railways in South Africa during the Boer War time when it was
the practice to place Boer civilians in cars at the head of a train to discourage sabotage. He was
responsible for the military control of railways and was knighted for his efforts, but was he
involved in this odious abuse of civilians? Later as Governor of Northern Nigeria, he evinced
the sentiments of a perfect Imperial peacemaker: "Every endeavour will be made to … stamp
out the internal conflicts which were depleting [native] numbers even more rapidly than slave-
raiding."[3] The few lines of dedication on the Royal Military College's Girouard Building, however, tell us little of his real triumphs as a colonial administrator and nation builder in some
of the most difficult countries in the world.

The glossy image of Canada's contribution to peacekeeping may be like Sir Percy's portrait. The reality is both less and more than it seems and yet less than it might be. Canada,s contribution is less than the proud boast of participation in every mission suggests, but it is greater than mere numbers would indicate. Nevertheless, it is still less than it should be—not for what we did, but for what we might have understood and for what we might have acted upon. Canada's contribution to peacekeeping is not the legacy it could be.

Speaking of Legacies

What would a peacekeeping legacy look like? A legacy is something of value passed on by previous generations, but it has another meaning related to functions of office holding derived from the responsibilities of papal and royal legates.[4] Consider a war-fighting legacy. Decades of careful American leadership, practice and scholarship have shaped military experiences—particularly German and American experiences of the Second World War—into a powerful and world-beating doctrine of manoeuvre warfare. It is not technology alone that gives American forces global pre-eminence. It is the synergy of a weapon forged from national will, wielded with a vision of national interest, binding together the threads of military power on land, sea and in aerospace. If American war-fighting prowess is a legacy, it is the legacy of countless men and women who bumbled through the 1942 Louisiana manoeuvres, crunched the numbers for operational research, interviewed thousands of veterans, fought the bureaucrats and the Colonel Blimps, struggled with new ideas and taught the next generation.[5] The keepers of the legacy reside in headquarters, staff colleges, research centres and academies—betimes-reviled repositories of intellectuals (sometimes a term of abuse).[6] It is their ability to distil experience into ideas about how to approach future problems and convey those ideas to people who need them that makes them legates of the past.[7]

The brief of a legate changes with the times. The *Times of London* introduced the term peace-keeper to modern political discourse in a story about the European scene in the time of Bismarck (6 September 1883): "Germany ... is the peace-maker and the peace keeper of Europe." In that era, keeping the peace meant policing order in the interests of the strongest party. Several United Nations peacekeeping missions had been in place for a number of years before the term appeared widely in connection with UN operations. The *Guardian* (24 October 1961, 8/3) wrote of "problems of a disarmed world, peace-keeping machinery . . ." The crisis in Cyprus seems to have popularized the use of the term, with the press using it more frequently. The *Daily Telegraph* wrote (17 January 1964, 12/2) "The sending of some international peace-keeping force has become a matter of extreme urgency." The *Manchester Guardian Weekly* reflected growing faith in the United Nations (5 March 1964): "If an international truce force went to the island [of Cyprus], Turkey would forego its right to intervene for three months . . . this is a rare declaration of faith in the United Nations as peace-keeper." The following year, *The Spectator* reflected the growing importance of peacekeeping for the United Nations (15 June 1965, 76/2): "Peace-keeping is the basic function of the United Nations." Dropping the hyphen again appears to have been a Canadian innovation; *Maclean's* Magazine (1 December 1965, 16) wrote that: "Lieutenant-General Burns was the first of a new breed of international trouble-shooters who now try to halt the escalators of war by policing cease-fires—the Canadian peacekeeper." The last citation in the *Compact Oxford English Dictionary* definition sounds a note of warning from the *Times of London* (17 September 1973, 16/8): "Peacekeeping is a purely temporary role: a permanently-active peacekeeper must in the end become an irritant."[8] Beyond dropping the hyphen, and becoming perhaps an irritatingly permanent peacekeeper, has Canada contributed more? I think it has. From before the time of Bismarck, Canada has been subtly shaped to contribute to peacekeeping.

The world has no coherent doctrine to end violent conflicts. In its abstract ideal, peacekeeping serves a global community, not the interests of a single state. In the service of the global community, the military machines of dominant powers have serious deficiencies. Yet, although there is now a United Nations Staff College, there is no repository for global peacekeeping experience. The UN Staff College in Turin focusses on fostering a "cohesive and effective management system" for the UN as a whole.[9] The UN Department of Peacekeeping Operations Military Training and Evaluation Service employs just eight people. Its informative bulletins help track some of the activities of member states, but its output is a drop in the ocean of professional military literature.[10] And so it remains largely for states to distil from collective experience the lessons of their efforts to preserve and enhance the peace from which we all benefit.

Canada brings a unique past to the common legacy of peacekeeping. Peace, order and good government are ideals that have shaped our military contribution. But while Canadian soldiers have tackled violence with methodical, low-key problem solving and stalwart, intelligent leadership, their narrow field of view or perhaps their modesty has blinded them to their real accomplishment. The real accomplishment has not been as an adjunct to bigger armies—first British and then American—fighting wars. The real accomplishment has been progress from winning wars to preserving peace, both in a complex divided society at home and in difficult situations abroad. It is here that we have fallen short of a legacy. With our eyes on the shiny technology of war wielded by our larger allies, we have ignored the equally important science of conflict resolution that has evolved steadily in the twentieth century, seemingly in a separate universe.

To explore Canada's progress toward techniques for restoring and preserving peace, I will reflect briefly on Canada's nineteenth century experience of Imperial policing, and our progression toward a more modern conception of internal security within a political framework. The fundamental difference lies in recognizing legitimate interests, and it is upon this recognition that the legitimacy of police or peacekeepers rests. I will then consider the contributions to various peacekeeping missions in the twentieth century. The military contribution to thinking and writing about peacekeeping, in contrast to the academic contribution, begins seriously only in the last ten years. The accomplishments of this brief span have so far escaped serious study from a conflict resolution perspective. From the inception of the *Journal of Conflict Resolution* in 1956, to the spate of peacekeeping conferences in the 1990s, the world of peace research was largely insulated from military operations by the education and experience of professional soldiers oblivious to it.

The early legacy of Peace, Order and Good Government

If Canadians can claim any special suitability to peacekeeping, it may stem from their early history—the political and social constraints on forces in Canada, and a practical approach to soldiering in the periphery of the British Empire. But there was also a tendency to want to emulate the power at the centre of the empire, which may have devalued the accomplishments of those not quite seen as real soldiers.

One of the earliest formal pronouncements of international peacekeeping doctrine was the *Peacekeeper's Handbook*, copyright 1978 by the International Peace Academy under the directorship of the Indian General, Indar Jit Rikhye. Central to the peacekeeping concept was that "some forms of military intervention can provide a stabilising factor in a conflict or violence situation, thereby allowing other agencies a better opportunity for dealing with the political and socio-economic problems that form the roots of the particular conflict. It is these latter problems that require resolution if a lasting solution is to be found."[11]

The idea that grievances underlie violent disputes got an early start in Canada. As early as 1829, William Lyon Mackenzie King argued, "let governments learn to be just to the people and they will find freemen both willing and able to protect their rights."[12] The 1837 Rebellion in Lower Canada was brutally suppressed by professional British troops supported by anglophone militias. But the aftermath of the rebellion was Lord Durham's call for responsible government and the righting of injustices. The first Red River Rebellion of 1870 was met with promises of reform that went unfulfilled, leading inexorably to the second rebellion in 1885. The lesson learned, social and economic causes of the conflict were more effectively addressed following the second rebellion. The story is not over. Louis Riel, hanged as a traitor, is now held up by some as a visionary leader and hero of the Métis nation.[13] It is, of course, a disputed history. Doyen of Canadian military historians Jack Granatstein rails against it.[14] But it is an evolution of perspective that reflects the Canadian tolerance of diversity and ambiguity—essential to peaceful conflict resolution.

By the 1880s, Canada was swept with the same spirit of Imperial adventurism that touched the rest of Victoria's realm, but a cautious government was reluctant to dispatch troops for Imperial ventures in distant Africa. The expedient of permitting Britain to recruit Canadian "voyageurs" directly for the Sudan expedition was a compromise—no direct commitment and nothing explicitly dangerous, but tacit logistical support for a rescue mission that could be described as humanitarian.[15] It was a pattern to be found in future commitments, for sound domestic reasons. The experience of Canadians under British command in Manitoba, the Sudan and South Africa tempered Imperial enthusiasm: "No matter what Englishmen may think of the Zulu, Boer, and Sudan campaigns, the rest of the world knows very well that [it all]… as well as in our own humble little affair, was a most disgraceful bungle."[16]

There was in our early military history another theme. Successive British Chiefs of Staff like Gascoigne and Dundonald sought to establish a regular expeditionary field force that would take its place in operations for the defence of the Empire. In opposition to this stood those who saw regulars as nothing more than a training cadre for a reliable militia under political control. Frederick Borden's reforms at the turn of the twentieth century enhanced the militia at the expense of the regular field force Gascoigne had wanted.[17] The militia, of course, was a good instrument for the scores of internal security tasks demanded of Ottawa toward the end of the nineteenth century.[18] The schizophrenia of an army torn between the small tasks of nationhood and the bigger dreams of Empire may date from this time. But the character of the Canadian army and its connection to society may have been better suited to police actions than were the continental armies of the day, with their eyes focussed on the next big war. The debate over "real soldiering" from the 1890s to the First World War had its echo in the detractors of peacekeeping during the Cold War and into the present day.[19]

The Commander of the first Red River expedition in 1870, the 28-year-old Lieutenant-Colonel Garnet Wolsely, found Canadians to be excellent officers: "They were thinking and yet practical men, without any of the pedantry which too often clings to the young officers of all Regular Armies."[20] The pedantry Wolsely decried may have had something to do with the regular officers' preoccupation with an imagined future war and foreign adventures, rather than the immediate tasks of a small army engaged in nation building. Practical Canadian officers brought real-world problemsolving rather than drill-book theory to their daily tasks.

Peacekeeping and internal security have a common denominator. They consist of the use of military forces for police actions under the constraints of law.[21] The Canadian army or militia was employed in 78 domestic interventions between 1897 and 1946.[22] Spread across a sparsely populated country, this represented the efforts of a large proportion of a small regular force and militia. The level of violence in these interventions was generally low and declined during the period. In most cases, civilian deaths and injuries (fewer than a dozen killed and forty wounded in the entire period) occurred before the deployment of military forces, whose task was to restore order.[23] Pariseau describes the intervention of senior officers who worked closely with civil authorities in almost every case. They relied on experience and good judgement to overcome the frictions inherent in these often delicate operations.[24] There were abuses and misapplication of the military; Pariseau documents several. Nevertheless, the record on the whole illustrates a tradition of restrained and co-operative use of military force to control and prevent violence, predating the United Nations.

Blue Flag and Cold War

The first Canadian peacekeeping deployment in the UN era consisted of two military observers sent to South Korea to observe and supervise elections as part of the UN Temporary Commission of Observers (UNTCOK) in 1947. From that year to December 2000 there were at least sixty-six missions that might be described as peacekeeping, fifty-nine of them launched by the United Nations. Canada has participated in all but seven of the UN missions.[25] Although our answer to the call is usually yes, the numbers of deployed military personnel have often been small. Of fifty-nine UN missions, twenty-six included a Canadian contingent smaller than 30 at any time. Using the peak Canadian strength for each deployment, the median has been just 12 military personnel, and only nine deployments have met or exceeded battalion strength. With Canadian Forces strength over 100,000 for most of the Cold War period, it was easy for these small detachments to keep a low profile.

Almost a third of all Canadian contributions to peacekeeping missions have consisted largely of technical support or logistics. Air transport in Pakistan, Congo, and West New Guinea or signals in Lebanon, Iran, and Central Africa have been more typical than battalions on the line in Cyprus and Egypt. While this sort of specialized assistance was essential for the success of the peacekeeping missions, there is little to set it apart from any other military mission. Technical competence and professionalism are required of the signallers, aircrew, logisticians, and other trades, but no special peacekeeping skills are called for. A radio relay or pallet drop are much the same in the Golan and Gagetown, New Brunswick. Only ten missions saw Canadian troops deployed in company strength or greater. Combined with minimal risk in most missions, and the clearly military threat in others (Congo 1960-1964 or Cyprus 1964-1965 and 1974, for example), Cold War peacekeeping experience supported the dogma that a well trained soldier could handle any sort of peacekeeping.

Senior Canadian officers held the top command or chief of staff positions at times in at least fifteen of the UN missions. Generals H.H. Angle, J. Dextrase, and E.L.M. Burns brought their Second World War experience to the missions of the 1940s, 50s, and 60s. But by the last decades of the Cold War, generals like Clive Milner and Mike Jeffrey had been shaped by the experience of NATO exercises in Germany and aid of civil power or assistance to civil authority tasks in

Canadian members of the UNEF on the border between Egypt and Israel, 1962.
(Photographer unknown. NA, PA-122737)

Canada. As the threat of superpower conflict receded with détente, it became easier for peacekeepers to take action on the local aspects of the conflicts they monitored.[26] The Austrian commander of UNFICYP, Major-General Gunther Greindl (1981-1989) and his Canadian successor Major-General Clive Milner (1989-1992) engaged Greek-and Turk-Cypriot commanders in protracted negotiations. The aim was to achieve the withdrawal of belligerents from the most dangerous parts of the Green line in Nicosia, where a separation of mere metres had led to numerous shooting incidents during the preceding decade. Success in 1990 was a tribute to persistent and methodical negotiation as well as careful consideration by the Cypriots of the military merits of withdrawal. Brigadier-General Mike Jeffrey was Chief of Staff for UNTAG in Namibia, the first UN mission with a unified military and civilian command and was identified by the Secretary General's Special Representative, Martti Ahtisaari, as a key leader in its success.[27]

There are countless examples of the contributions of Canadian units to the most difficult of peacekeeping circumstances. The Canadian Airborne Regiment was caught in the crossfire of the Turkish "peace operation" (their term) or "invasion" of July 1974 with Major David Harries commanding its rag-tag support company in the crucial area of the Nicosia airport.[28] Lieutenant-Colonel Michel Jones drove the 1st Battalion, Royal 22nd Regiment across Bosnia bulling past innumerable obstacles to relieve the UN headquarters under siege in Sarajevo. Lieutenant-Colonel Thomas Geburt traversed the Balkans from Croatia to the Srebrenica safe area, and on to Macedonia, reconnoitring and establishing UN safe areas and outposts with elements of 2nd Battalion, The Royal Canadian Regiment. Lieutenant-Colonel Glen Nordick prepared defensive positions with 3rd Battalion, Princess Patricia's Canadian Light Infantry to successfully face down the first serious attempt to overrun a UN safe area in January 1993. And Lieutenant-Colonel Mike Calvin and 2 PPCLI were engaged in the most significant combat action since the Korean War at Medak in Croatia in 1993.[29]

Commanders, specialists and staff officers have been no less active. The Canadian contribution to eleven of the sixty-six missions included specialists or technical experts. The International Commissions for Supervision and Control in Indochina introduced civilian observers assigned by the Department of External Affairs.[30] But innovation has been a hallmark of Canadian contributions even when the participants have not had special expertise. By their own accounts, Canadian officers on Observer Team Nigeria in 1969 were instrumental in drawing up the negotiations which successfully ended the mission. In Vietnam in 1973, "Canadians held the senior appointments in administration, communications, transportation, supply, investigations ... and press information." Wrote one retired colonel about the short-lived International Commission for Control and Supervision (ICCS). "They, in fact, ran the ICCS."[31] Lieutenant-Colonel Alex Morrison was at the forefront of new roles for the military within the United Nations. As a Minister-Counsellor at UN headquarters in New York during the crucial last six years of the Cold War (1983-1989), he was involved as the UN prepared for missions in Asia, Africa, and Central America.[32] Colonel George Oehring drove thousands of kilometres and held hundreds of hours of meetings to achieve the March 1993 "gentleman's agreement" ceasefire which presaged further progress in the seemingly intractable Bosnian conflict.[33] Canadian chaplain Captain Mark Sargent found a new military role in seeking practical inter-communal reconciliation in Bosnia in 1994.[34] General John Arch MacInnis, as deputy commander of the UN Protection Force (UNPROFOR) there in 1994-95, was the lynchpin to bring the civilian and military components of the headquarters together in the UN's most complex mission yet.[35] Colonels Andrew Leslie and Alain Forand protected 750 civilians by harbouring them in a UN camp at Knin in August 1995 despite shelling by the Croatian army.[36] As Force Provost Marshall in 1995, Colonel Patricia Samson introduced new investigative procedures to fight corruption in the UNPF.[37] The Canadian contribution to the UN Mission in Ethiopia and Eritrea in 2000 saw a significant innovation with the deployment of a Civilian Peacebuilding Advisor, Howard Wilson, to the military contingent. His work was helped by the newly established liaison position between DND and the Canadian International Development Agency.[38]

These vignettes are indications of a larger history yet to be written. Canadians do not have a monopoly on innovative contributions to peacekeeping. They have worked beside men and women of other nations and learned from them as much as they have led them. The stories of participants are evidence that the Canadian contribution is greater than indicated by the bare facts of histories such as Goodspeed's or Gardam's or the DND web site. Yet when all these experiences are recorded and retold in full, the Canadian contribution to peacekeeping will be less than what it might have been. Dr. Ken Eyre, a subaltern in Cyprus in 1967 and a company commander with the Canadian Airborne Regiment there in 1974 was for five years the Director of Research at the Pearson Peacekeeping Centre. He argues that "we don't learn from our experiences; we learn from thinking about our experiences. Like America's war-fighting legacy, our peacekeeping legacy will only mature with systematic thought and study."

Thought and Study about Peacekeeping—Two Solitudes?

Study relevant to peacekeeping has a long pedigree but it has not accumulated to the point of guiding policy, training and education. From the beginning it has been impeded by a schism between the peace movement, which renounces war, and the strategic studies community, which thinks seriously about military operations. It is really only with the growth of peace-keeping as a focus of military activity in the last decade that the middle ground of "conflict resolution" has provided a meeting place for soldiers and scholars with relevant expertise.[39] This is ironic, given that peacekeeping forces were born of the Suez Crisis in the same year, 1956, that Anatol Rapoport and Kenneth Boulding met to establish the *Journal of Conflict Resolution*.[40] The same dire threat of nuclear war and the need for better ways to manage conflict spurred both events. These two solitudes can be traced through the history of Canada's peace movement and her concurrent contribution to peacekeeping.

Historian Gary Moffatt has chronicled Canada's movement to 1969. He sees little of the peace movement's spirit in the original Six Nations Confederacy or in the interventions of the Jesuits, but he does find early evidence of pacifist isolationism in the French-Canadian reaction to Britain's Imperial wars. French-Canadian support for the British in the American Revolution was muted; because both sides had promised religious freedoms, the common sentiment was that Quebec had no stake in the outcome. Similarly, there was little enthusiasm among French Canadians for the Boer War or the First World War. The mounting casualties and increasing demands for manpower were met with mounting opposition, culminating in the conscription crisis of 1917.[41] The second similar crisis in 1942 met more organized resistance, including a vocal and well established group of pacifist women in Quebec.[42] Writing about conscription from the vantage point of the 1960s, nationalist André Laurendeau argued that during the war many French Canadians felt as if they were living in an occupied country.[43] It is arguable that the real threat to Canadian security and identity came not from the Boers, the Kaiser and the Nazis, but from the wars themselves—pitting anglophone against francophone on matters of policy and principle. From the very beginning of Canada's political history, negotiating a way around treacherous foreign conflicts has been vital to the preservation of national unity.

But the peace activists may not help us find a peacekeeping legacy. Moffatt's history of the peace movement bears out researcher Paul Redekop's description:

> The central difference between peace studies and conflict resolution studies is a differ-
> ence between position and process… The activities of interest to conflict resolution
> studies always involve processes and relationships… these processes are about
> change, rather than specific ends or outcomes. In contrast, peace studies activity
> involves taking a position on a particular issue, for something or against something.[44]

Being oppositional, the peace movement contributed little but an inadequate (though necessary) counterbalance to the prevailing military and strategic thinking that characterized the world wars and the Cold War. By limiting himself to organizations working for world peace, rather than for social and political change in general, Moffatt omits some of the useful thinking and research that was beginning to address the underlying causes of conflict. It has been easy for the security community—the armed services and defence industrial complex—to think of peace activists and protesters as a marginal irritant, one with little understanding of the real world. But it has also become increasingly apparent since the end of the Cold War that soldiers themselves do not understand conflict either at home or abroad; conflict like that of Somalia, Bosnia and Oka. Understanding conflict and conflict resolution processes is fundamental to peacekeeping and security, and this understanding has emerged from the study of conflict resolution—a field closer to peace studies than to strategic studies.

Expertise in conflict resolution cannot be considered marginal the security community. This is because building legitimacy and balancing interests make the difference between peacekeeping and coercion. Specialized techniques, knowledge and understanding make the difference between helping to resolve a conflict and allowing it to slide into escalating violence. We can borrow an analogy from the legacy of manoeuvre warfare.[45] Generals in the First World War attempted to incorporate the new technology of aircraft and armoured vehicles and aircraft into the same pattern of frontal assault and positional warfare that had led them to bloodbaths in the first place. It took another generation of thinking and practise before tanks, machine guns, aircraft and radios all came together to wage pure manoeuvre warfare. Generals on peacekeeping duty in the Balkans and Africa today, like their First World War counterparts, might be aware of the unreliable social technology of conflict resolution techniques and familiar with the buzz-words of peacebuilding, but they remain fixed on the practice of coercion, seeking robust force posture and superior firepower. The magnitude of the gap in our peacekeeping legacy is evident when we search for a yardstick to measure the operations alluded to above. Was Oehring's "gentleman's agreement" irrelevant? What did Nordick's defence of Sector West accomplish? Did a squadron of signallers in the Central African Republic make any difference at all? Were these only isolated and futile battles in the margins, or were they a part of campaigns leading to sustainable peace? Peacekeeping divorced from conflict resolution can be a deadend of pointless police actions—in the end, an irritant, as the *Times* suggested thirty years ago.

We need to go back, not quite as far as the Iroquois confederacy, but at least to the middle of the last century to see why military thinking about peacekeeping has evolved beside peace and conflict resolution studies without intersecting until quite recently. Pacifist internationalism was probably at its peak between the world wars. It took two forms: deterrence through non-violent resistance, built on the Ghandian model; and appeasement, in the hope that meeting reasonable demands would prevent further aggression. Both relied to some extent on the assumption of the reasonable opponent. Ghandi, himself a lawyer, depended on the rule of law in a Christian democracy to reduce the cost of resistance borne by his African and Indian followers. Appeasement of Germany was based on a widespread sense (outside France) of the unfairness of the Treaty of Versailles. The manifest failure of pacifism or appeasement to extend the promise of the "war to end all wars" was a serious blow to the credibility of peace activists. In Canada as in Europe, these policies were blamed not only for failing to prevent the Second World War, but also for undermining readiness to fight once fighting became inevitable. Pacifists were prosecuted and interned in Canada with a vehemence that left little room for rapprochement, even years after the war.[46]

Ironically, many of the peace activists on the political left had identified closely with the struggle against Fascism. They had supported collective security measures to resist aggression. Calls for a united front against Fascism came from the Seventh World Council of the Communist International and from the Canadian Youth Congress. The Canadian Communist Party established the League against War and Fascism, which had the support of groups outside the Communist Party. It split from the party in 1936, changing its name to the League for Peace and Democracy and actively supporting the Mackenzie-Papineau Brigade in the Spanish Civil War. The Trades and Labour Congress of Canada and a variety of moderate church groups were involved in the League but Communist Party involvement gave many Canadians the impression that it was a Communist front. After the May Day demonstrations of 1938 and the Ribbentrop-Molotov pact, the Canadian social democratic party—the Co-operative Commonwealth Federation, then with seven seats in Parliament -broke with the League. During the war, the Communist Party was outlawed and people expressing antiwar sentiments were summarily jailed under the Defence of Canada Regulations.[47] Members of the armed services were prohibited from writing to the press. The CBC was told to cancel a program on post-war problems, *Of Things to Come*, and customs officers confiscated books and pamphlets, including the Fellowship of Reconciliation's *Pacifist Handbook*.[48] This was the experience of men and women who formed the post-war peace movement of the 1950s in opposition to the security community's faith in alliances and deterrence. There was little desire for dialogue on either side. Yet both camps were seized with the idea of building institutions that would control conflict and prevent future wars.

Brigadier-General Lewis MacKenzie at the Sarajevo Airport, 1992. (CFPU CNL, ISC 92-4014(2A))

Between the mutual exclusion of peace activists and Cold War warriors we find more than fifty years of research that seeks to understand conflict with the aim of resolving it without violence. One of the earliest efforts to describe systematically the nature of "deadly conflict" was a mammoth undertaking begun in the 1920s by the British Quaker mathematician, physicist and father of meteorology, Lewis Fry Richardson, whose *Statistics of Deadly Conflict* was published posthumously. American political scientist Quincy Wright's equally ambitious undertaking, *A Study of War*, appeared in 1942. With the escalating destructive power of atomic weapons, intellectual efforts for peace burgeoned in the 1950s. British philosopher Bertrand Russell and German physicist Albert Einstein—with a coterie of intellectual notables—issued a manifesto in 1955 putting the case for conflict resolution: "In view of the fact that in any future world war nuclear weapons will certainly be employed, and that such weapons threaten the continued existence of mankind, we urge the governments of the world to realise, and to acknowledge publicly, that their purpose cannot be furthered by a world war, and we urge them, consequently, to find peaceful means for the settlement of all matters of dispute between them."[49]

American money brought Canada into the equation. Cyrus Eaton, trustee of the University of Chicago, invited Einstein and Russell to his summer home at Pugwash, Nova Scotia in 1955, the beginning of the Pugwash conferences on conflict and other global issues that have since taken their name from that setting. At the time of the celebrated first Pugwash conference, Russian-born mathematician and psychologist Anatol Rapoport was an assistant professor at the University of Chicago. He moved to the University of Michigan the following year, where he began to work with American economist Kenneth Boulding. In 1956, the year of the Suez intervention, they laid plans to establish the *Journal of Conflict Resolution*. Its first issues included articles on game theory and psycho-social aspects of conflict that were germane in their day, and seem remarkably prescient now. Ralph Dahrendorf's article "Toward a Theory of Social Conflict," (to name just one) is often cited by Balkan and African scholars to explain the civil wars of the 1990s. By 1959, Michigan had established the Center for Research on Conflict Resolution, and the International Peace Research Institute was established in Oslo, Norway. None of this made a ripple in Canada's foreign or defence policy. A 1957 publication by the Department of External Affairs, *Military Commitments Abroad*, viewed peacekeeping not as a

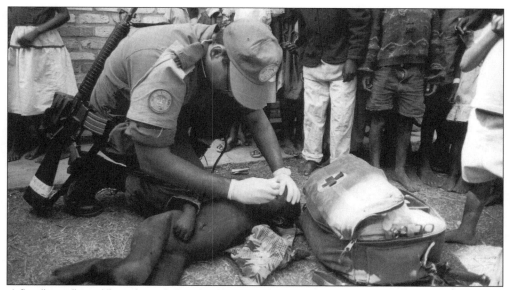
A Canadian medic providing assistance in Rwanda, 1994. (DND file photo.)

step toward conflict resolution but as a routine extension of military operations, all within an alliance framework and in opposition to a potential adversary.[50]

Conflict research continued to grow during the 1960s with the publication of Richardson's work and the foundation of new institutions. Dating from this period are the Polemological Institute in the Netherlands (Groeningen, 1962), the International Peace Research Association (Switzerland, 1964), the Institute for the Analysis of Conflict (London and later Kent, 1966) and the Richardson Institute for Peace and Conflict Research (London and later Lancaster, 1969). One of the most interesting counterpoints to Canada's peacekeeping legacy is the Tampere Peace Research Institute, established in 1969 by the Government of Finland. Like Canada, Finland had participated in the earliest peacekeeping missions, and had troops in the Middle East and in Cyprus. Like Canada, it sat uncomfortably between East and West during the Cold War. But the Tampere Peace Research Institute had a specific mandate for research on conflict resolution; it contributed to Finland's policy of engaging in peacekeeping as a means of suppressing and diverting dangerous international conflict. As the Cold War thawed in the 1980s, the institute tried to convert progress on the Helsinki Conference into a European security mechanism. Finland has been a quiet diplomatic workhorse for the Conference on Security and Cooperation in Europe and subsequently the Organisation for Security and Cooperation in Europe (OSCE). The longstanding relationship between Finland's citizen soldiers on peacekeeping duty and the Tampere support for Nordic peacekeeping training culminated in publication of the two-volume *Nordic UN Tactical Manual*.[51] At the strategic level, the Finnish institute has been important in the evolution of the OSCE's Vienna Centre for the Prevention of Conflict.[52] It is perhaps in the Nordic intellectual community and in neutral Austria that we find the closest relations between soldiers and academics in the conflict-resolution field during the Cold War.[53]

Canadian historian Sean Maloney describes Canada's peacekeeping contribution as a pursuit of Cold War objectives by other means.[54] In the 1960s, a standby battalion practised the complicated logistics of airlift for quick response to a UN or NATO call in the event of a crisis.[55] Training in paramilitary and internal security roles suitable for peacekeeping increased, but this was also related to the probability of internal deployments.[56] Officers for international duty with the UN were selected for experience rather than educated for anticipated tasks. After the Congo, there were only two new missions that called for significant numbers of observers –UNYOM in Yemen and UNIPOM in India-Pakistan.[57] Some of those selected participated in a new four-day course for UN observers run in Ottawa.[58] But this course had little to offer beyond area handbook information and the practical experience of those who had gone before. Since the first UN Special Commission in the Balkans in 1947, officers had been relying on their problem-solving abilities to investigate and resolve local incidents in accordance with delicate UN mandates.[59]

The conflict resolution literature of the early sixties did not address peacekeeping problems in a language that most soldiers could relate to. Dahrendorf did not appear to have been writing for the Cape Breton high school graduate on his way to the Kashmir in 1965. Since moving to the University of Toronto in 1974, Anatol Rapoport has contributed enormously to our understanding of game theory and the analysis of conflict, but his works are not widely read in military circles.[60] And although Hanna Newcombe's Peace Research Institute (established in 1976) has produced a vast compendium of empirical and theoretical reports in the *Peace Research Abstracts Journal*, this periodical has only recently been added to Canadian Forces libraries in Kingston, Ottawa and Toronto. Peace and conflict resolution research was beginning by the middle of the Cold War to assemble the social tools for conflict management. But if concepts of conflict and violence were becoming increasingly sophisticated and grounded in empirical research in the 1960s and 1970s, this was not always reflected in strategic thinking about peacekeeping, which continued to focus on pragmatic issues of diplomatic communication, national interests, finance, and logistics. Not until the end of the Cold War would soldiers begin to concern themselves with conflict resolution as it was understood in the academies.

Canadian Leadership in International Peacekeeping

Canada has a modest claim to leadership in international peacekeeping. Secretary of State for External Affairs Lester Pearson was awarded the 1957 Nobel Peace Prize not forproposing UN military forces but for "the powerful initiative, strength, and perseverance he has displayed in attempting to prevent or limit war operations and to restore peace."[61] The actual innovation of peacekeeping is credited to Dag Hammarskjöld, who received the 1961 Nobel Prize posthumously. Nevertheless, Ottawa was instrumental in fielding the first interpositionary UN force—the United Nations Emergency Force, later known as UNEF I—to the Sinai in 1956. The following year Prime Minister Diefenbaker spoke at the General Assembly in favour of a permanent UN police force. Pearson's first speech at the General Assembly after becoming Prime Minister in 1963 likewise supported a stronger UN peacekeeping capacity.[62] In December 1963, Pearson cited the example of Scandinavian and Dutch standby forces for UN duty in testimony to the Standing Committee on External Affairs.[63] In May of 1964 his ideas for international forces under UN peacekeeping mandates included advanced planning for their financial and logistic support.[64] In the same month, his Dag Hammarskjöld Memorial lecture at Carleton University called for a small military planning staff in the office of the Secretary General, and announced that confidential discussions with like-minded nations would begin shortly.[65]

In November 1964, Prime Minister Pearson hosted the Ottawa Peacekeeping Conference, attended by military officers of twenty-three countries that had contributed to UN operations or had designated standby forces.[66] It occurred against the background of Canadian diplomat Blair Seaborn's failure to bring about talks in Vietnam and mounting East-West competition in the Third World. Military attention was focussed on the German border and peacekeeping remained a marginal activity to maintain NATO solidarity (in the case of Cyprus—where two key allies confronted each other) and to shore up the periphery, where superpower conflict threatened to escalate. The deployment of Canadian troops to Cyprus had also been the occasion for Quebec's Réal Caouette of the Ralliement des Créditistes to recall Borden's attacks on French Canadians during the First World War. This was a reminder for the Liberal government of the constant balance that had to be struck between domestic constraints and international impulses.[67] But by the time the conference opened, opposition had subsided and there seemed to be a general domestic approval of Canada's peacekeeping role in Cyprus, Egypt, and the recently concluded Yemen operation.[68]

The sudden burst of peacekeeping in the 1960s, however, had demonstrated the weakness of ad hoc arrangements. Inter-communal violence surrounded the insertion of the UN force into Cyprus, and the friction over funding further complicated a mission with overtones of superpower confrontation. Within a year or two of the controversial Congo and Cyprus missions, scores of papers, pamphlets, conference proceedings and monographs had been produced on the problems of peacekeeping.[69] These were noted in Canadian military circles. Under the threat of nuclear war, decolonization and global governance were to the 60s and 70s what globalization and the end of the Cold War were to the 1990s. This was the backdrop to the "Meeting of Military Experts to Consider the Technical Aspects of UN Peace-Keeping Operations" held in Ottawa 2-6 November 1964. The conference was to be limited to matters such as composition, command and control, personnel administration, accounting procedures and legal problems. The wider political issues of authorization and financing would be left to discussions at the UN.[70] Despite its modest objectives, the conference appears to have been a disappointment, resulting in nothing more than a bland communiqué listing points of discussion. The conference demonstrated that although it was possible to discuss the technical aspects of peacekeeping while ignoring politics, it was not very fruitful to do so.[71]

The ponderously titled *Report of the Standing Committee on External Affairs and National Defence Respecting the United Nations and Peacekeeping,* published in May 1970, might be seen as the sum of what Canada had learned about peacekeeping in the 1960s. Ten meetings were held, visits to the UN were made, and witnesses were called from the academic, military, and non-governmental communities. The report is remarkable for its ignorance of conflict resolution theory and research that had been in wide circulation since the 1950s. The idea that peacekeeping was a form of third party intervention in conflict, and that it could apply conflict resolution tools, would appear in those terms in 1970, but not in Canada. The good offices of the Secretary General and the mediating role of the UN in concert with a peacekeeping mission are mentioned in the Canadian report. But neither this Parliamentary committee nor its UN precursor, the panel that wrote the *Comprehensive Review of the Whole Question of Peace-Keeping Operations in all their Aspects,*[72] addressed the full range of dispute resolution mechanisms open to the UN. They do not consider the implications of inquiry, good offices, mediation, conciliation, arbitration or judicial settlement, or resort to regional agencies in the context of field operations involving forces or observers working under UN auspices.[73] Although the UN handbook with this list of tools and techniques dates from 1992, the same list appears in League of Nations documents from the 1920s, and in treatises on diplomacy from even earlier.[74] The tools were not new, but the idea that they could be usefully applied at community level under the protection of a UN force had not yet emerged. The academic and non-governmental witnesses called by these committees had no personal experience of war-torn countries, and the soldiers had no knowledge of the previous twenty years of research and innovation.

Canadian soldiers in East Timor. (DND file photo.)

Peacekeeping stalled in the 1970s. Only the frustrating International Commission for Control and Supervision in Vietnam and three old conflicts in the well trodden Middle East drew new United Nations support (UNEF II, UNDOF, and UNIFIL). But with the continuing Canadian presence in Cyprus, these were enough to keep peacekeeping within view of Canadian policy makers, who stimulated some thinking, if not innovation, in peacekeeping. Innovation came largely from elsewhere, though not without Canadians involved.

Canadian Generals Leslie, Beatty and Yost, all with peacekeeping experience, had begun to make their presence felt in the International Peace Academy by 1970.[75] Ruth Forbes Young, a rich American with World Federalist sympathies, asked UN Secretary General U Thant what contributions she might make, and she was advised in 1969 to start a peacekeeping academy. The first seminars of the International Peace Academy Committee were held in elegant surroundings in Vienna the following year. Canadian Generals Leslie and Beatty rubbed shoulders with a former Chief of Staff UNFICYP, retired British Brigadier Michael Harbottle, and with peace researchers Asbjorne Eide, Chadwick Alger and Johan Galtung. Galtung was the principle consultant on peace research.[76] The Royal Institute of International Affairs had just published Harbottle's book on the military contribution to peacebuilding in Cyprus, *The Impartial Soldier*, and Harbottle was ready to take on new ideas like structural violence.[77] In 1974, Harbottle was asked by retired Indian Major-General Indar Jit Rikhye, the first president of the new academy, to compile and edit the *Peacekeeper's Handbook*.[78] Its publication in 1978 reflected workshops over four years in which the experiences of peacekeepers were collected and distilled.[79] Although the practical aspects of patrolling, logistics and communications overshadow the conceptual starting point, it is in the *Peacekeeper's Handbook* that we find the first doctrinal acknowledgement of the importance of the underlying causes of conflict to the practical peacekeeper. Here, too, is a seminal reference to Johan Galtung's distinction between physical and structural violence, along with definitions that had the potential to reshape military perceptions of peacekeeping:

Peace: A condition that exists in the relations between groups, classes or states
  when there is an absence of violence (direct or indirect) or the threat of violence.

Direct (Manifest) Violence: A condition that exists when human beings deliberately
  kill or physically injure other human beings.

Indirect (Structural) Violence: A condition that exists when the physical and psychological conditions of some groups, classes or states is inferior to those of others.

Peacemaking: An effort to settle a conflict through mediation, negotiation and other forms of peaceful settlement.

Peacebuilding: Social change that actively seeks to eliminate the likelihood of direct and/or indirect violence.[80]

Harbottle published *The Blue Berets* in 1971 and *The Thin Blue Line: International Peacekeeping and its Future* with Rikhye in 1974.[81] But it is in his description of the third party role of soldiers in peacekeeping (in *The Blue Berets*) and in the introduction to the *Peacekeeper's Handbook* that he came closest to the conflict resolution perspective. Subsequent seminars of the International Peace Academy included fewer peace activists, focussing more on matters of diplomacy and soldiering than on social engineering and peacebuilding.[82] When Brigadier Harbottle moved on to work with scholar Adam Curle at the Bradford School for Peace Studies and helped to found Generals for Peace in 1982, "many old regimental friends turned their backs."[83] Most Cold War soldiers could not yet think that far.

Public Discussion of Peacekeeping

Were Canadian military thinkers working on the problems of peacekeeping in the 1970s, 1980s and 1990s? Do we find the peacekeeping legacy in professional writing? Does it amount to a useable legacy for the conflicts of the twenty-first century? The dominant themes of military thought from the 1970s to the 1990s can be deduced from the catalogue of military publications and from professional military journals. The accumulated body of work up to 1995 is neither extensive nor very innovative.

The evolution of peacekeeping was tracked by *Canadian Defence Quarterly* under two successive editors—John Gellner and John Marteinson—from 1971 to 1995. Over the entire period of its publication, 55 articles of approximately 800 in the *CDQ* addressed peacekeeping. Of these, 42 appeared after 1989. In the very first issue in 1971, Brigadier Michael Harbottle reported on the work of the International Peace Academy, emphasizing the practical nature of its training. Ironically, his message may have been lost because people wilfully took "practical" to mean "practical soldiering." This meant the sort of patrolling, shooting and driving exercises that justified the expenditure of training funds in lean times for operational tasks like deployment to Cyprus.[84] But Harbottle did not mean the usual practical military tasks. He had a vision of something new:

> For years now, peace theory and conflict research institutes have existed for the specific purposes of studying the causes and effects of conflicts, and how they might be peacefully settled. But theory and research alone are incomplete without practical application…As a project [the International Peace Academy] had no counterpart since it would do what no research or theory institute could do, produce men and women trained for the practical field roles required in peacekeeping.[85]

A trickle of two or three Canadian officers a year continued to participate in the seminars and training sessions run by the IPA. But the field research centres suggested by Harbottle did not emerge, and the debate on applying conflict resolution theory to peacekeeping was not taken up by the military community in Canada. Only one subsequent article by a Canadian officer addresses the contribution of the IPA, and the importance of action-research, including off-the-record meetings of parties directly involved in disputes.[86]

By far the most numerous peacekeeping articles written by serving officers in *Canadian Defence Quarterly* are historical accounts or travel narratives. The better among them provide some political or strategic context for the mission, and some attempt to infer lessons with

Canadian soldiers use tear gas to disperse a riot in Dvar, Bosnia, 1998. (DND file photo.)

broader implications for peacekeeping policy. Some, however, served to reinforce the prejudice that peacekeeping was a bit of a holiday from the travails of soldiering in Gagetown or Wainwright: "The ICC flights were a memorable experience ... Life in Saigon was not unpleasant."[87] It was easy to dismiss this as less than real soldiering and not worthy of professional development.

Articles on the future of peacekeeping appeared intermittently. Professor Henry Wiseman suggested in 1975 that the Committee of 33, instigated by Pearson's 1964 Peacekeeping Conference, might yet breathe new life into peacekeeping. He reflected on the budgetary pressures of the 1970s and the utility of peacekeeping forces as barometers of tension and tools to slow escalation. In 1978, Brigadier-General E. Leslie (who had participated in IPA seminars) saw a broad peacekeeping future for Canada, with a wide range of different types of forces and expertise being required.[88] Lieutenant-Colonel James Allan disagreed in a subsequent issue of *CDQ*. He cited the IPA's own dictum of the need to resolve underlying causes of conflict to suggest that peacekeeping was ultimately a fallacy, serving only to freeze conflicts and lead to stagnation.[89] His litany of the technical problems of peacekeeping falls well short of Paul Diehl's perceptive analysis a decade later of what goes wrong when peacekeeping does not lead to peace.[90] After the fall of the Berlin Wall, bureaucrats and soldiers alike were bullish about the prospects for expanded peacekeeping roles, probably involving more use of force.[91] By this stage, policy advocates like Brian Urquhart and articles in *Survival* are being cited to add to the debate, but there is still little evidence of an intersection with the academic community.

The award of the Nobel Peace Prize to United Nations Peacekeeping Forces in 1988 no doubt contributed to a sense of excitement about Canada's contribution to an honourable cause. The autumn 1989 issue of *Canadian Defence Quarterly* was the first to be devoted completely to peacekeeping articles. They were mostly narratives and histories. Within three years a second special issue commemorated the completion of the peacekeeping monument in Ottawa. CBC productions and glossy coffee-table books appeared glorifying the image of the Canadian peacekeeper.[92] The soldier carrying a child to safety replaced the unsavoury image of the soldier killing. But unpleasant violence remained in the repertoire. Like poor Sir Percy Girouard's portrait at RMC, the grit of operations and the wrinkles of serious thinking were stripped away from the face of peacekeeping, leaving a vapid antidote to our Somalia trauma but little connection with the research or understanding needed to support future operations.

Conclusion

There are good historical and contemporary reasons for Canada's affinity with peacekeeping. Managing big wars abroad and small wars at home helps to keep the country together. Peacekeeping without effective conflict resolution, however, is a dead end. It evolves to interminable policing or escalating violence, as we have seen during and after the Cold War. There is a military role in conflict resolution that depends upon understanding the relationship between physical and structural violence, as peace researcher Johan Galtung taught peacekeeper Michael Harbottle 30 years ago. But the hard work of research, evaluation, experimentation, and professional self-examination has yet to follow our infatuation with the glossy image. We will honour our veterans by competence at preserving the peace. Canada's contribution to peacekeeping is not yet a legacy.

Notes for Chapter 18

1   I would like to thank Floyd Rudmin, Johan Galtung, Ernie Regehr, and Sgt Gary Kett of the Peace Support Training Centre for their kind assistance with the research for this chapter. Errors and omissions are all my own.

2   Major G.G.M. Carr-Harris, "The Girouard Story," in R. Guy C. Smith, *As You Were! Ex-Cadets Remember*, Volume 1 1876-1918 (Kingston: Royal Military College of Canada, 1983), 169.

3   Quoted from the Colonial Office Blue Book, 1907-8, by Carr-Harris, 174.

4   *The Compact Oxford English Dictionary*, Second Edition (Oxford: Clarendon Press, 1991), 958.

5   The Louisiana GHQ manoeuvres of 1941 occupy a special place in the evolution of U.S. war-fighting prowess, unprecedented and never since duplicated. Christopher R. Gabel, *The U.S. Army GHQ Maneuvers of 1941* (Washington, DC: Center of Military History United States Army, 1991), 194.

6   "Intellectually inclined officers must prove their combat credentials". Williamson Murray, "Thinking About Innovation," *US Naval War College Review*, Vol LIV, No. 2, (Spring 2001), 127.

7   Major Paul H. Herbert, *Deciding What Has to Be Done: General William E. DePuy and the 1976 Edition of FM100-5, Operations*, Leavenworth Papers Number 16 (Fort Leavenworth, Kan.: Combat Studies Institute, 1988), 95-98.

8   All examples of usage are from the *Compact Oxford English Dictionary*, op.cit., 1292.

9   *United Nations Staff College*, "About the Staff College: Our Mission," accessed 12 Aug 2001; available from http://www.itcilo.it/unscp/about/.

10 See *UN-DPKO News Bulletin* 3/2000 July/December 2000, and its successor, UN DPKO Military Training and Evaluation Service *News Bulletin* 1/2000.

11 International Peace Academy, *The Peacekeeper's Handbook*. Edited by Brigadier (Retired) Michael Harbottle (New York: Pergamon Press for the International Peace Academy, 1978), I/6.

12 Margaret Fairley, ed. *Selected writings of William Lyon Mackenzie* (Toronto: Oxford Press, 1960), 42.

13 David Kilgour, *Uneasy Patriots: Western Canadians in Confederation* "Eight: Louis Riel: Patriot without a Country," © 1990, 2001 -Last revised May 17, 2001, accessed August 2001, available from http://www.david-kilgour.com/uneasypatriots/8riel.htm

14 J.L. Granatstein, *Who Killed Canadian History?* (Toronto: Harper Collins, 1998), xiii.

15 Roy MacLaren, *Canadians on the Nile, 1882-1898: Being the Adventures of the Voyageurs on the Khartoum Relief Expedition and Other Exploits* (Vancouver: University of British Columbia Press, 1978).

16 Lewis Redman Ord, *Reminiscences of a Bungle by One of the Bunglers*, ed. by R.C. Macleod (Edmonton: University of Alberta Press, 1983 Ord kept a diary in 1885 and later revised and updated it), 98.

17 S.J. Harris, "The Permanent Force and 'real soldiering' 1883-1914," in Mark Milner, ed., *Canadian Military History: Selected Readings* (Toronto: Irwin, 1993).

18 Jean Pariseau, *Forces armées et maintien de l'ordre au Canada, 1867-1967: un siècle d'aide au pouvoir civil*, tome 1 (Montpellier : Thèse présenté au Centre d'histoire militaire et d'études de défense nationale, 1981), 401a.

19 Michael Harbottle wrote *What is Proper Soldiering?* 1990, which was adopted by British staff colleges as a reading in precisely this debate.

20 George Arthur, ed., *The Letters of Lord and Lady Wolseley, 1870-1911* (London: Heineman, 1922), cited by Roy MacLaren, 40.

21 David A. Charters, "From October to Oka: Peacekeeping in Canada, 1970-1990," Marc Milner, *Canadian Military History: Selected Readings* (Toronto: Longman, 1993), 370-372.

22 Pariseau, 401b.

23 Pariseau, 405-407.

24 Pariseau, 411a.

25 Canada did not send military observers or troops to the UN Commission for Indonesia, 1947-1951; the UN Special Commission on the Balkans, 1947-1952; UNAVEM I in Angola, 1989-1991; UNASOG between Sudan and Libya, 1994; UNMOT in Tajikistan, 1994 to the present; UNAVEM III in Angola, 1995-1997; and UNTAES in Eastern Slavonia, 1996-1998.

26 Détente is usually associated with Kissinger's initiatives in the early 1970s, SALT, the ABM treaty, and U.S. withdrawal from Vietnam. Charles R. Smith, "Cold War" in *Brassey's Encyclopedia of Military History and Biography*, Franklin D. Margiotta, ed., (Washington: Brassey's, 1994), 209-210. Missions most closely associated with the Cold War strategies of the superpowers—UNDOF, UNEF II, and the ICCS –displayed few local initiatives throughout the period. Others began to show evidence of autonomous decision making at theatre level, which may have had more to do with the increasing confidence and peacekeeping experience of commanders than the dynamics of the Cold War.

27 Although the structure was unified, the headquarters was split between two locations putting a special burden of co-ordination on the Chief of Staff. UN DPKO, "Nambia; UNTAG" available from http://www.un.org/Depts/dpko/co_mission/untagPT.htm accessed July 2001.

28 Major K.C. Eyre, "The Future of UN Interpository Peacekeeping under the 1956 Pearson-Hammarskjold Formula: Conclusions Drawn from Personal Experiences in Cyprus, in the Tragic Summer of 1974," *Canadian Defence Quarterly(CDQ)*, Vol 12, No. 1 (Summer 1982).

29 Interviews with participants and "MPs learn of Medak horrors," *The Calgary Herald,* 28 April , 1998, A2.

30 Mitchell Sharp (Secretary of State for External Affairs), "Viet-Nam: Canada's approach to participation in the International Commission of Control and Supervision October 25, 1972, March 27, 1973. (Ottawa: Information Canada, 1973) .

31 Gardam, 1992, 40, 44.

32 He was later founder and president of the Lester B. Pearson Canadian International Peacekeeping Training Centre. Lieutenant-Colonel Alex Morrison, "The Renaissance of United Nations Peacekeeping: Some Observations from New York,"*CDQ*, Vol 19, No. 1 (Summer 1989), 13-18.

33 Jeannie Peterson, CAC Sector South, "Weekly Briefing Notes for SRSG, Sector South, 30 July 1993: Political and Economic Issues" UNPROFOR files provided to author.

34 National Film Board of Canada, *Protection Force: In God's Command*, NFB Video 111c9195 102 (1996).

35 Interviews with Special Advisor to the SRSG, Zagreb, September, 1995.

36 Steven Edwards, "Two Canadian officers have testified that Croatia knowingly bombed Serb civilians in 1995," *National Post*, 9 Apr 1999, available from http://www.balkanpeace.org/cib/cro/cro03.html, accessed July 2001.

37 Minutes of the UNPF HQ Black Market Steering Committee, November 1995.

38 Communication with Susan Brown, Director of CIDA Peacebuilding Branch, 10 Sept 2001 and with Lieutenant-Colonel Murray Swan, DND Liaison Officer to CIDA, April 2001. See Howard Wilson, Civilian Peacebuilding Advisor (CPA) To United Nations Peace-Keeping Mission To Eritrea And Ethiopia (UNMEE) Report No: 1, 22-29/02/01.

39 Paul Redekop, "The Emerging Discipline of Conflict Resolution Studies," *Peace Research: The Canadian Journal of Peace Studies*, Vol 31, No. 1 (February 1999), 76-86.

40 Bradford School of Peace Studies, "History of Conflict Resolution," available from http://www.brad.ac.uk/acad/confres/dislearn/unit2.html#origins, accessed July 2001.

41 Gary Moffatt, *History of the Canadian Peace Movement Until 1969* (St. Catharines, Ont.): Grapevine Press, 1982), 6-17.

42 Simonne Monet-Chartrand, *Les Québécoises et le mouvement pacifiste (1939-1967)* (Montreal : Éditions Écosociété, 1993), 15-21.

43 André Laurendeau, *la Crise Conscription du Canada* (Montréal : Editions du jour, 1962), 157, cited by Moffatt, 14.

44 Redekop, 84-85.

45 White House Fellow and West Point Professor Major Richard D. Hooker's anthology, *Maneuver Warfare* (Novato, Cal.: Presidio, 1993) contains several articles on the intellectual heritage of manoeuvre warfare.

46 William Repka and Kathleen M. Repka, *Dangerous Patriots: Canada's Unknown Prisoners of War*. (Vancouver: New Star Books, 1982).

47 Moffatt, 18-22.

48 Moffatt, 23. I acknowledge that this abbreviated synopsis does not capture the full variety of the peace movement's contributions. In particular, the work of Moral Rearmament and the Caux conferences in seeking Franco-German reconciliation from 1946 to 1952 needs further exploration.

49 "The Russell-Einstein Manifesto," Issued in London, 9 Jul 1955, available at http://www.pugwash.org/about.htm, accessed July 2001.

50 External Affairs, *Military Commitments Abroad* (Ottawa: Government of Canada, 1957) cited by David Lenarcic, "Peacekeeping, 1965: The Canadian Military's Viewpoint," *Canadian Military History*, Vol 5, No. 1 (Spring, 1996), 105

51 Interview with one of the authors, Major Olli Viljaranta, October 1992, Nicosia, Cyprus.

52 Secretary General, Visit of the Director of the Conflict Prevention Centre to Tampere, Finland, on 1 August 2000; Minutes of the 296th meeting of the Permanent Council of the OSCE, 24 August 2000, available at http://www.osce.org/, accessed August 2001.

53 Notwithstanding one researcher's complaint: "At PRIO we invited [an upcoming] general to stay with us and pick up as much as he wanted … (he spent his time spying on us for the Norwegian secret police)."

54 See Sean Maloney's upcoming book on peacekeeping and the Cold War to be published in 2002 by Vanwell.

55 David Cox, "Canada's Interest in Peacekeeping: Some Political and Military Considerations," in *Peacekeeping: International Challenge and Canadian Response* (Ottawa: Canadian Institute of International Affairs, 1968) 53.

56 Dan Loomis, *Not Much Glory* (Toronto: Deneau, 1984).

57. The Observer Team to Nigeria engaged only four officers, and the Dominican Republic mission only one.

58 David Cox, "Canada's Interest in Peacekeeping: Some Political and Military Considerations," in Peacekeeping: International Challenge and Canadian Response (Ottawa: Canadian Institute of International Affairs, 1968), 53, cited by Gary Kett, 11.

59 Amikam Nachmani, *International intervention in the Greek civil war : the United Nations Special Committee on the Balkans, 1947-1952* (New York: Praeger, 1990).

60 His seminal works on game theory were produced at the University of Michigan, *Two-person game theory: the essential ideas* (Ann Arbor: University of Michigan Press, 1966) and *N-person game theory; concepts and applications* (Ann Arbor: University of Michigan Press, 1970). They influenced a generation of Pentagon strategists, particularly in the realm of deterrence. See Edward N. Luttwack, *Strategy: The Logic of War and Peace* (Cambridge,Mass.: Belknap Press of Harvard University, 1987) on deterrence and persuasion. His later work in Toronto provided more concepts for managing conflict, including crucial insights into co-operative processes; see *Conflict in man-made environments* (Harmondsworth: Penguin Books, 1974) and *The origins of violence: approaches to the study of conflict* (New York: Paragon House, 1989). They have circulated little from RMC's Massey Library. The only holding of Rapoport at the Canadian Forces College is in Toronto his edited edition of Clausewitz's *On War*.

61 Gunnar Jahn, "Speech by the Chairman of the Nobel Committee: The Nobel Peace Prize for 1957," Nobel E-Museum, available at http://www.nobel.se/peace/laureates/1957/press.html, accessed July 2001.

62. Girard, 316.

63 Ibid., 319.

64 Lester B. Pearson, "A New Kind of Peace Force—One of the Architects of NATO Sets Forth a Plan to Deal with Situations Like Cyprus" *Macleans,* 2 May 1964, 9-11.

65 Girard, 321.

66 Lieutenant-Colonel D.J. Goodspeed, Editor, *The Armed Forces of Canada, 1867-1967* (Ottawa: Directorate of History, 1967), 264.

67 The sense of Caouette's attack was isolationist: money should be spent at home on unemployment and social assistance, not on foreign military ventures of dubious worth. *Canada, House of Commons*, *Debates*, 21 Feb. 1964, 93-4.

68 Charlotte Girard, *Canada in World Affairs*, Vol XIII, 1964-5 (Toronto: Canadian Institute of International Affairs, 1978), 313-15.

69 World Federalists and the World Veterans Association were two of the organizations involved in promulgating the new ideas. For example, Dr. Kjell Goldmann, Peacekeeping and Self-Defence, Monograph No. 7, International Information Centre on Peacekeeping Operations (Paris: World Veterans Federation, 1968); Arthur I. Waskow, *Toward a Peacekeepers Academy: a proposal for a first step toward a United Nations Transnational Peacekeeping Force* (The Hague: Junk, 1967) was the result of a study initiated by the Association of World Federalists; Inis L. Claude, "The UN and the use of force," International Conciliation No. 532 (New York: Carnegie Endowment for International Peace, 1961).

70 Girard, 324.

71 Ibid., 327.

72 UN General Assembly, *Comprehensive Review of the Whole Question of Peace-Keeping Operations in all their Aspects*, Twenty Fourth Session, Document A/7742, 3 Nov. 1969.

73 UN *Handbook on the Peaceful Settlement of Disputes Between States* (New York: United Nations, 1992).

74 Albert E. Hindmarsh, *Force in Peace: Force Short of War in International Relations* (Port Washington, N.Y.: Kennikat Press, 1933).

75 Colonel R.D. Leech, "The International Peace Academy," *CDQ*, Vol 9, No. 2 (Autumn 1979), 21.

76 Communication with author, September 2001.

77 Michael Harbottle, *The impartial soldier* (London: Oxford University Press, 1970).

78 Eirwen Harbottle, "The Making of A Peacebuilder: The Story of Brig. Gen. Michael Harbottle, OBE, Ph.D." *Bearing Witness: The Journal of the Peacemaker Community*, Fall 2000, 10-15. Available at www.peacemakercommunity.org/English/hub/Journal/2000/Fall_Issue/BW_Fall_2000.pdf accessed August 2001.

79 Discussions with General Indar Jit Rikhye.

80 International Peace Academy, *The Peacekeeper's Handbook* (New York: IPA, 1978), I/6.

81 Michael Harbottle, *The Blue Berets* (London: Leo Cooper, 1971); Indar Jit Rikhye, Michael Harbottle, and Bjoern Egge, *The Thin Blue Line: International Peacekeeping and its Future* (New Haven: Yale University Press, 1974).

82 Eirwen Harbottle, 2000, 12.

83 Ibid., 13.

84 Jean Morin, DND Directorate of History, has raised this observation after beginning his research into the history of training for the Cyprus commitment. Communication with the author.

85 Brigadier Michael Harbottle, "The International Peace Academy: Training Not Theory," *CDQ*, Vol 1, No. 1 (Summer 1971), 56.

86 Colonel R.D. Leech, "The International Peace Academy," *CDQ*, Vol 9, No.2 (Autumn 1979), 21.

87 Lieutenant-Colonel G.D. Smith, "The Truce Supervision in Indochina, 1954-1973," *CDQ*, Vol 19, No. 1 (Summer 1989), 36.

88 Brigadier-General E. Leslie, "Some Thoughts on International Peacekeeping," *CDQ*, Vol 7, No. 3 (Winter 1977), 18.

89 Lieutenant-Colonel James H. Allan, "The Future of Peacekeeping in Canada," *CDQ*, Vol 7, No. 3 (Summer 1978), 30-37.

90 P.F. Diehl, "When Peacekeeping Does Not Lead to Peace: Some Notes on Conflict Resolution," *Bulletin of Peace Proposals*, Vol 18, No. 1 (1987), 7-53.

91 Louis A. Delvoie, "Canada and Peacekeeping: A New Era?" *CDQ*, Vol 20, No. 2, (Autumn 1990), 9-16, and Major-General (retired) John A. MacInnis, "Peacekeeping at the Crossroads," *CDQ*, Vol 25, No. 2 (December 1995), 10-13.

92 See, for example, J.L. Granatstein and Douglas Lavender, *Shadows of war, faces of peace: Canada's peacekeepers*, photographs by Boris Spremo (Toronto: Key Porter Books, 1992).

APPENDIX 1
Canadian Contributions to Peacekeeping Missions[1]

MISSION	LOCATION	DURATION	TYPE[2]	PARTICIPATION[3]	CANADIAN MISSION COMMANDER[4]	CONTRIBUTION[5]	
UNTCOK	Korea	1947-48	O	two UNMOs to South Korea to observe and supervise elections	—		L
UNCI[6]	Indonesia	Aug 47-Apr 51	G	None	—		O
UNSCOB	Balkans (Greece)	Oct 47-Feb 52	O	None	—		O
UNTSO	Lebanon-Syria-Israel	Jun 48-	O	Canada has participated in UNTSO since 1954. There are 11 Canadian Forces personnel assigned to UNTSO in the Middle East. Observers: Interviews indicate that there is a long history of Canadian observers gravitating quickly to key staff positions in headquarters. The term "observers" includes these staff positions. See note for ICCS.	MGen Burns, 54-56		L,C
UNMOGIP	India Pakistan	Jan 49-	O	UNMOGIP was established to monitor, in the State of Jammu and Kashmir, the cease-fire between India and Pakistan. Canada provided up to 39 military observers at any given time to UNMOGIP between 1949 and 1979. In addition, until 1996, Canada provided a CC-130 Hercules aircraft for the biannual rotation of the UNMOGIP Headquarters between India and Pakistan.	BGen Angle, Nov 49-Jul 50. Col Gauthier, Jan-Jul 66. LCol Bergevin, Jun 77-Apr 78. LCol Pospisil, Apr-Jun 78.		L,S,C
UN Command Korea	Korea	1950-53	F	In 1950, North Korea invaded South Korea and overran almost the whole of the country. To help South Korea defend itself, 16 nations contributed 932,000 troops to a UN force. UN Command Korea was created to co-ordinate the efforts of this force. Canada contributed over 6,100 soldiers, sailors and airmen at any given time, most of whom returned to Canada after serving a year in Korea. At the end of three years of fighting, 26,791 Canadians had served in the conflict, and 516 had been killed.[7]	—		T
UNCMAC[8]	Korea	1953-	O	Fighting ended in Korea in 1953 when representatives established UNCMAC as its collective representative at the subsequent peace talks. So far, no agreement has been reached. UNCMAC consists of ten senior officers from a number of UN member countries, one of which is Canadian.	—		L
ICSC[9]	Vietnam, Cambodia, Laos	1954-1974	O	Observers	— (Innovation of civilian observers from DFAIT)[10]		E
UNEF I	Israel Egypt (Sinai)	Nov 56-Jun 67	F	UNEF was the result of the Suez Crisis. The mission was created to secure and supervise the cessation of hostilities and the withdrawal of French, British and Israeli forces. Canada participated in UNEF for the duration of its mandate. Up to 1,007 Canadian military personnel were deployed at any given time, including a reconnaissance squadron, an infantry platoon, signals unit, engineers, logistics, as well as naval and air units. A medical detachment was also deployed for the first three years of the mission.	LGen Burns, Nov 56-Dec 58		S, C, T
UNOGIL	Lebanon	Jun 58-Dec 58	O	up to 77 UNMOs at any given time	—		—

Type: O=Observers, F=Force, P=Police, C=Civil Administration, E=Elections, G=Good Offices.
Contribution: O=no Canadian participation, L=fewer than 40 deployed at any one time, T=formed bodies of troops, E=experts on mission, S=support or logistics contribution, C=Canadian commander at some point.

ONUC	Congo	Jul 60-Jun 64	F,O	Canada participated in ONUC throughout the duration of this mission, with a maximum contribution of 421 personnel at any given time. The contingent included air and ground crew, staff personnel and signals.	(BGen Dextrase, COS)		S, C
UNSF and UNTEA	West New Guinea (West Irian)	Oct 62-Apr 63	F,O, P,C	2 Otter aircraft and crews (13 RCAF personnel to the UNSF's air unit for the duration of the mission).	—		S
UNYOM	Yemen	Jul 63-Sep 64	O	Canada provided up to 36 Canadian Forces (CF) personnel at any given time, including an air unit (fixed wing and helicopters) and UNMOs for the duration of this mission.	—		S, L
UNFICYP	Cyprus	Mar 64-	F,P	Canada contributed a battalion from 1964 to 1993. There are now three CF personnel with UNFICYP.	MGen Milner Apr 89-Jun 91		C, T
DOMREP	Dominican Republic	May 65-Oct 66	O	One observer, one year.	LCol Mayer, Jan- Oct 1966		C, L
UNIPOM	India-Pakistan	Sep 65-Mar 66	O	Canada provided UNMOs and an air unit for the duration of UNIPOM, with a maximum contribution of 112 personnel at any given time.	MGen Macdonald, 65-66		S, C
OTN[11]	Nigeria	Sep 68-Dec 69	O	2 observers, BGen Drewry and Maj Bristowe involved in drawing up peace negotiation.[12]	—		E
ICCS[13]	Vietnam	1973	O	Observers, Administration.[14]	—		S, C, E
UNEF II	Egypt-Israel (Sinai)	Oct 73-Jul 79	F	Canada participated in UNEF II between Nov 1973 and Oct 1979, contributing up to 1,145 personnel at any given time. The contingent included signals and logistics personnel, military police, headquarters staff and an air unit.	—		S, T
UNDOF	Syria-Israel (Golan)	Jun 74-	O	Canada has participated in UNDOF since 1974. There are approximately 185 CF personnel currently serving on the Golan Heights between Israel and Syria who provide second-line logistic support to the force, primarily supply and maintenance, and communications detachments to all UNDOF units.	BGen Yuill Jun 86-Jun 86		—
UNIFIL	Lebanon	Mar 78-	O	Canada provided up to 117 CF personnel between Mar and Oct 1978. The contingent included signals and movement control units.	—		—
MFO[15]	Egypt-Israel	Oct 81-	F,O	helicopters 86-90, staff	—		—
UNGOMAP	Afghanistan-Pakistan	May 88-Mar 90	G	5 UNMOs for the duration of this mission.	—		—
OSGAP[16]	Afghanistan-Pakistan	Mar 90-Jan 95	—	One military advisor to OSGAP from 1990 to 1992	—		—
UNIIMOG	Iran-Iraq	Aug 88-Feb 91	O	In addition to UNMOs, Canada provided a signals unit; up to 525 CF personnel were deployed at any given time.	—		—
UNAVEM I	Angola	Jan 89-May 91	O	None	—		—
UNTAG	Namibia	Apr 89-Mar 90	F,PC,E	Canada contributed logistics support, civilian police monitors and electoral supervisors throughout the duration of UNTAG. Up to 301 CF personnel were deployed at any given time, plus RCMP.	—	First use of RCMP in peacekeeping.	
ONUCA	Central America	Nov 89-Jan 92	O	Canada provided UNMOs and a helicopter detachment from Dec 1989 to Jan 1992. Up to 174 CF personnel were deployed to UNUCA at any given time.	BGen MacKenzie Dec 90-May 91		—
ONUVEH	Haiti	Oct 90-Feb 91	O,E	Canada provided 11 UNMOs to this mission, as well as Elections monitors.[17]	BGen Zuliani		—

UNIKOM	Kuwait	Apr 91-	O	Canada has participated in UNIKOM since its inception. Initial commitment was field engineer unit for demining. There are 4 CF members currently serving as United Nations Military Observers (UNMOs) in this observer mission.	—	—
UNSCOM[18]	Iraq/New York	Apr 91-	O	Up to 12 CF specialists are authorized to participate in UNSCOM. There are currently three CF members assigned to UNSCOM; two are posted to the UN Headquarters in New York and one is in Iraq as part of an UNSCOM weapons inspection team.	—	—
MIF	Gulf/Kuwait	Apr 91-	F	One ship on station as part of the Multinational Interception Force established following the liberation of Kuwait.	—	—
MINURSO[19]	Western Sahara	Apr 91-	O	A maximum of 35 CF personnel served at any given time as UNMOs, movement-control and staff personnel in the Western Sahara from May 1991 to Jun 1994.	MGen Roy, Jun 91	—
UNAVEM II	Angola	May 91-Feb 95	O	Canada participated in this mission from Jul 1991 to May 1993 and contributed up to 15 UNMOs during that period.	—	—
ONUSAL	El Salvador	Jul 91-Feb 95	O	Canada contributed up to 55 CF personnel at any given time, beginning in Jul 1991. Canada's last 5 UNMOs were withdrawn in Aug 1994.	—	—
UNAMIC	Cambodia	Oct 91-Mar 92	O,G	Canada provided up to 7 UNMOs between Nov 1991 and Feb 1992.	—	—
UNPROFOR	Former Yugoslavia	Mar 92-Dec 95	F,O	Over 2000 CF personnel served in the Balkans with UNPROFOR and UNPF, a logistics battalion, and as UNMOs and personnel within various headquarters positions. Canada also provided a Major-General who served as the Deputy Theatre Commander, UNPROFOR until 31 Mar 1995 and then as the Deputy Theatre Commander, UNPF until Jan 1996.	—	—
UNCOE[20]	Former Yugoslavia	1992-1994	O,P	Canada provided up to 7 Legal Officers and military police officers to UNCOE at any given time.	—	—
UNTAC	Cambodia	Mar 92-Sep 93	F,O,P, C,E	Approximately 240 CF personnel served at any given time for the duration of this mission. The Canadian Contingent included a 30-person naval observer element but the majority of the CF personnel provided transport services. In addition, there were approximately 121 Canadian civilians in Cambodia, including 67 assigned in various capacities to UNTAC and approximately 50 electoral observers.	—	—
UNOSOM I	Somalia	Apr 92-Mar 93	F	Canada contributed an advance party and headquarters staff between Oct 1992 and Mar 1993.	—	—
ONUMOZ	Mozambique	Dec 92-Dec 94	F,O	Canada provided up to 4 UNMOs from Feb 1993 to Dec 1994.	—	—
UNOSOM II	Somalia	Mar 93-Mar 95	F	Over the duration of the mission, Canada contributed up to 9 CF members at any given time, including headquarters staff and officers.	—	—
UNOMUR	Uganda-Rwanda	Jun 93-Sep 94	O	Canada provided 3 UNMOs between Jun and Oct 1993.	—	—
UNOMIG	Georgia	Aug 93-	O	—	—	—

ECMM	Balkan region[21]	Sep 93-	O	—	—	—
UNOMIL	Liberia	Sep 93-Sep 97	O	Brigadier General (Ret'd) Douglas participated in the UN Technical Reconnaissance of Liberia in1993. Canada did not, however, participate further in UNOMIL.	—	—
UNMIH	Haiti	Sep 93-Jun 96	F, O	Canada provided up to 750 military personnel and approximately 100 civilian police at any given time to UNMIH between Oct 1994 and Jun 1996.	—	—
UNAMIR	Rwanda	Oct 93-Mar 96	F	Canada participated in UNAMIR from Dec 1993 to Feb 1996, providing a logistics support unit of up to 112 Canadian Forces personnel at any given time.	MGen Dallaire, MGen Tousignant	—
UNASOG	Aouzou (Sudan/Libya)	May- Jun 94	O	None	—	—
UNMOT	Tajikistan	Dec 94-	O	None	—	—
UNAVEM III	Angola	Feb 95-Jun 97	F,O	None	—	—
UNCRO	Croatia	Mar 95-Jan 96	F,O, H[22]	Battalion plus support elements and staff (see UNPROFOR).	—	—
UNPREDEP	Macedonia	Mar 95-	F,O	Canada continues to participate in UNPREDEP with one CF officer serving as an UNMO to the mission.	—	—
UNMIBH	Bosnia-Herzegovina	Dec 95-	P,C,H,E[23]	Canada contributes a lieutenant-colonel to the position of military staff and liaison officer in the office of the UN Co-ordinator for Bosnia-Hercegovina and provides six CF personnel to the Mine Action Centre (UNMAC).	—	—
UNTAES	E. Slavonia, Croatia	Jan 96	F,O,C,E	None	—	—
UNMOP[24]	Prevlaka, Croatia	Jan 96-	O	One CF officer is currently serving as an UNMO.	—	—
MINUGUA[25]		Guatemala	Jan-May 97 —	Canada provided 15 Spanish speaking UNMOs to this mission between Feb and May 1997.	—	—
MONUA	Angola	Jul 97-Feb 99	O	None	—	—
UNSMIH[26]	Haiti	Jul 96-Jul 97	F,O,P	Canada provided civilian police and up to 750 military personnel at any given time for the duration of its mandate (see also UNMIH).	—	—
UNTMIH	Haiti	Aug-Nov 97	F,O,P	Canada contributed up to 750 personnel at any given time for the duration of the mission (see also UNSMIH).	BGen Gagnon Aug-Nov 97	—
MINURCA	Central African Republic	Apr 98-	F,E	Canada's contribution consists of a Signals Troop of 25 personnel and 4 staff officers in the Mission Headquarters. Twenty-two other CF personnel provide logistics and command support. Additionally, Canada contributed 32 signallers to support remote electoral sites for the period of the presidential elections.	—	—
MONUC	Congo	Nov 99-	O	Canada was prepared to provide a superior officer. Colonel Gaston Coté was designated as the COS Plans and Operations and was to assist in the establishment of the advanced headquarters. Canada also considered providing a small number of UNMOs to this new UN mission.[27] Among the recent observers was Major J. Howard, Detachment Commander from the 41st Canadian Brigade Group, Calgary. Nine other Canadian observers were on standby for deployment.[28]		
UNOMSIL	Sierra Leone	Jul 98-Oct 99	O	—	—	—
UNAMSIL	Sierra Leone	Oct 99-	F,O,P	—	—	—

MIPONUH	Haiti	Dec 97-	P	The Department of National Defence is providing six wheeled armoured personnel carriers to this mission as well as Canadian Forces driving instructors and Canadian Forces vehicle technicians.	—	—
INTERFET	East Timor	Sep 99-Mar 00	F,P	Canada will send about 250 ground troops to East Timor, September 30. The Royal 22e Régiment 3rd Battalion personnel, based in Valcartier, Que., will join the International Force for East Timor (INTERFET) for up to six months.[29]	—	—
UNTAET	East Timor	Oct 99-	C,O,E	The last of the three will leave in Mid-May 01, ending nearly two years of Canadian Forces presence in East Timor.[30]	—	—
UNMIK	Kosovo	Jun 99-Jan 01	C,P,E[4]	Battle group, helicopter sqn, recce sqn, and support assets, totalling about 1300, from Jun 99-Jan 00.[31]	—	—
UNMEE	Eritrea-Ethiopia	Dec 00-June 01	F,O	The 450-strong Canadian Task Force East Africa (TFEA) included a Company Group comprising the following elements: H Company of The Royal Canadian Regiment (three infantry platoons mounted in new LAV III armoured fighting vehicles); an engineer troop; a combat service-support platoon; and a company headquarters. The Company Group was complemented by a Canadian reconnaissance platoon, equipped with the Coyote armoured vehicle.[32]	—	—

Notes:

1. Sources: *Blue Helmets*, 3rd ed.; UN Web sites; and John Gardam, *The Canadian Peacekeeper* (Burnstown, Ont.: General Store Publishing, 1992). All UN missions from 1947 to the end of 2000 are listed, whether they had a Canadian contribution or not.
2. Type: O=Observers, F=Force, P=Police, C=Civil Administration, E=Elections, G=Good Offices.
3. Canadian Contributions to United Nations Peacekeeping Operations, http://www.dnd.ca/eng/archive/1998/apr98/contrib_a_e.htm and John Gardam, *The Canadian Peacekeeper*.
4. The list of commanders is incomplete after 1991.
5. Contribution: 0=no Canadian participation, L=fewer than 40 deployed at any one time, T=formed bodies of troops, E=experts on mission, S=support or logistics contribution, C=Canadian commander at some point.
6. Consular Commission for Indonesia and UN Commission for Indonesia.
7. "Canada's Military Legacy," available at http://www.dnd.ca/menu/legacy/global_90_e.htm#1991/94mission accessed August 2001.
8. United Nations Military Armistice Commission.
9. International Mission for Supervision and Control.
10. Gardam, 1992, 19. 25 percent civilians and 75 percent military.
11. Observer Team to Nigeria.
12. Gardam, 1992, 40.
13. International Commission for Supervision and Control.
14. Gardam, 1992, 44.
15. Multinational Force and Observers.
16. Office of the Secretary-General in Afghanistan and Pakistan.
17. OAS involvement in human rights and elections.
18. United Nations Special Commission is charged with the inspection and destruction of Iraq's ballistic missiles, chemical, nuclear and biological facilities.
19. Most recent entry in Gardam.
20. United Nations Committee of Experts.
21. Croatia, Bosnia, Yugoslavia, Macedonia, Romania, Bulgaria, Albania.
22. The Office of the N High Commissioner for Human Rights (UNHCHR) was established in 1994 and by 1995 routinely sent observers to field missions.
23. Elections Observers under OSCE auspices.
24. Most recent entry in *Blue Helmets*, 3rd ed.
25. United Nations Mission in Guatemala.
26. United Nations Support Mission in Haiti.
27. DND update, 7 Oct. 99.
28. Aline Dubois, "Operation Crocodile: Phase Two of UN mission in Congo imminent," http://www.dnd.ca/menu/Operations/Crocodile/html/ml3_27_05_e.htm .
29. "CF troops deployed on East Timor mission," http://www.dnd.ca/menu/maple/vol_2/Vol2_18/headline_e.htm .
30. "Termination of Canadian Forces contribution to East Timor," http://www.dnd.ca/eng/archive/2001/apr01/24timor_n_e.htm.
31. "Canada increases Contribution to Kosovo International Peace Implementation Force," http://www.dnd.ca/eng/archive/1999/jun99/11ContribKIPIF_n_e.htm .
32. DND Backgrounder, "Canadian soldiers helped pave the way to peace in Ethiopia and Eritrea," 6 June 2001.

APPENDIX 2
Canada and the Convergence of Conflict Research and Security Studies

Year	Key publications *denotes Canadian contributions	International Developments	Canada **denotes training initiatives
1920s			
1930s	Sorokin, P. 1937: *Social and Cultural Dynamics*	**1931**: Chair for the Study of International Institutions for the Organisation of Peace, University of Lyon, France	
1940s	Wright, Q. 1942: *A Study of War*	**1945**: Peace Research Laboratory, Missouri, USA	**No peacekeeping training or preparation
1950s		**1957**: Journal of Conflict Resolution, University of Michigan, USA **1959**: Center for Research on Conflict Resolution, University of Michigan; International Peace Research Institute (PRIO), Oslo, Norway	**1957**: **peacekeeping viewed as extension of routine military operations[1]
1960s	Richardson, L. 1960: *Statistics of Deadly Quarrels*. Sharp, G. 1973: *The Politics of Non-violent Action* Wehr, P. 1979: *Conflict Regulation* James, Alan. 1969. *The Politics of Peacekeeping* CIIA, 1968. *Peacekeeping: International Challenge and Canadian Response.* *Hill, R.J. 1968 *Command and control problems of UN and similar peacekeeping forces*	**1962**: Polemological Institute, Groningen, Holland[2]; Conflict Research Society, London, UK **1965**: International Peace Research Association **1966**: Centre for the Analysis of Conflict (University of London/University of Kent); Stockholm International Peace Research Institute **1969**: Richardson Institute for Peace and Conflict Research (London, then University of Lancaster); Tampere Peace Research Institute, Finland	**1964**: Ottawa International Peacekeeping Conference. Formalisation of the GPCT bias[3] **1965**: **standby battalion practised with RCAF for UN deployments; **1966**: **four day course for observers plus recommended self-study; training in paramilitary and internal security roles[4] (Was is IS training for Quebec?)[5] **1967**: Queen's CIIA Conference on Peacekeeping
1970s	International Peace Academy. 1978. *Peacekeeper's Handbook*	**1970**: International Peace Academy **1973**: Department of Peace Studies, University of Bradford **1979**: University of Ulster, Centre for the Study of Conflict (Northern Ireland)	**1979**: joint Canada/Norway Workshop on United Nations Peacekeeping at RMC
1980s	C.R. Mitchell. 1981. *The Structure of International Conflict*	**1982**: Carter Center: International Negotiation Network **1983**: National Conference on Peacemaking and Conflict Resolution, first conference in USA **1984**: Nairobi Peace Group (from1990, Nairobi Peace Initiative); United States Institute of Peace, Washington **1985**: International Alert, United Kingdom **1986**: Conflict Resolution Network, Australia; Harvard Law School, Program on Negotiation; Jean B. Kroc Institute for International Peace Studies, University of Notre Dame, USA **1988**: Institute for Conflict Resolution and Analysis, George Mason University, USA; Austrian Study Centre for Peace and Conflict Resolution/European Peace University	**1987**(-1990): Canadian International Institute for Peace and Security (CIIPS) **1988** International Centre for Human Rights and Democratic Development **1989** CDQ special peacekeeping issue (and ARMX supplement)

Year	Key publications *denotes Canadian contributions	International Developments	Canada **denotes training initiatives
1990s	Rikhye, Indar Jit and Kjell Skjelsbaek (eds).1990. *The United Nations and Peacekeeping: Results, Limitations and Prospects: The Lessons of 40 years of Experience* Dennis J.D. Sandole and Hugo van der Merwe, eds. 1993. *Conflict Resolution Theory and Practice: Integration and Application* Fetherston, A.B. 1994. *Towards a Theory of United Nations Peacekeeping* *Morrison, Alex with James Kiras and Stephanie Blair (eds). 1994. *The New Peacekeeping Partnership* Lederach, John Paul. 1997. *Building Peace: Sustainable Reconciliation in Divided Societies* Mackinlay, John (Contributing Editor). 1996. *A guide to Peace Support Operations* Oakley, Robert, Michael J. Dziedzic, and Eliot M. Goldberg (eds). 1998. *Policing the New World Disorder: Peace Operations and Public Security*	**1990**: Centre for Conflict Resolution,University of Bradford **1991**: First European Conference on Peacemaking and Conflict Resolution, Istanbul **1992**: *Agenda for Peace; Institute for Multi-Track Diplomacy, Washington ; Instituto Peruano de Resolucion de Conflictos, Negociacion, y Mediacion, Peru **1993**: *US Army War College Peacekeeping Institute; *UN planning team on SHIRBRIG; Berghof Research Centre for Constructive Conflict Management, Berlin ; Organisation of African Unity, Mechanism for Conflict Prevention, Management and Resolution ; University of Ulster/United Nations University: Initiative on Conflict Resolution and Ethnicity (INCORE) **1994**: The Conference for Security and Cooperation in Europe becomes the Organisation for Security and Cooperation in Europe, (OSCE), containing High Commissioner on National Minorities and Vienna Centre for Conflict Prevention; Carnegie Commission on Preventing Deadly Conflict, New York; Institute for the Prevention of International Conflict, Japan; UNESCO's Culture of Peace Programme **1995**: Supplement to Agenda for Peace; Kazakhstan Centre for Conflict Management **1996**: Dutch Centre for Conflict Prevention	**1992:** CDQ special peacekeeping issue **1993**: CDQ special peacekeeping issue **1994**: Pearson Peacekeeping Centre; ARMX replaced by "Peacekeeping 1994" **1996**: Canadian Peacebuilding Co-ordinating Committee; Ottawa Conference on Rapid Response (SHIRBRIG) **1997**: Ottawa process to ban landmines and Human Security Agenda[6]
2000s			

Notes:

1   External Affairs, *Military Commitments Abroad* (Ottawa: Government of Canada, 1957) cited by David Lenarcic, *A Case of Double Vision: Canadian Peacekeeping Policies in the 1960s*, (cited by Gary Kett).

2   What about French institute of polemology, which was more strategically oriented?

3   Department of National Defence, *Canadian Operations in Support of the United Nations: Organization and Training of Canadian Military Forces Earmarked for Service with the United Nations* (Ottawa: Canadian Forces Headquarters, April-May 1966), cited by Kett (2001) 5.

4   David Cox, "Canada's Interest in Peacekeeping: Some Political and Military Considerations," in *Peacekeeping: International Challenge and Canadian Response* (Ottawa: CIIA, 1968), 53 cited by Kett, 11.

5   Kett, 12, citing Loomis.

6   Robert J. Lawson, Mark Gwozdecky, Jill Sinclair and Ralph Lysyshyn, "The Ottawa Process and the International Movement to Ban Anti-Personnel Landmines," *To Walk Without Fear: The Global Movement to Ban Landmines* (Toronto: Oxford University Press, 1998), 160-184.

CHAPTER 19

GLUED TO ITS SEAT

Canada and its Alliances in the Post Cold War Era[1]

Joel J. Sokolsky

Introduction

IN 1989, just before the end of the Cold War, in an article entitled "Seat at the Table, Canada and Its Alliances," I wrote

> Canada's alliance relationships, the North Atlantic Treaty Organization (NATO) and the North American Aerospace Defence Command (NORAD) constitute nearly the sum total of Canadian defence policy. From the weapons acquired and the forces deployed to the very strategic and tactical assumptions under which the Canadian Armed Forces (CF) operate, the needs and perceptions of the Allies are dominant. Since both NATO and NORAD are American-led pacts, Canadian defence policy complements and is closely coordinated with U.S. global strategic interests and postures.[2]

Today, more than a decade into the post Cold War era, despite the disappearance of the Soviet threat, Canadian defence policy is more closely linked to that of the United States than at any other time in our history. Ottawa seems to be glued to its seat at the allied table. There are three related reasons for this: the Americanization of peacekeeping in the 1990s; trends within NATO; and the recent emphasis of the United States upon "homeland security," an emphasis that preceded but has been given the highest priority with the events of 11 September 2001. President Bush created a Cabinet level position to co-ordinate action in this new theatre of war. And, in its *Quadrennial Defence Review Report* issued on 30 September 2001, which makes direct reference to the attacks, the U.S. Department of Defense (DoD) declares that "homeland security" will now be the "highest priority of the U.S. military."[3] This emphasis will provide additional impetus to the deployment of a National Missile Defense system.

All three trends are related to the policy of the government of the United States to preserve and enhance its dominant position. As Michael Mastunduno has argued, since the end of the Cold War, "U.S. officials have in fact followed a consistent strategy in pursuit of a clear objective—the preservation of the United States' pre-eminent global position."[4]

The response of the Canadian military has been to stress the importance of interoperability with the United States, or the *1994 Defence White Paper* put it, Canada must be prepared "to fight with the best against the best."[5] On the land, at sea, in the air and in space, the CF has been scrambling to find the funds for the equipment and training to meet this objective. In *Shaping the Future of Canadian Defence: A Strategy for 2020*, this is made explicit. The CF must strengthen its "military to military relationships with our principal allies ensuring interoperable forces, doctrine and C4I (command, control, communications, computers and intelligence)." In particular it calls for expansion of "the joint and combined exercise program to include all environments and exchanges with U.S."[6] Given the history of the post Cold War decade which saw the CF deploy abroad along with the U.S. and its principal allies, in a host of UN and especially NATO operations, this approach is the only one that makes sense for the Canadian Forces. Interoperability is the direct military consequence of accepting unipolarity or at least American dominance.

From UN Blue to NATO Green:
Canada and the Americanization of Peacekeeping in the 1990s

In December 1997, the *Globe and Mail* had an article on Canada's "shrinking peacekeeping role." It noted that the 250 Canadian soldiers on various United Nations operations was the lowest number since Lester Pearson won the Noble Peace Prize forty years earlier. It also mentioned, parenthetically, that there were 1,300 Canadian troops in Bosnia. According to the article, these forces did not count because they were "part of a NATO... rather than UN force."[7]

In the following few years, the imbalance between Canada's UN and NATO peacekeeping commitments has become even more pronounced. As of 1 June 2000, there were some 2,756 CF personnel on overseas operations. Of these, 1596 were with the NATO Stabilization Force in Bosnia-Herzegovina and another 522 with the alliance's Kosovo Force (KFOR). In support of NATO operations in the Balkans, Canada had 118 personnel with the allied air forces at Aviano, Italy. If the ship's company of HMCS *Fredericton* (225) sailing with NATO's Standing Naval Force Atlantic is added, it means that ninety-three percent of all CF personnel overseas were deployed in support of NATO and its new peacekeeping operations.[8] In addition, Canada has continued to maintain a naval presence in the Persian Gulf, with HMCS *Calgary* deployed there. Only about 220 personnel, 190 of these on the Golan Heights and the remainder in small contingents of fewer than ten, were assigned to various UN activities.[9] Canada did send troops on a limited UN mission to Eritria, but they only served for six months. Forces were also dispatched to serve with NATO in Macedonia in August 2001.

The imbalance between blue and green operations is even more telling when it is considered that the CF has deployed its most advanced equipment to the NATO operations: CF-18 aircraft, Coyote reconnaissance vehicles, Leopard main battle tanks and the Halifax class patrol frigates.

In comparison to NATO's other middle powers, such as Belgium and Spain, Canada has a higher percentage of its available forces outside its borders, six percent as opposed to an average of two percent.[10] While the Prime Minister might declare that, generally speaking, we are "very reluctant to join an intervention that is not under the umbrella of the UN," the reality is otherwise.[11]

The discrepancy between the UN blue helmet commitments and the NATO green helmet commitments, organized and led by the United States, tells the whole story of international peacekeeping in the 1990s and what had happened to this quintessentially Canadian (and supposedly un-American) role for the CF. It also tells the story of what has happened to Canada's relationship to NATO and the American role in the alliance. In the 1990s, Canada has been over there, the classic "over there" Europe with Uncle Sam.

This is not how the future looked at the end of the Cold War. At the beginning of the 1990s, the Canadianization of U.S. defence policy seemed to be at hand as the UN, with considerable American support, launched a series of peacekeeping operations which in a few years saw nearly 80,000 blue helmets deployed to places ranging from Cambodia to the former Yugoslavia.[12] With American global security interests contracting and with the Security Council now able to reach a consensus more easily, peacekeeping offered Washington the prospect of the UN responding to regional crises and civil strife without a need for U.S. forces. The UN also undertook to intervene in countries on humanitarian grounds in response to starvation or atrocities brought on by these internal struggles. Despite some early successes, it soon became clear that UN peacekeeping forces were not able to deal with everything. In contrast to Cold War peacekeeping operations, the blue helmets were now being sent to areas where the fighting had not stopped, where in fact there was "no peace to keep."[13] Its forces soon became bogged down in Somalia and at serious risk in Yugoslavia.

This led to a new variation in UN peace efforts. Rather than sending in lightly armed multinational forces under UN command, the Security Council authorized a coalition of states, usually led by the United States, to intervene more forcefully into civil conflicts and impose a peace or at least a ceasefire. Such was the approach in Haiti and the NATO Implementation Force (IFOR) and the follow-on Stabilization Force (SFOR) sent into Bosnia after the U.S. brokered the Dayton accords. This new, more muscular peacekeeping very much reflected a shift in American policies. The earlier enthusiasm for peacekeeping evident in the senior Bush administration and initially under President Clinton was replaced by a growing opposition, especially in the Congress, to the UN and peacekeeping operations in general. Even though the American troops killed in Somalia had not been under UN command, many in Congress blamed the UN for the debacle and peacekeeping became a lightening rod for opposition to the Clinton administration's foreign policy, which seemed to place too much trust in the world body. In the spring of 1994, Presidential Decision Directive 25 (PDD-25) had set out strict conditions for American participation in UN operations and for U.S. support. More importantly, PDD-25 made it clear that if international action was required and American troops were to be involved, then Washington would lead the operation under a UN mandate but not under UN command and administration. It was not so much that the United States was not paying its peacekeeping assessments, although it was not; it was that Washington was taking steps to make sure that peacekeeping would be done the American way or not at all.

As the decade wore on, the number of peacekeeping missions declined. By mid-1996, there were just 26,000 troops in blue helmet UN operations.[14] At the same time, the U.S. was working through NATO and other "coalitions of the willing" to take the lead in implementing those UN mandates which it had helped sponsor and which were consistent with American policies and interests. It did appear that this approach was more effective in certain circumstances, for example in Bosnia and Haiti. For Canada, it was this Americanization of peacekeeping, not opposition to it by the U.S., which had the most profound impact.

Ottawa had supported Washington in the Gulf War, diplomatically and with forces. But it also eagerly embraced the renaissance of the UN and peacekeeping in the early 1990s. Within a few years, nearly 5,000 CF troops were abroad, most in the former Yugoslavia and with small numbers dispatched to Latin America and Cambodia. All of this reflected the long-standing Canadian desire to play an active role in international security affairs and a distinctively Canadian one. The *1994 Defence White Paper* stressed the importance of contributing to international security efforts and responding to humanitarian disasters. It stated that the CF would also maintain a global combat capability. With cuts to the defence budget and personnel, it became increasingly difficult to believe that Canada had anywhere near such a capability. Indeed, the heavy peacekeeping demands of the early 1990s had greatly strained the CF.

Even as Canada was increasing its contribution to UN efforts in the early 1990s, it was also taking part in NATO efforts in the former Yugoslavia. From the beginning, allied, including American, forces were supporting the efforts of the United Nations Protection Forces (UNPROFOR). Canada endorsed these allied efforts and the CF was involved in them. For example, the navy participated in NATO's maritime enforcement of the UN arms embargo in the Adriatic Sea. On the ground it was becoming evident that, despite helping to avoid even more widespread fighting and atrocities, UNPROFOR was not working. Indeed the force could not even protect itself. Canadian troops were threatened and in some cases taken hostage. While concerned about the deteriorating situation, Ottawa also worried about American calls for attacks on Serb forces lest they put UNPROFOR in greater danger. By the summer of 1995, the government was looking forward to withdrawing the CF. Then came the NATO air strikes and the Dayton Accords followed by the decision to deploy the Implementation Force. After some hesitation, Canada agreed to contribute forces to the NATO formation and these have remained for over three years. In a similar fashion, Ottawa—which had early on taken the diplomatic lead in pressing for UN action against the military government of Haiti—eventually endorsed and then participated in the American-sponsored intervention there.

Canada made a major commitment to IFOR and the follow-on Stabilization Force SFOR, supplying one of the largest national contingents. There were in excess of 1,200 troops as well as the continuing deployment of a ship to the NATO naval force in the Adriatic. In addition, to the extent that SFOR now focussed on post-conflict resolution and a wide variety of non-military activities to assist the population, the commitment was fully consistent with Foreign Minister Lloyd Axworthy's "Human Security Agenda."

Kosovo, however, represented the apogee of the Americanization of peacekeeping in the 1990s and thus a major departure for Canada. Although the operation could be justified on moral grounds and was consistent with the Human Security Agenda, the fact remained this was a war against a sovereign country without a UN mandate. Ottawa readily mounted up to join this latest American-led posse. Indeed, Canada mounted its largest overseas combat operation since the Korean War. In the Kosovo air campaign, "Canadian pilots flew 682 combat sorties, or nearly 10% of the missions against fixed targets" and they led half the strike packages they took part in, and were among only five countries delivering precision guided munitions."[15] The 1,400 personnel deployed to KFOR included an infantry battle group, a reconnaissance squadron, a tactical helicopter squadron and troops of engineers.

The Kosovo operations also showed that given sufficient warning, the army can move quickly overseas with vehicles and integrated helicopter units. The Edmonton-based Lord Strathcona's Horse was the second NATO force to enter Kosovo and the Pristina area, right behind the British:

> Less than 72 hours after rolling hundreds of military vehicles and containers off a freighter in Greece, the Strathconas were already spying on Russian peacekeepers and Serbian armoured units around Kosovo's only airport ... Some 24 hours after that, a U.S. Marine Corps Expeditionary Brigade that is supposed to specialize in quick deployments arrived in country.[16]

In the spring of 2000, Ottawa decided to consolidate its Balkan presence in Bosnia where a Canadian major-general would assume command of the Multinational Division Southwest. This region comprises forty-five percent of the total SFOR area.[17]

To be sure, neither Canada nor the United States have entirely abandoned UN peacekeeping. For example, in both Yugoslavia and Haiti, UN operations were mounted after or in conjunction with the American-led interventions. And some modest reforms have been made at UN headquarters to improve its capacity to deploy and sustain peacekeeping operations. Nevertheless, more sweeping changes, such as the Canadian suggestion for a greater multilateral standby capability, have received little U.S. support.

As a result of the Americanization of peacekeeping in the 1990s, the CF has been engaged in a number of near-war operations and foreign interventions alongside American forces. It would appear that with the defence of North America (mainly through NORAD) and that of Western Europe (through NATO) declining in relative importance, the focus of bilateral defence relations has shifted to what used to be called "out of area." From Washington's standpoint, Canada has been a welcomed contributor to NATO and other more vigorous peacekeeping operations which the U.S. has organized and led. To be sure, the Canadian contributions have been small in comparison to what the Americans can deploy. In a unipolar world the U.S. does not need the Canadian military contribution but politically it is important to involve other allies such as Canada. While the most the CF has often been able to send has been a ground unit of about one thousand, a squadron of six aircraft or a single ship, this level of support does compare favourably with that of other smaller allies. In addition, the CF brings to these operations an acknowledged professionalism and the ability to work closely with the Americans that is the result of years of allied co-operation.

This was not what the end of the Cold War was supposed to bring. Surprisingly, there has been little public comment. Whereas as recently as the 1980s, any hint of Canadian support for U.S. intervention abroad would bring protests from peace groups and compel the government to carefully word its response to the American action, Canadian deployments to IFOR, Haiti and especially KFOR occasioned no such domestic response. Indeed, there was widespread public support for the war against Yugoslavia.

The significant trends in peacekeeping in the 1990s have highlighted in the post Cold War era what has been a persistent duality in Canadian foreign and defence policy since the Second World War: the desire to play a more independent and distinct role through the UN *and* a strongly held instinct to join the U.S. and other traditional allies when unified western action was organized.[18] Both are the result of Ottawa's determination to remain active in international security affairs. During the Cold War, when it came to having to choose between collective security under the UN or some other multilateral umbrella and collective defence under NATO, Ottawa invariably sided with its traditional allies in NATO. And this has been the case again in the post Cold War era. In part, it is the result of the changing nature of peacekeeping. If Canada was to remain in the forefront of this activity, then it had no choice but to participate in the American-sponsored, NATO-based new peacekeeping. But it is also the result of the very fact that NATO has become what international political theorists say it cannot be, a collective defence organization *and* a collective security organization. And this is the direct result of a new international bargain which has come to characterize the alliance.

The United States and the Trans-European Bargain

Flexible Response was not simply the official name given to NATO's strategy adopted in 1967; it was, in a profound sense, the way the alliance approached all its seemingly intractable and inherently contradictory problems of a strategic and, above all, political nature. True to the messy nature of democratic government itself, this collection of democracies managed to surprise and confound its critics and achieve victory in the Cold War by adopting a series of initiatives that placed political compromise above military and strategic orthodoxy and intellectual rigour. The result was that the Allies stayed allied and in doing so achieved ultimate victory in the Cold War. The same approach has been followed in the post Cold War era, and this accounts for the continued centrality of the alliance in European and indeed global security.

The alliance was quick to respond to the breathtaking fall of the Warsaw Pact and then the Soviet Union itself. Beginning in the early 1990s, it revised its strategic concepts and then its very organization and structure. Most importantly, it immediately reached out eastward. A North Atlantic Cooperation Council was created to bring old adversaries (neutrals) into a consultative process. Special agreements were concluded with Ukraine and with Russia. As discussed below, the alliance became involved in the new peacekeeping and peace enforcement of the 1990s. Most importantly, the push was to expand, culminating in the admission of three new members, Poland, the Czech Republic and Hungary.

This is not to say all has gone smoothly, especially on the matter of an enlargement which extends the alliance's efforts to promote stability in the East while at the same time raising new concerns in Moscow. Then there is the question of whether in extending its membership eastward the alliance has truly guaranteed the security of the new allies. And whether the United States has in fact extended its deterrent over these countries or whether it has simply made more intractable its never resolved nuclear dilemma. True to its historic methodology of flexibility, the alliance has not paused to resolve these complications but rather has adopted a range of other initiatives to cope with them in the hope that in the post Cold War era as in the period that preceded it—stability will be its own reward and all will be well in the end.

The most important of these is the Partnership for Peace (PfP) program which has been viewed as a halfway measure between membership and exclusion. This may be the case. But given the difficulties of further expansion, PfP provides a mechanism for the involvement of more than thirty countries in European security through a web of military exchanges and exercises. It may be said that whereas NATO remains a collective defence organization, PfP's thrust is collective or co-operative security. In theory, it may not be possible for the alliance to be both. In practice, however, it *is* both, largely because of PfP.

The major reason for this is the fact that PfP has been championed by the U.S. In essence, this program has provided Washington with a multilateral institutional framework for the further extension of American influence into Europe in a way that diminishes the importance of the older, and especially smaller, Western European allies. It resembles in some ways the old transatlantic bargain whereby the U.S. guaranteed the security of Western Europe. In this new trans-European bargain, American links to the former Warsaw Pact members and Soviet republics extend directly across and over Western Europe. They now constitute the core of the new NATO, at least insofar as concerns the U.S.

The emphasis placed by Washington upon cultivating relations with the countries of Central and Eastern Europe, north and south, may be viewed as consistent with what Mastanduno has described as the American effort to "preserve the unipolar moment" in Europe through engagement.[19] But this begs the question of why the U.S. wishes to preserve and extend its influence in European security by fostering NATO expansion to the east. Two related rationales suggest themselves.

First, Washington shares with the countries closest to Russia uncertainty and the fear of the unknown. The Americans no doubt hope that Russia will evolve into a liberal democracy that eschews any revival of hegemonic aspirations along its western border. Much of American diplomacy and a good deal of money is directed at trying to promote this benign future. Yet, should the domestic situation in Russia deteriorate and bring to power an anti-American government, the firmer Washington's relations with the new democracies of Central and Eastern Europe are, the better the chances of deterring recklessness in Moscow. The U.S. is also interested in preventing miscalculation on the part of the countries in the region. In the meantime, Washington will—as critics in Russia surmise—be in a position to hold in check Russian influence in the region. America's close relations with Ukraine, for example, are meant "to counter any expansion of Russian power."[20]

The second reason for Washington's eastward thrust is that the Americans do not fully trust the Western European governments, either individually or collectively, to manage European security in the East, especially in a manner fully consistent with American interests. The record of the 1990s in the Balkans speaks for itself. Only by involving itself directly in the affairs of the East, using NATO as a justification both externally and domestically (for the purposes of public and congressional opinion), can the U.S. assure itself that further ethnic strife can be avoided. To this extent the new trans-European bargain can be seen as part of an American effort to sustain the relevance of the old transatlantic bargain. And the older NATO allies seem content to follow Washington's lead. At the same time, the shift of America's focus to the east is having an impact on the character of the alliance.

For the older members, NATO remains a collective defence organization. But given the absence of any kind of threat to Western Europe and the inability of the Western Europeans to develop any common policy toward the east, it is not surprising that the links now binding America to Europe run over and around these countries. Even the admission to the alliance of Hungary, Poland and the Czech Republic may be viewed as less the accession of these states to NATO and more the formalization of their security ties to the U.S. To be sure, the Western European allies and Canada are deeply engaged in the PfP process. Moreover, they are also concerned about the relationship between the countries of the east and the European Security and Defence Identity and the European Union. But their governments have been more or less compelled to go along with Washington's eastward push, or else risk undoing what remains of the transatlantic bargain.

All of this points to what Coral Bell has called the "pretense of concert in American national security policy in the post Cold War era." In the current international environment, America need only conform to the "pretense of concert." The Clinton administration has adopted the view that "the unipolar world should be run as if it were a concert of powers."

In a sense, the post-World War II "institutionalization" of diplomacy through the UN, NATO, the G-7, the WTO, the World Bank, the IMF, the OSCE and so on a has more or less imposed that strategy on policymakers. Resolutions must get through the Security Council and consensus must be sought in other organizations to "legitimate" the policies that are deemed to be in the U.S. national interest. Of course, the policies could be followed without seeking their legitimation by the "international community," but the advantage of securing it are worth the diplomatic labor it takes. A resolution or consensus eases consciences both in America and abroad, and helps protect U.S. allies from their respective critics at home (though not in Washington, of course).[21]

With regard to this new trans-European alliance, Canada, as always, is in a somewhat different situation, one that has nevertheless been affected by the new character of NATO. For Ottawa, the old transatlantic bargain provided the security in Europe it sought and did so without compelling Canadians to choose between their American and European allies. Although extended deterrence put Canada at risk, by bolstering the transatlantic ties it nonetheless fostered a stable strategic environment where war seemed less likely and thus Canada more secure. And it did so without placing high demands for conventional forces. Moreover, the politics of the alliance, with its formal equality of participation, offered Ottawa a seat at the most important international table consistent with its aspirations toward middle power status. Finally, there was always the hoped for, though not always achieved, counterweight objective: the Western European allies, especially the middle and small states, serve to balance the influence of the U.S. on Canadian defence policy.

The trans-European bargain also offers advantages to Canada. Its overwhelming political character accords with Ottawa's long-standing desire to obtain maximum participation at minimum commitment in defence expenditure. Thus while Canadian forces came out of Germany in 1993, Canadians have been active participants in the new NATO's eastward thrust and entire range of political activities. As with the U.S., there is a sense now that Canada's ties to European security extend through Western Europe to the emerging democracies of the East. Ottawa, for example has cultivated a special relationship with Ukraine and is educating officers and defence officials from many countries in the proper civil-military relations of a democracy.

At the same time, the new trans-European bargain, to the extent that it has generally diminished the role of the older Western European allies and enhanced the already dominant role of the United States, has certainly raised new questions about NATO serving as a counterweight to American influence on Canadian defence policy. This has been exacerbated by the apparent inability of the Western Europeans to deal with the problems of Eastern Europe on their own. Thus Canada finds itself caught between the European Union, to which it does not belong and which has proven ineffective in promoting stability in Europe on its own, and the unipolar superpower which believes it must step in to sort out the mess. Along with the older West European allies, Canada found itself pulled by the American emphasis on Eastern Europe and how Washington wishes to deal with the problems there.

Indeed, because of Washington's efforts to promote NATO's eastern emphasis, the Canadian Forces have been on active duty in Europe almost continually since the end of the Cold War. At the end of the 1990s, the CF had almost as many personnel in Europe as it had when the Cold War ended. More importantly, unlike the previous forty years, the CF has been involved in actual military operations, increasingly as the decade wore on, under NATO leadership. Not surprisingly, being able to operate with NATO allies, especially the U.S., has again become the focal point of military planning.

With NATO invoking Article 5 of the North Atlantic Treaty in the aftermath of 11 September, with the allies offering assistance to the campaign on terrorism out of area, and with dispatch of NATO Airborne Warning and Control System (AWACS) planes to patrol American skies over here, the alliance has become even more central to Western collective defence. The dispatch by Canada of a relatively substantial contribution of six warships, a battalion of troops and assorted aircraft suggests that NATO will continue to be an important part of Canadian security policy in the post Cold War era.

"A Very Important Piece of Real Estate": The Return of Homeland Defence

In one very important respect, however, Canada is unlike other allies and friends, new and old, who are enlisting in the war against terrorism. It is directly involved in the defence of the American homeland. This is nothing new, for strategic defence has long been the essence of the bilateral Canada-U.S. defence relationship.

In 1938 in Kingston, Ontario, President Franklin Roosevelt declared: "The Dominion of Canada is a part of the sisterhood of the British Empire. I give to you assurance that the people of the United States will not stand idly by if domination of Canadian soil is threatened by any other Empire." A few days later in response, Prime Minister Mackenzie King stated that Canada too had its obligations as a "good and friendly neighbour, and one of these is to make sure that our country is made as immune from attack or possible invasion as we can reasonably be expected to make it, and that, should the occasion ever arrive, enemy forces should not be able to pursue their way either by land, sea or air to the United States across Canada."[22]

The two declarations reflected the growing apprehension of Ottawa and Washington about the deteriorating international situation and the potential threat to both countries. They also bespoke the friendly feeling between the two countries and indeed between the two leaders. But they also reflected differing strategic perspectives based upon complementary but not identical national interests. For the United States, the problem was that Canadian weakness might endanger American security. Canada could not become a strategic liability in the defence of the U.S. homeland. For Canada, the problem was satisfying this legitimate concern without compromising, however benignly, its own national sovereignty. This could be accomplished by taking measures on its own to secure its territory, airspace and maritime approaches.

Although the focus was overseas, North America itself had lost the protection afforded by its ocean boundaries with the advent of nuclear weapons and long-range bombers. The United States could not hope to credibly extend its deterrent if the U.S. itself, and especially the deterrent, were vulnerable at home. Thus strategic air defence, shared between the Royal Canadian Air Force and the United States Air Force came to be the most important dimension of the bilateral defence relationship, although at sea (especially in the Atlantic) the Royal Canadian Navy and the United States Navy (USN) maintained and developed close collaboration in monitoring the maritime approaches to the continent. The Cold War brought about a situation wherein the North American continent came to be regarded as a strategic unity for purposes of defence. This made Canada, as John Foster Dulles once put it, "a very important piece of real estate."[23]

The end of the Cold War brought about a decline in the importance of traditional continental defence. But new concerns were even then arising. While the events of September 2001 raised this concept to the top of the American national security agenda, the trend in this direction has been evident since the collapse of the Berlin Wall.

In the early 1990s, the end of the Cold War brought about a marked scaling back of NORAD activities. To be sure, neither Washington nor Ottawa was prepared to dismantle the radar lines and disband the interceptor squadrons. Moreover, to the extent that NORAD's prime missions had become space surveillance and warning and assessment of missile attack, there was a continuing role for the combined command. Thus the agreement was renewed in 1991 and 1996. But the strategic value to the U.S. of Canadian airspace, which value had steadily declined throughout the Cold War in any case, was greatly diminished. Indeed, by the early 1990s, despite the NORAD renewals, there were suggestions in the United States that NORAD be dismantled. Some thought that its missile warning and attack assessment missions could be handed over to the United States Space Command or the United States Strategic Command, while the residual air defence role could be given to the USAF Air Combat Command, a component of the newly created United States Atlantic Command. The latter had responsibility for most of the defence of the continental United States.

Although the defence of North America was on the decline in the early 1990s, another paradox of the present era is that American overseas operations contributed to a revival of interest in missile defence as part of a revived concern with the defence of the American homeland—an interest that had not been seen since the early days of the Cold War. The revival in missile defence was initially the result of the Gulf War, when attention was focussed on Theatre Missile Defence or Ballistic Missile Defence (BMD), the need to provide protection for deployed forces and regional allies. In its 1994 white paper on defence, the Canadian government seemed to alter its position to accommodate a possible BMD role for NORAD:

> The Government will examine closely those areas which may require updating in
> accordance with evolving challenges to continental security. Canada will work
> towards an agreement that furthers our national interests and meets our defence
> needs, now and into the 21st century.[24]

Canada's potential role in ballistic defence will not be determined in isolation but in conjunction with the evolution of North American and possibly NATO-wide aerospace defence arrangements.[25]

The impetus for the new concern with BMD came from continued American activities abroad. Richard Betts observed that U.S. policies abroad may actually increase the danger to the American homeland. "Today, as the only nation acting to police areas outside its own region, the United States makes itself a target for states and groups whose aspirations are frustrated by U.S. power." It is "U.S. military and cultural hegemony, the basic threats to radicals seeking to challenge the status quo, that are directly linked to the imputation of American responsibility for maintaining world order. Playing Globocop feeds the urge to strike back."[26] This especially includes ballistic missile threats from so-called "rogue states." These states were developing or already had chemical, biological, radiological, nuclear and enhanced high explosive (CBRNE) weapons.

A new concern with homeland defence was emerging in the United States, one not seen since the 1950s. Paradoxically, again, these fears arose at a time when America's relative military power had never been greater. While fears about homeland defence were being pushed most forcefully by Republicans in the Congress, polls in the late 1990s conducted by the Chicago Council of Foreign Relations found that while "Americans feel secure, prosperous and confident," with "fear of armed threats from a rival superpower diminished, they are, nevertheless ... alarmed by violence at home and abroad. Moreover, they would "support measures to thwart terrorists, prevent the spread of weapons of mass destruction, and keep defense strong." While the vast majority of Americans did not see vital threats to U.S. interests abroad, fully eighty-four percent regarded "international terrorism" as the number one "critical threat" to American interests.[27] Here at least, the supposedly uninformed and disinterested American know-nothings knew something.

In what is now an eerily prophetic comment, the United States Commission on National Security in the 21st Century, the Hart-Rudman Commission, in a report subtitled *New World Coming* predicted in 1999 that

> America is becoming increasingly vulnerable to hostile attack on our homeland—and
> our military superiority will not protect us ... In fact there is a school of thought that
> American military superiority on the conventional battlefield pushes our adversaries
> towards unconventional alternatives. This school further postulates we are entering a
> period of "catastrophic terrorism" with terrorists gaining access to weapons of mass
> destruction including nuclear devices, germ dispensers, poison gas and computer
> viruses. States, terrorists, and other disaffected groups will acquire weapons of mass
> destruction, and some will use them. Americans will likely die on American soil, pos-
> sibly in large numbers.[28]

Yet another important indication of growing American concern with homeland defence was the renaming of the United States Atlantic Command in October 1999 to United States Joint Forces Command (USJFCOM). In addition to its responsibility to prepare U.S. forces for overseas deployment, the command's responsibility for "homeland defense" included "providing military assistance to civil authorities for consequence management of weapons of mass destruction (WMD) incidents within the continental United States, its territories and possessions."[29] It will also "support the WMD consequence management efforts of the other combatant commands" throughout the world. In setting up USJFCOM, Secretary of Defense William Cohen, appointed an Army National Guard Brigadier-General as the first commander of Joint Task Force—Civil Support (JTF-CS). "The JTF-CS will ensure Department of Defense assets are prepared to respond to requests for support from a lead Federal Agency such as the Federal Emergency Management Agency."[30]

In the wake of the events of 11 September, the U.S. military has made homeland security and defence "the highest priority." As the *Quadrennial Defence Review Report* notes:

> The United States will maintain sufficient military forces to protect the U.S. domestic
> population, its territory, and its critical defense-related infrastructure against attack
> emanating from outside U.S. borders, as appropriate under U.S. law. U.S. forces will
> provide strategic deterrence and air and missile defense and uphold U.S. commitments
> under NORAD. In addition, DoD components have the responsibility, as specified in
> U.S. law, to support U.S. civil authorities as directed in managing the consequences of
> natural and man-made disasters and CBRNE-related events on U.S. territory. Finally,
> the U.S. military will be prepared to respond in a decisive manner to acts of interna-
> tional terrorism committed on U.S. territory or the territory of an ally.[31]

It appears that as part of this new emphasis, the U.S. intends to again review the organization of its forces within the continental United States. The *QDR* calls for a continued examination of the "roles and responsibilities" of the active and reserve forces "to ensure they are properly organized, trained and equipped, and postured." It is clear, the report goes on, "that U.S. forces, including the United States Coast Guard, require more effective means, methods, and organizations to perform these missions. As part of this examination, DoD will review the establishment of a new unified combatant commander to help address complex inter-agency issues and provide a single military commander to focus military support."[32] The United States Marines expanded the scope of their special units to deal with attacks that might take place in the United States. Senior administration officials were suggesting revision to U.S. laws which restrict the use of the regular armed forces in civilian law enforcement.

This rising concern with homeland defence was already affecting the bilateral defence relationship, and indeed the character of overall relations between the two countries. As noted above, the American strategic interest in Canada is that it not become a strategic liability. In the Cold War, with both countries accepting shared threat, the strategic unity of the continent ensured that this would not be the case. But the real defence of the continent lay in the deterrent capabilities of the U.S., not in joint measures for direct defence. In the new security environment of the post Cold War era, and the dangerous uncertainties after 11 September, the value of Canadian real estate is increasing and the issue of BMD participation is again coming to the fore.

Even before recent events, Ottawa was accused of lax immigration procedures which may allow terrorists to make their way to America through the very real but very open and vast border with Canada. In December 1999, several individuals were caught trying to smuggle bombs into the United States. Canada has also been called "hacker haven" because of computer threats that originate there. Under pressure from Washington, Ottawa has been compelled to address these matters.

In addition, because of "perceived weakness in the Canadian arms export system," Secretary of State Madeline Albright in April 1999 endorsed revisions to the U.S. International Traffic in Arms Export Regulations. This had the effect of stripping Canada of its special status, "treating it like other allies."[33]

On National Missile Defence (NMD), the situation is somewhat different. Here, Canada's military weakness is of little relevance. The U.S. does not need Canadian forces or territory to mount the kind of limited BMD system now under consideration. The deputy commander of Space Command recently went so far as to suggest that if the Canadian government declined to endorse and participate in the anti-missile system, the United States might indeed "do nothing if a Canadian city is attacked."[34] Former Minister of Foreign Affairs and International Trade Axworthy warned that Canada would not be "stampeded by the Pentagon" into endorsing an "unproven anti-missile system without considering the broader implications for arms control."[35]

The implications for the future of NORAD should NMD be deployed are very specific and profound. This is because even without such a system NORAD still has the mission of warning of a nuclear attack on North America and "assessing its nature so that the appropriate response" can be taken by the President of the United States. NORAD calls this Integrated Tactical Warning and Attack Assessment (ITW/AA).[36] For this, NORAD relies on information drawn from American missile tracking and detection systems and from U.S. and Canadian air defences. Even though Canada makes no direct contribution to the detection and tracking of ballistic missiles and has reduced its air defences, it "remains at the very heart of NORAD operations as long as it remains part of the ITW/AA process." Canadian personnel help staff NORAD's operations centre which is shared with Space Command.

The U.S. military wants to incorporate the "decision-authority" to use any NMD into the existing ITW/AA process. It only makes sense to link the systems that detect and assess missile attack with those that would launch interceptors. What this means is that Canadians could be at the very heart of the American "national" missile defence system if it decides to stay in NORAD with an BMD role.

The United States has indicated that it would like Canada to participate in NMD within NORAD. As noted, America does not need Canadian air space or territory nor, despite the great respect it has for the CF, does it need Canadian personnel. Washington is not looking to Canada to fund NMD. But it is likely that it would ask Ottawa to increase contributions to other aspects of North American aerospace defence.[37] Canada has a record in space surveillance, although capabilities have declined in recent years. The military is working on "an ambitious $637 million project to give Canada a military presence in space and perhaps with it, a foothold" in NMD.[38]

What the United States appeared to want from Canada on NMD was not material or personnel contributions but rather political endorsement to bolster Washington's case for NMD—and the revision to the ABM Treaty that this would require—with other allies and with the Russians. As former U.S. Deputy Secretary of Defense John Hamre said in a speech in Canada in February 1999:

> I believe we are at an important pivot point in our relationship with each other. Unfortunately, I think that pivot point is going to revolve around the issue of national missile defence, and this is where we have to start having a very open and constructive dialogue with each other about what it means and why we're doing it .... Canada needs to take the lead ... in helping to communicate to the rest of the world why it is important to amend the ABM Treaty. If we fail to do it, I promise we are not going to not protect the United States. We are going to go ahead once the President decided the time is right. And we can do this, I hate to say it, by ourselves. We'd rather not do it by ourselves. It is part of a much bigger world ... So, I honestly and firmly believe it is Canada's unique opportunity, and I would say responsibility, to help us with our allies and to help us with the approach to understand it is in the world's interest to amend this treaty, so that we can proceed with a limited defence system that lets us protect everybody against rogue actors and still rely on the underlying deterrence that is the grounding and underpinning of the larger strategic security posture that we have. So, it's my plea, my plea for your help ... We have to work on this together. It's a shared responsibility.[39]

But it is precisely this kind of political endorsement which the Canadian government was reluctant to give Washington. The Canadian government recognizes the threat of weapons of mass destruction. Indeed it is for this very reason that Ottawa has been so active on non-proliferation issues. And Ottawa understands that if America is to continue to play an active role in global affairs, including when necessary intervening in regional crises, then it must not be deterred by a fear of strikes against its homeland. But Canada has not been entirely in accord with Washington as to the immediacy of the threat nor the efficacy and wisdom of NMD as a solution. Axworthy was more forceful in his criticism of this anti-missile system. After attending a UN arms control conference, he told Canadian reporters that NMD offers no protection against a range of other threats to North America, such as low-flying weapons and terrorist attacks. Moreover, Washington "risks provoking a Russian nuclear build-up" if it deploys NMD. It involves participating in an arms race that could result in the expansion of nuclear weapons.[40]

There has also been the concern that after an initial limited deployment, the momentum will be there for an expansion of the system into one that would indeed threaten the Russian deterrent. In addition, there is some speculation that future interceptors will kill incoming weapons with nuclear charges rather than by simply hitting them. If the attacking missiles are believed to carry chemical or biological warheads this might be necessary. This in turn raises Canadian fears about where the deadly debris would fall.

In the first six months of 2000, it appeared that Washington was pressing even more strongly for a deployment of a limited system. Based upon new assessments of the intelligence, the ballistic missile threat to the American homeland is said to have become much greater. This is said to be in part, the result of clandestine transfers of missile technologies from Russia and China to certain other states, including Iraq and Iran, enabling them to extend the range of their missiles. This is why the Ballistic Missile Defense Office wanted to press ahead with what it calls a "compressed high risk schedule," meaning that it wants to begin construction of the Alaska site without subjecting the program to the kind of rigorous and careful development that its critics say is necessary. This had to be done if the system was to be operational by 2005, the year in which the office believed the danger will be significant. In order to meet this deadline construction for the Xban radars had to start in the summer of 2001 and thus a decision had to be made in the fall of 2000. But tests in the summer of 2000 failed and the Clinton administration left to the new administration a decision on missile defence. In the meantime, Canada was able to obtain what it wanted, an early renewal of NORAD for a five-year period with no mention MND.

Indeed, despite the ongoing disagreement over NMD, Canada and the United States settled their dispute over the International Traffic in Arms Export Regulations, "resuming the special defense industrial relations they shared for more than 50 years."[41] And a DoD official has recently urged that the U.S. set up a "Canada-like" exemption to the ITAR "to speed up movement of munitions" with close American allies such as the United Kingdom and Australia.[42]

During the 2000 Presidential campaign, George W. Bush supported NMD but also called for a review of American strategy. Eliot Cohen has argued that missile defence must be part of such a review, which should deal with the whole question of homeland defence. He agrees that an "effective national missile defence may eventually require the United States to withdraw" from the AMB Treaty. However, he argues that "the moment for such a withdrawal has not yet arrived" Moreover, NMD

> has become a question of theology rather than policy, especially in an election year.
> President Clinton was probably right to defer the final decision on this matter, but
> sooner or later the difficult choice will have to be made. NMD will make sense only if
> it offers protection, not only against the odd missile from North Korea, Iraq or Iran,
> but against America's main rival, China.[43]

Upon coming into office, President George W. Bush renewed the call for NMD and asked allies to join in. It was, though, unclear whether he would be successful as new criticism arose from the Congress and the informed public. But this was before 11 September. While it can be argued that an anti-missile system will not protect the U.S. against determined terrorist threats, it seems evident that the wave of concern and action associated with homeland security will carry with it some kind of ballistic defence. Thus, the issue is again on the bilateral agenda.

The U.S. had indicated it will proceed with NMD with or without a revision to the Treaty, and since Washington would like to place the system under NORAD, the future of bilateral aerospace co-operation remains very much in question. This is mainly because if Canada does not want to participate in NMD "it cannot remain involved in the ITW/AA process, since the two will be linked." This would mean that Canada's role in North American defence would be diminished. It might be possible to maintain NORAD on a different basis, that is without responsibility for

Canadian Coyote reconnaissance vehicle, OP Kinetic, Kosovo, 1999. (DND file photo.)

missile warning, assessment and defence, as a somewhat hollow and marginalized organization. But according to Joseph Jockel, "without Canadian involvement in ITW/AA, maintaining
NORAD as a joint enterprise would have little to no point."

In such a case the U.S. would move to dissolve NORAD and shift ITW/AA, along with the operations of the missile defense, to an all-U.S. command. It would remain of some importance to the
U.S. to know what was occurring in Canadian airspace, but that could be readily resolved through
a fairly simple arrangement with the Canadian air force that did not involve a joint command.[44]

It might be argued that these doubts about Canada's future role in NORAD because of NMD
will intensify if the events of 11 September lead to an acceleration of the missile defence program. On the other hand, the tragedy may well afford Ottawa the rationale it needs to be more
receptive to an anti-missile role for NORAD, especially if these events bring about an agreement
with Russia on the ABM Treaty. Even if Ottawa (or Washington) decided that Canadian personnel would not be directly involved in NORAD's active missile defence role, both governments will
probably decide to maintain the unity of North American aerospace defence given recent events.
Indeed, with NATO surveillance planes contributing for the first time to the security of North
America, now would hardly be the time for the United States to ask one NATO ally to leave a
long-established joint command arrangement.

More importantly, with America now focussing more directly on homeland defence, the scope
and intensity of bilateral security relations, and the willingness to explore new avenues of collaboration, will likely increase. For example, the maritime defence of the continent, particularly
in the immediate ocean approaches, will heighten bilateral naval co-operation. And new efforts
will be made to co-ordinate responses to potential terrorist attack. In the wake of the attacks,
Ottawa announced that over a quarter of a billion dollars would be spent for "national security"
on a range of initiatives from more customs officers and police surveillance capabilities to measures to prevent terrorist organizations from raising funds in Canada. In this context, NORAD

will be just one among many joint undertakings and the political and strategic salience of missile defence will be diminished.

One factor which the CF and the Department of National Defence may be able to count on is that overall the Canadian public is favourably disposed to continued military co-operation with the United States. Indeed (and this is another paradox) the end of the Cold War has provided the government with a relatively permissive climate of public opinion in this regard. This may be the result of Canada joining the U.S. during the 1990s in what can only be described as a series of popular humanitarian interventions under the broad banner of peacekeeping. There was, for example, overwhelming public support for the action in Kosovo. Apart from arms control interest groups, general public opinion in Canada seems to be either indifferent to or positive about missile defence for North America. In the aftermath of 11 September, the Canadian public appears to be overwhelmingly predisposed to closer security co-operation with the United States.

Conclusion: A Traditional Response to a Non-Traditional Threat

It has been said repeatedly that everything has changed since 11 September. This is true in the sense that combatting international terrorism has now become the central focus of American foreign policy after a post Cold War decade in which no grand organizing principle similar to containment and deterrence emerged. During these years, many argued that the very definition of security had changed and expanded. No longer could it be viewed in strictly military or national terms. The economy, the environment, culture and especially "human" security now dominated international strategic relations. But combined with other trends in the 1990s the attack on America has brought back aspects of the Cold War world and catapulted traditional concerns about national security to the top of the agenda in order to deal with a non-traditional challenge. Indeed, Secretary of Defense Rumsfeld has cautioned the American people that this is to be a protracted struggle comparable to the Cold War. Here again, we have Washington asserting indispensable leadership against a threat which, because it is directed primarily against America, endangers the entire Western world. Once more, the NATO alliance is called upon to lend its material support and, more importantly, legitimacy and unity to American efforts. We hear another Presidential address to the American people asking like-minded nations in all parts of the world to join the United States in what we are told will be a "long twilight struggle."

It was the global character of America's Cold War policies which made the seat at the table so important for Canada. Sharing a continent as well as Washington's appreciation of the pervasiveness of the threat, it was essential that Ottawa also became concerned with its own national security and how its policies would be co-ordinated and adjusted to accommodate and support its closest ally.

After 11 September, Canada has once again been drawn into a global effort, one with even greater and more complex ramifications for bilateral security relations. Its response was to do what it has done in the past, joining the campaign alongside the United States and its Western allies. Along with NATO partners, it invoked Article 5 of the North Atlantic Treaty declaring the attack on America to be an attack on all alliance members. Ottawa dispatched forces overseas and turned anew to efforts to ensure that it did not become a security liability to the United States. Just as Canadians were glued to their television sets in early September 2001, so too have these events emphasized and reinforced the bonds of common strategic interests, concepts of world order and shared values that keep Canada firmly affixed to its seat at the table of the American led and dominated western alliance.

Notes for Chapter 19

1   Parts of this chapter have appeared in Joel J. Sokolsky, *The Americanization of Peacekeeping: Implications for Canada* Martello Papers 17 (Kingston, Ontario: Queen's University Centre for International Relations, 1997); Joel J. Sokolsky, "Over There With Uncle Sam: Peacekeeping, the 'Trans-European Bargain,' And the Canadian Forces," David G. Haglund, ed., *What NATO For Canada?* Martello Papers 23 (Kingston, Ontario: Queen's University Centre for International Relations, 2000); Joel J. Sokolsky, "The Bilateral Security Relationship: Will 'National' Missile Defense Involve Canada?" *American Review of Canadian Studies,* Vol 30 (2000), 227.

2   Joel J. Sokolsky, "A Seat at the Table: Canada and Its Alliances," *Armed Forces and Society,* Vol 16 (Fall 1989), 11.

3   United States, Department of Defense, *Quadrennial Defense Review Report* (Washington, D.C: 30 Sep 2001), 18.

4   Michael Mastanduno, "Preserving the Unipolar Moment: Realist Theories and U.S. Grand Strategy after the Cold War," *International Security,* Vol 21 (Spring 1997), 51.

5   Canada. *1994 Defence White Paper* (Ottawa: DND, 1994), 14.

6   Canada, Department of National Defence, *Shaping the Future of Canadian Defence: A Strategy for 2020* (Ottawa: June 1999), 10.

7   Paul Koring, "Haiti pullout reveals shrunken peace role," *Globe and Mail*, 15 Dec 1997, A1.

8   Current Operations, www.dnd.ca/menu/Operations/index_e.htm (9 Jun 2000).

9   "UN needs upgrade to keep peace: panel," *Kingston Whig Standard,* 24 Aug, 2000, 13.

10 David Haglund and Alen Sens, "Smaller NATO Members: Belgium, Canada Portugal and Spain," unpublished paper.

11 Kevin War, "Canadian troops could help EU army," *Kingston Whig-Standard,* 27 Jun 2000, 12.

12 United Nations Association of the United States, *Washington Weekly Report*, Vol 22 (14 June,1996), 4.

13 Major Brad Bergstrand, "What Do You Do When There's No Peace to Keep?", *Canadian Defence Quarterly,* Vol 23 (March 1994), 25-30.

14 "UN Oks Slashing Peacekeeping Budget," *Herald Sun* (Durham, N.C.), 8 Jun 1996, 2.

15 Canada, Department of National Defence, Speaking Notes for the Honourable Art Eggleton, Minister of National Defence. "Canadian Lessons from the Kosovo Crisis," Harvard University, 30 Sep 1999.

16 Mathew Fisher, "Allies in Kosovo envy Canada's hi-tech weaponry," *The Maple Leaf,* 14 Jul 1999, 16.

17 Operations Update, www.dnd.ca/menu/weeklybrief/jun00/01NwsConf_m_e.htm (1 Jun 2000).

18 It was a duality noted by Henry Kissinger; see *White House Years* (Boston: Little Brown 1979), 383.

19 Mastanduno, "Preserving the Unipolar Moment," 49-88.

20 Samuel P. Huntington, "The Lonely Superpower," *Foreign Affairs,* Vol 78, (March/April 1999), 47.

21 Coral Bell, "American Ascendancy And the Pretense of Concert," *The National Interest,* Fall 1999, p.60. Emphasis in original.

22 Cited by James Eayrs, *In Defence of Canada*, Vol II, *Appeasement and Rearmament* (Toronto: University of Toronto Press, 1965), 183.

23 As quoted in Joseph T. Jockel, *Security to the North: Canada-US Defense Relations in the 1990s* (East Lansing, Mich.: Michigan State University Press, 1991), 1.

24 Canada, Department of National Defence, *1994 Defence White Paper* (Ottawa: Minister of Supply and Services, 1994), 23.

25 Ibid,. 25.

26 Richard Betts, "The New Threat of Mass Destruction," *Foreign Affairs,* Vol 77, (January/February 1998), 28, 41.

27 John E. Rielly, "Americans and the World: A Survey at Century's End," *Foreign Policy,* Vol 114, (Spring 1999), 97, 99.

28 United States, Commission on National Security in the 21st Century, *New World Coming: American Security in the 21st Century* (Arlington, Va.: The Commission, 1999), 14.

29 "USA Com Redesignated to U.S. Joint Forces Command," *Marine Corps Gazette,* Vol 83, (November 1999), 8.

30 "Guard General to Command Joint Civil Support Task Force," *National Guard,* Vol 53, (November 1999), 12.

31 *Quadrennial Defense Review Report,* 18.

32 Ibid., 19.

33 Colin Clark, "U.S., Canada Agree on Cross-Border Arms Trade," *Defense News,* 8 May 2000, 4.

34 Jeff Salot, "Support missile project or else, Ottawa warned," *Globe and Mail,* 3 May, A1, A14.

35 Jeff Salot, "Don't Push missile defence on Canada, Axworthy says," *Globe and Mail,* 17 Mar 2000, A5.

36 Joseph T. Jockel, *The Canadian Forces: Hard Choices, Soft Power* (Toronto: Canadian Institute of Strategies Studies, 1999), 104.

37 Ibid., 107.

38 David Pugliese, "Canadians Forces back missile shield project. Military to spend $637 million to extend presence in space," *Ottawa Citizen,* 13 Mar 2000. (on-line edition).

39 Remarks as Delivered by Deputy Secretary of Defense John J. Hamre, Calgary, Alberta, Canada, 18 Feb 2000, www.defenselink.mil/speeches/2000/s2000218-depsecdef1.html.

40 Paul Knox, "Axworthy takes on U.S. over missile defence," *Globe and Mail,* 26 Apr 2000 (on-line edition).

41 Clark, "U.S., Canada Agree on Cross-Border Arms Trade," 4.

42 ADOD Memo Urges "Canada-like' Export Exemption for Closest Allies," *Inside US Trade,* 19 May 2000 (on- line edition).

43 Eliot A. Cohen, "Defending America in the Twenty-first Century," *Foreign Affairs,* Vol 79, (November/December 2000), 45.

44 Jockel, *The Canadian Forces,* 106.

CONTRIBUTORS

Lieutenant-Colonel David L. Bashow, a Canadian Air Force fighter pilot, is an Assistant Professor of History at the Royal Military College of Canada (RMC). He has written four internationally acclaimed military aviation history books.

Dr. Daniel Byers is a sessional lecturer at RMC. He recently received his PhD in history from McGill University in Montreal.

Dr. N.F. Dreisziger has been teaching in the Department of History at RMC since 1970. He has published extensively on Canadian and East Central European subjects.

Dr. Jane Errington is the Chair of the Department of History at RMC.

Lieutenant-Commander Gregg Hannah is a serving officer in the Canadian Forces who is presently teaching at RMC.

Dr. Ronald G. **Haycock** is a Professor of History and War Studies, as well as a former Dean of Arts, at RMC.

Dr. Michael A. Hennessy is an Associate Professor of History and War Studies at RMC specializing in issues of defence technology, intelligence, and naval and military strategic affairs.

Lieutenant-Colonel Bernd Horn, PhD, is the Commanding Officer of the First Battalion, The Royal Canadian Regiment and an Adjunct-Associate Professor of History at RMC.

Dr. Hal Klepak is a Professor of History and War Studies at RMC.

Dr. Jean Lamarre is an Assistant Professor of History at RMC specializing in American history and in transnational migration in the eighteenth century.

Major David Last, PhD, teaches political science at RMC and is on the faculty of the Pearson Peacekeeping Centre.

Dr. Roch Legault is an Assistant Professor of History at RMC.

Dr. Sean M. Maloney teaches War Studies and is the SSHRC Post Doctoral Fellow at the Royal Military College of Canada.

Professor B.J.C. McKercher, FRHistS, is Chair of War Studies at RMC.

Dr. Keith Neilson is a Professor of History at RMC.

Dr. Joel Sokolsky is a Professor of Political Science and Dean of Arts at RMC and Senior Fellow at Queen's University Centre for International Relations.

Michel Wyczynski is an Archivist with the Political Archives Section, Canadian Archives Branch of the National Archives of Canada.

INDEX